A History of
Modern Germany

A History of Modern Germany

1871 to Present

SEVENTH EDITION

Dietrich Orlow

Professor (Emeritus) of History
Boston University

PEARSON

Boston   Columbus   Indianapolis   New York   San Francisco   Upper Saddle River
Amsterdam   Cape Town   Dubai   London   Madrid   Milan   Munich   Paris   Montreal   Toronto
Delhi   Mexico City   Sao Paulo   Sydney   Hong Kong   Seoul   Singapore   Taipei   Tokyo

Executive Editor: Jeff Lasser
Editorial Project Manager: Rob DeGeorge
Editorial Assistant: Julia Feltus
Senior Marketing Manager: Maureen Prado Roberts
Marketing Assistant: Samantha Bennett
Production Manager: Fran Russello
Cover Administrator: Jayne Conte
Cover Designer: Suzanne Behnke
Editorial Production and Composition Service: Hemalatha/Integra Software Services Pvt. Ltd
Printer/Binder: Courier Companies, Inc.

Credits and acknowledgments borrowed from other sources and reproduced, with permission, in this textbook appear on the appropriate page within the text.

Many of the designations by manufacturers and seller to distinguish their products are claimed as trademarks. Where those designations appear in this book, and the publisher was aware of a trademark claim, the designations have been printed in initial caps or all caps.

Library of Congress Cataloging-in-Publication Data
Orlow, Dietrich.
   A history of modern Germany : 1871 to present / Dietrich Orlow. — 7th ed.
      p. cm.
   Includes bibliographical references and index.
   ISBN-13: 978-0-205-21443-3 (alk. paper)
   ISBN-10: 0-205-21443-6 (alk. paper)
   1. Germany—History—1871–1918.   2. Germany—History—20th century.
   3. Germany—History—1990–   I. Title.
   DD220.O67 2012
   943.08—dc23

                                                           2011017945

3 4 5 6 7 8 9 10 V092 18 17 16 15

ISBN-10:   0-205-21443-6
ISBN-13: 978-0-205-21443-3

Contents

~~~~~~

Maps

〰〰〰〰

Preface

Much of the history covered in this work seems to contradict the title of this book. For most of the second half of the twentieth century, Germany had been not one country, but two: West Germany, formally the Federal Republic of Germany, and East Germany, the German Democratic Republic. At first glance they seemed to have little in common. West Germany was (and is) a liberal democracy representing values of political and cultural pluralism and modified free enterprise. East Germany was a communist state whose leaders attempted to create a society founded on the principles of Marxism-Leninism. The two nations were integrated into opposing power blocs. West Germany is a friend of the United States and a member of the NATO alliance; East Germany was the Soviet Union's most important European ally and a member of the now-defunct Warsaw Pact. Relations between the two Germanies were strained, to put it mildly.

Yet, as if to illustrate that nothing in history is permanent, as this seventh edition of *A History of Modern Germany* goes to press, Germany has been reunited for two decades. When the text first appeared, more than twenty years ago, there seemed little likelihood that East and West Germany would be reunited. But the dramatic events of 1989 and 1990 led to the swift and unexpected collapse of the GDR. In a few short months, the East German communist regime fell from power, the hated Berlin Wall crumbled, and the East German people in a genuinely free election voted for reunification with the West.

Ironically, as a divided nation the two German states achieved much of what the German people sought in vain when they were last a united country: a long period of political stability, economic prosperity, and peace with their neighbors. Equally paradoxically, despite the existence of two German states, interest in the two countries' joint history seemed to increase. The reason is easy to see: The division of the country was the result of the course of German history in the years from 1871 to the end of World War II in 1945. For almost three quarters of a century, German history was synonymous with "the German problem," a shorthand way of indicating that Germany was an unstable and unpredictable factor in modern European history. A revolution, several coup attempts, and four constitutions gave the country political systems that ranged from monarchical authoritarianism to liberal democracy and Nazi totalitarianism, but no lasting stability. Closely related to political and social upheavals, the German economy experienced alternate periods of boom and bust. Twice in modern times the country reached the brink of economic and fiscal collapse.

Domestic upheavals in turn were related to repeated attempts by Germany's leaders to change the balance of power in Europe and the rest of the world. Having achieved national unity by victorious wars, the German leaders repeatedly attempted to use international aggression to provide the nation with domestic stability, economic prosperity, and respect abroad. The pattern culminated in Adolf Hitler's deliberate unleashing of World War II to realize his vast ambitions. At the end of that conflict, bombed cities; millions of dead, wounded, and homeless; and a divided nation subject to the whims of the victors represented the consequences of hubris.

Yet modern German history is more than Prusso-German authoritarianism, the Nazi dictatorship, military aggression, and the Holocaust. This account of the country's path from national unification in 1871 to political division in 1945 and reunification in our own day attempts to present these alternative aspects as well. Long-standing, if often submerged, traditions of political, cultural, and economic pluralism as well as left-wing radicalism existed side by side with right-wing authoritarianism. The surprisingly swift and strong establishment of Western pluralism and Eastern Marxism as societal values after World War II happened in large part because for many years these components in the German societal makeup, although not dominant, had been struggling for viability and recognition.

This is not a narrative history in the traditional sense. Many events have been omitted to keep the text "problem oriented." I have tried to retain the central focus on the dynamics in German society that led to both the volatility and unpredictability in the country's domestic policies and foreign relations, and to its impressive achievements.

The *"Im Mittelpunkt"* ("In the Spotlight") pieces, a new feature of the fifth edition, provide biographical capsules for a variety of prominent Germans from all walks of life. For this seventh edition some of the *"Im Mittelpunkt"* features have been replaced with new portraits, and others augmented with additional material. Another innovation concerns the illustrations. In addition to the caricatures and drawings featured in the first five editions, beginning with the sixth edition contemporary photographs were added. For this seventh edition several photos have been replaced and new ones added.

It is a pleasant duty to acknowledge the help that this book has received from a number of colleagues and friends. Werner T. Angress, Jeffrey Diefendorf, Werner Jochmann, Jean Leventhal, David Morgan, Arnold Offner, Norman Naimark, and Catherine Epstein all took the trouble to read portions of the manuscript. I would like to thank them for their valuable comments and suggestions. I am grateful to Eliza McClennen of the Boston University Geography Department for drawing all of the maps except for the one showing Germany since 1990. That one is reproduced courtesy of the periodical *Deutschland Magazine*.

A heartfelt thanks to the reviewers of earlier editions: Dan S. White, Nathan M. Brooks, Martin Berger, William Combs, David A. Meyer, Loyd Lee, Narasingha Sil, Rudy Koshar, Richard Breitman, David A. Hackett, Derek Hastings, Ronald J. Granieri, and S. Jonathan Wiesen. The book has also benefited from the comments of several anonymous colleagues who used the earlier editions in their courses and were kind enough to point out some factual errors and unclear interpretations in the earlier work.

As always, my wife Maria was an active collaborator and constructive critic in bringing out this seventh edition. Any shortcomings that remain are, of course, my own responsibility.

Dietrich Orlow
Bellevue, Washington

CHAPTER ONE

〰〰〰

The Founders' Generation

1871–1890

At the beginning of the nineteenth century, the territories that would eventually become "Germany" bore little resemblance either to the German Empire of 1871 or to the Federal Republic familiar to us today. For most of the century Germany was little more than "a geographic expression," as a contemporary statesman put it; Germany was the last of the European Great Powers to achieve national unification. The reasons were primarily political and diplomatic, although the country's geographic location in the center of Europe also constituted a handicap.

For Germans it has been a historical fact of life that the topography of their lands provides no real physical barriers either within the country or on the northern, eastern, or western frontiers of the territory, making travel—but also expansion and invasion—easy. Only in the south are there any mountains to speak of. Four major rivers—the Rhine, the Weser, the Elbe, and the Danube—dissect the plain, facilitate internal commerce, and provide access to international trade routes. The first three rivers are fully navigable for much of their course and empty into the North Sea, thus giving Germany ready access to the Atlantic trading routes. The Danube is commercially less useful. Not only is it a difficult river to navigate, but it empties into the Black Sea, a body of water in Eastern Europe that is connected to the Mediterranean Sea, not the Atlantic Ocean.

The balance sheet of economic resources is similarly mixed. Generally speaking, the quality of Germany's agricultural land is considerably better west of the Elbe than in the eastern regions. Traditionally, much of East Elbia was extensively rather than intensively cultivated, with rye, potatoes, and sugar beets the prevailing crops; the areas west of the river lent themselves to dairy and truck farming. Along the steep slopes of the Rhine and Mosel Rivers, winemaking has been a tradition since Roman times.

As for the raw materials needed for a modern industrial society, Germany possesses only coal in abundance; there are virtually inexhaustible

Map 1.1   Germany 1816–1866

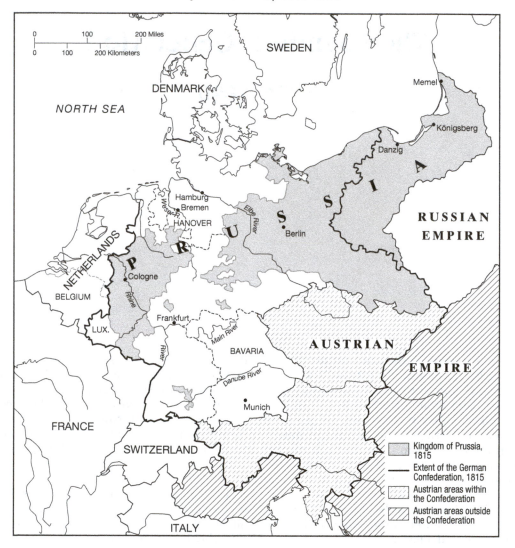

supplies of this resource in the Ruhr Valley and parts of Saxony and Silesia. The country has few iron ore reserves and virtually no oil deposits. Other metallic deposits are negligible.

Before unification, Germany's political and constitutional structure was that of a loose confederation of virtually independent states. Until 1806 Germany had been divided into some three hundred large and small states, organized in a fictitious entity called the Holy Roman Empire of the German Nation. With a stroke of his pen, Napoleon abolished this structure and substantially rearranged the boundaries of the German states. At the Congress of Vienna (1814–1815) the Great Powers, under the leadership of Prince Clemens von Metternich, the chancellor of the Austrian Empire, proceeded to revise Napoleon's revision. What emerged was the German

Confederation, composed of thirty-nine principalities and free cities. Among this group only five states (or *Länder*, as they are called in German) could, on their own, exercise major influence in the Confederation's affairs: the three southern states of Baden, Württemberg, and Bavaria, and the two largest entities in the Confederation, Prussia and Austria. Prussia especially benefited from the territorial rearrangement of the German states after 1815. It added the populous regions along the Rhine in western Germany, as well as a portion of Saxony to its earlier East Elbian holdings, thereby becoming the largest, wealthiest, and most populous member of the Confederation aside from Austria.

In the years 1848–1849, the German Confederation, like most of the western half of the continent, was shaken by a series of revolutionary upheavals. For a few months the dream of national unification and a liberal constitution seemed within reach. Confronted with widespread popular unrest in all of the German states, the rulers retreated to the sidelines and permitted popularly elected assemblies to write new constitutions embodying the liberal ideas of representative government and free enterprise. The revolutions eventually failed, and the princes and their allies returned to power. (At the height of the unrest the Prussian king, Frederick William IV, had promised, "Prussia will be absorbed by Germany," but he soon went back on his word.) The rulers promptly "revised" the liberal constitutions, shifting authority back to the executive, but in the process something of a political fault line emerged between the northern and southern German states. Whereas the southern Länder retained a number of liberal provisions in their constitutions, the northern states, led by Prussia, became bastions of authoritarianism.

Prussia gloried in its self-appointed role as champion of the conservative camp. Frightened by the virulence of the revolutionary upheavals, the Prussian king and the state's ruling elite, the land-owning aristocracy known as the Junkers, were determined to give Prussia a constitution that assured the permanent dominance of political conservatism in Germany's second-largest state.

A key element in Prussia's counterrevolutionary effort was the state's electoral system, the so-called three-class system of voting. These repressive provisions remained in effect until 1918, becoming an increasingly hateful symbol of Prussia's political backwardness. Briefly stated, the system worked as follows: For election purposes, Prussian voters, that is, males twenty-five years of age and older, were divided into three classes with membership in each determined by the amount of *direct* taxes an individual paid. Direct taxes really meant property taxes; Prussia did not levy an income tax at this time. Those voters contributing a third of an electoral district's direct tax revenue, regardless of the number of people involved, voted in the first class and had the right to choose electors, who in turn selected a third of the district's members of parliament. The second class consisted of those contributing the next third of the district's revenue from direct taxes; the last class was composed of voters whose taxes made up the last third of the tax income as well as all voters who paid no direct taxes at all.

The result was an extreme form of political discrimination: The very small number of voters in the first class, the somewhat larger number of voters in the second, and the vast number of voters in the third class were represented by the same number of parliamentary delegates. In practice the system resulted in a massive skewing of political power in favor of the rural and urban wealthy—as it was meant to do. In many of the East Elbian election districts the three-class system of voting meant that the landowner voted in the first class, the schoolmaster and pastor in the second, and all of the landowner's sharecroppers in the third.

The political result was an unfair advantage for conservative candidates for the state legislature during the next seventy years. As a rule, conservative candidates (especially in the rural areas of Prussia) received not only the votes

The Revolution of 1848: A contemporary rendering of clashes between civilians and soldiers in Berlin in March, 1848. (Source: akg-images.)

of those casting ballots in the first and second classes, but even those voting in the third class often had little choice except to support conservative candidates. Until 1918 there were no secret ballots in Prussian state elections, and fear of economic reprisals by landowners kept many sharecroppers from voting for opponents of Prussian authoritarianism. The long-term effects of the system may be gauged from the returns for the 1913 state election: The Conservative Party received about 17 percent of the popular vote and almost 50 percent of the seats in parliament; the Social Democrats received 28 percent of the popular vote and 2 percent of the parliamentary seats.

Germany's national unification in 1871 was the result of three short wars masterminded by the Prussian prime minister Otto von Bismarck. This may be a good place to introduce the man who was to dominate German history from 1862 to 1890. Born in 1815, Bismarck came from an ancient Pomeranian Junker family (he liked to boast that his ancestors had been in Prussia longer than the royal family, the Hohenzollerns), although his mother was the daughter of a Bremen merchant. Bismarck received a conventional administrative law education. He attended several liberal universities, but none of his teachers, conservative or liberal, had much of an impact on the young man. After graduation he joined the Prussian civil service, but soon resigned, finding the work simply too boring. For a few years he managed his Pomeranian estates (which his father had mismanaged almost to the point of bankruptcy), and it was here that he experienced the Revolution of 1848.

Bismarck wholeheartedly and publicly disapproved of the revolution. It was no surprise, then, that after the restoration of monarchical power the Conservatives identified Bismarck as a young man to be watched. In 1851 he was appointed chief Prussian delegate to the Confederation's Diet at Frankfurt. He seemed ideally suited to the task. Bismarck certainly supported the authoritarian regime in Prussia, but he had also indicated that he did not feel it was Prussia's place to challenge Austria's restored role as leader of the German Confederation.

All went well until the outbreak of the Crimean War. When Austria brought its proposal to the Diet to mobilize the troops of the German Confederation in support of the Habsburgs' self-serving mediation role in the conflict, Bismarck urged his government to reject the Austrian demand. He argued then and later that neither Prussia nor the other non-Austrian German states had vital interests in the Balkans. Bismarck recognized that particularly for Prussia, the Crimean War was a no-win situation; any involvement would alienate either the Russians or the Western powers. Bismarck's advice eventually prevailed, largely because the king's advisers in Berlin were badly split between those who wanted Prussia to support the Russians, and the liberals, who hoped Prussia would align itself with England and France. Given the deadlock, doing nothing, which Bismarck proposed, was a natural compromise.

With Prussia leading the opposition, the troops of the German Confederation were in fact never mobilized. As a result, Austria's clever scenario failed completely. At the end of the Crimean War, its international position was far worse than it had been when the conflict began. Russia resented Austria's ingratitude. (In 1849 Czar Nicholas I had sent Russian troops to Hungary to help the Austrians defeat the Hungarian Revolution.) France and England, equally annoyed at Austria's lack of action, were instrumental in helping Italy achieve national unification. Austria lost its possessions in northern Italy.

Bismarck was not in Frankfurt to experience the full triumph of his policy. Between 1859 and 1862 he served as Prussian ambassador to Russia and later to France. It was here that the king's request for Bismarck to become prime minister reached him. Bismarck readily accepted, assuring William that he could implement the military reforms the king desired without either yielding to parliament or provoking another revolution. As it turned out, Bismarck was right on both counts and when, a few years later, he also led the way to national unification, he was hailed as a political genius. Actually, the prime minister's reputation for prescience was undeserved. In retrospect, it is clear that when he assumed office, Bismarck had no long-range program except to stay in power and prevent the Prussian legislature from becoming the dominant player in the state's politics.

As far as domestic policy was concerned, the new prime minister relied on the loyalty of the reorganized Prussian army to carry him through. As he explained in his famous speech to the Prussian legislature's Ways and Means Committee in October 1862, "not by parliamentary speeches and majority votes are the great questions of the day determined— that was the great mistake of 1848 and 1849— but by iron and blood." The mostly liberal legislators fumed at this revelation, but they also recognized that Bismarck had the power to govern Prussia by administrative fiat while the impotent opposition occupied the legislature's time with meaningless debates and useless votes of no confidence.

A new ingredient was injected into what both sides had expected to be a long and bitter deadlock when the Schleswig-Holstein question once again stirred national passions. In essence, the issues in these North German duchies revealed the difficulty of combining the principles of modern nationalism with the remnants of feudal traditions. Since the later Middle Ages the two duchies of Schleswig and Holstein had been governed as personal fiefs by the kings of Denmark. A treaty of 1460 also provided that the two provinces should remain "forever undivided." In the Vienna settlement of 1815, the Great Powers decreed that the duchy of Holstein should become part of the German Confederation while Schleswig would remain outside. However, both duchies were still fiefs of the Danish royal house; they were not part of Denmark. In 1848 Danish liberal nationalists, no less nationalistically impassioned than their German counterparts, argued that the presence of a sizable Danish ethnic minority in northern Schleswig justified changing the status of that duchy: Instead of remaining a personal fief of the crown, the province should become an integral part of Denmark. German nationalists, bolstered by the indivisibility provision of the medieval treaty and the fact that a large majority of the population was German, insisted both Holstein and Schleswig become part of a unified Germany.

The conflict erupted into the only war ever declared by the German Confederation. In 1848 German nationalists from all political camps discovered that the Schleswig-Holstein question was a crucible of national self-determination and that Danish ambitions would have to be thwarted by force of arms. (Cynics pointed out that Denmark appeared to be the only potential enemy that could be defeated by the weak German forces; the German navy in 1848 and 1849 consisted of some chartered freighters.)

It soon turned out, however, that even a war with Denmark was no simple matter. The Great Powers—notably France, Russia, and Great Britain—became involved. Although Great Britain originally sympathized with the German liberals in 1848 (Prince Albert of Saxe-Coburg, Queen Victoria's husband, was a fervent supporter of the liberal cause), but expanding direct German control over Schleswig-Holstein would alter the balance of power in both the North and Baltic Seas and thereby affect vital British interests. It should have come as no surprise to the liberals that the Germans' territorial ambitions in the north turned England's sympathy for unification into something less than benevolent neutrality. The British political leader and later prime minister Disraeli spoke exasperatedly of "that dreamy and dangerous nonsense called German nationality."

As was to be expected, the war in 1864 was a one-sided affair. The Danes were quickly defeated, and the Great Powers, led by England, arranged a new settlement for the two provinces. The Danish crown lost all of Schleswig-Holstein; the two provinces became the personal property of the emperor of Austria and the king of Prussia. The two monarchs in turn agreed to administer their spoils so that Prussia would govern the northern province of Schleswig while Austria was in charge of Holstein. The arrangement ran into problems almost immediately. The emperor of Austria was anxious to be relieved of the burden of administering a territory some 600 miles from Vienna. Prussia, in contrast, was in no hurry to change the treaty provisions.

For the next two years, from 1864 to 1866, Prussia and Austria behaved a little like boxers seeking a good sparring position in the ring. Austria sponsored a number of federal reforms plans at the Diet. They included the creation of a new state of Schleswig-Holstein and the election of a national parliament. The Habsburgs also attempted to isolate Prussia by persuading at least the southern German states to join the Austrian protective tariff system, a transparent ploy to break up the *Zollverein,* the free-trade area that had encompassed all of the German states except for Austria since 1834. (Under Prussian leadership the Zollverein went in the opposite direction. It had recently, in 1862, concluded a commercial treaty with France, assuring virtual free trade between France and the members of the Zollverein.) Both Austria and Prussia also paid lip service to the ideal of German unification.

In 1866 the war of nerves and diplomacy turned into a shooting conflict. Again the military action was short and decisive. Using the advantages of improved logistics and better armaments that were the result of Prussia's recent military reforms, and relying on its efficient railroad system, Prussia swept through Austria's North German allies and then defeated the Austrians in a single encounter, the Battle of Königgrätz (now Sadowa in the Czech Republic). In the subsequent peace settlement, Prussia established its hegemony in all of Germany north of the Main River, severely punishing some of the states that had openly sided with Austria: The Kingdom of Hanover, parts of Hessen, and the free city of Frankfurt all became part of Prussia. The new superstate, along with a few smaller territories that had had the foresight to side with Prussia in the war, formed the North German Confederation. The German Confederation was dissolved and the medium-size southern German states were now entirely on their own. Austria lost no territory, but it had to agree to Prussia's annexation of Schleswig-Holstein, and, more important, it lost its predominant position in German affairs.

The North German Confederation is remembered chiefly for two reasons. One was that it was barely established when, less than five years later, it was replaced by the German Reich. The other remarkable event associated with the North German Confederation was the apparent capitulation of the Prussian liberals to Bismarck and the Prussian Junkers. Over the years historians have seen the first as evidence that Bismarck regarded the North German Confederation as a temporary entity, soon to be replaced by a unified Germany. The second seems to provide evidence of the liberals' spinelessness and their lack of commitment to strengthening parliament in the Prussian political system. At first glance it certainly does appear that Bismarck was the victor in the conflicts of the 1860s. Four years after he had become prime minister, the Prussian liberals hastened to pass a so-called Indemnity Bill in the Prussian legislature that retroactively gave parliamentary approval to the government's rule by decree since 1862.

Actually, neither did Bismarck intend the North German Confederation as a short-lived governmental structure nor was the defeat of the liberals as one sided as it appeared. It must be kept in mind that Bismarck in 1866 had no particular interest in German unification. He limited his ambitions to securing what he felt was Prussia's rightful place in German and European affairs. The North German Confederation admirably fitted this scenario: Prussia dominated all of northern Germany. Austria was effectively excluded from playing a major role in German affairs, and the southern German states were not sufficiently strong to challenge Prussia's preeminence. In effect, the North German Confederation represented the triumph of Prussian counter-revolutionary conservatism in the heartland of Germany. Bismarck and his king had reason to be content with the outcome of their policies.

That left the liberals. Politically, they were defeated. Had not the dreams of 1848 been ignominiously buried with the Indemnity Bill of 1866? In a sense, yes, but looked at in another way, the reformers realized a number of their long-term aims with the establishment of the North German Confederation. The new governmental entity had an elected parliament with powers to control the Confederation's taxes and budgets. Moreover, unlike the Prussian legislature, the Confederation's parliament was elected on the basis of universal male suffrage, at the time the most democratic manner of choosing parliamentary representatives. True, parliament's power existed more on paper than in practice. It had no control over the executive. (The Confederation had only one executive office anyway, that of chancellor. It was headed by Otto von Bismarck.) Parliament exercised control over the Confederation's budget, but that was largely meaningless because only about 5 percent of all public money outlays were included in this budget. The real power of the purse lay with state and local authorities, and the legislature of Prussia—the Confederation's largest and dominant member—continued to be elected by the three-class system of voting.

In fact, in 1866 the liberals sacrificed political gains for achievements in the areas of trade and economic policy. The North German Confederation combined the advantages of the Zollverein with the benefits of a single commercial code for the Confederation's states, thereby greatly facilitating the establishment of banking and industrial operations. The new commercial code even pleased the embryonic workers' organizations by removing the old Confederation's prohibition on labor unions. At the same time the Prussian and Confederation leaders remained solidly committed to a policy of free trade. Symptomatic of this decision was the appointment of Rudolf Delbrück, a liberal and fanatic free trader, as chief of staff in the Confederation's executive office. For the next ten years Delbrück remained the dominant figure in determining German economic policy.

The North German Confederation, then, was a genuine if somewhat unequal compromise. Bismarck and the Junkers achieved Prussian hegemony in northern Germany that assured their predominance over political liberalism and parliamentarism. The liberals obtained a democratically elected, albeit largely impotent, parliament and had the illusion that national unification was a step closer. Above all, however, the new Confederation removed the last legal and institutional barriers to Germany's rapid economic modernization.

Unforeseen changes in the international balance of power shortened the life of the North German Confederation. In a sense the chain of events began with some untidy ends left by the Austro-Prussian War. At that time France—in particular its emperor, Napoleon III—had hoped to use diplomatic pressure to impose a settlement on the two German powers. The swift Prussian military victory prevented Napoleon's diplomatic intervention, and for the next four years the French emperor, already beset by serious domestic problems, sought frantically to regain popularity at home by providing evidence of a diplomatic triumph abroad. Adroitly, Bismarck thwarted Napoleon's ambitions in Luxembourg and Belgium, until, by 1870 only the Spanish question remained to provide at least a negative French triumph.

Like the Schleswig-Holstein question, the succession to the Spanish throne provided massive opportunities for the intervention of the Great Powers. After a series of juntas and regents proved unable to provide political stability for the country, the leaders of the various Spanish factions agreed to go outside the country for a new ruler. Their eventual choice was Leopold von Hohenzollern-Sigmaringen, a member of the Catholic branch of the Prussian royal family. The prince was not in direct line of succession to the Prussian throne, but he was a nephew of King William I, and France was understandably concerned about the prospect of installing a Hohenzollern prince on the Spanish throne. Napoleon formally objected to Leopold's becoming king of Spain, and the prince did indeed withdraw his candidacy. The crisis seemed to be settled until both Napoleon and Bismarck (for reasons of domestic politics) decided to use the issue to inflame French and German public opinion. Bismarck proved to be far better in this game of nerves and public relations. France declared war on the North German Confederation in July 1870, at a time when the French military was in no way prepared for a major conflict.

The Franco-Prussian War was not only the longest of the three "wars of unification," it also had the most far-reaching and in many ways the most unfortunate results. The defeat of France led to Napoleon's abdication and the establishment of the French Third Republic. Under the terms of the Treaty of Frankfurt, which ended the conflict, France lost the provinces of Alsace and Lorraine, and it had to pay a large indemnity to the victorious Germans.

The founding of the German Empire was a direct consequence of Prussia's victory in the Franco-Prussian War. Unfortunately, the manner in which Germany was unified proved to be a major liability for future Franco-German relations and the development of democracy

Map 1.2   Germany 1866–1918

in Germany. The Franco-Prussian War was a war of nations. On both sides of the Rhine, nationalistic passions were raised to a fever pitch. After France had declared war on the North German Confederation, the southern German states, who were not members of the Confederation and therefore technically not parties to the conflict, were immediately pressured by public opinion in their territories to join Prussia and its allies in declaring war on

France. The concept of the *hereditary enmity* between Germany and France (a term that had been invented by French and German newspapers in the 1840s) was given a new lease on life. Even more tragically, the achievement of German unity became associated with the idea of a military victory over the neighboring nation. (The date of the decisive engagement in that conflict, the Battle of Sedan on September 5, 1870, became a national holiday in the new Reich.) Staging the ceremony that proclaimed the founding of the German Reich in the Hall of Mirrors at the Palace of Versailles on January 18, 1871, symbolized Germany's military triumph and France's humiliation.

But fears for the future certainly did not concern the Germans at the beginning of 1871. Seemingly all that mattered was that the nation had finally been united. After the initial triumph over Napoleon's armies, the southern German states joined with the North German Confederation in forming what became known as the Second German Reich. More precisely, the rulers of the southern lands negotiated with the king of Prussia and his allies to establish a union of princes that bore the name German Reich. (The term *Second Reich* was used to indicate that Bismarck's creation was the historic successor to the First or Holy Roman Empire, which Napoleon I had dissolved in 1806.) Here lay a major difference between the Reich of 1871 and anything envisioned at Frankfurt in 1848: The new Reich was the work of Bismarck and the princes; the German people had little part in determining the terms of its establishment. The German princes agreed that the king of Prussia and his heirs should be hereditary German emperors. In addition, Prussia's territorial gains of 1866 remained intact; the south did not challenge Prussian political and territorial hegemony in northern Germany. In a very real sense, the new Reich represented the ultimate triumph of the forces of the Prussian counterrevolution.

Contemporaries and historians have interpreted the significance of the events of 1871 in startlingly different ways. For most Germans the founding of the empire was evidence that providence had singled them and Germany out for special blessings. The military triumph over France, the annexation of Alsace-Lorraine, and 5 billion French francs (about 4 billion marks) in French reparations—here was clear evidence that God stood on the side of the Germans. As if to underscore the connection, the German victory and unity celebrations were permeated virtually everywhere by a tasteless amalgamation of chauvinism

and religiosity. Even the liberals seemed to have been converted to unabashed militaristic nationalism.

Later historians emphasized that unification was not the solution to the problems and tensions that beset Germany before and after 1871. Recent writings treat the years from 1871 to Bismarck's retirement in 1890 as a time in which German society should be looked on as a "patient" beset by serious ailments. The reasons for the contrasting views are not difficult to discern. Contemporaries looked back on a divisive past and consequently saw unification as the beginning of a great future. With the benefit of hindsight, later historians analyzed the faults of the Second Empire as forebodings of the disasters that would follow.

It was naive to believe, as most in the founders' generation did, that unification alone provided Germany with a magic key to cope successfully with the larger dilemmas affecting its society. Political unification certainly did not eliminate economic difficulties. After a two-year boom, for the next twenty years the Reich, despite some ups and downs in the economic indicators, experienced what was essentially a generation-long depression.

It was not entirely surprising, then, that the founders' generation, although celebrating the present, seemed strangely insecure about its future. These years were permeated with a wholly irrational fear of revolution, with the agents of upheaval successively identified as the French, the Catholics, and the socialists. Among intellectuals and artists a sense of pessimism about the future of humankind abounded. Friedrich Nietzsche, perhaps the most famous critic of the German society in the early years of the new empire, wrote bitingly about the foibles of his generation. His targets included everything from false religious fervor to the self-satisfied smugness of the German bourgeoisie. Similarly, Richard Wagner's operas, for all their surface nationalism, end in the *Götterdämmerung*, the destruction of the world of gods and humans. The Viennese poet Hugo von Hofmannsthal was not entirely facetious when he noted that the men and women of the 1860s and 1870s

A French cartoonist's view of the North German Confederation: A heavy-footed Bismarck is using the defeated German states as rungs on a ladder to reach unification under Prussian domination. (Source: akg-images.)

had left his own generation, that of the early twentieth century, two legacies: pretty furniture and hypersensitive nerves.

To be sure, gloom and doom did not replace joy and triumph. If the problems were real, so was the ability of the founders' generation to sublimate and escape them. A favorite device was to celebrate the glories of history. Professional historians did their part, but the country was also flooded with historical novels and romances—the latter often little burdened by any real knowledge of the facts. There seemed to be an insatiable market for highly fanciful treatments of every conceivable historic era from the Egyptians to the recent wars of unification. Life among the Germanic tribes and adventures located in the Middle Ages found a particularly appreciative reading public. Common to all was a "glittering national pride." Many a democrat who had played a prominent part in the events of 1848 now wrote a historical romance assuring readers that earlier longings had been fulfilled by the recent victory of Prussian arms. But while national synthesis replaced the earlier fictional accounts of conflicts among the Germans, nationality conflicts continued unabated in the stories of Germans and Poles in eastern Germany. Here a happy synthesis of German and Slavic cultures was not permitted to take place; German civilization had to triumph.

The desire for reliving imagined past glories was not restricted to literature. Like its European neighbors, German builders exhibited a peculiar inability to find an architectural style to express the functional changes brought about by the Industrial Revolution. All over Germany (and the rest of the continent) builders erected railroad stations that looked like pseudo-Gothic cathedrals and post offices that resembled Renaissance palaces.

Historical fiction and incongruous architecture were relatively harmless ways of denying the problems of the present. The consequences of the phenomenon that Gerhard Ritter has called "the militarization of the bourgeoisie" were far more serious. The phrase referred to the excessive awe in which the German middle classes held the military. Emotional dependence on the military expressed itself not only in such outward signs as excessive respect for uniforms, but above all through the transference of military forms of etiquette and thinking to civilian organizations and activities. Teachers attempted to model themselves after drill sergeants, and middle-age businessmen proudly displayed their reserve officers' commissions. In effect, the militarization of the bourgeoisie meant the acceptance by the German middle classes of the military's position at the apex of German society. The dictum was epitomized by the writings of the historian Heinrich von Treitschke. A former liberal, Treitschke beginning in 1879 published a multivolume *History of Germany in the Nineteenth Century,* setting out to prove that in the final analysis, military power alone determines a nation's destiny.

Even more disastrous for the future of the country was yet another manner of escaping the problems of modernity, anti-Semitism. Here, too, Treitschke served as an example. Like other intellectuals in Germany and elsewhere, he identified the alienating and negative aspects of modern industrialism with the influence of Jews in society. The anti-Semitism of the founders' generation was linked to the earlier sentiments of novelists like Gustav Freytag and Wilhelm Raabe, but the new anti-Semitism also borrowed heavily and ominously from the pseudoracial theories first introduced in France by the writings of Count Gobineau. Although the Jewish characters in Freytag's and Raabe's novels tended to be identified as recent immigrants whose personalities improved with assimilation, late nineteenth-century anti-Semitism attributed Jewish "evils" to the ethnic makeup of the Jewish people. For these writers the only solution to the "Jewish problem" was to reverse the progress of Jewish legal emancipation and immigration. Still, it should be pointed out that German anti-Semitism at this time was neither unique in Europe nor particularly pervasive or virulent.

As the depression continued and the social problems associated with it became increasingly difficult to ignore, there was a brief period during the 1880s when it appeared that a more realistic mind-set would prevail. There were some serious attempts to liberate the middle classes from their emotional dependence on the military and to persuade them to face realistically the problems of their own generation. In novels and musical compositions, specifically bourgeois forms and values emerged. A naturalist and realist style, largely borrowed from Emile Zola and other French writers, found its way into German literature. Instead of finding their heroes in the past, writers looked at the problems of their own time: rampant industrialization, urban slums, and the destruction of lives through inhuman conditions in the workplace. Authors like Theodor Fontane wrote brilliant, sympathetic, and moving descriptions of the fast-paced, pulsating life in the Reich capital. In music Johannes Brahms created compositions with a somber and specifically bourgeois character. Realism and naturalism even served as a counterweight to the militarization of society. Insofar as the naturalist authors were optimistic about the future of their society, they celebrated science rather than military power as the answer to its problems.

Unfortunately, as discussed in more detail later, the bourgeois revolt, if that is what it can be called, did not lead to any fundamental changes in the prevailing mood of German society. Fear of a Marxist revolution led most Germans to seek refuge once again in emotional and political association with militarism and nationalism. At the end of the 1880s, German society was no closer to facing its problems realistically or solving them than it had been twenty years earlier.

THE FABRIC OF SOCIETY: ECONOMIC AND POLITICAL POWER STRUCTURES

In 1871 Germany's 41 million inhabitants were living in a society that was on the threshold of changing from a primarily agricultural society to one dominated by industry and manufacturing. When the Reich was founded, about 50 percent of the workforce was still employed in agriculture. Ten years later most Germans worked in industrial or manufacturing jobs. Changes in the relative value of landed and liquid wealth accompanied the shift in employment patterns. Real property, at least in the form of agricultural holdings, decreased in relative worth while the value of liquid and industrial assets increased.

During the next thirty years, the modernization of Germany acquired a dynamic of its own. By 1907 three out of every four German workers were employed in industry. Most of them were blue-collar employees, but as industrial production became increasingly linked to higher technology, the number of white-collar workers grew rapidly as well. Less than 2 percent of the workforce in 1882, white-collar workers in 1907 comprised more than 6 percent of all German employees. In other words, within one generation, German society had assumed the social profile characteristic of highly developed capitalist societies.

Industrialization and modernization went hand in hand with urbanization and internal immigration. A steady stream of Germans moved from east to west, swelling the population of industrial centers in central Germany and those along the Ruhr and Rhine Rivers. It was not difficult to see the reason. Whatever the hardships of industrial labor, they were preferable to the bleak future facing a landless peasant on the estates of East Elbia. (In the East, German farm workers were replaced by increasing numbers of Polish migrant farm laborers.) Modernization had its effect on the spectrum of German political parties as well. The traditional Conservative and Liberal parties were joined by new organizations formed to address the conditions and problems associated with modernization and unification, notably a Catholic party and groups representing industrial labor.

For the German conservatives, modernization meant being confronted with the increasing irrelevance of their political ideas. Traditionally, Prussian conservatism—the dominant form of this political philosophy in Germany—had preferred Prussian particularism to German nationalism, favored agriculture over industry, and praised hierarchically determined responsibilities instead of individual freedoms. Conservatives had also insisted that political authoritarianism based on the union of throne, altar, and army should prevail over popular elections and parliamentarism. The world of 1871 hardly fit the conservatives' ideal. The unified Reich (dominated by Prussia, to be sure) had a government that espoused economic liberalism (which in those days meant a free-market economy, largely unfettered by government regulations, and an investor-friendly tax structure), as well as a national constitution that contained provisions for the election of a lower house of the national parliament (the Reichstag) on the basis of universal male suffrage.

Under the impact of the new situation, the Conservatives split into two groups, German Conservatives and Free Conservatives. The two groups were united in their unflinching defense of the authoritarian system established in Prussia after 1851, but they differed in their attitude toward the new Reich. Whereas the German Conservatives emphasized the need to preserve the old ways untainted by the innovations of modernism, the Free Conservatives endorsed national unification and industrialization as means of strengthening the power of Prussian conservatism in all of Germany.

Under the rules of universal male suffrage, the conservatives were at a decided disadvantage. (In Prussia, of course, the retention of the three-class system of voting assured them a dominant political position.) Traditionally, conservative voting strength came from the rural areas of Germany: Peasants and estate owners, Protestant clergy, and the inhabitants of small towns formed the heart of the conservative constituency. As Germany became increasingly industrialized, this support base was eroded through natural attrition. The rural population steadily declined; larger urban concentrations absorbed many small towns. The result was a precipitous decline of the conservatives' strength in the national parliament. By 1912 only about one in ten

German voters cast his ballot for one of the conservative parties.

The liberals also went separate ways. They split over the issue of the Indemnity Bill of 1866 (see earlier discussion, p. 7). The right-wing liberals, who gave themselves the name National Liberals, were willing to forgive Bismarck his high-handed and unconstitutional actions after he became Prussian prime minister in 1862; they wholeheartedly endorsed his engineering of the North German Confederation and after unification worked closely with the imperial chancellor and the German Conservatives in forging the new Reich. The left-wing liberals, or Progressives, were less forgiving of Bismarck's contempt of parliament; in the new national legislature they continued to press for increased parliamentary rights. Nevertheless, the estranged brothers drew closer together after unification: The Progressives supported national union under Bismarckian auspices as enthusiastically as their right-wing colleagues, and the divided liberals held similar views on a number of other issues as well. Until 1878 both liberal parties were unequivocally committed to major tenets of liberalism, including free trade, anticlericalism, and, with some variations in emphasis, civil liberties.

The two liberal parties appealed to many of the same voters, mostly various segments of the middle classes. The National Liberals were particularly strong among the upper bourgeoisie, especially the new "barons of industry." The Progressives, in contrast, did well among the ranks of the traditional *Mittelstand* and owners of family farms. (*Mittelstand* is one of those difficult-to-translate German words. In one sense it simply means middle class, but especially when used with modifiers such as "traditional" or "old" it refers primarily to occupational groups that existed before the advent of modern industrialization: the professions, small manufacturers, retailers, merchants, and independent artisans.) Neither party received much worker support, but only the Progressives were fitfully concerned about liberalism's lack of appeal among the industrial proletariat.

A shift in government policy in the late 1870s, away from free trade and in favor of protective tariffs (see a later section, p. 27), resulted in yet another liberal split. The Progressives unanimously rejected the new direction, but a majority of the National Liberal Party went along with the government's about-face. A minority among the National Liberals, however, regarded tariffs as a betrayal of a sacred liberal principle and seceded from the party. This group, which included a number of National Liberal leaders, formed several new political organizations that eventually merged with the Progressives.

When Germany was unified along *kleindeutsch* lines, Catholics not only became a permanent religious minority in the country, but they also confronted a rising tide of anticlericalism and anti-Catholicism from the liberal and Marxist parties. (The terms *kleindeutsch* [little German] and *grossdeutsch* [large German] derived from a bitter, if meaningless, dispute over German unification during the Revolution of 1848. The proponents of kleindeutsch wanted to exclude all of Austria-Hungary from any united Germany, whereas the advocates of grossdeutsch insisted the German-speaking parts of Austria had to be included in any future Reich.) One result of these concerns was the founding, in 1870, of the Center Party. (The name derived from its position in the center of the parliamentary seating chart.) Under the skilled leadership of Ludwig Windthorst, the last minister of justice of the Kingdom of Hanover before it was annexed by Prussia, the Center Party quickly established itself as an effective political voice for German Catholics. From the beginning, the party assumed an essentially defensive stance. It defined its primary task as safeguarding Catholic rights, particularly in the areas of education and public financial support for church institutions.

For virtually the entire span of its political life, the Center Party limited its appeal for members and voters to Catholics. It saw all German Catholics, from industrial laborers to landed magnates, threatened by an army of Protestants and anticlericals. The Center Party wanted to rally the entire Catholic constituency to what its leaders called the "Center Tower." It is true that from time to time voices within the party advocated transforming the group into a political organization that appealed to both Protestants and Catholics, but such proposals were always quickly silenced by the party's leadership. Although it was a political voice of Catholicism, the Center Party was not controlled by the clergy. Windthorst early on determined there was to be cooperation but not subordination. The Center Party remained at all times a Catholic lay organization with its own program and leadership.

The Center Party did not succeed in becoming the party of all Catholics, however. On the average, somewhere between 50 and 60 percent of those Catholics who voted cast their ballots for the Center Party. The percentage was highest among middle- and upper-class voters and in rural areas, lowest among industrial workers. Still, over the years these voting percentages also remained remarkably stable, so the party's leaders could count on roughly the same number of parliamentary seats after every national election.

If stability was the primary characteristic of the Center Party, explosive growth epitomized the development of the Sozialdemokratische Partei Deutschlands (Social Democratic Party of Germany, SPD). This political group had been formed in 1875 by the merger of two earlier organizations, the General German Workers' Association (Allgemeiner Deutscher Arbeiterverein), founded in 1863, and the Social Democratic Party, established in 1869. Although both groups saw themselves as representatives of the nascent industrial proletariat, originally the two organizations had quite dissimilar views of the political future of this segment of German society. Ferdinand Lassalle, the founder of the Workers' Association, favored kleindeutsch nationalism and cooperation with the state authorities in order to curtail the power of private enterprise, whereas the Social Democrats followed Karl Marx in rejecting narrow nationalism and identifying the bourgeois state as the handmaiden

of capitalist domination. The German socialists identified nationalism in any form as
part of the bourgeois "superstructure" of a
capitalist society. As a result they refused to
join in the rejoicing over national unification, whether kleindeutsch or grossdeutsch.
According to the socialists, only a political
revolution could liberate the proletariat from
the oppression of capitalism and the illusions
of nationalism.

In the new party, Marxist leaders and
ideas soon predominated. (Lassalle himself had in the meantime been killed in a
duel over a love affair.) At its founding congress in Gotha (1875), the party adopted a
program that was closer to the principles
Lassalle had enunciated earlier, but by 1891,
under the impact of Marx' fierce criticism
of the Gotha Program and Bismarck's Anti-
Socialist Laws (see the discussion on p. 30),
the SPD's platform followed the tenets of
Marxist orthodoxy. After 1891 the party was
committed to an ideology of revolution on
the basis of class struggle and dialectical
materialism. It contended the interests of
labor and capital were irreconcilable, and
capitalism, the dominant form of socioeconomic organization in the nineteenth century, would eventually be replaced by the
ultimate and highest form of human society,
socialism (and beyond that, communism) in
which common ownership of the means of
production would replace private capitalist
control. The instrument that would achieve
the transition from capitalism to socialism
was an act of revolution by the industrial
proletariat. In preparation for this revolution the workers had to organize themselves
politically in the Social Democratic Party
and economically through labor unions.
Theoretically, the two labor organizations
complemented each other: While the party
prepared the proletariat for the political
future, the unions sought to bring about
material improvements in the present.

The SPD was a class-specific organization.
Although many of its early leaders were middle-class intellectuals, the party proclaimed

that its goal was to obtain the votes and support of the industrial proletariat. Here the
party was remarkably successful. But the
SPD's support was never limited to Germany's
blue-collar workers. Even during the imperial
years a not insignificant number of middle-
class voters cast their ballots for the SPD. In
addition, it is clear from the electoral returns
that despite the party's anticlerical stance
(the Marxists also rejected organized religion
as part of the superstructure of capitalism), a
significant number of Protestant and Catholic
industrial workers consistently supported the
SPD rather than the Center Party or one of
the conservative groups supported by the
Protestant churches.

Catholic workers' and Protestant middle-
class support for an openly anticlerical and
revolutionary party illustrated what was to
become a growing problem for the SPD.
Almost from the day of its founding, the
SPD's revolutionary rhetoric contrasted
with its reformist behavior. As the socialists'
appeal grew, it became increasingly clear that
the party derived most of its mass support not
from the promise of political revolution, but
from its simultaneous advocacy of political
and social reforms and its close association
with the labor union movement. Because
most unions advocated parliamentary reform
and slow and steady improvements in wages
and working conditions, the party's revolutionary rhetoric became increasingly remote
from the members' day-to-day lives.

An overwhelming majority of German
voters supported one of the four group-
ings just discussed, that is, the conservatives, the liberals, the Catholics, and the
socialists. During the twenty years of the
founders' generation, the strongest parties
were the National Liberals and the Center
Party. The popular vote for the various conservative parties declined steadily, and that
of the Progressives fluctuated wildly. Still
the real success story was the SPD. At the
beginning of the Bismarck era, the Social
Democrats had one representative in the
national parliament; when the chancellor

left office, the number had risen to thirty-five. (The membership of the Reichstag was about four hundred.)

The constitutional structure of the Reich institutionalized what historians have called the Bismarck Compromise. It embodied three basic principles. To begin with, it maximized Bismarck's personal power. Second, it combined conservative authoritarian political ideas with liberal economic precepts. Finally, as a sort of corollary to the second principle, Bismarck rejected as "unconstitutional" demands for a share of political power by groups that became politically significant after the Compromise had been established, notably the Catholics and socialists. The constitution of 1871 was to benefit primarily conservatives and liberals. The document did not provide room for any post-1871 dynamics; it was designed to freeze the settlement of 1871 into permanence.

The constitution of 1871, modeled on that of the North German Confederation, was largely written by Bismarck and, with some changes, approved by the German princes. Its eventual adoption by the national parliament was pro forma. Under the terms of the document the German Reich became a hereditary monarchy with the imperial crown vested in the Prussian royal family. The king of Prussia was simultaneously German emperor. There was a national bicameral legislature, consisting of the Reichstag, elected on the basis of universal male suffrage, and the Bundesrat (Federal Council), which was composed of delegates sent by the various state governments. Prussia dominated the second chamber. The presiding officer of the Federal Council was always a Prussian government official, and the state controlled the largest block of delegates, seventeen out of fifty-eight. (Note that universal male suffrage applied only for election to the Reichstag. The states retained their own suffrage laws.)

The powers of the popularly elected parliament were severely restricted. There was no provision for ministerial responsibility, so the Reich chancellor and his cabinet served at the pleasure of the emperor, not parliament. Moreover, all federal legislation had to be approved both by the Reichstag and the Bundesrat, which gave the Prussian state government a virtual veto power over national initiatives. The Reichstag did have the power of the purse, but the federal budget, much like that of the North German Confederation, made up a very small part of the total public expenditures in the Reich.

At the time of its founding, the Second Reich had an embryonic national executive. In fact, originally there were only two cabinet offices, those of the Reich chancellor and foreign minister. Bismarck held both portfolios. Not until the late 1870s were additional cabinet-level offices created. There was also virtually no federal civil service. Federal legislation was commonly administered by the state bureaucracies, which meant in practice that the Prussian bureaucracy was in charge of implementing Reich laws in most of Germany.

The German Constitution and the terms of the Bismarck Compromise placed major decision-making power in the hands of a small and sociopolitically homogeneous circle of men. An estimated twenty individuals made all major political decisions in the years 1870–1890. This elite group, as well as their two hundred or so associates who headed the major administrative offices in the empire, came from essentially similar social backgrounds. They belonged to the aristocracy or, if not originally noble, were rewarded with a noble title in the course of their careers. They all went through roughly the same educational system and joined the same select group of fraternal organizations.

It has often been noted that the terms of the Bismarck Compromise were heavily influenced by the chancellor's experiences during the Prussian constitutional conflict. Nowhere was this more apparent than in the position of the military under the constitution of 1871. In times of peace there was no federal armed force, only the armies of the individual states. (In practice, except for Bavaria and Württemberg, most of the states' armed forces were integrated into the Prussian army structure.) The national parliament had no influence over the command structure or the composition of the officer corps in any of the units of the armed forces. Once war had been declared (in the nineteenth century it was axiomatic that civilized nations did not fight wars without formal declarations), the state armies were federalized under the command of the emperor, who was, of course, the king of Prussia.

Except for its power of the purse, parliament was to have no substantive say in military affairs, but the Reich's leaders expected little resentment from the public at large. They hoped that after the victories of the Franco-Prussian War, public opinion would agree that the army was entitled to special privileges, and for the most part they were right: The German military, and particularly the Prussian army, had reached an unprecedented level of prestige and popularity. In 1871 most Germans probably agreed with the assessment by the Prussian minister of war, General von Roon, that "an efficient army is the only conceivable protection against both the red and the black specter [that is, international Marxism and Catholicism]. If you ruin the army, it is goodbye to Prussia's glory and Germany's greatness."

Constitutions are skeletons for the political and social life of a country. Ideally, the document should not only be well designed for the time during which it was written, but, perhaps even more important, it should allow for the possibility of amendments as political conditions change. Bismarck's constitution of 1871 failed on both counts. It was seriously flawed from the beginning, and it provided virtually no flexibility for the future. One glaring shortcoming was the fact that Bismarck had designed it specifically to ensure his own personal power. The constitution, in other words, was not designed to permit political life to evolve, but to keep one individual in power.

The inadequacies of the constitution became apparent very soon. To begin with, industrialization brought with it the need for expanded governmental structures at the federal level. As a result, between 1877 and the end of the decade, three new federal cabinet posts were created: the Ministry of the Interior, the Ministry of Justice, and the Treasury Department. However, all were headed in "personal union" by cabinet officers who chaired the analogous Prussian state ministries, so the expansion of the federal bureaucracy did not diminish the influence of the states in federal affairs.

Bismarck was also concerned about military–civilian relations within the executive. Although for the most part Bismarck and the military agreed on major policy decisions, the chancellor recognized the military's ambitions for power aggrandizement and sought to contain them. A number of prominent officers thought the military should make policy decisions independent of the chancellor's office, subject only to the dictates of the emperor, but Bismarck insisted on the priority of the civilian executive. The chancellor vigorously opposed plans to create the office of federal minister of war, arguing the chancellor should remain the emperor's only constitutional adviser on all federal military policies.

Bismarck and the military quickly joined forces, however, when it came to minimizing the Reichstag's influence over military affairs. A conflict between parliament and the military emerged soon after the Reich was established. In 1874 the federal government introduced a so-called eternity bill (*Äternat*). Under its provisions the Reichstag would have agreed to provide the military for their federal duties with appropriations at current levels of funding in perpetuity, provided the numerical strength of the armed forces remained unchanged. In effect, the Reichstag would have abdicated even the rudimentary controls over the military budget that the constitution allotted it. Even in the heady days of the mid-1870s, the majority of the national parliament was unwilling to go this far. The government eventually had to settle for a "seven-year law" (*Septennat*), which gave the military a monetary free hand until 1881, but not in perpetuity.

The conflict of 1874 was symptomatic of what was perhaps the greatest problem with the Bismarck constitution of 1871. As noted earlier, it made no provisions for adapting to the shifting dynamics of German political life. Bismarck had agreed to a democratically elected national parliament largely because he felt the legislature itself could be ignored as a factor in the political decision-making process. It soon became clear to both Bismarck and his opponents, however, that parliament would play a crucial role in Germany's evolving political life. Bismarck himself early on recognized his "mistake" in agreeing to universal male suffrage as the method for electing the Reichstag and repeatedly considered proposals for amending the constitution to provide for a third federal legislative chamber. He hoped that a body composed of representatives elected from the membership of occupational and professional groups, a so-called economic parliament, would have a more conservative outlook than the popularly elected members of the Reichstag.

When these and other efforts at diluting the strength of the democratically elected national parliament failed, Bismarck increasingly resorted to other means to influence the domestic balance of power in his favor. He created artificial confrontations in which he attempted to rally the original supporters of the Bismarck Compromise against a succession of imagined "enemies of the Reich."

THE KULTURKAMPF

One of the more quixotic episodes in German history was the Kulturkampf, or "culture war." This bitter and unnecessary altercation pitted two unlikely allies, Bismarck and the liberals (who coined the term *Kulturkampf*), against the clerical and political leadership of Germany's Catholic minority. Although Bismarck and the liberals were allied in the Kulturkampf, their motives for pursuing the struggle were quite different, a factor that became increasingly significant as the altercation went on. For Bismarck the Kulturkampf was a political battle to defeat what the chancellor saw as a challenge to his Compromise. For the liberals, however, the Kulturkampf was a classic nineteenth-century conflict between church and state, in which the liberal ideas of "progress, science, and rationality" were arrayed against the dark forces of "superstition and clerical reaction."

Bismarck and the liberals always maintained that the conflict was initiated by the Catholic Church, and in a way they were right. Faced with a rising tide of anticlerical modernism in the second half of the century, church leaders, including the aged Pope Pius IX, felt it was necessary to reestablish church authority in the areas of doctrine and morals. As a result, the leaders hoped, the church would be able to provide more effective guidance to Catholics as they confronted what church leaders saw as the errors and temptations of the secular world. This was one of the considerations that led to the promulgation of the dogma of papal infallibility at the first Vatican Council in 1870. According to this doctrine, when speaking ex cathedra ("from the chair [of St. Peter]"), the pope's rulings on matters of faith and morals were binding on all Catholics.

The theological validity of the doctrine was sharply debated both before and during the Council sessions, and among the opposition to the new dogma were a number of German bishops and professors of Catholic theology. They opposed the majority view partly on theological grounds, but also because they felt it concentrated too much church authority in the hands of "ultramontane" (literally, "beyond the mountains," that is, the Alps) officials, in other words, the Vatican bureaucracy. After the Vatican Council had made its decision, however, virtually all German Catholic leaders accepted the new doctrine.

The promulgation of the papal infallibility dogma came at about the same time Germany achieved its unification, and it could be argued that for the Catholic leadership a Germany dominated by a Protestant majority constituted one of the dangers that the new doctrine was designed to combat. Similarly, Bismarck and the liberals were convinced that the founding of the Center Party in December 1870 was designed to provide the pope with yet another weapon to combat the newly united Germany. Actually, there was no direct link between the dogma of papal infallibility, the establishment of the German Catholic political organization, and the unification of the Reich.

Bismarck and the liberals contended that through the infallibility dogma and in cooperation with the leaders of the Center Party, the pope was attempting to undermine the political balance of power established in the Bismarck Compromise of 1871. Consequently, they argued the German Catholics, or at least those who supported the Center Party, were acting against the interests of the Reich; they had become "enemies of the Reich." Because Catholics welcomed national unification no less enthusiastically than other Germans, it is difficult to see any evidence of a Catholic conspiracy against Bismarck's handiwork. In fact, there was none. To be sure, it was true that in 1871 Catholics constituted a potentially volatile minority in the country. The Reich's Catholic population was composed of three ethnic groups: Germans along the Rhine, in southern Germany, and in Silesia; Poles in East Elbia and, increasingly, the industrial west; and, after unification, the French of Alsace-Lorraine. Understandably, the Poles and the French were not enthusiastic about their inclusion in the German Empire, and Bismarck was not totally wrong in expecting them to use religion for nationalistic and political purposes. But as far as the German Catholics were concerned, Bismarck had Prussian rather than Reich worries. He profoundly distrusted and disliked the Center Party's national leader, Ludwig Windthorst. In turn, Windthorst left no doubt about his own bitterness over the annexation of Hanover by Prussia.

The problem was compounded by the close intertwining of church and state in nineteenth-century Germany. Separation of church and state existed neither in theory nor in practice. Public schools were segregated along religious lines; religious instruction was part of the compulsory curriculum. Professors of theology were state civil servants, just like other university teaching personnel. The states, or technically the princes, had a say in ecclesiastical appointments. Finally, both the Protestant and Catholic churches were supported by public taxes and subsidies.

Bismarck's ire focused on the Center Party. His answer to the imaginary danger was simple: The pope had created the Center Party, and it was up to the pope and the ecclesiastical authorities to control and prevent the party from organizing Germany's Catholics as a political pressure group. (What Bismarck and the liberals had in mind was a papal decree dissolving the Center Party.) This view of the situation was profoundly naive. It completely misjudged the nature of the Center Party. The party was a grassroots organization of the laity over which the German bishops, much less the pope, had only very limited influence. Consequently, even if the pope had wanted to control the German party, it is doubtful that he could have done so, particularly because the infallibility dogma did not cover political matters.

Bismarck and the liberals interpreted the pope's unwillingness to act as resistance that would have to be broken. Bismarck left it to the liberals to choose the specific means of breaking the Catholic "resistance," and not surprisingly they turned to the legislative arsenal typical of conflicts between church and state in nineteenth-century Europe: a series of laws designed to increase secular control over church affairs. Most of the legislation came at the state level because under the German federal system, educational and ecclesiastical matters were subject to state rather than federal control. One exception to this rule was a federal law of 1872 that legislated the expulsion from Germany of all foreign members of the Jesuit Order.

As the largest state, Prussia led the way. Under the leadership of the vehemently anticlerical minister of education, Adalbert Falk, the state legislature passed a package of legislation that became known as the May Laws of 1873. They stipulated the appointment of lay inspectors for public schools, provided for compulsory civil marriage (in addition to, not as a substitute for, a church ceremony), and instituted state supervision of seminaries and monastic orders. These laws applied to the Protestant churches as well, but they tended to be enforced only against Catholics.

The reaction of the papacy and Germany's Catholics was strong, and from Bismarck's point of view, completely counterproductive. In one of the last acts before his death, Pope Pius IX in May 1875 declared the entire package of Kulturkampf laws invalid and morally not binding on Catholics. Prussia responded by expelling priests and bishops from their parishes and sees, leaving a large number of vacancies. Eventually in 1878 Prussia cut off all financial subsidies (but not the regular income from church taxes) to the Catholic Church. All in vain. Catholics neither deserted their church, nor did they cease their support of the Center Party. Rather, the discriminatory legislation forged a closer alliance among laity, political organization, and clergy. Symptomatic of this development was the increase of the Center Party vote. The party obtained fifty-eight seats in the Reichstag elections of 1871, before the Kulturkampf began in earnest, but in the 1874 contest, after the May Laws had been in effect for almost two years, the figure rose to ninety-one. It stayed at this level, with only minor fluctuations, until the end of the empire.

Still, as the decade of the 1870s wore on, Bismarck and the church authorities concluded that it was in the interest of both to end the animosity. A turning point came with the death of Pius IX in February 1878. Partly because of his own bitter personal experiences with the Italian liberals, Pius IX had come to regard the anticlericalism of the liberals as the primary danger facing the Catholic faith. His successor, Leo XIII, was less concerned with liberalism and more worried about the challenge from the emerging Marxist organizations. As a result, he was anxious to end the altercation with Bismarck and the German liberals in order to concentrate the church's defensive efforts in Germany on combating the influence of Marxism. Bismarck, too, was concerned about the rising Marxist tide. In addition, the Protestant churches were growing uneasy over the blatant anticlericalism of the liberal proponents of the Kulturkampf.

Confidential negotiations between representatives of the German and Prussian governments and the papacy to end the Kulturkampf began in 1876. Three years later the parties reached an agreement. With the exception of the ban on foreign Jesuits and the law on civil marriage, the government agreed to either rescind or no longer enforce all of the anti-Catholic measures. This was a clear victory for the German Catholics, but the chancellor came away satisfied as well. The agreement with the papacy permitted Bismarck to claim that he was not defeated by a domestic opponent but had reached an accord with a foreign power, the Holy See. Formally, the Bismarck Compromise remained intact; the German Catholics had not been able to break the political power monopoly of the liberals and conservatives. For this reason the Kulturkampf left a lasting and bitter legacy. Germany's Catholics continued to feel that they were second-class citizens, never quite accepted by the Protestant majority. And they were not entirely wrong. As late as 1918 personnel records of the Prussian civil service were replete with judgments like "although a Catholic, he is a quite decent fellow." At the end of the 1870s, Catholics had ceased being "enemies of the Reich," but they never quite became the empire's friends.

Im Mittelpunkt   **Ludwig Windthorst (1812–1891)**

The quintessential outsider, Ludwig Windthorst came to be a thorn in the flesh of many a prominent personality during the course of his long life. He is best known, of course, as the leader of the Catholic opposition during the Kulturkampf, but at a later time his devout Catholicism did not prevent him from clashing with the Pope.

Windthorst was a round peg in a square hole almost from his birth. He was born into a Catholic middle-class family in an area of Germany, Hanover, which was and still is overwhelmingly Protestant. Windthorst studied administrative law at the University of Göttingen (the same institution from which Bismarck obtained his degree), and for a time he followed the traditional career of a Hanoverian civil servant. In the course of his career he had both legislative and executive functions. He was a member of the Hanoverian parliament in 1849 but quickly switched to the executive branch. From 1851 to 1853 and again from 1862 to 1865, he served as the state's minister of justice, the first Catholic member of the Hanoverian cabinet. Windthorst's politics were those of a fervent and rather conservative particularist. Throughout his long life, he attempted to be a loyal subject of the Hanoverian king.

Windthorst's life and career changed abruptly in 1866. During the Austro-Prussian War Hanover sided with the Austrians and as a consequence the state was annexed by Prussia. Windthorst never forgave the Prussians and especially Bismarck for what he regarded as a naked act of aggression. During the negotiations between the Prussian government and the Hanoverian royal house over a financial settlement for the deposed king, Windthorst acted as the monarch's legal adviser.

The unification of the Reich filled Windthorst with new resentments against Prussia. He looked on the unified Reich as a Prussified Germany, dominated by a Protestant majority and a Protestant royal house. Determined to safeguard the rights of Germany's Catholic minority, Windthorst was one of the founders of the Center Party in 1870. He quickly rose to become its undisputed leader and for the rest of his life ran the party with a tactful but strong-willed hand. Although Windthorst had hoped the Center Party would become the political home both of Germany's Catholics and disaffected anti-Prussian elements of all religious persuasions, he was unable to take the party "out of the [Catholic] tower." He could not persuade the other Catholic leaders of the Center Party to reach out to members of the Protestant community, and until after World War II the party remained an almost exclusively Catholic institution.

ECONOMIC AND SOCIAL DEVELOPMENTS

Between 1871 and 1890 the German economy went through wildly fluctuating boom-and-bust periods. The era began with a brief "hyper-boom." Germany's political unification came during a long period of upswing that had begun in the 1850s. The already bullish economy received a concentrated infusion of investment capital from the French reparations. France paid off its debts within two years, and in Germany the rapid influx of money set off a wave of speculative fever that touched virtually all sectors of the economy.

By the end of 1872, there were clear signs that the economy was becoming overheated, and in mid-1873 the speculative bubble burst. Numerous banks and businesses failed, and unemployment soared. For the next twenty years, despite some ups and downs, the German economy did not again achieve the impressive growth rates of

During the 1870s Windthorst and his party became embroiled in a fierce struggle with Bismarck and the Prussian and federal governments. Whereas Windthorst saw the Center Party as the spokesperson for the legitimate rights of Germany's Catholics, the Reich chancellor was convinced the Center Party was spearheading a drive to destroy the newly united Reich and its constitutional system. As a result, Bismarck during the Kulturkampf repeatedly labeled Windthorst and his associates "enemies of the Reich."

The outcome of the Kulturkampf was a clear victory for Germany's Catholics, although Windthorst was disappointed that Pope Leo XIII chose to end the Kulturkampf through a diplomatic agreement between the papacy and the German Reich, rather than permit the Center Party to savor a political triumph in German domestic politics. The pope, for his part, resented that Windthorst always took great care to keep the Center Party independent of orders from the clergy and the papacy.

During the Kulturkampf Windthorst fought Bismarck and the chancellor's liberal allies in the only arena that was open to him, the national parliament. In the course of the altercation, "the little excellency" (the nickname derived from his small stature) became a highly skilled parliamentary tactician and orator, gaining the respect of friend and foe alike.

Windthorst's clash with the pope did not end with the settlement of the Kulturkampf. He continued to oppose the reactionary policies of Leo XIII. Despite strong pressure from the papacy, the Center Party in 1878 refused to vote for the Anti-Socialist Laws, arguing that it set a dangerous precedent for political action against a minority that could in the future just as easily be turned against Germany's Catholics.

At the end of his life, Windthorst could look back on many parliamentary and political successes. With few weapons at his command but his skills in parliament and his ability to encourage Germany's Catholics to stand fast against the onslaught of the Prussian state, Windthorst successfully resisted Bismarck and the formidable array of weapons at the chancellor's disposal. Windthorst failed, however, in his other lifelong quest— to restore Hanover as a separate *Land* within the German Reich. That development had to await the end of World War II.

Still, it was ironic that at the time of his death Windthorst, the former "enemy of the Reich," was accorded the honor of a state funeral.

the early 1870s. The depression was particularly severe in 1877–1878. That low was followed by a modest upturn and a new plateau in the mid-1880s, but then came another recession, which reached its nadir toward the end of the decade. Not until the mid-1890s did the economic indicators return to the levels of 1872.

In spite of the uneven economic performance, German society as a whole in the next ten years moved toward economic modernization and urbanization. The population of the country grew steadily. Death rates dropped, and emigration, after reaching a peak in the early 1880s, decreased markedly. In the mid-1880s, when the economy experienced one of its brief upturns, Germany became a country of net immigration. Foreign workers, primarily from Italy and Russian Poland, poured into the country. At the same time, the number of people moving from the eastern areas of Germany to the industrialized west reached unprecedented levels.

Im Mittelpunkt   Gerson Bleichröder (1822–1893)

The label "Bismarck's banker," which is often applied to Bleichröder, is true, but it hardly does this complex personality full justice. In many ways Bleichröder epitomized the transition from traditionalism to modernity in German society. A successful private banker at a time when his profession was increasingly replaced by joint stock financial institutions, he was also a devout Jew in an age in which many of his coreligionists chose at least the veneer of assimilation into Christian society. He also mixed the roles of private financier and public diplomat, a tradition among bankers in the nineteenth century that reached its culmination with the Rothschilds, yet he was thoroughly modern in his use of public relations methods to advance his financial and political goals.

Bleichröder came from a family of private bankers, and there was apparently never any question that he would follow in the footsteps of his ancestors. In 1855 he took over the reigns of the Bleichröder Bank from his father. By 1859 he managed Bismarck's private investment portfolio, and when the Pomeranian *Junker* became Prussian prime minister he turned to Bleichröder to finance the state's operation during the years in which the state legislature refused to pass a budget. In this context Bleichröder financed the "Wars of Unification." He did this not only because it benefited his banking establishment but also because he shared many of Bismarck's political views. Like his illustrious client, Bleichröder was a political conservative, who distrusted democratic institutions and the rule of parliament.

After the founding of the Reich, the symbiotic relationship between Bismarck and his banker intensified. Bleichröder took full advantage of the economic boom years that followed Germany's unification; a good portion of the French reparation payments were invested through his bank. As was true for the Rothschilds in France and Great Britain, Bismarck also used Bleichröder on a number of quasi-diplomatic missions. Here the banker acted as the voice of the Reich and Prussian governments, although his lack of official status also gave Bismarck "deniability" if that was needed.

As far as Bleichröder was concerned, these missions increased the reputation of his house, and they enabled him to discover opportunities for profitable investments that benefited both the bank, and, not incidentally, augmented Bismarck's own personal portfolio. (Note that the concept of insider trading had not yet been invented. Statesmen and politicians routinely mixed public and private finances.)

In due course Bleichröder and his high-ranking patron amassed immense fortunes, which Bleichröder, at least, used to achieve laudable political ends. While the banker remained silent on outbreaks of German anti-Semitism and quietly practiced his faith, behind the scenes he attempted to use his financial clout to improve the conditions of Jews in Eastern Europe, especially in Romania and Russia.

The personal relations between Bismarck and Bleichröder were complex and paradoxical. They certainly socialized with each other and had a great deal of respect for one another, but they never became intimate friends. The worlds of the Prussian *Junker* and the Jewish banker were simply too far apart. Their lives, however, remained connected almost to their deaths. Bleichröder and Bismarck died within a year of each other.

The occupational profile of the country was also changing rapidly. Agricultural employment remained essentially stable, but the number of people employed in industry almost doubled. Industrialization created thousands of new factory jobs, but the modernization of the German economy also established numerous white-collar and skilled blue-collar positions.

Both Marxist analysts and small businessmen's associations postulated that with increasing industrialization independent artisans and small businessmen as a class would disappear. Thousands, so the propaganda of the trade associations claimed, lost their livelihood and had no choice but to seek a wage position in industry. In fact, industrialization did not mean the disappearance of the German Mittelstand. The economy demanded new craft skills, and the total number of independent artisans and small businessmen actually increased. At the same time, positions opened up as well in the technical government services. The increasingly complicated economy required a diversification of technical officials (such as mining and building code inspectors, health inspectors, railroad officials) at all levels of government.

German society was in the midst of social and physical flux, but its class relations remained highly stratified. Germans were divided by both status and income into lower, middle, and upper levels. Like other European industrialized societies in the last quarter of the nineteenth century, German society was characterized by a very small upper class, a somewhat larger middle level, and a sizable lower class. The prevailing income and tax structure produced extremely wide variations in the standard of living between the well-to-do and the poor. A large percentage of the population continued to live near subsistence level while the upper-middle and upper classes could easily afford luxuries. It is also true, however, that the standard of living for most Germans, with the notable exception of the East Elbian landless proletariat, was rising fairly steadily. In other words, although the relative gap between rich and poor remained vast, the standard of living for both was rising.

A few typical prices and wages from the decade of the 1870s may illustrate the reality of stratification. In 1876 a machinist living in Munich earned about 270 marks a year, an elementary school teacher about 1,600, and a lawyer with his own practice 34,000 marks. The variations in standards of living became even more pronounced because of the prevailing price patterns. Generally speaking, basic foodstuffs were very expensive, particularly in comparison to what we would regard as luxury items. Thus a loaf of bread cost 36 pfennigs (there were 100 pfennigs in a mark), which meant the machinist would have to work about a third of a day for this basic necessity of life. A pound of butter was 1.10 marks, requiring one and a third day's labor from the machinist. (As a result, butter consumption among the lower classes was infrequent; they relied on lard as their primary source of fat.) In contrast, a pound of caviar cost 1.50 marks, so this item, which we would clearly consider a luxury, made a very small dent in the budget of the well-to-do lawyer. In practice, the price and wage patterns meant that those at the lower end of the socioeconomic scale spent almost all of their earnings on the necessities; they had virtually no discretionary income. In contrast, the well-to-do could afford a wide variety of luxuries without actually regarding such expenditures as extravagant. The society, then, was characterized by vast gulfs not just in income levels, but in attitudes toward money and expenditures as well.

For a number of enterprising entrepreneurs, the boom of 1871–1873 provided the opportunity to make sizable fortunes. The level of investment activity in these two years can be gauged from the increase in the money supply: Despite negligible inflationary pressures, between 1871 and 1873 the German money supply increased by more than 50 percent. The ready availability of capital had a multiplier effect that reverberated throughout the economy. In accord with classic economic theory, direct investment in high-growth industries, such as export-oriented and manufacturing enterprises, indirectly stimulated equivalent activity in services and products not specifically related to the original investment target.

The boom also marked the last chapter in the long cooperation between Bismarck and the liberals. At the beginning of the Bismarck era there was still widespread support for the classic doctrines of economic liberalism in the business sector. Under the guidance of Rudolf Delbrück in the Reich chancellery and his liberal allies in the Prussian state cabinet, the Reich and Prussian governments continued the policy of free trade and minimal governmental intervention in the marketplace. Free trade was obviously beneficial to Germany's export-oriented enterprises. These included the chemical, textile, and nascent electrical industries. Agricultural interests, too, continued to favor free trade during the boom years. At the beginning of the 1870s, Germany was still exporting sizable quantities of agricultural products to Great Britain. Competition from America and Russia was not yet a major factor. Moreover, duty-free importation of iron products kept prices for farm implements low.

In addition to accelerating the modernization of the German economy, the hyper-boom of 1871–1873 also inaugurated profound changes in the German banking and capital investment system. Before unification, the German banking community had been characterized by a large number of local private banks. The availability of tremendous amounts of capital for investment made possible the modern forms of German banking. So-called universal banks established branches throughout the country and handled all financial transactions from checking and savings accounts to stocks and bonds and mutual funds. Moreover, because the Reich government channeled the French reparation payments into the economy primarily through financial institutions located in Berlin (as we saw, much of the money went through the hands of Bismarck's personal friend, the banker Gerson Bleichröder), the banks in the Reich capital assumed a dominant position in the German economy. By the end of the decade, Berlin had become both the political capital of the Reich and its banking center.

The crisis of 1873 accelerated the trend toward centralization in Germany's banking system. In the fall the crash of the Viennese stock market led to difficulties for a number of German financial institutions. Far more serious, however, was the collapse of the Jay Cooke Bank in New York; many German private banks held obligations from the New York firm in their portfolios. During the next few years, as many of the smaller private banks were forced out of business, four major universal banks emerged as controlling forces in the German banking and investment community: the Deutsche Bank, the Dresdner Bank, the Darmstädter Bank (this was also known as the Industrie- und Handelsbank; it was the forerunner of the present-day Commerzbank), and the Discontogesellschaft. It was symptomatic of the new era that two of the four, the Deutsche Bank and the Industrie- und Handelsbank, had not existed before 1871.

By the mid-1870s the crisis had affected all sectors of the economy. The overall impact of the depression may be gauged by the precipitous fall of prices and wages: Between 1873 and 1878 wages fell between 50 and 70 percent and prices between 50 and 60 percent. At the same time, in part because of technological improvements in the production processes, the output of goods did not decrease proportionately, so a constant surplus of unsold products delayed the onset of recovery. This phenomenon, the existence of a large volume of unsold goods, led in the second half of the decade to a passionate debate over one of the kingpins of German economic policies, the system of free trade.

The crisis depressed the entire economy, but some sectors obviously suffered more than others. Among those particularly adversely affected were agriculture, iron and steel, and textiles. As we saw, before the depression German agriculture had supported the free-trade policies of the government. However, the situation changed abruptly in 1875–1876 with the collapse of international grain prices. The recovery of American agriculture from the ravages of the Civil War and increased worldwide production depressed prices, all but eliminating the higher priced German products from competition on the international market. To make matters worse, Germany's growing urbanization forced it, much as had been true of England forty years earlier, to import grain, and under the policy of free trade, cheap food imports could enter the country without restriction. German agriculture feared it would be shut out even from its home market. By the mid-1870s German farmers were clamoring for a protective tariff.

Agriculture was actually the third link in a chain of economic interests demanding massive changes in Germany's traditional economic policies. The first sector of the economy that had called for protection was the iron and steel industry. With the onset of the depression, its products were increasingly unable to prevail over foreign competition, and heavy industry formed a lobbying organization, the Verband Deutscher Eisen und Stahlindustrieller (Association of German Iron and Steel Industrialists), which worked both publicly and behind the scenes for a protective tariff. Its arguments were in part strategic (without a viable heavy industry, Germany in times of war would be dependent on imports from potential enemies) and partly economic and social. The spokesmen for heavy industry claimed that without protective tariffs they would be unable to pay their workers a living wage.

Another sector of the economy joining the cries for protectionism was the textile industry. Its membership in the protectionist front added not only numbers but also geographic diversification. The supporters of lobbying efforts for heavy industry and agriculture came primarily from Prussia, whereas the Reich's textile works tended to be located in southern and central Germany. The textile manufacturers, handicapped by the technologically backward state of their facilities and the decentralized nature of their business, were unable to compete with cheaper imports from England and America. Like their colleagues in heavy industry, the textile manufacturers claimed that excessive foreign competition prevented them from paying higher wages to their workers. To coordinate their lobbying efforts, the textile and

iron and steel manufacturers joined in 1876 to create yet another and larger lobbying organization, the Zentralverband Deutscher Industrieller (Central Association of German Industrialists).

By 1878 the protectionists had mobilized sufficient support to overcome the fierce opposition of the export-oriented industries; the major German seaports, such as Hamburg and Bremen; and the Prussian Ministry of Commerce. (Especially that ministry had been staffed with enthusiastic free traders ever since the days of the North German Confederation.) By the end of the decade, Germany had joined the growing list of European countries abandoning free trade. (After 1880 Great Britain was virtually alone among the European countries in continuing a policy of complete free trade.) The Reich instituted relatively modest tariffs on iron and steel and textiles and somewhat higher levies on agricultural products.

The shift to protectionism had ramifications far beyond the field of economic policy. The decision to institute tariffs also brought about a profound political reorientation. One analyst has called it "the equivalent of re-founding the Reich." It involved a major shift in the focus of power within the framework of the Bismarck Compromise. Instead of working together primarily with both liberal parties, the chancellor now forged an alliance between the Conservatives, the National Liberals, and, to a lesser extent, the Center Party. This became possible because many of the landowners and industrialists who demanded tariffs aligned themselves politically with the Conservative, National Liberal, or the Center Party camps. The change in economic policy of 1878–1879 determined the economic and political priorities for the next ten years. The tariff decision facilitated the union of the Junkers, with their interests in large-scale agriculture, and the industrial barons who dominated heavy industry. The chancellor also began replacing a number of prominent liberal officials with more conservative bureaucrats. During the latter part of the Bismarck years, Germany was well on its way toward assimilating the industrial interests into the basic power structure of the conservative counterrevolution. The only major

During the long depression (1873–1893) thousands of Germans left the country to seek their fortunes in the New World. This 1874 drawing from *Harper's Weekly* shows German immigrants embarking on a steamer in Hamburg for their journey to New York. (Source: Harper's weekly, 1874 Nov. 7, pp. 916–917/Library of Congress Prints and Photographs Division [LC-USZ62-100310].)

factor left out of the new politico-economic equation was labor, which grew in both numbers and organizational strength in direct proportion to the advancing industrialization of the country. To deal with the problem, Bismarck and his new partners once again invoked the concept of the "enemies of the Reich."

SOCIAL LEGISLATION AND ANTISOCIALIST LAWS

Social and labor policies were another example of the persistently asymmetrical patterns of modernization in Germany. In the 1880s the Reich began instituting what was to become the model for all systems of social legislation. Simultaneously, however, it began a full-scale attempt to suppress the political organizations that represented those most likely to benefit from the social legislation. True, to some extent political repression and social concern sprang from the same ideological sources. A number of religious and political leaders were genuinely appalled by the social consequences of rapid industrialization, but, like Bismarck, they were also worried about the stability of the Reich if industrial labor gained significant political or economic power. Political tactics during the tariff debates also entered into the equation. At least some of the industrialists favoring protective tariffs felt that by advocating some social legislation to benefit their employees, they could gain the support of labor organizations and social reformers for their primary goal, tariff legislation. From the employers' point of view, labor support for protective tariffs would undercut the organizing efforts of the Marxist SPD, part of whose political platform was free trade.

What emerged from this dual effort to alleviate the workers' worst suffering while suppressing their efforts to gain political power was a strange set of allies. Some of the genuine social reformers were also political anti-Semites. This was particularly true of Adolf Stöcker, a Protestant minister who was later to become imperial court chaplain. Stöcker, who had close ties to the German Conservative Party, was convinced that Jews were primarily responsible for both the excesses of rampant industrialism and the ideas of Marxism. He hoped that social reforms would lead the workers away from supporting Marxism and draw them toward conservatism and the Protestant churches. Other proponents of anti-Marxism, however, showed little interest in social reforms and concentrated on finding ways to use police power and the courts to destroy the workers' economic and political organizations.

In the first decade after the founding of the Reich, the groups that would eventually arouse so much concern among Germany's leaders played a very minor role in German social and political life. To be sure, the boom years of 1871–1873 spurred the growth and militancy of the labor movement. Six years after the founding of the empire, the SPD vote had risen from 100,000 to 493,000, but the party's twelve seats in the Reichstag hardly made it a significant power bloc in German politics. The same was true of the socialist labor unions. It is estimated that of the roughly 5 million industrial workers in 1875, only about 25,000 were organized in unions affiliated with Marxist organizations. By 1877–1878 the number had grown to 47,000, but then the membership declined sharply during the hard times of the 1880s. In the early 1870s there had been an increase of strikes to gain higher wages and better working conditions, although even during the boom years few of these work actions involved more than a thousand workers. With the onset of the depression, the strike wave soon dissipated.

Nevertheless, in the government and among many employers with their traditional *Herr im Hause* ("lord of the manor") attitude, the memories of a militant labor movement lingered.

For Bismarck and his allies, then, the Marxists constituted a real, if embryonic, threat on three fronts. Marxism was a movement whose revolutionary ideology did not preclude collective violence in the eventual overthrow of capitalism, although the socialists resolutely rejected the use of individual terror or assassination. The Social Democratic Party's 1875 program proclaimed that the organization would work for the overthrow of capitalism by all "lawful means." The SPD also proudly maintained ties to workers' organizations in other countries, proclaiming the need for all proletarians to cooperate in their struggle against capitalism. Partly because of this, Germany's governmental leaders tended to lump all socialist thinkers together; they were part of an international terrorist conspiracy whose aim was to foment a Marxist and anarchist revolution so as to destroy the European political and economic fabric of society. Finally, Bismarck had never forgiven the German socialist leaders for their grossdeutsch stand during the years of unification. The two most prominent German socialist leaders, Wilhelm Liebknecht and August Bebel, had bitterly opposed Bismarck's military road to unity, favoring instead a united Germany that was not dominated by Prussian authoritarianism.

By 1875 German socialism and the empire's leaders were on a collision course. Bismarck inaugurated a program of administrative repression, which systematically sought to prevent socialists and socialist ideas from entering the officer corps and the ranks of the civil service. (The latter, of course, included public school teachers and university professors.) In a stock phrase much used in socialist campaign oratory, this was the era in which a Social Democrat could not even become a night watchman in a German government building. Bismarck also began thinking seriously about banning the German

Socialist party altogether. In the spring of 1878, the government introduced such legislation in the Reichstag (laws against political parties had to be introduced at the federal level because most parties were organized throughout the Reich), but the bill failed to pass. Both the liberals and the Center Party refused to back such a blatant attempt at political repression.

The government's desire for persecution and parliament's concern for constitutional liberties hung in uneasy balance for a few months until two assassination attempts on the emperor tipped the scales in favor of the government. On May 11, 1878, an unsuccessful attempt was made on the life of the seventy-eight-year-old emperor, by then a much venerated and genuinely popular figure. The monarch was not hurt, but there was an outcry of indignation; Bismarck immediately blamed the socialists for the crime, although even the government prosecutors could find no link between the assassin and any organized political group.

Unfortunately, less than a month later a second assassination attempt was almost successful. This time a physician with anarchist leanings, Dr. Nobiling, shot the emperor as he was riding in an open carriage through a Berlin park and seriously wounded the monarch. Nobiling was clearly mentally unbalanced. In fact, the Prussian Ministry of the Interior proposed that the physician be sent to an asylum for the criminally insane rather than stand trial. Bismarck, however, persisted in his linkage theory, citing Nobiling's onetime attendance at a socialist meeting as proof that the assassination attempt was part of an SPD-controlled terrorist campaign. The government dissolved parliament and called for new elections. Because the last Reichstag had just been elected a year earlier, it was obvious that the chancellor hoped the voters' sympathy for the severely wounded emperor would result in a Reichstag majority favorable to the government's repressive aims.

Bismarck had judged the mood of the German electorate well. After a brief campaign characterized by near mass hysteria, the voters elected a national parliament whose majority agreed with Bismarck that the socialists were a threat to the stability of German society. The new Reichstag passed the Anti-Socialist Laws. The legislation forced the Socialist Party and its affiliated unions to disband. Also prohibited was any printed matter or meetings that in the opinion of the police advocated socialist doctrines. The penalties for violation were jail sentences and fines, as well as "internal exile," which meant that the police could keep anyone convicted of "socialist crimes" from residing in the town in which he had committed his offense. There was only one part of the legislation package that even this Reichstag refused to approve. Bismarck had wanted the parliament to expel its socialist members and preclude the voters from casting ballots for SPD candidates in future elections. Here the majority of the Reichstag felt that the fundamental right of parliament to determine its own membership was at stake, and that part of the legislation was voted down. The remainder of the package, however, passed, initially for three years. The Anti-Socialist Laws were periodically renewed until 1890, although the Reichstag majorities voting for the laws grew progressively smaller.

In the short run, Bismarck had scored a major political triumph; in 1878 public opinion was clearly on his side. At the same time, the Anti-Socialist Laws politically ostracized the fastest growing segment of German society. For the remainder of the Bismarck years, the SPD became an outlawed organization subject to constant harassment by local police officials. As in the case of the Kulturkampf, the repression did not destroy the organization. On the contrary, while the Anti-Socialist Laws were in effect, the SPD's strength increased continuously. Twelve years after the repressive laws were put on the books, the party's dozen deputies in the Reichstag of 1877 had grown to thirty-five.

For the socialists themselves, the effect of the Anti-Socialist Laws of 1878 was paradoxical:

On the one hand, the laws provided evidence for those within the socialist movement who argued that the liberation of the working class could never come in cooperation with the elite of the empire, but only through its complete overthrow. At the same time, however, the laws led the SPD to focus its political activities on parliamentary elections because parliamentary campaigning and getting elected was the only form of political agitation not prohibited by the legislation.

Social reform legislation was a corollary to the Anti-Socialist Laws, although significantly, repression preceded reform. Germany embarked on government-sponsored social reforms at the beginning of the 1880s. There was little doubt that help was needed. The depression was nearing its climax, and times were particularly hard for industrial workers. Pleas for social activism from both Protestant and Catholic clerics increased. Adolf Stöcker founded the Christian Social Movement to give organizational force to his views, and in Catholic circles the Archbishop of Mainz, Emmanuel von Ketteler, developed a full-fledged social gospel program. Incidentally, Catholic thinking was a not insignificant factor as far as Bismarck was concerned. In the waning days of the Kulturkampf, paying at least lip service to Catholic doctrines on social reform would clearly facilitate a rapprochement with the Center Party.

The first indication of governmental interest in social reform legislation came in 1881 as part of a speech from the throne by the emperor. The monarch spoke of his concern for the sufferings of industrial laborers and endorsed the principle of social legislation. At the same time, in accord with Bismarck's strategy, he stressed that social reforms would be an effective antisocialist strategy: Workers would recognize the government's concern for their welfare and turn away from the Marxist doctrine of revolution. For a variety of reasons ranging from political opportunism to genuine social concern, the emperor's initiative was widely welcomed in the Reichstag. During the final vote only the German Conservatives, the Social Democrats (because the laws were designed to

destroy them politically), and the Progressives opposed the government bills; even the Free Conservatives voted for the measures.

Between 1883 and 1889 the government introduced three major pieces of reform legislation. Together they were the beginnings of a "social net" designed to catch those hurt by economic developments through no fault of their own. The first bill inaugurated a national health insurance scheme. Through a system of employer and employee contributions, the beginnings of a comprehensive healthcare system were created. A year later, in 1884, national accident insurance provided aid for workers hurt on the job. Finally, as a sort of capstone, in 1889 Germany's system of social security was established. Under the provisions of the law, an initially relatively small number of workers were guaranteed a very modest pension on reaching the retirement age of sixty-five.

The Anti-Socialist Laws and the social reform legislation were meant to work in tandem, and in a sense they did, although hardly in the manner expected by the government. The social legislation in no way achieved its avowed aim of persuading the German proletariat to abandon Marxism. By 1890 the SPD's vote had grown to 1.4 million compared to 493,000 twelve years earlier. The increase was all the more impressive because it came during a time of increasingly severe administration of the Anti-Socialist Laws. The campaign of repression against labor organizations reached a climax of sorts in 1886, during the so-called Puttkamer era. Robert von Puttkamer, an archconservative Prussian minister of the interior who symbolized the reactionary regime of Bismarck's last years, even attempted, unsuccessfully, to eliminate by administrative fiat labor's right to strike.

In more subtle ways, however, the social legislation did affect the workers' view of imperial Germany's society. Although all members of the Social Democratic Party and its affiliated unions worked to defeat the antisocialist legislation, the social reforms called forth a different reaction. Especially toward the end of the 1880s, some leaders in the SPD and even more in the unions argued that the reforms demonstrated that improvements in the workers' lot could come through further changes within the capitalist system rather than by relying primarily on the hope of political revolution. In introducing his repressive measures against the socialists, Bismarck had hailed the legislation as the solution to the Marxist "problem." In a sense the reverse was true: Not the Anti-Socialist Laws, but the reform legislation would change the nature of the German Marxist movement.

FOREIGN RELATIONS

Although Bismarck's reputation as the architect of German domestic stability has become increasingly tarnished, the years since 1871 have done little to diminish the Iron Chancellor's prestige in the area of foreign policy. Here he has retained his reputation as a statesman who almost single-handedly established an international balance of power that kept peace among the European Great Powers for more than forty years. In fact, our contemporary terminology on international relations is permeated with words and concepts invented by Bismarck. The terms *Realpolitik* and *honest broker* are two examples. It is also true that a number of modern-day statesmen have consciously modeled their policies on those of the Iron Chancellor. Bismarck's success in laying the basis for long-term peace among the Great Powers seems all the more remarkable because without the experience of two world wars and the prospect of nuclear holocaust to haunt them, the thought of military action to settle disputes was in no way abhorrent to European decision makers.

Before turning to a more detailed discussion of Germany's foreign relations in these years, the problem of priorities in Bismarck's foreign policies needs to be addressed. Were the chancellor's foreign policy aims dictated by the Reich's geopolitical position or was the conduct of Germany's foreign relations designed primarily to maintain authoritarianism at home? Bismarck himself and most German historians writing before

1945 tended to support a "priority of foreign policy" (*Primat der Aussenpolitik*) thesis. Confronted by France's desire for revenge, the Reich had no choice but to maintain a large military establishment and to secure France's diplomatic isolation. At the same time, the constant foreign threat prevented Germany from undertaking major domestic political reforms because this would endanger domestic stability and weaken the Reich's military preparedness.

After the collapse of the empire in 1918, a school of younger historians, led by Eckart Kehr, increasingly challenged Bismarck's claim that his foreign policy was dictated by the givens of Germany's geopolitical position. This, they contended, was a myth deliberately fabricated by Bismarck and his supporters to mislead the German public. The new school of interpretation argued that in reality a "priority of domestic concerns" (*Primat der Innenpolitik*) determined Germany's foreign policy. To preserve political authoritarianism in Germany and prevent democratization, Bismarck invented a military threat from France and allied the new Reich to Austria and Russia, the countries with the most reactionary domestic systems among the European Great Powers. At the end of World War II, a new generation of historians, such as Hans Ulrich Wehler, rediscovered the writings of Kehr and others (which had been largely ignored after World War I and suppressed by the Nazis) and buttressed them with new documentation.

Most contemporary historians accept many of the positions of the "domestic priorities" school. There is no doubt that Germany's unique geographic position in Central Europe had profound repercussions for the conduct of its international relations. But it is equally true that the conduct of Germany's foreign policy was designed to help preserve the authoritarian system at home, and Bismarck's shift in foreign allies, as we will see, was often little more than a reflection of changing political partnerships at home.

Bismarck never tired of elucidating the idea that under his leadership Germany's

A cartoon from a September 1878 issue of the British magazine *Punch*. The reference is to the Anti-Socialist Laws. Bismarck is trying to stuff socialism back into the box. (Source: akg-images.)

foreign policy was based on a set of simple and unchanging principles. One was the promise that Germany had no territorial ambitions beyond those achieved in 1871; the Reich was a "satiated" state. Second, the military victories of 1871 had given Germany the right to exercise hegemony in Central Europe; that is to say, it would not tolerate a second major power on the central European plain. Third, Bismarck (quite wrongly) rated conservative and monarchical regimes as inherently more stable factors in international relations than democratic and republican states. Consequently, he sought to create alliances among the three conservative empires of Germany, Austria-Hungary, and Russia while isolating France as the least stable and most volatile among the Great Powers. Bismarck's only exception to the "democratic equals unstable" rule was Great Britain, which the chancellor did regard as a constant element of stability in the international balance of power. Bismarck's three axioms led him to conclude that Germany should cooperate with Austria and Russia to preserve authoritarianism on the continent while working together with England to isolate France. Germany itself, as the most stable, satiated, and powerful nation on the continent, was uniquely qualified to play the role of "honest broker," mediating disputes among the Great Powers and preserving peace among them.

Bismarck's assumptions contained a fundamental flaw. The chancellor was convinced the rearrangement of the international balance of power in 1871 had created an essentially static and permanent set of relationships that could be frozen into perpetuity. He refused to recognize that domestic pressures in Germany and the other Great Powers would result in constantly changing balances among the great nations of Europe.

Bismarck's choice of allies to preserve the stability of the European balance of power illustrated the error of his assumption. The two countries that Bismarck regarded as the Reich's most reliable partners, Austria and Russia, were countries in domestic turmoil. Consequently, rather than being bastions of stability, their domestic difficulties led them to pursue aggressive and risky foreign policies. From Bismarck's point of view, it was particularly unfortunate that Austria and Russia could achieve their foreign policy aims only at the expense of each other. This meant that for the most part rather than cooperating with Bismarck to stabilize the post-1871 balance of power, they sought his support to change it to their own advantage.

Bismarck was more fortunate in the choice of his primary Western ally, Great Britain. Not only was England genuinely interested in stabilizing the post-1871 international balance of power, but also the relative absence of domestic tensions in Great Britain meant that the conduct of its foreign policy was singularly stable and predictable. As a result, Anglo-German relations were for the most part harmonious, until, beginning in the 1880s, Bismarck's own response to domestic pressures in Germany led to a cooling. As we saw, to forge his new domestic alliance with the conservatives, Bismarck agreed to endorse their demand for tariffs. In addition, the chancellor heeded the call for colonial possessions, a demand voiced primarily by the National Liberals. Inevitably, this led to questions in Great Britain about the Reich's future role in world affairs. Would Germany be content with its function as a Continental power, or would it embark on a quest for overseas possessions and become England's rival in extra-European affairs? The chancellor recognized the pitfalls of imperialism and was reluctant to pursue colonial ventures. Nevertheless, for purely domestic reasons, the Reich in 1884 began its unfortunate career as a colonial power.

The decision of 1884 was symbolic of the increasing intertwining of domestic and foreign policy in the second half of the founders' era. After 1878 the evolution of Germany's domestic politics increasingly influenced the conduct of the Reich's foreign policy. To be sure, even earlier the Kulturkampf and Bismarck's alliance with the Liberals had created some tensions with Austria, a country that traditionally relied on the Catholic Church as one of the pillars of domestic stability for its multinational empire. The end of the Kulturkampf improved relations between the Hohenzollerns and the Habsburgs. Bismarck's endorsement of the principle of protective tariffs improved the climate still further because Austria-Hungary had always opposed a free-trade policy. But Bismarck's support of tariffs on agricultural products had profound repercussions for Russo-German relations. After 1879 Russian grain exports were increasingly excluded from the German market. In their anger the Russians were quick to remind Bismarck that they had potential alliance partners outside the conservative empires: There was always France.

Bismarck's failure to recognize the seriousness of the rivalry between Austria and Russia and his determination to maintain the domestic terms of the Compromise of 1871 resulted in a foreign policy that was by no means free from elements of instability and inconsistency. However, the chancellor's strategic errors were balanced by his tactical skills in negotiating a series of multilateral alliances and bilateral treaties. In fact, these tactical skills for a long time preserved his reputation as a master of Realpolitik and the controlling agent of the European balance of power.

The construction of Bismarck's alliance system began, logically enough, with what the chancellor hoped would be the bedrock of the post-1871 balance of power: agreements of friendship and cooperation among the three conservative empires. Two years after the founding of the Reich, the Three Emperors' Alliance was signed among the rulers of Austria, Germany, and Russia. It was the embodiment of Bismarck's belief in the viability of the monarchical principle in the conduct of foreign relations: The alliance was a personal agreement between the individual monarchs.

The irreconcilable differences between Austria and Russia over the future of southeastern Europe soon turned partnership into mutual antagonism and suspicion. Russia supported the territorial and political ambitions of the Slavic nations in the Balkans against the Ottoman Empire, while Austria regarded pan-Slavism as a threat to the stability of the Habsburg realms. Germany was caught in the middle with no direct interest in southeastern Europe (Bismarck had said repeatedly that the Balkans were not worth the bones of a single Pomeranian grenadier), but the chronic and growing Austro-Russian tensions made the Reich's self-defined role as the arbitrator of the post-1871 balance of power in Europe increasingly difficult.

This became apparent as early as 1875, during what Bismarck called the "war is in sight" crisis. The potential war he referred to was one between France and Germany, with Russia at least diplomatically ranged on the side of France. Actually, Bismarck wildly exaggerated the dangers of a diplomatic and military realignment in Europe at this time. The occasion for Bismarck's melodramatic outburst was Russia's frustration with the Three Emperors' Alliance. Only two years after the solemn signing of this agreement, the Russian foreign minister went so far as to indicate publicly that better relations between the czar and France were not out of the question. Although no concrete agreements followed these musings, Bismarck became exceedingly nervous: He had clearly failed in his quest to create a new balance of power on the basis of the long-term cooperation of the conservative empires.

Relations among the three emperors grew even worse with the outbreak of actual hostilities in the Balkans. In 1875 and 1878 Bulgaria went to war with the Ottoman Empire. During the conflict Russia openly supported the Bulgarians, while Austria and Great Britain gave diplomatic backing to the Turks. Once again, Germany was caught in the middle, although Bismarck was also presented with a perfect opportunity to exercise his self-chosen role as honest broker. In the summer of 1878, the chancellor invited all interested parties to an international conference, the Congress of Berlin. The chancellor hoped that under his leadership the congress would be able to settle the Turkish–Bulgarian conflict and create a new and stable order in southeastern Europe. However, he found it very difficult

A portrait of Otto von Bismarck in his later years. He is wearing the uniform of a Prussian officer. (Source: Courtesy of National Archives and Records Administration.)

to play the part of honest broker. Austria and Russia were too far apart on most issues, and especially the Russians felt Bismarck did not act as "honest broker."

Without admitting that his own actions were instrumental in destroying the original premise of the Three Emperors' Alliance, after the Congress of Berlin Bismarck ended his tightrope walk between Russia and Austria and instead began to forge a closer bond between Germany and Austria. The result was the Dual Alliance of 1879. In this treaty Germany agreed to aid the Habsburg monarchy militarily and diplomatically if Russia attacked Austria.

Although the Dual Alliance was a defensive pact—if Austria went on the attack Germany obligated itself only to observe benevolent neutrality toward the Austrians—the treaty was not universally popular in Germany. To overcome some residual opposition to the Dual Alliance among the Conservatives (many of whom wanted both tariffs and to preserve Germany's special relationship with Russia), the diplomatic treaty with Austria was supplemented by a new trade agreement between Austria and Germany that provided for a mutually advantageous protective tariff system.

Three years later the Dual Alliance was expanded to include Italy. Bismarck's aim in this Triple Alliance was to encourage the Italians to pursue their imperialist ambitions in Africa, where they might clash with France, rather than press for political and territorial demands in southeastern Europe, where Italy's aims would run counter to Austria's.

The permanently stabilizing effect that Bismarck had hoped would be provided by the Dual and Triple Alliances lasted less than five years. Italy remained an uneasy partner in the Triple Alliance and certainly did not give up its Adriatic ambitions. More significantly, domestic developments in Germany disturbed the Reich's traditionally good relations with Great Britain. Bismarck's new partnership with industrialists and Junkers tied him to forces that looked on England as a commercial and imperialist rival. By the end of the 1880s, the Reich felt it necessary once again to adjust

its alliances. In 1887 Bismarck, never a modest man, negotiated a new agreement, the Reinsurance Treaty, with Russia that the chancellor regarded as a stroke of genius, but which his critics tended to see as a move just short of deliberate deception and duplicity.

A crisis in France provided the immediate impetus for the Reinsurance Treaty. In 1887 it appeared likely that a conservative and *revanchiste* military leader, General Boulanger, would become president of the French Republic. In Germany the government asked for and obtained authorization to increase the strength of the army; the Reich staged military maneuvers in Alsace to alert France to Germany's military preparedness. For nervous minds, war was again just around the corner. Understandably, the last thing that Germany wanted in 1887 was a rapprochement between Russia and France. The Reinsurance Treaty was a desperate effort to preclude such a possibility.

As was typical of most alliances in nineteenth-century Europe, the Reinsurance Treaty was a secret accord whose terms were not announced either to the general public or to the members of parliament. The chain of events that led to the Reinsurance Treaty began with an initiative by a high-ranking Russian diplomat, Count Peter Shuvalov, suggesting the renewal of formal treaty ties between Russia and Germany. Because Germany was already bound to Austria under the specific terms of the Dual Alliance, Bismarck proposed an accord in which Russia secretly promised to remain benevolently neutral if France attacked Germany in an "unprovoked" manner. As a quid pro quo, in a "top secret" clause, Germany promised to remain benevolently neutral toward Russia if the czarist government took action to change the status of the Dardanelles and Bosporus Straits, which meant increasing Russia's military presence at the eastern end of the Mediterranean.

At first glance, Bismarck had succeeded in squaring a diplomatic circle. Germany had now obtained promises of benevolent neutrality from Russia in case of a French attack. At the same time, its special relationship to Austria under the terms of the Dual Alliance remained in effect because the Reinsurance Treaty covered only Russian actions in the Straits, not an attack on Austria. The impression that all was well among the three Eastern powers was confirmed a year later when the emperors of Austria, Russia, and Germany renewed their promise of mutual consultations on all matters of common interest in yet another treaty, a second Three Emperors' Alliance.

In reality, the Reinsurance Treaty was a hollow triumph, and the new Three Emperors' Alliance demonstrated the limitations of personal agreements among heads of state in the conduct of international relations. In the long run, the Reinsurance Treaty was not really viable; Germany could not undertake to support both Russian and Austrian aims in the Balkans. The Reich's promise to remain neutral as Russia moved on the Straits violated at least the spirit of its general promise to aid Austria's efforts in stopping Russian ambitions in southeastern Europe. Bismarck's explanation to the Austrians that the "top secret" clause of the Reinsurance Treaty would actually aid the Habsburgs' interests, because any Russian moves toward Constantinople would call forth fierce British opposition and consequently bring England closer to the partners in the Dual Alliance, was not very convincing.

As this explanation showed, in some sense Bismarck himself recognized the fatal flaw of his diplomatic strategy. The assumption that the conservative empires in Eastern and Central Europe had compatible interests just because they were authoritarian systems was simply wrong. Within two years after the signing of the Reinsurance Treaty, Bismarck's entire system of alliances was in serious disarray. Germany's new emperor, William II, refused to extend the Reinsurance Treaty when it came up for renewal in 1890. Russo-German relations deteriorated accordingly. More significantly, the new monarch, unlike his grandfather, was determined to expand Germany's role as an imperialist power, thereby setting the Reich on a diplomatic collision course with

Great Britain. By 1890, then, Germany's foreign policy was at a crossroads. Far from having stabilized the international balance of power, the Reich's system of alliances was subject to severe stresses and weaknesses, and Germany's self-selected position as honest broker had lost much of its credibility.

THE END OF THE ERA AND BISMARCK'S DISMISSAL

Twenty years after the empire had been established amid pomp and martial ceremonies at the Palace of Versailles, the founders' generation looked back with pride on the past, and seemingly, with confidence into the future. Rising economic indicators suggested that the long depression was nearing its end. By 1890 the German economy had reached a new stage in its development: Germany was now a major capital exporter. Domestic stability seemed assured; there certainly was no real danger of revolutionary upheavals to overthrow the Bismarck Compromise. And in the field of foreign policy, Bismarck's triumph in resurrecting the Three Emperors' Alliance had apparently secured Germany's continued hegemonic position on the Continent.

And yet there was a prevailing sense that all was not well. The malaise had numerous manifestations. Brahms' and Bruckner's somber compositions reflected a sense of pessimism about the future that could not be entirely dispelled by the simultaneous popularity of frothy Viennese operettas. In literature the turn of the decade saw the brief flowering of the German naturalist and realist schools. Typical was the novel *Effi Briest* by Theodor Fontane, published in 1895. The story is that of the tragic death of a young noblewoman, who, after committing a single naive indiscretion, is crushed by the weight of societal prejudices and lack of compassion. Like much of German society the novel exudes a sense of being trapped without a way out. Politically, this feeling manifested itself through a

PUNCH, OR THE LONDON CHARIVARI—March 29, 1890.

DROPPING THE PILOT.

One of the most famous cartoons of all times, "Dropping the Pilot," was a
Punch comment on William II's dismissal of Bismarck. It appeared in an
1890 issue of *Punch*. (Source: 19th era/Alamy.)

precipitous rise in political anti-Semitism. A flurry of short-lived anti-Semitic parties gained notoriety and some popularity by linking the evils of modernization with the emancipation and influence of the country's Jews.

At the level of high decision making, concern about modernization took a different form. By the end of the decade, it had become clear that the terms of the Bismarck Compromise needed major revision. The Anti-Socialist Laws had not banished the specter of revolutionary Marxism; on the contrary, as the economy recovered, new members flocked to both the SPD and the unions. Parliament was increasingly unwilling to accept its lack of real power under the constitution, pressing instead for a greater say in running the affairs of the country.

We now know that in response to the obvious tensions, Bismarck himself was contemplating redrafting the Compromise of 1871. There are indications that he hoped to invoke the doctrine of the "state of constitutional emergency." As a solution to the "emergency" he apparently envisioned either a military coup or, more likely, a renegotiation of the princes' compact that had led to the creation of the Reich in 1871. The latter scenario would have involved a decision by the states' rulers to rewrite the constitution of 1871. The new constitution, so Bismarck felt, should significantly reduce the rudimentary powers of the Reichstag while increasing the authority of the chancellor.

Even more than a hundred years later, it is difficult to tell how serious any of these plans for constitutional revisions were. Bismarck was a master of the art of disinformation; much of what emanated from his office was designed more to mislead than to inform. In the end, it did not matter; all of the chancellor's maneuvers came to naught because of a feature in the constitution of 1871 that Bismarck had originally included as the keystone of his own power: the special relationship of the chancellor and the emperor. When Bismarck became prime minister of Prussia in 1862, he regarded himself as the "loyal servant of William I." As far as he was concerned, that

relationship did not change for the remainder of his life; he chose the same phrase as the inscription on his tombstone. However, in 1888, death brought an end to the special partnership: in March, William I died at the advanced age of ninety-one. He was succeeded by his son, Frederick III, then fifty-seven. At the time of his succession to the throne, however, Frederick III was already dying of cancer of the throat. His death occurred in June, so 1888 became a three-emperor year. Within the space of four months Frederick III had been replaced by his twenty-nine-year-old son, William II, the man who was to be the last German emperor.

As crown prince, Frederick III, and even more his wife, Princess Victoria, a daughter of Queen Victoria of Great Britain, had reputations as friends of liberalism and political modernization. For years Bismarck had lived in fear of Frederick's accession to the throne. The chancellor's concerns proved groundless because, except for dismissing the extremely unpopular Prussian minister of the interior, Robert von Puttkamer, Frederick made no personnel or policy changes during his brief reign.

The situation was entirely different with his son, William II. The new monarch was an energetic, arrogant, impulsive man determined not only to look like a head of state but also act the part. Within a few months after becoming emperor, he was confronted with both the necessity and opportunity for deciding two fundamental policy issues. One involved the renewal of the Reinsurance Treaty and the other the extension of the Anti-Socialist Laws. In both cases William did not hesitate to reach his own decisions, and both times his judgment was diametrically opposed to Bismarck's.

Like many experts in the Reich foreign ministry, William became convinced that in signing the Reinsurance Treaty, Germany had maneuvered itself into an impossible position with respect to its obligations to Austria under the Dual Alliance. Consequently, against Bismarck's advice, the emperor decided the Reinsurance Treaty should not be renewed when it lapsed in 1890.

A second conflict between the aged chancellor and the young monarch arose over the future of the Anti-Socialist Laws. The year 1890 was also the time for the triannual renewal of this repressive legislation. Here Bismarck, in line with his "constitutional emergency" plans, proposed not only a simple extension of the legislation originally passed in 1878 but a tightening of the screws that was a clear affront to the tradition of immunity from political prosecution for members of parliament. The government submitted a bill to the Reichstag that would have permitted the police to arrest all socialist members of the Reichstag as common criminals. The chancellor was fully aware that it would be impossible to obtain parliamentary backing for the entire package. A majority of the delegates was willing to extend the Anti-Socialist Laws in modified form, but that majority would not agree to emasculate the rights of members of the Reichstag. In retrospect it appears that a parliamentary defeat of the legislation was part of Bismarck's strategy. He apparently planned to dismiss the Reichstag after the antisocialist bill had been defeated and to schedule new elections. If, as expected, the elections produced another antigovernment majority, a state of constitutional emergency could be declared, and the Reichstag permanently prorogued.

To his credit, the emperor was unwilling to go along with such an artificially induced constitutional crisis. He favored negotiating a compromise with the parliamentary majority in order to obtain support for a weakened version of the Anti-Socialist Laws. Bismarck decided to turn the conflict between himself and William into a contest of wills. He threatened to resign unless the emperor agreed to maintain a hard line on the Anti-Socialist Laws. (Incidentally, threatening to resign was nothing new for the chancellor. He had used threats of resignation with good effect on a number of occasions during his career.) The young monarch not only disagreed with Bismarck on the substantive issue involved, but he also called the chancellor's bluff. Determined in any case to escape the tutelage of the grand old man, he quickly accepted the chancellor's resignation. The long era of Bismarck's domination of German affairs came to an abrupt end in March 1890.

CHAPTER TWO

Wilhelminian Germany

1890–1914

The years from Bismarck's dismissal in 1890 to the outbreak of World War I in 1914 present a series of contrasting and contradictory images to the historian. Germany had achieved the "place in the sun" that the emperor William II demanded for his nation. However, although the country had finally "arrived" as a great power, Wilhelminian Germany was a society divided against itself. The outwardly secure authoritarian political climate hid vacillation and paralysis in the decision-making processes behind the scenes. Germany's foreign policy was erratic. Years of patient negotiations for stable alliances were negated by impetuous and heavy-handed actions by the emperor and other leaders.

The contradictions inherent in Wilhelminian society were perhaps most noticeable in the areas of culture and values. Pervasive militarism in the society reached its high point. Led by the emperor, Germans from the aristocracy to the lower middle class delighted in uniforms and the aping of officers' mannerisms. At the same time, the Victorian stodginess

in dress and manners was challenged by thousands of young Germans, who donned simple clothing, joined hiking clubs, and longed for the romantic simplicities of life.

Historians generally agree that Germany's problems were related to the phenomenon of telescoped and asymmetrical modernization. Wilhelminian Germany was undergoing very rapid economic and technological development. In 1890 a little less than half of all Germans were still employed in agriculture. At the end of the decade, after the depression had run its course, an unprecedented industrial boom began; by 1914 only a third of the German workforce worked on the land. Drawn by the economic opportunities in industry, the population continued to move westward and from rural to urban areas. Between 1870 and 1914, 2 million Germans moved from the agricultural areas of East Elbia to settle in Berlin and the urban centers of western Germany.

Not surprisingly, along with the shift in occupation and locale came demands for greater political participation—but here the old ruling classes and their supporters balked. Although they pursued policies that encouraged modernization in economic life, they rejected modernism in politics. The emperor in many ways epitomized this attitude. On the one hand he was genuinely concerned about the social problems of industrial labor, yet when workers demanded more political power, William II called them "a mob not worthy of the name human."

Art and literature also reflected the contradictions of the age. Official art—the styles approved by the academies and the country's social and political leaders—favored philistine paintings and bombastic statues of military heroes. But increasing numbers of painters and sculptors, following the lead of their French colleagues, "seceded" from the officially approved styles. Instead of pseudorealism and sentimental romanticism, a new generation of artists favored expressionism and impressionism. Similarly, Wilhelminian architecture was characterized by a decorative style that delighted in stucco sculptures at the most unlikely places on the outside of buildings; bric-a-brac and over-stuffed furniture were hallmarks of interior decorating. Yet here too there were signs of revolt. A German form of art deco known as the *Jugendstil* increasingly dotted the urban landscape with lean forms and graceful lines.

Developments in literature ran along parallel paths. Heroic novels, farces, and light revues found a ready audience but so did thoughtful works highly critical of Wilhelminian society. Gerhard Hauptmann's dramas of social realism played to packed audiences, and Thomas Mann's early novels, with the erudite but telling criticism of nineteenth-century middle-class smugness, became best sellers almost overnight. Most educated Germans had a handy supply of quotes by Friedrich Nietzsche ready for all occasions, but few actually grasped the philosopher's underlying message of biting cultural criticism.

Wilhelminian Germany, then, was a time of contradiction, conflict, innovation, and rapid change. Many Germans recognized that between 1890 and 1914 their society was at a crossroads, but most Germans wanted it both ways: modernization and traditionalism.

PARTIES, LOBBIES, AND PATRIOTIC ORGANIZATIONS

Some of the most bitterly fought controversies in Wilhelminian Germany involved issues of political reform and restructuring. Perceptible shifts in electoral strength led to much internal soul searching among the four major German parliamentary groups: the conservatives, liberals, Catholics, and Social Democrats. Generally speaking, as the country became more urbanized and industrialized, the voters' allegiances shifted to the left of the political spectrum. Hardest hit were the conservatives. The two conservative parties continued to dominate in their traditional strongholds in East Elbia, and the three-class system of voting in Prussia secured their iron grip on the Reich's largest state. In the Reichstag elections, however, the conservatives steadily lost ground. By 1912 (the year of the last national election before the outbreak of World War I) the conservatives had been reduced to about 10 percent of the national popular vote. The German Conservative Party was represented by only forty-five delegates in the Reichstag (in 1890 the party still had seventy-three), while its more moderate cousins, the Free Conservatives, were reduced to fourteen instead of the twenty delegates.

Unfortunately, in their efforts to halt the erosion of their popular support, the conservative leaders increased the intransigence of their programs and the demagoguery of their campaigns. Attempting to undercut the competition from Stöcker's Christian Social Movement (see the discussion on p. 29) and a bevy of anti-Semitic parties that arose cometlike in the early 1890s, the German conservatives in 1892 adopted a new manifesto, the Tivoli document. In this program, the German Conservative Party embraced anti-Semitism while rejecting parliamentarism

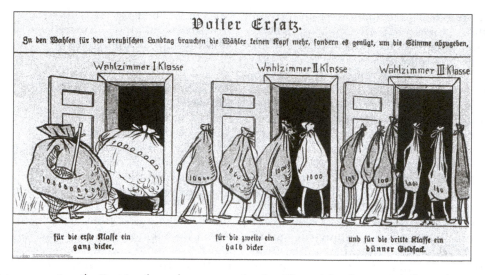

A biting comment on the Prussian three class system of voting. The weight of a voter's ballot is determined by his wealth. (Source: akg-images/Interfoto /Sammlung Rauch)

and social democracy as incompatible with Germany's national interests or political character.

In one sense, the conservative tactic was successful. The anti-Semitic parties disappeared as quickly as they had risen. They reached their peak in the election of 1893, when they obtained 2.9 percent of the national vote and sent sixteen delegates to the Reichstag. Ten years later, when the long depression of the 1880s and 1890s had run its course, the anti-Semitic parties were represented by only three delegates in the national parliament. But the demise of the anti-Semitic parties represented not the decline of anti-Semitism but rather its diffusion into other forms of articulation. Even so, the conservatives' demagogic tactics could not prevent the party's decline at the polls.

Liberalism, too, suffered from political stagnation. The two liberal parties, the right-of-center National Liberals and the left-of-center Progressives, together sent 118 delegates to the Reichstag in 1890; by 1912 that number had fallen to eighty-seven.

The Progressives suffered a disproportionate share of the decline, while the National Liberal strength held steady at about 10 percent of the popular vote—still a far cry from the halcyon days of 1874 when the National Liberals alone had 152 members in the Reichstag. The National Liberals were torn between supporting the status quo and increasing the party's electoral popularity by presenting a viable alternative to the authoritarianism. They were unable to resolve the dilemma. Instead, two powerful factions within the same party increasingly went their own ways.

A growing dichotomy emerged between the party's Reichstag delegation and its colleagues in the Prussian state legislature. All National Liberals enthusiastically supported such nationalistic causes as colonialism and navalism; they also formed the backbone of such government-sponsored chauvinistic efforts as the Naval League (see the later discussion on p. 51). But on domestic policy the National Liberals did not see eye to eye. In Prussia the National Liberals continued their alliance with the Conservatives, rejecting any changes in the Prussian electoral system, but in the Reichstag a new generation of National Liberal leaders was increasingly dubious about tying the party's fortunes to the authoritarian system. A group of Reichstag delegates, which included the party's future chairman, a young lawyer from Saxony named Gustav Stresemann, organized themselves as Young Liberals in 1900 and urged the party's leadership to loosen National Liberalism's ties to the increasingly reactionary conservatives.

The Progressives' fortunes were hampered by a series of party splits. A united Progressive Party did not emerge again until 1910 and by that time intraparty sniping had eroded much of the left-wing liberals' strength. In addition, the Progressives were also divided on the future of German politics. Most of them favored increased powers for parliament, substantial changes in the Prussian electoral system, and some were even willing to break the pariah barrier around the Social Democrats. In the election of 1912, a few Progressive Party organizations concluded electoral alliances with the SPD that committed Progressive and Social Democratic candidates not to oppose each other in runoff elections. (Under the German election laws, if no candidate obtained a majority of the popular vote in a district, a runoff contest between the two highest vote getters was required.)

But there was another side to the Progressives as well. The left-wing liberals were also caught up in the mentality of imperialism and chauvinism. Like the National Liberals, the Progressives were enthusiastic supporters of naval armament and imperialist expansion. A prominent leader, Friedrich Naumann, who worked hard to integrate social democracy into the German political fabric, also did much to propagandize Germany's need for a sphere of influence in southeastern Europe.

The Catholic Center Party and the Social Democrats were political success stories. In every national election during the Wilhelminian years, the Center Party obtained between 14 and 16 percent of the popular vote, which translated into a solid block of around a hundred delegates in the Reichstag (some 20 percent of the total), so that the votes of the party were decisive on many issues that came before the national parliament. In addition, Catholic leaders used extraparliamentary organizations to mobilize public opinion among their constituents. A large lay organization, the Popular Association for Catholic Germany (*Volksverein für das katholische Deutschland*), founded in 1890, mobilized Catholic public opinion on educational questions and issues of church autonomy. At the same time, a growing Catholic union movement drew support especially from miners and metalworkers in western Germany.

Still, all was not harmonious in the Catholic camp either. Shifting population patterns affected Catholics even more than Protestants, and the Center Party's share of the total potential Catholic vote fell as Catholics moved from the countryside to the cities. The result was intensified debate over the Center Party's social and political goals. The party's national leaders were proud of their gradual acceptance by the Reich's Protestant authoritarian establishment and generally supported imperialism and the military. A growing minority, however, felt that the price of "governmentalism" was too high because it tended to alienate the increasing number of left-wing Catholics and thus hurt the party at the polls. Some younger leaders in the party, such as Matthias Erzberger (who, when he was first elected to the parliament in 1903, was twenty-eight and the youngest member of the Reichstag) and the future chancellor Joseph Wirth, urged their party to endorse social activism and reforms of Germany's authoritarian political structure.

Rapid changes in German society led to debates on other intraparty controversies as well. The decision to serve as the political voice only of German Catholics inevitably condemned the Center Party to permanent minority status among Germany's political parties. With little danger of a new Kulturkampf, some of the party leaders demanded that the Center Party "leave the [Catholic] tower" (*Heraus aus dem Turm*) and become a party that would be attractive to both Catholic and Protestant voters. The Center Party's national leadership, however, resolutely rejected such a course as too risky.

While the bourgeois parties were concerned about declining popularity or stagnation, the Social Democrats went from triumph to triumph. In 1890 the party sent thirty-five delegates to the Reichstag. Twenty-two years later almost a fourth of the members of the national parliament, 110 in all, were Social Democrats. And even this figure was not fully representative of the party's popularity among German voters. In 1912 every third German voter cast his ballot for the SPD, but failure to redraw the districts since 1871 and the requirement for runoff elections, which allowed the bourgeois parties to combine their forces against a Social Democratic candidate, kept the party's strength in the Reichstag disproportionately low.

The SPD's problems were not lack of success at the ballot box but growing internal divisions over the future of the party's ideological and tactical direction. By 1895 both Marx and Engels had died, so the party had to find its way without the guidance of its intellectual founders. The end of the depression and the lapse of the Anti-Socialist Laws presented the SPD with a paradox. On the one hand, the number of Social Democratic voters and members and the strength of the socialist unions were growing rapidly. At the same time, the boom years after 1897 clearly signaled that the collapse of capitalism was not imminent. In essence, then, the SPD had to decide how to use its popular strength in the age of high capitalism.

The conflict over the party's relationship to capitalism would eventually lead to the split of the German Marxists into Social Democrats and Communists, but that development was still some years away. The debate over the need to adapt Marx's predictions to fit the reality of conditions at the turn of the century began innocently enough with the publication in 1898 of a small volume entitled *Foundations of Socialism and the Tasks of Social Democracy*. The author was

Eduard Bernstein, a forty-eight-year-old Social Democratic newspaper editor and former bank clerk. Bernstein, who was one of the executors of Engels's literary estate, intended to update Marxism, but in the process he gave some radically new interpretations to such accepted Marxist concepts as the class struggle and dialectical materialism. Nevertheless, Bernstein never abandoned his belief that socialism would eventually replace capitalism as a higher form of human societal organization.

The thrust of Bernstein's argument was that the road to socialism would be evolutionary rather than revolutionary. Consequently, he urged the SPD to work for the improvement of the workers' lot within the context of capitalism and not expect an early demise of the hated system. The unions should press for improved wages and working conditions, and the party should work for reforms leading to greater political democracy. To this end, Bernstein urged the SPD to exploit the tactical possibilities of parliamentarism both by using the proletariat's voting strength and by forging alliances with the more reform-minded segments of the bourgeoisie.

Especially the leaders of the rapidly growing socialist unions welcomed Bernstein's analysis because it stressed the importance of labor's struggle for better wages and shorter hours. But there was also fierce opposition to "revisionism," as Bernstein's proposals came to be called. Led by Rosa Luxemburg, a brilliant writer and for many years one of the most popular teachers at the SPD's training center for party functionaries, left-wing socialists disagreed with Bernstein on virtually every point. Luxemburg and others argued that the advent of imperialism demonstrated that capitalism was not only reaching its highest but also its final phase, so that Social Democrats should be preparing the proletariat not for coexisting with capitalism but for the revolution that was coming sooner rather than later. Instead of concentrating on bread-and-butter issues (important as these might be in the short run), the unions should plan for the general strike with which the workers would seize revolutionary power.

If carried to their logical conclusion, the disagreements between revisionists and anti-revisionists would have split the party. Because this was an outcome both sides were anxious to avoid, most Social Democratic activists rallied around a third faction in the party. This group, called the centrists, included the SPD's longtime and much respected national leader, August Bebel, as well as Karl Kautsky, the SPD's chief theoretician. (Kautsky wrote the theoretical sections of the party's official program, the Erfurt Program; Bernstein, the parts on day-to-day tactics. As a result, the platform was a contradictory mix of Marxist revolutionary rhetoric and tactical suggestions for reforms within the context of capitalism.) The centrists argued that speculations about the future of capitalism should not deter the party from addressing its most pressing current concern: the need to forge a powerful working-class organization that would press forward Social Democracy's demands on both fronts, political and economic. The party organization itself thus became a primary goal.

The ideological struggle between revisionists and their opponents emerged into open conflict at the party's 1905 national congress. Here the left-wing radicals introduced a resolution putting the party on record as endorsing the concept of the political use of the general strike. The resolution was defeated, largely because the unions (who traditionally sent a large bloc of delegates to the SPD's national congresses) opposed it. Until World War I, the SPD stayed ideologically on the fence. The official (and contradictory) party platform remained the Erfurt Program of 1891.

Efforts to organize public opinion outside the parameters of the parties were particularly important during the reign of William II. In fact, the 1890s might well be described as the decade of the mass lobbies. Dissatisfied with the effectiveness of the political parties, which, with the exception of the SPD, mostly lay dormant except when activated at election time, middle-class economic and social-interest groups established lobbying organizations to plead their causes.

The influence of the extraparliamentary pressure organizations on the evolution of the German political scene is difficult to assess. Some historians contend that groups like the Agrarian League and the Naval League (see the later discussion on p. 51) were instrumental in preventing further political modernization in Germany at a crucial time. Other analysts caution against overestimating the popularity and influence of the nationalist organizations, pointing out that far more Germans joined the SPD than even the most successful of the nationalist organizations, the Naval League. As usual, the truth lies somewhere in between. The extraparliamentary organizations did not control politics, but they did mobilize middle- and upper-class public opinion around certain emotion-laden issues, such as tariffs, imperialism, and navalism. In addition, the lobbying groups helped to delay political modernization because all of the important ones were in favor of preserving Prusso-German authoritarianism.

The prototype of a successful extraparliamentary mass mobilization effort was the Agrarian League (*Bund der Landwirte*—BdL). Founded in 1893, the Agrarian League launched an effective multimedia public relations campaign against the liberal agricultural tariff policies of the Caprivi government (see the later discussion on pp. 59–60). The BdL was initiated and led by East Elbian landowners, but the appeal for tariff protection sparked an immediate response from farmers all over Germany, and the Agrarian League quickly grew into a large organization. By 1914 it had some 300,000 members. The BdL was officially a nonpartisan organization, but—not surprisingly in view of its political stand—it maintained close ties to the leadership of the conservative parties. It also succeeded in placing some of its friends in important government positions.

The BdL formed an alliance with another economic interest group, the Central Association of German Industrialists (*Centralverband deutscher Industrieller*—CdI).

Im Mittelpunkt Eduard Bernstein (1850–1932)

Bernstein was one of the most influential but also most vilified of the Social Democratic leaders who tried to adapt Marxism to the realities of European economic life after Marx's death in 1873. The son of a Jewish locomotive engineer, Bernstein started out as an apprentice bank teller, but he soon struck out on his own. When he was twenty-two years old, he joined the SPD, and although he had little formal education, the party leaders asked him to be editor of the party's major newspaper, *Der Sozialdemokrat.* After the passage of the Anti-Socialist Laws in 1878, Social Democratic newspapers were forbidden to be published in Germany, and Bernstein spent much of the years between 1878 and 1890 in exile, first in Zurich and later in London. He was still the editor of *Der Sozialdemokrat*, although the paper now had to be smuggled into Germany from abroad.

While in London Bernstein met Friedrich Engels, who asked him to be one of the executors of the Marx–Engels literary estate. The association with Engels might have led Bernstein to become an orthodox Marxist determinist, but there was a countervailing influence. Bernstein was also in contact with the English Fabian Society. Acutely concerned about the problems of capitalism as it existed in Great Britain at the turn of the century, the Fabian Society was a group of intellectuals and writers, such as George Bernhard Shaw, who were determined to improve the lot of the country's industrial workers. However, they rejected the Marxist idea that this could be done only through the class struggle and a violent revolution. Instead, they advocated nonviolent reforms. After his sojourn in England, Bernstein, too, concluded that a number of Marx's assumptions about the evolution of capitalism were wrong. It was not true, for example, that as capitalism reached its higher stages, the lives of the industrial workers would become more and more destitute. Like the Fabians, Bernstein was also convinced that if a country had a full-scale political democracy, capitalism could be reformed and changed without violent upheavals.

After he returned to Germany, in 1905 Bernstein published a slim volume that was to become a bombshell in Social Democratic circles. In *The Foundations of Socialism,* Bernstein argued that in the industrialized countries of Western Europe at the turn of the century, capitalism was a far more complex phenomenon than Marx had predicted. Bernstein never abandoned his conviction that socialism would eventually replace capitalism as humankind's dominant economic and social value system, but he questioned both the means of achieving socialism and the final purpose of a socialist society. For Bernstein, capitalism was not a monolithic entity but a variety of interest groups, some of which were more or less "progressive." "Progressive" capitalists would accept social reforms; "reactionary" ones would not. Bernstein also insisted that working for socialism was primarily an ethical mandate, not a way of installing a dictatorship of the proletariat.

Bernstein insisted that by working together with "progressive" capitalist forces, it was possible to achieve important improvements in the lives of the industrial workers even before capitalism was

When it became clear that even after the depression ended, heavy industry would remain a fairly stagnant part of the economy, the leaders of Germany's heavy industry also opposed the Reich's free-trade policy and insisted on permanent protection from foreign imports. By the end of the Wilhelminian years, cooperation between conservative farmers and the leaders of heavy industry, colloquially known as the alliance of "iron and rye," was well established.

Unlike agriculture, where the BdL dominated lobbying efforts, German industry did not speak with a single voice. Germany's replaced by socialism. The means of achieving this end was not a violent revolution but a political system that established full-scale democracy. As a result he insisted that the primary task of the Social Democratic Party was not to prepare the proletariat for a violent revolution but to strive for political democracy as a way of voting in socialist reforms and eventually socialism itself.

The reaction to Bernstein's book (and his subsequent writings) in Marxist circles was, at least on the surface, overwhelmingly negative. Vladimir Lenin, the leader of the Bolshevik Party in Russia, accused Bernstein of betraying the socialist cause. For Lenin "Bernsteinianism" and "revisionism" became epithets hurled at anyone who advocated reform rather than revolution. In Germany Rosa Luxemburg became Bernstein's primary ideological adversary. She bitterly denounced her party comrade as criminally naive for advocating that capitalism would allow itself to be voted out of power. Delegates to the SPD's national conventions routinely passed resolutions reaffirming the necessity of a proletarian revolution.

Actually, Bernstein's ideas were far more influential than it appeared at first glance. The German labor unions readily endorsed a theory that allowed them to negotiate collective bargaining agreements limited to bread-and-butter issues. The SPD, too, although rejecting Bernsteinianism in theory, actually pursued policies that put the party's weight behind establishing democracy in Germany rather than preparing for revolution.

Ironically, during World War I Bernstein and Luxemburg both joined the *Unabhängige Sozialistische Partei Deutschlands* (Independent Socialist Party of Germany, USPD) (see below, p. 89), although they did so for entirely different reasons. For Luxemburg the USPD represented the revolutionary side of German Marxism, whereas Bernstein, a lifelong pacifist, agreed with the USPD's demand for an immediate end to the fighting. After the armistice Bernstein rejoined the SPD in 1919 and continued to be an active member until his death. From 1902 until 1928, he was a member of the Reichstag, although he was not a very faithful legislator; his activities remained primarily in the areas of writing and speaking.

In the 1920s Bernstein's ideas seemed to enjoy a brief period of acceptance in the SPD. The 1921 Görlitz Program embodied many of Bernstein's ideas, although his name was never mentioned in the document. The programmatic endorsement of revisionism was a brief interlude, however. The party's next statement, the Heidelberg Program of 1925, again showed the heavy hand of orthodox Marxists, although its passionate revolutionary rhetoric did not match the SPD's day-to-day reformist politics. It was not until after World War II that Bernstein's ideas were acknowledged and accepted by the German and West European Social Democratic parties. The SPD's 1959 Bad Godesberg Program is permeated by Bernsteinianism, and it is fair to say that the ideas of Eduard Bernstein are now part of the ideological foundations of all of Western Europe's social democratic parties.

rapidly growing electrical, chemical, and banking interests did not need to fear foreign competition. On the contrary, they benefited from a policy of free trade that facilitated exports. In addition, they were opposed to agricultural tariffs that would increase consumer prices and consequently the price of labor, which was a major cost factor in industries employing a large number of skilled workers. Politically, these growth-oriented industries wanted to modify those parts of the authoritarian system that permitted the stagnant agricultural and heavy industry segments of the economy to retain a disproportionately large share of political power. In 1909 representatives of Germany's major banks joined leaders of the electrical and chemical industries to form the Hansa Association (*Hansabund*) as a rival to the CdI. Unlike the Agrarian League and the CdI, the Hansabund supported a policy of relatively free trade and demanded modifications of the Prussian three-class system of voting. Some members of the Hansabund even initiated modest efforts to integrate the moderate forces among the Social Democrats into Germany's social and political fabric.

The most strident linkage of politics and economics came in the decade before the outbreak of World War I. In 1904, frightened by the growing membership of the socialist unions and the SPD's electoral successes, the Agrarian League, the CdI, and the Association of Small Businessmen (*Mittelstandsvereinigung*) united to launch yet another public relations effort, the National Association against Social Democracy (*Reichsverband gegen die Sozialdemokratie*). Nine years later, the same groups attempted to create a new umbrella bourgeois political lobby, called the Cartel of Producing Estates (*Kartell der schaffenden Stände*). The cartel's program consisted of demands to reduce the power of the Reichstag and to place restrictions on the activities of labor unions. The group demanded right-to-work laws, a continuation of the prohibition on nationwide collective bargaining agreements, and a new set of antisocialist measures.

Much of the businessmen's lobbying activities were a response to the changing power dynamics in the marketplace resulting from the growing strength of Germany's unions. During the boom years organized labor increased rapidly in membership and militancy. Between 1890 and 1914 German union membership as a whole grew from 357,000 to 2.5 million—an almost sevenfold increase in twenty-four years. The largest gains were registered by the socialist unions: 278,000 members in 1890; 2.1 million in 1914. The socialist unions also streamlined their organizational structure. In 1890 they formed a new umbrella organization, the General Commission (*Generalkommission*). It was designed to improve coordination and cooperation among the various craft unions, which had been virtually autonomous until then. Catholic and liberal unions did not join the General Commission, but employers derived little comfort from this. As the experience during a number of bitter strikes showed, workers from all three wings of the union movement often cooperated in forcing concessions from the employers.

The various business lobbying groups differed on many political and economic issues, but they were united in their support of Germany's imperialist ventures. As we see later (in the discussion on p. 73), the Reich's authoritarian leaders eagerly used the widespread enthusiasm for acquiring colonies and naval armaments to neutralize demands for political and constitutional changes and create instead a common front of support for the government's policies.

The enthusiasm for imperialism resulted in large part from the success of the most influential supra-economic lobbying groups in Wilhelminian Germany, the Colonial League (*Kolonialverein*) and especially the Naval League (*Flottenverein*). Founded in 1897, the Naval League was a truly "modern" lobbying group. Whereas traditional militarism had directed veneration toward the Prussian army, the Naval League lobbied for a branch of the armed forces that had an all-German rather than Prussian focus. The Naval League also gave expression to some specifically Wilhelminian values. It openly celebrated of Germany's quest for a "place in the sun": As a major imperial and industrial power, the Reich needed a strong navy to protect its overseas trade and colonial possessions. Celebrating the navy also fit in well with rapid industrialization because the navy would epitomize the superiority of German technology and industry.

The initiative for the establishment of the Naval League came from the government itself. From the beginning, the driving force behind the organization was the state secretary (i.e., minister) for naval affairs, Admiral Alfred von Tirpitz. The admiral was convinced the navy could become the spark that would rekindle the sense of patriotism he felt had been sadly declining since 1871. Enthusiasm for the navy would unite the nation behind the government's policies and generate pressure on the Reichstag to pass the naval construction bills that Tirpitz submitted at regular intervals to the national parliament. The admiral was one of the first to recognize the importance of the military–industrial complex in modern society. Although the league sought both individual and corporate memberships, it was financed primarily by corporate contributions.

Once launched, the organization became a rapid success. Within a few years it had a membership of more than 100,000. With its official sponsorship, the Naval League became part of the social and club scene in many communities. High school teachers served as secretaries of numerous local chapters. The league maintained an ambitious public relations program, ranging from public lectures by naval officers on their journeys to faraway places to providing slanted teaching materials for use in the public schools.

The Naval League was not the only extra-parliamentary organization to plow the fertile field of nationalist agitation. Influential behind the scenes was the Pan German Association (*Alldeutscher Verein*). The guiding spirit of the Pan Germans was a former official in the Prussian ministry of justice, Heinrich Class. In 1912 Class, using a pseudonym, published a pamphlet with the provocative title, *Wenn ich der Kaiser wär'* ("If I Were the Emperor") in which he urged William II to reduce democracy and "Jewish influences" at home and press for greater German power abroad. The Pan Germans not only demanded that the Reich be more aggressive in gaining overseas territory, but they also wanted Germany to incorporate the German-speaking parts of Austria-Hungary. But such public efforts were not the essence of the Pan Germans' activities. Class emphasized working in secret to influence the views of the Reich's industrial, military, and political leaders. He had a tendency to overestimate his own persuasiveness, and the Pan German program never became German government policy, although the monarch as well as a number of his personal advisers and leaders of the conservative parties were sympathetic to the Pan Germans' basic program, including its strident anti-Semitism.

POLITICAL ISSUES AND PERSONALITIES

Politics in Wilhelminian Germany, as in any other modern society, was a product of organizations, issues, and personalities. The members of the Reich and Prussian cabinets, the chiefs of the Prussian general staff, the leading administrators of the state governments, and some key personal advisers of the emperor constituted the Reich's oligarchy of decision makers. It was a small group. It was also a politically and socially homogeneous circle, with shared family and educational experiences. Almost all the leading men in the empire possessed titles of nobility, although few were Junkers in the strict sense of the word. For the most part the chancellors, military chiefs of staff, and cabinet ministers came from families that had their roots west of the Elbe or even outside of Germany. Unfortunately, it is also fair to say that as a group, the German oligarchy of leaders, with their rural heritage, narrow social perspective, traditional education, and conservative political outlook, was not well qualified to lead the country into the twentieth century.

Titular and symbolic head of this small group of decision makers was the man who gave the era its name, Emperor William II. Like the times in which he lived, William was a study in contrasts. Born with a physical disability that left him essentially without the use of his left arm, he was an overachiever whose personality traits were, at one and the same time, weakness of character, arrogance, intolerance, charm, quick-wittedness, and lack of perseverance. He was a man who needed constant reinforcement. Bismarck described William as someone "who wanted to have a birthday party every day of his life."

Although unsure of his opinions and anxious for popular and peer approval, the emperor insisted he was a leader who made his way undeterred by considerations of popularity or politics. It will come as no surprise that he selected friends and associates who were sycophants rather than honest advisers. They included such men as the romantic and sentimental aristocrat Count Philipp zu Eulenburg; a mediocre general, Count Alfred von Waldersee; and a reactionary industrialist, Baron Carl Ferdinand von Stumm-Halberg. But there was also another side to the emperor. Among the monarch's longtime friends was Albert Ballin, the Jewish head of a successful shipping firm, the Hamburg-America Line, and a man of unquestioned personal integrity.

Under the terms of the Bismarckian constitution the emperor presided over a three-layered executive structure. In addition to privy councils on military and civilian affairs, he appointed the Reich chancellor and federal ministers, as well as, in his capacity as king of Prussia, that state's prime minister and the other members of the Prussian cabinet. (Except for the years 1892–1894, all the Wilhelminian chancellors also served as Prussian prime ministers.) Constitutionally, none of these appointments were subject to parliamentary approval, although the Reich and Prussian cabinets had to deal with their respective legislatures to get their budgets approved. In practice, the Reichstag's role as partner of the executive was expanding throughout the Wilhelminian years. Unwilling to countenance massive public disapproval, the Reich executive worked hard to obtain a supportive parliamentary coalition on most major issues.

It was not easy, however, to find government leaders who worked well within the strictures of this system of "parliamentary authoritarianism." As Reich chancellors the government leaders had to work with the increasingly left-leaning Reichstag. But in their capacity as Prussian prime ministers they were required to maintain good relations with the conservative majority in the Prussian Landtag. And if this split were not difficult

enough, they also had constantly nurse the emperor's inflated ego. Few men could do this for any length of time. The contradictory requirements help explain the succession of relatively short-term chancellors during the Wilhelminian years.

From 1890 to 1894 the chancellor was Leo von Caprivi, a professional soldier who, to everyone's surprise, turned out to be a natural political talent. In contrast to his immediate predecessor, Caprivi, at fifty-nine, was virtually a young man at the time of his appointment. But Caprivi fell afoul of conservative opposition to his economic policies (see the discussion on pp. 59–60), and after four years he was succeeded by a seventy-five-year-old Bavarian aristocrat, Chlodwig von Hohenlohe-Schillingsfürst. The chancellor's advanced age made it difficult for him to carry the burdens of office. In addition, Hohenlohe was unfamiliar with Reich and Prussian issues. Most of his career had been spent in Bavarian politics, and before going to Berlin he had been governor of Alsace-Lorraine. Originally the emperor and his adviser Philipp zu Eulenburg intended that the aged Hohenlohe should serve as transition leader until they could turn to Bernhard von Bülow, the man they regarded as Caprivi's ideal successor. The Hohenlohe era lasted rather longer than anticipated, largely because the chancellor refused to resign, and the emperor was not willing to face the political crisis that an outright dismissal would have caused.

In 1900 William II exclaimed, "Bernhard has arrived, and I know all is well." In fact, all was not well for very long. The new chancellor, Bernhard von Bülow, was fifty-one years old and in the prime of his life. He also had charming manners, a facility for languages, and an extraordinary ability to feed William's ego with subservient memoranda. But he had spent all of his professional career in the German diplomatic service and had no experience in dealing with either parliament or domestic politics. When in 1906 Bülow proved incapable of preventing parliamentary investigations into some scandals in the Reich colonial office (see discussion on

Emperor William II strikes a pose as commander in chief of the Prussian army. The portrait dates from 1912. (Source: Courtesy of Library of Congress.)

p. 60), relations between the emperor and his erstwhile favorite turned sour, and three years later William used Bülow's failure to obtain the Reichstag's approval for a package of tax reforms as a welcome opportunity to dismiss the facile charmer.

As Bülow's successor the emperor chose an able but colorless Prussian bureaucrat, Theobald von Bethmann Hollweg. The new chancellor had spent his entire career in the Prussian civil service, rising to the post of minister of the interior in 1906. In contrast to Bülow, he was an able administrator and familiar with domestic issues, but Bethmann Hollweg had no foreign policy experience—a serious handicap at a time of rising international tensions.

Given the importance of the military in Wilhelminian Germany, the chief of staff of the Prussian army enjoyed a position of great influence and power. Here, too, practices during the Wilhelminian era contrasted sharply with those of the Bismarck era. When William II became emperor in 1888, he replaced the incumbent, General Helmuth von Moltke, who had been chief of staff since the Prussian constitutional crisis of the 1860s, with a personal favorite, the fifty-nine-year-old General von Waldersee. The contrast between the two men was striking—and not just in terms of age and length of service. Unlike the brilliant Moltke, Waldersee was by all accounts a mediocre military talent. Moreover, whereas Moltke was taciturn and aloof, Waldersee enjoyed political intrigue and hosting lavish parties at his Berlin home. (The latter would have been impossible on the modest salary of a Prussian officer, but Waldersee had had the foresight to marry an American heiress.)

Unfortunately for Waldersee, his social graces could not compensate for his lack of military capabilities. After only two years in office, Waldersee was replaced as chief of staff, although he remained a member of the emperor's personal entourage. Waldersee's successor came from the Moltke mold. General Alfred von Schlieffen, fifty-nine years old in 1892, was a distinguished strategist with a long record of staff appointments behind him. Unlike Waldersee, Schlieffen felt politics and the military should not mix, or, more precisely, he assumed political considerations should at all times be subordinated to military plans and strategies.

Schlieffen retired in 1906, and the emperor, no doubt hoping that history would repeat itself, selected another Moltke as the next chief of staff. The "younger" Helmuth von Moltke (he was fifty-eight at the time of his appointment) was the namesake and nephew of the "great" Moltke. Unfortunately, he had inherited only the name, not the skills of his uncle. Another mediocre talent, he failed completely when his leadership was tested during World War I. Within a year after the outbreak of the conflict, Moltke resigned his post.

Running through the length of the Wilhelminian years were a number of specific political controversies, all of them concerned with a fundamental problem: the redistribution of political power as the Reich made the transition from a rural traditional society to one dominated by industrial and urban lifestyles. To be sure, the issue was seldom stated so crassly. Instead, the debates over the basic problem of power tended to appear as high-minded discussions of political philosophy and values.

To begin with, there was the "federal problem," or to be more exact, the relationship between the Reich and its largest state, Prussia. Twenty years before, Bismarck had created a united Reich dominated by Prussia, and Prussia in turn was the political domain of the East Elbian Junkers. By 1890 it was clear that the Junkers were headed for economic decline and political isolation. Should this group continue to dominate Prussia, and, if so, should Prussia continue to exercise hegemony over the affairs of the Reich? The Junkers' own answer to this legitimate question was a resounding "yes," but that hardly settled the issue.

In this struggle for control of state and Reich, the Prussian ruling classes were not without political assets. The emperor agreed with their contention that Prussian authoritarianism was the key to the Reich's past and future greatness. As king of Prussia, William appointed well-known conservatives to a number of key Prussian positions. Ernst von Köller, the minister of the interior from 1894 to 1895, became hated for his reactionary appointment policies in the Prussian civil service and for his efforts to resurrect the laws against the socialists. Similarly, the state's prime minister from 1892 to 1894, Botho zu Eulenburg, a cousin of Philipp, sought to preserve the conservatives' power monopoly in Prussia; he single-handedly sabotaged efforts to achieve greater cooperation with the Catholic Center Party. The Prussian ministry of agriculture became a virtual branch office of the Agrarian League. The minister for most of the 1890s, Baron Ernst von Hammerstein-Loxten, as well as his successor Freiherr von Schorlemer-Lieser, had been active in the BdL before their appointments to the cabinet. The Central Association of Industrialists also managed to have its voice heard at the Prussian cabinet table. The minister of trade, Ludwig Brefeld, was a man with good connections to the industrialists' lobbying group.

But Prussian internal politics were only one side of the federal issue. There was also the interaction of the Reich and Prussia. In spite of his boast that he would go his own way, undeterred by shifts of public opinion, William knew that he could not isolate Prussia from the political pressures of the Reichstag nor, in the long run, continue to impose Prussia's authoritarian ways on the Reich as a whole. Köller's plans for a new set of antisocialist laws in Prussia were shelved, for example, when it became clear that they had no chance of being passed in the Reichstag. As the fulcrum of the German political spectrum continued to move left in the next twenty-four years, Prussia became politically more and more isolated, and relations between the state's ruling circles and the rest of the country grew increasingly strained. Unfortunately, this development also intensified the determination of Prussia's political leaders to maintain their control over the state at all costs.

A number of issues were involved in the Reich–Prussian relationship, but after 1890 the political debate centered largely on reforms of the Prussian electoral system as the key to changing Prusso-German authoritarianism. For good reason. The three-class system of voting enabled the Junkers and their allies to control politics in three fifths of the Reich; if the rules of universal male suffrage, under which the Reichstag was elected, prevailed in Prussia as well, the Conservatives' domination of Prussia would end. By 1900 polarization on the electoral issue was virtually complete. Progressives and Social Democrats as well as some National Liberals and Center Party leaders demanded major reforms in Prussia.

In contrast, Conservatives, most National Liberals, and a majority of Prussian Center Party leaders, as well as spokesmen for the Agrarian League and heavy industry, insisted that the Prussian electoral system should be left unchanged. Indeed, they claimed that the real problem was universal male suffrage as practiced in national elections. They demanded property qualifications as a condition for the right to vote in all state and national elections, or—a plan Bismarck had also toyed with—a parliament composed of representatives selected by economic-interest groups to take the place of the Reichstag. Most of the time the emperor and his advisers recognized that the clock of political modernization could not be held back. They tried to thread their way cautiously—too cautiously—between the intransigence of the Prussian conservatives and the demands for change by most other Germans.

As Prussian prime ministers, both Bülow and Bethmann Hollweg introduced electoral reform bills in the Prussian Landtag. The proposals did not envision the abolition of the three-class system, but they would have mitigated some of the most glaring discrepancies between the popular vote and parliamentary representation under the system established in 1851. All in vain. Until 1918 the Conservatives and most National Liberal and Center Party representatives in the Prussian legislature consistently voted down all efforts to realize electoral reforms. William in turn was not willing to use his powers as king to impose his will on the Prussian Conservatives. As a result, the gap between the politically dominant groups in the state and public opinion in Germany as a whole continued to grow. By 1914 the state that had united Germany was increasingly isolated from its own creation.

Another problem was the need for obtaining Reichstag backing for proposals by the federal government. There were two ways of achieving this goal: The government had to work either with "floating majorities" for each specific bill it wanted passed, or it could attempt to create a long-term alliance of parties that supported the executive because it agreed with the government's basic policy aims. From the Reich cabinet's point of view the latter was certainly preferable because it promised long-range stability in the relations between executive and legislature. But there was a major difficulty: The growing strength of the SPD and the left wing of the Center Party steadily decreased the size of the delegate block that endorsed the authoritarian status quo as a matter of political philosophy.

Nevertheless, the Reich governments attempted to create a "cartel of parties" that would support the executive in the Reichstag. Major disagreements emerged, however, over the membership of such a political cartel. The driving force behind one particular form of cartel, called the *Sammlungspolitik* ("collection policy"), was the Prussian minister of finance from 1890 to 1901, Johannes von Miquel. The minister, an old National Liberal-turned-Conservative, consistently advocated a resurrection of the coalition of Conservatives and National Liberals with which Bismarck had governed after 1878. Such a combination could be expected to support protective tariffs, imperialism, and a strong navy—and forcefully oppose reform in Prussia.

Miquel's scenario contained a major flaw, however: The Conservative-National Liberal alliance represented only a minority—and a declining one at that—of the Reichstag votes. For this reason, astute politicians like Caprivi rejected Miquel's Sammlungspolitik unless it included the Center Party and preferably the Progressives as well. Such a coalition would still support imperialism, but it opposed other issues on the conservative agenda. The Progressives were against protective tariffs. They also demanded constitutional reforms, and the Center Party refused to join the cartel if the government insisted on reinstituting repressive laws against either Catholics or socialists.

Caprivi was willing to pay a high price for Progressive and Center Party cooperation, but the conservatives were not. When the chancellor in 1892 introduced restoration of church control of the public elementary schools as a gesture of goodwill toward the Center Party, the conservatives protested against the bill's implications

for the "nationality struggle" in the east. Church control of elementary schools would have meant that in East Elbian regions with a predominantly Polish population, Polish Catholic priests would have been in charge of the Prussian public schools. The controversy demonstrated the difficulty of "collecting" a politically viable cartel. The conservatives' opposition to the school bill was a major factor in Caprivi's decision to resign as Prussian prime minister.

Hohenlohe and his successors recognized the futility of reviving the coalition of 1878. Increasingly, the Reich government relied on the Center Party as the pivot of its parliamentary support in the Reichstag. As a result, the Reich cabinet could expect solid majorities for its policies of imperialism and some support for protective tariffs but not for plans to turn back the constitutional clock. On the contrary, the growing strength of the Center Party's left wing was reflected in 1906 and again in 1908 when the Catholics took the initiative in pushing through Reichstag hearings on governmental abuses that seriously embarrassed the Reich executive. Bülow's angry attempt to rebuild the cartel of 1878 through gerrymandering and a media blitz in the election of 1907 had no lasting effect.

Bethmann Hollweg learned from his predecessor's errors. He abandoned the Conservative-National Liberal alliance at the Reich level and attempted instead to forge a coalition of all bourgeois parties. But this coalition was also a house divided against itself. The bourgeois groups were in full agreement only on a need for a strong defense and imperial activism. On most domestic issues the views of the Progressives, the Conservatives, and parts of the Center Party were often diametrically opposed.

By 1914 the attempts to "collect a cartel" had largely failed. Or, more precisely, they had succeeded only in the areas of defense and imperialism. This is the essence of what has become known as the primacy of domestic politics in Wilhelminian foreign affairs:

Bebel, August; German politician of the Social Democratic Party (SPD); Deutz, Cologne 22.2.1840-Passugg (Switzerland) 13.8.1913.-"Der rabiate August". (August Beber, the fiery leader of the SPD, holding a speech at the Reichstag).-Caricature by G. Brandt. From: Kladderadatsch, 1903. (Source: akg-images.)

Prince Bernhard von Bulow (1849-1929) 1917 (oil on canvas), Liebermann, Max (1847–1935). (Source: Hamburger Kunsthalle, Hamburg, Germany/© DACS/The Bridgeman Art Library International.)

The conduct of the Reich's global politics was to a large extent an attempt by the Reich's decision makers to maintain support for the country's domestic authoritarianism. Because the emperor and the ruling oligarchy were unwilling to countenance a political opening to the left, the chancellors felt they had no choice but to use an aggressive and activist foreign policy as a basis for preserving domestic stability.

One of the obstacles standing in the way of building a stable coalition was the attempt to link social reform and renewed repression of the Social Democrats. Soon after coming to the throne, William II, who regarded himself as a modern if patriarchal ruler, inaugurated what he called a New Course in social policy. Under this catchword the government proposed (and the Reichstag passed) improvements in the system of state arbitration tribunals, factory safety inspections, and laws governing the maximum number of work hours for women and children.

But the New Course had a political purpose as well. Like his grandfather, William expected that improvements in the lives of workers would lead them to abandon their allegiance to the Social Democrats. When it again became clear that industrial labor could not be bought off with kindness, the emperor ordered the Reich cabinet to submit a new series of antisubversion bills to the Reichstag. It was a futile effort. A majority of the national parliament voted down all such proposals until the government finally gave up the quest in 1899.

Stymied by the Reichstag's majority on the antisubversion laws, some of William's advisers, including Philipp zu Eulenburg, toyed with the idea of forcing a change in the Reich constitution to give the emperor greater control over parliament. William was not only flattered by such scenarios, but he also recognized the political impracticality of any Bonapartist coup. Not only was the vast majority of public opinion opposed to a rewriting of the Reich constitution, but so too were the emperor's fellow rulers in the German states.

As was to be expected in a rapidly changing society, tax reform was another major domestic controversy. Like many industrializing countries, Germany had a problem of private wealth and public poverty. The states' operations were financed by property taxes and the income from state-run commercial enterprises, with the bulk of Prussia's revenues before World War I coming from the profits of the state railroad. In contrast, the federal government and the localities had no adequate tax base to finance their growing obligations. Specifically earmarked for the federal government were only the incomes from tariffs, some consumers' taxes, and users' fees. The situation was even worse at the local level. The cost of constructing sewers, streets, and public transportation systems for the rapidly growing urban centers during the 1890s far outstripped the income from the municipalities' traditional tax base of levies on local commercial activities. The result was budgetary poverty at the Reich and local levels while the states produced large budgetary surpluses. Since 1871 the Länder, through their representatives in the Bundesrat, had voted biannual subsidies to the Reich. Quite aside from the anomaly of having the Reich come hat in hand to its subdivisions every two years, these *Matrikularbeiträge* (literally, "inscription contributions"), as they were called, brought no relief at all for the cities.

By 1890 few in or out of government questioned that Germany's tax system needed

an overhaul, but the financial and political implications of any reform package suggested aroused bitter controversy. Prussia had the most restrictive electoral system, but many of the other German states also had laws that linked the political weight of a voter's ballot to the amount of taxes he paid. Consequently, any major shifts in the forms and amounts of taxation would involve changes in the class allocation of voters and bring with it alterations in the political balance of power.

Leo von Caprivi's tax reform bill focused on the problem of the municipalities. Under the government's proposals, the cities would benefit from a progressive income tax, rising to a maximum of 4 percent on annual income of 100,000 marks or more. Caprivi also suggested as part of his tax reform package that in Prussia the division of voters into electoral classes should be undertaken at the precinct rather than the district level. Under this scheme, relatively wealthy voters in poorer precincts would be classified in one of the first two classes, rather than the third class. Conversely, voters of moderate income in wealthy areas would be classified as voters in the last class.

Not surprisingly, the Prussian conservatives protested against the political implications of Caprivi's proposals. As a result, although the tax reforms were eventually adopted, they brought no changes in the Prussian electoral system. The allocation of voters into classes remained at the district level, leading to an increasingly glaring discrepancy between the popular vote and political representation in the Landtag.

The flow of governmental revenues during the boom years after 1897 carried Germany through the years of Hohenlohe's chancellorship, but Bülow was again confronted with a financial crisis. This time the problem was at the Reich level. Expenditures for the naval buildup and the rising costs of federal social welfare programs had raised the Reich's public debt by 1907 to 5 billion marks. For an age that regarded debts in any amount as a blight on public finances, this was a matter that could not be ignored.

Because tax reform inevitably endangered the cohesion of Bülow's fragile "bloc" of supporters, the chancellor waited as long as possible before tackling the problem. By 1908, however, it was clear that to balance the federal budget the Reich would need an additional 500 million marks annually for a number of years. To make good the shortfall, Bülow proposed 300 million marks from increased Matrikularbeiträge, an additional 100 million in the form of new consumer and indirect taxes, and finally, 100 million from the proceeds of a new Reich inheritance tax. On June 24, 1909, the Reichstag passed the first two parts of the package, but Conservatives and Catholics combined to defeat the proposed inheritance tax. (It was this legislative setback that William used to dismiss Bülow.)

Closely related to taxes was another perennial issue in German domestic politics: tariffs. When Caprivi assumed office, agricultural prices had been rising for some years, and the chancellor felt that Germany's tariff structure should reflect what was expected to be a lengthy period of price stability. At the time most German farmers agreed. As a result, they raised only minimal objections to a series of twelve-year trade treaties that the Caprivi government negotiated with Germany's major international trading partners between 1890 and 1892. The treaties provided for low tariff rates for both agricultural and industrial imports.

Neither the Reich's farmers nor Caprivi foresaw the collapse of the international grain market in 1893. Newly organized in the Agrarian League, Germany's farmers now clamored for renegotiation of the Caprivi treaties to protect them from cheap agricultural imports from America and Russia. The farmers failed to raise the Reich's tariffs (particularly because the terms of the Caprivi treaties continued to benefit the rapidly growing export industry), but they did obtain relief in the form of export subsidies. Nevertheless, the landowners' unhappiness was instrumental in forcing Caprivi's resignation less than a year later.

The tariff issue came to a head during Bülow's administration when the Caprivi treaties expired. In 1902 Germany's tariff situation had become exceedingly complicated. A growing percentage of the Reich's wealth came from the exports of Germany's manufacturing industries, particularly chemicals and electrical products. At the same time, the significance of agriculture in the national economy was steadily decreasing. From a national point of view, then, tariffs that protected farmers but endangered the flow of German exports abroad made no economic sense. But, as always, there was the political dimension. As we saw, the German farming community was dominated by East Elbian landowners, who were also the backbone of Prusso-German authoritarianism.

Confronted with a clear dilemma, Bülow equivocated. The chancellor was fully aware that Germany's exports were by now the lifeblood of the economy, but he also felt he had to appease the agricultural lobby. Consequently, the new tariff treaties his government negotiated provided for somewhat increased rates on agricultural and industrial imports, but Bülow also made sure the rates were not so high as to provoke retaliation by Germany's trading partners against the growing volume of the Reich's industrial exports. Instead of getting all the tariff protection it wanted, agriculture was temporarily bought off by increased export subsidies and cheaper credit.

Taxes and tariffs involved conflicting economic interests; repeated clashes between the government and the Reichstag over the question of executive privilege and the role of the emperor as commander in chief of the Reich navy and the Prussian armed forces concerned the even more fundamental question of the evolution of the Reich constitution.

At first glance, the battles over executive privilege often concerned seemingly esoteric items. One was the Prussian code of military justice. Traditionally, the military establishments of Prussia and the other German states conducted courts-martial in secret, with the accused neither present nor able to respond to the charges. By 1896 most German states had changed their codes of military justice to give the accused the right to be present at his own trial. Prussia, however, lagged behind, and the emperor made reform of the code a major issue of executive privilege. He announced melodramatically that he owed it to his ancestors to maintain the Prussian system of military justice unchanged. It is indicative of the changing balance of power in German politics, however, that in the face of opposition from a majority of the Reichstag, William and his military advisers yielded. By the beginning of World War I, Prussia, too, had a reformed code of military justice.

An issue of executive privilege involving parliament's power of the purse arose in 1906. For this fiscal year the Reich government asked the Reichstag for a supplemental appropriation of 24 million marks to pay for unexpected expenses incurred in putting down a rebellion in the German colony of South-West Africa (present-day Namibia). Prodded by the energetic young Center Party delegate Matthias Erzberger, parliament voted to hold hearings on abuses in Germany's colonial administration before appropriating the funds. The emperor objected strongly, claiming that such a step interfered with his powers as commander in chief of the armed forces, but the Reichstag did not yield. In fact, the hearings seriously embarrassed the German colonial office. Erzberger and his colleagues exposed a cesspool of corruption in the administration of Germany's African colonies.

If the emperor needed additional evidence that the military's claim to be a law unto itself was increasingly out of step with the mood of the country, it was provided by a celebrated incident involving military–civilian relations in the town of Zabern (Saverne) in Alsace in the fall of 1913. Here the commander of the local garrison, a lieutenant, without consulting the civilian authorities, had ordered force to be used against a group of French demonstrators. A number of demonstrators were illegally arrested and some maltreated and wounded. This time it was the crown prince (also named William) who inflamed public opinion. He dispatched a public telegram to the lieutenant in Zabern congratulating him on his forceful action, but in a subsequent debate a majority of the Reichstag protested the military's (and indirectly the crown prince's) high-handedness.

The crown prince was not the only member of the royal family whose personal intrusion into the processes of shaping policy repeatedly caused constitutional crises. The emperor, too, became the center of controversy. The most celebrated incident was the *Daily Telegraph* affair of 1908. Here William involved himself in a misguided attempt to take a personal hand in improving relations between Great Britain and Germany. In an interview he told the Berlin correspondent of the London newspaper *Daily Telegraph* that during the war between Great Britain and the Boers of South Africa, he, William, had stood firmly on the side of the British—although he knew that most Germans regarded the Boers as the underdogs and England as the bully in the conflict. After it was published, the *Daily Telegraph* interview led to a Reichstag debate during which the emperor's "personal rule" was attacked from all sides. Every political group, including the Conservatives, demanded that the emperor be more circumspect in the future. The parliamentary outcry did not abate until William in a published letter to Bülow promised that in the future he would refrain from further efforts at personal policy making without consulting his constitutional advisers.

The imperial family's actions were symptoms rather than causes of the severe political and constitutional crisis in which Germany found itself on the eve of World War I. Chancellor Bethmann Hollweg, who had a perceptive eye for the domestic political situation, recognized that the political polarization in the country could only be bridged by meaningful reforms that would lead to greater parliamentarization and democratization. Beating the patriotic drums would not, in the long run, halt the decline of the Conservatives' and National Liberals' share of the popular vote.

ECONOMIC DEVELOPMENTS

The dominant themes in Wilhelminian economic life were an accelerated pace of industrialization and a period of sustained prosperity. Except for two brief recessions in 1901–1902 and 1908–1909, times were good for most segments of the population. Although life for many was hard and the gulf between rich and poor did not narrow, in the absence of significant inflationary pressures the standard of living for the majority of Germans increased markedly.

Prosperity was a by-product of the Reich's continuing industrialization. The number of those employed in industrial or manufacturing jobs rose steadily while the agricultural segment of the workforce declined. In line with this development, agriculture's contribution to the gross domestic product fell from 37 percent in the time span 1885–1889 to 25 percent at the end of the Wilhelminian years.

Contemporary observers recognized that capitalism came to permeate all facets of German life. The economist Werner Sombart described the purpose of a new journal for research in the social sciences that he founded in 1903 as the "historical and theoretical analysis of the cultural significance of capitalism." High capitalism also meant managerial capitalism. The industrial sector of the economy in particular was now largely controlled by what were essentially professional managers. The economic historian Hans Jaeger has provided us with a "group profile" of Wilhelminian executives. Often of humble background, they were proud of their accomplishments and thoroughly comfortable with the conventions of morality, decency, and authority prevalent in the late Victorian age. Strong personalities, they expected obedient employees, wives, and children, although in their own eyes they were caring business leaders, fathers, and husbands. The ideal of the *Bildungsbürger* (a well-educated citizen), celebrated earlier by novelists like Gustav Freytag and Wilhelm Raabe, held little attraction for them. Their interests were largely confined to their businesses. By their own lights the

managers were also apolitical. "Naturally" they were "nationalists," "patriots," and "anti-Marxists," but politics as such, they claimed, interested them only insofar as it affected their businesses.

These executives were managers of what was now the typical form of large-scale enterprise in Germany: the limited liability corporation. Close ties existed between major banks and industrial corporations because most stock certificates issued by German corporations were held as part of bank-owned portfolios. Yet another characteristic of German high capitalism was the growing number of industrial cartels and trusts. Firms in various branches—notably iron and steel—created both vertical (control of the manufacturing process from raw materials to final product) and horizontal (marketing and pricing agreements) trusts to stabilize prices and maximize profits. Such developments were actually encouraged by the country's political leaders; there was no anti-trust legislation in Wilhelminian Germany. Finally, the electrical and chemical industries pioneered the use of scientific research for product development. Large corporations routinely established in-house scientific laboratories specifically to design new products and improve manufacturing techniques.

Industrialization and a rising standard of living encouraged further population growth and mobility. Germany's population grew from about 48 million in 1890 to slightly over 60 million twenty years later. Interestingly, the increase occurred while birthrates were declining. The growth was due instead to longer life expectancy that resulted from the welfare policies introduced since the 1880s, as well as improvements in hygiene and health care. Emigration declined, but the internal population movement continued undiminished. The primary migration pattern was still from east to west, leading to problems of urban crowding in the cities of the west and shortages of cheap agricultural labor on the estates of East Elbia.

Internal immigration was facilitated by the completion of Germany's national rail network. In 1879 a number of private companies operating in Prussia and the adjoining states had been merged into the Prussian-Hessian State Railroads. The new system served all of Germany, except for areas of Württemberg and Bavaria; these southern German states retained their own railroad systems. For both economic and strategic reasons the Prussian-Hessian State Railroads focused on rapid east–west connections. Trunk lines linked the industrial areas of western Germany to the seaports of Rotterdam, Bremen, and Hamburg, as well as the agricultural regions east of the Elbe. These same lines were equally capable of carrying fast-running troop trains from the French and Belgian frontiers to East Prussia and Silesia, enabling the rapid movement of troops in case the Reich's nightmare of a two-front war became a reality.

Virtually all Germans enthusiastically supported the development of railroads, but the construction of canals aroused bitter controversy. Ever since the 1850s economists and industrialists had advocated building a network of canals to supplement the railroads and make the shipment of bulky goods such as coal and grains more economical. The heart of the proposed system was the Mittellandkanal, a waterway that was intended to connect the industrial areas of the Rhineland and Westphalia with the seaports of Bremen and Hamburg. Although the project had the enthusiastic endorsement of transportation experts and the emperor, it was not finished until long after the empire had fallen. The East Elbian agrarians, who dominated the Prussian Landtag, saw the canal network not as a boon but as a threat to their economic future. They argued especially the Mittellandkanal would increase competition from foreign grain imports by significantly reducing shipping costs from the ports of entry to consumers in the west. In addition, they argued that construction of the canal itself would aggravate the labor problem in the east because thousands of agricultural laborers would undoubtedly prefer work on the canal to laboring on Junker estates.

The agrarians managed to delay the construction of the Mittellandkanal, but their efforts did not seriously hinder the rapid expansion of German industry. By the end of the Wilhelminian years, industrial patterns that are still apparent in present-day Germany had been well established. Heavy industry was concentrated along the Rhine-Ruhr Valley. Cities like Essen, Duisburg, Hamm, and Düsseldorf became major metropolises; firms like Krupp, Thyssen, and Gutehoffnungshütte, household words. The rapidly expanding chemical industry, whose explosive growth was based primarily on the chemistry of coal tar and aniline dyes, settled somewhat farther south along the shores of the Main. This branch of the economy was also already dominated by firms that are still giants of the industry: Hoechst, Bayer, BASF. In central Germany, the rich deposits of brown coal became the basis of a concentration of medium-size manufacturing firms, specializing in textiles, machinery, and building products. Somewhat later, the region around Halle and Merseburg developed into a major center for the refining of petroleum products and the manufacture of cement.

Another growth sector in the German economy, the electrical industry, found its home in Berlin. This branch was also dominated by large-scale firms, notably Siemens and the Allgemeine Elektrizitäts-Gesellschaft (General Electric Corporation). In the seaports of Hamburg and Bremen processing industries for imported raw materials like coffee, cocoa, and tobacco were established. Germany also built a sizable merchant fleet. Originally, the primary business of the two largest firms, the Hamburg-America Line in Hamburg and the Norddeutscher Lloyd in Bremen, had been created to carry immigrants to America, but with the decline in emigration and a corresponding growth in the volume of German exports, they emphasized worldwide shipping and passenger service instead.

The most visible sign of Germany's exploding economy was the volume of the country's trade. The volume of the Reich's exports between 1889 and 1910 increased by 81 percent, in monetary terms from 825 million marks to 1.5 billion annually. Despite the impressive export statistics, Germany's imports, mostly in the form of raw materials and agricultural goods, increased even faster. The scissors were closed by another feature characteristic of high capitalism, the growing volume of German investment abroad. By 1910 Germany was no longer a net capital importer but a sizable capital exporter. The country's firms and banks held investments of some 35 billion marks abroad, earning annual returns of 1.8 billion marks.

Investment at home and abroad, of course, strengthened the role of the banks in the economy. The trend toward concentration of financial power in the hands of the four "D" banks—Discontobank, Deutsche Bank, Dresdner Bank, and Darmstädter Bank—continued; on the eve of World War I they controlled some 65 percent of all stock in German corporations. These banks were also the major conduit for German investment abroad. As we saw earlier, Germany's "full-service" banks traditionally acted as their own brokerage houses, and by the beginning of the century the German stock markets were essentially mechanisms for the banks to buy and sell stocks from the portfolios they controlled. Independent investors played only a minor part in stock market transactions.

There is little doubt that businessmen fared well in the years before World War I. A basically unregulated marketplace provided unprecedented opportunities for expansion and profits. Nevertheless, businessmen complained bitterly about what they saw as the growing welfare state. They attacked the whole concept of *Sozialpolitik* (social policy)—which included everything from government inspectors who reported violations of the occupational safety laws to old-age pensions—as unwarranted interference by the state with the system of free enterprise.

The condition of labor under high capitalism is less clear. Before the end of World War I, a self-serving conservative historiography portrayed workers as increasingly prosperous and content with their lives. Their sense of well-being was disturbed only by the activities of socialist agitators. During the 1920s and especially since World War II, a revisionist school concentrated on doing empirical research into the real living conditions of Germany's industrial labor. Their conclusions often paint a bleak picture of economic exploitation and social misery. Weekly hours were long (fifty-seven was the average in 1914) and wages, by today's standards, low. The average annual wage (adjusted for inflation) in 1913 was 1,163 marks, as compared to 5,675 marks in 1959. Dark and dank housing in urban slums and poor nutrition led to the spread of such diseases as tuberculosis and rickets. Social problems like petty crime, alcoholism, and domestic violence were widespread.

But there was another side to the picture as well. Labor did benefit from the boom of the Wilhelminian years. Real wages were rising fairly constantly for most German workers; the annual average wage of 1,163 marks in 1913 represented a 61 percent increase over the corresponding figure of 711 marks for 1890. As union membership grew, so did labor militancy and the number of industrial workers covered by collective bargaining agreements. Labor union membership reached 2 million in 1913, 18.5 percent of the total industrial workforce. (For comparison, the figure for the United States in 2009 was 12.3 percent.) Living conditions for the industrial proletariat, then, although still harsh and bitter for most, were also significantly better in 1914 than they had been when the Wilhelminian years began.

Present-day historians have centered their attention on the growth of large-scale enterprises and organized labor during these years, but the contemporary discussion of economic developments seemed far more concerned about the future of a third component, the Mittelstand. Actually, this segment of society was by now composed of two rather distinct groups, the old and new Mittelstand, with the new Mittelstand (see the earlier discussion on this group, p. 14) growing far more rapidly than the old. The Mittelstand propagandists, however, focused almost entirely on the old "middle estate." They saw independent artisans, members of the professions, retailers, owners of apartment houses—in fact, small businessmen of all kinds—threatened by the rise of big business and big labor.

Like the agrarians and the industrialists, members of the old Mittelstand organized a lobby to press their case. But the Mittelstand's public relations efforts were seriously hampered by the group's inability to agree on the best way to ensure the future prosperity of Germany's small businessmen and artisans. There were those who longed for the utopian past of guild restrictions and legal limitations on the growth of big business. Others recognized the futility of turning back the clock. They argued that the future of the Mittelstand was at the side of big business in that industrialization would provide new opportunities for small businessmen as well as large corporations. (Incidentally, the second group was right: The number of independent artisans and small businessmen was significantly higher in 1914 than in 1890.) Unable to reach a compromise, spokesmen for the old Mittelstand concentrated their venom on the one enemy on which they could agree: the Social Democrats. Convinced that unionization of their employees raised labor costs to levels that drove many small businessmen into bankruptcy, they endorsed right-to-work laws and the aims of the National Association Against Social Democracy. On the eve of World War I the Mittelstand lobby was firmly allied with the political right.

Despite the general level of prosperity in Wilhelminian Germany, there was one glaring weakness in the economy: agriculture in general and East Elbian agriculture in particular. The full extent of the structural problems in the east did not become apparent until after World War I, but acute observers recognized the signs of the structural agricultural crisis long before then. As early as 1900 the industrialist Siemens pointed to the heavy debt burden of East Elbian agriculture as a serious mortgage on the future. The causes of the problems were not difficult to identify. In anticipation of continuing high agricultural prices, the East Elbian agrarians had borrowed heavily to finance machinery and speculate in land. But, as we saw, beginning in 1893, prices on the international market fell precipitously. German agriculture was driven not only from the world markets but undersold on the home market as well. (U.S. grain imports to Germany, for example, increased from 406 million tons in 1890 to 1.2 billion in 1906.)

The agrarians refused to recognize their problems as a structural crisis; they insisted instead that the issue was one of unfair competition. As a result, the home-made problems of East Elbian agriculture were not significantly addressed during the Wilhelminian era, and within a few years the foundation of the Junkers' economic strength would collapse under the weight of its accumulated debt.

Overall, the years from 1890 to 1914 brought the German economy to the stage of high capitalism. Rapid industrialization meant opportunities for expansion and profit, and despite hardships for the laboring classes, the standard of living for all those connected with industrialization rose. Fears of a Mittelstand in demise were greatly exaggerated; small business flourished as suppliers and spin-offs of industrialization. The only really weak sector was East Elbian agriculture, an increasingly less significant sector of the economy. Nevertheless, the agricultural sector had a disproportionately large impact on the country because of the political influence that its spokesmen wielded.

LITERATURE, ART, AND SOCIETY

The strains and stresses of modernization characterized the era's cultural and social life as well. Wilhelminian Germany exhibited two distinct, although overlapping, states of mind. The "establishment," that is to say, the men—and Germany, like all of Western society at this time, was dominated by males—who gave official or social sanction to the accepted values and art forms were proud of their accomplishments and secure in their values. This group of social and political leaders also had few doubts about the wisdom of the dicta it sought to transmit to future generations through a rigid educational system. In fact, critics of the establishment focused their attacks on Germany's high school teachers, the *Oberlehrer,* as symbols of the system's sclerosis and arrogance. Perhaps the most famous such portrayal was in Heinrich Mann's novel *Professor Unrath,* the book that later became the basis for the movie *The Blue Angel* starring Marlene Dietrich.

The established culture of the age was a closed and static system in which sentimentality, militarism, narcissism, literary hero worship (centered mostly around Goethe and Schiller), and uncritical acceptance of vulgarized versions of Wagner's and Nietzsche's messages predominated. As we noted earlier, pseudo-military forms dominated social life in much of Wilhelminian society. High school teachers proudly displayed their military decorations in class every September 5, the day commemorating the Battle of Sedan in 1870, and the bourgeois man had "arrived" when he obtained his reserve officer's commission.

Much in the established cultural norms was contradictory and paradoxical. Many Germans had lost faith in the religious message of Christianity. Revealed truths were replaced by the presumed certainty of scientific and technological knowledge. At the same time, the establishment insisted that the churches remain the moral arbiters of society. Consequently, the major religious bodies became increasingly identified with the values of the establishment; they became social and cultural rather than religious institutions.

The Wilhelminian cultural establishment was arriviste, bourgeois, and aristocratic. It was questioned and opposed by at least two other sets of cultural and social values, one raised within the establishment's own ranks, the other outside its class parameters. Social Democratic organizations, of course, proudly rejected the establishment's norms as outgrowths of capitalist decadence. They contrasted official Wilhelminian culture with a class-conscious "proletarian" culture, an effort that always remained more potential than actual. Looking back it is clear that despite

their social and cultural isolation within Wilhelminian society, even socialist workers accepted a good deal of the establishment's value system.

A more serious threat to the official culture came not through class antagonism but from the generational conflict in the ranks of the Wilhelminian bourgeoisie. Not surprisingly, criticism of the establishment by the younger generation focused on the schools and the family. What would eventually become organized as the Youth Movement objected specifically to the rigidity of the school curriculum, patriarchal dominance in the family, the prevailing repression of sexuality and bodily freedom, and more generally what these critics called the "materialism" of the society. A favorite figure in Youth Movement fiction was the young idealistic hero who, as a result of societal pressures, turns into a crass materialist.

The Youth Movement was never a monolithic, tightly knit organization. What came to be called a movement was originally little more than a vague feeling of dissatisfaction with the prevailing norms of society. Even those who decided to organize themselves did so in numerous small groups that were only very loosely coordinated at the national level.

The revolt of Wilhelminian youth began innocently enough with the efforts of a university student from the Berlin suburb of Spandau, Karl Fischer. He was determined to provide an antidote to what he saw as the deadening effects of the German educational system. In 1901 he founded an organization he called the *Wandervögel.* (Literally, "migratory birds," but "backpackers" is probably a better translation.) The purpose was to encourage peer group interaction and physical activity in the form of weekend camping trips to the countryside in the Mark Brandenburg surrounding Berlin. From the beginning the Wandervögel preached and practiced what they regarded as antimaterialistic and antihierarchical values. On their hikes they emphasized an informal lifestyle that stressed comfortable clothing, natural foods, and youthful equality. (The Wandervögel routinely used the *Du* rather than the *Sie* form of address.)

The Wandervögel movement spread rapidly throughout Germany; within a few years there were hundreds of local clubs in all parts of the Reich. Even more than Fischer's ideas, the appearance of a book of songs, *Der Zupfgeigenhansl* ("The Guitarist's Companion"), late in 1908 spurred the growth of the movement. The collector and arranger of this edition of folk songs—which, incidentally, did a great deal to rekindle interest in German folk traditions—was Hans Breuer, a friend of Karl Fischer. The songs had a practical purpose as musical accompaniment on the hikes, but the tunes were also intended to reduce the popularity among German teenagers and college students of the sentimental and banal rags and polkas of the day. The *Zupfgeigenhansl* became an immediate best seller. Within seven years of its initial publication the book had gone through twenty-six editions.

The Wandervögel were both part of and forerunner of the actual Youth Movement. The latter, however, had a far broader purpose than the earlier organization. The Youth Movement intended to organize the "young" (who were defined as sixteen- to thirty-five-year-olds) to change the basic values of the Wilhelminian establishment. Unfortunately, the Youth Movement's ideals themselves were not free of either contradictions or dangerous prejudices. The movement rejected materialism but embraced nationalism as the highest form of idealism. Many, although not all, of the groups endorsed anti-Semitism, personifying Jews as the embodiment of materialism. The rejection of materialism also covered Marxism and Marxists, further widening the gulf between bourgeois and proletarian youth groups. The Youth Movement stressed democracy and equality in its own ranks but regarded parliamentary democracy as interest-group politics without an idealistic purpose. Many in the movement were sharply critical of the pervasive militarism in Wilhelminian society, yet their intense, if "idealistic," nationalism did not make them immune to the siren calls of the same Wilhelminian imperialism and militarism.

The Youth Movement reached the pinnacle of its organized visibility in October 1913 when thousands assembled at a national festival on the mountain peak of the Hohen Meissner, in Hessen. This celebration of the German Nation was deliberately intended to present a peaceful and spontaneous contrast to the militaristic and bombastic official commemoration of the hundredth anniversary of the Battle of Leipzig, staged at the same time. (The Battle of Leipzig had begun the series of setbacks for Napoleon that culminated in the Battle of Waterloo.) Yet the Hohen Meissner festival also revealed the limitations of the youth revolt. Those making the trek to the mountain peak were overwhelmingly male, middle class, and Protestant. The Youth Movement had no answer for the class or religious divisions in Wilhelminian Germany. Moreover, the movement's vision of the future was an idealized, utopian view of the past: a romanticized Germany made beautiful by the patina of age. Finally, it was bitterly ironic that many of the thousands who proclaimed their love of peace on the Hohen Meissner less than a year later enthusiastically rushed off to war.

The ideas of the youth revolt were rapidly disseminated in a society in which mass media in the modern sense—with the exception of the electronic variety—had become commonplace vehicles for the distribution of art, literature, and information. The trend toward ever-wider proliferation of newspapers and periodicals accelerated. Aside from newspapers, whose circulation was helped by the advent of photojournalism, products targeted for specific audiences, especially women's magazines, became successful as leisure time among the middle and upper classes increased.

In line with the broad attacks on the values of the establishment, it was a golden age for political satire and muckraking journalism. The weekly *Simplizissimus,* published in Munich and edited by the publicist Thomas Theodore Heine, was one of the most widely circulated satirical periodicals. No person or institution in authority was spared in its biting and clever drawings. Maximilian Harden's

Zukunft was a muckraking periodical that combined the features of investigative journalism with the sensationalism of a tabloid. Harden's exploits led to both increased circulation for his journal and a number of short-term jail sentences for the editor after convictions for libel and lèse majesté. His most famous case came in 1906 when Harden published a series of articles accusing the emperor's personal friend Philipp zu Eulenburg of homosexuality. (At this time homosexuality even among consenting adults was, of course, a criminal offense.) Eulenburg sued for libel but died before the case was finally decided. Far less lurid, although equally significant, were several journals of opinion, literary criticism, and fiction targeted for an audience of intellectuals. Especially notable among these was *Hochland,* ("Highland") which soon became the most influential journal among educated Catholics, and the *Deutsche Rundschau,* ("German Panorama") which performed much the same service for an audience of Protestant intellectuals.

Both so-called highbrow and mass consumption literature flourished. It was the great age of the novel. In 1890, 1,731 works of fiction were published; by 1909 the figure had reached 4,297, an increase of 148 percent. To be sure, much of this production was what the Germans called *Trivialliteratur,* but the themes of both serious literature and the "trivial" variety reflected the battle between the values of the establishment and the forces of reformism. Stories with a regional focus remained popular, although novels about foreign travel and adventures located in exotic colonial areas sold even better. Not incidentally, the latter also fit in well with the propaganda of the Naval League. As would be expected in an age of increasing technology, science fiction novels found a ready audience but so did fiction with mystical and occult themes. Much of the Trivialliteratur consisted of books that were forerunners of today's "modern romances." Mostly written by women authors, many appeared first in serialized form in women's magazines. By far the most popular were the stories of aristocratic social life by Marie von

Ebner-Eschenbach. Karl May was by far the most popular author writing Trivialliteratur.

Above all, however, playwrights and authors put the city, its problems, and throbbing life at the center of their works. Indeed, by 1910 literary critics were already complaining that German literature was in danger of becoming monopolized by big-city themes. Many of the novels were not so much celebrations of urban life as warnings against the city's unhealthy influence. Some authors, like Theodor Fontane, described the entirety of urban life of Berlin in loving if critical detail, but many others populated their books with prostitutes, vagabonds, and other victims of urban conditions. Most authors were pessimistic about the future of the bourgeoisie and its materialistic values. Heinrich Mann, one of the most noted German novelists during this time, wrote bitter satires of the dehumanizing effect that industry and money had on society. Less strident in tone, but no more optimistic about the future of traditional bourgeois values, was Heinrich Mann's younger brother Thomas. His novel *Buddenbrooks,* published in 1901 when the author was twenty-six years old, became an immediate best seller and firmly established Thomas Mann's reputation as a major literary talent. *Buddenbrooks* is at one and the same time a celebration of the traditional German middle class, its family-oriented and humanistic values, and the story of the inevitable decline of these values. Using the experience of his own upbringing in the city of Lübeck, Mann traces the history of one north German family from the 1830s to the beginning of the twentieth century. By the end of the novel the reader, if not the remaining Buddenbrooks, realizes that the old bourgeois values celebrated by Freytag cannot survive the challenge of alienation, industrialization, and rampant materialism. Among dramatists there was only one towering figure, Gerhart Hauptmann. In a series of plays, such as *Die Weber* ("The Weavers"), he used naturalist techniques to depict the human tragedies that followed in the wake of industrialism and materialism.

Particularly evocative of some authors' anti-establishment stand were two other themes,

Im Mittelpunkt   Karl May (1842–1912)

No one personified the popular cultural ideals of the founders' generation and the Wilhelmenian years better than Karl May. Born in 1842, May was a prolific novelist and essayist as well as a difficult and controversial personality. He was certainly not an instant literary success. In fact, May spent much of his early adulthood from 1865 to 1874 in jail for a variety of petty crimes.

The author did not discover his true calling until 1874, but when he did he hit all the hot buttons for literary popularity in late nineteenth- and early twentieth-century Germany. Taking advantage of the booming market in illustrated periodicals, May wrote serialized novels and short stories for this medium—more than a hundred before he died. The locales and characters of his fiction varied widely, but his most popular stories were adventure novels set in what at the time were exotic places like the Orient and especially the American "Wild West."

May's most enduring contribution to the genre of *Trialliteratur* were the adventures of the fictional Apache chief Winnetou and his German friend and collaborator, Old Shatterhand. (Like May, his fictional hero was from Saxony.) In these stories Winnetou is the noble savage, and Old Shatterhand the exceptional white man who is not greedy and duplicitous.

Like many authors of his time, May did not base his descriptions of far-away locales on actual experience. For the American West he relied on maps, guidebooks, travel accounts, earlier fictional treatments like the novels of James Fenimore Cooper, and, above all, his own lively imagination. The author did eventually visit the United States in 1908, but he got no further west than Buffalo, New York.

May was a very modern self-promoter. Like today's authors and their book tours, May went on extensive lecture tours promoting his works. He also had himself photographed in costume as Old Shatterhand and that character's Oriental counterpart, Kara ben Nemsi (Karl the German). The photos were then sold by the thousands as postcards.

In later years, May turned increasingly toward mysticism and pacifism. His writings became allegorical texts on the theme of raising mankind from evil to good. Typical was his lecture in Vienna a week before his death in 1912, entitled, "Upward to the Realm of Noble Man." It was perhaps fortunate for May that he did not live to see the outbreak of World War I.

The author's enduring popularity rests especially upon his adventure stories set in the American West. Generations of German, Austrian, and Swiss-German adolescent boys grew up (and are still growing up) reading about Winnetou and Old Shatterhand, and playing cowboys and Indians based upon their adventures. Hitler was a great fan, but so was Albert Einstein.

Long after his death May lives on in his books (which are constantly republished), in movies, and in summer festivals. Between 1912 and 1968 twenty-three films based upon his stories were produced with international stars playing Old Shatterhand and Winnetou: The American Lex Barker portrayed Old Shatterhand in several films and the French star Pierre Brice played Winnetou.

Today there are three summer festivals devoted to producing stage versions of May's stories. The two most famous are in West Germany, one in Bad Segeberg in Schleswig-Holstein and the other in Lennestadt-Elspe in North Rhine Westphalia. In the latter location Pierre Brice for ten years reprised his movie characterization of Winnetou. After the reunification of Germany a third outdoor venue for May's tales was established in Rathen, Saxony, close to the village of Radebeul where May lived most of his life. He also died there in his villa, named appropriately enough, Old Shatterhand.

sexual repression and dehumanization in the military. Frank Wedekind was the best known of a group of writers specializing in "student tragedies": stories in which the young protagonists die because society refuses to acknowledge their awakening sexuality. Similarly blunt in their criticism of establishment values were works about the brutality and mindlessness of German military training and the arrogance of the Prussian officer corps.

Unlike the print media, painting, sculpture, and architecture traditionally did not arouse mass interest. Perhaps precisely for this reason, the conflict between old and new values in art was not muted but erupted into bitter, if contained, controversy. Wilhelminian "official" art, that is, the styles that received private and governmental commissions, was dominated by heroic and sentimental realism. As one wag has put it, this was the taste of an age that had no taste. It was certainly the taste of William II, himself something of an amateur drawing talent.

"Official" art, however, was rejected by a growing number of mostly younger painters and sculptors. Increasingly, French impressionism and, somewhat later, expressionism, influenced Germany's artists. In 1894 a group of painters in Munich refused to accept the decisions of the Academy of Art as to which pieces should be displayed in the officially sanctioned annual show. They "seceded" from the academy and decided to exhibit the rejected works on their own. A few years later a similar revolt racked the Berlin art world. Incidentally, as if to demonstrate that aesthetic and chronological youthfulness need not coincide, the secessionists in Berlin were led by the dean of German painters, the fifty-year-old Max Liebermann.

The secessionists initiated the triumph of impressionism and expressionism in German art; a short time later the "rebel" Max Liebermann was awarded an honorary doctorate from the University of Berlin, whose art faculty was dominated by traditionalists. The new aesthetic brought a fundamental change in both styles and themes. There was no place for sentimentality or pseudorealism.

Impressionist painters took as their subjects the play of light in nature and scenes from urban and rural bourgeois life; singularly absent were pictures of battles and conventional portraits. In contrast to impressionism, which as Gerhart Masur has pointed out, "lacked any note of social protest," German expressionism, led by groups of painters such as "The Bridge" in Dresden and "Blue Rider" in Munich, delighted in shocking the establishment by portraying the seamy side of life or by deliberately offending the prevailing moral codes.

"Secession" in architecture was more difficult to achieve. The means needed to finance architectural projects were obviously considerably greater than those required for completing a painting, and most major buildings were commissioned by agencies that approved of the official Wilhelminian styles: a heavy-handed grandiosity overladen with useless decoration. The streets of Berlin became impressive, but oppressive, facades reflecting the desire for grandeur in the capital. The overall effect was not pleasing. Unlike the Ringstrasse in Vienna, Berlin did not grow as an organic whole. Instead, each major new construction project tried to be impressive on its own.

Still, the prevailing prosperity brought about a building boom, and here and there new visions became apparent. Even some "official" architecture, like the Museuminsel, the cluster of buildings in Berlin that houses the major museums in the capital (see the fuller description in Chapter 11), achieved a pleasing neoclassical effect. More important, toward the end of the 1890s the Jugendstil was making inroads into both architecture and interior decorating. Lean, uncluttered buildings that combined gracefulness with functionality were making their appearance in German cities. As was true of the visual arts, in architecture, too, the age of modernism had arrived.

There are striking parallels between political and cultural developments during the Wilhelminian years. Culturally, too, the old and the new vied with each other. In art, literature, and social life new values of openness, spontaneity, and free expression existed side by side and in competition with the rigidity and pseudoheroism of Prusso-German authoritarianism. By 1914 the outcome of the struggle was not yet determined, but clearly the new and young were gaining the upper hand.

FOREIGN RELATIONS

At the end of 1913, Curt Riezler, a friend and adviser of Chancellor Bethmann Hollweg, noted, "the danger of war in our time is greatest from those countries where a weak government is confronted with a strong nationalistic movement." Riezler, who was thinking of Austria and Russia rather than Germany when he made these remarks, also accurately described Germany's foreign relations dilemma. Unfortunately, the empire's decision makers did not recognize themselves in Riezler's mirror. The leaders of the Reich, knowing that support for their authoritarian system was waning, hoped to rally public opinion in support of an aggressive foreign policy to stabilize the domestic situation. They were convinced that Germany would not only remain stable domestically, but that the Reich was in a favorable position to manipulate the international balance of power as well. They cited a number of reasons—all wrong as it turned out—for their optimistic assessment.

Ever since the end of the Napoleonic Wars, it had been an axiom of European diplomacy that the position of Great Britain was the key to the balance of power. During most of the nineteenth century, except for the Crimean War, England had stayed out of Continental entanglements and remained in "splendid isolation." There were increasing signs, however, that isolation was becoming counterproductive for Great Britain and the country would have to conclude alliances with one or more Continental powers to safeguard its overseas empire. The German leaders, and that meant especially Bülow, the man who shaped the Reich's foreign policy for more than a decade after 1897, were convinced that in view

of England's rivalries with Russia and France, Great Britain had no choice but to ally itself with Germany. Consequently, they argued, the Reich was in a buyer's position and could exact a high price for accommodating Great Britain. Strategic confidence supplemented Germany's diplomatic illusions. The Reich's military leaders were convinced that the strategic concept known as the Schlieffen Plan (see the discussion on pp. 80–81) provided a fail-safe method for winning any military confrontation with Russia and France. In addition, Bismarck's nightmare of a two-front military conflict seemed to be less of a threat than it had been earlier. The Russo-Japanese War of 1904–1905 had demonstrated Russia's military weakness and the Revolution of 1905 its domestic instability.

All of this reasoning was faulty, although admittedly there was an element of verisimilitude about it. Great Britain did have a sincere desire for an alliance with Germany, and, as World War I would reveal, the Russian empire was a tottering colossus. Nevertheless, the reasoning of the Reich's decision makers contained a fundamental flaw. For England, Germany's desirable position as a diplomatic partner was based on a continuation of Bismarck's view of the German empire as a satiated power. That assumption, however, ran counter to the imperialist ambitions of the Wilhelminian leaders. Consequently, Germany's role in the balance of power was changing radically. The state secretary in the foreign ministry, von Oerenthal, put it well when he noted that Germany's global ambitions changed its diplomatic position from that of a bride to that of a suitor. Tragically, the leaders of Wilhelminian Germany failed to recognize the Reich's changed circumstances. In the decade before the outbreak of World War I, Germany's foreign policy grew increasingly erratic, eventually resulting in Germany's virtual isolation in the concert of powers.

The key to Germany's problems was its unwillingness to restrict its role as a great power to the Continent. That decision in turn was linked to the Reich's leaders' encouragement of an imperialist mentality as a major element in their efforts to prevent progressive constitutional reforms. True, imperialism and navalism were hardly German inventions. In fact, the most prominent popularizer of navalism was an American, Admiral Alfred Thayer Mahan. The impact of his book *The Influence of Sea Power on History*, published in 1895, was as great as the author's historical reasoning was dubious. Being a navy man, Mahan argued that history demonstrated that civilizations based on sea power were superior to those that relied on land forces. As a result, Mahan forecast a glorious future for Great Britain and the United States, while he was pessimistic about countries like Russia.

For both the public and the leaders in Germany (as well as other Western societies), navalism and imperialism went hand in hand with another popular theory, that of social Darwinism. This doctrine was essentially a vulgarization and distortion of Charles Darwin's theory of evolution. Whereas Darwin argued that nature determines the survival of the fittest through random selection, social Darwinists linked the struggle among nations and individuals to the need for deliberate decisions that aid nations and individuals to survive as the "fittest." In its most blatant form, social Darwinism justified both laissez-faire capitalism and imperialism. As far as Germany was concerned, the ideas associated with imperialism, navalism, and social Darwinism convinced the country's leaders that the Reich had a mission as a global rather than merely a Continental power. To take its place among the "fittest" of nations, Germany required both a navy and an overseas empire.

In a sense, Germany's global ambitions were formally announced in a speech by the emperor on January 18, 1896. In his address commemorating the founding of the empire, traditionally a high point of patriotic fervor in Germany, William II signaled that under his leadership the Reich would demand to be consulted when it came to deciding the fate of both Europe and the rest of the world. Germany, like England and France, would intensify its efforts to obtain overseas colonial possessions.

The concrete results of Germany's global policy fell far short of its aspirations. Before the Reich was stripped of all its colonial possessions at the end of World War I, the German flag flew in the Pacific over some islands (the Marshall Islands and the Bismarck Archipelago) and Kiaochow off the coast of China. In Africa the Cameroons, Togoland, German South-West Africa (now Namibia), and German East Africa (now Tanzania) were controlled by the Reich. The German colonies were of little strategic value and singularly unattractive to German settlers. Far from being economic assets, their administration required constant subsidies from the Reich treasury. As for Germany's membership in the global club of imperialist nations, the Reich never achieved more than associate status. Western imperialism continued to be dominated by the British and French, as well as, after 1898, the Americans.

Still, in terms of domestic politics the colonies proved to be a major asset. Along with the growing volume of Germany's trade they were used to justify a major change in the Reich's military policy. In 1897 Admiral Alfred von Tirpitz, the Reich secretary of the navy, proclaimed the need to construct what he called a "deterrent fleet" (*Risikoflotte*). Until then Germany's minuscule navy had consisted of some coastal defense vessels, but Tirpitz claimed that the Reich's role as a global power required a fleet that was strong enough so no other naval power (and that meant essentially the British) would risk attacking it. Specifically, the admiral, backed by the emperor, proposed that the Reichstag appropriate funds to build a force of fifty destroyers for coastal defense, and nineteen "ships of the line." The latter category included battleships and their support vessels. The construction program was to extend over the next twenty-five years, and, according to the government, would require no additional outlays of money: Revenues obtained from the sustained growth of the German economy (1897 marked the end of the depression) would be sufficient to finance the construction of the fleet.

Map 2.1   Germany's Colonial Possessions, 1914

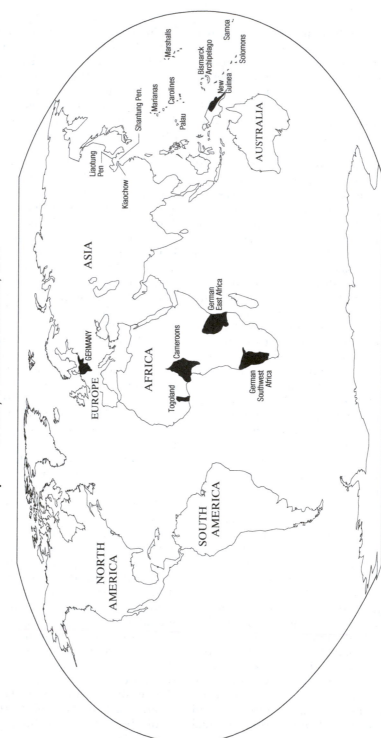

Tirpitz's proposals, which were vigorously endorsed by the Naval League, aroused massive enthusiasm among most middle-class Germans, although the illusion that the navy could be built without additional burdens on the Reich treasury lasted only three years. The supporters of navalism felt sufficiently sure of continuing public enthusiasm for their cause that they proposed an augmented construction program in 1900. Arguing that both Great Britain's recent diplomatic defeat of France (in 1898 France had yielded to England in Africa, freeing the way for British control of Egypt and the Sudan) and the U.S. victory in the Spanish-American War demonstrated the decisive importance of naval power, Tirpitz and the government proposed increasing the German deterrent fleet to forty "ships of the line." Even the navy's leaders no longer contended that sustained economic growth would be sufficient for the expanded construction program. Instead, the fleet was to be financed through bonds, in other words, an increase of the Reich debt. The outlay was now portrayed as an investment in Germany's future because the fleet would protect the nation's merchant fleet and the growing volume of the Reich's overseas trade.

Within six years the construction of a new class of battleships by the British navy, the Dreadnought class, had rendered all previous naval construction plans obsolete. Despite the immense costs involved in pursuing the dream of a German deterrent fleet under the changed conditions, the Reich's leaders and a majority of the Reichstag decided to meet the British "challenge." After 1906 Germany, too, began to build Dreadnoughts. That decision did not diminish England's naval superiority, but it did significantly increase Germany's national debt. More important, the growing financial sacrifices for the navy made the fleet construction program an increasingly important factor in maintaining the domestic balance of power. As long as politicians could be found who agreed with the judgment by one of Tirpitz's subordinates that "everything in Germany including the constitution would have only one purpose: to serve the needs of the navy," the Reich's leaders would be tempted to use navalism to stabilize the domestic situation regardless of the international consequences.

Incidentally, it was indicative of the emotional mystique of navalism that public opinion and the Reichstag were far more critical of increases in the land forces. When the Caprivi government proposed raising the peacetime strength by 84,000 men, an increase that corresponded to the growth of the population, the Reichstag refused to vote appropriations for more than 59,000 men. It was not until 1913, in the face of changes that increased the de facto strength of the French army, that the German land forces were significantly augmented.

The fleet-building program (and even more the rhetoric that accompanied it) provided a background cacophony that insistently disturbed the harmony of Germany's diplomatic relations. As noted earlier, Germany wanted good relations with Great Britain. Unfortunately the Reich demanded a diplomatic price from England that the island nation was not willing to pay: The Germans insisted not only on their recognition as a major imperial power but also on tying any Anglo-German treaty to British support of Austro-German ambitions for attaining hegemony in central and southeastern Europe.

Negotiations between Germany and Great Britain began in 1898; they continued intermittently until 1912. At times the negotiators seemed to come close to an agreement, but eventually both sides admitted failure. The main difficulty was the Reich's stubborn insistence that Germany continued to operate from a position of strength, whereas in reality a series of alliances and agreements among the other Great Powers produced major shifts in the balance of power that undermined Germany's initially strong position.

Partly as a reaction to the Reich's failure to renew the Reinsurance Treaty (see the earlier section, pp. 37ff), the French and the Russians in 1894 concluded a mutual defense alliance. Frustrated by the unproductive Anglo-German negotiations, Great Britain, too, eventually turned elsewhere for allies. The result was a series of agreements between England and Japan (1902), France (1904), and Russia (1907). By the end of the decade Germany was diplomatically all but isolated; only Austria-Hungary, a country beset by increasing domestic problems, could be counted as a firm ally. Italy, the third partner in the Triple Alliance of 1882, drifted closer to France and away from the Austro-German camp.

In the face of the front of Great Powers diplomatically aligned against Germany, its foreign policy after 1904 became increasingly erratic and frantic. In repeated efforts to weaken Anglo-French and Anglo-Russian ties, the Reich between 1905 and 1913 attempted to exploit the diplomatic crises that periodically resulted from the emergence of power vacuums as "the sick man of Europe," the Ottoman Empire, declined.

In 1905 the first Moroccan crisis began as a test of wills between France and Germany, but it quickly turned into an Anglo-German crisis as well. France, which had long pursued economic interests in Morocco, at the end of the century moved to establish a formal protectorate over the area. Germany, suddenly discovering its interest in the rights of self-determination for the weak Sultan of Morocco, protested France's unilateral moves and called for an international conference to determine the fate of Morocco. The other powers agreed, but the meeting became a diplomatic defeat for Germany. With the exception of Austria, all of the Great Powers supported France. The Reich's position was certainly not helped by the dilettantish efforts of William II. He attempted (and failed) to weaken Russia's ties to France by personally negotiating a treaty of alliance with Czar Nicholas II of Russia.

Despite the earlier setbacks, during a second Moroccan crisis six years later, Germany again attempted to force international intervention. This time the Reich government even dispatched a naval vessel to the port of Agadir to underscore the Reich's concern for the fate of Morocco. Diplomatically, the result was another defeat for William. At a second conference the

German and Austro-Hungarian empires were again isolated, although as a face-saving gesture, Germany was awarded part of the Cameroons in Africa.

In the meantime, the focus of crisis management efforts by the concert of powers had shifted to southeastern Europe. In 1908 Russia and Austria agreed to end Turkey's nominal control of the province of Bosnia-Herzegovina (now the Republic of Bosnia-Herzegovina, one of the successor states to what was formerly Yugoslavia), and Austria annexed the territory. Russia's prize in the bargain was to have been increased rights of passage for its naval forces through the Straits of Constantinople, but Great Britain refused to agree to a change in the Strait's regime.

Three years later, a Turkish-Italian War seemed to signal the final demise of the Ottoman Empire. Not only did Turkey lose further territory in North Africa (Libya), but its military weakness put the control of what remained of its European possessions in doubt. This was of considerable interest to Germany, whose growing investments in the Ottoman Empire (especially in connection with a "Berlin to Baghdad" railroad project) gave the Reich a vital interest in preserving the territorial integrity of the Ottoman Empire. Turkey's Balkan neighbors, in contrast, had no interest in preserving the Ottoman Empire. A series of so-called Balkan Wars in 1912–1913 pitted Greece, Serbia, Bulgaria, Rumania, and Montenegro first against the Turks and then against each other, with Russia and Austria attempting to manipulate rival alliance systems behind the scenes.

Acting on behalf of the concert of powers, the ambassadors of the Great Powers in London, including the German emissary Prince Lichnovsky, met under the chairmanship of the British foreign minister Lord Grey. The diplomats eventually restored temporary peace in the Balkans, but Germany's diplomatic position on the eve of World War I remained precarious. From the Reich's point of view, the balance sheet of Wilhelminian foreign relations was not favorable. Largely isolated in the concert of powers, Germany had little to show for its global ambitions except the ruins of failed efforts and persistent illusions.

GERMANY ON THE EVE OF WORLD WAR I

William II celebrated his silver jubilee as emperor in 1913. As was to be expected, the occasion was marked by great pomp and circumstance and in many ways it accurately reflected the mood of both the nation and its leader. The standard of living of most Germans was rising, the economy strong and expanding. Germans took pride in their country's technological and scientific accomplishments. Even the path toward nonviolent political modernization seemed to have been cleared. The election of 1912 had demonstrated the strength of the forces that favored convergence rather than increasing polarization. The extreme right and left were losing strength among the voters; most Germans clearly supported the moderate center and left. On the right side of the spectrum, conservatism was reduced to a permanent and small minority. On the left side, there were clear signs that the ostracism (both self-imposed and inflicted from the outside) of the socialists was weakening. Votes by the SPD in support of budgets submitted by "bourgeois" governments in some southern German states, which broke a long-standing taboo in the party, represented a major victory for the revisionists in the SPD.

But there was another side to the picture. Optimism, pride, and consensus existed side by side with pessimism, alienation, and polarization. The late nineteenth century marked the final triumph of science, rationalism, and materialism, but there was also a growing feeling that something vital had been lost. As we saw, sometimes the reaction to the materialism of the Wilhelminian establishment took the form of a rebellion for modernity and self-proclaimed idealism. More often, the response was a sense of pessimism and fatalism.

The signs of sociopolitical convergence, too, were not unambiguous. True, by 1913 William and his advisers had given up any thought of a coup from above to halt the erosion of political authoritarianism at the Reich level. At the same time, the failure of efforts to reform the three-class system of voting in Prussia demonstrated that the forces opposed to political modernization in Germany were fortifying their Prussian redoubt. The road to full modernization in Germany would certainly not be smooth.

The international scene also provided a set of contradictory indicators. On the positive side of the ledger was the restoration of the balance of power by the end of 1913. Although differences among the Great Powers persisted, the peace treaties imposed on the belligerents in the Balkan Wars and an Anglo-German agreement on economic spheres of influence in the Middle East just before the outbreak of World War I showed that the concert of powers was still capable of functioning well. Beginning in 1906 a flood of books appeared in Germany and other European countries attempting to prove that war was impossible and perpetual peace among the Great Powers inevitable.

But again, there were countervailing tendencies. International conflicts and crises had clearly been on the rise in the last ten years, and there was increasing discussion of the "unthinkable": a military confrontation among the Great Powers. Helmuth von Moltke, the chief of staff of the Prussian army, remarked during a military appropriations debate that "eternal peace is a pipe dream, and not a very pleasant one at that."

His sentiments were shared by many Germans and other Europeans. These elements convinced themselves that war promised an end to materialism and decadence. In 1912, the same year in which much pacifist literature appeared, a retired general, Friedrich von Bernhardi, wrote a best seller with the prophetic title *Deutschland und der nächste Krieg* ("Germany and the Next War"), in which he described military conflict as not only inevitable but also beneficial because it would end the age of materialism and selfishness, heralding a new era of heroism and self-sacrifice.

Most important, perhaps, were the signs that some groups in Germany longed for war as a way to stop Germany's political modernization. In 1913 the editor of the *Deutsche Arbeitgeberzeitung* ("Germans Employers' Newspaper"), the organ of the country's employers' associations, decided a war was "the cure for [our] diseases." It is certainly true that the Reich's responsible leaders did not actively pursue policies in this direction, but when an occasion arose in which an unforeseen terrorist act presented them with the choice of dampening or heating up the conflict, they chose escalation. Their decision was motivated primarily by military and diplomatic considerations, but the German leaders were not unaware that war would at least for a time unite the nation in support of an otherwise crumbling system of authoritarianism.

CHAPTER THREE

~~~~~~~~~~~~~~~

World War I

1914–1918

Few events have changed the course of human history as profoundly as World War I. Directly or indirectly, the hostilities affected all Germans as well as most Europeans and Americans. By the time the war ended in November 1918, much of the old order in Germany and Europe had disappeared. Two revolutions in Russia ended the rule of the czars, and Austria-Hungary disintegrated into several new nation-states. In Germany Prusso-German authoritarianism was overthrown, and the country lost its status as a great power. William II abdicated and went into exile in Holland. He remained there until his death in 1941 and never visited Germany again.

The human costs of the war were staggering. World War I was the first modern "total" war. Increasingly sophisticated (and destructive) armaments and mechanized warfare were not only very wasteful of human resources on the battlefield but also required mobilization of economic and human resources on the "home front" to an unprecedented degree. The results were enormous casualty figures and

major societal dislocations. Germany suffered more than 6 million dead, wounded, and missing soldiers. An additional 750,000 people are estimated to have died from war-related malnutrition and diseases.

THE OUTBREAK OF THE WAR

After World War I had ended, politicians and scholars on both sides of the Atlantic began a search that has continued until our own times for the persons or developments that had been "guilty" of starting the conflict. In the treaty that ended the war, Germany was forced to acknowledge its responsibility for unleashing the conflict, but during the 1920s most Germans—but also many scholars in the Allied countries—supported the "revisionist" view that the German government had played only a minor part in the outbreak of the war.

Interest in the war-guilt issue waned as Europe was plunged into World War II. (There were no doubts about Nazi Germany's responsibility for unleashing that conflagration.) In 1961, however, the publication of a massive new study by the German historian Fritz Fischer reopened the debate. Fischer's book, *Germany's Aims in the First World War* (the German title of the work, *Der Griff nach der Weltmacht* ["The Grasp for World Power"], expressed the author's thesis even better), argued that an unholy alliance of Germany's military, industrial, and political leaders deliberately maneuvered the country into war to maintain the power of authoritarianism at home and extend German hegemony abroad.

At least part of Fischer's thesis has stood the test of time. As we will see, Germany's leaders were certainly not dragged into the conflict against their will; rather they saw the war as a domestic and foreign policy opportunity. But that leaves the question of Germany's actual war guilt. Fischer also contended that the imperial government and the Prussian general staff deliberately set out to wage war in 1914 to achieve aims laid out long beforehand. But here the evidence is less clear. On balance, it appears the "guilt" of Germany's political and military leaders lay not in planning a conspiracy to wage war but in the failure to recognize the consequences of their decisions during the crisis that led to the outbreak of hostilities.

On June 28, 1914, the heir to the throne of the Austro-Hungarian Empire, Archduke Franz Ferdinand, was on an official visit to Bosnia-Herzegovina, a territory that Austria had formally annexed six years earlier. The itinerary of the archduke and his wife that day included an inspection of an army regiment and a reception by the mayor of Sarajevo, the capital of the province. As they were leaving the town hall, the royal couple, seated in an open car, was assassinated by a young Bosnian Serb, Gavrilo Prinšip.

This act of terrorism stood at the beginning of a chain of events that would eventually precipitate World War I, although initially few expected such an outcome. Political assassinations were regrettably common in late nineteenth- and early twentieth-century Europe. In 1881 Czar Alexander II was killed by a bomb Russian terrorists had placed under his carriage. In 1898 Franz Ferdinand's aunt, Empress Elizabeth, was assassinated by an Italian anarchist. The motives of Prinšip and his six accomplices were also familiar then and now. The assassin and his fellow conspirators, young students and self-proclaimed intellectuals, belonged to an organization called Young Bosnia. The avowed aim of the group was to liberate Bosnia-Herzegovina from Austrian rule so that along with Serbia and other South Slav states it would become part of a new and larger country, Yugoslavia.

The assassination became a crisis rather than just a tragedy when the Great Powers, and particularly Austria, saw their vital interests threatened. Interrogations of Prinšip and his accomplices (all of the conspirators were quickly captured by Austrian police) convinced the Austrian authorities that Young Bosnia was far more than a club of misguided youths. The Austrian officials learned that the terrorists had been provided with weapons, passports, and safe conduct routes from Serbia into Bosnia by a secret Serbian terrorist and political organization, The Black Hand. It was also known that the leader of The Black Hand was the chief of the intelligence section of the Serbian general staff, Colonel Dragutin Dimitrijeviš. From this information the Austrian authorities deduced (wrongly) that the Serbian government must have known of Prinšip's plans and that the assassination was in fact a case of state-sponsored terrorism.

Austria-Hungary refused to believe Serbia's protestations of shock and innocence; the Habsburg government was determined to strike back. The only question was how, or, more precisely, whether retaliation should take the form of diplomatic or military measures. For some years prior to 1914 a so-called war party in the Austro-Hungarian government had been advocating a preventive military strike against Serbia. This group, led by the chief of the Austro-Hungarian general staff, General Franz Count Conrad von Hötzendorff, was not only convinced that Serbia was attempting to destroy the Austro-Hungarian Empire, but that Serbia was little more than a tool of Russia in this effort. Consequently, Hötzendorff and his allies argued that only Serbia's military defeat by Austria would convince Russia and Serbia to end their efforts at undermining the political and territorial integrity of the Austro-Hungarian Empire.

Until the assassination of the archduke, Hötzendorff and his supporters had been restrained by a "peace party" led by the Hungarian prime minister, Count Tizsa. This group countered Hötzendorff's offensive military strategy with warnings about an Austro-Russian conflict. After the murder at Sarajevo the "war" and "peace" parties repeated their arguments more forcefully. Tizsa and the "peace" party continued to oppose military operations, pointing out that military action would leave Austria isolated. Hötzendorff, arguing for military operations, proposed that the Austrians send a diplomatic mission to Berlin to ask for German support.

Austria's decision to involve the Germans was made on July 3. Two days later, a high-level Austrian delegation went to Berlin to request Germany's support for whatever Austria determined was necessary to "punish" Serbia. In submitting their case to the Germans, the Austrians did not indicate what specific action they had in mind, although military action was clearly not ruled out. William II met personally with the head of the Austrian delegation, Count Hoyos, and gave him assurances that the emperor and his government would back the Austrians in any actions they might take. Without consulting either the chancellor or the military chief of staff, William II had issued a blank check to the Austrians. (Chancellor Bethmann Hollweg was informed subsequently; the following day he amplified William's views in a conversation with the Austrian ambassador.)

"A Chain of Friendship"—"If Austria attacks Serbia, Russia will fall upon Austria, Germany upon Russia, and France and England upon Germany." (*The Brooklyn Eagle*, 1914. Professor Oron J. Hale provided the cartoon.)

Interlocking alliances of 1914. (Source: Courtesy of Library of Congress.)

There were a number of reasons for William's overly hasty and unnecessary decision to sign the "blank check." The emperor was an impulsive man, inordinately proud of his ability to reach quick and "instinctively correct" judgments. The monarch also felt there should be no doubts that Germany would stand by its one remaining ally. Balance-of-power considerations entered into his decision. As noted earlier, both Austria and Germany were determined that Russia should not be allowed to threaten Austria's and Germany's position in central and southeastern Europe. Finally, there were the implications for domestic politics. When he promised his support, William was clearly not contemplating a world war, but he also felt that a military triumph in a limited theater of operations would unite the nation behind him and Prusso-German authoritarianism.

William's blank check enabled the "war party" in Austria to win its case for a "preventive" military strike against Serbia. As of July 7, Austria was determined on military rather than diplomatic humiliation of its neighbor to the south. To be sure, the decision was kept secret from the other Great Powers (including Germany) for another two weeks. Not until July 23, when Austria dispatched an ultimatum to Serbia, did the tragedy of Sarajevo become a full-scale international crisis. Although the Serbian answer to Austria's ultimatum was a model of accommodation (Serbia rejected only one of the ten demands made by Austria), the Viennese government determined that the Serbs' reply was unsatisfactory, and on July 28 Austria-Hungary declared war on Serbia.

Austria's move was a surprise to virtually everyone in Europe. William II, for one, had earlier expressed his opinion that the Viennese government would be satisfied with Serbia's apologetic reply to the Austrian ultimatum. The declaration of war also changed the dimensions of the crisis entirely. The expected defeat of Serbia by Austria would have significantly altered the balance of power in the Balkans, something Russia was unwilling to accept. In response to Austria's declaration of war on Serbia, Russia put its troop contingents facing the Austrian border on alert. The Austro-Russian altercation in turn led France to begin mobilizing its troops under the terms of the Franco-Russian alliance, while Germany mobilized its troops to comply with the terms of the Dual Alliance. It was this aspect of the crisis, the mobilization timetables, that caused the Reich's military leaders to panic. In the midst of frantic last-minute diplomatic efforts (mostly by Great Britain) in the final days of July to defuse what was now clearly the worst international crisis since the war scare of 1875, Moltke, the chief of the German general staff, telegraphed Hötzendorff asking his Austrian counterpart to ignore all further political and diplomatic attempts to delay military preparations and to begin immediate full-scale mobilization.

The Austrian decision to declare war on Serbia and Moltke's precipitant action bypassing the political and diplomatic efforts to contain the rapidly growing crisis made a decisive struggle among the Great Powers inevitable. What had begun as a tragedy for the House of Habsburg and developed into a diplomatic crisis was about to become the first military confrontation since the Napoleonic Wars involving all of the Great Powers.

MILITARY DEVELOPMENTS

It is a truism among historians that military planners tend to base their strategies for future conflicts on the presumed lessons learned from the last war. The pattern certainly fit the German strategy in World War I; it was intended as an adaptation of the plans that had succeeded so well during the Franco-Prussian War of 1870–1871.

For land warfare Germany originally had only one strategic concept, the so-called Schlieffen Plan. Named for its originator, the chief of the Prussian general staff in the 1890s, General Alfred von Schlieffen, it was designed to meet the worst-case contingency of a two-front war in which Germany had to wage military operations simultaneously against the French in the west and the Russians in the east. It was well known that the Russians, who were hampered by an inadequate transportation system, required far longer to move their troops to the front than was true for the Western powers and Germany. Consequently, Schlieffen's concept envisioned immediate and massive offensive operations against France, which would result in the defeat of Germany's western neighbor six weeks after war had been declared. Once France had been eliminated from the conflict, the Germans would move the bulk of their forces to the eastern front just in time to face and defeat the lumbering Russians as they drew near the borders of East Prussia.

The Schlieffen Plan is still recognized as a bold and brilliant military concept, although in practice, as we will see, it failed ignominiously. A recent "revisionist" study contends that Schlieffen has been unfairly maligned for the failure of "his" plan. The author of this new thesis, Terence Zuber, claims that the "Schlieffen Plan" was actually an invention of the Prussian General Staff after the war had ended to cast blame for Germany's defeat on the former (and now conveniently dead) chief of the General Staff. According to Zuber, Schlieffen himself was far more cautious than his successors; he favored a defensive strategy with limited counteroffensives.

Regardless of the plan's authorship, the German military strategists in 1914 were determined to use Germany's advantages in staff organization and speed of troop deployment to offset the Russians' superior numerical strength while offensive moves were designed to outwit the French defensive strategists. French military planners, for their part, interpreted the lessons of 1871 to mean that France needed to strengthen the defenses on its eastern border. As a result, the French after 1871 built a string of fortifications across the traditional invasion routes from Germany, thereby effectively precluding a repetition of the German operations that had succeeded in 1871. To bypass the French defenses, the German strategy stipulated an alternate invasion route. Instead of confronting the French directly, the German armies would march through Belgium. The French armies, seeing themselves outflanked, would then have to withdraw major units from their original defensive positions, enabling the Germans to overrun the French fortifications. But the strategy's military advantage was also its political fatal flaw. In blithely contemplating marching through Belgium, the German military leaders felt that military considerations had to take priority over the political and diplomatic repercussions of violating Belgian neutrality: Since 1839 that country's neutrality had been guaranteed by all of the Great Powers, including Prussia and later Germany.

The declaration of war triggered the immediate implementation of Germany's offensive strategy; within three weeks some 2 million German soldiers were ready for battle. The German land forces were divided into eight armies. After mobilization, seven advanced against France and Belgium while one guarded the borders in the east. German troops did cross the Belgian frontier according to schedule, but contrary to what Germany expected, Belgium refused the Reich's request for unhindered passage. Instead, the Belgians put up stiff resistance, actually halting the German advance for a few days. Still, Belgium was obviously no military match for Germany. At the end of August, the German armies advanced from Belgium into northern France, inflicting severe losses on the weak French and British troops positioned there.

The German strategy soon ran into difficulties, however. The French were able to regroup, and at the Battle of the Marne (September 1914) the German advance was halted—permanently as it turned out. What had been planned as a war of swift movements in the west became a war of

Im Mittelpunkt Erich Ludendorff (1865–1937)

It could be said that Erich Ludendorff was destined for a military career almost from the day of his birth. The son of an army officer, Ludendorff was born in West Prussia, an area that is now part of Poland. At age ten, he entered a Prussian cadet school, traditionally the first step on the road to becoming a career Prussian military officer. Even at this early stage, Ludendorff's teachers noted his acute intellect and organizational skills; he was especially good at military history and tactics.

There was, however, the matter of the missing "von." Ludendorff did not come from a noble Prussian family, and, as a result, the most prestigious branches of the army, such as the cavalry, were closed to him. Nevertheless, his well-recognized skills secured him an appointment to the General Staff in 1894; by 1904 he headed the Deployment Section of the General Staff.

While Ludendorff's career consisted mostly of staff appointments, he did, briefly, see action in World War I. As a brigade commander, he led the assault on the Belgian city of Liège. For this feat he was awarded the *Pour le Mérite*, Prussia's highest military decoration. Shortly afterward, Ludendorff was sent to the eastern front to join General von Hindenburg's staff. This began the long association of the two men, who were to dominate the Supreme Command of the Armed Forces (*Oberste Heeresleitung*—OHL) and the German government in the latter part of the war. For the moment, they earned the gratitude of the emperor and most of the German people for their brilliant victory at the Battle of Tannenberg. At Tannenberg, Ludendorff demonstrated his superb handling of logistics and supplies, and in August 1916 he was appointed quartermaster general of the German armed forces.

Ludendorff was never one to oppose mixing politics and the military or, more precisely, he insisted politics had to be subordinated at all times to the needs of the military. Because he found Germany's civilian leader at the beginning of the war unwilling to accept this dictum, Ludendorff and Hindenburg agitated forcefully to have Chancellor Bethmann Hollweg dismissed. They succeeded in reaching their goal in 1916, but military rule could not guarantee the "victory peace" the OHL promised.

After 1916, with a supine emperor and civilian government leaders unwilling to stand in their way, Ludendorff and Hindenburg pursued an all-or-nothing military strategy that succeeded in defeating the Russian Empire, only to fail on the western front. By October 1918 Ludendorff acknowledged that the war was lost. He resigned from the officer corps and fled to Sweden.

---

attrition. For the next three and a half years, defensive operations were far more effective than offensive sallies. At the end of 1914, an elaborate system of trenches, stretching from the English Channel in the north to the Swiss border in the south, separated by no-man's-land, dominated the strategic picture in the west. For the soldiers, the war became long years of boredom, filth, and disease punctuated by periodic offensives involving hundreds of thousands of men on both sides, but until mid-1918 these efforts were largely futile. Major innovations in weaponry, notably permanently mounted machine guns, enabled defenders to inflict heavy casualties. Offensive forces had no comparable weapons until the beginning of 1918 when tanks became operational on a large scale and tipped the balance in favor of the offensive. Only rarely was the fighting interrupted by moments of commonsense humanity. One such event occurred in December 1914 when along one section of the western front German and Allied soldiers met in the no-man's-land between the lines and celebrated Christmas together.

He returned to Germany shortly after the armistice and immediately began dabbling in a variety of extreme right-wing organizations and plots. Ludendorff passionately hated the Weimar Republic, and he never saw a conspiracy to destroy the German democratic constitution that he did not like. He supported the Kapp putsch and joined Hitler in the Beer Hall putsch. Ludendorff was tried alongside Hitler after that failed coup, but the lenient and sympathetic judges acquitted him. Hitler persuaded him to run for president in 1925, but Ludendorff came in as a distant third behind his old colleague Hindenburg and the candidate of the democratic parties, Wilhelm Marx.

After that disaster, Ludendorff largely withdrew from active political life and devoted himself to an organization he founded in 1925, the Tannenberg Association, better known as the Ludendorff Movement. Although Ludendorff was the titular head of the group, the brains behind this politico-religious sect—which never had more than a few thousand members—was his second wife, Mathilde. The Ludendorff Movement worked tirelessly to expose what it claimed was a tripartite conspiracy that had engineered Germany's defeat in World War I and was now working to destroy the entire German race: Jews, Catholics, and Free Masons.

Hitler's coming to power was a bittersweet experience for Ludendorff. On the one hand, he enthusiastically welcomed the destruction of the Weimar Republic and the Nazis' anti-Semitic measures, but on the other, he soon discovered the Nazis had little use for his movement's anti-Catholic venom. Anxious to secure the goodwill of Germany's Catholics and the papacy, the Nazi regime quickly limited the publications of the Tannenberg Association, and the Nazi-controlled press was prohibited from publicizing Ludendorff's views and activities. It was also symptomatic of the Nazis' campaign to keep Ludendorff out of the public eye that he was not invited to attend Hindenburg's funeral in 1934, although it is doubtful he would have gone even if he had been invited. The two men had long since become bitter enemies. Ludendorff always resented that Hindenburg had been unwilling to join him in resigning from the military in October 1918, and he never forgave his old colleague for serving as the republic's president.

Ironically, the Nazis decided to grant Ludendorff the honor and respect in death that they had denied him in life. The former general died in December 1937, and Hitler promptly ordered an elaborate Nazi funeral for him.

Within two months after the start of the war, Germany's strategy for winning a two-front confrontation had failed. (The emperor's eldest son, Crown Prince William, admitted privately in November 1914 that Germany could not win the war.) One reason for the setback in the west was the unexpectedly early arrival of the Russians in the east. During the Battle of the Marne, the Germans had to send two army corps (about 60,000 men) from the western front to the eastern front to deal with the surprisingly swift arrival of the Russians on the borders of East Prussia. Tactical mistakes by the commander on the eastern front, General von Prittwitz, aggravated the situation. Almost in desperation, in mid-August command of the eastern front troops was transferred from Prittwitz to General Paul von Hindenburg. The new commander in turn selected General Erich Ludendorff as his chief of staff.

Hindenburg was then sixty-seven years old and the scion of an old-line Junker family when he assumed command in the east. Ludendorff, some fifteen years Hindenburg's junior, was a far less popular and venerable figure. He did not belong to the nobility, nor

Map 3.1 Military Operations of World War I

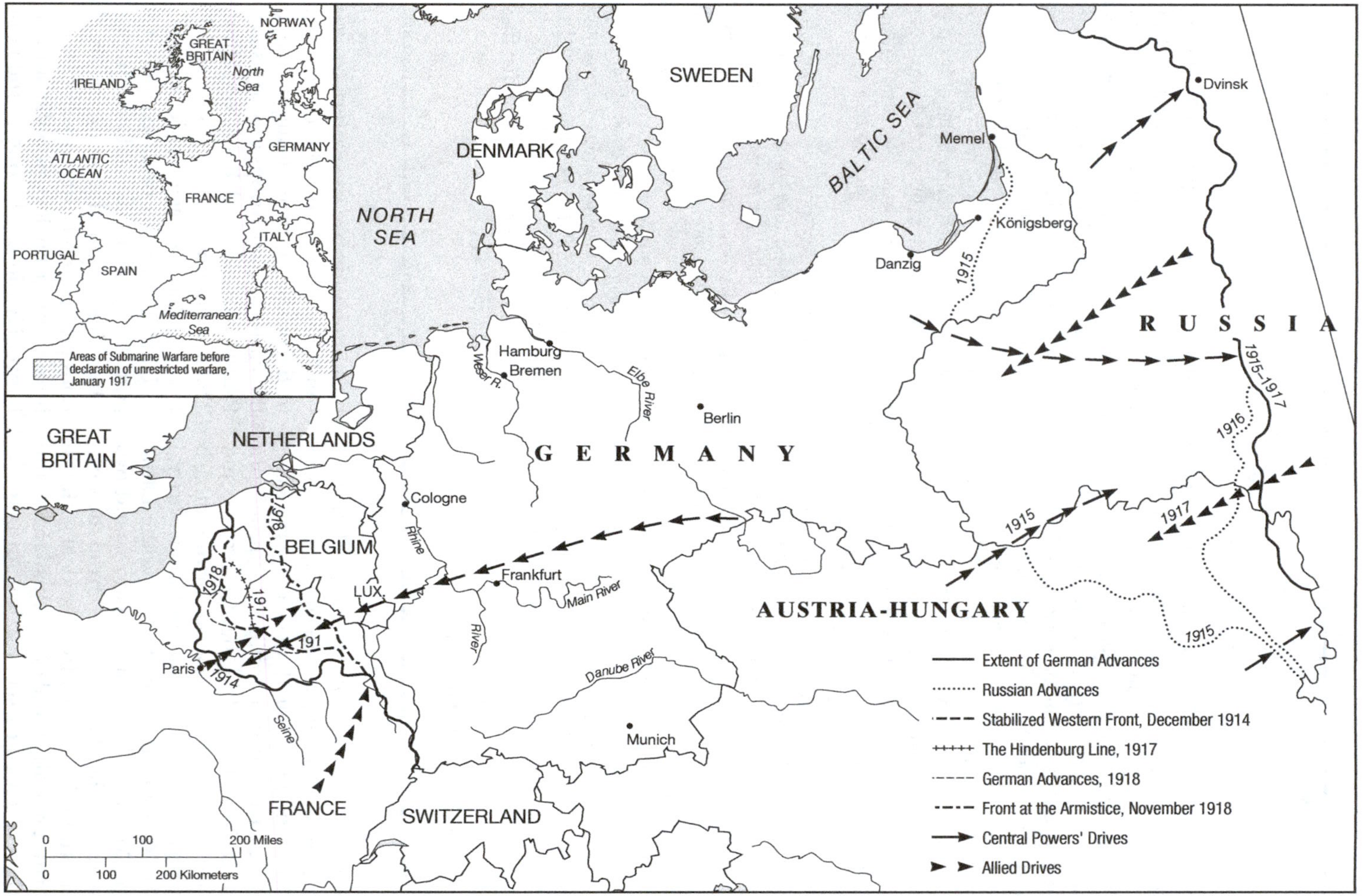
NORWAY
GREAT BRITAIN
IRELAND
North Sea
GERMANY
ATLANTIC OCEAN
FRANCE
ITALY
PORTUGAL
SPAIN
Mediterranean Sea
Areas of Submarine Warfare before declaration of unrestricted warfare, January 1917
NORTH SEA
DENMARK
SWEDEN
BALTIC SEA
Memel
Königsberg
Danzig
Dvinsk
1915
RUSSIA
1915–1917
1916
1917
1915
Hamburg
Bremen
Weser R.
Elbe River
Berlin
GREAT BRITAIN
NETHERLANDS
GERMANY
Cologne
Rhine
BELGIUM
1918
1917
1918
191
LUX.
Frankfurt
Main River
River
Paris
1914
Seine
Danube River
Munich
AUSTRIA-HUNGARY
FRANCE
SWITZERLAND
0 100 200 Miles
0 100 200 Kilometers
Extent of German Advances
Russian Advances
Stabilized Western Front, December 1914
The Hindenburg Line, 1917
German Advances, 1918
Front at the Armistice, November 1918
Central Powers' Drives
Allied Drives

had he served in one of the guard regiments that were the traditional grooming grounds for Prussian generals. In fact, Ludendorff had made his career in the quartermaster corps, the least prestigious branch of the military but one that suited his own capabilities singularly well: Ludendorff's major strengths were organization and planning. The two men immediately demonstrated their military acumen in the Battle of Tannenberg. A brilliantly executed pincer movement managed to surround the invading Russians. In the resulting battle the Russians suffered more than 120,000 casualties and were forced to retreat more than 130 miles back into Russian territory. Hindenburg and Ludendorff had become instant heroes. William II talked of the team of "Wotan and Siegfried."

Ironically, what had begun as a serious problem in the east promised, after the victory at Tannenberg, to become part of the solution to Germany's military dilemma. While operations in the west bogged down into trench warfare, the eastern theater provided opportunities for large-scale offensive operations that could be converted into optimistic press reports. For image and public relations purposes, the victory at Tannenberg soon overshadowed the far more important defeat on the Marne.

While Hindenburg's and Ludendorff's stars were rising, the defeat on the Marne ended the military career of Helmuth von Moltke. In September 1914 he resigned as chief of staff. Moltke was succeeded by the Prussian minister of war, General Erich von Falkenhayn. The new chief of what was now called the Supreme Command of the Armed Forces knew that in spite of the optimistic press releases put out by the government's propaganda machine, the overall military situation was far from favorable. On the western front the war of attrition produced heavy casualties. The blockade, which the British had imposed at the outbreak of the war, prevented needed imports from reaching Germany. Finally, as Napoleon had discovered a century earlier, large-scale operations on the Russian plain did not necessarily mean that Russia had been defeated.

As his answer to the impasse, Falkenhayn advocated what came to be known as the Verdun strategy. Specifically, the new chief of the OHL proposed a siege of the key French fortress of Verdun. Falkenhayn anticipated one of two outcomes: Either the Germans would capture the fortress, thereby decisively weakening the French defensive line, or the constant German pressure on the fortress would force the French to deploy a steady stream of defenders to the area, who would then become casualties of the constant German artillery barrages. It all sounded good on paper, but Falkenhayn lost sight of the fact that at the beginning of 1916 the Reich did not have the military resources to maintain the steady and uninterrupted pressure on the fortress that would have been required to make Falkenhayn's Verdun strategy a success.

In the meantime, Germany's overall strategic situation was steadily deteriorating. Italy's decision to join the war on the Allied side in the spring of 1915 had already put additional pressure on the Austro-German southern flank. The blockade had increasingly severe repercussions for the German home front. At the beginning of June 1916, a Russian offensive, although eventually stopped, achieved initial gains. The attack on the fortress system at Verdun began in February 1916. For the rest of the year the area was a constant battleground. To be sure, France's military commanders decided to defend Verdun at all costs (the fortress was never taken by the Germans) and the French suffered heavy casualties as a result, but the German losses were not significantly lower.

Like Moltke, Falkenhayn failed to produce a winning strategy and in August 1916 the emperor accepted Falkenhayn's resignation as chief of the OHL. He was succeeded by the two military leaders who symbolized victory for most Germans: Hindenburg and Ludendorff. At the beginning of June 1916, a Russian offensive, although eventually stopped, achieved initial gains. In July 1916 the Germans were forced to send major reinforcements to the Somme front, where the Allies had begun an offensive that cost further thousands of lives on both sides. The Battle of the Somme lasted until November when winter and mud halted the operations.

The failure of the Verdun strategy was compounded by almost simultaneous setbacks suffered by the German navy. In strategic terms, the navy's primary responsibility during World War I was to break or at least loosen the British blockade. To accomplish its task the German navy relied on blockade runners, the high seas fleet, and a new type of weapon, the submarine.

In imposing their blockade, the British attempted to prevent virtually all imported materials from reaching Germany. At first the Germans were relatively unconcerned about the blockade. The military leaders expected the war to end before the British naval measures could have much effect. However, as the conflict dragged on the German war effort was increasingly affected by Britain's naval superiority.

Germany's single effort to engage the British surface fleet came in May 1916 when the British and German fleets met almost accidentally off the coast of Denmark. The outcome was a German tactical victory and a strategic defeat. The British suffered a loss of fourteen ships and 6,100 casualties; the Germans lost only five ships and 2,500 men. At the same time, these figures were meaningless in strategic terms. As darkness fell on May 16, the remainder of the German high seas fleet returned to port, leaving the British naval hegemony (and the effectiveness of the blockade) intact.

From now on, Germany's efforts to break the British blockade and impose interdictions of its own were essentially reduced to attempting to establish a counterblockade by the use of submarine attacks on British shipping. However, this effort soon led to diplomatic complications, particularly with the United States. The rules for imposing a blockade had been laid down by international agreement in 1856, at a time when no power possessed submarines as part of its naval arsenal. Under the rules of 1856, a ship suspected of attempting to run a blockade

could not be sunk until it had been stopped by a "shot across the bow," an inspection of its cargo had determined that it was carrying contraband of war, and provision had been made for rescuing the crew. World War I submarines were singularly unsuited for this sort of ritual. The early submarines were small vessels whose hulls could be easily pierced by naval gunnery or, for that matter, a machine gun mounted on the deck of a freighter. As a naval weapon, submarines were effective only if they could rely on stealth and fire their torpedoes without warning.

The German government claimed that the blockade rules of 1856 were impractical for twentieth-century warfare. The Reich announced a counterblockade around the British Isles and contended that submarines had the right to sink ships suspected of violating the German blockade without the usual warning in the prohibited area. The United States—which so far had not only remained neutral in the war but was also Great Britain's major trading partner—vigorously protested Germany's announced disregard of the traditional block-ade rules. Conflicts between the two powers over this issue surfaced repeatedly. The most famous incident was the sinking, by a German submarine, of the passenger liner *Lusitania* off the Irish coast in April 1915. The steamer was a British-owned and -operated passenger ship that traveled regularly from New York to Liverpool and back. On this particular voyage, the ship carried about 1,900 passengers, including some Americans, and a load of munitions intended for the British army. The Germans justified the sinking by pointing to the munitions on board, while the Americans protested the loss of innocent life that followed the attack.

For the first two years of the war, German submarine warfare was "restricted"; that is to say, the Germans attempted to avoid attacks on neutral and particularly American vessels. In the latter part of 1916, however, as the failure of the Verdun strategy became apparent, the Reich's military leaders turned to grasp at the straw of intensified submarine warfare to turn the tide of military fortune. In January

1917 the German government yielded to the pressure of the OHL and proclaimed a policy of unrestricted submarine warfare. The Reich declared the waters around the British Isles to be a war zone. Any ship, whether enemy or neutral, found within the zone would be presumed to be carrying contraband and consequently subject to attack without warning. The government knew that the new policy would in all likelihood bring the United States into the war on the side of the Allies, but the German military strategists regarded the political risks as acceptable. In their view unrestricted submarine warfare would succeed in bringing Great Britain to its knees before America's contribution to the war effort could become effective.

As had been true of the original battle plans and the Verdun strategy, Germany's third attempt "to go for broke" also failed. To be sure, German submarines did sink a large number of freighters bound for the United Kingdom, but unrestricted submarine warfare never came close to threatening the British economy or preventing U.S. troops and supplies from reaching Europe after America declared war on Germany on April 6, 1917. In the last year of the conflict, the United States significantly aided the Allied war effort with men and matériel.

By the end of 1917, Germany's military situation on the western front was no more favorable than it had been three years earlier. At home things were far worse. Signs of deteriorating morale were becoming apparent throughout the fabric of German society. In addition, the Germans' only significant ally, Austria, had made it clear that it would not be able to survive another winter.

Recognizing that Germany was unable to force a decision in the west, the OHL increasingly pinned its hopes for a military reversal on developments in the east. In December 1916 Austrian and German troops inflicted a severe defeat on Russia's major Balkan ally, Rumania. A series of setbacks on the battlefront and two revolutions in the course of 1917 ended Russia's participation in World War I. Vladimir Lenin

(for whom the OHL had provided transportation from Switzerland to Russia) and the Bolsheviks came to power in November 1917. They were determined to conclude peace with Germany and Austria at any cost to safeguard the revolution in Russia and make preparations for its export to the rest of Europe. The result was the Treaty of Brest-Litovsk (March 1918), a decidedly one-sided pact by which Germany and Austria intended to secure their permanent control of eastern and southeastern Europe.

The OHL had anticipated that victory in the east would enable the Germans to launch a new and final offensive in the west in the spring of 1918. Hindenburg and Ludendorff admitted that such an offensive would be very costly in both men and matériel—a casualty figure of 600,000 men was "precalculated"—but they argued that the eventual military gains would force the Allies to agree to peace on Germany's terms. Once again, the OHL was "going for broke." The Reich's military leaders knew that if the offensive did not succeed in ending the war, Germany would have no resources left to withstand an Allied counterattack.

The spring offensive began in March 1918. For some days, the Germans made impressive territorial gains, but soon lack of supplies and reserves slowed the forward momentum before any of the strategic goals could be reached. Instead, the Allies regrouped and began a counteroffensive. In July the German defensive lines were pierced to a distance of some 4 miles. This breakthrough was the beginning of the end. On August 8 another Allied thrust on the Somme front led large numbers of German troops to flee in panic. Hindenburg and Ludendorff concluded that the Reich's military resources were now insufficient to stop an Allied invasion of German territory; on September 29 they advised the emperor to negotiate an armistice as quickly as possible. It went into effect on November 11, 1918.

Military historians have argued endlessly over the details of strategic decisions, personnel appointments, and missed opportunities among all of the belligerents in World War I, but they are generally agreed that the final outcome could have been predicted in September 1914. After the German defeat in the Battle of the Marne, time was increasingly on the side of the Allies. With only the relatively weak Austrians, Bulgarians, and Turks at its side, Germany did not have sufficient human or economic resources to defeat the powers arrayed against it. The Wilhelminian attempt to challenge the global balance of power was bound to end in military disaster.

DOMESTIC POLITICS: REFORM, REPRESSION, AND REVOLUTION

Germany's wartime leaders expected the war to eliminate domestic political division and for a time their expectations were fulfilled. When the emperor announced on August 4, 1914, that for the duration of the war a *Burgfrieden* ("peace in the castle") would end domestic conflicts and political divisions, most of his subjects enthusiastically welcomed the prospect of genuine national unity. At the beginning of the war the vast majority of Germans rallied behind the Reich's political and military leaders, convinced that Germany was fighting a just and legitimate war against a host of aggressors.

The mood of August—epitomized by flower-draped soldiers singing lustily on their way to the front and railroad cars marked "to Paris" on their sides—was predicated on two premises: that the war would be both victorious and short, and that the Reich's leaders were committed to instituting domestic political reforms. Neither premise turned out to be true. As the war dragged on and the possibility of a negotiated peace—let alone victory—became increasingly remote, political differences not only reemerged but also dominated political life.

Politics in wartime Germany involved the interaction of four major institutions. To begin with, there were the Reich and Prussian executives, headed by the emperor. In 1914 both the Reich and Prussian cabinets were led by the man who had been chancellor since 1909, Theobald von Bethmann Hollweg. Secondly, the Reichstag assumed an increasingly active role as the need for appropriations to finance the war effort forced the government to go to parliament frequently to obtain authorization to borrow money. Germany's military leaders constituted a third group in the country's political interaction process. Finally, as hardships at home and at the front increasingly polarized the country, new extraparliamentary pressure groups emerged on both the right and left of the political spectrum.

Bethmann Hollweg attempted to preserve national unity by pursuing what he called "the politics of the diagonal." By this the chancellor meant steering a course that lay "diagonally" between the demands of the conservatives, who insisted the war was being fought to maintain the status quo at home and increase the Reich's power abroad, and the "reformers," who argued that keeping up the national war effort required meaningful changes in the political structure to make it more accountable to the people. Bethmann Hollweg maintained his balancing act with considerable skill for almost three years, but in the end, isolated and without support from any quarter, he had to admit failure.

Wartime politics focused on three major issues. One was the question of "war credits," which meant granting the government authority to issue bonds to finance the war. A second issue involved constitutional reforms that would change the Prussian electoral system and introduce responsibility to parliament for the Reich and Prussian cabinets. Finally, the formulation of Germany's war aims became an increasingly divisive issue.

Voting for war credits was a traumatic experience, particularly for the Social Democrats. Until August 4, 1914, the SPD in the Reichstag had never voted for a defense appropriation. After an emotional caucus debate, the members of the SPD's Reichstag delegation were split, seventy-eight to fourteen, in favor of war credits. To preserve the appearance of unity, the party decided to cast its ballots unanimously for war credits. The party did so in the firm belief that not only was the Reich fighting a defensive war but also that a victory for Germany's enemies, who included czarist Russia—for socialists the most hated symbol of political repression— would mean a setback for the future of socialism in Europe.

Still, a number of Social Democratic delegates even in August 1914 doubted the government's protestations of a purely defensive war effort. As the war dragged on, and the nature of German authoritarianism did not substantially change, the number of dissenters increased. A growing minority in the party either opposed voting for additional war credits altogether, or at the very least they demanded immediate, concrete political reforms as the price of further votes for war credits. In December 1914 the divisions in the party became public when Karl Liebknecht, a leader of the party's left wing, broke party ranks and cast his vote in the Reichstag against a new government request for military appropriations.

In the course of 1915, signs of a split within the party became increasingly visible. At the end of the year, twenty SPD Reichstag delegates openly voted against war credits. The government exacerbated tension and bitterness in the Social Democratic ranks still further by ordering the arrest, in 1916, of Rosa Luxemburg for sedition and of Karl Liebknecht for high treason. Spearheaded by a group of left-wing labor leaders calling themselves Revolutionary Shop Stewards, 55,000 marched in Berlin to protest Liebknecht's court-martial. (The socialist leader had in the meantime lost his parliamentary immunity because he was drafted into the army.)

By 1917 the dissidents formed a separate party, the Independent Social Democratic Party of Germany (*Unabhängige Sozialdemokratische Partei Deutschlands*—USPD). To be sure, the founding of the USPD did not threaten the existence of the parent party. Most SPD activists and especially the rank and file of the socialist unions remained loyal to the SPD. The USPD's organizational strength was restricted to a few areas—notably Berlin, the port cities of Hamburg and Bremen, Saxony, and parts of the Rhine-Ruhr region. The USPD also suffered from excessive ideological diversity. Both Rosa Luxemburg and her longtime political opponent Eduard Bernstein were members of the party; they were united only by their joint opposition to a continuation of the war. Finally, the USPD was very loosely organized. Many of the USPD's leaders had long objected to what they regarded as excessive centralization and bureaucratization in the old party. Consequently, the USPD permitted various intraparty caucuses to have a great deal of organizational autonomy.

The most important among these were the Revolutionary Shop Stewards and the Spartacus League. Founded at the beginning of 1916 and led by Luxemburg and Liebknecht, the Spartacus League argued that Germany had reached a protorevolutionary stage and urged workers to make active preparations for a violent revolution. This stand, however, was not shared by many of the USPD's national leaders who hoped to achieve a socialist revolution by nonviolent means.

One political reform on which the SPD and USPD were in full agreement was the demand for immediate changes in the Prussian electoral system. This issue also became the most important crucible of success for Bethmann Hollweg's politics of the diagonal. For the reformers, changes in the Prussian electoral system were a litmus test of political modernization, just as the Prussian conservatives regarded its preservation the cornerstone of authoritarianism. The chancellor attempted to follow a careful and slow course between these incompatibles, but his efforts were in vain. It required a great deal of persuasion on the part of Bethmann Hollweg (and the example of the February revolution in Russia) before the emperor agreed to announce publicly in the so-called Easter Message of 1917 that after the war he would propose changes in the Prussian electoral system to align it more closely with the system of universal male suffrage used for

Reichstag elections. But the Easter Message came far too late. The long months of delay had eroded virtually all of Bethmann Hollweg's credibility among the reformers. Moreover, the emperor's public pronouncement had no effect on the intransigence of the Prussian conservatives and their allies. They continued to block all concrete reform proposals in the state legislature.

Although the issue of Prussian electoral reforms had long dominated political discussions, the problem of ministerial responsibility was an issue born of the war experience. Before 1914 only the Social Democrats and, with some reservations, the Progressives had favored changing the Reich constitution to make the Reich government formally responsible to the Reichstag. But dissatisfaction with the government's handling of the war and growing distrust of the Reich leaders' ultimate war aims increased demands for legislative control of the executive among other parties as well. At the beginning of 1917, the parliamentary leaders of the Center Party, the right-wing Social Democrats, and the Progressives agreed to form a Multipartisan Committee (*Interfraktioneller Ausschuss*) to pressure the emperor and the Reich executive into recognizing an expanded role for the Reichstag majority in making national policy decisions. Representatives from the National Liberals eventually joined their colleagues on the Multipartisan Committee, so that by the end of the year only the conservatives and the USPD stayed aloof. The former rejected any liberalization of the Bismarckian constitution, and the latter was convinced that reforms would merely perpetuate a capitalist system that needed to be swept away in its entirety.

The war aims issue became increasingly important in the face of rapidly declining morale at the front and at home. As the war continued, the reformist groups in the Reichstag insisted that parliament must be given a voice in formulating Germany's conditions for a negotiated peace. In all of the belligerent countries discussions of war aims involved two sets of political considerations. One was the determination by each country's leaders of the economic and territorial gains they felt would be necessary to ensure the nation's self-determined place in the balance of power. This aspect of the process of formulating war aims meant give-and-take among the major economic, political, and military interest groups in the various warring nations. In addition, there was a second, mass psychological aspect to the problem. This concerned the relationship between sacrifices and hardships on the one hand and "rewards" for the sacrifices on the other. It seemed axiomatic that the larger the deprivations endured at home, the more these sacrifices would have to be compensated by concrete territorial and economic gains at the end of the war. The industrialist Alfried von Krupp expressed this simplistic view well when he wrote to the chief of the emperor's privy council at the end of July 1915: "Germany must win a prize which makes worthwhile the blood shed by our sons and brothers."

But, as Krupp also recognized, that goal could be obtained only if "peace terms are dictated to our enemies." Here, as far as Germany was concerned, was the Achilles' heel of the quest for peace terms that correlated with the country's sacrifices. As the hardships continued, new items were added to the list of war aims, but that equation also made a negotiated peace increasingly remote. Only a clear military victory could break the vicious cycle, but, as more and more government leaders admitted privately, there were fewer and fewer chances of winning the war militarily.

Still, the Reich's leaders insisted on compiling long lists of unattainable and counterproductive war aims. The "shopping list" really constituted an amalgamation of the territorial changes desired by the military to improve Germany's strategic position and demands by the Reich's industrialists to reduce Germany's dependence on imported raw materials while improving its competitive role in international commerce.

In the west the military wanted to retain control of Belgium, including the naval bases on the English Channel. In addition, the generals also insisted on "rectifications" of the Franco-German border, so that, for example, the string of fortifications around Verdun would fall to Germany. The industrialists wanted to join the iron-rich French industrial area of Longwy-Briey with the coal-producing regions of the Ruhr to create a vast steelmaking basin. In the east the Germans were particularly interested in Russia's Polish and Baltic possessions. Poland was to become independent of Russia and linked to either Germany or Austria. In November 1916 Germany actually established an "independent" Kingdom of Poland, but this empty gesture fooled no one; the country remained under German occupation and control. As for Russia's Baltic provinces—the areas that are now Lithuania, Latvia, and Estonia—the German war aims envisioned severing these areas from Russia and associating them as autonomous regions with the Reich. In southeastern Europe the military leaders were uncharacteristically modest (this was, of course, the area of primary strategic interest to Austria-Hungary), but the industrialists and the diplomats demanded German economic hegemony in the Balkans and the Ottoman Empire.

Although mostly hidden from public view because of wartime censorship, the war aims issue occasioned bitter debates between "moderates" and "extremists" among the Reich's wartime leaders. From the perspective of Germany's enemies, the difference between the two groups may have been minimal because both wanted to establish permanent German hegemony on the European continent, but the varying views had major implications for the future evolution of German domestic politics.

The extremists, who included the leaders of the OHL, anticipated that the imposition of a "victory peace" on the Allies would not only achieve the Reich's military aims but would also secure authoritarianism at home for the foreseeable future. The moderates, in contrast, wanted to link domestic reforms with the territorial and economic war aims. Only such a linkage, they reasoned, would

preserve national unity and maintain the morale necessary for continuing the war effort. In addition, the moderates, particularly as Germany's military position worsened, advocated a more flexible stand on such issues as the future of Belgium and Poland.

Against the background of the relentlessly continuing war, debate over Germany's conditions for peace—even in the abbreviated form permitted by the censors—increasingly polarized the country. In June 1915 left-wing socialists advocated immediate and unconditional peace negotiations, but 1,347 "celebrities," including almost 500 university professors and clergymen, insisted that Germany would have to be guaranteed "political, military, and economic control of Belgium" as well as "large reparations" before agreeing to peace.

While the battle for public opinion took place in the pages of the press, the leaders of the OHL after August 1916 pressured Bethmann Hollweg and the emperor to commit themselves to a full set of maximal war aims. The chancellor warned against giving credence to Hindenburg's and Ludendorff's predictions of an early military breakthrough, and it was not until the spring of 1917, after the Russian March Revolution had significantly increased the chances for a military turnaround in the east, that the military succeeded in convincing the emperor to accept its terms for a "victory peace" and, not incidentally, withdraw his support from Bethmann Hollweg.

The circumstances surrounding Bethmann Hollweg's resignation in the summer of 1917 led to a major, if unacknowledged, constitutional crisis. Formally, of course, the chancellor served at the pleasure of the emperor, but in terms of practical politics he needed the support of a majority of the Reichstag if only to secure further votes for war credits. The OHL's interference in the constitutional balance of power completely ignored the political dimension of the chancellor's position. The issue was not so much support for Bethmann Hollweg—by this time he had few friends anywhere—as it was a disregard of the Reichstag in the process of choosing a successor to the hapless Bethmann Hollweg.

The leaders of the military considered Admiral von Tirpitz and ex-chancellor Bülow for the position, but the emperor rejected both. Hindenburg and Ludendorff then insisted on the appointment of Georg Michaelis (until that time the deputy minister for agriculture in Prussia) as the new Reich chancellor. Michaelis was not a felicitous choice. He had no previous national political experience; indeed, his only qualifications for the job were the confidence of the OHL and a reputation as an able administrator of the food-rationing system in Prussia. His lack of political experience was a serious handicap in dealing with a restive Reichstag.

Hindenburg and Ludendorff were convinced that their goals could be accomplished only if the civilian war effort was more effectively regimented than it had been in the first two years of the war. To this end, they had already proposed the Patriotic Auxiliary Service Law, which the Reichstag passed in July 1916. Under this legislation, the government, through a supercoordinating agency, the War Office, received wide-ranging authority to control wages, production levels, and prices, as well as restrict the free movement of labor. The legislation severely curtailed the bargaining rights of labor unions, but in line with the OHL's attempt to ignore parliament and the parties and deal directly with economic interest groups, the law assigned the unions an institutional role in administering the law. Union representatives became ex-officio members of various regional commissions that determined wage scales, worker mobility, and conditions of labor. The military leaders hoped that in return for these economic gains, the unions would forgo their support of demands for political reform.

The OHL was not content just to interfere in the economy. Hindenburg and Ludendorff also wanted to mobilize public opinion in favor of the OHL's political aims and peace terms. A major vehicle for this propaganda effort was the Fatherland Party, which was founded with the OHL's blessing in September 1917. Led by one of Germany's minor territorial princes, Duke Johann Albrecht of Mecklenburg, and that former master of mass propaganda, Admiral von Tirpitz, the Fatherland Party had no parliamentary ambitions. Its sole purpose was to lobby for imposing a "Hindenburg Peace" on Germany's enemies and maintaining Wilhelminian authoritarianism at home. The label "Hindenburg Peace" was symptomatic of yet another effort to bypass the regular constitutional channels of politics. The OHL openly encouraged a cult of personality around the figure of the aged field marshal. During the last two years of the war, the German propaganda machine increasingly portrayed Hindenburg as the personification of the war effort and the guarantor of victory. His kindly and venerable face with the caption "Let us help him do the job right" appeared on thousands of posters and millions of postcards.

Extraparliamentary activism was not limited to the supporters of authoritarianism and the Hindenburg Peace. Indeed, the deliberate efforts by the OHL and the political right to ignore the growing signs of war weariness facilitated the organizing activities of the far left. The first political strikes occurred in mid-1916, at the time of the Battle of Verdun. Despite the opposition of union leaders, during 1917 and 1918 a wave of political strikes—often organized by the USPD, the Revolutionary Shop Stewards, or the Spartacus League and encouraged by the revolutionary successes in Russia—enveloped the country. The most dramatic evidence of the country's polarization was a major strike of munitions workers in Berlin in January 1918. In defiance of their union leaders, 120,000 workers staged a walkout lasting several days to demonstrate their support for peace and an immediate end to the Prussian three-class system of voting.

The increasing signs of domestic polarization were not lost on the leaders of the Reichstag, who recognized that they might lose control of the situation in the streets. Spearheaded by the energetic young Center Party Reichstag delegate Matthias Erzberger, the Social Democrats, the Center Party, and the Progressives introduced a joint resolution in the Reichstag in July 1917, calling for immediate peace negotiations on the basis of no reparations and no annexations. It passed easily.

The resolution was naive and impractical (by this time the Allies had no intention of returning to the status quo before the war), but the effort demonstrated the cooperation among the reformist parties while revealing the isolation of the conservatives and the ineptness of the new chancellor. Michaelis, who used the debate on the peace resolution to make his maiden speech in parliament, gave ample evidence of his lack of political skills. Someone who regarded the Hindenburg Peace as a set of moderate terms was clearly out of touch with most of German public opinion, and his clumsy attempt to endorse the peace resolution "as I interpret it" (which he explained to the crown prince meant that the resolution enabled the government to conclude peace on any basis it wished) merely underscored his general untrustworthiness.

Michaelis's initial performance in the Reichstag did much to ensure an early end to his career as Reich chancellor. Less than three months after he came into office, even the OHL had to recognize his incompetence. His successor, Count Georg von Hertling, was a seventy-eight-year-old Bavarian conservative. (Having learned a lesson from the Michaelis fiasco, the emperor sounded out some Reichstag leaders before Hertling's appointment.) Hertling was a Catholic and in earlier years had been an influential voice in the Center Party, so his appointment at least indirectly ensured a closer relationship between the executive and a leading group among the reformers in the Reichstag. In addition, Hertling's appointment brought movement to the deadlocked political situation in Prussia. As a south German, Hertling was unfamiliar with Prussian affairs, and although he served as Prussian prime minister in name, the actual head of the Prussian cabinet after October 1917 was now the deputy prime minister, Robert Friedberg. Before he moved to the executive office, Friedberg had been the parliamentary leader of the National Liberal Party in the Prussian legislature.

Hertling came into office at a time of mounting evidence that the German political consensus was breaking down. In addition to the signs described earlier, political anti-Semitism had been on the rise for some time, and the OHL at least indirectly encouraged this particularly virulent form of political emotionalism. In 1916, responding to what the military said were complaints about the disproportionately large number of Jews serving in rear echelons, rather than at the front, the OHL commissioned an inquiry and then promptly refused to publish the results on the grounds that to do so would encourage further anti-Semitic sentiments. Needless to say, that announcement only led to more rumors and innuendoes. (The actual results of the survey, as Werner T. Angress has shown, revealed no significant differences in the military assignment of Jews and Gentiles.)

Hertling, then, knew that the time for domestic reforms was at hand. Spokesmen for the reformers made it clear that the new chancellor would face a very hostile parliament unless he implemented reforms of the Prussian electoral system. The emperor, of course, had given such assurances in his Easter Message of 1917, but so far no concrete measures had followed his words. Now, however, both Hertling and Friedberg assured the Reichstag leaders that a bill significantly modifying the electoral system in Prussia would be introduced in the Prussian state legislature.

Hertling and Friedberg kept their word, but the measure was immediately voted down by a majority of the Prussian Landtag. The group of diehards included the conservatives, about two-thirds of the National Liberals (who thereby rejected the initiative of their former leader), and a substantial portion of the Center Party delegates. There the issue remained until the end of the war: a festering sore in German political life and a constant reminder of the failure of the reformers.

A final clash between old guard and reformers was postponed by Germany's military victories in the east. The defeat of Russia and Rumania permitted the military and the industrial interests to realize part of their maximal war aims in the Treaty of Brest-Litovsk. Under this Austro-German *Diktat*, Russia lost some 1 million square kilometers of territory with a population of 50 million. In addition, Russia was deprived of more than 90 percent of its coal mines, a third of its agricultural land, and virtually all of its known oil fields. Germany and Austria-Hungary extended their economic and military hegemony eastward from Königsberg and Cracow to Kiev. The Treaty of Brest-Litovsk rallied most Germans behind the banner of chauvinism for the last time. In the Reichstag, the USPD opposed the agreement and the majority socialists abstained from voting, but all the bourgeois parties, including the Progressives and the Center Party, supported the treaty.

The Reichstag's reception of the Treaty of Brest-Litovsk convinced the Reich's political and military leaders that victories on the battlefield provided the most effective means of defusing demands for domestic reforms. Unfortunately for them, the corollary to victory in the east, a successful offensive in the west, was unattainable. The failure of the Ludendorff offensive in the spring and summer of 1918 ushered in both Germany's military defeat and the collapse of the conservatives' domestic political strategy.

In mid-August the emperor for the first time privately acknowledged that the Reich would have to end the war. At the beginning of October, Ludendorff, now in a state of panic, dispatched his military aide, Colonel von dem Bussche, to inform the leaders of the Reichstag that armistice negotiations had to begin within forty-eight hours. The news sent shock waves through parliament; most of the political leaders had little inkling of how serious the military situation actually was. The military leaders, for their part, were unwilling to take responsibility for acknowledging the defeat. As a result, they now insisted on a step that until then they had strenuously resisted: They placed responsibility for ending the war and guiding Germany's political future in the hands of the Reichstag

leaders, or, more precisely, the leaders of the reformist parties in parliament.

The reformers, in turn, used their newly won power not only to begin negotiating an end to hostilities but also to implement the domestic reforms that they had been demanding since before 1914. The consequence was a package of constitutional changes that transformed Germany from an authoritarian into a parliamentary monarchy much like Great Britain. The proposals were certainly not new ones in German politics, but their hasty implementation at the behest of the OHL and their association with the parallel acknowledgment of military defeat was not fortuitous. Moreover, in their rush to present results, the reformers left many constitutional problems unresolved. For example, the October reforms did not eliminate the Reich-Prussian dualism. In addition, although the emperor had promised the reformist parties he would agree to a parliamentary Reich cabinet and work to bring the Prussian electoral system in line with that of the Reich, there was no indication what steps the monarch would take if the Prussian Landtag continued to block reform legislation. Similarly, while the Reichstag obtained power to control the military in wartime, the peacetime relations between parliament and the military remained unclear. (Recall that in peacetime, the national armed forces reverted to their status as state armies, which meant largely Prussian contingents.) Still, on paper the reformers had succeeded in transforming the Reich into a constitutional monarchy.

Some major personnel changes also seemed to signal the beginning of the new era. In late October, Ludendorff resigned. He was replaced by the former head of the War Office, General Groener (see the later discussion, pp. 91–100). To Ludendorff's surprise, Hindenburg did not join him in resigning but stayed on as chief of the OHL. Hertling left his post as chancellor and Prussian prime minister. He was succeeded by a politically moderate aristocrat, Prince Max von Baden, a cousin of the reigning duke of Baden. The new chancellor had close ties to the leaders of the Progressive Party, and he refused to take office until he had received a full vote of confidence from the majority parties in the Reichstag. Moreover, he insisted that delegates of all the reformist parties, including the right-wing Social Democrats, be represented in his cabinet.

There is no doubt that for most Germans, the October reforms satisfied their demands for political change. All over the Reich rallies were organized with speakers from the reformist parties celebrating the democratization of Germany's political system. Only the conservatives on the right and the radical left rejected the constitutional changes.

The hopes for an orderly transition to political democracy were dashed by precipitous action on the part of the emperor. William and the leaders of the OHL had agreed to the October reforms in a moment of panic. For a few days the monarch wavered between accepting his new role as figurehead of the Reich and marching into Berlin as the head of "a few loyal regiments" to undo the reforms he had just approved. Eventually, his authoritarian and irrational leanings won out. On October 29, rather than oversee the implementation of the constitutional changes and work with the Baden government to guide electoral reform through the Prussian Landtag, the emperor suddenly left Berlin and traveled to the OHL's headquarters in Spa, Belgium. There was no military necessity for this step; it was an impetuous gesture to demonstrate that William II still identified himself with "his" generals rather than the democratic politicians. In all likelihood, his flight from Berlin and his association with the most authoritarian part of the old regime also ensured that the emperor himself was swept away when the entire Prusso-German authoritarian system collapsed less than a week later.

WAR AND SOCIETY

Like its enemies, Germany entered the age of twentieth-century global warfare woefully unprepared. World War I was the first "total war" in which victory depended as much on a country's economic and social resources as on the military skills of its armies at the battlefront. Germany's military strategists were justly famous for their general staff work, but in planning for the eventuality of war they had completely neglected the economic and social implications of a drawn-out conflict among the Great Powers. Anticipating a short war, all of the military's plans assumed that the outcome of the conflict would be determined by one or two decisive battles.

As far as German life on the home front was concerned, the most important neglected factors in this scenario were the cumulative and debilitating effects of the British blockade, the lack of mechanisms to manage the war economy during the first two years of the conflict, and the pressures of inflation.

The blockade and the constantly increasing demands of the military quickly brought on an economy of chronic shortages. The primary victims both in terms of reduced supplies and higher prices were civilian consumers because in wartime the needs of the military always came first.

The economy of scarcity as such put pressure on the social consensus, but even more important for the breakdown of morale at home was the uneven impact on the various sectors of German society. Some groups were hit particularly hard; others, at least in relative terms, actually benefited from the situation. The defense-related sectors of the economy understandably did best. The military decided that production was more important than cost consciousness, and manufacturers of war matériel were essentially able to charge whatever prices they wished. This not only resulted in vast profits for this sector of the economy (with no meaningful taxation to skim off the excess profits), but labor in defense industries indirectly benefited as well. For the first three years of the war, manufacturers outbid each other for the services of skilled laborers in frantic efforts to obtain lucrative army contracts.

In contrast, sectors of the economy oriented primarily toward the civilian market bore the brunt of the hardships. Farmers were one of the first sectors of the economy to be subjected to tight price controls. In an effort not to alienate consumers in the cities, the government early in the war decided that prices for basic foods should remain low, regardless of market conditions. With some justification, farmers claimed that the government-set prices were considerably below production costs; fertilizer, animal feed, and farm machinery were obtainable (if at all) only at price levels vastly above those of prewar times. The consequence was a ubiquitous black market in foodstuffs, fueled, ironically, in part by the decision to encourage the production of war matériel regardless of price considerations. Purchasing agents of the defense industries routinely paid inflated prices for agricultural goods on the black market to provide additional supplies for their workers as hiring incentives or fringe benefits. Such practices in turn reduced the supply of farm labor; farmers constantly complained that high wages paid in war-related industries led many agricultural workers to seek jobs there.

Manufacturers of consumer goods were hurt in two ways: First, they were increasingly unable to obtain raw materials. Either they could not compete with the defense industries on the open market, or, after centralized allocation agencies were established (see p. 99), their requests were always assigned a lower priority than those of war matériel manufacturers. In addition, they could generally not afford to pay the wages offered by defense industries because the government, again with an eye toward maintaining morale in the urban areas, attempted to maintain low prices for such consumer goods as were available. The labor problem was aggravated as casualties mounted, and the military dipped ever deeper into Germany's reserves of draft-age men. Although war-related industries could often get their labor exempted from the draft, applications from manufacturers of civilian goods were generally turned down. As was true of food, a thriving black market in consumer goods was the inevitable result of these conditions.

Finally, there was the service and retirees sector of the economy. Civil servants (who in Germany included teachers at all levels of education), professionals, old-age pensioners, and most white-collar workers had little bargaining power in the scramble for benefits in the economy of scarcity. For the most part living on fixed or even declining incomes (upper-level civil servants actually suffered significant salary cuts), they were largely excluded from participating in the black market economy. For most Germans, then, the war at home meant shortages of food, poor health conditions, housing in chronic need of repair, and a general deterioration in the quality of life.

Food was undoubtedly the greatest problem. Before the war Germany imported large amounts of agricultural products, including grains, animal feeds, meat, dairy products, as well as such items as coffee, cocoa, and tea. Most of the imports came from overseas areas, notably the United States, Canada, Australia, and Latin America. Once war was declared, German trade with all these areas virtually stopped; the British blockade effectively prevented overseas goods from reaching the Reich. Before 1914 Germany had also imported large amounts of Russian grain and meat. The war also disrupted this trade as well. For most of the war, then, Germany could import agricultural goods only from Holland and the Scandinavian countries (these nations remained neutral), but even here the British exerted constant pressure to reduce the level of exports to the Reich.

Although the discovery of artificial nitrates by the chemist Fritz Haber eased the fertilizer shortage, any illusions that Germany's own farmers could replace the lost imports were soon dashed. The effects of the blockade were felt almost immediately. In October 1914, faced with a shortage of grain, the government authorized the baking of "war bread," a product composed of a mixture of 80 percent flour and 20 percent potato starch. It was the beginning of what would soon be an all-pervasive *Ersatz* ("substitute")

An example of the cult of personality surrounding von Hindenburg. A poster urging the purchase of war bonds bears his picture and the caption, "The times are hard, but victory is assured." (Source: Paul Bruno/ Library of Congress Prints and Photographs Division [LC-USZC4-11806].)

economy. (The term *ersatz* actually came into both German and English usage at the time of World War I.) By the summer of 1917, 837 nonmeat substitutes for sausage and cold cuts had been patented.

The food situation grew more severe with each year of the war. Far worse than the often only tasteless ersatz products was the growing lack of actual food commodities. The shortages culminated in the so-called turnip winter of 1916–1917. By this time the longtime staples of the German diet grain and potatoes, were in very short supply. The only available, relatively abundant substitute was turnips, or more precisely, rutabagas, and even these were rationed. The official weekly rations for an adult living in Berlin in January and February 1917 consisted of between 2 and 6 pounds of turnips (or, if available, 2 pounds of bread), less than 2 ounces of butter, and 1 ounce of margarine. In August of that year, when the new harvest had come in, the weekly allotment had only increased to 5 pounds of potatoes, a half pound of meat, and three quarters of a pound of sugar.

The economy of shortages substantially changed gender relations in the country. The influx of women into the workforce (replacing the men sent to the front), both in the industrial workforce and the service sector, radically changed the Victorian image of womanhood: homebound and subject to the dictates of her father or husband. Increasingly, women were not only gainfully employed but became the primary breadwinner in the family. In addition, the unaccustomed presence of many women outside the home changed sexual mores and increased the incidence of venereal disease.

But for many women, emancipation remained a rather abstract blessing. Food shortages brought on malnutrition-related diseases, such as tuberculosis, rickets, dysentery, and typhoid fever. At the same time, housing and transportation facilities deteriorated through delayed maintenance while rents, despite government efforts to control them, skyrocketed as landlords attempted to keep up with inflation.

The reality of the hardships contrasted sharply with the government's upbeat and simplistic propaganda about conditions on the home front. Official statements praised the German inventive spirit for producing ingenious ersatz products of every kind. Government propaganda claimed as late as February 1917 (at the height of the turnip winter) that the various shortages had no measurable effect on public health. The people knew better. By 1917 "lack of enthusiasm" (to use the term employed by a government report) among the poorer classes had turned to despair and revolt. Official admonitions not to dwell on the hardships at home when writing to the soldiers at the front had little effect. The rising number of strikes was an indication of the growing frustration with the economic and political conditions.

However, not all of the German people went in a straight line from enthusiasm to alienation to despair and revolution. A far truer picture would reveal the increasing polarization of the society. For almost the entire duration of the conflict, there were many, especially among the upper and middle classes, who continued to believe the war was necessary and perhaps even morally uplifting. If strikes and grumbling on food lines were indications of disillusionment, much wartime literature was "pro-war." Most of the genre was, as one postwar literary critic has said, "not worthy of the greatness of the subject." The books, full of soldiers' humor and vulgarity, presented a world of black-and-white contrasts, in which noble-minded officers (in these novels the heroes are almost invariably officers) are fighting selflessly to defend their homeland and Western civilization against the onslaught of Russian, French, Belgian, and British barbarians.

Above the level of *Trivialliteratur,* two themes dominated wartime literature. One was the myth of the *Fronterlebnis,* the experience of being at the front. Veterans, such as Ernst Jünger in his book *In Stahlgewittern* ("The Storm of Steel"), would later (the work was published in 1920) use their wartime experience to create the figure of the soldier sui generis. In this picture the war molded civilians from all walks of life into new human beings standing apart from and in a sense above the day-to-day cares of peacetime Germany. The experience of the front and especially what Ernst von Salomon would later call the "high of battle" alienated the soldier from the old society and made him a harbinger of a new revolutionary morality and ideology.

The other theme was the conflict of civilizations. Jünger was by no means the only intellectual who professed to find a larger meaning in slaughter and conquest. The June 1915 "Manifesto of Celebrities" demonstrated that much of the intellectual establishment supported the OHL's aim of a victory peace. Gerhart Hauptmann, the naturalist playwright who had been highly critical of Wilhelminian society before the war, published a famous open letter to the French writer Romain Rolland in which he defended Germany's role in the war, including the invasion of Belgium. Perhaps the most famous instance of German intellectual chauvinism was the publication, in 1918, of Thomas Mann's *Betrachtungen eines Unpolitischen* ("Observations of an Apolitical Man"). In this book-length essay, Mann, the best-selling author of *Buddenbrooks,* angrily contrasted the materialistic "civilization" of the British and French bourgeoisie with the German *Bürger's* ideal of "culture." Whereas Western civilization produced peoples with a narrow materialist outlook, German culture formed an educated, idealistic citizen of the world.

For intellectuals, too, the year 1917 represented something of a watershed. For many a feeling of disillusionment set in. A typical example was Walter Flex's *Wanderer zwischen beiden Welten* ("Wanderer between Two Worlds"), a book that was to become something of a youth cult novel in the 1920s. Published at the end of 1918, the novel is a memorial to the author's wartime friend who died in battle. It is also a heart-wrenching portrayal of a sensitive man's reaction to the horrors of war. A far more radical rejection of the values of wartime chauvinism was the Dada movement, a form of cultural nihilism. Launched in a Zurich café in the summer of 1916 (the founding ceremony was repeated in 1917 in Berlin), the Dada movement was less important for the artistic products it inspired than for the antiestablishment sentiments of its philosophy: "Dada means nothing. It is the significant nothing which has no meaning at all. We want to change the world with nothing, we want to alter poetry and painting with nothing, and we want to end the war with nothing."

For some time it appeared as if the Reich's leaders regarded war and society as largely separate entities. True, prodded by executives from the large Berlin electrical manufacturing firm, AEG, the Prussian ministry of war established a War Raw Materials Section (*Kriegsrohstoffabteilung*) at the beginning of the war. The AEG's chairman, Walther Rathenau, became its director. The new office was given authority to monitor and control the use of scarce raw materials. But aside from this initiative, during the first two years of the conflict, other than building a propaganda apparatus and instituting food rationing, the German government made little effort to coordinate and manage the wartime economy. This situation did not change until Falkenhayn's failure at Verdun. Now a rapidly expanding war-management bureaucracy was built up. Numerous allocation boards handling everything from textiles to shoelaces issued vast amounts of paper in a largely vain attempt

to ensure some fairness in the distribution of increasingly scarce supplies.

A new stage in mobilizing the resources of the home front came with the so-called Hindenburg Program. When Hindenburg and Ludendorff took over leadership of the OHL in August 1916, they demanded a 100 percent increase in small-arms ammunition and a 300 percent increase in artillery shells and machine guns by the spring of 1917. These goals, which were completely unrealistic, required extensive control of industrial production and the total mobilization of the German labor force, including persuading thousands of women to take on industrial jobs. Bethmann Hollweg, if not the OHL, recognized that the momentous shift in manufacturing priorities envisioned by the Hindenburg Program would seriously endanger the frayed social and political consensus. In an attempt to give the mobilization effort the appearance of a consensual rather than a dictatorial decision, the government proposed the establishment of a War Office. Headed by General Groener, the War Office, which had overall charge of the economic mobilization effort, was particularly instrumental in trying to give the war effort the appearance of a cooperative venture of the military, government officials, and representatives of industry and labor.

Consensual management of the war economy was a victim along with the politics of the diagonal in the cold coup of August 1917. Like Bethmann Hollweg, Groener was dismissed. The War Office itself was largely dismantled and its functions decentralized under the overall direction of the so-called deputy commanders. These commanding generals of the reserve forces in Germany's military districts, mostly officers unsuited for frontline commands because of old age or infirmities, tended to be particularly insensitive to the morale problems of the home front. Their answers to strikes and demonstrations were usually a single-minded decision to draft strike leaders and send them to the front. Relations between the army and the reformist forces, including the labor unions, deteriorated accordingly.

By the end of the war, the military for most Germans was symbolized by the figure of the deputy commander, whose only answer to war weariness was repression.

Although Germany did attempt to develop mechanisms for managing a totally mobilized war economy, the problem of financing the conflict was ignored almost completely. This neglect was to haunt the country for years after the lost war. In addition to the horrors of physical destruction and death, World War I was also a totally unexpected financial burden for all of the belligerents. As far as Germany was concerned, the cost of conducting the war rose from roughly 36 million marks a day at the beginning of the war to 136 million per day at the end. Because the German national debt was already sizable in 1914, the government had no reserves with which to finance the conflict.

But government expenditures can be met in only two ways: taxes and credits. Taxes are unpopular, particularly in wartime, although ironically, the excess of money over goods that is characteristic of an economy of scarcity makes it economically sensible to raise taxes. All of the belligerents relied on war bond drives and other forms of credit to finance a good deal of their war expenditures, but the Germans attempted to finance almost the entire war effort with credits. Part of the reason was unjustified confidence that the expenditures would be quickly recovered from the defeated enemies. (The example of the 5 billion marks in French reparations after the Franco-Prussian War of 1870–1871 came readily to mind.) Then, too, the government was encouraged by the enthusiasm with which the early war bond drives were received. During the first bond drive between August and October 1914, 1.2 million Germans subscribed a total of 4.5 billion marks. Subsequent bond efforts were less successful, but the expectation that the government credit was good and the money would be repaid with interest remained strong.

The success of the bond drives and the expectation of victory led the government to spend with little regard for actual resources. The cost of the Hindenburg Program was particularly staggering. As already noted, the military did not hesitate to pay vastly inflated prices and permit employers to pay very high wages to obtain the needed war materials. A balanced budget, a frequently invoked if often breached article of faith before the war, became an illusion, and Germany's public finances essentially operated in an Alice-in-Wonderland world. There were some efforts to cut wages and prices in early 1918, but by that time inflation had acquired an unstoppable dynamic of its own. At the end of the war, the mark was worth about half of what it had been in 1914. The implications were particularly severe for many middle-class Germans who had anticipated that their retirement years would be financed largely from the proceeds of lifelong savings and war bonds. The German financing of World War I, then, failed in every sense: It burdened the country with a vast debt, and, by eroding the value of the mark, it dashed the hopes for financial security in old age of a whole generation of Germans.

CONCLUSION

In November 1918, the Reich's new leaders inherited a staggering legacy of destruction, despair, and uncertainty. The armed forces had suffered more than 6 million casualties, including 1.6 million war dead. At home malnutrition-related diseases brought massive increases in the death rate. Germany faced peace with an exhausted population, worn-out industrial facilities, and a vast national debt. (The total cost of World War I for all belligerents is estimated at about 1 trillion marks [about $238 billion] in 1914 prices; Germany's share of that sum was 175 billion [about $42 billion].)

These "material" consequences of the war had grave implications for Germany's future, but in a sense, perhaps even more ominous were the less tangible social and political results of the conflict. In at least three ways, World War I shattered important aspects of the implicit prewar national consensus.

One was the implied promise of continuing prosperity and upward social mobility. The war ended abruptly the sustained high growth rates that would later give the years before 1914 the glow of a "golden age." During the war, the standard of living as a whole not only declined rapidly but the burden of the conflict was also very unevenly distributed among the various segments of the population.

Shattered, too, was the illusion that Germany was advancing toward greater political modernization. The emperor's announcement of a *Burgfrieden,* his Easter Message of 1917, and Bethmann Hollweg's politics of the diagonal had all raised expectations that the Reich's political and military leaders would cooperate in the effort to reform Prusso-German authoritarianism. The OHL's "silent dictatorship," the emperor's shortsightedness, and the intransigence of the conservatives destroyed that hope. The enactment of the October reforms came about only because the OHL and the emperor acknowledged—briefly—that they had lost their gamble to preserve authoritarianism at home through military victories abroad. The constitutional changes of 1918 did not result from a national consensus but from the bankruptcy of the old regime.

Finally, a third shattered consensus was the promise of the correlation between sacrifices and rewards. Like the inhabitants of all the belligerent countries, the Germans (encouraged by the OHL's relentlessly upbeat propaganda about the military situation) were fully convinced that the coming peace would somehow make the sacrifices during wartime "worthwhile." This part of the national consensus held as late as the spring of 1918 during the debate on the Treaty of Brest-Litovsk. A few months later that bubble, too, had burst. The reaction was anger, disbelief, and alienation.

In November 1918 Germany was an exhausted, deeply polarized nation in need of a new national consensus. What the ingredients of that new consensus would be was largely unclear. The Germans were united for the moment only in their desire for peace and their determination to maintain the Reich's territorial and political integrity.

CHAPTER FOUR

~~~~~~~~~~~~

Revolution, Inflation, and Putsches

The Search for a New Consensus, 1918–1923

The armistice ending World War I took effect on November 11, 1918. Most Germans welcomed peace, although few appreciated the magnitude of the problems that lay ahead. The failure to achieve economic recovery, social and political polarization, and Germany's inability to secure a place in the international balance of power repeatedly brought the Reich to the brink of political and economic collapse in the years immediately after World War I.

REVOLUTION

We have already seen how the emperor's flight from Berlin undermined the credibility of the reformers. Most Germans had assumed that after the October reforms, the majority party leaders would work together with the emperor and his old advisers to put the new constitutional monarchy in place. When this proved illusionary, the initial euphoria that virtually all Germans felt in October was quickly followed in November by a profound distrust of all existing authorities and institutions. The distrust was most widespread among the soldiers and sailors. At the beginning of November, following the example of their contemporaries in Russia, German army and navy units established a German version of the soviets, the soldiers' councils (*Soldatenräte*). (As was initially true of the Russian soviets as well, the German term for "council" [*Rat*] referred to an institution, not a political ideology.) Originally, most of the councils addressed issues that were of immediate concern to the lower ranks of the armed forces: better food rations, putting an end to arbitrary disciplinary measures, and preventing officers from sending units on useless suicide missions in the last days of the war.

The first of these councils was established on November 4, in the Baltic seaport of Kiel, headquarters of the German naval command. Throughout the war complaints about conditions on naval ships had been endemic. Sailors resented the harsh discipline and the highly visible differences in living conditions and food rations between officers and men. In 1917, there had already been a major mutiny, which the naval command had brutally suppressed. Twelve of the mutineers were sentenced to death, and two were actually executed.

The developments in Kiel in early November 1918, must be seen against this background. It was a matter of common knowledge that the armistice was only days away. At the same time, it was an ill-kept secret that the leaders of the navy planned to send the fleet on a last engagement against the British that would save "the honor of the navy." When the naval command issued orders to some units to prepare their ships for a "routine training mission," coal stokers on a number of vessels, realizing they were being sent on the planned suicide mission, refused to obey the orders. Shipyard and dockworkers in Kiel went on strike in support of the mutineering sailors. Together with the sailors they elected representatives to form the Kiel workers' and soldiers' council.

Faced with widespread support for the strike and mutiny, the mayor of the city and the commanding admiral of the Baltic Naval Station agreed to cooperate with the workers' and soldiers' council. In addition, at the request of the sailors and workers two Reichstag delegates, Gustav Noske, who was the SPD's spokesman on military and colonial affairs, and Hugo Haase, the national chairman of the USPD (Independent Socialists), arrived in Kiel on November 5. It was Noske who quickly took charge of the situation. Elected chairman of the workers' and soldiers' council, Noske persuaded the military and civilian chiefs of administration formally to recognize the authority of the council. The result was a curious dual system of government. Orders from the military commander and regulations from the civilian authorities went into effect only after

they had been approved and countersigned by the chairman of the workers' and soldiers' council. Surprisingly, perhaps, the two chains of command worked reasonably well together; the naval command abandoned the planned suicide sortie, and the council helped prevent looting and restored at least a modicum of discipline to the ships.

The system of dual lines first established in Kiel quickly became the model for the institutionalization of revolutionary authority throughout most of Germany. News of the events in Kiel spread rapidly as sailors took advantage of the opportunity to leave their ships and go home. In the next few days workers' and soldiers' councils sprang up in the urban areas of western and central Germany. Here, too, the councils generally did not attempt to take the place of the regular administrations but permitted the established civilian and military administration to continue functioning under the general supervision of the councils.

While the councils helped preserve law and order in most of Germany, in Bavaria events took a more radical turn. At the beginning of November the decidedly left-wing chairman of the USPD in Bavaria, Kurt Eisner, sensed that conditions were ripe for the overthrow of political authoritarianism in the state. On November 7, Eisner managed to turn an antiwar rally in Munich into a massive demonstration demanding the abolition of the Bavarian monarchy. The regent hastened to renounce his throne. Eisner proclaimed the establishment of the "Free State of Bavaria," which was to be governed by the state leaders of the SPD and the USPD in association with the workers' and soldiers' councils until elections for a constitutional convention could be held.

The fall of the Wittelsbach dynasty, which had ruled Bavaria for more than a thousand years, sent political shock waves through the country as the workers' and soldiers' councils recognized that the old regimes were virtually without popular support anywhere in Germany. In the next two days, all of the territorial princes, with the exception of William II, the emperor and king of

Prussia, abdicated, leaving their states' affairs in the hands of new provisional governments and the workers' and soldiers' councils. For the most part, the German revolution was a bloodless and very moderate upheaval. The princes were not physically harmed; several even received formal expressions of gratitude from the workers' and soldiers' councils for their past services to the state. In turn, the old rulers routinely requested that the states' civil servants stay on the job and cooperate with the new authorities. The revolutionaries also made no attempt to alter the federal structure of Germany. In fact, one of the motivating factors for revolution in many of the Länder was the desire to escape the wartime tutelage of the central government in Berlin.

Remarkably, throughout the first week of November the Reich capital remained an island of seeming calm. As late as November 8, Berlin was quiet, public services and transportation functioned normally. Even the stock market was in operation. Berlin's status as a white spot on the revolutionary map changed abruptly on November 9. On this cold and wet Saturday, thousands of Berlin workers demonstrated to demand an immediate armistice and the abdication of William II as German emperor and king of Prussia. As had been true in Munich two days earlier, they met no resistance; on the contrary, soldiers and police readily fraternized with the demonstrators.

The Reich chancellor, Max von Baden, and his government had been urging William II to abdicate in favor of one of his younger sons, but the emperor hesitated until it was too late. The chancellor, seeing the milling thousands almost literally outside his office window, felt he had to act on his own. He made two decisions: one largely symbolic and the other with far-reaching constitutional implications. On his own authority he announced the emperor's abdication. (William actually relinquished his imperial crown a few hours later, but he did not formally abdicate as king of Prussia until November 28.) At the same time Max von Baden asked the leader of the SPD, Friedrich Ebert, to succeed him as Reich chancellor.

Baden, of course, had no constitutional authority to name his own successor. Since the October reforms that power rested with the Reichstag, and on November 9, parliament was not in session. But Baden also recognized that the demonstrators were clearly not in the mood for appreciating constitutional niceties. After a brief conference with the leaders of his party, Ebert accepted the chancellor's offer; just before noon on November 9, Germany had its first Social Democratic Reich chancellor.

Ebert and his colleagues in the SPD realized that their position would be extremely difficult without the cooperation of the USPD. The Berlin district of the SPD had traditionally been dominated by the left wing of the party, and after the split Berlin became one of the strongholds of the USPD. Indeed, key segments of the Berlin proletariat sympathized with the far-left Revolutionary Shop Stewards movement. For this reason, the SPD's leaders, immediately after accepting Baden's offer, proposed to the USPD that the two parties share power and positions equally in the new Reich government.

The SPD's completely unexpected proposal left the USPD in a quandary. Some left-wing radicals like Karl Liebknecht and Rosa Luxemburg were passionately opposed to working together with the right-wing socialists. At the same time, many in the USPD also feared that if the governmental infrastructure broke down completely, the mass starvation, civil war, and widespread random violence that followed the Bolshevik revolution in Russia would be repeated in Germany. In addition, the commitment by the German Marxists to preserving the Reich's national unity should not be underestimated. Like their colleagues in the SPD, many USPD members were, as one USPD local in East Prussia put it, "German to the marrow of our bones."

For these reasons a majority of the USPD's leadership voted to accept the SPD's offer to form a new provisional national government, called the Council of People's Plenipotentiaries. The CPP would be composed of six members, with the two socialist parties' national leaders, Ebert and

Haase, serving as cochairmen. The other four members were Emil Barth, the head of the Revolutionary Shop Stewards in Berlin; Wilhelm Dittmann, a moderate USPD leader; Otto Landsberg, one of the SPD's experts on constitutional questions; and Philipp Scheidemann, the leader of the SPD's Reichstag caucus. With the exception of Max von Baden, the incumbent ministers of the old cabinet stayed in office. They were to act as "technical aides" of the CPP.

The provisional government faced both immediate and long-range policy decisions. The two socialist groups agreed that the most pressing need was the conclusion of an armistice to end the fighting, but on other issues they were sharply divided. For example, the USPD members wanted to press ahead with the socialization of certain sectors of the economy, especially coal mining, banking, insurance, and parts of the steel industry. The SPD argued that the economy would have to recover before any sectors could be socialized.

While the party leaders debated the future of the country, the revolution in Berlin developed a dynamic of its own. At about 2 o'clock in the afternoon on November 9, Philip Scheidemann, the head of the SPD's Reichstag group, announced "the people had won" and proclaimed the formal establishment of the "German Republic." Scheidemann had no constitutional authority to make his pronouncements, and neither did Karl Liebknecht, who, two hours later in another part of the city, proclaimed the founding of the "German Socialist Republic" in which "all legislative, all executive, all judicial power" would be in the hands of the workers' and soldiers' councils rather than the CPP.

On the following day the Berlin workers' and soldiers' councils refused the role Liebknecht had envisioned for them. A citywide meeting of elected representatives from the local workers' and soldiers' councils gave the CPP a vote of confidence, and rejected a motion sponsored by the Spartacus League (modeled after the famous Army Order No. 1 adopted by the Petrograd [now St. Petersburg] soviet) to give the workers'

and soldiers' councils direct command over the police and military forces in Berlin. To be sure, the delegates also demanded that the CPP take immediate steps to implement the "socialization" of the economy and the "democratization" of society.

With the decisions in Berlin on November 10, the first stage of the German revolution ended, and it became possible to assess how much of a revolution there had been. On the surface the changes seemed profound. Dynasties that had ruled in Germany for centuries had been swept away. The new leaders of the national and state governments were socialists, sometimes allied with left-wing progressives and Catholics. A completely new set of institutions—workers' and soldiers' councils—at least in theory was the final arbiter of decisions on public policy.

Yet much remained as before. The old civil service continued to function. The new authorities took pains to protect private property and to prevent looting and arbitrary expropriations. The armed forces remained under the command structure of the old officer corps, despite the presence of elected soldiers' councils. Terms like *socialization* and *democratization* had made their way into the political jargon, but little had been done to implement concrete reforms. In essence, the upheavals of early November 1918, had swept away the prewar constitutional structures. Germany could now move in a variety of directions, from following the Bolshevik example in Russia to building a Western-style pluralist society, but as yet it was entirely unclear which path the Reich would take.

In theory, making the important decisions was the job of the constitutional convention. Actually, a series of tactical arrangements and agreements in the second half of November, severely restricted the range of possible future decisions. To begin with, the new rulers agreed to respect "the well-earned rights" of the civil servants, virtually precluding any large-scale purge of the old imperial officials.

In mid-November, representatives of the unions and employers' organizations established a Central Cooperative Working Group

Im Mittelpunkt Friedrich Ebert (1871–1925)

Although they were members of the same party for many years, it is difficult to imagine a sharper contrast than that between Rosa Luxemburg and Friedrich Ebert. On the one hand, the sharp-witted intellectual who excelled in debates on the lacunae of Marxist ideology, and on the other the party functionary and Reichstag deputy who had little interest in the theories of dialectical materialism.

Friedrich Ebert was born as the son of a tailor in Heidelberg. His formal education ended with the eighth grade when he began to learn the trade of a leather worker and saddle maker. He became active in the socialist union movement at an early age, however, and in 1891 moved to Bremen, where he established himself as a pub keeper. At the end of the nineteenth century, neighborhood taverns in the working-class districts of Germany's major cities were both places for socializing and locations where workers could get advice on the details of Germany's growing body of social legislation. Like many pub owners, Ebert became a self-taught expert in helping his customers get as much out of Germany's social legislation as possible. Without putting it in those terms, he was practicing Bernsteinian reformism.

Ebert also became a respected figure in the working-class movement. He was elected to a series of union positions, and during his stay in Bremen from 1891 to 1905, he served as an elected member on the city's parliamentary body, the *Bürgerschaft*. Eventually, Ebert's organizational skills also came to the attention of the SPD's central leadership. In 1905, he moved to Berlin to begin working full time as a functionary at the SPD's central headquarters, and in 1912, he was elected national chairman of the party.

At the outbreak of World War I, Ebert led the majority faction of the party, which looked on the German war effort as a justified defense against the threat of Russian czarism, to vote in favor of the government's request for war credits. (Rosa Luxemburg, of course, passionately opposed that decision.) Aside from his fear of Russian expansionism, Ebert's motivation for supporting Germany's authoritarian regime was twofold. He was a genuine German patriot (whenever his patriotism was questioned in later years, he pointed out "I gave two sons to this country," referring to two of his children who were killed in action during the war), and he hoped that as a reward for the SPD's willingness to support the war effort the emperor and his government would institute the reforms that would establish a true democracy in Germany. Specifically, this meant ministerial responsibility at both the federal and state levels, and the abolition of the three-class system of voting in Prussia in favor of universal suffrage. (All factions in the SPD had long demanded the women's vote.)

As evidence mounted that the OHL and the emperor were unwilling to grant meaningful reforms, the left-wing faction of the SPD abandoned the course charted by Ebert and founded the USPD. Ebert, however, never wavered in his conviction that the progressive forces in the Reichstag would be able to lead Germany peacefully to democracy. As the empire collapsed in the fall of 1918, Ebert worked hard to contain the radicals and maintain law and order under very trying

(*Zentrale Arbeitsgemeinschaft*—ZAG), which concluded a national collective-bargaining agreement covering most industrial workers. Labor won some major concessions, such as the eight-hour day, higher wages, and the promise that returning veterans would be rehired without loss of seniority. But the collective-bargaining agreement also precluded the implementation of any governmental plans to alter the structure of the circumstances. He feared the Reich's disintegration, and he was determined that Germany should not suffer the fate of Russia and succumb to communist rule. For these reasons, Ebert did not hesitate to accept the position of cochairman of the Council of People's Plenipotentiaries (CPP), and he used all of his persuasive powers to get the chairman of the USPD, Hugo Haase, to join him as cochairman.

As cochairman of the CPP, Ebert made one of his most fateful and controversial decisions. The so-called Ebert-Groener Pact, actually an oral agreement between Ebert and General Wilhelm Groener, Hindenburg's successor as head of the OHL, provided that the OHL would send a contingent of troops loyal to the government to help the CPP maintain law and order in Berlin. In return, Ebert agreed to respect the autonomy of the armed forces, which meant the CPP would not control appointments to the officer corps. The agreement benefited the army far more than the civilian government. The troops Groener sent quickly proved unreliable, but the agreement set the stage for what was to be the future republic's major problems, the armed forces' position as a state within the state.

Ebert wanted the new Germany to be a true political democracy. For this reason he and the CPP selected Hugo Preuss, a left-wing liberal, to write a draft of the new German constitution. Rejecting any plans for a dictatorship of the proletariat, Preuss attempted to combine the best features of the American, French, and British constitutional practices in the constitution of the Weimar Republic.

In February 1919, the Constituent Assembly elected Ebert provisional president of the republic, and in 1922, he began serving a regular term in that office. His tenure there was not a happy one. These were the years of extreme instability with frequent attempts by both the extreme left and the extreme right to overthrow the constitutional system. Ebert repeatedly invoked his emergency powers under Article 48. The result was a stream of vilification from all sides. The Communists never forgave Ebert for standing in the way of their Bolshevik-style revolution, and they held him responsible for the deaths of Rosa Luxemburg and Karl Liebknecht. The extreme right accused him of being a traitor who led the revolution that had "stabbed the armed forces in the back."

There was no truth in either charge, but Ebert felt it necessary to defend himself against the charges, especially from those of the extreme right. In a series of lawsuits, he attempted to clear his name by obtaining indictments against his critics for slander and libel. It was a largely futile and tactically counterproductive move. The lawsuits enabled his opponents to repeat the charges over and over again in open court before judges that were far more sympathetic toward the far right than the democratic left and center.

Ebert died prematurely in 1925, in the midst of one of his perennial judicial battles. He was ill with appendicitis but delayed getting the necessary operation in order to assemble some court documents. As a result, he suffered a ruptured appendix and died, only fifty-four years old.

economy significantly without the approval of both labor and management.

A second agreement with equally far-reaching implications involved a tactical partnership between the CPP and the OHL. On November 10, General Groener, Ludendorff's successor in the OHL, contacted Friedrich Ebert and offered him a deal: In return for keeping the officer corps free from "political" (that is to say, parliamentary) interference

and supporting efforts to limit the activities of
the soldiers' councils, the OHL would assist
the CPP in maintaining order at home and
administer the demobilization of the troops
at the front. Ebert, without consulting his
colleagues in the CPP, agreed to what became
known as the "Ebert-Groener Pact."

Most historians have been severely critical
of Ebert's decision to accept Groener's
offer. After all, granting the army continued
autonomy as "a state within the state" seemed
both counterproductive and unnecessary
at a time when the military's prestige and
self-confidence were at their lowest point in
a century. With the benefit of hindsight it
is easy to see the force of these arguments.
Ebert, however, had his eye on a number of
short-term problems. One was the necessary
demobilization of the frontline troops. He
knew that as part of the armistice agreement
the Allies would insist all German troops
leave French and Belgian soil within two
weeks. That meant transporting 2 million
war-weary, exhausted, and bitter soldiers
back to the Reich. Ebert was convinced
that moving that many people in good
order could only be done with the help of
the army's corps of staff officers. And it was
true: Germany's retreat was not marred by
the scenes of looting and pillaging that had
characterized the Russian demobilization
earlier in the year.

Ebert's second consideration was the
problem of internal security, especially in
Berlin. When Groener made his offer, the CPP
had already come to realize that there was no
really reliable force in the capital that could
protect the national government. The regular
Berlin police force was in disarray, and the
new—self-appointed—police chief was a man
who sympathized with the Spartacus League.
There were numerous self-styled militias
in the capital, but all of them tended to
disappear whenever confronted with any real
challenge. Groener's offer to dispatch some
reliable troops to Berlin was tempting; Ebert
could not know that the OHL's "trustworthy"
force would turn out to be just as unreliable
as all the others.

A third area in which the freedom of future
decision making was severely curtailed was the
federal structure of the Reich. For many years
the Social Democratic programs had demanded
a "unitary" Reich structure, with a strong central
government and weak states. In fact, the socialists proposed that many of the small Länder
should be abolished altogether. However, once
in power, the socialist Länder governments
turned out to be enthusiastic supporters of
states' rights. German particularism had come
through the revolution alive and well.

In the meantime, the CPP had begun its
work. One of the first disagreements among
the members of the CPP and their respective parties was setting the date for electing delegates to the national constitutional
convention. The SPD advanced tactical
and ideological reasons for early elections.
The party hoped that the voters, grateful
for peace and democracy, would be more
likely to vote for one of the socialist parties
while the memories of injustices under the
old regime were still fresh. In contrast, the
USPD contended that a period of "education" and measures to democratize especially the army and the civil service were
needed before the voters could be entrusted
with sanctioning the new order.

The members of the CPP agreed to leave
the final decision on the election date to a
national congress of workers' and soldiers'
councils. Meeting in Berlin in mid-December
1918, the decision of the congress was a severe
disappointment to the USPD; by heavy majorities the delegates endorsed the SPD's position on setting the date for national elections.
Indeed, although the SPD members of the
CPP had proposed a date in early February,
the congress scheduled national elections for
January 19, 1919.

Still, the national congress of workers'
and soldiers' councils did not merely rubber-
stamp the positions of the right-wing Social
Democrats on the CPP. The delegates were
sharply critical of the government's relations with the OHL and adopted a series of
resolutions, the so-called Hamburg Points,
designed to curb the autonomy of the officer

corps and enlarge the scope of activities of the soldiers' councils. The congress endorsed the collective-bargaining agreement negotiated earlier by the ZAG, but the delegates also voted to appoint a Socialization Commission and charged it with investigating the feasibility of nationalizing major sectors of the German economy.

Nevertheless, the congress's decision on the election date destroyed the basis of the tactical partnership between the USPD and the SPD. The Independent members of the provisional government resigned at the end of the year; they were replaced by three new SPD leaders. But the left-wing socialists still faced a basic dilemma. Should they attempt to argue their case during the deliberations of the constitutional convention, or should they work to propel the revolution forward? Most of the USPD decided on the former course of action, but some of the party's more radical elements were determined to stage a "second revolution."

On December 30, 1918, the founding convention of the German Communist Party (*Kommunistische Partei Deutschlands,* KPD) met in Berlin. Against the advice of Rosa Luxemburg and Karl Liebknecht, the leaders of the Spartacus League, a majority of the delegates voted to boycott the national elections and instead stage a Bolshevik-style revolution. "Spartacus Week," as the radicals' uprising from January 5 to 12, came to be known, was both a misnomer and a pitiful and amateurish attempt at a revolution. Most of the action took place in Berlin, where some thousand armed men, led by an unwieldy executive committee of fifty-three, attempted to overthrow the CPP. They had no chance of success. The uprising was quickly and bloodily put down by regular army troops and government-paid volunteer vigilante groups—all under the nominal command of Gustav Noske, one of the new members of the CPP. (The vigilante groups, the so-called *Freikorps,* were to play a major role in the counterrevolutionary uprisings of the early 1920s; they are discussed in more detail later, pp. 127ff) The only legacies of the "second revolution" were the imprinting

of a lasting fear of "Marxism" among the German middle classes and embittered relations between the Majority Socialists and their former comrades. Not without reason the left-wing forces blamed the SPD for tolerating the brutality of the Freikorps units; one of the vigilante groups murdered Luxemburg and Liebknecht.

THE WEIMAR CONSTITUTION

The elections of delegates to the constitutional conventions (in addition to the national constitutional convention, many of the states, including Prussia, also elected state assemblies) were held under rules determined by the CPP. They provided for equal and universal suffrage for all Germans twenty years or older; for the first time women as well as men had the right to vote.

The introduction of a truly democratic voting system meant that no political party could rely on the effects of the Prussian three-class system of voting to assure it a disproportionate share of political power. The bourgeois parties especially hastened to present a new image as parties of the people. In fact, the word "people" itself (in German, *Volk*) suddenly became part of most middle-class party labels.

Democracy confronted the conservatives with particularly difficult challenges. Their role as an oligarchic leadership group had come to an abrupt end. The conservatives met the new challenge boldly. In November 1918, the wings of the prewar movement formed a new organization, the German National People's Party (*Deutschnationale Volkspartei—* DNVP). Although the new party continued to be led by the old conservative notables, it attempted to broaden its voting appeal to include white-collar workers, professionals, and businessmen. The party also expanded its geographic base to all sections of the country, although it remained strongest in Protestant northern Germany.

In 1919, the DNVP presented an image of progressive conservatism to the voters. The party stood for the traditional bourgeois

Im Mittelpunkt Rosa Luxemburg (1870–1919)

Rosa Luxemburg was a Marxist ideologue who literally died for her convictions. She was also a political activist who was both admired and vilified—although much of the adulation was posthumous, whereas most of the attacks came during her lifetime.

She was born as the daughter of a rabbi and timber merchant in the small town of Zamosc, in what was then the Russian part of Poland. After her family moved to Warsaw she attended the Russian Secondary Gymnasium for Girls, where she demonstrated her brilliant intellect and her rebellious personality in about equal measures. After running afoul of the school authorities several times, she was forced to leave Poland in 1889, and moved to Zurich, where she began her studies at the university. While there she quickly established contact with many of the German Social Democrats who had also been forced into exile in Switzerland as a consequence of Bismarck's Anti-Socialist Laws.

In 1898, Luxemburg moved to Berlin, and from then until her death she immersed herself in Social Democratic politics. She became one of the few women who was regularly elected to the SPD's national conventions, and she was also a frequent delegate to the congresses of the Socialist International. Much of her work for the party took place at the SPD's training school for party functionaries. She would have won a teaching award every year if there had been one; even her later political opponents remember her as a brilliant and empathic teacher.

Ten years after moving to Berlin, Rosa Luxemburg and Eduard Bernstein began their intellectual feud. Luxemburg passionately opposed all of Bernstein's revisionist ideas because she was convinced they would blind the socialist movement to the need to prepare it and the working class for the proletarian revolution. In contrast to Bernstein, Luxemburg argued that capitalism, despite its robust appearance, was already in its last stages. In her famous phrase, imperialism "was the highest and last stage of capitalism." Because capitalism was already tottering under the weight of its own contradictions, concentrating on bread-and-butter issues instead of the ultimate revolution would merely delay capitalism's overdue demise. Luxemburg argued the party and the labor unions should organize the workers to use the weapons at their command—especially the general strike—to stage the proletarian revolution and establish the dictatorship of the proletariat.

Luxemburg's analysis of imperialism paralleled the thoughts of Vladimir Lenin in Russia, but there was one issue on which she and the Bolshevik leader sharply disagreed. Luxemburg passionately believed in intraproletarian democracy—that is to say that within the SPD and the union

values of free enterprise, protection of private property, and Christian ethics. It not only rejected all experiments with "Marxist collectivism," but it also muted its traditional anti-Semitism. Still, the DNVP's openness to the new times did not last long. Within a year the party was denouncing the republic, democracy, parliamentarism, and Jews while demanding a return to the rule of the Hohenzollerns.

The National Liberals emerged after the upheavals of 1918–1919 as the German People's Party (*Deutsche Volkspartei*—DVP). In January 1919, however, the party was only a shadow of its former self. In most areas of Germany it had no real organization, and the movement, the members should be free not only to express differing points of view but also freely elect their leaders. Luxemburg totally rejected Lenin's "vanguard theory," whereby a small group of professional revolutionaries acted in the name of the proletariat.

Rosa Luxemburg saw the outbreak of World War I as the long-expected cataclysmic civil war among the capitalist nations that signaled the end of this hated system. Along with other left-wing socialists (including Lenin) she supported the Zimmerwald Movement, which encouraged all workers to oppose their nations' war efforts by whatever means possible, including sabotage, strikes, and mutinies. She sharply criticized the SPD's decision to support the war effort and openly urged German workers to refuse to serve in the military and to sabotage the manufacture of armaments. As a result, she was tried for sedition and spent most of the war years in jail. As might be expected, she joined the USPD as soon as it was founded. She was also an active member of the extreme left-wing Spartacus group.

Released from jail in October 1918, she immediately resumed her agitation against the majority SPD. She argued against establishing the Council of People's Plenipotentiaries and vehemently opposed the USPD's decision to join the provisional Reich government. Instead, she demanded that all power be put in the hands of the workers' and soldiers' councils as a first step leading to the dictatorship of the proletariat.

At the end of December 1918, Luxemburg, along with Karl Liebknecht, was one of the founding members of the German Communist Party (KPD). As editor of the party's newspaper, *Rote Fahne*, she spewed a continuous stream of venom against the provisional Reich government, but she opposed the decision by the KPD to stage a second revolution to overthrow this government in January 1919. Rosa Luxemburg argued that the party had neither the resources nor the manpower necessary for a successful revolution. (During the debate on this issue at the KPD's founding convention, she exclaimed, "Comrades, you are taking this business of making a revolution a little too lightly.") Nevertheless, true to her democratic convictions, she accepted the vote of the majority and loyally supported what she knew would be an unsuccessful and amateurish attempt.

She paid with her life for her convictions. During the so-called Spartacus Week, both Luxemburg and Liebknecht were arrested by one of the extreme right-wing vigilante groups that the government had authorized to fight against the left-wing insurgents. The two Communist leaders were severely beaten before being murdered. Their bodies were thrown into the *Landwehrkanal* in Berlin.

membership was reduced to a few followers of the party's new chairman, Gustav Stresemann. As a result, the DVP faced a difficult campaign in the election of 1919, particularly because it was hard to distinguish the DVP from the DNVP. The new party's voting appeal was directed primarily toward the urban upper and middle classes. The DVP had particularly strong support among industrialists and business executives.

The DVP made a striking comeback in 1920. Middle-class voters, disappointed by the ineffectiveness of the Progressives and the DNVP's support for the counterrevolutionary upheavals of March 1920 (see the discussion on pp. 128–29), turned instead to Stresemann's party. Unlike the conservatives, who refused to become reconciled to the republican form of government, the DVP leaders, including especially Stresemann himself, adopted a middle-of-the-road stance. They became "pragmatic Republicans" (*Vernunftrepublikaner*). By this they meant that although in their hearts they remained monarchists, for the foreseeable future political reason dictated that the republic would have to be accepted as Germany's legitimate constitutional form.

For a brief span, the old progressives were the largest bourgeois party. The progressives were the only group that incorporated their support of democracy into their new name; they became the German Democratic Party (*Deutsche Demokratische Partei*—DDP). The Democrats appealed to a wide cross section of middle-class Germans, from industrialists and professionals to white-collar workers and farmers. During the 1919 campaign, the DDP portrayed itself as the party that could gain the trust of the SPD while at the same time holding the socialists' radical tendencies in check.

The DDP's political glory vanished as quickly as it came. The party was unable to assimilate its early massive voting support into an effective organization. The death of the party's venerated leader, Friedrich Naumann, in 1919, left it without either direction or a coherent program. After the spring of 1919, large numbers of disappointed voters and members deserted the DDP and turned to the DVP instead.

The Center Party had the fewest adjustments to make. It toyed briefly with a new name (in 1919, the party campaigned as the Christian People's Party [*Christliche Volkspartei*]), but the Catholic party quickly abandoned such efforts to be fashionable and reverted to its old name of Center Party. The party's prewar core of right-wing Catholic leaders made way for men from the populist left-wing faction of the party. The new leaders readily accepted democracy as the basis of Germany's constitutional system. They also emphasized the party's concern for industrial workers and improved social welfare programs. At the same time, the party did not neglect its concern for safeguarding Catholic interests, especially in the fields of public education and civil service appointments.

The dispute over war credits and other issues had shattered the already-fragile unity of German social democracy. Until 1922, three separate and largely antagonistic socialist organizations competed for the votes of the German industrial proletariat. All three professed to be guided by Marxist ideology as a blueprint for transforming present-day capitalism into future socialism. The Majority Socialists remained the largest of the three Marxist parties. The SPD was dominated by right-wing leaders who saw the establishment of political and economic democracy as the necessary (and sufficient) instrument for protecting the interests of Germany's industrial workers. The party remained equivocal about the future of the workers' and soldiers' councils. The SPD was willing to accord them a role as spokesmen for the workers' economic interests, but it rejected their institutionalization as legislative or executive bodies.

The Independent Socialists, the USPD, regarded the SPD's vision of the road to socialism and genuine democracy solely through the ballot box as naive and contrary to Marxist principles. There was certainly something to this criticism, and in recent years the USPD's vision of a "third way," avoiding the mistakes of the Majority Socialists and the brutality of the Bolsheviks, has received much praise from historians.

The USPD argued that as long as the capitalists controlled the "commanding heights" of the economy and public administration, the socialists' popularity at the ballot box was meaningless. For this reason, the left-wing Social Democrats wanted to retain the workers' and soldiers' councils as vehicles of proletarian control to implement the structural changes in German society necessary to transform it from capitalism to socialism.

In the second half of 1919, and the first months of 1920, it appeared that many German workers shared the USPD's vision of proletarian democracy. The USPD experienced a veritable explosion of members and votes in the wake of the counterrevolutionary activities that culminated in the Kapp putsch of 1920 (see the discussion on pp. 128–29). Unfortunately for the party, it was the illusionary glow of health in a political organism already in the process of disintegration. In October 1920, the party split over the question of affiliating with the Russian-dominated Communist (Third) International (Comintern). Most of the Independent leaders did not favor affiliation with the Comintern, but the bulk of the membership did. As a result, a majority of the USPD's rank-and-file members joined the Communist Party, the KPD. What remained of the USPD eventually rejoined the SPD in 1922.

The Communist Party was the most radical of the three Marxist groups. The communists were committed to Marxism-Leninism in that they regarded the Bolshevik revolution in Russia (and the Bolshevik party's role in these events) as the basic model for all future proletarian revolutions. They resolutely rejected democracy in its bourgeois sense (one delegate at the KPD's founding convention noted "ten proletarian fists are worth ten thousand votes"), and proclaimed the need for the dictatorship of the proletariat, exercised through the KPD as the vanguard of the proletariat. The KPD remained a largely sectarian splinter group until the fall of 1920, when the disintegration of the USPD enabled it to become a genuine mass party.

The national elections of January 19, 1919, showed continuity of a trend that had been apparent before the war: the growing strength of the reformist groups. Voter participation was again high: 85 percent in the last Reichstag election in 1912; 83 percent in 1919. The share of the Social Democrats' vote rose from 34.8 percent in 1912 to 45 percent in 1919 (37.9 percent for the SPD; 7.6 percent for the USPD). The KPD, of course, did not run. The DDP became the strongest bourgeois party. The Democrats (formerly Progressives) obtained 18.5 percent in 1919, compared to the Progressives' 7.7 percent in 1912. The

Center Party, benefiting from increased voter participation among Catholics, also increased its popular vote somewhat, from 16.4 percent in 1912 to 19.7 percent in 1919. The National Liberalism under the guise of the DVP obtained a mere 4.4 percent of the popular vote. Finally, the conservatives' core voter constituency remained what it had been before the war: about 10 percent of the popular vote. The combined vote of the conservative parties in 1912, had been 9.2 percent; in 1919, the DNVP did only slightly better—10.3 percent. The most striking result of the election of 1919, then, was the vote of confidence given the reformist parties. The SPD, Center Party, and DDP together received 76 percent of the popular vote in 1919, a figure substantially higher than the 58.9 percent they had obtained in 1912.

The National Assembly (*Nationalversammlung*) that was to write Germany's new constitution met not in Berlin but in Weimar, an inconspicuous but famous town in the state of Thuringia. The reason was partly symbolic: In the eighteenth and early nineteenth centuries, Weimar had been the residence of Germany's greatest literary figure, Johann Wolfgang von Goethe. In addition, Berlin was still experiencing some aftershocks of the "Spartacus Week," and it was felt that the delegates' physical safety might be endangered in the capital.

The National Assembly had a dual function. It was both a provisional Reich legislature and a constitutional convention. One of its first decisions was to legitimize the political changes that had occurred since November and to replace the makeshift CPP and what remained of the workers' and soldiers' councils with a Reich president and a national cabinet. Friedrich Ebert was overwhelmingly elected president by the Assembly; the Majority Socialist Philipp Scheidemann became chancellor of a coalition cabinet composed of ministers from the SPD, the Center Party, and the DDP.

But the National Assembly's main task, clearly, was to write a new constitution. Two issues in particular aroused long and passionate debates. One was the nature of the Reich's future political system, the other concerned revisions in Germany's federal structure. In December 1918, the CPP had asked Hugo Preuss, a distinguished scholar of constitutional law and a member of the DDP, to write a draft constitution. There was no doubt about Preuss's position on the two basic questions. His draft envisioned a full-scale parliamentary democracy, modeled on those of France and Great Britain. Universal suffrage and proportional representation provided for national and state parliaments that were fully reflective of the voters' opinions. The executive was subject to control by the popularly elected Reichstag; the Reich cabinet served only as long as it had the confidence of the national parliament. The National Assembly accepted this part of Preuss's draft constitution. In Preuss' draft the second chamber of the national legislature, the *Reichsrat*, was not popularly elected. As was true before 1919, its delegates were appointed by the state governments.

In later years, the Weimar constitution would be much criticized for the peculiar position that it accorded the Reich president. Preuss had in mind an essentially ceremonial figure, who would stand above party strife and be representative of all the people. For this reason he proposed a popularly elected president. The president's seven-year term was designed to ensure that he was in office longer than the members of the Reichstag, who had to be elected every four years. Preuss's draft limited the president's powers to little more than nominating the Reich chancellor, but the National Assembly went beyond this and inserted what became Article 48 of the constitution. This gave the president the right to declare an emergency and govern the Reich or a Land for a limited time without parliamentary approval. The delegates to the National Assembly had the "Spartacus Week" upheavals of 1918–1919 in mind when they included Article 48 in the constitution, but in later years the powers of this article would be used to undermine the very democratic system it was meant to strengthen.

Preuss's draft also proposed far-reaching revisions of Germany's federal structure.

To strengthen the powers of the federal government he proposed the division of the Prussian superstate into a number of separate Länder. The delegates in the convention proved unsympathetic toward Preuss's ideas on federalism. Prussia remained intact. In fact, with the exception of merging three former mini-principalities in central Germany into the state of Thuringia, there were no significant territorial changes among the German states during the fifteen-year span of the Weimar Republic.

The balance of power between the federal government and the states did shift in favor of the Reich, however. The new constitution transferred control of the armed forces, the *Reichswehr,* to the national government and expanded the role of the federal judiciary. Above all, the Reich was no longer dependent on the states to finance the federal government's day-to-day operations. Under the guidance of Matthias Erzberger, the minister of finance in the Scheidemann cabinet, the National Assembly voted to reverse the prewar pattern of revenue allocations. Most direct taxes, including personal and corporate income taxes, were now earmarked for the federal government while the states were left with property taxes and some indirect sources of revenue. Erzberger's reforms reversed the system of the states' supporting the Reich through the *Matrikularbeiträge* (see an earlier discussion, p. 59). Under the Weimar constitution the federal government returned a portion of the income tax it collected to the Länder.

The Weimar constitution reflected the thinking of the reformist forces in Wilhelminian Germany. It was not a revolutionary document. Instead, given the self-imposed limitations of Wilhelminian reformism, the Weimar constitution provided something for everyone. The right wing of the SPD had long demanded a fully democratic voting system, and this goal was realized in the constitution's provisions for proportional representation. The Democrats were pleased by the constitution's strong emphasis on parliamentary control of the executive and the safeguards for civil rights and private property. Finally, the Catholics were able to write provisions into the document that ensured a continued institutional role for the Catholic Church in public life and the de facto maintenance of public schools segregated by religious affiliation.

At the same time, adoption of the constitution also marked the beginnings of future conflicts. Like the Bismarck constitution of 1871, the document written by the National Assembly did not create a national political consensus. True, the Weimar constitution had the support of three out of four German voters in 1919. However, the remaining one-fourth, the political "outs," constituted a potent mix of the new and old right, the National Liberals, the left-wing socialists, and the Communists. These elements objected not only to specific provisions of the constitution, but for a variety of contradictory reasons also denied the validity of the entire work of Weimar.

The seemingly unbridgeable gap between the new "ins" and "outs" occasioned some bitter debates during the convention over what were essentially symbolic issues. The one arousing the most deep-seated emotions was the choice of national colors. The conservatives favored retaining the old imperial colors of black, white, and red to symbolize Germany's past glories, but for the Socialists, Democrats, and parts of the Center Party, black, white, and red stood for the rule of Prussian authoritarianism. They voted for black, red, and gold, the colors of national and political liberation during the revolution of 1848. The radical left rejected both and proclaimed their allegiance to the red flag of socialism. The National Assembly eventually adopted black, red, and gold as the republic's colors (with significant exceptions for shipping and the army), but the flag controversy was to mar Germany's political life throughout the Weimar years. The political right disdained the national colors as "black, red, and yellow" and continued to march behind the old imperial flag.

The flag issue was symptomatic of the republic's deeper problem of alienation. Almost from the moment of its founding some important groups in society identified the new regime

with the loss of their privileged status and the end of the empire's glory. The segments included the officer corps, high-ranking civil servants, industrialists, members of the judiciary, and many among the educated middle classes, the *Bildungsbürgertum.* In what turned out in retrospect to have been a grave mistake, the political leaders of the republic for the most part left the "rejectionists" in positions of influence. It was thought that the old officials and leaders would serve the new regime as loyally as they had the old, and would in time become sincere republicans as well. That decision contained a twofold error. During the next few years the old guard, with some laudable exceptions, did not rally to the republic but used its control of key positions to undermine the new order. The regime's failure to remove these opponents of democracy from power in turn created a second alienation problem: The republic quickly lost much of the support of the forces on the left who had been instrumental in overthrowing the authoritarianism of the empire.

THE TREATY OF VERSAILLES

One of the most important decisions facing the National Assembly was whether to accept or reject the terms of peace that the Allies presented to the Germans in May 1919. The debate not only polarized German public opinion but also left a bitter legacy for the future. The peace treaty between Germany and the victorious "Allied and Associated Powers" has become known as the Treaty of Versailles, from the place of its eventual signing, the Hall of Mirrors at the Palace of Versailles. The Allies' choice of locale was deliberate: The German Empire was to suffer its final humiliation in the same chamber in which it had celebrated its initial triumph in 1871. As was the case for the earlier Treaty of Brest-Litovsk, which the Germans and Austrians had imposed on the Russians, the Treaty of Versailles was a one-sided pact; it embodied the victors' visions of a new balance of power in Europe and the world.

The final terms were negotiated among the leaders of the major Allied nations, principally

David Lloyd George for Great Britain, Georges Clemenceau for France, and Woodrow Wilson for the United States, rather than between the Allies and their former enemy. President Wilson returned to America in February 1919, and thereafter most of the work was done by Clemenceau and Lloyd George and their aides. In May the finished draft was handed to the Germans for their comments. The Scheidemann government drafted a lengthy reply, objecting to almost every paragraph in the document, but the Allies rejected virtually all of the Germans' counterproposals, leaving the Reich government in June with only two choices: to accept the Allied terms or reject them and risk a new war.

When the draft treaty was handed to the Reich government, a feeling of shock, even betrayal, over the presumed severity of the terms permeated German public opinion. Chancellor Scheidemann spoke for the nation when he originally rejected the treaty with words that were to haunt him for the rest of his career, "What hand would not wither when it signed such a treaty?" The reaction of other political leaders was even stronger. Otto Braun, the Social Democratic prime minister of Prussia, had visions of resuming military resistance from the state's East Elbian redoubt, much as Prussia had done after its defeat by Napoleon a hundred years earlier, but such political grandstanding was completely unrealistic. As the government learned from Germany's military leaders, the Reich did not have any military resources with which to resist an Allied invasion and consequently no choice but to accept the treaty. As for the conservatives, they now blamed Germany's defeat and the insulting treaty on the political upheavals in November 1918. Forgetting that the OHL had acknowledged military defeat and demanded that Germany ask for an armistice, the conservatives and their allies suddenly discovered that Germany's armies had been "victorious" until they were "stabbed in the back" by the revolution of 1918.

The Germans' shock and dismay at the treat terms was based in large part on the illusionary belief that the Allies would treat a democratic

Germany more leniently than one still ruled by the Junkers and their associates. Germany's enemies, however, took a different view. Quite aside from the fact that some of the men prominent in the republican government had until recently been staunch supporters of Germany's maximal war aims, the basic purpose of the treaty as far as the Allies were concerned was unrelated to the change of regimes in Germany. The Allies' avowed goals were to effect a change in the global balance of power that would prevent further aggression on the part of Germany and assure the payment of sufficient reparations from the Reich (and its partners in the war) to help the Allies recoup their wartime expenses. The Allies also insisted the Versailles Treaty would inaugurate a new sense of morality and justice in the conduct of international relations.

The disagreements over whether to accept or reject the peace treaty led to the young republic's first cabinet crisis. The DDP, hopelessly deadlocked on the issue, dropped out of the government, and Scheidemann resigned as chancellor. The new cabinet was a coalition of SPD and Center Party ministers, headed by Gustav Bauer, a Social Democratic union leader. Eventually a majority of the National Assembly voted for acceptance, but the margin for approval was narrow and the sense of outrage and bitterness pervasive throughout the house.

In the Treaty of Versailles, the goal of changing Germany's role in the European balance of power was implemented primarily by reducing the Reich's territory and population and by placing restrictions on its military strength. Germany lost about a tenth of its prewar territory and population. In the case of many, though by no means all, of the territorial changes mandated by the treaty, the inhabitants of the areas in question were asked to vote whether they wanted to remain in the Reich or become citizens of a neighboring state. Most of the German territorial losses involved areas in the east that had mixed or predominantly Polish populations. Parts of the former Prussian provinces east of the Oder were incorporated into the newly established republic of Poland.

Other boundary changes involved the return of Alsace-Lorraine to France and smaller transfers of territory and populations to Denmark and Belgium. Although the territorial changes were often in accord with the wishes of the inhabitants, the new boundaries did at times create an odd patchwork of overlapping jurisdictions. The province of East Prussia, for example, which had voted to remain German, was physically separated from the rest of the Reich by a large strip of Poland, the so-called Polish Corridor. Germany also lost all of its colonies. These were technically turned over to the League of Nations but actually administered by individual Allied powers as "mandates" of the League.

Ostensibly as a prelude to worldwide disarmament (one of the Allies' nods to the new era of morality) but actually to reduce Germany's military power, the treaty put severe limitations on the size and quality of Germany's military establishment. The German army was to be reduced to a force of 100,000 men. (The prewar strength had been 750,000.) In addition, the Reich was forbidden to continue universal military service, build military airplanes or submarines, maintain naval ships larger than 10,000 tons, or possess offensive land weapons. Essentially, the military sections of the Treaty of Versailles were designed to give Germany an army that was no match for Allied forces, although it would be sufficiently strong to maintain order at home. The treaty also provided for Allied troops to remain in occupation of the left bank of the Rhine for fifteen years.

The economic provisions of the treaty were to become the most controversial part of the pact. The Allies wanted Germany to reimburse them for at least part of the staggering sum of $150.5 billion (in 1914 values; the figure in 2010 terms would be $3,250,032,450,000) that the war was estimated to have cost them. To this end, they forced Germany to pay reparations. The treaty did not actually specify a sum. Rather, in accepting the terms of peace the Reich agreed to sign a promissory note for an as yet unspecified amount. Other economic provisions were designed to give Allied businesses a competitive advantage over the Germans. The

Reich, for example, could not impose tariffs on imports from the Allied countries until 1925. But there were also forms of petty harassment, such as the prohibition of labeling German sparkling wines "champagne," and the transfer without compensation of German patents and trademarks to Allied owners.

The most innovative feature of the Treaty of Versailles and its companion pacts with Germany's wartime partners was the strong emphasis on morality in the future conduct of international relations. The guiding spirit here was the U.S. president Woodrow Wilson. He hoped that the principle of self-determination would eliminate many of the nationality conflicts that had led to war in Europe in the past. As a corollary, the American president also insisted that the concept of the League of Nations, which he envisioned as a sort of permanent international parliament, be made an integral part of the peace treaties.

There is no doubt that the concept of self-determination redressed a number of ancient wrongs. It made possible the reestablishment of an independent Poland after 150 years of partition as well as the creation of Czechoslovakia and the union of the South Slav peoples in the state of Yugoslavia. Unfortunately, in practice the proclaimed ethical values in the Treaty of Versailles at times also bore a marked similarity to the old power politics. Strategic considerations dictated that the principle of self-determination be set aside in the case of Austria. The German-speaking population of the former Habsburg Empire voted to join the new German republic, but the plebiscite was ignored by the Allies. From the German perspective, even the League of Nations was part of the victors' alliance; the Reich was not permitted to become a member until 1926. (The United States never joined the League, but here the reason was self-imposed isolation, not ostracism.)

In German eyes the attempt to link the treaty's economic provisions with the Allies' professed concern for ethics in international relations seemed particularly hypocritical. The economic sections of the Treaty of Versailles were preceded by a short sentence that was to dominate discussion of the treaty throughout the 1920s: Article 231. In this paragraph, which was also part of the peace treaties with Austria and Hungary, Germany and the other Central Powers recognized the Allies' moral right to impose reparations because they, the Central Powers, had been solely responsible for unleashing World War I. Article 231 was the "war-guilt clause."

Since 1919 the Treaty of Versailles has had a curious historiography. The debate over the justification for Article 231 began almost immediately after the Germans had grudgingly signed the treaty in June 1919, and eventually produced a sizable literary industry. Many scholars wrote "revisionist" histories, arguing that the Reich and its partners were not solely responsible for the outbreak of the war.

Map 4.1   Germany after World War I

The publication of John Maynard Keynes's *The Economic Consequences of the Peace* in 1919, severely criticized the economic terms of the treaty. The British economist contended that by subjecting Germany to excessive hardships, the peace terms had destroyed the bases for postwar European prosperity. The Great Depression of the 1930s, and the rise of Hitler seemed to provide evidence for this argument.

However, the disastrous consequences of appeasing Hitler and the experience of World War II did much to discredit the earlier revisionists. During the 1970s, the treaty debate was rekindled by a new generation of scholars. Following Fritz Fischer this group of "re-revisionists" argued there was an organic link between Hitler's and the OHL's war aims. Others took up this theme and contended that the Treaty of Versailles did not impose impossible terms. These scholars claimed that the Reich's insistence that Germany could not meet its financial obligations was a smokescreen invented by political leaders who became quite ingenious in using a variety of subterfuges to escape honoring the Reich's treaty obligations. The real victors of World War I in this view were not France and Great Britain but Hitler and the Nazis. The Allies' leniency made possible the later rise of totalitarianism.

A balanced assessment of the Treaty of Versailles is difficult without agreement on the terms on which the issue ought to be discussed. On the one hand, it is true that the treaty failed to change permanently the balance of power in Europe; Germany rose again. On the other hand, the treaty provisions, by not smoothing the path of the democratic republic into the family of nations, aided the rise of its enemies. As far as the long-standing argument over the severity of the reparations is concerned, it is impossible to extract this issue from its political implications. There is no doubt that Germany had the ability to pay the sums demanded. But there were two difficulties. Politically, it was impossible for a succession of Reich governments to justify the additional burden of the reparations on a country already suffering from severe problems of postwar economic readjustment. In addition,

most Germans, including many well-meaning republican leaders, were convinced that the primary object of the reparations was not to make Germany pay but to ruin the Reich's economy as a prelude to destroying Germany's political and territorial integrity. This argument was given verisimilitude by some of the hidden, additional costs of the reparation burden. Conan Fischer has pointed out, for example, that for every 100 gold marks credited to the reparations account, Germany had to pay an additional 74 gold marks as a "clearing payment," a charge comparable to the "transaction fees" imposed by modern financial institutions. This latter payment was not credited to the reparations account. Perhaps it is not so surprising that Germany would attempt to evade the imposed peace terms.

ECONOMIC AND SOCIAL PROBLEMS

Four years of war had severely disrupted Germany's social fabric and left the economy with a host of short- and long-term problems. Even a casual observer could not help but notice the evidence of malnutrition, rundown transportation and production facilities, and the general decline in public morality. Nor did the signing of the armistice end shortages and black-market activities. For some weeks after the fighting had stopped, the Allies continued the blockade while they and the Germans argued over the Reich's ability to pay for needed imports in gold or hard currency. The blockade deadlock was eventually resolved, but the terms of the armistice themselves compounded Germany's economic difficulties. The Reich had to agree to turn over to the Allies a significant number of trucks, production machinery, and railroad rolling stock to aid in the recovery of the devastated areas of France and Belgium. Similarly, much of Germany's shipping tonnage was transferred to Great Britain.

But by no means could all of Germany's problems be blamed on the Allies. The end of the war brought a new sense of militancy to the workers of the country. Segments that had not benefited from the war economy wanted to catch up. Railroad workers, whose already low standard of living had rapidly eroded during the war, turned especially militant. Recognizing their strong bargaining position, the railroad workers and other groups of employees in the public sector staged a wave of authorized and wildcat strikes in the winter of 1918–1919, to press for immediate wage hikes.

However justified, higher wages also compounded the problem of inflation. Despite the later claims of the political right, the revolution did not cause Germany's inflation. The imperial government had decided to finance the war almost entirely with credits. By the end of the war, the German mark had fallen from a value of 4.2 to the dollar in July 1914 to 8.9 in January 1919. In 1918, the interest on the national debt was higher than the whole federal budget had been in 1913. In the long run, the erosion of the mark would reduce the value of savings and pensions, but for the moment most Germans felt the result primarily in the increased costs of imports and higher outlays for social services. To be sure, in a fully functioning international economy higher prices for imports would be offset by a competitive advantage for German exports, but for some years after the end of hostilities normal patterns of international trade were disrupted. In the meantime, the country spent increasingly large sums to pay for imports of raw materials and agricultural goods and to meet the demands for higher wages and veterans' benefits.

The problems of the German economy were real, but much of the discussion about what caused them was not. The Reich's postwar decision makers tended to ignore the effects of long-term structural changes and their own misguided policies as reasons for Germany's difficulties. Instead, they blamed the effects on the peace treaty. This argument ignored that most of the lost lands were located in the poorer agricultural areas of East Elbia, which had been regions of chronic economic difficulties for years. Similarly, the population losses for the most part involved unskilled farm labor rather than skilled industrial workers. Setting aside emotional and nationalistic arguments, the Allies had inadvertently enabled the Germans

to write off some of their prewar problems. This was especially true of the overseas possessions. All of the chauvinistic hand wringing about the loss of the colonies could not hide the fact that before the war the administration of the colonies had required constant subsidies from the Reich budget. In economic terms, the most serious effects of the peace treaty were the loss of 75 percent of Germany's prewar iron ore reserves and a significant portion of its coal mining capacity in the areas of Silesia, Alsace-Lorraine, and the Saar.

While Germany's economic and political leaders heaped scorn on the Treaty of Versailles, they cast a blind eye on a number of economic and social harbingers of change that were largely unrelated to the peace terms. War and revolution had caused tremendous shifts in the relative wealth and status of various groups in the society. By 1918, segments that had enjoyed high status and relatively secure economic positions in 1914—such as officers, high-level civil servants, teachers, professionals, urban landlords, and pensioners—suffered hardships while other groups benefited. Among the latter were some categories of blue- and white-collar workers and many large-scale industrialists. Under the provisions of the ZAG (see the earlier discussion on p. 106) most industrial workers and white-collar technical and clerical employees, the so-called new Mittelstand, were now covered by a blanket collective-bargaining agreement that provided for increased wages, preferential rehiring of veterans, and the realization of such long-term demands as the eight-hour day. In addition, the ZAG, the Weimar constitution, and eventually a National Law on Industrial Councils of February 1920, enlarged the scope of workers' participation in managerial decisions. Through elected industrial councils, which became mandatory in all firms with twenty or more employees through their union representatives, had a voice in decisions affecting safety and efficiency in the production process, as well as hiring, firing, and wage determinations. At least on paper German businessmen had lost some of their traditional rights as "lords of the manor."

At the same time, there were reciprocal benefits for the industrialists. The trend toward private cartel and trust agreements continued unabated; the lack of real competition in turn enabled the industrialists simply to pass on increased labor costs in the form of higher prices. Many industrialists were also not overly concerned about inflation. The devalued mark enabled them to pay off prewar debts at a fraction of their original cost; the larger enterprises in particular often had hard currency deposits outside of Germany, enabling them to avoid paying for imports of raw materials in marks.

For farmers and urban landlords war and revolution presented a mixed picture. Initially, large-scale farmers and house owners benefited from the effects of the inflation. For the first time in several generations most East Elbian estates and many apartment houses were debt free, their mortgages wiped out by inflation. Nevertheless, both groups still felt they had reason to complain. Farmers and landlords bitterly resented what they saw as unfair government measures to benefit urban consumers. Farmers rejected price controls on farm products; landlords railed against rent controls.

Changes in relative social standing did not alter the fact that the economy as a whole was experiencing severe difficulties. Industrial production, to take the most important indicator, had declined from an index figure of 100 in 1913 to 56 in 1918 and 37 in 1919. Business, labor, and politicians all agreed that something needed to be done. The obvious answer to the problem was the successful transition to a peacetime economy and the restoration of the international economic order. There was also widespread agreement that massive infusions of investment capital were needed to rebuild the economic infrastructure. Creating a favorable climate to attract capital from German and foreign investors would require currency stability, and that in turn meant curbing the inflation and providing for political stability. Finally, the structural problems of East Elbian agriculture were no closer to a solution after the war than they had been before the conflict began.

Identifying the milestones on the road to recovery proved considerably easier than overcoming the practical and political obstacles that stood in the way. In fact, a number of politically astute decisions had economically counterproductive consequences. Guaranteeing veterans an immediate return to their old jobs defused a potentially volatile social problem, but it also saddled employers with unneeded labor and precluded necessary geographic and occupational shifts in the workforce. Similar objections could be raised against some of the immediate postwar wage settlements. The increased wage scales for public-sector employees, such as railroad workers, inflated government budgets at a time when they were already out of control. Until the fiscal year 1925, government budgets at all levels—federal, state, and local—showed annual and growing deficits. Chronic budget deficits in turn had an adverse effect on the German economy's ability to raise investment capital. Government borrowing not only competed for investment money along with the private sector, but the deficits fueled the inflation, which led to further political unrest and subsequent discouragement especially of foreign investment.

The Germans attempted to address their immediate postwar dilemma in two ways. One stood the test of time, although it had little immediate impact; the other had only disastrous short- and long-term consequences. The solution with long-term benefits involved a new revenue system: As we saw, the National Assembly adopted a much needed restructuring of the Reich's system of taxation and revenue allocation. By shifting the bulk of taxation from property and consumer revenues to personal and corporate income taxes, the National Finance Act of 1919 created a more rational and less regressive system of taxation. Unfortunately, these changes in the tax structure did not significantly increase the amount of revenue gleaned from an impoverished country. Recognizing the desperate need for capital, the Reichsbank, the German equivalent of the Federal Reserve System, made what in retrospect was a disastrous move: It printed money in the hope that the economic recovery would mitigate the obviously inflationary consequences of this decision. Indeed, the bank authorized the printing of a great deal of money. In the period 1919–1921, the money in circulation increased each year by 50 percent over the previous year.

For reasons that were numerous and complex, economic recovery did not materialize. Certainly, Germany's political instability (see the discussion on pp. 127ff.) was a major factor. In addition, it proved difficult to restore the traditional trade patterns. Some partners and competitors, like the United States, had benefited from the wartime absence of the Germans on the international markets. Quite generally, Germany's trading partners protected their home markets with tariff legislation, and the Reich inadvertently encouraged such retaliation by shortsightedly engaging in large-scale dumping practices. The low value of the mark, of course, made German exports relatively cheap, but this advantage was more than offset by the rapidly rising cost of raw materials and foodstuffs on which the German economy remained heavily dependent. The country's economic difficulties can be readily gauged by the mark's declining value relative to the dollar, the strongest postwar currency: From January 1919 to October 1922, the value of the mark fell from 8.9 to 4,500 to the dollar.

The Germans certainly recognized the problem, but until the fall of 1923, they also largely ignored it. The primary reason was the ready availability of a scapegoat for inflation and economic difficulties: reparations. Basically, the Allies intended the reparations imposed on Germany to be simple financial transactions to compensate the victors for some of their wartime expenses in the form of cash and goods. In practice, things were considerably more complicated. To begin with, there was disagreement among the Allies on which losses the payments should cover. They agreed that Germany should pay for the recovery of the areas in Belgium and France that had been devastated by war and compensate the British for the loss of freighters sunk by submarines. Such a view of reparations was a fairly narrow and traditional one. But there were also those in the Allied countries who argued that reparations should encompass a much wider scope. Germany, for example, should be responsible for underwriting the pensions of Allied war veterans.

Then there was the question of the link between the German reparations and the inter-Allied war debt problem. The latter issue in turn had two major dimensions. Before and during the war, France (and to a lesser extent Great Britain) had made large loans to czarist Russia. When the Bolsheviks came to power, these sums became bad debts; the new Russian government refused to accept responsibility for them. While the European Allies had loaned money to Russia they had in turn borrowed heavily from the United States. The American government and banks insisted that these loans would have to be repaid with interest. The European Allies, however, found themselves in a difficult position. With the Russian loans lost, the German reparations remained the only readily accessible source of assets both to generate recovery in the Allied countries and enable them to meet their obligations to America.

In April 1921, the Allies presented Germany with a reparations bill of 132 billion gold marks ($31.4 billion in 1914 terms) to be paid over a number of years in the form of both money and goods. The initial German reaction was to reject this sum as far too high and patently unjust. There was almost universal agreement among German labor, business, and government leaders that Germany's gross national product was simply not large enough to bear additional obligations of 132 billion gold marks. But after another government crisis and the occupation by French troops of the city of Duisburg, the Reich government agreed to yield to the Allied dictum.

The Allies were less than sympathetic toward Germany's cries of poverty. There was clear evidence that although the German government might have been poor, the Germans were considerably more wealthy. That is to say, the Allies complained that the German government was something less than forceful in taxing the often sizable assets that remained in private hands. The French in particular suspected that the Germans were husbanding their resources to regain their military strength. Allied control teams reported that there seemed to be secret paramilitary groups all over Germany, often trained by regular army officers, with hidden caches of arms. (The Allied officers tended to overlook, however, that much of this activity was not directed against a foreign enemy but constituted preparations for overthrowing Germany's democratic government.)

Although the Allies presented a united front toward Germany on the reparations issue, they differed on the best approach for collecting the German debt. Generally speaking, Belgium, France, and Italy formed a hawkish bloc while Great Britain took a more dovish approach. The reason for England's differentiated attitude was not so much credence in Germany's claims of poverty as concern for the revival of international trade. Increasingly, Great Britain recognized that without German recovery there would be little hope of a return to Europe's prewar prosperity. The Germans, of course, were aware of England's disagreement with the other Allies and tended to harbor quite unrealistic hopes that England would "mediate" the dispute.

The Germans grasped at the British straw at least in part because they had so few other options. True, a few diehard armchair strategists envisioned a scenario in which Germany would simply refuse to honor its reparations obligations, but more responsible leaders recognized that this would have meant the rapid disintegration of the Reich. To demonstrate its earnestness on the reparations issue, the Reich government turned to something called the "fulfillment policy." This strategy was the brainchild of two men: Joseph Wirth, a left-wing Center Party leader who served as Reich chancellor from May 1921 to November 1922, and his minister for recovery (and later foreign minister), Walther Rathenau.

The fulfillment policy was not mere subterfuge on the part of Rathenau and Wirth. These leaders were truly convinced that the country did not have the resources to continue reparations payments for any length of time. In his capacity as minister for reconstruction, Rathenau took the lead in attempts to negotiate a series of agreements with the French that would have converted some of Germany's cash payments into alternative forms of compensation, such as supplying German laborers for construction work in the devastated areas of France. The fulfillment policy was also a deliberate and dangerous gamble. Its supporters hoped an honest and committed effort on the part of the Germans to pay their bills for a time would convince those on the Allied side with a truly open mind that even with the best of intentions the reparations system was not workable.

The fulfillment policy did not succeed. In Germany inflation continued unabated. The mark fell from 4,500 to the dollar in October 1922 to 18,000 in January 1923. In part to escape its diplomatic isolation (see the discussion on pp. 135–36), the Reich concluded a friendship pact with Soviet Russia. The Treaty of Rapallo (April 1922) contained a clause providing for the mutual cancellation of debts. In French eyes this was an attempt on the part of the Germans to set a precedent for escaping the Reich's obligations toward the Allies. Even more disastrous for the continuation of the fulfillment policy was the murder of Walther Rathenau in June 1922 by extreme right-wing terrorists.

The unequal struggle over reparations came to a head in the Ruhr crisis of 1923. Wirth had been succeeded by Wilhelm Cuno, a Catholic shipping magnate with close ties to the right wing of the DVP and wide-ranging prewar connections to American and English shipping interests. In December 1922, the Germans were, once again, behind in their reparations payments. (At issue was a shipment of telegraph poles.) The right-of-center French government, headed by a conservative, Raymond Poincaré, distrusted Germany's intentions and asked the reparations

Im Mittelpunkt Walther Rathenau (1867–1922)

Walther Rathenau experienced both the triumph and the tragedy of Germany's Jews before the Holocaust. He was a true Renaissance man: a successful industrialist, brilliant wartime administrator, as well as a profound thinker and mystic. He was a Jew who was at times highly critical of his fellow Jews, especially the Zionists, whom he held responsible for much of the anti-Semitism of his age. And yet as a Jew he was also hated by the right-wing extremists, who would eventually assassinate him.

Rathenau was born in 1867. His father had founded the Allgemeine Elektrizitäts-Gesellschaft (AEG), a major manufacturer of electrical appliances and electrical engineering products. Rathenau joined the AEG's board of directors in 1899, and became CEO of the company after his father's death in 1915. Under Rathenau's leadership the AEG became Germany's most important electrical products company, in many ways comparable to the General Electric Company in the United States.

A fervent German patriot, during World War I Rathenau helped the war effort in a variety of ways, most notably as head of the War Ministry's Raw Materials Department, the office which was responsible for allocating Germany's scarce resources in the most efficient manner possible.

After the war Rathenau became active in politics. He joined the liberal German Democratic Party, and in 1921, served as minister for reconstruction in the cabinet of Josef Wirth. As a member of the cabinet, Rathenau was the primary architect of the failed "fulfillment policy." He wanted Germany to demonstrate the sincerity of its effort to pay the reparations, but he was also convinced the payments which the Allies imposed constituted an unfair and impossible burden on the young republic.

In 1922, Wirth, who was Rathenau's close friend, asked the industrialist to serve as Germany's foreign minister. In his new position Rathenau continued his efforts to establish better relations with the Western powers, but his short tenure in the job was most notable for improving relations between the Weimar Republic and the Soviet Union. In the spring of 1922, Rathenau and the Soviet foreign minister Chichirin negotiated what became the Treaty of Rapollo. With this pact Germany and the Soviet Union agreed to recognize each other diplomatically and to cancel their mutual financial obligations.

For the sick minds of two extreme rightists, Erwin Kern and Hermann Fischer, here was indisputable proof of the international Jewish conspiracy: The German Jew Rathenau and the Russian Jew Chichirin had forged a pact to put Germany and Europe under Jewish control. In June 1922, the two men killed Rathenau as he was riding in an open car in Berlin.

The assassination unleashed a tremendous wave of popular sympathy for the foreign minister. It also led to one of the most dramatic and moving speeches in German parliamentary history. In the eulogy for his slain friend, Chancellor Wirth dramatically pointed to the right side of the Reichstag, proclaiming "there is the enemy. The enemy is on the Right." Wirth was convinced—rightly so—that the persistent anti-Semitism of the DNVP had sown the seeds of hatred that resulted in Rathenau's death.

The assassination did have one positive consequence. Shocked by the wave of home-grown terror, the Reichstag passed the Law for the Protection of the Republic, which set in motion substantial and successful efforts to punish political crimes in all of the German states, except Bavaria.

commission, a body consisting of representatives from France, Belgium, Italy, and Great Britain that monitored the reparations schedule, to declare the Reich in default of its treaty obligations. By a vote of three to one (the British representative cast the negative vote), the commission declared Germany in default and authorized France and Belgium

The disastrous effects of the 1923 hyperinflation. A housewife starts the fire in her kitchen stove with worthless banknotes. (Source: Courtesy of Library of Congress.)

to take punitive action. In early January the two countries moved a contingent of engineers, accompanied by a small military force, into previously unoccupied parts of the Ruhr region to oversee the operations of the coal mines in that area. Ostensibly, their purpose was to ensure that coal earmarked for France and Belgium was actually shipped.

There was something rather tragicomic about the coming test of wills. To begin with, by the time the Allied engineers (the

delegation went by the acronym of MICUM, *Mission interalliée pour la contrôle des usines et des mines* [Interallied Control Commission for Factories and Mines]) arrived on the scene, there was not a great deal to supervise. Anticipating the vote of the reparations commission, the Germans had transferred the records of the German coal syndicate from Essen to Hamburg some days before the French and Belgians moved into the Ruhr. In addition, the Germans were convinced the real aim of the French was to sever the Ruhr area from the Reich and consequently destroy Germany's national unity. As far as Poincaré and the French government were concerned, this was not true, and the Germans' misreading of French and Belgian intentions led to what in retrospect turned out to be a disastrous overreaction. Recognizing the Reich's inability to oppose the Allied moves with military force, the German government resorted to a policy of passive resistance. This meant political and economic leaders in the Ruhr, with the full support of the Reich and Prussian governments, called on the population of the occupied area to stage what amounted to a general strike. Less coal was mined in the months from January to September than in the first ten days of the year.

While passive resistance inconvenienced the occupiers, their difficulties were minor compared to those the Germans caused for themselves. The Cuno government supported the idle population of Germany's industrial heartland with federal cash grants-in-aid. In effect, passive resistance was financed by authorizing the indiscriminate printing of money. The result was to open the floodgates of uncontrolled inflation. Between early January and November 15, 1923, when inflation was finally brought under control, the German mark in relation to the U.S. dollar fell from an already unprecedented 18,000 to the dollar to an astronomical 4.2 trillion. The social and economic consequences of state-sponsored inflation were enormous and disastrous. Tax collections (and government budgets) became meaningless as money lost its value by the hour. Worse, lifetime savings vanished overnight while economic life was reduced to barter.

Passive resistance was a game of chicken played with unequal resources and for the highest stakes. The Cuno government gambled that once passive resistance had demonstrated Germany's resolve, the French and Belgians would recognize the failure of their adventure in the Ruhr and reopen negotiations on the reparations question. And even if the French proved stubborn, surely the British would make them see the folly of their ways. Neither scenario came true. The French and Belgians showed no signs of weakening for nine long months, and although the British remained critical of hawkish policies, they were not about to abandon their wartime allies and back the Germans. In the meantime, the German situation was growing desperate. Inflation and the obvious lack of political leadership brought within sight the day in which the country would sink into chaos.

On September 23, the Germans called "chicken." The Cuno cabinet resigned, and a new "grand coalition" Reich government headed by Gustav Stresemann and composed of ministers from the DVP, the DDP, the SPD, and the Center Party announced the end of passive resistance. Simultaneously the government declared a state of emergency throughout the Reich to deal with the political and economic aftermath of the Reich's diplomatic capitulation.

Stresemann and his minister of finance, Hans Luther (who had no party affiliation), recognized that the end of passive resistance would have to be followed by immediate currency restabilization. Unlike their predecessors, they succeeded. Drawing on ideas that had been floated earlier, the Stresemann cabinet authorized the establishment of a new bank, the *Rentenbank* (Mortgage Bank). The new agency in turn issued certificates of credit (*Rentenmark*) that had the force of money. The certificates were backed by a mortgage on Germany's agricultural and industrial assets, which was assigned to the Rentenbank. In a sense, it was a psychological trick because foreclosure of such a "mortgage" was unrealistic, but, largely because the evils of inflation had become so patently obvious, no one pointed out that the new currency was an emperor without clothes. On November 15, 1923 (ironically, it was the day on which the old mark reached its lowest exchange value of 4.2 trillion to the dollar), the new Rentenmark officially replaced the old mark; it was pegged at the prewar value to the dollar of 4.2.

Four years after the end of the war Germans surveyed the ruins of failed recovery policies. Problems brought on by the war had been compounded by runaway inflation. Severe social dislocation and further political polarization pursued each other in a vicious cycle of cause and effect. The seeming miracle of restabilizing the currency in the fall of 1923, was at best a first step toward revitalizing an economy that had for almost ten years lived beyond its means.

COUNTERREVOLUTION

The first four years of the Weimar Republic were extraordinarily unstable times, characterized by widespread political violence. Both the extreme left and the radical right engaged in political violence, but right-wing activities constituted the more acute danger to the Weimar Republic. A primary cause of the chronic political unrest on the right was the unwillingness of many individuals and groups in the society to accept the new democratic and parliamentary constitutional system. They became part of the "counterrevolutionary" movement that sought to undo the "revolution" of November 1918. It mattered little to them that the upheavals of 1918, hardly deserved the name of revolution. The counterrevolutionaries were rebelling against an imagined present evil to restore either a mythical past or bring about a utopian future.

The mentality of counterrevolutionaries had a number of sources. Many in the generation that fought in World War I had a sense that the reality of peace fell short of the promise of war. The conflict destroyed their faith in progress, rationality in human affairs, and the desirability of civilian comfort and security. Intellectuals among them agreed with the conclusion of Eckert von Sydow's book, *The Culture of Decadence*, published in 1921, that periods of decadence and turmoil were also eras of heightened creativity.

Metaphysicians, of course, were relatively rare among the counterrevolutionaries. Most joined their ranks for more mundane reasons, although these, too, could be intellectualized. Complaints that the world of individual honor and courage had been replaced by union bosses, war profiteers, and masses acting through their undisciplined weight of numbers could also be read as resentment, particularly among the ranks of younger officers, that the republic had failed to provide them with peacetime positions they felt were commensurate with their service and sacrifices to the nation.

Ironically, the republican government provided the organizational format with which the counterrevolutionaries would attempt to overthrow parliamentary democracy. At the end of 1918, and well into the next year, the republican state and federal cabinets authorized and financed the organization of volunteer military units, so-called *Freikorps* (Freecorps). The Freikorps were envisioned as a strictly stop-gap measure to supplement the inadequate regular armed forces in order to deal with the January 1919, "second revolution" and Polish encroachments in the east. The Freikorps ranged in size from a few hundred men to eight thousand; the leaders were for the most part junior- and middle-level officers of the old army. Eventually, the combined number of these vigilante forces reached some 280,000 men organized in 200 Freikorps. The fighters were recruited from a quite narrow age and social spectrum. Members of the middle and upper middle classes predominated, with high school and university students, military cadets, and sons of farmers particularly strongly represented. Blue-collar workers were noticeably underrepresented in the Freikorps.

Unfortunately, many members of the volunteer units, and particularly some of the groups' leaders, were not content to limit their political and military activism to short-term emergency service. With varying degrees of sincerity and sophistication, a minority among them—their number is estimated to have been about thirty thousand—came to believe that their experiences in the war and their success in "saving Germany from Bolshevism" had lifted them to a higher stage of consciousness, that of political soldier. The prose writings of Freikorps leaders are often confused, but two leitmotifs are contempt for the civilian pursuits of political compromise, career, and comfort, and calls for action to create "the future century of other-directed totality," as Ernst von Salomon put it.

Some of these politicized soldiers were attracted to Germany's embryonic version of fascism. Especially in Bavaria a large number of *völkisch* political organizations sprang to life. (Translating the word *völkisch* into English has always represented something of a problem. Literally, it refers to "people" or "folk," but in political terms those who identified themselves as völkisch used the term with clear implications of chauvinism, racism, and anti-Semitism.) Although one group, the Nazi Party (*Nationalsozialistische Deutsche Arbeiterpartei*—NSDAP), would eventually eclipse its rivals, it was originally only one of some forty völkisch counterrevolutionary organizations active in Munich in early 1919. Moreover, there was little to distinguish the various groups from each other. All professed an ideology that was essentially an amalgam of anti's: They were all antidemocratic, anti-Marxist, antiparliamentary, and anti-Semitic. The last programmatic feature was a reflection of the fascists' conviction that there was an international Jewish conspiracy responsible not only for Germany's defeat in World War I but also for Germany's own revolution and all other left-wing revolutions.

The distinct minority of political soldiers among the Freikorps and the as-yet lunatic fringe fascist groups would not have been strong enough to cast Germany into four years of unending revolutionary turmoil. This became possible only because of the support these elements received from parts of the mainstream conservative political forces and elements of the regular army. Support came in various forms: editorial, organizational, financial, and, especially in the case of the Reichswehr, weapons and training. The sym-

pathizers supported the aims (if not always the means) of the counterrevolutionaries, because they, too, looked on parliamentary democracy as the ruin of Germany. In addition, these circles were also convinced the country lived under the constant threat of a Bolshevik-style revolution.

Ironically, the Communists' own activities gave an air of verisimilitude to these irrational fears. We have already noted the attempt by Spartacus and the Revolutionary Shop Stewards to stage a "second revolution" in January 1919. A few weeks later, Bavaria was thrown into turmoil after Kurt Eisner was murdered by a member of the extreme right-wing Thule Society. The eventual results were two Bavarian "soviet republics," one dominated by some anarchists in Munich and the other by the Communists. The first lasted for a week, the second for two weeks before both were bloodily put down by Freikorps and regular army troops, but the brief experience left a lasting impression on many middle-class Bavarians.

The communist threat did not seem to lessen after 1919. In the spring of 1920, left-wing socialists and Communists organized the "Red Army of the Ruhr." Again, with great cruelty, regular army units and Freikorps put down the uprising. In the spring of 1921, Communists were responsible for more political violence; the "revolution" was now centered in the central German region of Halle-Merseburg. This time it required only regular Prussian police forces to restore order.

The Ruhr crisis of 1923, seemed to provide the "Bolsheviks" with yet more opportunities. The Communists had gained a political base of operations by joining coalition governments with the SPD in the central German states of Saxony and Thuringia, and the growing economic problems increased the appeal of left-wing extremism among blue-collar workers. Still, it was all bluff. In the fall of 1923, Saxony and Thuringia were taken over by a federal executor backed by Reichswehr troops. There was another outbreak of violence in October 1923 in the city of

Hamburg, but this, too, was an ill-prepared, localized affair. Order was quickly restored by the police.

An even more powerful catalyst in providing support for counterrevolution from the right were the myths and realities surrounding the Treaty of Versailles. The peace treaty formed a large component in the political mythology of the right. Its spokesmen incessantly claimed not only that the pact was unjust but that Germany's own democratic government was guilty of treason for agreeing to sign the onerous treaty. The Freikorps also opposed the Treaty of Versailles because under its provisions the Reich government was committed to disbanding these units by April 1920. At least some members of the vigilante groups were determined to overthrow the republican government rather than accept the end of their paramilitary careers.

The politicized Freikorps, then, were united in their stand against Versailles, democracy, and dissolution. The first serious threat to the republic from the right came during the Kapp-Lüttwitz putsch ("putsch" can be translated as "coup") just before the April 1920 dissolution deadline. This episode—and it was little more than that—was named after the two principal activists in the drama, General Walther von Lüttwitz, the commander of the Reichswehr's Berlin district, and Wolfgang Kapp, a frustrated politician and East Prussian agricultural official. Lüttwitz was a simpleminded officer who was convinced a military dictatorship would solve all of Germany's problems; Kapp was something of a professional conspirator, who delighted in drawing up grandiose plans and inventing secret codes. Both men, and the bevy of DNVP and DVP politicians with whom they were in contact, relied on one of the most politicized among the Freikorps, the Ehrhardt Brigade, to carry out the actual putsch.

This unit, named for its commander, the former marine commandant Hermann Ehrhardt, was stationed at Döberitz, a major army post located only some 20 kilometers from the capital. In its politics the Ehrhardt Brigade clearly sympathized with extreme rightist and völkisch ideas. In the early morning hours of March 13, 1920, the brigade, as well as some regular army units under Lüttwitz's command, seized control of Berlin. There was no resistance from either the police or other Reichswehr troops; the army leadership declared it would remain at "parade rest." Initially, the coup seemed to be an instant success. The Reich ministers hurriedly left the capital. Kapp appointed himself Reich chancellor and named Lüttwitz as minister of defense.

The Kapp-Lüttwitz putsch soon demonstrated, however, that far-right conspirators were no less amateurs than their rivals on the extreme left. The rule of Kapp and Lüttwitz was marked by confusion and ineptitude, and the supporters of the republic did not remain idle. A paralyzing general strike, called by all three branches of organized labor a few hours after the Ehrhardt Brigade had marched into the city, shut off utilities in Berlin and made travel all but impossible. The Reich and Prussian civil service refused to carry out the conspirators' orders. After five days the putsch collapsed; the coup's leaders took refuge in more hospitable climates. The old government seemed to return almost as quickly as it had been overthrown. With a few new faces, a cabinet of the Weimar coalition parties (SPD, DDP, and Center Party) was returned to power.

Despite its swift collapse, the Kapp-Lüttwitz putsch had important consequences for the future development of the counterrevolution in Germany. Although the coup failed in northern Germany, a parallel effort succeeded in Bavaria. The commander of the Munich *Reichswehr* district, General Arnold von Möhl, forced the democratically elected Bavarian state government to resign. In its place moved a commissioner of the army's choosing, Gustav von Kahr. The new Bavarian leader was an old-line Catholic conservative whose major political goal was the restoration of the Bavarian monarchy. Because he saw the existence of the German Republic as an obstacle to realizing this plan (the Weimar constitution guaranteed a republican form of government in all federal states), Kahr

A poster urging passive resistance during the Ruhr crisis. A tough German worker defies French soldiers. The caption reads, "No! You won't subdue me!" (Source: akg-images.)

welcomed as allies the counterrevolutionary forces that were equally determined to overthrow democracy, albeit for different reasons. Under the state commissioner's rule, Bavaria became a haven for extreme right fugitives from justice. (After the putsch, Ehrhardt, for example, lived openly in Munich.) In addition, the Kahr regime welcomed the activities of Bavaria's numerous indigenous extreme rightist groups, including the fledgling Nazi Party.

Putsches were not the only means used by the extreme right to destabilize democracy. Counterrevolutionary rightists also resorted to individual acts of terror. Both Matthias Erzberger, the former Reich minister of finance, and Walther Rathenau were murdered by assassins with clear ties to the extreme right scene. However, the death of Rathenau, the popular Jewish Reich foreign minister, in June 1922 also spurred the Reich government to take effective countermeasures. Rathenau's friend, Chancellor Wirth, took advantage of the spontaneous outcry of revulsion against the right-wing terrorists and persuaded the Reichstag to pass the Law for the Protection of the Republic. The measure made it a crime to engage in antirepublican activities and set up a special federal court to try those violating the new statute.

Unfortunately, national legislation could do little to curtail the activities of the counterrevolutionaries in Bavaria. The Kahr regime argued that the Law for the Protection of the Republic violated Bavaria's states' rights, and in any case the new federal court duplicated the work of the state's own People's Courts, which had been established in 1919 to try leftist revolutionaries. With the Ruhr crisis looming on the horizon, the Reich government was unwilling to risk a conflict over states' rights, so that in practical terms, Bavaria remained an exceedingly friendly environment for right-wing counterrevolutionary groups and plots.

The extreme right welcomed the Ruhr crisis as a boon to its cause. During the period of passive resistance, the counterrevolutionaries engaged in acts of sabotage against the occupation forces and the minuscule pro-French separatist organizations in western Germany. Above all, however, they expected that the end of passive resistance would enable them to move against the republican government because they would now be able to claim that the democratic leaders had given in to the foreign enemy and failed to save Germany from imminent communist revolution.

Their hopes remained unfulfilled. Contrary to what the extreme right had expected, the Stresemann cabinet's swift declaration of a state of emergency preserved law and order in most parts of the Reich. Under the terms of the decrees, responsibility for administering the state of emergency was in the hands of both the Reichswehr and the states' civilian authorities. In contrast to its behavior in 1920, the Reichswehr in 1923, remained actively loyal to the Weimar constitution—at least in the states outside of Bavaria.

These developments were not welcome news for the Bavarian conspirators. They had been actively planning the overthrow of the republic throughout the spring and summer of 1923. The numerous völkisch parties mounted a massive propaganda campaign to mobilize public opinion against the democratic Reich government. Simultaneously, paramilitary organizations sent their members on training missions and field maneuvers. The expectation was that when the signal for the uprising came, various paramilitary organizations, units of the Reichswehr, and the Bavarian government would cooperate in deploying the counterrevolutionary forces on their march to Berlin. On paper, the whole operation was very much modeled on Benito Mussolini's successful march on Rome a year earlier.

The political side of the planned Bavarian putsch for the first time focused widespread public attention on the leader of the Nazi Party, Adolf Hitler. The chairman of this small völkisch group was born on April 20, 1889, in the Austrian border town of Braunau. Orphaned as a teenager, Hitler had ambitions to become an artist but did poorly in school and eventually drifted to Vienna and later Munich. In 1914, Hitler volunteered for the

German army and served with some distinction in a Bavarian regiment. The future Nazi leader was mustered out as a lance corporal in 1918, but he remained a civilian employee of the army. In this capacity he lectured in a political indoctrination program, which some officers organized for their soldiers to "immunize" them against leftist political ideas.

In addition to his duties as a military propagandist, Hitler was also responsible for reporting on the activities of the various völkisch groups in Munich and recommending to his military superiors those that warranted receiving subsidies from secret army funds. In the course of his observations of Munich's völkisch scene, Hitler became acquainted with the *Deutsche Arbeiterpartei* (German Workers' Party—DAP), a minuscule group that had been founded by a Munich toolmaker in the spring of 1919. Hitler joined the party, quickly becoming its chief of propaganda and leading speaker. In 1920, the party was renamed the National Socialist German Workers' Party (NSDAP), and in

July 1921, Hitler became the real leader of the Nazi Party. Although he quit his job with the army, the Nazi leader continued to enjoy excellent relations with the Bavarian military.

Hitler's undeniable rhetorical talents quickly propelled him to the forefront of Munich's völkisch scene, and the Bavarian counterrevolutionary leaders selected him to coordinate the political and propagandistic preparations for the planned putsch. All seemed ready for the enterprise at the beginning of November 1923. However, at the last moment the counterrevolutionaries' conservative allies in Bavaria decided to withhold their support when the commander in chief of the Reichswehr, General Hans von Seeckt, who had ambitions of his own, indicated that he would not permit the army to cooperate with the putschists at this time. Hitler and his associates, who included Ludendorff and Captain Ernst Röhm, the former commander of a key Reichswehr unit in Munich, felt betrayed by what they regarded as the cowardice of

An advertisement for a Freikorps. The soldier is drawn in the expressionist style, and the text reads: "Protect your homeland. Join the Freikorps Hülsen." (Source: Julius E. F. Gipkens/Library of Congress Prints and Photographs Division [LC-USZC4-11607].)

Kahr and his military allies. Hitler decided to stage the "National Revolution" without the conservatives' cooperation, although he still hoped that the state commissioner and the Reichswehr would jump on the bandwagon once the popularity of the putschists' cause had been demonstrated.

The effort failed. Hitler and some members of the NSDAP's own paramilitary unit, the Stormtroopers (*Sturmabteilung*— SA), literally crashed a rally organized by Kahr in a Munich beer hall to explain the state commissioner's decision to delay the expected putsch. Von Kahr and the Bavarian Reichswehr commander, General Otto von Lossow (he had succeeded von Möhl in late 1922), briefly agreed to join Hitler, but within hours both changed their minds. In addition, Seeckt, when informed of the events in Munich, ordered Lossow's arrest. Hitler and Ludendorff led a demonstration of thousands through the streets of Munich on the morning of November 9, 1923. This last effort to demonstrate to the Reichswehr the counter-revolution's grassroots support failed when shots, probably fired by nervous police officers, caused panic and dispersed the crowd. Ludendorff was arrested immediately. The other conspirators, including Hitler (who was slightly injured in the melee), fled, but they were eventually rounded up and tried for treason before the Bavarian People's Court. The judges proved lenient. Recognizing the "patriotic motivation" of the defendants, they imposed extremely light punishments. Ludendorff was acquitted and Hitler sentenced to only five years in prison. The Nazi leader was paroled after serving nine months of his sentence in a very comfortable apartment at the fortress of Landsberg.

In later years Hitler's "Beer Hall putsch" was to occupy a large place in Nazi mythology, but in reality, like the Kapp putsch, it was a dismal failure. Why did the counterrevolution fail? One reason, clearly, was the ineptitude of the counterrevolutionaries themselves. The Kapp-Lüttwitz coup was badly organized, and the Hitler-Ludendorff putsch was a hastily improvised alternative after the original premise proved unworkable. In addition, the republic had some powerful supporters. The loyalty of the labor unions proved decisive in 1920; their activism was not needed in 1923. Most significant, however, was the attitude of many mainstream conservatives in the army and the civil service. Much as they desired the end of democracy, many recoiled when confronted with the choice of taking up arms against the Reich government and risking the danger of civil war. Hitler, who in 1923, had no qualms about such a step, complained eloquently about the fickleness of the conservative establishment. The experience was a bitter lesson for him but one from which he learned well.

FOREIGN RELATIONS

The Reich's defeat in World War I not only ended Germany's dream of becoming a decisive factor in the global balance of power but also deprived the country of the hegemonic position in Central Europe it had held since 1871. For the foreseeable future, the Reich would be an object of, rather than a partner in, the conduct of international relations.

In the months between the signing of the armistice and the announcement of the peace terms, German foreign policy was essentially limited to dampening the fires of dissatisfaction in the Reich's border areas and eliciting sympathy abroad for the new Germany's difficulties and aims. The effort was not without success. The various separatist and autonomist movements had little popular support, and it soon became clear that the Allies, too, had no interest in dismantling the Reich. Indeed, in the Baltic areas of Estonia, Latvia, Lithuania, and parts of northern Poland, Freikorps and regular army units operated for some time with the tacit approval of the Allies. Their ostensible purpose was to prevent Bolshevik incursions into the region, but it was an open secret that the German government was equally concerned about the growth of Polish power.

As we saw earlier, the territorial losses imposed by the Treaty of Versailles were not as onerous as they might have been. True, Alsace-Lorraine was lost to the Reich, but the Allies did not permit Poland to extend its western borders to the Oder-Neisse line (present-day Germany's border with Poland), nor was a new Confederation of the Rhine constituted. In addition, a number of plebiscites in areas of mixed population proved gratifying to the German cause. The bulk of East Prussia, a considerable portion of Silesia, and much of Schleswig voted to remain in Germany. In fact, it could be argued that with two notable exceptions Germany's post-1918 boundaries reflected the true wishes of the populations concerned.

The exceptions were Silesia and Austria. In the first case the Allies, in partial violation of the results of the plebiscite, decreed that for economic reasons the bulk of coal-rich Upper Silesia should go to Poland. In the case of Austria the people had voted overwhelmingly to join the German republic, but the Allies prohibited the union because they felt a Reich that included both Germany and Austria would endanger the new balance of power in southeastern Europe.

After the Reich had grudgingly agreed to sign the peace treaty, Germany's and France's roles in the dynamics of European power relations were essentially reversed from what they had been in 1871. As the new hegemonic power in Central Europe, it was now in France's interest to isolate Germany diplomatically. In the next few years, France established an intricate system of alliances, the *cordon sanitaire* ("belt of safety"), between itself and the newly independent powers of eastern and southeastern Europe. France obligated itself to come to the aid of Poland, Rumania, Czechoslovakia, and Yugoslavia if the territorial or political integrity of these nations were threatened either by Germany or a power allied to the Reich. The latter provision was directed against both a resurrected Habsburg Empire and the possibility of a Russo-German rapprochement.

Much as France had done after 1871, Germany sought to break out of the diplomatic isolation the Treaty of Versailles had imposed on it. Realistically, only two paths were open to accomplish this aim: One was reaching a modus vivendi with one or more of the Western Allies, and the other involved an arrangement with the other pariah in international relations, Soviet Russia. Both scenarios contained considerable risks. An agreement with the West would give additional impetus to the counterrevolutionary right because France in particular would not accept Germany back into the family of nations unless the Reich acknowledged it was no longer a Great Power. An entente with Soviet Russia involved relations with a power whose avowed aim was the spread of revolution throughout the world.

The foreign policy of the early republican governments toward the Western Allies was not notably successful. France remained distrustful of German intentions. A much-heralded international conference at Genoa in April 1922, attended by Germany and its former enemies including the United States and Soviet Russia, failed to break the deadlock over the linkage of reparations and inter-Allied war debts. As we saw, the Ruhr crisis of 1923, was a severe economic and diplomatic defeat for Germany. The Reich's attempts to drive a wedge between England and France were unsuccessful; Great Britain remained firmly on the side of France.

At first glance, Russo-German relations took a more promising turn. Substantively, however, the results were rather less impressive. To begin with, the two powers had little to offer each other besides mutual commiseration as international outcasts. The Russian civil war had brought that country's economy to the brink of collapse, so its role as a trading partner was negligible. The German government continued to be suspicious of the close relations between Soviet Russia and the German Communists. Nevertheless, increasing frustrations over its failure to achieve a modus vivendi with the Western Allies led Germany, in 1922, to play the Russian card.

A thoughtful Hitler glances out from his comfortable quarters at the Landsberg prison after the failed Beer Hall putsch. Note that he is not required to wear prison garb but could continue to wear his regular clothes. (Source: Courtesy of Library of Congress.)

The move was a reactive maneuver rather than a bold new initiative. Russian overtures suggesting the normalization of relations between the two countries had been forthcoming for some time. They culminated in the draft of a treaty that the Soviet foreign minister G. V. Chicherin presented to the Germans when he stopped in Berlin on his way to the Genoa Conference. After the failure of the reparations conference, the Wirth government, with the full approval of Reich president Ebert, authorized Rathenau to initial the Russo-German draft treaty.

The resulting Treaty of Rapallo (Rapallo is a suburb of Genoa) implied far more than it delivered. The agreement contained no secret clauses and its published terms were innocuous enough. Germany and Russia accorded each other diplomatic recognition, agreed to a mutual cancellation of debts, and resumed normal commercial relations. These provisions were significant, but they hardly changed the balance of power in Europe. The diplomatic impact of the Treaty of Rapallo was related to what the pact was rumored to contain: a secret military alliance directed primarily against Poland. Such Russo-German cooperation clearly would have had implications for the strength of the cordon sanitaire and the viability of the Versailles system. In fact, the treaty contained no such provisions, but from the perspective of the Western Allies, and particularly France, the Treaty of Rapallo was yet more evidence that Germany was continuing its efforts to escape the consequences of its defeat in World War I. (Incidentally, France's distrust was not entirely unjustified. Even before the Rapallo Treaty the Red Army and the Reichswehr agreed to cooperate, and throughout the 1920s, the Reichswehr used the Russian connection to develop military hardware prohibited under the terms of the Treaty of Versailles. The Germans also made use of training facilities in Russia.)

On balance, the treaty probably brought more disadvantages than advantages to the Reich. It undoubtedly increased France's distrust of Germany's foreign policy aims. France's desire to demonstrate its strength was one factor in its decision to occupy the Ruhr in early 1923. Domestically, the counterrevolutionary right in Germany saw the Treaty of Rapallo as further evidence of the workings of the international Jewish conspiracy: This myth contributed to the assassination of Rathenau two months after he had signed the Treaty of Rapallo.

The foreign policy record of the republic's first five years, then, was not impressive. Despite some sincere attempts to face realistically Germany's new position as a lesser power, successive Reich governments had not been able to achieve Germany's reintegration into the family of nations. A largely symbolic pact with a destitute and weak Soviet Russia was clearly no substitute for achieving this primary objective.

CONCLUSION

Looking back on the preceding five years, few Germans in late 1923, felt good about the immediate past or confident about the future. Politically, the period had been marked by almost constant internal strife. Partly as a result of the turmoil, the republic was held in low esteem by many Germans. The elections of 1919, seemed to show the strength of the reformist parties—SPD, DDP, and the Center Party—but that support eroded quickly. The Reichstag election of June 1920, already showed evidence that the Weimar Republic was destined to be a "democracy without democrats" as the right-wing Social Democratic speaker of parliament, Paul Löbe, put it. The 1920 contest showed major gains for the forces of the right—notably the DNVP and the DVP—and antiparliamentary groups on the left—the USPD and the KPD. True, these statistics were somewhat deceptive. The shock of the Kapp putsch persuaded the DVP to leave the ranks of the intransigent parties; in 1923, the right-wing liberals joined the DDP, SPD, and Center Party in a grand coalition government that ended passive resistance in the Ruhr. On the left the USPD disintegrated, but the party's dissolution hardly strengtheneds the cause of parliamentary democracy. Most of the former USPD members joined the Communists. The völkisch forces suffered a setback with the failure of the Hitler-Ludendorff putsch, but the DNVP remained a hard-line antidemocratic party, whose popularity was growing rather than declining.

The country's political developments, of course, were linked to its economic problems. Germany emerged from the war burdened with a huge internal and external debt. The Reich was also increasingly unable to control its runaway inflation. At the end of 1923, the country managed to stabilize its currency, but all of the well-known structural problems still awaited solutions.

At the same time, the last five years had also demonstrated that although the republic did not have a surfeit of enthusiastic supporters, most Germans rejected as well the available alternatives to parliamentary democracy. Repeated efforts by left-wing extremists to stage a "second revolution" failed dismally. But so did counterrevolutionary attempts by the extreme right, such as the Kapp-Lüttwitz and the Ludendorff-Hitler putsches.

In the area of international relations, all of Germany's attempts to evade accepting the consequences of the Versailles system had failed. Stonewalling the reparation demands led to France's exacting "productive guarantees" in the form of occupying various German cities. The Rapallo Treaty was a factor in France's decision to occupy the Ruhr. As we saw, this crisis resulted in economic disaster and diplomatic humiliation for Germany.

The main tasks for the future, then, were twofold: to translate recognition that there was no viable alternative to the republic into positive support for parliamentary democracy and to gain acceptance for the new Germany abroad. Reaching the first goal required a period of sustained prosperity, and a change in the country's mentality: the ideals of western pluralism had to be endorsed by the country's intellectuals and permeate Germany's *Bildungsbürgertum* much as Wilhelminian authoritarianism had done before the war. As far as foreign relations were concerned, Germany had to regain its membership in the international community, but that meant genuinely accepting its role as a second-rate power. At the end of 1923, the prospects for realizing either or both aims did not appear favorable.

CHAPTER FIVE

Fools' Gold: The Weimar Republic

1924–1930

The six years between the currency stabilization in 1924 and the resignation of the last parliamentary Reich cabinet in March 1930 were the "golden years" of the Weimar Republic. For many contemporaries, this was a time of renewed optimism for the present and hope for the future. In politics, the strength of the antidemocratic extremists seemed to be ebbing. Some sectors of the economy were finally showing signs of genuine recovery. Germany's acknowledgment in the Treaty of Locarno (see the discussion on p. 154) that it accepted the legitimacy of its 1919 western boundaries promised to inaugurate a period of goodwill between Germany and France. Membership in the League of Nations and the award of a permanent seat on the League's Council of Ten, the equivalent of the UN Security Council, signaled that—at least on paper—the Reich was no longer ostracized in the community of nations. Finally, the "golden years" are indelibly associated with a time of remarkable productivity and brilliance in Germany's cultural and artistic life.

The apparent return of stability and prosperity understandably induced a sense of self-satisfaction among those who had brought about the new order in 1918–1919. Although they had been on the defensive for the preceding five years as the republic staggered from crisis to crisis, they now took naive pride in their accomplishments. In his account of the revolution of 1918, written ten years after the events, the right-wing Social Democratic leader and Reich chancellor Hermann Müller expressed concern that his readers would take the blessings of democracy for granted. Müller should have directed his concerns elsewhere. Two years after the publication of his book entitled *Zehn Jahre Deutsche Geschichte, 1918–1928* (Ten Years of German History), parliamentary democracy in Germany was no longer functioning; the Reich president—not the Reichstag—made and unmade Reich chancellors. A few months later, the Nazis—sworn enemies of democracy but until then the butt of numerous political jokes—had become the second strongest party in the national parliament.

Unfortunately, there was another side to Weimar's golden years: Much of the glitter was fools' gold. Politically, the strength of the extremists declined, but it was only a temporary lull. Moreover, even when the extremists had little parliamentary representation, the moderate forces were never able to forge a permanent national republican consensus that might have sustained parliamentary democracy when it was faced with the problems that loomed ahead. The economic disasters to come also cast their shadows in the so-called golden years. The German economy lived on borrowed time, and the brief years of prosperity hid chronic structural difficulties and pockets of lingering recession.

In international relations "the spirit of Locarno," which sought better relations with France, was only one side of the picture. Far from welcoming Franco-German cooperation, the extreme right parties and paramilitary groups continued to foment hatred against what they called the Reich's "hereditary enemy," France. The Reichswehr, for its part, continued its efforts to escape the disarmament provisions of the Treaty of Versailles by intensifying its clandestine cooperation with the Soviet Red Army. And Weimar culture was also a culture of alienation. Germany's intellectuals and artists excelled in a variety of media, but few used their talents to support the republic and its values.

In essence, then, the golden years represented a brief hiatus before a period of new and worse crises. As we will see, the years of optimism were cut short by the advent of the Great Depression and Germany's inability to deal with the economic, political, and social consequences of this unforeseen disaster.

THE SEARCH FOR THE ELUSIVE CONSENSUS

In the middle period of the Weimar years, politics were characterized by a number of seemingly contradictory developments. The center of the political spectrum shifted to the right in national elections, but for the legislatures and governments in the major Länder the voters appeared to prefer a more leftward tilt. The parliamentary strength of the extreme right declined to virtual insignificance, but paramilitary and extraparliamentary rightist groups continued to flourish.

In May 1924 Germany held its first Reichstag election since June 1920. As was to be expected, the results reflected the political backlash from the country's economic hard times. The parties of the moderate center—SPD, DDP, Center Party, and DVP—suffered substantial losses while the extremists gained. The Communists received 3.7 million popular votes, and the Nazis, despite their leader's recent conviction for attempting to overthrow the government, obtained almost 2 million votes and sent twelve deputies to the Reichstag.

But the successful introduction of the new currency quickly eroded the electoral strength of the extremists. The national parliament elected in May proved incapable of choosing a stable government, and in December the voters were again called to the polls. This time they elected both a new Reichstag and Prussian Landtag. The new results were considerably more gratifying to the supporters of parliamentary democracy. The Nazis and the Communists each lost more than a million votes.

In the spring of 1925 a new Reich president had to be elected. At the end of February 1925 the republic's first leader, Friedrich Ebert, died. Under the provisions of the Weimar constitution, a successful candidate initially had to obtain a majority of the votes cast to be elected. Given the fragmented political scene in Germany, such an outcome was highly unlikely, and for this reason the constitution provided for a runoff election. This time a plurality of votes sufficed for victory. Furthermore, in a misguided attempt to assure as much freedom of choice as possible, the framers of the constitution did not limit the candidates in the runoff contest to those who had participated in the first round of balloting. Parties were free to nominate new candidates.

Not surprisingly, none of the candidates received the necessary majority in the first round, which was held in March. For the runoff contest, the SPD, DDP, and Center Party agreed to put forth the chairman of the Center Party and then Reich chancellor, Wilhelm Marx, as their joint candidate. In the initial contest the Communists had nominated their chairman, Ernst Thälmann, and the Nazis' candidate was Erich Ludendorff. In the runoff election the KPD refused to support the pro-republican ticket; Thälmann stayed in the race and by doing so undoubtedly helped defeat Marx. After Ludendorff's dismal showing in the first round (he received 200,000 votes out of 27 million cast), the general did not compete in the runoff. The DVP and DNVP had been expected to renominate their lackluster choice in the first contest (Karl Jarres, the mayor of Duisburg), but at the last moment they dropped Jarres and turned instead to the retired hero of World War I, Field Marshal Paul von Hindenburg. Although the seventy-six-year-old field marshal did virtually no campaigning, the old-line Junker and avowed monarchist narrowly won the election.

There were some fears that with the field marshal's election the counterrevolutionaries had accomplished peacefully what they had failed to do with violence in March 1920: turn back the clock to 1914. There is no doubt that many of those who had proposed him for the presidency hoped that, once elected, Hindenburg would pave the way for a military coup, the restoration of the monarchy, or both. Hindenburg, however, took his oath to the republican constitution seriously, and until the constitutional crisis of 1930, he exercised the functions of his office in a constitutionally correct manner. In addition, the national leaders of the DNVP for a time made their peace with the republic. During the next few years, conservative leaders actually held ministerial posts in a number of right-of-center coalition governments.

Stability in the center of the political spectrum contrasted with divisiveness and strife among the extremists. Like other European Communist parties, the KPD was deeply affected by the struggle for power among the Russian Bolshevik leaders that followed Lenin's death in 1924. Ultraleft, centrist, and rightist factions purged each other with dizzying speed in response to the Comintern's and eventually Stalin's directives. Turnover among the membership was high. A semblance of stability did not return until the end of the decade when the Stalinization of the German Communist Party was complete. In the meantime, the KPD was no serious threat to the stability of the Reich.

The Nazis and other völkische groups were also experiencing organizational difficulties. After Hitler went to jail most NSDAP members dropped out of politics, while the activists who remained disintegrated into a number of feuding sects or joined other völkische groups. Hitler himself briefly attempted to control developments from inside his prison apartment, but he soon recognized the futility of the effort and concentrated instead on writing the first volume of his autobiography *Mein Kampf* ("My Struggle").

When the Nazi leader was paroled in February 1925, he immediately set to work rebuilding the shattered party. It was an uphill struggle. Hitler essentially had to organize a new party. For some years after 1925, his primary goal was not size, but exclusivity. The NSDAP was a small, even insignificant group, but it was also very much Hitler's own party. "The Hitler Movement," as the Nazi Party now increasingly subtitled itself, had no formal ties to other völkische groups, and Hitler refused to permit party members or Stormtroopers (the Stormtroopers were the paramilitary wing of the party) to hold simultaneous memberships in any other political or paramilitary groups. (Multiple memberships were common in the völkische camp.) Hitler also benefited from Ludendorff's political self-destruction. After the general's pathetic showing in the 1925 presidential election he vanished into political oblivion.

Although Hitler successfully guarded his political turf and the NSDAP was even able to absorb a number of rival völkische groups,

Henrich Himmler in 1925 when Hitler appointed him head of the still minuscule Schutzstaffel (SS) in Bavaria. (Source: Courtesy of National Archives and Records Administration.)

during the golden years the Nazis remained a political fringe group. Since 1925 the NSDAP had concentrated its organizing efforts in the urban areas of northern Germany, but in the Reichstag elections of May 1928 the party did particularly poorly in these regions.

Supporters of the republic were also encouraged by developments in some of Germany's major Länder. In Prussia the parties of the Weimar coalition—SPD, DDP, and Center Party—retained comfortable majorities in the legislature. Indeed, in Germany's largest state in 1928, well over 60 percent of the voters cast their ballots for one of the moderate groups. As a result, Prussia was spared the frequent government crises that characterized the national scene. Otto Braun, the leader of the state's SPD, served as chief executive continuously for almost twelve years, from 1920 to 1932.

Democracy also returned to Germany's second-largest state, Bavaria. Heavily implicated in the preparations, if not the implementation, of Hitler's Beer Hall putsch, the Kahr regime was forced out of office after the coup failed. The state again became a political fief of the Bavarian People's Party (*Bayerische Volkspartei*—BVP), a staunchly Catholic and conservative, but parliamentary, group. It governed Bavaria for the remainder of the republican years.

Right-of-center cabinets were the rule for the national executive. Short-lived coalitions stretching from the DDP on the left to the Center Party and sometimes the DNVP on the right provided most of the federal cabinets. The chancellor was almost invariably a man from the Catholic Center Party; Wilhelm Marx, the chairman of the Center Party, headed four Reich governments in the span of four years.

The national elections held in May 1928 could be seen as additional evidence of the country's return to political stability. The big winner was the SPD, the staunchest pillar of democracy in Germany; the Social Democrats obtained almost 30 percent of the popular vote. Together the parties of the Weimar coalition almost reached a majority,

47 percent, and if the DVP were added, the mandate for the moderate groups was a comfortable 56 percent of the popular vote. The big losers were the antidemocratic forces on the right; the Nazis were essentially marginalized. The new Reichstag for the first time since 1923 elected a cabinet of the great coalition. Ministers from the SPD, DDP, DVP, and the Center Party formed a government under a right-wing Social Democratic chancellor, Hermann Müller.

Unfortunately the portents of continued stability were misleading. The election returns of 1928 also showed that a true republican consensus remained an elusive goal. To begin with, the strength of the Weimar coalition parties was very uneven. Although the SPD regained much of its earlier popularity, the two liberal parties continued their downward trend. The DDP was badly hurt; its overall share of the popular vote fell to less than 5 percent.

Equally ominous were the internal developments within the DNVP. Many of the party's regional leaders and most of its rank-and-file members rejected the national leadership's decision to steer the party in the direction of political moderation. At the end of 1928 the moderate national leadership, headed by Count Kuno von Westarp, was forced out by an intraparty maneuver led by the industrialist and owner of a film and newspaper empire, Alfred Hugenberg. The new leader was a fanatical opponent of parliamentary democracy. He saw the DNVP's path to power at the side of the extreme rightists, rather than in cooperation with moderate bourgeois groups.

The republic was also weakened by the premature death of Gustav Stresemann, the leader of the DVP (the right-wing liberals) in August 1929. His successor, Eduard Dingeldey, had neither the charisma nor the will to continue Stresemann's course. Instead, the DVP veered sharply to the right, attempting to occupy a position on the political spectrum that the DNVP under Hugenberg had vacated.

Above all, the basis for agreement on substantive issues among the pro-republican groups was tenuous, to say the least. For example, a major political furor arose in 1928 over defense appropriations. The specific controversy concerned the advisability of building a so-called pocket battleship, which the navy had requested. Battle cruisers were permitted under the terms of the Treaty of Versailles, although their military usefulness was the subject of fierce debates among political and military experts. The Social Democratic Reich ministers and the Prussian government both opposed the appropriation, but the bourgeois ministers, who held a majority in the Reich cabinet, insisted on the naval appropriations. When the budget proposals were made public, the traditional grassroots distrust of the military erupted into a revolt of the SPD's rank-and-file members against the party's leadership. The dissatisfaction among the membership forced the Social Democratic Reich ministers, including Chancellor Müller, into a highly embarrassing position: Their party insisted that as members of the Reichstag they vote against the budget proposals that they had endorsed as members of the Reich cabinet.

Another disquieting symptom of Germany's political malaise was the persistent presence of numerous paramilitary groups even during the republic's golden years. They represented all political camps, but most of them supported the far right. Masquerading under the guise of veterans' organizations (actually, anyone, veteran or not, who liked to turn out on Sunday afternoons to demonstrate against the republic could join), members and leaders of the right-wing paramilitary groups were contemptuous of democracy and convinced that Germany should not and need not accept the political consequences of the lost war. Instead, they hoped for the return of authoritarianism or the triumph of a "nationalist revolution." The largest and most influential of the ostensible veterans' groups was the "Steel Helmet—Association of Frontline Veterans" (*Stahlhelm—Bund der Frontsoldaten*). At one point the Steel Helmet had a membership of more than 5 million. It was also a thoroughly "respectable" organization; the Reich president himself was the *Stahlhelm's* honorary national chairman. At the same time, the group's politics were the same as those of the Hugenberg wing of the DNVP, and, like Hugenberg, in later years the Steel Helmet joined forces with the Nazis.

The problem of alienation among the aging veterans could be explained by the residual effects of the war, but this was not true for the republic's failure to win the allegiance of large numbers of Germany's high school and university students. The Weimar Republic was plagued by a chronic problem of right-wing political radicalism among its student population. Many students were active in the paramilitary groups, and as early as 1927 the German National Student Organization, following the example of its Austrian counterpart, voted to include a clause in its bylaws that would have excluded Jews from membership in the organization. The intervention of the Prussian minister of education prevented the vote from having any practical effect, but the resolution was symptomatic of the popularity of völkische ideas among the students. Long before the Nazis scored a major victory in national elections, Hitler's supporters dominated student governments in many of the German universities.

The emergence of a viable parliamentary democracy was also hindered by the proliferation of single-issue parties in the wake of the economic disasters of 1923. In some Reichstag elections, voters filling out their ballots had to make their way through a list of twenty-six parties. To be sure, few of these groups were able to obtain the 60,000 votes needed to send a representative to the national parliament, but single-issue parties did receive more than 10 percent of the national vote in the 1928 and 1930 Reichstag elections. Most of these parties pressed for economic relief of specific interest groups. Typical was the largest and politically most successful of the single-issue parties, the Economics Party (*Wirtschaftspartei*—WiP), which gave itself the subtitle "Reich Party of the German Mittelstand." In fact, the Economics Party was little more than a lobbying group for real estate interests.

The WiP demanded an end to rent control, the abolition of subsidies for the construction of public housing, and lower property taxes. Because the democratic parties had voted for all of these social welfare measures, until the final years of the republic the WiP's leaders opposed parliamentary democracy. The party's political success (in 1930 the WiP received almost 1.4 million popular votes, 4.5 percent of the total) came primarily at the expense of the left liberals, the traditional political voice of the urban middle classes.

Farmers, too, in increasing numbers deserted the traditional political parties in favor of single-issue organizations. As the crisis in agriculture foreshadowed the advent of the Great Depression (see the discussion on p. 146) numerous peasant parties appeared on the political scene, all insisting that agriculture needed protection in the form of tariffs and cheap credit. Their combined strength cut significantly into the vote of the major parties, especially the already-decimated liberals. The DNVP was less severely affected because the Agrarian League in eastern Germany continued to maintain its close ties to the conservatives.

The balance sheet of political developments during the republic's golden years, then, presented a decidedly mixed picture. It is true that ideological differences, for the most part, were carried out with political means; the republic was secure from military coups or revolutionary violence. Moreover, there were indications that the moderate groups in the center of the political spectrum were gaining strength as the economy recovered and so-called normal times returned. But allegiance to the democratic system had not yet laid down firm roots in much of German society, and even the pro-republican groups remained divided on fundamental policy issues. Democracy in Germany needed time and continued prosperity to integrate many of those now distrustful of the republican system. Unfortunately, as it turned out, parliamentary democracy in Germany had very little time in which to demonstrate that it was the better system.

ECONOMIC AND SOCIAL DEVELOPMENTS

The Ruhr crisis represented an economic watershed in the Weimar years. No recovery of the German economy was possible until confidence in the stability of the Reich's currency had returned. The creation of the Rentenmark in the fall of 1923 was an important first step toward this goal, but long-term stabilization depended on reaching agreement on a complex set of political and economic issues. These included the rebuilding of the international credit system and Germany's recognition of the territorial and financial provisions of the Versailles settlement.

The Rentenmark was without any real metallic backing—the Reich had virtually no reserves of gold or silver—so that the actual foundation for a stable German monetary system would have to be hard currency reserves, especially U.S. dollars. Those could come only in the form of loan packages subscribed to by private investors in Germany and, more important, the United States. It was obvious, however, that the Reich would remain a poor credit risk so long as large and chronic deficits were the rule at every level of government and Germany continued to attempt to evade the financial obligation imposed by the Versailles Treaty.

A breakthrough on this complex issue came in 1924, by the simultaneous retirement of the Rentenmark and the introduction of a new permanent national currency (the *Reichsmark*) that led to negotiations on a new reparations agreement between Germany and its former enemies. To demonstrate their seriousness of purpose, all levels of government in Germany made drastic budget cuts for the fiscal year 1924. For the first time since the end of the war, Germany's local, state, and federal governments presented balanced budgets to their respective legislatures. At the same time, the Reichsbank, under its new president, Hjalmar Schacht, severely restricted credit and kept interest rates high. (Throughout the remainder of the decade, German interest rates were consistently higher than those of other major industrialized nations.)

These moves brought about immediate social and financial consequences. The budget balancing act was accomplished largely at the expense of state and federal employees. Because entitlement programs, such as the social security system, traditionally were self-carrying insurance schemes and not part of the annual budgets, personnel costs were the single largest item of both state and federal budgets. (Self-carrying insurance schemes use actuarial methods to achieve a balance between the income from premiums and the payment of benefits to the participating beneficiaries.) Hardest hit were blue- and white-collar workers and public school teachers (who, you will recall, are state employees in Germany) with little seniority. Prussia, Germany's largest state, laid off some 14,500 teachers between the end of 1923 and mid-1925, a development that severely aggravated an already serious unemployment problem among college-educated youth. Tenure rules protected the jobs of other civil servants, but even senior bureaucrats had to accept substantial pay cuts. But the high interest rates and Germany's fiscal austerity program made the country attractive to foreign investors. Between 1924 and 1930 foreign creditors invested 20.5 billion Reichsmarks ($4.9 billion) in the German economy.

Putting Germany's domestic fiscal house in order was one prerequisite for economic recovery, but it would remain a hollow gesture unless it were supplemented by an agreement on reparations. In the summer of 1924, a committee of fiscal experts from the Allied countries, led by Charles Dawes, the president of the First Bank of Chicago, submitted a new proposal to the Germans. The Dawes Plan did not alter the actual total of the reparations bill (it remained at 132 billion marks), but the scheme eased Germany's fiscal position in a number of significant ways. To begin with, the Allies arranged for an initial loan to Germany of $200 million by a consortium of American banks to provide the Reich with much-needed hard currency reserves. This and other measures have led some historians, like Stephen Schuker, to severely criticize the Allies' post-Versailles treatment of the Reich, and to complain that in the end the Americans paid reparations to the Germans. (The loan was secured by the assets of the German national railroad system.) The Reich's annual reparation payments were pegged at the modest sum of 2.5 billion Reichsmarks. More important, under the Dawes Plan Germany's creditors abandoned the policies of "productive guarantees," that is to say, the occupation of German cities as a punishment for nonpayment. Instead, the Dawes Plan contained provisions designed to ensure that the transfer of payments did not endanger the stability of the new Reichsmark. A reparations agent, the American banker Parker Gilbert, established an office in Berlin to oversee the transfer of payments and report to the Allies on German economic and fiscal policies.

Although the Dawes Plan was a decided improvement over the policies that had led to periodic confrontations in earlier years, many among the political right rejected the new scheme because of the continued shackles on Germany's fiscal and economic sovereignty. Still, even the right was not blind to the practical advantages. In August 1924, exactly half of the DNVP's Reichstag delegates voted with the government majority, thereby ensuring the votes necessary to give approval to the Dawes Plan.

The republican authorities had acted swiftly to create a stable currency, but, important as this was, it did not solve the problem of the aftermath of the ruinous inflation. Clearly, some equitable way had to be found to "revaluate" long-standing commercial obligations, savings, and bonds that had been calculated in what were now worthless marks. Not surprisingly, this issue became a major political controversy. Pensioners, creditors, and holders of savings accounts wanted to protect their assets while debtors insisted "a mark is a mark." After all, it was not their fault that the collapse of the currency had enabled them to pay off their obligations cheaply. In the end, the Reich Supreme Court and the Reichstag reached a conclusion that pleased neither side. Liquid assets were "revalued" at

15 percent of their original worth while real property retained its full value. Because this decision gave a relative advantage to owners of real property, a special tax, earmarked for the construction of public housing, was levied on house owners. Angered by what they saw as an unfair burden on their properties, real estate interests were instrumental in the establishment of an anti-republican party, the Economics Party (WiP), discussed earlier.

A stable currency and a good credit rating led to a steady, albeit uneven, expansion of the economy. Aided by the flow of foreign investments, industrial production in 1928 rose to an index figure of 114 (comparing favorably to 1913 when the figure was 100), while corporate profits increased from 5.1 percent of equity in 1924–1925 to 7.2 percent in 1928–1929. But there was a darker side here as well. Domestic investment activity never regained the levels of 1913 and neither did exports. From 1910 to 1913 exports composed 17.5 percent of the German GDP; by 1925–1929 the figure was only 14.9 percent.

The boom also created and hid a number of important structural changes in the economy. In the industrial sector, the most noticeable development was the accelerated trend toward "rationalization," that is to say, the reorganization of the manufacturing process to save labor costs. Particularly in labor-intensive, export-oriented industries, machines increasingly replaced human labor. The result was not only a 25 percent increase in productivity and a rise in real wages in some industries but also a depressingly high rate of overall unemployment. From 1924 to 1929 unemployment never fell below 6.8 percent. The problem was particularly severe in older industries like iron, steel, textiles, and coal mining. Here, labor–management relations were chronically acrimonious, as employers sought to cut wages, increase the workday, and replace skilled male workers with unskilled (often female) laborers. In 1928, a lockout in the steel industry, which affected 80 percent of the workforce, created a great deal of bitterness in the Ruhr area.

Large numbers of unemployed workers (incidentally, this was a problem that plagued other industrialized countries as well) were only one indication of profound changes in the structure of Germany's economic and social life. The role of government changed dramatically. It became increasingly common for government arbitrators to settle labor disputes. At the same time, the country's *Sozialpolitik*, that network of insurance schemes and legal safeguards designed to protect employees from hardships, was knitted considerably tighter. The most important addition was the introduction of compulsory unemployment insurance in 1927. Overall, annual government expenditures for social services at all levels increased from 1.8 billion marks from 1910 to 1913 to 2.6 billion in the 1925–1929 period. Veterans' pensions and disability payments required large sums. In 1927 the federal government used its sizable surplus to restore a good part of the salary cuts for civil servants that had been enacted in 1923–1924. In the period 1925–1930, expenditures for public housing construction, largely financed by the receipts from the inflation-related tax on real property, were twice as high as those for defense. But the easy availability of credit also tempted many cities and states to float bond issues with which to finance a variety of improvements in their infrastructure.

Despite the economic upturn, the recovery left large pockets of structural distress. Agriculture remained a chronic trouble spot. Farm debt climbed from the equivalent of 3 billion Reichsmarks in 1923 to 12 billion seven years later, while prices for agricultural products, after reaching a postwar high in 1926, continued to fall beginning in 1927. Although experts recommended cutbacks in planting, farmers for the most part attempted to increase production. To become more efficient they purchased expensive machinery, a decision that turned out to be counterproductive because it aggravated their indebtedness while the augmented production depressed prices still further. Before long Germany's farmers were again demanding tariff protection.

The Mittelstand—small businessmen, retailers, independent professionals—also complained about continuing hardships. Spokesmen for these interest groups described the "crisis of the Mittelstand" in vivid terms: Not only were their savings wiped out by the inflation, but the recovery passed them by as well. There is no doubt that some parts of the Mittelstand suffered relative deprivation in the redistribution of income during the Weimar years. Small businesses had a harder time obtaining credit than did large export-oriented industries, and many retail establishments were hurt by the growing competition from chain and department stores. Compared to the years just before the war the Mittelstand's share of the GNP fell while that of labor and corporations rose. The real income of the traditional white-collar employees (retail clerks, secretaries, and so forth) declined while the wages of blue-collar workers rose.

At the same time, the plight of the Mittelstand must not be exaggerated. For many small businesses and independent artisans, the effect of the inflation had been cushioned by their ownership of real estate. During the second half of the decade, the number of new businesses increased rapidly. Equally important, the members of the new Mittelstand, such as technically skilled white-collar workers, benefited from the rationalization measures in some industries. On balance, most members of the Mittelstand remained better off than many blue-collar workers and civil servants. In objective terms, then, the Mittelstand's complaints were not justified. In reality, members of this group mourned the loss of status and relative standing in the society that they associated with the Wilhelminian era.

By the end of the decade, the German economy, despite some chronic problems, gave cause for optimism. Even the reparations did not seem to present a major difficulty. The annual payments consumed about 10 percent of the federal budget—not an exorbitant sum, particularly because most of the money was derived from foreign loans. The expectation of continued prosperity led the Reich and its creditors in June 1929 to agree on a new repayment plan. The Young Plan (named for the American banker who chaired the negotiations between Germany and the Allies) was a monument to economic hopes and illusions. The ink on the agreement was hardly

dry when the collapse of the New York stock market ushered in the Great Depression, and with it an entirely different set of problems. Still, the Young Plan does illustrate what might have been. The new agreement set up a schedule of fifty-nine annual payments ranging from 1.6 to 2.4 billion Reichsmarks ($381–$571 million). In addition, all international controls on German economic life were removed, and the Allies agreed that the last French and Belgian troops would leave German soil in 1930.

The Young Plan did not cause the depression, but when the effects of the economic downturn were felt in Germany, the plan became an object of fierce political attacks. The anti-republican forces concentrated their venom on the plan's long-term payment schedule: While millions of Germans suffered hardships, the Republican authorities had obligated themselves to continue reparations for another sixty years to pay for a war that few Germans felt personally responsible for either beginning or losing. Such attacks ignored the fact that overall Germany paid only a little over 10 billion marks in reparations in the years between 1924 and 1930.

Looking back from the depths of the Great Depression, most Germans could see little good even in the golden years, but we should remember that the second half of the decade produced important, and, on the whole, positive changes in German economic and social life. There were continuing structural problems—agriculture, young academics, depressed regions—but these years were also a time in which the GDP grew rapidly, much of German industry was modernized, and the "social net" was more tightly knit.

WEIMAR CULTURE

The glitter of the Weimar era's golden years was particularly dazzling in area of culture broadly defined. Moreover, although economic recovery and political stability proved to be short lived, the patina of Weimar culture has endured. From architecture to films, from the novel to interior design, the Weimar years continue to influence our own times.

The artistic flowering during these years was not just the result of fortuitous circumstances. Convinced that a spiritual and cultural regeneration would provide a vehicle for Germany's return to greatness, the republic's political leaders consciously set out to provide a fertile environment for the country's renaissance of culture. Symptomatic were the public expenditures for education and the arts: Until the Great Depression forced cutbacks, budgetary outlays for education and the arts at all levels of government were substantially higher than during the Wilhelminian years.

Still, money alone cannot create culture; art and literature are produced by artists and other creative talents. With important exceptions, Bismarckian and Wilhelminian Germany were not noted for either. Why then the cultural explosion during the Weimar years? Why was such an extraordinary number of outstanding talents singularly productive during a very brief time span? In part Weimar's glow derives from contrasting it with the cultural dark age that followed. Weimar culture ended abruptly when the Nazis came to power. After 1933 many of the Weimar artists, now in foreign exile, their careers destroyed or at least interrupted, remembered the years before the Nazis as having had the quality of an artists' Camelot.

Such remembrances contained a good deal of subjective selectivity. Nevertheless, there was more to Weimar culture than false memory. The extraordinary flowering of artistic endeavors in Germany came about largely because of the interaction of three factors: the technical and stylistic originality of many of the works produced, the importance of Berlin as the center of cultural modernism, and the eclecticism of the German artistic scene.

During the 1920s, Germany had a cultural capital for the first time in modern history. To be sure, artistic life in the provinces did not die out—then as now even moderate-size cities maintained municipal theaters and opera houses—but as a concept Weimar culture was

to a large extent synonymous with the capital. As if by a magnet aspiring artists were drawn to Berlin; feared and famous critics on the city's daily newspapers determined the fate of books and theater productions. And, equally important, in Berlin there existed an audience for virtually any innovative concept, no matter how outrageous. The result was an intellectual and artistic hothouse atmosphere that provided not only a great deal of mutual support and encouragement, but also, it must be admitted, a sense of freneticism and sensationalism.

More than anything else, Weimar culture was a genuine multimedia phenomenon. The artists and writers of the 1920s were fortunate in that they worked at a time when new media and new mass audiences for artistic endeavors—notably the cinema—were becoming available. During the Weimar years, films outgrew the status of novelties shown at carnivals and became a recognized art form suitable for mass audiences. Weimar artists took enthusiastically to the new medium. Germany was flooded with good and bad films, and actors and actresses became household words overnight. Marlene Dietrich achieved instant stardom in her first major film role, the wanton Lola in *The Blue Angel*. An early horror film, *The Cabinet of Dr. Caligari*, demonstrated the effectiveness of expressionism (see the discussion on p.152) as a cinematic style. Moreover, the influence of Weimar filmmakers was not limited by the German borders. When the Nazis came to power, many leading artists and directors left Germany and found a new home in Hollywood.

In addition, the experience of the war had done much to weaken the influence of established techniques and values in such traditional fields as painting, architecture, sculpture, music, and literature. The atonality of Arnold Schönberg and his students dominated "serious" music while the influence of American jazz enriched popular music. The black American jazz singer and dancer Josephine Baker became the toast of Berlin when she performed in the capital. The first German musical, *The Three Penny Opera*, with lyrics by Bertold Brecht and a score by Kurt Weill, was an instant hit when it was first performed in 1928. In painting and sculpture the sentimental realism of the Wilhelminian years was replaced by a variety of schools, ranging from neorealism to cubism. In literature, expressionism and neorealism dominated.

For all its eclecticism, Weimar artistic life was also remarkable for some attempts to fuse the various visual and handicraft art forms into a coherent statement that expressed both the functionality and aesthetic of modernism. That effort was particularly epitomized by a unique school, the *Bauhaus* (House for the Building Arts). It was founded in 1919 through the efforts of the architect Walter Gropius and a number of leading painters and craftsmen, including Wassily Kandinsky, Paul Klee, and Oskar Kokoschka. The Bauhaus attempted to create a teaching and work atmosphere in which the lines between functionality and aesthetics and those between art and craftsmanship were fluid. Furniture and buildings were to be no less works of art than paintings or pieces of sculpture. Without imposing any strictures on its associates, the Bauhaus faculty developed a style of design for furniture and interior decorating that remains a model of uncluttered leanness. These ideas found concrete expression in some of the public housing projects built in the 1920s. Even today some of these large-scale constructions, like the *Hufeisensiedlung* (Horseshoe Settlement) in Berlin (the apartments were built in the form of a horseshoe surrounding an ornamental pond), remain models of well-designed and yet functional low-income housing. The Hufeisensiedlung has been aptly described as a building that "reconciled the spirit of a garden city with the necessities of an urban housing project." Like so much else that was original in Weimar culture, the Bauhaus aroused the ire of the Nazis. They criticized the Bauhaus style as "degenerate" and "*unvölkisch*" and forced the school's closing in 1933.

Political didacticism reached high levels of sophistication during the Weimar years. Two media forms, investigative journalism and the political cabaret, attracted particularly outstanding contributors. Carl von Ossietsky, the editor of the journal *Die Weltbühne* ("The World Stage"), succeeded in exposing many vestiges of authoritarianism in German politics (he earned the hatred of the far right by revealing some of the Reichswehr's secret rearmament activities) and attacking the philistinism of the republican authorities. A frequent contributor to Die Weltbühne was Kurt Tucholsky, a brilliant satirist who ridiculed the German political and social establishment in numerous prose and poetry pieces. It should be noted that although Weimar's political authors justifiably attacked many current abuses, they also helped undermine confidence in the democratic and parliamentary system by their seeming unwillingness to make distinctions between the shortcomings of the supporters of democracy and those who worked actively to overthrow the republic.

Ironically, although Weimar culture constituted an outburst of artistic creativity, the most pervasive theme in literature was a profound sense of cultural pessimism: The end of Western and particularly German civilization was at hand. A typical representative of this mood was the historian Oswald Spengler. His two-volume work, *The Decline of the West* (the first part was published in 1918, the second in 1922), attacked hedonism and materialism as the forces that were hastening the end of Western civilization. Authors of fiction echoed Spengler's theme of decay. Hermann Broch's novel trilogy *The Sleepwalkers* (published in 1931 and 1932) documented the disintegration of Wilhelminian values. Whereas Broch emphasized the progressive emptiness of prewar society, Josef Roth's *Radetzkymarsch* (1932) provided a more sympathetic, seriocomic, and nostalgic view of the vanished Habsburg Empire. Thomas Mann's *The Magic Mountain* (1924) also exuded a sense of death and disease. Mann chose as the locale for his novel a tuberculosis sanitarium in the Swiss Alps. Here, the hero, a young Hamburg engineer, surrounded by slowly dying fellow patients, is exposed to a variety of philosophical systems, none of which he regards as satisfactory explanations for the state of the world.

Im Mittelpunkt   Kurt Weill (1900–1950)

If any two names personified the brilliance of Weimar cultural and artistic life, they were surely those of Kurt Weill and Berthold Brecht. The two men collaborated on a number of musical productions, with Brecht supplying the lyrics and the libretti and Weill the music. Their most famous and enduring collaboration, of course, was *The Three Penny Opera*, which premiered in 1928 and became an instant hit.

Weill came from a Jewish family and was born in Dessau in Thuringia. His musical talents were recognized very early, and he studied composition with two famous musicians of the day, Engelbert Humperdinck (the composer of the opera *Hansel und Gretel)* and Ferruccio Busoni, but Weill's compositions quickly departed from the neoclassical tastes of his teachers. In 1926 Weill married Lotte Lenya, a singer who was to originate many of the roles that Weill created. Lenya was, for example, the original Jenny in *The Three Penny Opera*.

During the Weimar Republic, Weill was one of the most politically engaged but also most successful artists. On his own, Weill specialized in cabaret songs. While the music combined elements of jazz with catchy tunes, the biting lyrics attacked capitalism, militarism, and the reactionary right. Weill collaborated with Berthold Brecht in creating a series of musicals. Weill's music for these productions, such as *The Rise and Fall of the City of Mahagonny,* was modern and original but also accessible. The political messages paralleled those of the cabaret songs. Although a number of Weill's musicals are still in the modern operatic repertoire, none of the Brecht-Weill collaborations equaled the success of *The Three Penny Opera*.

Weill's politics as well as his Jewish ancestry made him an object of Nazi attacks even before Hitler came to power. Nazi thugs on several occasions tried to disrupt performances of *The Three Penny Opera* and other Weill productions. He recognized soon after the Nazis came to power that there was no future for him in Germany, and in 1934 he and his wife fled the Third Reich, moving first to Paris and then to New York.

In the United States, Weill (as well as Lotte Lenya) was one of those refugees from Hitler's Germany who had a successful second career in his adopted homeland. Having already used jazz forms and the style of the American musical in his earlier compositions, Weill fit in well with the musical trends prevalent in American musical theater in the 1930s and 1940s. His American musicals, such as *Knickerbocker Holiday* (1938), *Lady in the Dark* (1940), and *One Touch of Venus* (1943), were hits on Broadway, and they have remained staples of the American musical theater repertoire. They were successes at least in part because the American Weill dropped his left-wing political stance entirely. His American productions contain no political messages.

It was a great loss to German cabaret music and to the German and American musical theater that Kurt Weill died at the early age of fifty from respiratory ailments.

The authors' pessimism about the future of the West and Germany derived in large part from their conviction that alienation was the most prominent characteristic of modern society. Alienation came in a variety of forms. In Alfred Döblin's epic novel, *Berlin Alexanderplatz* (1929), a "good man" who has run afoul of the law is destroyed by the cruelties of bourgeois society. The figure of the *Spiesser*, the self-satisfied, middle-class boor, often portrayed as a heartless war profiteer, became a staple of Weimar literature. On the political left, authors like Bertold Brecht and Heinrich Mann, artists like George Grosz, and investigative journals like *Die Weltbühne* attributed the slaughter of World War I and the rampant materialism of Weimar Germany to the greed and insensitivity of capitalism and capitalists.

In contrast, artists sympathetic to the political right identified the bourgeoisie with rationalism, modernism, and lack of völkisch consciousness. Hans Grimm's best seller, *Volk ohne Raum* ("A People without Space"), set in Africa, celebrated the victory over an alien culture and a physically harsh environment. Möller van den Bruck's *Das Dritte Reich* ("The Third Reich") looked to the future to overcome the distasteful modernism of his day, while Oswald Spengler called for a return to "Prussian socialism," which he identified with German society during the time of Frederick the Great. For some artists antimaterialism was synonymous with anti-Americanism. They claimed to find ready fodder for their prejudices in contemporary developments in Germany, such as the rationalization movement in industry. Dubbed "Taylorism" (after its primary promoter, the American engineer Frederick Winslow Taylor) or "Fordism" (after Henry Ford), many intellectuals identified such efforts to modernize the economy as symbolic of America's shallow and heartless materialism.

More common than accounts of class or national alienation, however, were tales of fictional characters feeling individually isolated because they were unable to relate to the society around them. Often the struggle took on epic dimensions. In Robert Musil's *Der Mann ohne Eigenschaften* ("The Man without Qualities"), published between 1930 and 1943, the hero attempts (and fails) to find a bridge between his own intellect and the consciousness and values of prewar Austro-German society. Undoubtedly, the most famous case of multiple alienation was Franz Kafka. Although he died young, at the age of 41 in 1924, the emotional intensity of his novels and short stories has made the adjective "Kafkaesque" a synonym for the state of total alienation, which the author himself felt keenly. As a son, Kafka felt estranged from his father. As an author writing in German, he was alienated from the Czech culture of his native city of Prague, yet as a Jew he also felt alienated from the German culture around him. For Kafka, as for many Weimar artists, existence was "baseless" and "contextless."

Not surprisingly, World War I had a major impact on German cultural life during the 1920s. Some artists celebrated the war as the crucible that transformed men into heroes for a new age. Ernst Jünger's wartime diaries, *In Stahlgewittern* ("The Storm of Steel"), published in 1920, were particularly influential in creating the myth of the *Fronterlebnis*. Ernst von Salomon's *Das Buch vom deutschen Freikorpskämpfer* ("The Book of the German Freikorps Veteran"), which appeared in 1928, carried the same theme forward to the counterrevolutionary upheavals of 1918–1919.

Celebrations of the war experience were rushed into print soon after the conflict ended, but the two most famous antiwar novels, Erich Maria Remarque's *Im Westen nichts Neues* ("All Quiet on the Western Front") and Ludwig Renn's *Krieg* ("War"), were not published until a decade later. Then, however, both of these powerful statements on the senselessness and dehumanization of war became immediate best sellers. Remarque's novel was also turned into a major film.

Value confusion as it related to youthful adjustment to adult life, already a staple of prewar literature, was an equally prevalent theme in Weimar culture, especially as Sigmund Freud's ideas found a wider audience. Notable (amid much titillating sensationalism) were the stories of Arnold Zweig, an author who was famous for his portraits of the female psyche, and Hermann Hesse's novels of youthful escapism to exotic places and states of mind.

Not surprisingly, in the early 1930s numerous authors used the Great Depression as a theme. Hans Fallada's 1932 novel, *Kleiner Mann—was nun?* ("Little Man, What Now?"), became an instant best seller; millions of copies in twenty languages were sold. Fallada's particular concern was the impact of the Great Depression on the *Stehkragenproletariat,* the lower-middle-class white-collar workers. Unaccustomed to unemployment, and insecure in their status, the depression crushed them psychologically even more than materially.

The themes of Weimar culture were to some extent universal ones, but the styles of the age had unique features. Undoubtedly, expressionism was the most important stylistic contribution of Weimar culture. *Expressionism* began as a prewar phenomenon (the term was first used in 1901), but it was not until World War I and its immediate aftermath that the style came to dominate virtually all art forms. Expressionism was a revolt against rationalism. Its followers rejected artistic portrayals of empirical reality and sought instead to "express" an inner reality of emotion. As a consequence, artists and authors stressed pure emotion and their subjects' character makeup at the expense of plot development and representation.

In films, where expressionism was particularly important and its influence continued longer than in other media, the elements of the style resulted in visual shock treatments to create an emotional impact. Expressionist filmmakers were particularly fascinated by portraying human madness on the screen—both individual and in the form of mob hysteria.

Despite its wide-ranging influence, expressionism did not remain the dominant stylistic form for long. Most writers became frustrated by expressionism's lack of emphasis on plot and story. In drama, audiences found it hard to identify with generic characters like "father," "son," "man," and "woman." In the second half of the 1920s, expressionism increasingly lost ground to neorealism and neosentimentalism. Neorealism, or "new objectivity" as it was known in Germany, brought renewed emphasis on empiricism in literature and functionality or abstraction in the visual arts. The Bauhaus effort was one example of successful modified modernism. In contrast, some of those rejecting modernism turned from expressionism to pre-industrial forms and values. Often the

result was unabashed sentimentalism and völkisch kitsch, but in one field, architecture, the controversy yielded very positive results. The 1920s saw a genuine renaissance of German architecture with buildings inspired by Bauhaus functionalism standing next to edifices that aimed at a romantic revival of earlier styles. In aesthetic terms, examples of both were highly successful.

Weimar culture, like all of German society during the golden years, was divided and poised at a crossroads. A variety of voices and forms clamored for attention. Unfortunately, eclecticism did not result in tolerance and pluralism so much as in politicization and mutual distrust. As the society became destabilized with the onset of the Great Depression, the various schools of artists sought an exclusivity for their themes and styles that in the end undermined all of them, much as the republic that had enabled them to flower was destroyed by Nazi totalitarianism.

FOREIGN RELATIONS

As was true of the economy and cultural life during the republic's golden years, Germany's foreign relations too took a turn for the better. Largely through the efforts of Gustav Stresemann, the Reich foreign minister from 1923 until his death in 1929, Germany emerged from its postwar diplomatic isolation and achieved a degree of reconciliation with its former enemies, notably France.

Although Stresemann's six-year tenure as foreign minister provided much-needed continuity in this important post, he was never without critics. The German Nationalists, ironically Stresemann's coalition partners in the Reich cabinets of 1924 and 1927, bitterly attacked the foreign minister's efforts at Franco-German reconciliation, characterizing them as appeasement and a sellout.

The foreign minister also had considerable difficulties with his own party, the DVP. Stresemann remained the uncontested national chairman of the right-wing liberals, but the influential right wing in

Im Mittelpunkt Marlene Dietrich (1901–1992)

The actress, chanteuse, and media phenomenon Marlene Dietrich was born Marie Magdalene Dietrich in December 1901 in Berlin. Her family was solid middle class; her father, who died in 1911, was a lieutenant in the Berlin police force. Dietrich went to an elite Gymnasium, the Auguste Victoria School for Girls (named after the wife of Emperor William II), where she developed an interest in pursuing a career in music. However, her ambitions to become a concert violinist were cut short by a wrist injury. Instead, she turned to the stage and the new medium of moving pictures.

During the 1920s she appeared in both live theater and a number of movies. Her breakthrough came in 1929 when the director Josef von Sternberg cast her as Lola in the film *The Blue Angel*. In the movie, which was based upon a novel by Heinrich Mann, Dietrich plays a seductive femme fatale who destroys the life and career of a respectable school director, played by one of the most famous German actors of the time, Emil Jannings.

The Blue Angel also marked the end of Marlene Dietrich's German career, and the beginning of her successes in the United States. Her mentor, Josef von Sternberg, had moved to Hollywood and he asked Dietrich to follow him. She did and between 1930 and 1935 the team made a number of outstanding films for Paramount Pictures.

When the Nazis came to power, the propaganda minister, Joseph Goebbels, recognized Dietrich's star power and attempted to entice the actress to return to Germany, but she refused. She despised the Nazis and their anti-Semitic policies. She stayed in Hollywood and in 1939 became an American citizen. During World War II Dietrich supported the Allied war effort in a number of ways. She performed in live shows for American soldiers, and she was also one of the first media celebrities to raise war bonds for the Allied cause. In 1945 Dietrich was awarded the Presidential Medal of Freedom for her wartime contributions.

After the war Marlene Dietrich reinvented herself as a cabaret performer, recording artist, and touring singer. She was quite successful in these endeavors, in large part because her musical arranger, Burt Bacharach, took full advantage of her deep and sexy contralto voice. Dietrich returned to Germany for a concert tour in 1960, and while there was some criticism for her war-time activities, all of her concerts were sold out. She was also warmly received by the Federal Republic's political leaders, including Willy Brandt. Dietrich's artistic career ended in 1965, when she broke a leg while performing in Sydney, Australia. Four years later she published her autobiography *Nehmt nur mein Leben* ("Just Look at my Life.")

She spent the last eleven years of her life as a bedridden, virtual recluse in an apartment in Paris. One of her few regular visitors was her daughter, the actress Maria Riva. Dietrich died at age ninety in May 1992. Despite her many years in America and later in Paris the actress never lost her emotional affinity with the city of Berlin, the place of her birth and early triumphs. She asked to be buried there, and now rests quite close to her mother in a cemetery in Berlin-Schöneberg.

The bulk of Dietrich's artistic and literary estate—some 100,000 pieces of correspondence—is also in Berlin. It forms the core of the holdings of the Film Museum, Berlin. In addition, the city of her birth honored her by naming a square after her in 1998 and making her an honorary citizen in 2002. The Federal Republic issued a postage stamp in her honor in 1997.

the DVP consistently put pressure on the foreign minister to abandon his policies of reconciliation with the Western Allies and draw closer to the DNVP's position.

Stresemann's overall foreign policy aim was to "revise" the consequences of the Treaty of Versailles. Concretely, this meant ending Germany's diplomatic isolation, removing the remaining occupation troops from its territory, and eliminating the Allied Control Commission's monitoring of German disarmament. To this end Stresemann was willing to pay the "price of Locarno." The Locarno treaties were the keystone of Germany's foreign relations in the second half of the decade. At the suggestion of Lord D'Abernon, the British ambassador in Berlin, the German government at the beginning of 1925 proposed to Great Britain and France that the Reich would be willing to recognize the legitimacy of its western boundaries if the Allies agreed to a withdrawal of their occupation troops from German soil before the scheduled date of 1935 and readmitted Germany into the family of nations on an equal footing.

The British responded positively, but the French were less eager to take up the German offer. After waiting six months before replying, the French countered Stresemann's proposal with a demand that Germany also recognize the legitimacy of its eastern borders and that the entire treaty package be guaranteed by a mutual assistance pact among France, Great Britain, and Italy.

It took several months of negotiations in Locarno, Switzerland, between Stresemann, his French counterpart Aristide Briand, and their staffs, before the treaty package could be initialed in October 1925. Even then the "Eastern Locarno" proved unattainable. Not only were the Germans unwilling to recognize the legitimacy of their 1918 boundary with Poland (although the Reich agreed to forgo any use of force in attempting to change the boundaries there), but also the British refused to accept any responsibility for guaranteeing the boundaries in the east. In the final treaty the Reich only agreed not to challenge its

new boundaries in the west, and Great Britain and Italy in turn guaranteed the inviolability of these territorial changes. Germany was also accepted as a member of the League of Nations. The Allies for their part speeded up the removal of some of their occupation forces and withdrew the Inter-Allied Control Commission. In 1930 the last French soldiers left Germany.

Although Germany gained much from the Locarno agreements, the treaties became the subject of a bitter debate within the country.

After originally supporting the Locarno initiative (the DNVP was a member of the Reich cabinet when the negotiations began), conservatives and the völkische groups soon attacked Stresemann because he had failed to achieve the impossible: They demanded that he should have insisted on the return of Alsace-Lorraine to Germany and obtained from the Allies an agreement to rescind the war-guilt clause of the Versailles Treaty.

Although for Stresemann reconciliation with the Western powers was a primary goal of his foreign policy aims, the foreign minister was careful to balance the agreement with the West by good relations with Soviet Russia. In April 1926 the Reich and Soviet Russia signed the Treaty of Berlin. In this agreement, the two partners confirmed the terms of the Treaty of Rapallo and agreed that if either were attacked by a third power the other would remain neutral. The Russians were also pleased that before taking its seat in the League of Nations, Germany had issued a declaration announcing that in its disarmed state it could not be expected to participate fully in any sanctions that might be imposed against the Soviet Union by the League. Finally, although the new agreement with the Soviet Union was silent on this point, good relations with Russia made it possible for the Reichswehr to continue testing armaments forbidden in Germany under the terms of the Versailles Treaty.

The third pillar of his revisionist foreign policy was rearmament. To be sure, in contrast to the *revanchistes* of the radical right, the foreign minister had no wish for a renewed armed conflict with France. He was convinced, however, that a true European balance of power was impossible if Germany remained defenseless. For this reason, Stresemann not only supported all rearmament measures that were legal under the Treaty of Versailles—such as the construction of the pocket battleship—but he also approved of the Reichswehr's clandestine activities, including the ongoing cooperation with the Soviet Red Army.

Stresemann's foreign policy demonstrated both the usefulness and the limitations of the "spirit of Locarno." The treaty package did begin a process of removing some of the mutual suspicion between Germany and its former enemies. At the same time, the "spirit of Locarno" was not able to bring about an era of real peace based on mutual trust. Neither the Allies nor the Germans could escape thinking in categories of national policies and national rivalries. Stresemann wanted to use the Locarno agreements to regain Germany's Great Power status. The French in turn remained suspicious about the Germans' motives and were consequently reluctant to give up their "productive guarantees."

Stresemann died in 1929. In ill health for some years, he was finally worn down by the incessant attacks of his domestic political foes—both among the radical right and in his own party. At the time of his death his foreign policy remained uneasily poised on the road to reconciliation with Germany's former enemies.

THE COLLAPSE OF THE ECONOMY AND THE END OF PARLIAMENTARY DEMOCRACY

At first glance 1929 was in many ways the republic's best year. Industrial production exceeded the prewar high set in 1913. The "spirit of Locarno" had returned Germany to international respectability, and the Young Plan promised a final and relatively painless settlement of the vexing reparations issue. Weimar Germany's Berlin-centered cultural and artistic life glittered and dazzled.

Actually, as we now know, Germany (and indeed all of Europe) stood at the edge of a precipice. The signs of optimism in the heady days of 1929 hid a host of unresolved problems that had been left in the wake of World War I. Germany's and Europe's economic growth lagged behind such "takeoff" areas as the United States. Despite the impressive recovery in the second half of the decade, Europe had lost its position as the pivot of the international economic system.

Germany's chronic economic problems, especially the difficulties in agriculture and labor unrest, caused tensions in the grand coalition, but they remained manageable until the fall of 1929 when the financing of unemployment compensation caused a battle over principles among the coalition partners. When the German national system of unemployment compensation was established in 1927, it was intended to be a self-perpetuating insurance scheme financed by contributions from employees and employers. It worked well until the particularly severe winter of 1928–1929 when unexpectedly large numbers of unemployed had required subsidies from the Reich budget to keep the insurance fund solvent. The crisis seemed to be over when the economy picked up again in the summer of 1929, but less than a year later with the onset of the Great Depression the insurance system collapsed entirely. Disagreements over financing unemployment compensation led to the fall of the government in March 1930 and the beginning of the republic's final constitutional crisis.

Economic historians continue to debate the long- and short-range causes of the Great Depression, but there is little disagreement about its devastating impact. The seeming suddenness of the downturn, its rapid spread, and its depth and duration created a political and social crisis from which no Western society was immune but which reached disastrous dimensions in Germany.

The depression caused interdependent fiscal, credit, and confidence crises that brought economic life to a virtual standstill and plunged Germany into a political and

A campaign poster of the Bavarian Party. The text reads: "The Bavarian Party, the bridge to reconstruction." Note the iconic imagery of the Bavarian people striding confidently into the future while below the bridge a raging river sweeps away the powerless Nazis. (Source: akg-images/Interfoto/Pulfer constitutional catastrophe. The fiscal impact came first, and it was linked to American investment in Germany. During the golden years, American investors had channeled billions of dollars into the private and public sectors of the German economy. With the crash of the New York stock market in October 1929, that flow of capital came to an abrupt end. In fact, caught short by the market crash, American investors hastened to cash in many of their short- and medium-term obligations in Germany, leading to a massive flight of capital.

The first to be adversely affected by the shortage of foreign capital were the German cities. During the golden years, numerous municipalities had floated bonds on the American money markets to finance improvements in their infrastructures. The rapid withdrawal of these obligations, coupled with decreasing tax receipts and increased expenditures for social services that resulted from the economic impact of the Great Depression, led to the bankruptcy of many cities. The municipal fiscal crisis in turn had repercussions for the states because under German law the latter were responsible for the cities' debts.

The fiscal crisis in the public sector was both caused and compounded by a credit crisis in the private sector. Here, too, foreign and domestic investors abruptly withdrew their monies in the fall of 1929. The downward spiral continued with a crisis of confidence leading to precipitous declines in production and consumption while business failures and unemployment simultaneously climbed to unprecedented levels.

How to cope with rapidly rising unemployment was the issue that converted the economic difficulties into a political crisis. In the winter months of 1929–1930, unemployment, which had been a chronic irritant until then, was rapidly transformed into a national obsession. At the end of 1929, 1.9 million (8.5 percent of the workforce) were out of work; a year later the figure was 3.1 million (14.0 percent of the workforce). In the Reich cabinet a classic debate pitted

the DVP as the party of business against the SPD as the voice of labor.

In March 1930, the Reich cabinet faced a decision on how to meet the rapidly growing deficits of the unemployment insurance program. The SPD ministers (and especially the secretary of labor, Rudolf Wissell) favored subsidies from general revenues while the DVP demanded an increase in payroll deduction taxes of 0.25 percent for employers and employees. Unable to compromise on this issue, the Reich cabinet submitted its resignation. The differences seemed narrow on the surface (and indeed many SPD leaders criticized Wissell's obstinacy), but in reality the two sides were at odds over a fundamental issue: Labor felt that recovery should not be accomplished on the backs of those who suffered immediate hardship, whereas businessmen increasingly came to believe that the high cost of unemployment compensation and social services in general prevented an upturn in the economy.

The Müller cabinet was the last government of the Weimar era supported by a majority of the Reichstag. After March 1930, the fragile consensus of republican forces was replaced by what Eberhard Jäckel has called the "mutual paralysis of forces." No combination of political and socioeconomic groups was strong enough to govern Germany under the rules of parliamentary democracy, but a number of them did have sufficient strength to block the coming to power of rival coalitions. Political life in the last years of the Weimar Republic was characterized by increasing street violence of competing political armies and efforts by a variety of interest groups—from the army to industrial lobbies—to influence decisions through extraparliamentary means.

The paralysis of parliament elevated the Reich president to a position as supreme arbiter of the nation. For the next three years, the president—rather than parliament—would determine the fate of chancellors, cabinets, and legislation to cope with the Great Depression. Unfortunately, the incumbent, Paul von Hindenburg, was singularly ill equipped to shoulder the burdens that fell to him. Now eighty years old, Hindenburg's mental and physical powers were rapidly deteriorating. In addition, he had little knowledge of the complex economic and political problems facing the country. In fact, he was a virtual prisoner of the advisers and friends that surrounded him in the presidential palace and on his East Prussian estate. In Berlin, Hindenburg's personal advisers were, for the most part, conservative politicians, Reichswehr officers, and his son Oskar von Hindenburg, who was then a major in the army. Among the Reichswehr officers, General Kurt von Schleicher, the chief of the defense department's Political Bureau, played a key role in the president's entourage. In East Prussia, the president socialized with his Junker neighbors, most of whom supported Hugenberg's DNVP.

Hindenburg's—or rather his advisers'—choice as chancellor to succeed Hermann Müller was Heinrich Brüning. At first glance, Brüning seemed to bring a number of important assets to the job. He was a leading member of the Center Party, the political group that had supplied more Weimar chancellors than any other party. At age forty-five he was relatively young, energetic, and ambitious. For some years he had served with

distinction as the chairman of the Reichstag's Ways and Means Committee, earning a well-deserved reputation as an expert on the intricacies of the federal budget.

But there was another side to Brüning. Like the president and his entourage, Brüning had long-standing reservations about the democratic constitutional system and the revolution of 1918 that had brought it about. Brüning rejected continuing the federal coalition with the Social Democrats; he readily promised the president to appoint only members of the bourgeois parties to his cabinet. Above all, however, Brüning would work to weaken parliamentary democracy. Despite some recent efforts by his admirers to refurbish Brüning's image as a democrat, there is little doubt that the new chancellor favored the restoration of the monarchy and the return of at least a modified form of authoritarianism. The chancellor agreed with the conservatives surrounding the Reich president that the Weimar constitution would have to be amended so as to curtail severely the powers of the Reichstag. Brüning, then, promised to use the economic crisis to make fundamental changes in Germany's democratic constitutional system. It was this goal that made him acceptable to the president's advisers.

CHAPTER SIX

From Authoritarianism to Totalitarianism

1930–1938

Historians agree that Heinrich Brüning's appointment as Reich chancellor ended parliamentary democracy in Germany, but there is considerably less consensus on the relationship between the advent of the "presidential regimes" in 1930 and the coming to power of the Nazis in 1933. Did Brüning and his two successors, Franz von Papen and Kurt von Schleicher, pave the way for totalitarianism, or were they the last, ineffective, barrier stemming the Nazi tide, as they claimed? Certainly, the change from the "New Conservatism" of the presidential governments to the totalitarianism of the Nazi regime was fluid rather than abrupt. A number of New Conservatives thought of the Nazis as their natural allies and, as we will see, some among them were instrumental in helping Hitler come to power. Both groups rejected parliamentary democracy as a political system. They were also united in their opposition to Stresemann's policy of international reconciliation and compromise; they placed more faith in diplomatic confrontation and bluff. Instead of free trade and priority for overseas exports, both groups pursued economic autarky—that is to say, national self-sufficiency—and regional trading systems. It should come as no surprise, then, that in the first five years of their rule the Nazis also continued many of the New Conservatives' constitutional, economic, and foreign policies.

THE RULE OF THE NEW CONSERVATIVES

Parliamentary democracy ended in March 1930. For the next three years, Germany was governed by forces that ruled without parliamentary control: the civil service, the army, and, to a lesser extent, major business and agricultural groups. Politically, these forces subscribed to ideas that for want of a better name have been labeled "New Conservatism" while administratively they relied on the authority and charisma of the Reich president.

In the last years of the Weimar Republic, the spectrum of German politics shifted considerably. Both the liberal and the traditional conservative parties failed to retain a significant following among the German voters, and they all but disappeared from the political landscape. Political Catholicism and the two Marxist parties did much better in keeping the allegiance of their supporters, but their mutual antagonisms prevented effective cooperation among them. The Communists regarded the Social Democrats (SPD) as a "social fascist" organization, and the leader of the Center Party elected in 1928, Monsignor Ludwig Kaas, was determined that political Catholicism should become a right-wing nationalist movement opposed to cooperation with all forms of organized Marxism.

Despite impressive strength at the polls and in the streets, the Communists' hope for revolution and the dictatorship of the proletariat was always an illusion. The expectations of the German Communist Party (KPD) that the Great Depression signaled the final collapse of capitalism in Germany was not only wishful thinking but politically counterproductive as well. Under the Comintern-dictated doctrine of defining the Social Democrats as "social fascists" (which was not dropped until 1935), the KPD concentrated its efforts on weakening the SPD, which the KPD's masters in Moscow regarded as the real vanguard of fascism. The result was a paralyzing fraternal conflict among the German working classes that, in the final analysis, benefited only the Nazis in their quest for power. The KPD's incendiary rhetoric also helped strengthen the Nazis by persuading large numbers of Germans, especially among the middle classes and the well-to-do, that only Nazism could block the victory of Bolshevism in Germany.

The Nazis' recipe for curing Germany's ills was in some ways the mirror image of the communist path. The Nazis agreed with the Communists that Germany could only choose between Nazism and communism. Both, therefore, sought to evoke an apocalyptic atmosphere, but in contrast to the communist appeal to proletarian revolution, Hitler's movement promised to overcome class divisions and create a genuine "national community" (*Volksgemeinschaft*) (see the fuller discussion below, pp. 179–81) that would enjoy economic prosperity and national greatness. To achieve this goal, the Nazis demanded the destruction of democracy, the elimination from power of those forces that in their view had brought ruin to Germany—Jews, Marxists, democrats, and republicans—and their replacement by Adolf Hitler and his followers.

Among the practitioners of the antidemocratic "new politics," the New Conservatives had the least popular appeal. While the Communists and Nazis steadily increased their voting support as the Great Depression deepened, the electoral success of the New Conservatives remained minuscule. But this was of little concern to them; their aim of restoring authoritarianism to Germany depended on the support of the traditional "natural" elites that had governed Germany before World War I. In addition, many New Conservatives were not opposed to cooperating with a force that had demonstrated its mass appeal: the Nazis. They were convinced that the Nazis, for all their rabble-rousing talents, needed the guidance of the old elites if they hoped to share in exercising political power.

The New Conservatives would eventually discover that in their relationship with the Nazis they were the tail rather than the dog; but for almost three years, from March 1930 to the end of January 1933, control of the Reich lay in the hands of the New Conservatives. Three presidential chancellors followed each other in quick succession. We have already met Heinrich Brüning, the right-wing conservative Catholic who succeeded Hermann Müller. He was followed, in May 1932, by Franz von Papen, nominally another member of the Center Party. Papen was a Westphalian aristocrat and wealthy landowner who had been a cavalry officer and diplomat in World War I. His political views were those of an extreme conservative; since 1925 he had urged German Catholics to renounce cooperation with the Social Democrats in any form. Finally, for a brief two months, in December 1932 and January 1933, the chancellor's office was occupied by the man who was in many ways a political father of New Conservatism: General Kurt von Schleicher. This master of intrigue was a major force behind the scenes in every one of the presidential cabinets. It was Schleicher who recommended both Brüning and Papen to Hindenburg.

The three presidential chancellors shared a common outlook on Germany's political and social future. At the heart of their political strategy lay the conviction that the Depression and the political paralysis of the early 1930s presented Germany not only with massive social and economic problems but also with unique opportunities to solve what they termed the country's "constitutional emergency" and its diplomatic impotence. The reality of political polarization and the threat of societal disintegration would, they felt, enable them to change Germany's constitutional structure from democracy to authoritarianism while simultaneously forcing the Allies to restore the Reich to the status of full equality in the concert of powers. The presidential cabinets were determined to use the "constitutional emergency" to replace, in Brüning's words, a "senseless form of parliamentarism" with a "healthful, limited democracy." Concretely, the domestic plans of the New Conservatives involved a strengthened Reich executive, severe curtailments of the powers of the Reichstag, and reforms of Germany's federal structure to reduce the residual powers of the Länder. The key to realizing this reform program was the Reich president's unwavering support of "his" chancellor, unity among the "natural" elites, and the continuing paralysis of the democratic forces.

At the same time, the presidential cabinets hoped that Germany's deflationary policies (see the following, pp. 165–67) would enable the Reich to throw off what they regarded as the key to the debilitating shackles of the Versailles system: the reparations payments. The belt-tightening measures they imposed were at least in part designed to convince the Allies that Germany simply had no resources with which to continue reparations payments. In the short run, then, the New Conservatives were not overly concerned about the country's economic problems; on the contrary, they actually expected the country's growing social misery to advance their long-range domestic and foreign policy goals.

By the time Heinrich Brüning moved into the chancellor's office, the worrisome credit and investment crisis had become a major recession. It would continue to grow worse throughout Brüning's chancellorship; by the summer of 1931, the crisis had become a full-scale depression. Germany's industrial production decreased by 50 percent between 1927 and 1933; exports declined from 26.9 billion marks in 1929 to 10.4 billion in 1932. Despite the decline in production, there continued to be a surplus of unsold goods. Business failures and farm indebtedness multiplied dramatically, and that in turn caused massive liquidity problems for many banks, including some of the Reich's largest. In July 1931 the government was forced to declare a banking holiday for almost two weeks to prevent panic withdrawals.

These structural symptoms of economic dislocation were real enough, but the average German was more concerned with the immediate social consequences of the depression: both actual and feared unemployment, and the decline in the standard of living. Unemployment was the most visible and immediate manifestation of economic difficulties. Lack of jobs had been a chronic problem for many even in the so-called good years of the Weimar Republic, but during the Great Depression unemployment grew to catastrophic levels. In 1930 the official statistics registered 3.1 million without work. In the summer of 1932, that figure had risen to 6.2 million; a third of the workforce was without a job. The unemployed included mainly blue-collar workers and those just starting their careers.

An example of the cult of personality around Brüning. A 1930 Center Party campaign poster shows Communists and Nazis struggling in vain to overcome "Brüning, the last defense of liberty and order." Hitler is the man pictured at the extreme lower right-hand corner. (Source: akg-images.)

But the growing unemployment figures had an adverse effect even on those lucky enough to keep jobs. Repeated wage cuts and loss of benefits were a fact of life for virtually all members of the workforce. Moreover, white-collar workers, professionals, and management-level employees were particularly susceptible to a psychological "fear effect." Unlike blue-collar workers, for whom at least temporary layoffs were not an unfamiliar experience, the salaried segments of the workforce were unaccustomed to being laid off, and they associated unemployment not only with a decline in their standard of living but, worse, with a loss of status as well.

As we will see, the presidential Reich cabinets seemed singularly blind to the social and economic consequences of the depression. To be sure, they were aware of the rising misery index, but Brüning and his successors were also convinced that efforts to address the social problems directly (other than through charity and minimal welfare payments) were both economically and politically counterproductive. In agreement with most experts in Germany (and other industrialized nations), the New Conservatives regarded the depression in economic terms as a "cleansing crisis" by which the market forces rejuvenated themselves after a period of imbalance caused by hyperactivity.

Remarkably, even politicians and union leaders politically opposed to the New Conservatives did not give their highest priority to finding jobs for the unemployed. Even many union leaders regarded fiscal orthodoxy and balanced budgets as articles of economic faith. Not until late 1931 and 1932, when the number of jobless was already more than 5 million, did the German labor unions endorse public works programs as countercyclical measures. As far as incentives for the private sector were concerned, it was not until the brief chancellorship of Kurt von Schleicher that a modest program of tax relief for employers who hired new workers was tried.

For the New Conservatives, the principal role of government during the "cleansing crisis" was to prevent the erosion of the value of the German currency. They were convinced that only faith in the mark's stability would persuade private entrepreneurs to invest their money in the Reich's economy and thus start the cycle of economic recovery. In practice this meant a rigid policy of deflation. Regardless of the social consequences, public expenditures would not be allowed to outpace current tax receipts. (This was also the reason the Reichsbank and especially its president, Hans Luther, fiercely opposed any public works program that involved deficit financing.) Balanced budgets, of course, can be produced in only two ways: cutting costs or increasing revenue. The Germans did both. The reductions focused on civil servants' salaries (between 1930 and 1932 civil servants' wages were reduced by 20 percent) as well as unemployment and welfare payments. Still, with tax receipts steadily declining as the Great Depression grew worse, these measures to balance the budget failed. The presidential governments (and, pressured by them, state and local authorities as well) increasingly resorted to raising taxes. The revenue-enhancement measures ranged from income tax surcharges to a series of consumption taxes. The latter imposed levies not only on luxury items and alcoholic beverages, but also on such everyday necessities as sugar, salt, and meat. The most resented of the new taxes was actually a throwback to premodern times, a "head tax" levied on every adult German regardless of income. To keep German industry competitive in the shrinking world market, the government also put pressure on the private sector to cut wages and prices. Both were to be cut by 10 percent, but for prices the indexing began with the levels of December 1931, whereas the 10 percent wage reduction was based on the wage levels of 1927. (The government argued that between 1927 and 1931 wages had outpaced increases in productivity.)

Politically, the economic measures not only benefited the Nazis and the Communists, but they also alienated forces whom Brüning and his successors regarded as their natural political allies. This was certainly true for the East Elbian and especially

Im Mittelpunkt Heinrich Brüning (1885–1970)

The first of the so-called presidential chancellors remains one of the most controversial figures in modern German history. The question whether Brüning was the last hope of democracy or acted as the gravedigger of the Weimar constitution remains unresolved, in large part because the chancellor himself supplied contradictory evidence for his thoughts and actions.

Brüning was born in Münster in Westphalia, and he died in exile in Norwich, Vermont. He came from a very devout Catholic family of merchants and small businessmen. The future chancellor's personality did not seem to be suited for a political career. He was highly intelligent, gifted with superb organizational skills and an unmatched ability to master intricate details. He was also, however, a poor orator, lacked any sense of humor, and remained a lifelong bachelor with few intimates or friends. To the outside world, he exhibited a cold and efficient demeanor with no deep emotions. But this was a mask. In reality Brüning was a highly sensitive man with a number of underlying passions that he repressed until he wrote his memoirs long after retiring from public office.

Brüning was one of the many Germans of his generation for whom World War I became a crucial turning point. To the end of his life, Brüning was marked by his *Fronterlebnis*. When the war broke out, he volunteered immediately for military service, in spite of a physical ailment that would have kept him out of the army. He served with great distinction on the western front, and almost to the end of the conflict he remained convinced that Ludendorff and Hindenburg could achieve victory for Germany.

Brüning hated the Revolution of 1918 and all it stood for. As an officer, he was personally humiliated by members of a workers' and soldiers' council. In an assessment characteristic of his mind-set, he regarded the upheavals of 1918–1919 as evidence of a lack of self-discipline and moral failing on the part of the revolutionary leaders. The experience also reinforced his conviction that Marxism was not only a wrong-headed political ideology, but also a moral evil.

In 1919 Brüning became active in the Catholic trade union movement, in part because he wanted to do his part to prevent Catholic workers from joining the Socialist unions. From 1920 to 1930 Brüning was the general secretary of the Catholic trade unions. In 1924 Brüning became a member of the Reichstag as a deputy of the Center Party. His organizational talents were quickly recognized, and he became the chairman of the Reichstag's Ways and Means Committee where he rapidly earned a reputation as an expert in the intricacies of budget making. Ideologically, Brüning was a supporter of the right wing in the Center Party. Unlike Wilhelm Marx and the leaders of the Prussian Center Party, Brüning warmly welcomed Ludwig Kaas's election as chairman of the Center Party in 1928.

After the onset of the depression and the failure of the democratic parties to form a parliamentary government, President von Hindenburg asked Brüning to become Reich chancellor. Among the reasons for this choice—which had been engineered by a group of Hindenburg's advisers, including Brüning's longtime ally, General Kurt von Schleicher—were not only Brüning's reputation as a fiscal expert but also his willingness to exclude the Social Democrats from any federal cabinet and his unspoken, but well-known, conviction that Germany was better off as a monarchy than as a republic.

As chancellor, Brüning immediately embarked on a policy of deflation and budget cutting. His decision reflected his innate fiscal conservatism, but he also had political reasons of his own. In part these were a throwback to the concept of the "primacy of foreign policy." The chancellor was convinced that Germany's reparations burden and the disarmament clauses of the Versailles Treaty were the primary obstacles that prevented the Reich from regaining its status as a Great Power. He was therefore determined to convince the Allies that Germany's domestic system would become destabilized unless they accepted his foreign policy demands. In addition, Brüning was convinced that, in moral terms, the depression was at least in part a deserved punishment for the hedonism and excesses of the 1920s.

Brüning abhorred Nazism as much as Marxism, and he did all he could to prevent Hitler from controlling the powers of the national government. However, like most conservatives, he thought it was best to defuse the Nazi threat by co-opting Hitler's movement and saddling it with government responsibility. To that end, he attempted to persuade the leaders of the Prussian Center Party to agree to a coalition with the Nazis in the state government. The Prussian Center Party leaders refused, although Brüning continued to work on this project virtually until the day Hitler became Reich chancellor.

Ironically, Brüning reached the pinnacle of his career in the Center Party just as the life of Germany's political parties was ending. In May 1933 Brüning succeeded Monsignor Kaas (who had been called to Rome to take a position in the Vatican administration) as national chairman of the Center Party, only to preside over the party's dissolution. Brüning was not physically harmed during the early months of the Third Reich, but the increasing number of threats against him persuaded him to leave Germany in May 1934. This was a wise decision because a number of prominent Catholic politicians were murdered during the days of the so-called Röhm affair. The former chancellor eventually made his way to the United States, and from 1939 until 1950 he taught in the government department at Harvard University.

Brüning undoubtedly hoped that after the end of World War II he would be able to resume his political career in Germany. But that was not to be. Konrad Adenauer, the leader of the Christian Democratic Union (the successor of the Center Party), was determined to prevent the men he regarded as the failed politicians of Weimar from playing a significant role in Germany after 1945.

Brüning did teach at the University of Cologne from 1951 to 1954, but then he returned, a bitter man, to the United States. For the rest of his life, he devoted himself to writing his memoirs, but he insisted they should not be published until after his death. When the book appeared, it caused a sensation because it opened a whole plethora of old controversies and wounds. Brüning openly avowed his monarchist feelings and his distrust of parliamentary democracy. Above all, he revealed himself a man who was emotionally dependent on Hindenburg and the Neo-Conservatives. In long passages, Brüning repeatedly asserted his loyalty to the dead Reich president while mourning Hindenburg's injustice to the former chancellor. All in all, the memoirs certainly confirmed that Adenauer was right that Brüning should not play a major role in Germany's public life after 1945.

East Prussian landowners. Throughout the 1920s the chronically depressed agricultural areas of the east had benefited from an "Aid for the East" (*Osthilfe*) program, which provided cheap credit to East Elbian farmers and businessmen. Until 1930 the program was largely financed by federal money but administered by Prussian state agencies. The Prussian authorities applied fairly stringent criteria before applicants could qualify for subsidized loans. The state administrators were generally not willing to waste money on estates that were so heavily indebted as to be unsalvageable even with government credit. (East Elbian landowners had long complained that the Prussian administrators of the Osthilfe used excessively strict standards in judging credit applications.)

The depression vastly increased not only the need for subsidies but also the number of farms threatened by bankruptcy. The Junker spokesmen for East Elbian agriculture appealed to Hindenburg—a fellow East Prussian landowner—to force a liberalization of the aid program. Brüning was aware of these concerns, and before becoming Reich chancellor he promised the Reich president he would take steps to ease the credit crisis in the east. He kept his promise by gradually pushing Prussian state agencies out of the administration of the Osthilfe. But even these measures were not enough to satisfy Hindenburg's friends and neighbors; they denounced the chancellor as an "agrarian Bolshevik" who was trying to destroy the Junkers as a social class. Their criticism was echoed by the Agrarian League and the DNVP, both of whom grew increasingly strident in calling for Brüning's dismissal.

The first phase of the New Conservative era came to an abrupt end in the spring of 1932. Hindenburg's term of office as Reich president ended in April of that year, and Brüning had hoped that the major parties, including the Nazis and the DNVP, would agree to Hindenburg's reelection by acclamation. The moderate groups agreed, but the DNVP,

the Nazis, and the Communists refused. There would have to be a full-scale election. Eventually the DNVP nominated Theodor Duesterberg, the second in command of the Stahlhelm; Hitler became the Nazi Party's candidate; and the Communists again put up their own leader, Ernst Thälmann. Brüning and the moderate Weimar parties (including the SPD) supported Hindenburg. After a bitter campaign the former field marshal was reelected, but the country he headed was more polarized than ever.

Soon after the presidential election, Hindenburg withdrew his support from Brüning. Kurt von Schleicher and other New Conservatives close to the president persuaded him that the Center Party chancellor, for all his good intentions, had been too accommodating to the forces of democracy and parliamentarism, especially the Social Democrats. Franz von Papen, who had initially welcomed Brüning's appointment as chancellor, promised to have fewer scruples. His goals for constitutional reform were not significantly different from those of his predecessor, but his political tactics were far less subtle. Whereas Brüning had at least adhered to the letter of the constitution and attempted to find a consensus in the Reichstag for his policies, Papen reveled in his near-total lack of support in parliament. Papen's continuation in office and the realization of his program completely depended on the Reich president and the men around him.

Papen moved quickly to translate the New Conservatives' ideas on constitutional "reforms" into practice. With the stroke of the Reich president's pen, the chancellor obtained the destruction of major parts of the German federal structure. State elections in April 1932 had produced a parliamentary deadlock in Prussia. The state legislature was unable to elect a new government, and under the terms of the Prussian constitution the old cabinet remained in office as a caretaker government. Both the New Conservatives and the Nazis had long regarded the Prussian cabinet, in which Social Democratic ministers headed key departments, as a major obstacle to their long-range plans. The Prussian government, for example, had been instrumental in persuading the Brüning cabinet to order the dissolution of the two primary causes of the escalating street violence, the Nazi Stormtroopers and the Communists' Red Front Fighters Association.

Papen, soon after coming into office, revoked the ban on the Nazi Stormtroopers (the ban on the communist paramilitary organization remained in force), permitting the Nazi thugs to resume their activities on Germany's streets. When the level of political violence predictably increased, Papen claimed that the Prussian government was unable to maintain law and order. On July 20 the Reich cabinet issued a presidential order placing the administration of Prussia under federal control, with Papen himself serving as Reich commissioner for Prussia. For the remainder of the year Papen and the Reich minister of the interior, Baron von Gayl, an old-line Hugenberg conservative, carried out a purge of the Prussian civil service. Dozens of pro-republican administrators were dismissed or retired and replaced with men who sympathized with the New Conservatives.

Papen's decision to rescind the dissolution order against the Stormtroopers was a gesture of appeasement toward the Nazis. Like Brüning, Papen at this time regarded Hitler's movement as a potential ally, not an enemy, of New Conservatism. For this reason, the New Conservatives had not been unduly alarmed when, as a result of the national elections in September 1930, the Nazis became the second largest party in the Reichstag. Instead of the twelve deputies elected in 1928, there was now a sea of 107 brown shirts in the national parliament. The Nazis' attitude during the presidential election of 1932 eventually convinced Brüning that he could not deal with Hitler, but Papen was still sure he could secure the goodwill of both the DNVP and Hitler's party. There were no difficulties with Hugenberg, the leader of the DNVP. The DNVP provided most of the ministers in Papen's "cabinet of barons" (so called because of the large number of aristocrats in the government) and the only real

parliamentary support for the second presidential chancellor. Papen also had the support of most East Elbian landowners and a large section of the business community. As for the Nazis, Papen (and Schleicher) followed the same course that had led Brüning to disaster. Papen agreed to Hitler's demand for new national elections in July 1932 when the Great Depression had reached its full impact. The results were yet further losses for the moderate parties and the DNVP, while the Nazis more than doubled their representation in the Reichstag. They were now the largest party in parliament; their parliamentary leader, Hermann Göring, was elected speaker of the house.

In return for these political gifts, Papen and Schleicher thought they had Hitler's agreement to support, or at least tolerate, the New Conservative regime. Here they were very much mistaken. The Nazis were not willing to become Papen's junior partners. In August Hitler demanded that Hindenburg appoint the Nazi leader as chancellor with powers to run the country by decree—much as Brüning and Papen had been doing since 1930. On Papen's advice, the Reich president refused, and that decision ended, at least for a time, the honeymoon between the new chancellor and the Nazis. In a desperate attempt to gain time, Papen called for new elections only four months after the July Reichstag had been elected. The results of the November 1932 contest brought significant losses for the Nazis, although they remained the strongest party in the Reichstag. In view of what the New Conservatives called the continuing "constitutional emergency"—that is to say, a Reichstag that refused to cooperate with the New Conservatives—Papen then asked the Reich president to suspend the constitution and establish a temporary military dictatorship.

Papen made his new "reform" proposal in November, but by that time the man behind the scenes, Kurt von Schleicher, felt he had a better alternative. The general knew that Hindenburg would be reluctant to agree to the blatant destruction of the constitution that he had sworn to uphold. In addition, Schleicher argued that Papen's plan for a military dictatorship was both politically risky and unnecessary. The general felt he had found a way out of the constitutional impasse that would accomplish the basic goals of the New Conservatives without resorting to open dictatorship. Schleicher offered to head a Reich government that he claimed would, unlike his predecessor's, be able to work harmoniously with a majority of the Reichstag.

Kurt von Schleicher's brief tenure as chancellor revealed a third variant of the New Conservative scenario. The new chancellor was hardly a flaming democrat. Like Brüning and Papen, the general was disdainful of parties and parliamentary democracy. He differed from his immediate predecessors only in that he envisioned an extraparliamentary populist corollary to the basic authoritarian structure that he was convinced Germany needed. The core of Schleicher's plans—and little more is discernible even now because the general was given to great secrecy but little systematic thought— seems to have been to ally the forces of New Conservatism with big business, organized labor, and the Nazi Party. To secure the support of these groups, he offered the employers tax relief, the unions an expanded public works program, and the Nazis a share of governmental power; Gregor Strasser, the number-two figure in Hitler's party, would become vice-chancellor in Schleicher's cabinet.

Schleicher's scheme failed ignominiously and rapidly. Some spokesmen for the business community reacted positively, but most union leaders were unwilling to trust a political general who, in the past, had made no secret of his animosity toward organized labor and Social Democracy. As for the Nazis, Gregor Strasser was willing to go along with Schleicher's plans, but Hitler was not. When the Nazi leader rejected Strasser's advice for the NSDAP's future course of action, the Nazis' second in command resigned all of his party offices. He also issued a statement urging all those who sympathized with his views not to follow his own example, but to remain loyal to Adolf Hitler. By the end of December 1932, Schleicher, too, fell back on the proposal of a military dictatorship as the only way out of the constitutional impasse. Hindenburg still refused.

After almost three years in power, the balance sheet of New Conservatism was not impressive. The presidential chancellors had destroyed parliamentary democracy and a good part of the German federal structure, but they were unable to put into place constitutional changes that would restore authoritarianism permanently to the Reich. But all was not yet lost. Papen, who had by now recovered from the shock of his dismissal and betrayal by his old friend Kurt von Schleicher, had yet another plan for realizing the New Conservatives' political goals. He claimed the scheme would not violate the letter of the Weimar constitution, it would secure the Nazis' cooperation, and it would keep the New Conservatives in positions of real power.

THE NAZIS' RISE TO POWER

After he became chancellor in 1933, Adolf Hitler often included in his interminable speeches a section that came to be dubbed his "party history." Invariably lasting about half an hour, the party history expressed the Führer's conviction that providence had selected him, the unknown soldier of World War I, to overcome all obstacles and create first a powerful political movement and then the Third Reich.

Actually, Hitler's rise to power reflected more mundane factors at work. One of these was German history itself. The Nazis did not burst on the German political scene without warning. They were the inheritors and beneficiaries of deep and ill-hidden strains of anti-Semitism, antimodernism, and antiparliamentarism in German society. This was the fertile soil that had nurtured völkisch movements since the 1890s. The lost war and the disappointments many Germans felt with the lackluster performance of the Weimar Republic provided further nourishment. Still, with all these factors present, the Nazis received less than 3 percent of the popular vote in 1928.

It required the depression to transform the National Socialists from a fringe group to a major political force. The political effects of the economic disaster—the paralysis of the parliamentary system, the government's seeming unwillingness to deal with the steadily worsening economy, the rising strength of the Communist Party—persuaded many Germans that only Hitler and his party provided hope for the future and an alternative to the triumph of Bolshevism. The Nazis scored their first success in the Prussian local elections of December 1929 and then, roughly paralleling the continuing downturn of the economic indicators, went from victory to victory until in the depths of the depression 37 percent of the German electorate cast their ballots for Hitler's movement.

To make effective use of the influx of members and voters that the depression brought to the party, the Nazis used a system of three parallel organizational structures, each with separate but complementary functions. The party proper was divided into regional units called *Gaus* (a *Gau* was an old Germanic territorial unit), each headed by a *Gauleiter* (Gau leader). The Gaus's boundaries for the most part corresponded to the Reichstag electoral districts, and the primary function of the activists in the Gaus was to campaign and get out the vote.

A second organizational rung consisted of affiliates (*angeschlossene Verbände*) in which Nazi sympathizers (and party members) were organized according to economic and professional interest groups ranging from farmers to the "National Socialist Association of Munich Coal Dealers." Their purpose was to spread the Nazi influence among the various economic interest groups and, if possible, turn them into agencies of political support for the Nazi cause. The party was particularly effective in organizing farmers, retailers, university students, and physicians.

Finally, there was the most visible element of the Nazi Party, the paramilitary groups, notably the Stormtroopers (*Sturmabteilung*—SA). (The organization that was later to become the dreaded symbol of the regime—the *Schutzstaffel* [Protection Squad—SS]—was still in an embryonic stage of development.) During the last years of the Weimar Republic, the SA, with a membership of about 400,000

at the end of 1932, was undoubtedly the most important part of the Nazis' political strategy. The Stormtroopers put up posters, protected the party's rallies from disturbances by political rivals, and terrorized opponents and innocent bystanders alike. The Stormtroopers effectively symbolized both the Nazis' militancy and their brutality.

The Nazis' triple organizational structure and their eclectic and opportunistic program were well designed to reap political benefits from an atomized and fearful German electorate. Blatantly copying the practices of Mussolini's regime in Italy, in literally hundreds of rallies, the Nazis practiced a typically fascist style of campaigning: masses of swastika flags and patriotic symbols, stern-looking uniformed guards, martial music, and histrionic speakers. At the same time, the omnipresent Stormtroopers, who were involved in daily brawls with Communists and other political opponents, impressed particularly the German middle and upper classes with their dedication to saving Germany from the—imaginary—imminent Bolshevik revolution. The Nazis were also sophisticated politicians; Hitler was the first modern political leader to make extensive use of the airplane during his campaigns.

The NSDAP's message in its rallies was always the same. The party's speakers insisted that Germany's political and economic problems had personified causes—Jews, "November [1918] criminals," Marxists—and that the only solution was the elimination from power of the evildoers and of the system of parliamentary democracy that, the Nazis claimed, had enabled these elements to come to power. But Adolf Hitler and his party did not limit themselves to attacking the Weimar Republic. They also promised relief from want and fear to virtually every segment of German society. It did not seem to matter that some of the proposals were mutually contradictory or that the party could show no realistic means of financing its various giveaway plans. The message repeated ad nauseam was that once the Nazis came to power, all of the difficulties would be automatically resolved.

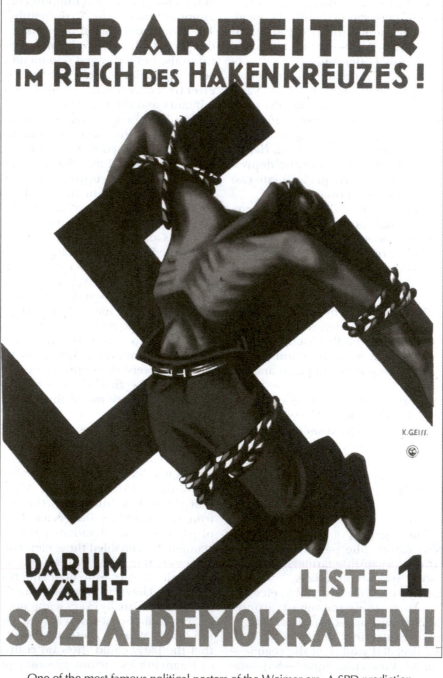

One of the most famous political posters of the Weimar era. A SPD prediction during the Reichstag election of July 1932: If the Nazis come to power, the workers of Germany will be crucified on the swastika. (Source: Photos 12/Alamy.)

For a time, these methods worked well. Desperate times produced desperate reactions. The spectacular Nazi successes in the September 1930 Reichstag elections (18 percent of the popular vote) were only a first step. In the next two years, the Nazis increased their vote in almost every local, state, and national election. Eventually, more than three out of every ten voters cast their ballots for the Nazis, enabling the party to control a number of state and local governments.

The question as to who joined and voted for the Nazis has long fascinated historians. For some years, it was accepted as axiomatic that the Nazis obtained most of their support from the lower middle class, but newer studies have demonstrated that they made significant inroads into all segments of German society. Still, there were differences. Among the party's members and activists, the lower middle class was heavily overrepresented relative to its share of the population. In contrast, blue-collar workers, particularly if they lived in large cities, were underrepresented. As far as the voters were concerned, Catholics cast fewer Nazi ballots than Protestants. Small-town and rural inhabitants were more likely to vote Nazi than those who lived in large cities. In terms of occupation and social class, there was a positive correlation between income and status and the Nazi vote. That is to say, Nazi support was strongest among the well-to-do. The old Mittelstand (small businessmen, retailers, civil servants, and academics) cast the highest proportion of the Nazi vote.

The NSDAP's chauvinistic, anti-Marxist, antidemocratic, and anti-Semitic message generated massive popular support, and for that reason the New Conservatives were eager to use Hitler's movement for their own purposes. As a result, the Nazis and the New Conservatives joined forces in a number of anti-republican ventures. Supported by glowing editorial comments in the publications of Hugenberg's media empire, the Nazis and Stahlhelm in November 1929 launched an initiative campaign against the Young Plan. In August 1931 the Nazis and a variety of New Conservative groups met in Harzburg in the state of Brunswick (the Land Brunswick was by now under the control of a Nazi–New Conservative coalition government) to inaugurate the "National Opposition," or "Harzburg Front," promising to cooperate in destroying the Brüning government and parliamentary democracy.

Hitler was undoubtedly gratified by the enthusiasm of the thousands who packed his rallies and by the interest that the leaders of Germany's "natural" elites took in his movement, but he also recognized the political limitations of his situation. The NSDAP's New Conservative allies were quite content to permit the NSDAP its rallies and often violent street demonstrations, but they had no intention of yielding real power to the party. The Reich president twice—in August and November 1932—categorically refused to give Hitler dictatorial authority as the head of the Reich government.

The road to power through the ballot box presented similar obstacles. Without a clear majority at the polls, the Nazis—as the party's leader in Berlin and later Reich minister for propaganda, Joseph Goebbels, recognized—were in danger of "winning ourselves to death." In late fall 1932 it became obvious that the Nazis' popularity had crested. The noticeable decline of the party's popular vote in the November Reichstag elections was accelerated in the state and local contests that followed.

As it lost its momentum, the party developed serious organizational and financial problems. By the end of the year, it became difficult to maintain the party's cohesion. Especially the Stormtroopers were becoming restless and anxious to obtain the spoils of power. There had been a regional revolt in Berlin as early as March 1931, and extraordinary efforts on the part of Adolf Hitler were required to subdue the rebellious foot soldiers. Hindenburg's refusal to appoint the Nazi Führer chancellor on August 13 forced the SA to delay again the long-expected "night of the long knives," during which the Stormtroopers would be able to take revenge on their political and personal opponents without worrying about the legal consequences.

Finances presented another pressing problem. Both contemporaries and some scholars have argued that corporations and individual businessmen supplied large sums to the NSDAP in the 1920s and especially after the party's impressive showing in the September 1930 elections. Actually, as Henry Turner and others have demonstrated, support from these sources did not represent a major factor in the Nazi Party's finances. The NSDAP for the most part financed its activities on a pay-as-you-go basis through membership dues and various money-making schemes. It is true, however, that as victory seemed in sight in 1932, the party had gone heavily into debt, and the political setbacks in the fall of that year made it difficult for the Nazis to repay these loans. For a variety of reasons, then, contemporary observers as well as some later historians concluded that at the end of 1932 the NSDAP was on the verge of disintegration.

The party's political and financial difficulties persuaded Gregor Strasser—whose position as the NSDAP's chief of administration provided him with good insight into the party's true situation—to recommend that Hitler accept Schleicher's offer and permit Strasser to join the general's cabinet as vice-chancellor. As we saw, the Nazi leader refused; he wanted all or nothing. From the vantage point of December 1932, it looked very much as though it would be the latter.

The Nazis' further decline was halted not by destiny but by Franz von Papen and some of the other New Conservatives. The last phase of Hitler's rise to power is not the story of elemental forces in the electorate, but of backstage intrigues, blind ambition, and political naiveté among a small group of men. The ex-chancellor wanted revenge for Schleicher's cold coup, which had forced Papen out of office. Almost as soon as Papen cleared out his desk he began to send out feelers to Hitler and his associates. The efforts intensified in mid-December as it became

clear that Schleicher's scheme for securing the Nazis' cooperation had failed.

By early January 1933 a series of secret meetings involving Papen, Hitler, and a number of go-betweens had worked out what amounted to a backstage deal for a new coalition. Hitler would become chancellor in a cabinet composed of Nazis and New Conservatives. Papen, who intended that he would be the real power in the government, reserved for himself the posts of vice-chancellor and Reich commissioner for Prussia. In addition, the New Conservatives would have a clear majority in the cabinet; there were to be only three Nazi ministers. Papen's scheme promised a squaring of the political circle. If Hitler agreed, the new cabinet would be able to obtain a vote of confidence in the Reichstag and thus relieve the Reich president of the necessity of violating the letter of the constitution. At the same time, the proposed distribution of cabinet seats seemingly guaranteed New Conservative domination of the government. Incidentally, as Papen should have known, Hitler had no interest in collegial government. The number of cabinet meetings steadily declined from 72 in 1933 to 12 in 1935, 6 in 1937, and 1 in 1938. After 1938 the Reich cabinet never met again.

There remained only two obstacles: securing the cooperation of the Reichswehr and persuading Hindenburg to accept the scheme. The first difficulty was resolved by selecting General Werner von Blomberg as the minister of defense in the new cabinet. Blomberg, a career officer and personal friend of the president's son, was known as a Nazi sympathizer. Hindenburg's approval for a cabinet headed by Hitler was a little more difficult to obtain. The president had a personal dislike for Hitler, and Schleicher had been arguing—quite correctly—that the Nazis had lost their momentum, so all that was needed was to await their disintegration. Papen countered by pointing to the Nazis' recent success in the state elections in the minuscule Land of Lippe (with a total population of about 20,000), which Papen maintained showed the NSDAP was still a force that needed to be tamed. (Papen did not mention that the Nazis' success in the Lippe elections was the result of concentrating all of the party's resources on this agrarian backwater or that the moderate parties had done proportionately much better than Hitler's movement.)

Papen's arguments won out over Schleicher's. Hindenburg agreed to appoint Hitler chancellor, and on January 30, 1933, the new Reich cabinet was ready to take the oath of office. In addition to Hitler as Reich chancellor, there were only two other Nazi cabinet members: Hermann Göring served as Reich minister without portfolio and acting Prussian minister of the interior, and Wilhelm Frick, an old Bavarian associate of Hitler's from the days of the Beer Hall putsch, became Reich minister of the interior. They were joined by what appeared to be a formidable array of prominent New Conservatives including—in addition to Papen—Hugenberg, who became Reich and Prussian minister of economics and agriculture, and, as Reich minister of labor, the head of the Stahlhelm, Franz Seldte. The rest of the cabinet consisted of civil servants with conservative leanings, some of them holdovers from the Brüning cabinet.

GLEICHSCHALTUNG: THE ESTABLISHMENT OF NAZI TOTALITARIANISM

Adolf Hitler was determined to subject the Reich to permanent and total Nazi control. Germany was to become the instrument with which he would accomplish his long-established domestic and foreign policy goals. The Nazis, who were masters at creating bureaucratic euphemisms and double-speak, termed the first step in the process "synchronization," or *Gleichschaltung*. In essence, Gleichschaltung constituted a series of measures that prohibited all organized political activity other than that of the Nazi Party, established an increasingly efficient system of state-sponsored terror, converted the country's vestigial parliamentary democracy into

Hitler's personal dictatorship, and attempted to infuse all traditionally nonpolitical activities with Nazi values and ideas.

Hitler's foreign policy goals were based on two idées fixes that he pursued single-mindedly in the face of all setbacks and contrary empirical evidence. The Nazi leader's *Weltanschauung* (literally "worldview," that is to say, his ideology)—spelled out in considerable detail long before 1933 in innumerable speeches, his autobiography (*Mein Kampf*), and a second, unpublished manuscript (which was published after World War II under the title *Hitler's Second Book*)—rested on twin foundations: race and space. Hitler's "solution to the racial question" was the elimination of the Jews from Germany and Europe, although in 1933 it was not clear—perhaps not even to Hitler—if that meant forced emigration or physical extermination. There was no doubt, however, that "space" referred to the conquest of Russia and Eastern Europe to obtain the vast new *Lebensraum* (living space) that Hitler insisted Germany needed.

On the domestic side the two most immediate goals of the self-styled "government of national resurgence" were the attainment of a monopoly of political power for the "nationalist parties" and getting people back to work. Ironically, the Nazis' Gleichschaltung program was implemented largely by the New Conservatives who had originally intended that Hitler and the Nazis would play roles as junior partners in fulfilling the triumph of New Conservatism. The reason was that at least in the early stages of the Gleichschaltung, the New Conservative goals matched Hitler's own: destruction of democracy, rearmament, revision of the Versailles system, economic recovery.

During the drive for power, the Nazis' economic proposals had often been the object of derision by their opponents. Such ideas as abolishing interest in all banking transactions (one of the articles in the party's official 1920 program) were clearly ludicrous in a highly developed industrialized economy. During their many political campaigns, Hitler and his associates also did not hesitate to promise relief measures to virtually all segments of the economy: Farmers were assured that under Nazi rule tariffs would be sufficiently high to keep out foreign competition while small retailers could expect legislation forcing department stores out of business. Once in power the Nazis' economic radicalism was seemingly abandoned. Neither interest rates nor department stores disappeared. In fact for the most part, the chancellor during the first few months of 1933 left economic policies pretty much in the hands of his New Conservative minister of economics, Alfred Hugenberg, and the president of the Reichsbank. They in turn kept up the price, wage, and currency controls that Brüning had begun and Papen and Schleicher continued.

Nevertheless, there was a noticeable shift in priorities and, after a few months, major personnel changes as well. In contrast to his predecessors, Hitler determined that the government's first priority was not to safeguard the value of the mark but to reduce unemployment: The Führer immediately insisted on massive government-sponsored public works programs. Simultaneously he launched an unprecedented arms buildup. Within a week after becoming Reich chancellor, Hitler announced to his cabinet that during the next four to five years the regime's top priority would be providing the armed forces with whatever they needed. There were no objections from his New Conservative allies: Defense appropriations, which had constituted 4 percent of all public outlays before 1933, rose to 50 percent by 1938. The most dramatic and visible link between the public works effort and rearmament was the construction of the system of strategic superhighways, the *Autobahnen*. The emphasis on "getting things done" in turn contributed to the Nazis' undeniable popularity in the early years of the Third Reich. Here were leaders who seemingly did not let the country drift; they acted to lift Germany from the morass of economic turmoil. And the results were dramatic: The number of unemployed, which had stood at 6 million in January 1933 fell to 4 million by the end of the year.

Public works and rearmament programs are quite costly. Fearful of the inflationary effect of spending money the government did not have, Hitler's predecessors had consistently refused to embark on the path of deficit financing. The Nazis, however, had no patience with theories about orthodox public finance. The Reich chancellor demanded that the Reichsbank advance the government funds with which to revitalize the economy and begin the rearmament program. Since the president of the Reichsbank, Hans Luther, was known as an extreme fiscal conservative, Hitler asked him to resign. (Luther became ambassador to the United States.) His successor was Hjalmar Schacht, a former president of the Reichsbank whom the Republican government had dismissed early in 1930 when Schacht endorsed the Nazis' and New Conservatives' critique of the Young Plan. In September 1933 Hugenberg was maneuvered out of the cabinet. His successor as Reich economics minister was Kurt Schmitt, an insurance executive. The personnel change was more significant in Hugenberg's other position in the cabinet, that of minister of agriculture. Here his successor was R. Walther Darré, the NSDAP's specialist for agriculture.

In insisting on deficit financing, Hitler was not guided by any economic theories; he simply refused to let fiscal considerations stand in the way of his political goals. Schacht went along, not because he shared Hitler's political ambitions, but because like John Maynard Keynes in England, he was convinced that the German economy had so much unused capacity in 1933 that loosening the credit screws did not pose an inflationary danger. He agreed to advance the government an initial 600 million marks. They were followed in the next five years by an additional 12 billion marks. Especially in the first two years of the Nazi era, the pump-priming funds were not given in outright grants but channeled through what was formally a private corporation. Established in 1933 the Corporation for Metallurgical Research (known by its acronym as the Mefo Corporation) was a phantom business enterprise that awarded government contracts to various private companies, especially in the defense sector. The work contracted was paid for in advance by "Mefo credits," that is to say, bonds backed by the Mefo Corporation. The Mefo credits were guaranteed by the Reichsbank and could be exchanged for actual marks at any German bank.

Although some New Conservatives may have been skeptical about deficit financing, the dissolution of the independent labor unions had their full approval. On May 2, 1933, the government dissolved all labor unions and seized their assets. In place of an independent labor movement the Nazis established the German Labor Front (*Deutsche Arbeitsfront*—DAF). The new organization was an affiliate of the Nazi Party. Reflecting the Nazis' vision of the Volksgemeinschaft (see later, pp. 179–81), membership was compulsory for both employees and employers. The DAF had neither the right to strike nor the power to bargain collectively. The head of the new giant organization was Robert Ley, Gregor Strasser's successor as the NSDAP's chief of administration.

The government's ongoing efforts to attain self-sufficiency in raw materials and foodstuffs also continued earlier New Conservative policies. Like many on the political right, Hitler was convinced that the Allied blockade in World War I had been decisive in creating a seedbed for the revolutionary upheavals of 1918. Brüning and his successors had already raised tariffs on agricultural goods to protect Germany's farmers, but the Nazi regime went much further. The Law on Hereditary Landholding (*Reichserbhofgesetz*) and the establishment of the *Reichsnährstand* (Reich Food Estate) not only protected farmers against foreclosures but also severely regimented them. They were prohibited from selling their land; to link "blood and soil" in the Third Reich, farms had to be passed intact to a male heir. Inaugurated in September 1933, the administration of the Reich Food Estate controlled agricultural prices, production quotas, and imports. The goal was to raise agricultural production by providing farmers with a closed market and stable prices.

The drive for autarky and the one-sided emphasis on rearmament changed the traditional equilibrium of the German economy, a development that, ironically, soon threatened the success of the rearmament program itself. As we saw, since the founding of the empire, German economic growth was fueled primarily by exporting finished goods and importing food and unprocessed raw materials. The new government's economic policies resulted in a sharp decline of the country's exports and a corresponding loss of foreign currency income to buy needed imports. It soon became clear that without exports, the Reich would not be able to pay for the import of raw materials and agricultural commodities indispensable for armaments production and feeding the country's industrial workers.

A scheme of Schacht's, the "New Plan," seemed to provide a solution for a time. Schacht, who replaced Schmitt as economics minister at the beginning of 1935, proposed that rather than trading on the open world market, Germany should orient its trade relations toward those nations willing to conclude bilateral agreements that would bypass the hard currency problem. The cost of exports and imports would be calculated in the two national currencies, rather than in an international medium of exchange like the U.S. dollar or the British pound, and the accounts settled through "clearing agreements." Germany concluded a series of these bilateral agreements in the next few years, but because the United States and Great Britain refused to enter into international trade pacts on this basis, the Reich lost many of its traditional markets in North America and Western Europe. Instead, its trade was increasingly diverted toward eastern and southeastern Europe and South America.

The New Plan prevented the collapse of Germany's international trade in the early Nazi years, but it could not keep pace with the needs of the rearmament program. By the beginning of 1936, the Reich faced a very severe hard currency crisis; at one point the Reichsbank had on deposit only 88 million

A Nazi attempt to have Hitler ride on Hindenburg's coattails. The caption reads, "The marshal and the corporal are struggling alongside us for peace and equality." (Source: Photos 12/Alamy.)

marks in hard currency—enough to finance Germany's imports for one week. In addition, Germany's lack of strategic raw materials threatened Hitler's rearmament plans. As noted earlier, with the exception of coal, the Reich had virtually no significant amounts of commercially viable mineral resources. Hitler, however, was determined to achieve autarky in this area as well.

In August 1936 the Führer proposed that Germany develop a Four Year Plan—so named because it was to enable the Reich's army and economy to wage war within four years. He wrote a long memorandum that began by reiterating the inevitability of armed struggle against Bolsheviks and Jews and concluded with the demand that top priority be given to making Germany self-sufficient in strategic foodstuffs and raw materials. With a vast new bureaucracy, headed by Hitler's long-time associate Hermann Göring, the Four Year Plan administration set out to exploit the marginal raw material resources available in Germany regardless of the prohibitive costs involved. The Four Year Plan also financed the manufacture of synthetic substitutes for matériels needed to wage war, such as artificial rubber and gasoline extracted from coal.

The financial implications of the Four Year Plan led to a break between Hitler and his wizard of economic recovery, Hjalmar Schacht. In the past, private industry had shown little interest in developing Germany's mineral resources because of the costs involved; it was far cheaper, for example, to import iron ore from Sweden than to mine Germany's own low-grade deposits in Lower Saxony. Under the Four Year Plan, the huge costs involved in mining iron ore in Germany would be borne by the government (eventually a new nationalized state-owned conglomerate, the Reich Works "Hermann Göring," was set up for the purpose), and Schacht protested the inflationary consequences of this decision. When Hitler ignored his advice, Schacht at the end of 1936 resigned as head of the Reichsbank and as Reich economics minister. He was replaced by Walther Funk, a spineless former journalist who left economic decision making to Göring and the bureaucrats in the Four Year Plan administration.

The Four Year Plan was not a success. At the beginning of World War II, Germany's dependence on imported raw materials and foodstuffs was not significantly different than it had been in 1936. When the Four Year Plan was launched, its advocates claimed that Germany could save 464 million marks annually in hard currency spent on imports, but the actual figure in 1939 was closer to 150 million marks, and most of the revenue improvements came not from reduced imports but from increased exports in 1937 and 1938 as the worldwide Great Depression abated.

The Nazis also did not "cure" the depression, although the combination of price, wage, and currency controls along with deficit financing and the public works and rearmament programs probably enabled Germany to come out of the depths of the depression somewhat faster than was true of some other industrialized countries. Most visible (and constantly taunted by Nazi propagandists) was the dramatic drop in the number of unemployed. As we saw at the end of 1933 there were 4 million people without jobs; three years later that figure had dropped to 1.6 million. By 1938 the German industrial index had risen to 125 from a base figure of 100 in 1929.

The Nazis' economic policies were variants of measures that were also adopted by other countries, but, as David Schoenbaum and Pierre Ayçoberry have pointed out, the regime also set out to fundamentally alter politics and social relations in Germany. To be sure, even here the Nazis fell far short of their goals. One of their stated aims, for example, was the elimination of women from the labor force. A woman's natural place, the Nazis claimed, was in the home raising a family. In reality, however, the number of gainfully employed women rose from 4.2 million in 1933 to 5.2 million five years later. And the trend continued. During World War II, Germany had a higher percentage of women in the civilian workforce than Great Britain.

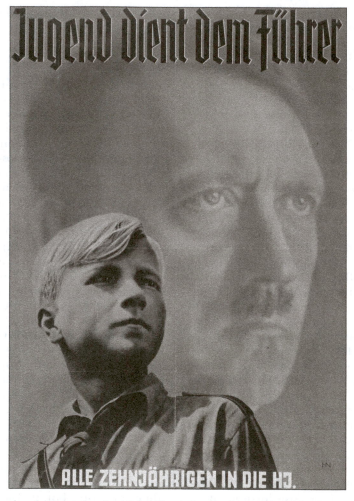

Jugend dient dem Führer

ALLE ZEHNJÄHRIGEN IN DIE HJ.

An advertisement for the Hitler Youth attempting to instill in Germany's youth the ideal of service to Hitler. The original text translates as "Youth serves the Führer; all ten-year-olds belong in the Hitler Youth." Note also the idealized features of the "Aryan" youth in the poster. (Source: Courtesy of Library of Congress.)

Nevertheless, the Nazis had a vision of German society that differed radically from the pluralistic and individualistic ideals that had characterized the imperial and Weimar years. The Nazis called their new entity a Volksgemeinschaft (people's community). Like virtually everything the new rulers undertook, the Volksgemeinschaft was part propaganda, part reality. The basic idea was the creation of a society in which the "racially" and politically "positive" elements would work together in harmony for the common good. At the same time the Volksgemeinschaft resolutely excluded groups in society that the Nazis classified as "racially" and politically "unhealthy" elements. These included not only Jews, Gypsies, and foreigners in general but also all political opponents, homosexuals, and the mentally ill. These groups had no rights and received no benefits; they remained outside the Volksgemeinschaft. Even for the in-group this did not mean a classless society, although the Nazis, and especially Hitler, felt the lives of the common people should be improved at the expense of the well-to-do. To this end the new rulers shifted more of the tax burden to the rich and instituted a variety of subsidies to benefit the economically disadvantaged members of the Volksgemeinschaft.

How important was the Volksgemeinschaft in creating support for the regime? Some historians, notably Götz Aly, claim that the Volksgemeinschaft, both as a propagandistic ideal and a set of social policies, was the key to Hitler's and the Nazis' popularity. Most Germans, according to Aly, did not look upon the Third Reich as a regime of terror and repression, but as a sort of "feel good dictatorship." Others, including the dean of German social historians, Hans-Ulrich Wehler, vigorously dispute Aly's claim. According to this group, the Volksgemeinschaft was nothing but propaganda and illusion.

Volksgemeinschaft brought benefits to some segments of German society, but essentially neglected the problems of others. Among the various social groups, labor suffered the most severe decline in rights and privileges, if not in standard of living. During the Weimar Republic, German workers had obtained a position of legal and financial security through a closely knit mesh of social legislation. Under the Nazis, as we saw, independent labor unions were eliminated outright on May 2, 1933. Their place was taken by the DAF, which instituted a variety of symbolic and cosmetic benefits. The Strength through Joy movement provided vacations to foreign lands for a relative few, day trips for many more, and improvements in the workplace for almost everyone. These benefits were certainly not equitable substitutes for the right of collective bargaining and protection from arbitrary dismissals, but it is true that many workers and their families

were appreciative of the fact that the regime seemed concerned about humanizing the work environment and providing holidays for groups that had not enjoyed such privileges before. These benefits, seemingly, were examples of the Volksgemeinschaft in action. In addition, the wages of some highly skilled specialists rose to such an extent that in 1936 the government determined excessive wage increases were creating inflationary pressures and decreed a wage freeze. Still, as a group, labor was undoubtedly worse off than during the good years of the Weimar Republic.

In sharp contrast to labor, large-scale industrialists, particularly those in heavy industry and armaments manufacture, were the real beneficiaries of the regime's policies. Iron and steel, portions of the chemical industry, and segments of what was then high technology (manufacturers of bomb sights, optics, and so forth) all gained at the expense of consumer industries. Farmers and some professionals also benefited, at least in economic terms, during the Nazi era. Although the basic problems of German agriculture were not addressed by the Nazis (German and European agriculture to this day suffers from inherent structural difficulties), farmers were undoubtedly better off than they had been during much of the Weimar and depression eras. Protection against foreclosures and the establishment of a regulated market, along with price subsidies, enabled many farmers to hold on to their land. Benefits for professionals came mostly at the expense of some of their colleagues when the Nazis' political legislation prohibited political opponents and Jews from practicing law and medicine or holding government jobs (see the later discussion, pp. 183–84).

Perhaps the most remarkable feature of the regime's social policies was the relative absence of benefits for a group that had supported the Nazis' struggle for power in disproportionately large numbers, the commercial and retailing sector of the old Mittelstand. Although Nazi propaganda continued to praise the small businessman as the personification of the "honest" merchant, and contrasted him with the avaricious Jewish "peddler," when it came to actual practice, the government gave preference to large-scale businesses. As had been true of the controlled economy during World War I, small businesses simply could not compete with the giant corporations in either prices or wages.

The Nazis' attempt to reshape German society culturally and politically went far beyond the timid efforts of the New Conservatives to return the Reich to authoritarianism. An integral part of this effort was the use of terror and repression against groups and ideas that the Nazis defined as incompatible with the Volksgemeinschaft.

Quite literally, Germany's first experience with what Ernest Fraenkel has called the "dual state"—that peculiar parallelism of government-sanctioned Nazi Party activities and party-approved government acts—was a wave of random political terror early in 1933. One of Hermann Göring's first decisions as acting Prussian minister of the interior was to dismiss most of the incumbent chiefs of police in Germany's largest state. With few exceptions, they were replaced by high-ranking SA leaders who immediately deputized hundreds of Stormtroopers as auxiliary police, ostensibly to prevent communist violence and ensure that "law and order would be maintained" during the campaign for a new Reichstag, to be elected on March 5.

There were virtually no Marxist disturbances, but during and after the campaign the SA used its semiofficial status to settle old and new scores. The country was soon dotted with unofficial concentration camps in which the SA (and in some cases SS units) incarcerated and maltreated their political opponents. In Prussia alone, between 25,000 and 30,000 persons were taken into "protective custody" in March and April 1933. Other Stormtroopers roamed through the streets engaging in random acts of violence against the property of Jews and political opponents. The SA was determined to have its "revolution."

After a few months, the government put an end to this phase of more or less spontaneous violence by the Stormtroopers. At the beginning of June, Hitler announced the Nazi revolution would continue for a thousand years, so there was no need for rash actions. Understandably, the Stormtroopers, and especially their ambitious chief of staff (nominally Hitler was head of the SA), Ernst Röhm, were not content to be relegated to the position of an honorific Sunday afternoon marching society. Röhm had larger ambitions for his SA. He hoped to destroy the autonomy of the Reichswehr and drown the army in a "sea of brown shirted militia."

Conflicts among the SA, the army, the SS, portions of the government, and the Nazi Party leadership simmered under the surface from the beginning of the regime. It is now clear that the SS and the Reichswehr cooperated in amassing evidence (much of it fabricated) that persuaded Hitler that Röhm and his associates were planning a putsch against the government and the NSDAP's civilian leadership. At the end of June 1934, Hitler ordered a purge of the Stormtroopers. Between June 30 and July 2, eighty-five prominent SA members, including Röhm and most the SA's provincial leaders, were summarily shot without trial by SS execution squads. At the same time, the driving forces behind the purge—Göring, Goebbels, and Hitler's secretary Rudolf Hess (who was appointed deputy Führer for party operations in the summer of 1933)—also decided on the death of some longtime political opponents who clearly had no connection to the SA or its possible ambitions. Gregor Strasser, Gustav von Kahr, Kurt von Schleicher and his wife, Papen's private secretary, and scores of others were all executed by the SS killers.

The purge of the SA leaders was followed almost immediately by a less violent but equally significant turnover in the ranks of the NSDAP's administrators. About 20 percent of the party's functionaries who held office in January 1933 were dismissed in the summer and fall of 1934. Most of them were replaced by new party members—that is, those who had joined the NSDAP since January 1933.

Under the leadership of Heinrich Himmler and Reinhard Heydrich, who headed the NSDAP's own espionage service (*Sicherheitsdienst*—Security Service, SD), the SS took the place of the Stormtroopers as the regime's primary instrument of terror. By 1936 the traditionally decentralized German police administration was nationalized and centralized, with Heinrich Himmler, who had begun his rise to power by seizing control of the Bavarian state police in 1933, appointed "head of the SS and chief of the German police," a position that left him only nominally subordinate to the Reich minister of the interior. The Nazis' terror apparatus included a national secret police (the infamous Gestapo), which replaced the states' political police units, and a regularized system of concentration camps that would eventually include the notorious extermination camps of World War II. The network of camps initially included three large institutions—Dachau near Munich, Sachsenhausen near Berlin, and Buchenwald near Weimar—and several smaller camps. They were run by a special unit of the SS, the Death Head Formations, under the command of Theodor Eicke, an old-line Nazi and the first commandant of Dachau. In 1937 the number of inmates was about 10,000, but the power of terror went far beyond the actual number imprisoned. Increasingly, the SS took justice into its own hands. Despite the efforts of some judges to preserve judicial autonomy, the Gestapo claimed the right to keep in "protective custody" even those who had been acquitted of all crimes by the regular courts.

Sadly, there were few protests from Hitler's New Conservative allies against the obvious violations of legal safeguards during and after the Röhm affair. (In a rare show of civil courage, Papen in a sense triggered the Röhm purge with a public speech in which he condemned the regime's many illegal acts.) To a large extent the reason for silence lay in the illusions that many New Conservatives had about the nature of Nazism. By destroying the SA, the leaders of the Reichswehr and the New Conservatives felt Hitler had eliminated the most "radical" element in the NSDAP. With what in retrospect can only be called

criminal naiveté, Hitler and the SS were seen as forces of moderation.

To be sure, Hitler deliberately cultivated such illusions about his "moderation." An important clue to Hitler's seeming willingness to cooperate with the old elites was the treaty with the papacy, for which negotiations began early in 1933. (The concordat itself was signed in July.) In return for a promise to stay out of politics and dissolve the Center Party, Germany's Catholics were permitted relatively free exercise of their religion and—a touchy subject throughout the Weimar years—the retention of segregated Catholic public schools. The price paid by the Catholic Church, however, was high: The concordat constituted at least tacit approval of the Nazis' dictatorship. In addition, the Nazis began to violate the terms of the agreement almost immediately, and we now know that one of Hitler's long-range goals was the destruction of both the Catholic and the Protestant churches. As Joseph Goebbels, after April 1933 the Reich minister for propaganda, put it, "we want to become our own church."

The New Conservatives were also grateful to the Nazis for seemingly stopping the Bolshevik revolution before it could begin. Here the Nazis took advantage of a fortuitous incident. On February 28, 1933, the Reichstag building was set on fire. The government immediately announced that the fire had been set by the Communists as a signal to launch the Bolshevik revolution. Within hours the Reich president, citing the communist menace, signed a decree authorizing the arrest of all members of the Communist Party as well as suspending civil liberties for the entire country. Today it is known that the Reichstag fire was not the work of the Communists. The arsonist was a deranged Dutch citizen, Marinus van der Lubbe, who had no connection to the KPD. Historically, the importance of the incident was not the fire, but its political consequences. The decree destroying civil liberties was supplemented by an Enabling Act in March 1933 that gave the government power to rule by decree for the next four years. With the exception of the SPD, all parties in the Reichstag voted for the law, thus ensuring the two-thirds majority amending the constitution. (All of the Communist deputies had either fled the country or been arrested, so that they were unable to vote.)

Political Gleichschaltung now moved into high gear. The decree of February 28 and the Enabling Act provided the legal authority for dissolving the Social Democratic Party soon after the KPD had been prohibited. A few months later, in July 1933, all parties except the NSDAP became illegal, and the Nazi Party was declared the "foundation of national authority." The various right-wing but non-Nazi paramilitary groups were merged with their Nazi counterparts.

By the end of 1933, the NSDAP had achieved a monopoly on political power in Germany, but the Nazis were not content with the destruction of political pluralism and individual civil liberties. On the first anniversary of Hitler's appointment as Reich chancellor, German federalism was destroyed. Instead of autonomous Länder, the German states were reduced to subunits of the central government. They were now headed by

Im Mittelpunkt Heinrich Himmler (1900–1945)

Heinrich Himmler was the personification of everyman as evil. Unprepossessing, pedestrian, and pedantic, Himmler was nevertheless in charge of implementing one of the worst crimes in all of history, the Holocaust. In 2008 the German newsmagazine *Der Spiegel* characterized Himmler as "the greatest mass murderer of all time."

Himmler was born in October 1900 into a solid, middle-class Bavarian family. His father, Joseph Himmler, was principal of the prestigious Wittelsbacher Gymnasium in Munich and private tutor to Prince Heinrich of Bavaria. The prince also became Himmler's godfather. Himmler attended school in Landshut, and while he did well academically, he was singularly inept in athletics. Nevertheless, perversely, he was determined to pursue a military career. Himmler served in the 11th Bavarian infantry regiment during the last two years of World War I, but the end of the conflict also effectively ended his ambitions to become a professional officer. He would eventually be in command of vast armies, but his role was that of a political soldier, not a regular officer.

After World War I Himmler enrolled in the agronomy department of the Technical University of Munich with the goal of becoming an agricultural estate manager. He failed in this endeavor, and was equally unsuccessful as a chicken farmer. His political career showed more promise. During his student days Himmler had become interested in extreme right-wing organizations and their racist and anti-Semitic ideology. He joined one of the most extreme of these groups, the Thule Society. Himmler also began his lifelong obsession with Nordic mythology and folklore.

Himmler became a member of the Nazi Party and the Stormtroopers while still a student in Munich, and he participated in the failed Beer Hall putsch. After Hitler was released from jail, Himmler joined the fledgling Schutzstaffel (Protection Squad, SS), becoming head of the SS in Bavaria. At this time the SS was a small (some 280-member) subunit of the much larger SA. The members of the SS were used primarily as bodyguards for Hitler as he campaigned throughout Germany.

By 1929 Himmler headed the SS in all of Germany. He now set out to mold the organization into an association of supposedly racially superior beings. Although Himmler himself did not look like the ideal Aryan (Albert Forster, the Nazi Gauleiter of Danzig, who did have blue eyes and blond hair, in a fit of anger once shouted, "if I looked like Himmler, I wouldn't talk about race"), he was determined to make the SS into the Nordic-Aryan order of the future. He instituted strict

Reich plenipotentiaries, most of whom were Nazi Party Gauleiters. In their new positions as government officials, the party's provincial leaders worked under the supervision of the Reich minister of the interior but, typical of the dual state, as Gauleiters they remained Hitler's direct subordinates.

The most important constitutional change, however, came after the death of the Reich president in August 1934. Hindenburg's demise had been expected for some time, and both Hitler and the New Conservatives had plans for the future. It was no secret that many of the New Conservatives hoped for a restoration of the monarchy after Hindenburg's death. Hitler, of course, had no intention of sharing power with an emperor. Instead he hastened to secure the support of the Reichswehr, potentially the most important autonomous power factor in the country, for his future plans. The scheme worked. Hitler's gift to the army in the form of rendering the Stormtroopers politically impotent persuaded most of the Reichswehr's leaders that their organizational future was secure under Hitler's leadership. They raised

membership rules for the SS, designed to exclude all applicants with Jewish or "racially inferior" ancestors. These rules also applied to prospective wives of SS members.

All this playing with eugenics did not propel the SS into a position of power in Nazi Germany. That began in 1933 when Himmler in his capacity as the newly appointed chief of the secret police in Bavaria began a system of concentration camps that incarcerated the regime's political enemies. In the next years Himmler added ever more positions and titles, all part of the Nazi system of state-sponsored terror. A major step forward in his career came in July 1934, when the SS demonstrated its loyalty to Hitler (the motto of the SS was "my honor is loyalty") by executing dozens of its comrades in the SA for their participation in a nonexisting plot to overthrow Hitler.

During World War II it was only natural that Hitler delegated to Himmler the task of subjecting the Third Reich's supposed racial enemy, the Jews, to "special treatment" (*Sonderbehandlung*), the Nazi code word for extermination. There is no doubt that Himmler implemented the Holocaust for reasons of ideological conviction. In a speech in October 1943 to high-ranking SS officers he proclaimed that the SS should be especially proud of its role in the Holocaust. He also insisted that without the extermination of the Jews in Europe, every Jew would become a spy and saboteur, determined to undermine the German war effort—just as they had done during World War I.

In the last weeks of World War II Himmler had delusions of a different sort. He recognized that Germany could not win the war, but he also thought he would be able to negotiate an alliance between the Third Reich and the Western allies against the Soviets. The British and the Americans, of course, refused to have anything to do with Himmler.

When Hitler found out about Himmler's overtures, he flew into a rage. On the day before he committed suicide the Nazi dictator stripped Himmler of all his state and party offices and expelled him from the Nazi Party. After Germany's unconditional surrender Himmler tried to disguise himself as a simple soldier in order to escape detection in the chaos of the immediate postwar days. He did not succeed. He was captured by British forces who soon discovered his true identity. Before he could be interrogated Himmler committed suicide by biting on the cyanide pill which all high-ranking SS officers had been issued in the final weeks of the war. The former SS leader is buried in an unmarked grave somewhere on the Lüneburg Heath.

no objections when immediately after Hindenburg's death Hitler added the functions of the Reich president's office to his other duties. On the contrary, the army's relationship to Hitler was cemented by an oath of personal loyalty to the Nazi leader in his new capacity as Reich president. As of mid-1934, Hitler's power rested on the triple authority—of his function as Reich president, Reich chancellor, and head of the Nazi Party.

Along with the political transformation of the country, the Nazis enacted measures designed to eliminate Jews and political opponents from the Volksgemeinschaft. As early as April 1933, a euphemistically named "Law for the Reestablishment of a Professional Civil Service" provided for the dismissal of all political opponents and Jews from any civil service positions. The initial exemption for veterans of World War I was soon eliminated from the law. In quantitative terms, the subsequent purge of the civil service involved some 1–2 percent of Germany's public employees (between 15,000 and 30,000 people), but in the higher ranks of the civil service the percentage of those dismissed or demoted was as high as 12 percent.

At the same time, the most notorious Jew baiter among the Nazi provincial leaders, Julius Streicher (the Gauleiter of Franconia), with Hitler's personal approval, organized a nationwide boycott of Jewish businesses. Negative international reaction to Streicher's boycott—in the form of countermeasures against German exports in the United States and other foreign countries—as well as the SA's uncontrolled violence, soon brought an official end to the anti-Jewish boycott but not to further anti-Semitic measures. The regime simply turned to legislation instead of party-sponsored "spontaneity." Meeting in a special session at the 1935 Nazi Party congress, the thoroughly gleichgeschaltete Reichstag passed the Nuremberg Laws. This series of measures attempted to define "Jewishness" on the basis of a person's ancestry: Thus persons having one or more Jewish grandparents were categorized as Jewish or of "mixed

race." Marriages between non-Jews and Jews were prohibited, and Jews lost their German citizenship; they became aliens in their own country.

These essentially negative measures destroyed all forms of pluralism in German society. They were also a prerequisite for what the Nazis saw as the positive building blocks toward the establishment of a true Volksgemeinschaft. "Positive" steps included above all the politicization of all cultural and artistic life. An important development in this respect was the establishment of a new cabinet post, the Reich ministry of propaganda and public enlightenment. Headed by Joseph Goebbels, the Gauleiter of Berlin and longtime propaganda chief of the NSDAP, the new ministry, staffed by a massive bureaucracy, made sure that nothing was published or exhibited that was not approved by the propaganda ministry. To ensure that unsuitable literature did not reach the eyes of the public in the future, the propaganda ministry and various party offices issued monthly lists of prohibited and approved books. The propaganda ministry also issued daily guidelines to the German press, complete with suggested editorials and instructions on how to treat various stories.

Long before they came to power, the Nazis had promised that under their rule German cultural and artistic life would experience a new burst of creativity. "Folk-related" and "race-conscious" arts and literature were to take the place of "Jewish decadence" and "liberal philistinism." The Nazis' cultural program, in short, was a revolt against modernism. As was true of most of their endeavors, the Nazis proved far more adept at destruction than creativity. The new era of cultural flowering began, appropriately enough, with black listings and book burnings. In May 1933 university students in various German towns, with the full approval of Goebbels and other leaders, staged an auto-da-fé in the capital and other cities during which they committed to the flames literary symbols of Germany's supposedly decadent Jewish and liberal past: books by Heinrich Heine and the Mann

Hitler, Göring, and Goebbels taking the salute at a parade. The picture probably dates from the early days of World War II. Hitler and Goebbels are giving the Nazi salute while Göring is lifting his jewel-encrusted Reich marshal's baton. (Source: Courtesy of Library of Congress.)

brothers, the plays of Bertolt Brecht, and the works of Sigmund Freud, among many others. These authors were then officially banned in the Third Reich; their works disappeared from bookstores and library shelves.

In the visual arts, too, the focus of the regime's efforts was negative rather than positive. To be sure, in July 1937 a new museum, the House of German Art (after 1945 it became the House of Art), opened in Munich. Designed to look like a neoclassical temple, the new museum staged annual shows of "German" paintings and sculptures; Hitler himself made the final selections. For paintings he invariably chose idealized neorealistic depictions of farm life, battles, and Nazi leaders, himself included. The Führer's favorite sculptures were oversized, idealized, neoclassical nudes representing heroic abstractions ("The Army," "The Party," "Motherhood").

For example, the main entrance to the new Reich chancellery, which the architect Albert Speer designed to Hitler's specifications, was flanked by two monumental male nudes by Arno Breker, the dictator's favorite sculptor. One, holding a torch, represented "The Party"; the other, brandishing a sword, symbolized "The Armed Forces."

But in his address celebrating the opening of the House of German Art, Hitler devoted most of his time to what one analyst has aptly called "a declaration of war on modernism." The Nazi leader ranted, "cubism, Dadaism, futurism, impressionism etc. have nothing to do with the German people. All of these concepts are simply the pretentious stammering of human beings whom God denied true artistic talent and instead gave the gift of gab and the ability to deceive."

Not surprisingly, the Nazis defined painting and sculpture from expressionism to abstract art as "degenerate." They insisted these works be removed from the walls of German museums. The artists were forbidden to practice their craft. The equivalent of book burning for the visual arts was a traveling show enti-tled "Degenerate Art," which toured Germany under the sponsorship of the Nazi Party in 1937. For this purpose the Nazis selected a number of modern—especially expressionist—paintings and sculptures and by clever use of lighting and labeling attempted to demonstrate the works' lack of artistic merit.

Through the Nazi purge of all forms of modernism, German intellectual life suffered a tremendous bloodletting. Because univer-sity professors were civil servants, the Law on the Restoration of a Professional Civil Service applied to them as well. About sixteen hun-dred Jewish and liberal university teachers were dismissed; many went into exile, espe-cially to the United States. Nazi attempts to replace them with "racial scientists" or to have something called "German physics" replace Einstein's "Jewish Theory of Relativity" were of course laughable. After the 1933 Nobel Peace Prize was awarded to a well-known paci-fist, Carl von Ossietsky (who was already in a concentration camp at the time), Germans were prohibited from accepting further Nobel Prizes. Instead, the regime created the German National Prize, whose first recipient was the NSDAP's semiofficial theoretician, Alfred Rosenberg.

Literature, too, suffered a precipitous decline. Many of Germany's best-known authors—the Mann brothers, Bertolt Brecht, Alfred Döblin—were forced into exile. In their place moved völkisch hacks, who pro-duced an endless stream of novels and short stories extolling the virtues of farm life and military combat. Only in the area of the cin-ema did productions of the Nazi era attain a technical quality that in some cases was greater than that of the Weimar years. This is not surprising, for film was particularly suited as a propaganda and mass-entertainment medium.

Propaganda and—literally—uniformity were the real essences of Nazi culture. From the attempt by the SS to create perfect physi-cal specimens in its elite ranks (members of the SS had to submit themselves and their prospective brides to a "racial examination"

before they could marry) to compulsory membership in the Hitler Youth after 1936 for all girls and boys over the age of ten, uniforms characterized the Nazis' projected image. The most impressive manifestation of the Nazis' self-projection was the NSDAP's national congresses, staged each September in Nuremberg. Here hundreds of thou-sands of Germans—all arrayed in a variety of uniforms—paraded before Hitler in an unending series of marches and ceremonies. Albert Speer designed massive neoclassical reviewing stands and arranged for special pyrotechnic effects. The purpose was to evoke the impression, for both participants and observers, of a unified nation subject to the total control of its godlike Führer.`

Apart from these incessant spectacles (the Nuremberg congresses had their counterparts on a smaller scale in the form of numerous regional rallies) what was daily life like for the average member of the Volksgemeinschaft? It was a combination of normality, fear, and conformity. The Nazis set out to establish a "totalitarian" regime in Germany, and to a large extent they succeeded. Lack of political freedom and complete control over all forms of public life constituted a yoke that bore heavily on those who valued their political and intellectual liberty. Yet there was another side to the Third Reich as well. For many Germans life under the Nazis was not all that different from what it had been before Hitler came to power. For the average, apolitical German—and this category included the vast bulk of the population—it was accommodation and conformity rather than a complete change of lifestyle that was expected. Gestapo and party agents (aided by numerous denunciations from the public at large) listened and looked intently for signs of nonconformity. Did one forget to put up a swastika flag on a national holiday? Did a *Volksgenosse* (people's comrade) consist-ently refuse to use the greeting "Heil Hitler"? But most Germans learned quickly to restrict their honest language to family members and trusted friends. Displaying a swastika flag on the many Nazi holidays and contributing money to the numerous party-sponsored collections were

In April 1933 Julius Streicher and the Nazi party organized a short-lived nationwide boycott of Jewish stores. The photo shows a Stormtrooper posted at a Jewish locksmith's shop to discourage customers from entering the store. The sign reads, "Germans! Fight back! Don't buy at Jewish [stores]!" (Source: Courtesy of National Archives and Records Administration.)

usually all that was necessary to show that one was a good member of the Volksgemeinschaft. In a very real sense, the society continued to function because most Germans, including many in the traditional elites—scientists, intellectuals, technocrats—did their jobs as they had done before. Even some opponents of the regime were permitted to live relatively unmolested for long periods of time once they agreed to refrain from political activity.

In particular the economy was subjected to relatively few restrictions. Despite currency controls, until the outbreak of World War II much of the free-market economy prevailed. Businessmen were free to make (and lose) money. During the peacetime phase of the

Third Reich there was no commodity rationing in effect, and although workers lost many
of their rights, notably that of collective bargaining, most could still change jobs without
undue difficulties. At the same time a price-
and-wage freeze introduced in 1938 helped
control inflation. From 1936 to 1944, inflation
was less than 2.9 percent per year.

FOREIGN RELATIONS

The foreign policy aims and tactics of the
Nazi regime were distinctly different from
those of the Weimar governments and the
New Conservative chancellors. All of the
Reich cabinets after World War I attempted
to "revise" the terms of the Versailles Treaty
to improve Germany's relative position in
the international community. The parliamentary foreign ministers—which meant
principally Gustav Stresemann—sought to
realize their revisionist ambitions primarily
(although not exclusively) through bilateral
and multilateral agreements with Germany's
former enemies. As we saw, these efforts
culminated in the Treaty of Locarno and
Germany's membership in the League of
Nations. The foreign policy of the new presidential cabinets did not abruptly reverse
Stresemann's tactics of accommodation, but
there was a distinct change in atmosphere.
Increasingly, the "Spirit of Locarno" was
replaced by confrontation and diplomatic
bullying.

The presidential governments pursued
three immediate foreign policy goals: ending reparations, reestablishing the Reich's
freedom of diplomatic action, and securing Germany's right to parity in armaments.
Eventually, they hoped to restore to Germany
the hegemony it had enjoyed in central and
southeastern Europe before 1914.

The results of their efforts were mixed.
Brüning's most spectacular bilateral initiative,
the Austro-German Customs Union of August
1931, was a complete failure. France immediately used its financial leverage in Vienna to
force Austria to withdraw its signature from

the treaty. The New Conservatives did somewhat better in the area of armaments and
reparations. In 1931 President Herbert Hoover
declared a one-year moratorium on inter-Allied
debts. Great Britain and France in turn agreed
to a suspension of the payments Germany
owed them. The moratorium actually ended
reparation payments permanently; Brüning
and Papen could take credit for lifting the
reparations burden from Germany. Germany
never resumed payments after 1932. In the
fall of 1932, the International Disarmament
Conference at Lausanne, Switzerland, recognized in principle Germany's right to
equality in armaments. On balance, the New
Conservatives had a right to be pleased with
their tactics. As Gerhard Weinberg has pointed
out, in 1932, given the Soviet Union's relative
weakness, Germany's position among the Great
Powers did not compare unfavorably with that
of 1914.

Some historians have interpreted Hitler's
foreign policy ambitions as a continuation of
the goals of Germany's leaders during World
War I and their New Conservative successors.
In reality, however, there was an essential
qualitative difference between the two sets
of objectives. The Nazi dictator, almost from
the moment he became chancellor, was not
content to regain the boundaries of 1914,
even if augmented with German control of
Belgium and Holland. In line with his fixa-
tion on race and space, Hitler regarded such
objectives as completely inadequate. He aimed
at the military conquest of Eastern Europe and
the Soviet Union, eventually to be followed
by the establishment of German global
hegemony. The pursuit of peaceful territorial and political "revisions" of the Versailles
settlement resulted from purely tactical considerations. The Nazi leader wanted to place
the Reich in a more favorable position to wage
war while precluding Allied moves against
Germany when the Reich was still in the early
stages of rearming.

Still, this meant that for the short term
the New Conservatives and Hitler agreed on
tactics and interim goals. They differed only
in their ultimate aims and these, even Hitler

recognized, were some years off. For the moment, the new regime was served well by the old diplomats. (The common goals help explain, for example, why only one German ambassador, Friedrich von Prittwitz und Gaffron, the envoy in Washington, resigned his post in protest over Hitler's appointment as chancellor.) Even Hitler's views on Germany's friends and foes among the Great Powers were not all that different from those of the New Conservatives. For the Nazi leader, the primary enemy was always Russia; there lay the vast expanses that Hitler insisted Germany was destined to conquer. Few of the New Conservatives shared Hitler's racial interpretation of history, but because Russia in 1933 meant the Soviet Union, the Führer's passionate anti-Bolshevism had their full approval.

Hitler and most New Conservatives also shared a deep-seated dislike of France. To be sure, for Hitler the humiliation of France was a mere sideshow compared to the ultimate battle with Soviet Russia. But he and the New Conservatives agreed that in the long run France remained an enemy power with which reconciliation was impossible. As far as Great Britain was concerned, Germany since 1918 had attempted to maintain good relations with England, primarily as a counterweight to France. Hitler continued this policy, although he remained ambivalent about the island nation. Hitler admired Britain's domestic stability and its ability to control a vast empire with limited human and material resources, but the Nazi leader despised British democracy and England's traditional policy of maintaining a balance of power on the Continent.

Neither Hitler nor the New Conservatives had shown much interest in the United States (except for the reparations issue) during the 1920s, although Hitler at times seemed convinced—based on the U.S. immigration laws then in force and the practice of segregation in the South—that America's ruling classes shared his concern about suppressing inferior races. After Franklin Delano Roosevelt's election as president and his open opposition to Nazism, Hitler abruptly changed his mind. He now claimed that America was increasingly dominated by Jews and blacks.

Italy was the only Great Power that Hitler consistently regarded as Germany's natural ally. This conclusion derived less from a rational assessment of the country's strength and interests than from unabashed admiration for Mussolini. To achieve a German-Italian alliance Hitler was even willing to violate his own dictum that all German-speaking minorities in Europe should be brought within the territorial boundaries of a Greater German Reich. As early as 1927 he agreed that the German-speaking population of the southern Tirol, an area that had been ceded to Italy in 1919, should remain under Italian control.

For the Nazi dictator, his twelve-year rule constituted a continuum in which the "peaceful" years were diplomatic preparation for his ever-present, long-range strategic goals. In his speeches to government and military leaders, Hitler made no secret of his ultimate ambitions. Four days after he became Reich chancellor, he addressed the leading generals of the Reichswehr on the need for rearmament, Lebensraum, and the conquest of Eastern Europe.

Still, for the first six years of Nazi Germany's history, the crises were diplomatic rather than military. They followed a constant pattern. After articulating a particular territorial or political demand, there would be a delay after which Hitler in a surprise move seized the object of his ambitions. The Führer then invariably proceeded to calm the resultant furor among the other powers with a solemn announcement that this had been his last revisionist demand.

Because this pattern was repeated several times between 1933 and 1939, the question arises as to why the Allies and particularly France and Great Britain permitted Hitler to use this ploy successfully time after time. The answer lies in a number of factors, including the Western leaders' conviction that their military defenses were sufficient to defy any real German aggression and Hitler's willingness to take large risks. Above all, however, the Nazi leader cleverly and rather more consistently than his parliamentary predecessors used two of the fundamental principles that were the basis of the Versailles Treaty system, national self-determination and anti-Bolshevism, to justify his revisionist demands.

The "government of national resurgence" established its line of diplomatic activism early and forcefully. In October 1933 Germany withdrew from the League of Nations, the second major power to do so; Japan had abandoned the international body in May 1933. Hitler and his associates claimed that the principle of equality in armaments, which the Allies had conceded in 1932, had remained a paper declaration. Hitler also knew the decision to leave the League of Nations would be popular at home. Most Germans regarded the League as part of the hated Versailles system.

The Nazis were particularly effective in using their image as champions of anti-communism for diplomatic ends. Friction between Germany and Poland had been endemic during the Weimar years, but in February 1934 Hitler put German-Polish relations on a new footing by signing a ten-year nonaggression and friendship pact with Poland. The Nazis would violate the treaty with impunity five years later, but in 1934 the agreement solidly established the new government's anticommunist credentials. In place of the traditional entente between Germany and Russia, the Nazis joined another fiercely anti-Russian power to guard Europe against Russian expansionism. Equally important, the treaty signaled to France that the much vaunted cordon sanitaire in Eastern Europe could be breached.

France's position was also weakened by the return of the Saar early in 1935. Under the Treaty of Versailles, France was given the right to administer this territory for fifteen years. At the end of this period, the inhabitants were to vote on their future status. Because the population was (and is) overwhelmingly German, it was not surprising that the people of the Saar voted by a heavy majority to rejoin the Reich.

The Nazis effectively exploited the measures that the Allies took to counter the Reich's diplomatic offensive. At the beginning of 1935, France, clearly worried by the agreement between Germany and Poland, and even more by the pace of German rearmament, signed a treaty of mutual assistance with the Soviet Union. Hitler responded quickly by using the agreement as justification for the reintroduction of universal military service, a measure that was a blatant violation of the Treaty of Versailles. The German government argued the move was necessary to block the Bolsheviks' advance westward.

A few months later, the Franco-Soviet Pact again served as an excuse for a second, even more audacious move by Hitler. After much public controversy the French parliament ratified the Franco-Soviet Pact early in 1936. For the Nazis this development was a welcome chance to employ, for the first time, military means in attaining a foreign policy objective. Arguing that the ratification of the Franco-Soviet agreement threatened Germany's national security, the Reich government on the morning of March 7, 1936, dispatched troops into the demilitarized Left Bank of the Rhine, thereby violating both the Treaty of Versailles and the Treaty of Locarno. Initially, the French response was vigorous (eighteen divisions were put on full alert), but Hitler won his gamble. The French government appealed to Great Britain for joint action against Germany, but the British cabinet refused. England's conservative prime minister Stanley Baldwin felt any military confrontation between Germany and the Western Allies would only benefit the Soviet Union. Because the French were unwilling to take action on their own, the Allies limited their response to a formal protest, and Hitler had triumphed. The reoccupation of the Rhineland was, moreover, a victory that was particularly impressive in the eyes of the New Conservatives. After all, previous German governments had negotiated for years just to get the French troops removed from German soil, whereas Hitler in the course of one Saturday morning reestablished German military sovereignty over the Reich's western borders.

By no means were all of Hitler's initiatives instant successes, however. One serious setback was the Nazis' crude move in Austria. In July 1934 the Austrian branch of the Nazi movement attempted to overthrow the pro-Italian government of Chancellor Dollfuss and pave the way for the annexation of Austria by Germany. Although the putsch was planned by the Austrian Nazi Party, the NSDAP's headquarters in Munich were fully cognizant of the sister party's plans. The insurgents succeeded in murdering the Austrian chancellor but not in toppling his regime. When Mussolini rushed troops to Italy's border with Austria to demonstrate his country's concern for Austria's independence, Hitler backed off immediately and made no attempt to challenge the Italian dictator. For another four years, Austria retained its independence.

The initial reaction to Germany's unilateral reintroduction of universal military service appeared equally strong. Italy, France, and Great Britain—allies since 1915—responded by forming the Stresa Front and promising to act jointly in thwarting any further violation of the Versailles system. Coupled with the Franco-Soviet Pact and the Soviet Union's apparently growing willingness to join a collective security system against the Nazis, Hitler's ambitions seemed to be confronted with formidable obstacles.

But the barriers were without substance. What appeared on paper as a phalanx of diplomatic agreements arrayed against the Nazis was in fact little more than a collection of meaningless "statements of principle." The reason for the breakdown of collective security was simple: The partners did not trust each other. Italy, which had single-handedly stopped Hitler's attempt to annex Austria in mid-1934, increasingly veered toward Germany when Great Britain and France—halfheartedly—opposed Mussolini's ambitions in Ethiopia and his support of the Nationalist side in the Spanish Civil War. Germany, in contrast, stood solidly behind Italy; by the fall of 1936, the Stresa Front had been replaced by the Rome-Berlin Axis. As for the Franco-Soviet Pact, it, too, had a major Achilles' heel. Even the French government that negotiated the agreement was less than enthusiastic about its alliance with the forces of international Bolshevism.

Above all, however, Great Britain developed growing doubts about the value of collective security. Hitler's claim that his ambition was only to fulfill the principle of national self-determination and that a strengthened Germany meant a stronger bulwark against the spread of Bolshevism found willing ears among members of the British government. Propagandistic actions on the part of Germany—like the 1936 Summer Olympics in Berlin and the signing of the Anti-Comintern Pact between Germany and Japan in the same year (Italy joined the pact in 1937)—also impressed the British. (Incidentally, most of the rituals which we now associate with the Olympics Games—such as the torch relay from Greece to the site of the particular games—were invented for the 1936 event. They were chosen with a view toward their cinematic effect in Leni Riefenstahl's film *Olympia.*) As early as the spring of 1935, Germany and Great Britain negotiated a bilateral agreement on naval armaments that permitted the Nazis substantially to exceed the limits set down in the Versailles Treaty. England's inaction during the Rhineland crisis was another symptom of its alienation from the principle of collective security. Hitler was undoubtedly gratified when Lord Halifax, who was to become the British foreign secretary in February 1938, assured the German dictator in November 1937 that the British cabinet was convinced Hitler's actions against the German Communists had saved Western Europe from Bolshevism. Halifax also let it be known that there would be no objection on the part of his government to further territorial changes in Hitler's favor provided they would be achieved by diplomacy rather than war. Hitler listened well: He had been given the green light for what was to become a year of crises in 1938.

Cuando la División española regrese un día a su país, no podremos darle a ella y a su valeroso general otro certificado que el del reconocimiento de su fidelidad y valor hasta la muerte.

An official portrait of Hitler at the height of his power. The caption reads, "One People, one Reich, one Führer." (Source: *Anschläge,* no. 116.)

CONCLUSION

Adolf Hitler was convinced it was his destiny to rule Germany and Europe, and, by the end of 1937, the dictator had traveled a considerable distance toward reaching his goal. The Nazis had established a totalitarian "dual-state" regime that controlled all aspects of public life from art to sports. An efficient terror machine assured that there was no organized opposition in the country.

In international affairs the balance sheet was clearly in Hitler's favor. Germany had regained its position as an equal among the Great Powers. Hitler managed to break up both the Locarno and Stresa fronts. Germany's support of Mussolini's military activities against Ethiopia and the Reich's and Italy's joint intervention on the Nationalists' side in the Spanish Civil War persuaded the Italian dictator to veer increasingly toward the German orbit. A state visit by Mussolini to Germany in September 1937 formally cemented the Rome-Berlin Axis. Earlier, an Anglo-German naval agreement and Great Britain's inaction during the Rhineland crisis had revealed serious cracks in the Franco-British relationship.

Still, for different reasons, neither Hitler nor the Germans felt satisfied at the end of 1937. In fact, the regime was in the midst of a serious malaise. As far as the German people were concerned, the euphoria about the Third Reich had dissipated quickly. The early economic measures of the regime had given it genuine popularity among most Germans, but the reality of restrictions, terror, and repression turned enthusiasm into passivity and sullenness. In August 1934 only 84.6 percent of those voting in a plebiscite staged to approve Hitler's assuming the powers of the Reich presidency cast their ballots in favor; dictatorships are accustomed to affirmative voting in the 99th percentile. A few months later, DAF-sponsored national elections for factory shop stewards were so disastrous for the Nazis that the results were not published; we now know that despite immense pressure only 30–40 percent of the workers voted for the Nazi list of candidates. Even more ominous from the

NSDAP's point of view, when the party permitted Germans to apply for membership in the Nazi Party again (the membership rolls had been closed since March 1933), the results were a severe disappointment: the number of those applying for party membership fell far short of expectations.

Hitler was fully aware of the impotent unrest among the people he ruled (the Gestapo had a quite efficient net of agents to report on the mood of the country), but he was dissatisfied for his own reasons as well. The German dictator was convinced both that his ultimate goals could be accomplished only with military force and that he alone could lead the Reich in this war of conquest. At the same time, he was sure he would die an early death. The realization that he would be fifty years old in April 1939 persuaded him that he needed to accelerate the pace of his actions, rather than remain content with his accomplishments.

This was the background for a meeting with his top military and diplomatic advisers that Hitler called on November 5, 1937. His select audience included the Reich's military chiefs, Blomberg (Reich minister of defense), Fritsch (army), Göring (air force), and Raeder (navy), as well as the Reich foreign minister, Konstatin von Neurath. In the course of his interminable, four-hour-long monologue, the Führer reiterated his view that race and space determined the fate of empires and peoples and that to fulfill its destiny Germany would have to undertake military operations in the near future.

The significance of this November 1937 conference did not lie in Hitler's general remarks but in the concrete conclusions that he drew from his analysis of the world situation. His listeners were intimately familiar with the racist litany that he repeated yet again. However, whereas in the past the Reich's need for Lebensraum in Eastern Europe was foreseen as a more long-range aim, this time Hitler demanded immediate military preparations to enable Germany to annex Austria and conquer Czechoslovakia by "lightning fast actions." Hitler dismissed the risks involved: The Western Allies were weak entities that would not seriously resist Germany's drive to the east and southeast.

After he had concluded his address, Hitler discovered to his dismay that although the Reich's military and diplomatic leaders did not object to the Nazi dictator's long-range goals, they had serious reservations about Hitler's assessment of the diplomatic and military risks involved. They did not share his view that the Western Allies would not resist continued German efforts to change the map of Europe. But objections of the military and civilian leaders did not shake Hitler's convictions. On the contrary, more than ever he was determined to move fast. On December 22, 1937, the general staff began preparing plans for "Case Green," the code name for military operations against Czechoslovakia. Equally important, Hitler recognized that to accomplish his goals he would have to part company with some of those New Conservatives who had served him so well during the first five years of his rule.

CHAPTER SEVEN

~~~~~~~~~~~~~~~~

Conquest, Death, and Defeat

1938–1945

In the brief time span covered by this chapter, the German Reich reached its pinnacles of power and territorial expansion, but the Germans also experienced unprecedented depths of defeat and despair. Announcing that "Germany will be a world power, or it will vanish," the Nazi dictator dropped the mask of peaceful revisionism and unleashed World War II. With the end of that conflict, the second part of Hitler's prophecy had come true: For all practical purposes, Germany was no more. In 1945, Germany, as Andreas Hillgruber has remarked, stood not at the level of 1939 or 1914, but—in terms of sociopolitical development—closer to 1815. Adolf Hitler's rule had set German history back 150 years.

Compressed into these momentous years are three interconnected themes. The first is the accelerated growth of totalitarianism and terror in Germany. The groups that had retained a measure of autonomy during the first five years of the Third Reich increasingly became subject to further controls and

infiltration. The Nazis' drive to conquer all of Europe and their parallel attempt to physically exterminate Europe's Jews and other so-called inferior races constitute a second theme. The Holocaust, then, was not incidental to the war effort but a major theme and integral part of Hitler's war of conquest. Finally, the disintegration of the Reich presents a third theme of this chapter. When Hitler realized he had lost his gamble for world conquest, he unleashed a process of self-destruction that led Germany to the brink of societal disintegration.

FURTHER GROWTH OF THE NAZI FÜHRER STATE

During the first five years of the Third Reich, Hitler and the Nazi Party had destroyed democracy in Germany and secured a monopoly of political power. By 1938, no major societal interest group openly opposed the Nazis, but some segments retained a measure of organizational autonomy. The most important among these were the diplomatic establishment (the Reich foreign minister Konstantin von Neurath had been in office since 1932), the Wehrmacht, portions of the civil service, the Catholic and Protestant churches, and the nation's business leaders.

At the beginning of 1938, Hitler and the Nazis were not particularly concerned about the last three groups on the list. It did not appear that the business leaders or the civil servants had either the means or the desire to challenge the Nazis' future plans. The churches remained an unknown factor in the long run, but for the immediate future they represented no threat to Nazi rule. However, Hitler was concerned about the military and diplomatic leaders: The dictator recognized that the realization of his far-reaching plans needed the cooperation of the Reich's diplomatic establishment and of the leaders of Germany's armed forces. Until now the members of both groups—with negligible exceptions—had backed Hitler's goals, but their leaders' lukewarm reception of Hitler's plans for war in November 1937 indicated to the Nazi leader that the symbiosis was coming to an end.

The opportunity for expanding Nazi control over the diplomatic and military establishments came unexpectedly in February 1938. Nazi Party organs had attempted to meddle in the conduct of the Reich's foreign policy since 1933, but their efforts had not been notably successful. Alfred Rosenberg, the self-styled guardian of the NSDAP's ideological purity, set up a "Foreign Policy Office" that established ties to various fascist groups outside of Germany, but these initiatives were hampered by Rosenberg's usual ineptitude and dilettantism. Considerably more important was the "Bureau Ribbentrop" that operated within the organizational framework of the Office of the Deputy Führer for Party Operations. Joachim von Ribbentrop was a relative newcomer to the party, having joined the NSDAP only in 1932. He also had no diplomatic experience, but as an international wine dealer before the Nazis came to power, Ribbentrop possessed wide-ranging

foreign contacts. With funds provided by the Nazi Party treasurer, Ribbentrop assembled a motley group of amateur diplomats that attempted to "Nazify" German foreign policy.

The regular foreign service officers complained bitterly about the unwanted competition, but Ribbentrop quickly gained the approval of the one who counted. His successful handling of negotiations that led to the Anglo-German Naval Agreement of 1935 convinced Hitler that Ribbentrop was the Nazi Bismarck, with skills far superior to those of Germany's professional diplomats. It was no surprise, then, that Hitler appointed Ribbentrop as Reich foreign minister in February 1938, replacing the—from the Führer's point of view—no longer satisfactory Neurath.

At almost the same time, a string of fortuitous circumstances enabled the Nazis to purge the ranks of the armed forces. In this case the initiative came not from Hitler but from Heinrich Himmler and Hermann Göring. Both held long-standing resentments against the traditional leaders of the Wehrmacht: Himmler felt the old-line Prussian officers were hampering the expansion of the SS, and Göring was convinced that they did not appreciate the importance of a large air force in modern warfare.

Fortunately for the two conspirators, personally damaging material seemed to be available against two of Germany's most important military leaders, General Werner von Blomberg, the Reich minister of defense since 1933, and the commander of the land forces, General Werner von Fritsch. Until now neither had given the Nazis any trouble. Blomberg had been an early, consistent, and enthusiastic supporter of Hitler's rearmament program, and Fritsch prided himself on being "just a soldier" who did not interfere in political decisions. Both men were alarmed, however, by Hitler's plans for what they regarded as risky and premature military adventures.

Under these circumstances, real and manufactured revelations of Blomberg's and

Fritsch's personal misconduct came at an opportune time. Blomberg, a widower for some years, had remarried in 1937; Hitler and Göring had been witnesses at the wedding ceremony. Blomberg's bride was then a secretary in his office, but a few months later Himmler produced evidence from police files that some years earlier the new Mrs. Blomberg had posed for pornographic pictures. Blomberg was quietly permitted to resign. Fritsch, however, was the victim of a deliberately organized frame-up. Reinhard Heydrich, the man in charge of the Reich Security Main Office (*Reichssicherheitshauptamt—RSHA*) of the SS, brought forward an individual who swore (falsely) that he had had homosexual relations with Fritsch. The frame-up was later exposed, and a court of honor exonerated the general, but by that time Fritsch had already been forced to resign from his post. Despite the verdict of the court of honor, Hitler refused to reinstate him.

In the wake of the Blomberg and Fritsch affairs, Hitler took personal control of the armed forces. Hermann Göring, who held the position of air force commander among his many jobs, suggested himself as Blomberg's replacement as head of the ministry of defense, but the Führer rejected the proposal. Instead, Hitler abolished the ministry altogether and replaced it with the High Command of the Armed Forces (*Oberkommando der Wehrmacht*, OKW), a structure comparable to the U.S. Joint Chiefs of Staff. As head of the new agency, Hitler did not select a distinguished officer but a military cipher: Wilhelm Keitel was a thoroughly colorless and nondescript officer who, like Ribbentrop, had no ambitions except to carry out Hitler's wishes. In effect, then, the Nazi dictator became his own minister of defense. Keitel's chief of staff was Alfred Jodl, an able but also thoroughly Nazified officer. Fritsch's replacement was equally symp 2 tomatic of the growing Nazi influence in the officer corps. As the new commander of the army, Hitler selected Walther von Brauchitsch, an opponent of Göring but also one of the earliest and most enthusiastic Nazi fellow travelers among the Wehrmacht officers.

A few months later, the army's chief of staff, General Ludwig Beck, was also dismissed. Beck, who would later become one of the leaders of the military conspiracy against Hitler (details of this story are covered in Chapter 8, pp. 229–33), had voiced political and tactical objections to the Führer's plans to invade Czechoslovakia. Beck's place was taken by Franz Halder, an officer in the Fritsch mold of "just a soldier."

The Nazification of the armed forces and especially Hitler's personal control of the military operations accelerated during the war itself. The dictator held the pliable commander of the army Brauchitsch responsible for the German defeat in the Battle of Moscow in December 1941. To the accompaniment of a great deal of propaganda fanfare, Hitler now took over day-to-day supervision of military operations, deciding everything from grand strategy to minor tactical decisions at the regimental and company level. (For a discussion of the military operations in World War II, see the next section of this chapter, p. 207 ff.)

As the tide turned and the German setbacks multiplied, Hitler increasingly vented his frustrations on the officer corps. Between 1942 and 1945, the Führer appointed and dismissed four army chiefs of staff. And tenure was barely more secure in less exposed positions. By the time World War II ended, Hitler had dismissed half of all officers who held the rank of general at the beginning of the war.

What little remained of the Wehrmacht's organizational autonomy was destroyed in 1944. When it became clear that the conspiracy against Hitler in July 1944 involved a number of high-ranking officers, the Nazis conducted a full-scale purge of the armed forces. Dozens of officers were summarily executed. The dictator appointed Himmler commander of the reserve forces. In addition, although the expansion of the officer corps since 1933 had already led to the appointment of many pro-Nazi officers in all branches of the Wehrmacht, Hitler now insisted that German army units be provided with so-called National Socialist Leadership

Officers. Modeled on the political commissars in the Soviet army, their function was to motivate the soldiers in their charge with Nazi political fanaticism. Needless to say, at the end of 1944 with the German armies in full retreat on virtually every front, such desperate measures had no practical effect.

The erosion of autonomy in the military sphere had its counterpart in the progressive Nazification of the Reich's civilian administration. In the course of the war, Hitler and the party leaders vastly expanded their control over the Reich's administrative apparatus and the processes of political decision making. In June 1942, during what was to be its final session in the Third Reich, the thoroughly Nazified Reichstag passed legislation giving Hitler full authority to issue laws as well as the power to dismiss civil servants, judges, and prosecutors who, in the Führer's opinion, "were not doing their duty."

As the fortunes of war turned against the Third Reich, Hitler increasingly delegated authority to the only men he felt he could fully trust, the Gauleiters of the Nazi Party. Most of these "old fighters" had been serving as chiefs of the Länder administrations since 1933, but in 1942 the Führer gave eighteen of them additional functions as "Reich Defense Commissioners." In this capacity they were the civilian counterparts of the commanding generals in the Reich's military districts, responsible for all aspects of the civilian administration. Other Gauleiters were entrusted by Hitler with far-reaching authority to administer large policy areas. The Gauleiter of Saxony, Fritz Sauckel, was given the task of securing foreign workers as replacements for the Germans who were drafted into the army in ever-larger numbers. Sauckel began with material and propagandistic inducements but, when the results were unsatisfactory, he turned to terror and force. In the latter war years the Germans, with the help of the collaborationist regimes in the occupied areas, simply rounded up able bodies and transported them to the Reich. Joseph Goebbels, the Gauleiter of Berlin and Reich propaganda minister, reached the apex of his powers in 1943 when Hitler appointed him "Plenipotentiary for the Total War Effort," with authority to coordinate all civilian aspects of the German war effort.

The process of assigning additional spheres of power to certain party leaders had a dual effect: It created a jungle of overlapping jurisdiction that enabled Hitler to continue his longtime practice of playing his various underlings off against each other, and it produced some clear victors and losers among the various Nazi Party leaders and organizations. The most notable beneficiaries of the growth of the Nazi Führer state were an individual, Martin Bormann, and an organization, the SS. Since 1933, Bormann had been the chief of staff for Rudolf Hess, the Deputy Führer for Party Operations. When Hess flew to England in May 1941 (see p. 209), Bormann made the most of the opportunity. Taking charge of the organization of the Deputy Führer (now renamed the "Party Chancellery"), he remained physically close to Hitler at all times and eventually served as a funnel through which all access to the dictator took place. Hitler trusted Bormann explicitly; the chief of the Party Chancellery became Hitler's alter ego, carrying out without question the Führer's wishes and commands.

Ironically, the SS rose in importance as the power of the Third Reich declined. Under the determined, if pedantic, leadership of Heinrich Himmler, the Nazi elite organization had always regarded itself as the true embodiment of Nazism, but the SS owed its rise to power more to its efficient management of terror than to Himmler's muddled racial endeavors.

The SS had begun to lay the groundwork for its expanded activities long before the war, but with the start of military operations the SS succeeded in merging ever-larger blocks of party and state functions under its control. Only four weeks after World War II had begun, the SD and the state political police (Gestapo) were combined into a single organization, the "Reich Security Main Office," headed by one of Himmler's most vicious subordinates, Reinhard Heydrich. During the war Heydrich and his successor, the former head of the Austrian SS, Ernst Kaltenbrunner (Heydrich was assassinated by Czech resistance fighters in 1942), rapidly expanded their network of state-sponsored terror. Himmler, too, continued to amass additional state titles and functions. In August 1943 he became Reich minister of the interior, and thus nominal superior of all German civil servants, and, as we saw, a year later the chief of the SS was appointed commander of the German army reserves.

Although the Nazification of the civil service and the armed forces proceeded at an accelerated pace, Hitler remained curiously apprehensive about challenging the autonomy of the churches. Especially in the early months of the Third Reich the regime had toyed with the idea of endorsing a Protestant fringe group called the *Deutsche Christen* (German Christians). This organization wanted to purge Christianity of its Jewish heritage, and substitute an "Aryan Christianity," headed by Jesus as a non-Jewish, Nordic warrior-hero. Eventually Hitler recognized how little support the German Christians had, and the group was abandoned. At the regional level, there were also repeated attempts by some Gauleiters to subordinate the churches in their provinces to direct Nazi control. During the war Hitler ordered the cessation of efforts to suppress the churches because he feared a new Kulturkampf might turn public opinion against the regime.

The moral power of the churches was demonstrated by their opposition to a program that had been assigned a high priority in the Nazi catalog of racially motivated measures. In 1938, the Nazis had begun a program of killing mentally ill individuals who were kept in state institutions. These "mercy killings," which a number of authors have identified as a practice run for the Holocaust (see later, pp. 216 ff.), were justified on the grounds that they would prevent hereditary genetic defects from perpetuating themselves in the German racial stock. Rather belatedly, in 1941 the Catholic archbishop of Münster, Count Galen, publicly protested the practice.

As a result, although the killings were never abandoned altogether, the regime took greater care to shroud them from the public. Unfortunately, by the time Galen took to the pulpit, some eighty thousand mental patients had already been murdered.

The Nazis' soft glove approach toward the churches during World War II did not apply to Nazi–church relations in the areas of Eastern Europe under Nazi control. In Nazi-occupied Poland, many Catholic clerics were murdered as part of the effort to deprive the Poles of their intellectual and moral leaders. Similarly, in the German border area with Poland, the Warthegau, the Nazi Gauleiter Arthur Greiser had Hitler's full approval for his systematic campaigns of persecution against the clergy and practicing members of both Christian churches.

When the Third Reich collapsed in May 1945, Germany had been subjected—on paper at least—to a full-fledged totalitarian system in which virtually all power rested in the arbitrary hands of Adolf Hitler and his henchmen in the Nazi Party. The German wartime experience constitutes a case study in the transformation of a modern pluralist society into what Robert Koehl has called a neofeudal dictatorship without institutional safeguards for the rights of either individuals or groups.

TRIUMPH AND FALL

The Diplomacy of Appeasement

One of Hitler's unshakable idées fixes was to wage a war of conquest that would result in the subjection of the European continent to Nazi rule. The year 1938 marked an important watershed in the pursuit of Nazism's ultimate goals. During the first five years of the Third Reich, the Nazi leaders had claimed that Germany wanted only to be treated as an equal among the world's Great Powers; the Reich merely sought a revision of the "unfair" portions of the Treaty of Versailles. At the beginning of 1938, however, the Nazis dropped the mask of peaceful revisionism. Instead, Hitler made it clear that he expected the other Great Powers to acquiesce to Germany's control of territories that lay beyond the Reich's boundaries of 1914. Some of these lands, it is true, were inhabited by German-speaking populations, and for a time, Hitler justified his territorial ambitions by the doctrine of national self-determination. However, by the fall of 1938 even this pretense had to be dropped. Hitler's aims were revealed in their stark reality: conquest and control, not fairness and international justice.

At the meeting of the regime's top military and diplomatic leaders in November 1937, the Führer insisted Germany now needed to take advantage of its head start in rearmament to begin a series of military operations before the French and British rearmament programs had a chance to catch up. Hitler also left no doubt about the progression of the Nazis' victims: Austria, then Czechoslovakia, and finally Poland and Russia. At the same time, the German dictator thought in global terms; he wanted to coordinate his conquest of Europe with Japanese expansions in Asia, which were already under way. Consequently, German foreign policy gave up its traditional tilt toward China in favor of a political and military alliance with Japan.

Austria, the Nazis' first new territorial objective, was particularly well chosen to mark the transition from revisionism to conquest. The country was (and is) German in both language and culture, and at the end of the 1930s, its political independence rested on increasingly precarious foundations. Since the unsuccessful Nazi putsch in July 1934, Austria had been ruled by an "Austro-fascist" regime led by Kurt von Schuschnigg. The Austrian leader's government relied on Mussolini to protect it from German aggression and on restrictions on the political freedom of its own people to control opposition at home. Both the Austrian Social Democrats and the Nazis were prohibited; the only party allowed in Austria was the government-sponsored Fatherland Front.

Unfortunately for Schuschnigg and his regime, the Italian dictator abandoned his concern for Austrian independence in favor of strengthening the Rome-Berlin Axis. In Austria itself, the contrast between the country's economic stagnation and the pace of economic recovery in Germany led to a sizable increase in the support for the illegal Nazi movement, especially among younger Austrians.

Consequently, Hitler held two trump cards in his hands when in February 1938 he all but ordered Schuschnigg to come to the Führer's mountain retreat at Berchtesgaden on the Austrian border. During their meeting, the German leader insisted that Schuschnigg reorganize his cabinet by including some of the leaders of the outlawed Austrian Nazi Party.

Recognizing the weakness of his position, Schuschnigg did not reject the German demand outright, but he did attempt to counter Hitler's pressure with a public relations coup of his own. The Austrian government announced that it would stage a plebiscite on the question of Austria's independence on March 12, 1938. It was, to be sure, a rigged election. For example, the Austrian voting age was raised from twenty-one to twenty-five just for the plebiscite to keep many younger Nazi sympathizers from casting ballots. Nevertheless, the outcome of the election might not have supported the German Nazis' contention that the overwhelming majority of Austrians were longing to "come home to the Reich."

Hitler was determined to prevent the plebiscite from taking place. The German government reacted to Schuschnigg's announcement by demanding not just the cancellation of the plebiscite but also Schuschnigg's resignation in favor of the leader of the Austrian Nazis, Arthur Seyss-Inquart. If the terms of the ultimatum were not accepted, Hitler threatened military action against his homeland.

After a frantic and futile effort to secure Mussolini's help, Schuschnigg resigned on the evening of March 11, 1938, yielding power to Seyss-Inquart. In a telegram actually written in Berlin, the new leader of Austria promptly asked that German troops be sent to Austria to help him "maintain law and order." On the morning of March 12, German units crossed the border; they were met with what appeared to be near-universal acclaim by the Austrian population. One day later, Hitler himself "came home." He began a triumphant tour of the country that culminated in a rally staged in the square in front of the old imperial castle in Vienna. Here an audience of 100,000 cheering listeners heard Hitler "report before history" that his homeland had returned to the Reich. For the Nazi dictator, the *Anschluss* (annexation), as the union of Austria and Germany is called, was a political, diplomatic, and even economic triumph. Politically, Hitler had created the Greater German Reich, a feat not even Bismarck could rival. In addition, a look at the map showed that German territory now surrounded Czechoslovakia like a vise. In economic terms, the Reich's chronic lack of hard currency was temporarily eased by the quite substantial Austrian gold reserves. Above all, however, Hitler had seemingly proved himself to be a master at diplomatic blackmail. His "instincts" about the reaction of Great Britain and France turned out to be far more accurate than the fears of some of his advisers.

After World War I, the Allies—and especially France—had repeatedly moved to prevent what they saw as threats to Austria's independence, but in 1938 France and Great Britain limited their action to diplomatic protest notes and quickly accepted the fait accompli of Austria's annexation. Mussolini, another former champion of Austrian independence, simply washed his hands of the whole affair.

The Allies' surprising lack of vigorous reaction was a consequence of the policy of appeasement, the diplomatic strategy that the leaders of Great Britain and, to a lesser extent, France adopted in the hope that it would both respond to and contain Hitler's "revisionist" ambitions. We now know that appeasement encouraged rather than contained Hitler's drive for power. Appeasement failed to preserve Austria's independence, and a few months later, the Western Allies in the name of this misguided policy would present Czechoslovakia to Hitler on a silver platter as well. Why, then, did the foreign policy leaders of Great Britain and France persist in holding on to what was clearly an unsuccessful diplomatic strategy?

The term *appeasement* will always be associated with the name of Neville Chamberlain, the British conservative politician and prime minister who was the most enthusiastic advocate and practitioner of the policy. For Chamberlain appeasement was a way of accommodating Nazi Germany's "legitimate" desires for revision of the post–World War I international balance of power while at the same time safeguarding Great Britain's and France's vital interests. The diplomatic strategy of appeasement was based on two major premises, both, as should have been clear at the time, fundamentally false. One assumed that Hitler was as anxious to avoid a new world war as the leaders of the Allied countries, and the second postulated that the Nazi leader's desire for changes in the balance of power was motivated primarily by his opposition to the spread of Soviet communism. That is to say, the appeasers saw a fundamental union of values between themselves and Adolf Hitler. From this it followed that Nazi Germany—as Western civilization's major bulwark against communist expansion—was justified in its demands for substantial revisions of the terms of the Versailles system.

Unfortunately, Hitler's interpretation of Nazi Germany's legitimate ambitions had nothing in common with those of his diplomatic partners and adversaries. To be sure, he was fundamentally opposed to Bolshevism and intended to subjugate Soviet Russia, but he planned that fate as well for France and most of Continental Europe. Moreover, for Hitler, appeasement was proof that democracy was a political system that produced leaders who were cowards and consequently wanted to avoid war at all costs.

The Czechoslovak crisis during the fall of 1938 demonstrated particularly well both the folly and the illusions associated with the

Map 7.1   Germany's Expansion 1933–1939

policy of appeasement. After his triumphs in Austria, Hitler lost no time in turning to his next victim, Czechoslovakia. At the end of May, he issued secret orders to draft plans for the "obliteration" of Czechoslovakia.

Both politically and economically, Czechoslovakia was a success story among the various states that resulted from the breakup of the Austro-Hungarian Empire. This new Central European nation, with its developed and well-balanced economy, was the only one among the successor states of the Habsburg Empire to establish and maintain a viable parliamentary democracy. Czechoslovakia even managed to defuse conflicts among its various ethnic minorities; the country was noteworthy for its enlightened policies on cultural pluralism. Although some 3 million

Germans (known as Sudeten Germans because most of them lived in the area of the Sudeten Mountains) and thousands of Poles and Hungarians remained within the boundaries of Czechoslovakia, relations between them and the majority Czech and Slovak peoples were largely free of friction during the 1920s and early 1930s.

Unfortunately, the multinational harmony broke down with the advent of the depression. Some of the areas with large German-speaking populations were particularly hard-hit by the economic downturn. A government-sponsored policy that favored hiring Czechs for civil service jobs over members of the ethnic minorities aggravated the situation. In the meantime, much as had been true in Austria, the seemingly rapid recovery of Germany under Nazi rule led to increased support for a pro-Nazi group, the Sudeten German Party (*Sudetendeutsche Partei*—SdP). Publicly, the SdP demanded only increased political and cultural autonomy for the Sudeten Germans, but in reality the party and its leader, Konrad Henlein, worked for the annexation of the Sudeten areas by the German Reich.

In the spring of 1938, Hitler began using Henlein and his group to stir up friction between Germany and Czechoslovakia. The SdP was ordered to wage a campaign of violence accompanied by constantly escalating demands. The object was to put the Czechoslovak government on the defensive while enabling the German propaganda machine to create the myth that the Sudeten Germans were an oppressed people longing for union with the Reich.

Initially, the Czechoslovak government refused Henlein's demands outright. The reason for the Czechoslovak's courageous resistance in the face of a much stronger power lay in the fact that, on paper at least, the country had some very powerful friends. In 1924, France and Czechoslovakia signed a military alliance that obligated France to come to Czechoslovakia's aid if the latter were attacked by a foreign power. Czechoslovakia negotiated a similar agreement with Soviet Russia,

although the Russians insisted on a clause that their commitments would come into effect only if France honored its obligations. Great Britain and Italy, however, were not directly committed to protecting Czechoslovakia, and they took the lead in initiating the diplomatic maneuvering that would eventually sacrifice Czechoslovakia's very existence on the altar of appeasement.

The Nazis used the NSDAP's annual congress in early September 1938 to bring the tensions between Czechs and Germans to a frenzied climax. Characterizing the Czechoslovak government as a friend of Soviet communism, Hitler demanded that the Sudeten Germans be given the right of self-determination immediately. If the "oppressive" Czech regime remained unyielding, he would take matters into his own hands. The Czechoslovaks, relying on the promises of protection incorporated in their alliance system, made it clear that they would resist by force any German invasion. War seemed inevitable.

For Neville Chamberlain, the prospect of war in Central Europe was unthinkable. He remained convinced that such a conflict would only aid the cause of world communism. In mid-September he flew to Berchtesgaden to plead with the German dictator to restrain his use of military force a little longer; in the meantime Allied diplomats would attempt to find a diplomatic solution to the crisis. Hitler agreed that he could probably resist the pressure of German public opinion for action on his part for a few days longer. Chamberlain in turn praised Hitler's moderation and regarded his visit as a triumph of appeasement.

Chamberlain completely misjudged Hitler's character, for the Führer always looked on concessions as a sign of weakness. Within days Hitler announced that the Sudeten area would have to be turned over to Germany without a vote. In addition, the Germans became solicitous of the Hungarian and Polish minorities. They, too, should be permitted to join their respective motherlands. Because the Czechs still remained unyielding, Europe again seemed poised on the brink of war.

Only Chamberlain had not lost hope. He went to Germany a second time to renew his pleas for a peaceful solution. After another week in which war hysteria mounted, his efforts appeared to be successful. The leaders of Germany, Italy, France, and Great Britain agreed to meet at a summit conference on September 29. The meeting was held, appropriately enough, at the *Führerbau*, part of the complex of buildings that formed the national headquarters of the Nazi Party in Munich. Without consulting either the Czechs or the Russians, the participants accepted a "compromise" proposal offered by Mussolini as a diplomatic solution to the Sudeten crisis. The document was actually an Italian translation of Hitler's latest demands. By this "compromise" Czechoslovakia was forced to yield the Sudeten area to Germany. If the Czechoslovaks refused to accept the dictum of the Four Power Conference, France would refuse to honor its treaty obligations. Should Czechoslovakia accept the judgment, however, the Four Powers agreed to "guarantee" the territorial integrity of what remained of Czechoslovakia. The proposal was a cynical sellout to Nazi Germany, but Chamberlain returned home having achieved what he proclaimed was "peace in our time."

Having gotten his way at Munich, Hitler initiated a dual course of action. The German government solemnly announced that the Reich had no further territorial ambitions anywhere in Europe. To give additional credence to this declaration, the German foreign minister Joachim von Ribbentrop at the beginning of December 1938 traveled to Paris and signed a joint declaration with France; the Reich again renounced any ambitions to regain Alsace-Lorraine. But at the same time, hidden from public view, Hitler issued orders to "take care of the rest of Czechoslovakia."

The second Czechoslovakian crisis came in March 1939. The Nazis pressured some right-wing Slovak political leaders to declare their independence from Czechoslovakia, thereby dismembering the country. Slovakia became an ostensibly independent country, although it was actually a satellite of Nazi Germany. As for the Czech part of the country, the Germans reduced it to a colony of the Reich. Threatening the Czechs with bombardment and military invasion, the Nazis bullied the Czech leaders into asking that their lands be placed under German "protection." What remained of Czechoslovakia became the Reich Protectorate of Bohemia and Moravia. The first Reich "protector" was Konstantin von Neurath, the man Hitler had dismissed as foreign minister in February 1938.

The Nazis' cynical destruction of Czechoslovakia five months after they had agreed to guarantee its continued existence brought a swift and ignominious end to the policy of appeasement. Instead of seeking to accommodate the Nazi dictator's further ambitions, Great Britain and France now issued guarantees of support to Hitler's most likely next targets, Poland and Rumania.

The Nazi leader was not impressed. He regarded the guarantees as a bluff and proceeded to initiate the next crisis. Immediately after the dissolution of Czechoslovakia, Germany proposed bilateral talks with Poland on boundary rectifications. Compared with the destruction of Czechoslovakia, the Germans' initial demands seemed modest: The autonomous city of Danzig (today Gdansk in Poland), which did have a largely German population, should be returned to the Reich and an extraterritorial road should be built through the Polish Corridor to facilitate access to the German exclave of East Prussia. In return, Hitler offered to extend the 1934 German-Polish nonaggression pact for another twenty-five years. The Germans also tried to lure the Poles with hints of joint German-Polish moves against Soviet Ukraine. The Polish leaders, with the fate of Czechoslovakia (in whose dismemberment they had participated) vividly before their eyes and emboldened by the Franco-British guarantee, resolutely refused to yield to the German demands.

Hitler was not overly concerned by the impasse. At the beginning of April, he ordered plans for "Case White," an attack on Poland; it was originally scheduled to begin on August 20, 1939. The Nazi leader's confidence came partly because his "infallible" adviser on foreign policy, Ribbentrop, assured the Führer that Great Britain would not go to war over Poland. In addition, Germany's diplomatic position seemed to be improving rapidly in the spring and summer of 1939. The conclusion of the Pact of Steel in May between Italy and the Reich bound the two fascist states to support each other in all endeavors. However, a far more dramatic shift in the balance of power was the conclusion of a nonaggression pact between Nazi Germany and the Soviet Union in August.

The Nazi-Soviet agreement was an alliance between two most unlikely partners. Hitler had made something of a career of anti-Bolshevism, and the Russian leader, Joseph Stalin, although distrustful of all of his Western neighbors, had in the past poured particular venom on Hitler and the Nazis. However, the policy of appeasement (and especially the Allies' behavior at the Munich Conference) revived Stalin's fears that the Western powers were encouraging Hitler to seek territorial and political gains at the expense of the Soviet Union. Hitler, too, for all his anticommunist bravado, saw an opportunity in the summer of 1939 to strike a tactical bargain with his fellow dictator. After some months of not very secret negotiations, Ribbentrop and his Soviet counterpart Molotov signed two agreements on August 23, 1939. One was a public document—a nonaggression pact—in which each partner promised to remain benevolently neutral toward the other in case of war with third countries. The benefits to Germany were obvious. Not only were the Nazis relieved of Bismarck's nightmare of a two-front war, but in case of conflict with the Western powers Germany could make use of the Russian land route to obtain needed imports from Asia and Russia itself, thereby undermining the effect of any British blockade.

Far more important in the short run, however, was the second agreement, a secret codicil that envisioned a fourth partition of Poland and a full-scale territorial rearrangement of Eastern Europe. Under the terms of this secret agreement, Russia essentially regained the lands it had lost in 1918. Germany agreed that the Soviet Union could seize control of the independent Baltic states of Lithuania, Estonia, and Latvia, the eastern parts of Poland, and Bessarabia. In addition, the Germans acknowledged that Finland was part of the Soviet hegemonic orbit. In return, Russia agreed to German control of the remainder of Poland. In effect, then, Hitler was free to annex the bulk of Poland.

Military History of World War II

The Nazi-Soviet Pact effectively undercut the Anglo-French guarantees of Poland, and Hitler felt free to attack Germany's eastern neighbor with impunity. Ignoring Mussolini's lack of enthusiasm about a Europe-wide conflict and qualms by some of the Nazi leaders, including Hermann Göring, the Führer ordered a full-scale attack on Poland beginning at dawn on September 1.

The Polish campaign introduced two new elements into warfare that were to become characteristic of Nazi operations in World War II. One was the strategy of the *Blitzkrieg* (lightning-fast war). Taking advantage of technical improvements in armaments, the Germans subjected Poland and subsequently other opponents to massive and coordinated attacks by waves of fighter planes, massed tank assaults, and swiftly moving infantry. The Poles resisted valiantly but ineffectively. Less than a month after the war began, Poland capitulated. But the Polish campaign, as would be true of the war in Russia later, was also a *Weltanschauungskrieg*—a clash of ideologies and values in which the Nazis' aim was not just military victory but extermination or subjugation of an entire people.

After the German military operations in Poland had been concluded, and Soviet troops had moved into the parts of eastern Poland assigned them by the Nazi-Soviet Pact, Poland disappeared from the map. The Germans annexed outright much of the country and converted the rest into a colonial entity called the "General Government" (*Generalgouvernement*). As governor-general, Hitler chose an old-time Nazi and his own personal legal counsel, Hans Frank.

The military operations against Poland testified to the effectiveness of the Nazi rearmament program, but Hitler's expectation that the Western Allies would now write off the East European state much as they had Czechoslovakia earlier did not come true. Two days after Germany moved into Poland, both France and Great Britain declared war on the Reich. This move confronted Hitler with a genuine dilemma. Not only had his (and Ribbentrop's) "instinct" betrayed him, but the Nazis had no strategic plans for immediate military operations against the Western Allies. At first, the Nazi dictator attempted to revive the ploy that had succeeded so well in the past. On October 6, 1939, he repeated his longing for genuine peace and renounced any further conquests in Europe. But Great Britain and France ignored Hitler's so-called peace offer.

This forced Germany for the rest of the war to improvise a strategy or, rather, a series of strategies. The result was what Andreas Hillgruber has called the "global blitzkrieg." Concretely, Hitler determined that he would attempt to repeat the successful operations in Poland by similar lightning attacks on other continental targets, notably France in the West and later the Soviet Union in the East. (The fate of Great Britain remained unclear; Hitler continued to harbor hopes of a bilateral agreement with England that would temporarily divide the world into British and German spheres of influence.) In each case the campaigns were envisioned to last no more than a few weeks or, at most, months. There were no German plans for either a conflict of attrition or drawn-out defensive operations because Hitler was convinced that each successful blitzkrieg would be sufficient to persuade his remaining enemies to accept peace on the Nazi dictator's terms.

Hitler's scenario also assigned roles to his principal allies, Italy and Japan. Mussolini was to conduct operations in the Mediterranean area, cutting the British supply lines to India and the Far East. As for the Japanese, Hitler urged them to direct their military operations against British and American targets in Asia. This strategic advice was in line with Japan's own intentions, but for Hitler it was self-serving. The Führer hoped that Japanese pressure on South Asia would force the British as well as the Americans to divert their resources to the Far East instead of Europe.

The strategy of the global blitzkrieg had no chance of success. It seriously underestimated the inherent weaknesses of the Axis powers, including Germany. The Japanese did conclude a neutrality pact with the Soviet Union in April 1941 and challenged the United States directly by bombarding the U.S. naval base at Pearl Harbor (Hawaii) in December of the same year, but U.S. resources proved sufficient for prosecuting the war effort on both the Pacific and Atlantic fronts. Italy's weakness became glaringly apparent in the fall of 1940. Without informing Hitler, Mussolini staged an unprovoked and ill-timed attack on Greece, but the Italian troops were swiftly driven back into Albania. (Albania was under Italian control at this time.) The Italians had to be rescued by the intervention of German units. If Italy was unable to prevail over Greece, it was clearly no match for British strength in the Mediterranean and North Africa. Germany, for its part, did little better. Despite Göring's boasts, the Nazis failed to achieve air superiority over the British Isles during the Battle of Britain. Later, the Third Reich's inability to defeat the Soviet Union (see pp. 212 ff.) in the most important part of the global blitzkrieg sealed the fate of Nazi Germany.

But these developments lay in the future. In the fall of 1939, Hitler was confronted with the necessity of continuing the war in the West. On October 9 he ordered the OKW to submit plans that would result in the "definitive military annihilation of the Western powers." The German generals feared another war of attrition on the western front because defeating France or Great Britain was clearly not the same as overrunning Poland. (Virtually all of the high-level German officers had, of course, served in World War I.) The planners' qualms and poor weather conditions delayed the attack in the West until May 1940. Just prior to this, the Germans had launched a successful amphibious operation that led to Nazi control of Denmark and Norway. Outracing the British, who had similar designs, the Scandinavian operations assured that Swedish iron ore would continue

One of the most famous cartoons of the British caricaturist David Low. Hitler and Stalin meet across a dead Poland. Stalin inquires if he is indeed meeting the "bloody assassin of the workers" (as Soviet propaganda had titled Hitler before the Nazi-Soviet Pact) and Hitler assumes he is correct in facing "the scum of the earth," as the Nazis had been fond of labeling the Soviet dictator. (Source: Interfoto/Alamy.)

to reach German ports. (Sweden remained neutral throughout the war.)

Like the North Sea operation, the blitzkrieg against France was a master stroke of military maneuvering. The Germans bypassed the massive French defensive positions, the Maginot Line, and attacked from the north as Ludendorff had attempted to do in the summer of 1918. This meant violating Dutch and Belgian neutrality, but Hitler was never one to concern himself about international law and treaty obligations. This

Map 7.2   Military Operations of World War II: The German Offensives, 1939–1942

time, there would be no years of trench warfare in the West. Six weeks after the attack began, France suffered a humiliating defeat. Underscoring their vengeful triumph, the Nazis forced the French to sign the agreement to end hostilities in June 1940 in the same railroad car that had been used to finalize the armistice ending World War I. (Since then the car had been housed in a French museum; the Nazis had it shipped back to the Forest of Compiègne.) Under the 1940 armistice, France was divided into a northern zone under German military occupation and an ostensibly independent southern zone. The latter would be governed by a collaborationist regime led by the eighty-four-year-old French "hero of Verdun," Marshal Philippe Pétain.

After the defeat of France the Nazis were in virtual control of the Continent west of the Russian borders, but contrary to Hitler's expectations, Great Britain still refused to negotiate a peace treaty with the Third Reich. On the contrary, Neville Chamberlain's replacement by Winston Churchill as Great Britain's prime minister on May 10, 1940—the same day the Germans launched their offensive on the western front—signaled that England was more determined than ever to defeat the Nazis. Churchill had opposed the policy of appeasement, arguing—quite correctly—that dealing with Hitler was not possible. German aerial bombardment of England, including the destruction of many civilian targets, stiffened British resistance still further.

Although defeated in the Battle of Britain, Hitler did not yet abandon his attempts to subdue the island nation. The Luftwaffe continued bombing attacks to terrorize the population, and Hitler ordered the construction of a huge fleet to fight the British and the Americans. (It was never built.) At the same time the Nazi dictator turned his military machine against Russia. In July 1940, he ordered work to begin on plans for a full-scale attack on the Soviet Union in the spring of 1941. Aside from pursuing his lifelong ambition of conquering Lebensraum in the East, the Nazi leader reasoned that the defeat of the Soviet Union in yet another blitz-krieg would finally persuade the British that they could not win the war, and consequently they would accept Hitler's plan for a global division of power between Germany and Great Britain.

Deluded hopes for sharing global power with Great Britain were apparently also involved in one of the more bizarre episodes of World War II—the flight of the Deputy Führer for Party Operations, Rudolf Hess, to England in May 1941. Hess decided he would make a personal effort to persuade the British to come to terms with Hitler. He was as unsuccessful as his master. The British, after determining that he had no military secrets to reveal, interned the Deputy Führer for the duration of the war while the Germans declared Hess insane.

Any attack on the Soviet Union would, of course, be a blatant violation of the Nazi-Soviet Pact, but Hitler insisted that the

Map 7.3   Military Operations of World War II: The Allied Offensives, 1943–1945

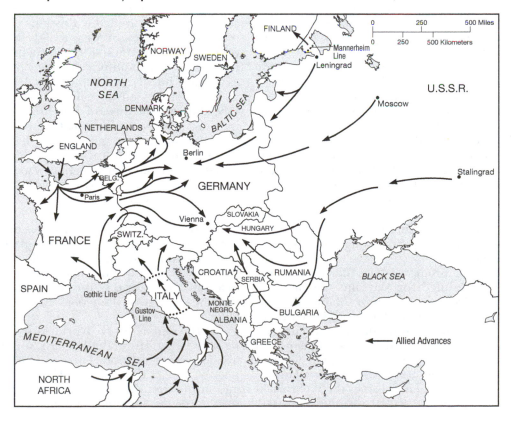

normal rules of international relations had no place in wars for Lebensraum and battles of Weltanschauungen. At the height of his power in the summer of 1940, Hitler felt that he no longer needed Stalin's friendship. Moreover, talks involving Hitler, Ribbentrop, and the Soviet foreign minister, Vyacheslav Molotov in November 1940 revealed fundamental differences with the Russians over the future of the Soviet Union's hegemonic status in Europe. While Hitler, however insincerely, was tempting Russia with visions of conquest in the direction of Iran, Iraq, Afghanistan, and India, Molotov insisted that the Soviet Union was more concerned about the Balkans, the eastern end of the Mediterranean, and the Baltic Sea—all areas that Hitler included in his definition of Germany's indispensable Lebensraum.

Since the fall of France, Stalin had been pursuing his own version of appeasement with Germany, so the Nazis' attack in June 1941, intended as yet another blitzkrieg operation, was completely unprovoked. (Incidentally, in recent years some revisionist historians, pointing to evidence in testimony made available after the fall of the Communist regime in Russia, have argued that Stalin was planning to attack Germany, so that Hitler was actually launching a preventive strike. However, the evidence for this scenario is very unpersuasive.) A force of 3 million soldiers (153 infantry and 19 tank divisions) and 2,700 airplanes launched a three-pronged attack directed at St. Petersburg (then called Leningrad), Moscow, and Kiev. The strategy was designed to bring the Soviet Union to its knees after a campaign lasting no longer than four months.

The beginnings of "Plan Barbarossa" had been scheduled for May, but the Germans had to divert some units to subdue what was then the Kingdom of Yugoslavia first, and the actual attack on Russia did not start until June 22. Initially, the campaign seemed a repeat of earlier Nazi successes. The German troops advanced hundreds of miles a day. In a series of encirclement battles the Wehrmacht wiped out entire Russian armies and took more than a million prisoners. By July 4, 1941, Hitler was convinced the Soviet Union had been irrevocably defeated; the Führer was already thinking of new campaigns in India, Afghanistan, and, closer to home, Switzerland and Sweden.

Ironically, many Western military experts and political leaders agreed. The Atlantic Charter, Churchill's and Roosevelt's 1941 joint manifesto on the liberation of the oppressed peoples from the Nazi yoke, made no mention of the Soviet Union, seemingly accepting its defeat by the Nazis as a fait accompli. Hitler and the experts were wrong. The Russian campaign began the downfall of the Third Reich; the Führer and his generals—like Napoleon earlier—had vastly underestimated the strength of the Russians. Not only were the Soviet armaments—especially the T-34 tank and Russian field artillery—far more effective than the Nazis anticipated, but German intelligence seriously underrated the Russians' overall manpower reserves. In August 1941, the chief of the army's general staff noted ruefully that the Soviets had about twice as many divisions as German intelligence had reported.

The German advance began to slow in July, although the forward movement was still impressive. By December it had come to a halt. Long logistical lines and effective harassing of German communications by a growing Soviet partisan movement seriously weakened the German positions. The Nazis laid siege to Leningrad but could not capture the city. Their situation was even more precarious in the central sector of the front. A brilliant Soviet counterattack during the Battle of Moscow at the beginning of December for the first time in the war put the Germans on the defensive. At the end of the year, it was clear that the strategy of the global blitzkrieg had failed.

By December 1941 World War II had become what Hitler had always sought to avoid, a war of attrition. There was little prospect of defeating the Soviet Union quickly, and in the west the Nazis faced a new adversary. After the Japanese had attacked Pearl

Harbor, Germany immediately declared war on the United States. Hitler took this step not only to demonstrate support for the Japanese, but also because he was convinced that eventually he would have to battle the United States for global supremacy in any case.

There are indications that early in 1942 the Führer realized that rationally the Third Reich had little hope of winning the war. Hitler and the other Nazi leaders increasingly placed their faith in the fanaticism of the German soldier, which would somehow prevail over the Allies' manpower and matériel superiority. Equally unrealistic, Hitler expected the wartime alliance of the Soviet Union, Great Britain, and the United States to break up before the end of the conflict. Irrationally, Hitler still hoped for an Anglo-Nazi partnership. He was convinced Great Britain would object to an expanded U.S. role in Asia and turn to the Nazis for support against America. Above all at the beginning of 1942 the racial Manichaeanism (a struggle between racially defined absolutes of good and evil) of Hitler's vision of world conquest took priority. As the dream of carving out a conquered Lebensraum faded, the Nazis carried out Hitler's other priority, the systematic extermination of the Jews.

Stopped in the north of Russia, the Germans launched another major offensive in the summer of 1942. The objectives were the southeastern regions of Russia and especially the oil fields of Baku. In late July, Rostov-on-Don fell, and Hitler ordered Army Group B to seize the city of Stalingrad (now Volgagrad), in southeastern Russia.

The Battle of Stalingrad and an attempt to regain the initiative in the Kursk offensive a few months later were the last large-scale Nazi offensives on the eastern front and the costliest; between November 1942 and February of the following year the Germans lost more than 800,000 men. In strategic terms, the Soviet victories at Stalingrad and Kursk (July 1943) turned the tide of the war. The back of the Nazi war machine had been broken. Hitler reacted with a succession of futile "no retreat" and "scorched earth"

orders by which he sought to delay the end and gain time for the Holocaust. Even during the Battle of Stalingrad, transportation facilities for shipping Jews to the death camps had priority over those supplying troops on the eastern front.

Heavy manpower losses (some 2 million men by the summer of 1943), coupled with inadequate reserves and the failure of German submarines to interdict Allied transatlantic supply lines, enabled the Allies to take the initiative on all fronts. In the West, the Allied landings in North Africa (November 1942) and Sicily (July 1943) ended the German dream of cutting the British lifeline to India and, instead, established bridgeheads for an Allied counteroffensive on the European Continent. In May 1943 the last units of the German *Afrika Korps* under General Erwin Rommel, sent to aid the faltering Italians, surrendered to British forces commanded by Field Marshal Alexander. Finally, the long-awaited Allied landings on the French coast in June 1944 inaugurated the liberation of Western Europe and, at the end of the year, brought the war to Germany itself. Hitler's hope about recently developed "miracle weapons," especially the V-2, an early form of ballistic rocket directed toward England from launching sites in northern Germany, was illusionary. The weapons had little effect on Allied operations. (The V stood for *Vergeltung*, the German word for "retaliation.") Far more effective were the constant nighttime and later daytime bombings of German cities by British and American air forces.

Whatever hope Hitler had of a falling-out among his enemies faded rapidly. In January 1943, the United States and Great Britain had announced the policy of "unconditional surrender," precluding a negotiated peace as an end to the war. Stalin, too, endorsed this policy, particularly after what were apparently tentative feelers for a separate peace between Germany and Russia were decisively rejected by Hitler in December 1942.

The last German offensive operation was the Battle of the Bulge in late 1944 and early 1945. The unsuccessful initiative had the objective of reconquering the seaport of Antwerp in Belgium in order to disrupt Allied supply lines and dividing American and British troops in the West to delay their advance into Germany. After some initial ground advances, Allied air superiority and lack of fuel for the Germans' motorized elements quickly blunted the offensive. In retrospect, this concentration of resources in the West undoubtedly contributed to the collapse of the central part of the eastern front, enabling the Russians to speed their final advance toward eastern Germany and the Elbe.

In the spring of 1945, the European part of World War II came to an end. For some weeks after the Battle of the Bulge, Hitler still sent phantom armies into battle, fantasized about new miracle weapons, and clung to the hope that the Allied coalition would fall apart at the last moment. He briefly interpreted Roosevelt's death in April 1945 as such a turning point, but the dream of world conquest had ended. On April 30, after marrying his longtime mistress, Eva Braun, Hitler and his new wife committed suicide. Before he died, the dictator named Grand Admiral Karl Dönitz, the commander of the German submarine force and a Nazi fanatic for many years, to succeed him as Reich president. Joseph Goebbels was named Reich chancellor; Himmler and Göring, both of whom had made contact with Allied authorities in the last days of the war, were dismissed for defeatism. (Dönitz accepted his appointment. Goebbels, in one of the most macabre acts during the death throes of the Third Reich, had his children put to death before he and his wife committed suicide shortly after Hitler took his own life.) Espousing his racial fanaticism to the end, Hitler left a political testament admonishing the German people above all to continue the struggle against "international Jewry."

On April 25, 1945, American and Russian troops joined up at Torgau on the Elbe. On May 7 the German forces on the western front surrendered to the Allied commander in chief, General Dwight D. Eisenhower. And one day later, General Wilhelm Keitel, on behalf of the High Command of the Armed Forces, signed papers of unconditional surrender at the headquarters of General Zhukov, the commander of the Russian forces, in Karlshorst just outside Berlin.

NAZI RULE IN EUROPE

The Nazis' goal of permanent mastery over Europe was always an illusion, but for almost four years much of continental Europe was under direct or indirect Nazi control. As was true of their military strategy, Hitler and his henchmen did not develop specific long-range plans for German rule in Europe before or during the conflict. Nevertheless, it is possible to delineate some leitmotifs in the hegemonic thinking of Hitler and various other Nazi leaders. Essentially, the Continent would have been divided into three categories of territories subject to varying degrees of German control. An engorged Greater German Reich constituted the planned core of Nazi Europe. In addition to the areas that Germany had already absorbed—Austria, the Czech parts of Czechoslovakia, parts of Poland—Nazi planners were anxious to incorporate the remaining "Germanic" areas of Europe, such as Holland, Denmark, Norway, and the Dutch-speaking parts of Belgium. Second, particularly in western and south-western Europe, the Nazis envisioned areas that would be dotted by German military bases and the presence of Nazi troops but that would be accorded some rights of autonomy and ruled by indigenous collaborationist regimes. Finally, there were the vast areas of Eastern Europe and the Soviet Union. Under all Nazi scenarios these territories were listed as objects of pure colonial exploitation, without any rights of self-government.

Although most of the Nazi plans for the postwar future can only be reconstructed from Hitler's monologues (the so-called table talks) and the musings of other Nazi leaders, the fundamental differences between the German occupation policies in Western and Eastern Europe were apparent even during the war. Some areas in Western Europe, like Belgium and northern France, remained under military administration throughout the conflict. In the rest of France, as well as in Holland and Denmark, the Nazis for a time permitted apolitical or non-Nazi right-wing groups to administer the countries under German supervision rather than install the minuscule proto-Nazi groups that offered themselves as collaborators. In Norway, however, the Nazis appointed as leader of the government a man whose name became a synonym for treason, Vidkun Quisling, the head of the small Norwegian Nazi Party.

Although the German occupation was obviously never popular, initially some collaborationist and caretaker regimes in Western Europe were welcomed as a way of dealing with the reality of defeat after the failure of the previous governments. In the first months of Nazi rule, resistance in western and southeastern Europe was relatively unimportant. Collaborators—using the word to include everyone who was willing to deal with the Nazis—far outnumbered resistance fighters.

The picture changed rapidly as the Nazis' true intentions became clear. Although Hitler had declared repeatedly (the last time five days before the outbreak of the war) that Germany had no designs on Alsace-Lorraine, the Reich forced the French to give up the two provinces as part of the armistice agreement. The Germans similarly annexed Luxembourg and a small section of Belgium. Moreover, the Nazis were not content simply to reincorporate these territories; they implemented a policy of "ethnic cleansing" by expelling thousands of people whom the Nazi racial experts judged to be "un-German."

Dislike of the Nazi occupation and the collaborationist regimes the Germans had installed in Western Europe increased rapidly when the Nazis inaugurated their three most disastrous policies—the Holocaust, the requisition of forced labor, and the large-scale execution of hostages. By the time the German troops had been driven out of Western Europe, both they and their collaborationist regimes had earned the hatred of the vast majority of the people of Western Europe.

Resistance increased rapidly as thousands of young men went underground rather than face deportation as forced labor to the Reich. (The Communists of Western Europe remained quiescent or even cooperated with the German occupation authorities during the period of the Nazi-Soviet Pact, but they spearheaded the resistance after the German attack on the Soviet Union.) Indiscriminate taking and execution of innocent hostages fueled the flames of resistance even further. In 1942, the Nazis murdered the entire male population of the Czech village of Lidice in retaliation for hiding the assassins of Reinhard Heydrich, the SS official who was then serving as "Reich Protector" of Bohemia and Moravia. Two years later in an equally infamous incident, the village of Oradour in France was wiped out to avenge the killing of two SS officers by French resistance fighters. As for the collaborationist regimes, they were indelibly tainted with the more or less willing participation in the reign of horrors that the Germans unleashed on all the occupied areas.

The question of collaboration or resistance, which constituted a major dilemma for many in Western Europe, never posed itself in the occupied areas of the East. In Poland and Russia, the Nazis had no interest in cooperative governments; the sole goal was naked exploitation and repression. Here the Nazis planned (and began implementing) a form of colonial rule that would have forced Eastern Europe back into the Dark Ages.

The administration of occupied Russia quickly became a confused melee of overlapping jurisdictions. The Nazis established a ministry for the occupied eastern territories headed by the Nazi theoretician Alfred Rosenberg. (The new minister's sole qualifications were his background as a Russian-speaking Baltic German; he was born in Riga and had been a student in Moscow.) Territorially, occupied Russia was to be divided into four administrative zones, called Reich Commissariats: Moscow, Crimea, "Eastland" (the Nazis' collective name for the three Baltic countries of Lithuania, Latvia, and Estonia), and Ukraine. Because the German armies were unable to conquer either Moscow or southern Russia, only the viceroys for Eastland and Ukraine took up their positions. As administrator for Eastland Hitler chose Hinrich Lohse, the Gauleiter of Schleswig-Holstein; Erich Koch, the Gauleiter of East Prussia, reigned in Ukraine.

What looked like a rational chain of command for the occupied Russian zones on paper was in fact administrative chaos. Although Lohse and Koch were technically Rosenberg's subordinates, as Gauleiters they had direct access to Hitler. In practice they paid little attention to their nominal superior, who in any case maintained his well-deserved reputation as an incompetent administrator and ineffective infighter. In addition, neither the Reich commissioners nor the minister had any real authority over the SS, which had exclusive jurisdiction in the area of "security affairs" in Poland and Russia, a mandate that included everything from dealing with guerrilla warfare to the extermination campaigns against the Jews.

Neither Hitler nor Himmler, nor many of the Wehrmacht leaders, felt the rules of "civilized conflict" applied to occupied Russia and Poland. Instead, the concept of "racial war" justified systematic attempts to physically eliminate the indigenous Slavic elites. Even before the actual attack on the Soviet Union, the High Command issued an infamous "commissar order" to all Wehrmacht units. It authorized the troops to execute all captured "Bolshevik leaders and Red Army commissars" rather than send them to prisoner-of-war camps. Throughout the years of Nazi rule, the *Einsatzgruppen* (Special Units) of the SS roamed the occupied areas of Poland and the Soviet Union executing those whom the SS arbitrarily labeled as "Jews and Bolsheviks."

For the long-range future, the Nazis had plans for a new *Drang nach Osten* ("Thrust toward the East," the term used to describe the centuries-long process of expanding the areas of German settlement in Central and Eastern Europe). They intended to force much of the Slavic population of Russia to resettle east of the Ural Mountains. Those who remained in European Russia would be reduced to slavery in the service of the thousands of "Germanic" settlers—Germans, Dutch, Scandinavians—who would populate what the Nazis regarded as the vast empty spaces in Eastern Europe.

In view of the Nazi practices during the occupation, it was not surprising that German rule in Eastern Europe quickly developed into open warfare between ruler and oppressed. Even where German troops and officials had been welcomed as liberators from the Bolsheviks (this was especially true in the Baltic countries), the feelings of sympathy quickly turned to hatred as the reality of Nazi rule became apparent. The Russians were able to establish a large-scale partisan movement, whose guerrilla tactics effectively harassed the German lines of supply throughout the war.

In the final analysis, then, Nazi rule in Europe demonstrated the same nihilism that characterized the regime's rule in Germany. In the end the Nazis brought nothing but subjugation, oppression, and terror to the peoples under their control.

THE HOLOCAUST

It is impossible to think of the history of the Third Reich and Nazi rule in Europe without at the same time taking account of the Holocaust. This systematic program of genocide was not an incidental aspect of the Nazis' drive for power but an essential part of their program. During the Holocaust, the Germans and their collaborators in the occupied areas selected and murdered millions of people. The victims singled out for extermination included groups as diverse as Polish priests and Hungarian Gypsies. But there was never any doubt that the Holocaust was directed primarily against Europe's Jews: Six million Jews, about two-thirds of all Jews living in Europe in 1939, would eventually perish at the hands of the Nazis.

The Holocaust put into gruesome practice the racial Manichaeanism that Hitler had enunciated as early as 1919. Nazi measures against the Jews can be divided into two phases. During the first five years of the Third Reich, the Nazis enacted a variety of measures designed to reverse the emancipation of Germany's Jews that had begun at the onset of the nineteenth century. Between 1933 and 1938, Jews were systematically subjected to a variety of discriminatory measures: They were prevented from engaging in their chosen business or professional activities; the Nuremberg Laws of 1935 prohibited intermarriage between Germans and Jews and deprived Jews of their German citizenship. The legal status of Jews became that of resident aliens in the Reich.

Paralleling the legal discriminatory acts were periodic outbreaks of violence, ranging from the nationwide boycott of Jewish stores in April 1933 to random harassment of individual Jews. Nevertheless, after the April boycott, anti-Semitism was, for the most part, more verbal than violent. When it served their purpose, the Nazis even temporarily rescinded some of the anti-Jewish measures. During the Summer Olympic Games of 1936, when thousands of foreign tourists flocked to Germany, villages and towns were quietly ordered to take down their "no Jews allowed here" signs. The overall object of the Nazis' campaign against the Jews in this first phase was to force Germany's Jews to leave the country. It was not, however, a benign exodus. Jews who did leave Germany were required to leave most of their property and assets behind.

The beginning of the second part of the Nazis' campaign against the Jews was coupled with the onset of the aggressive phase of Nazi territorial expansion. The first public and very violent manifestation came in the fall of 1938. On November 7 Herszel Grynszpan, a young Polish Jew living in Paris, assassinated Ernst vom Rath, a diplomat attached to the German embassy in Paris. Grynszpan acted on his own; the Jewish community in France neither knew of his plans nor approved of the murder.

The Nazi leaders, however, pretended that Grynszpan's act of personal desperation was part of an international Jewish conspiracy. Hitler and his associates decided to stage a vicious nationwide pogrom. The result was the "Reich Night of Crystal" (*Reichskristallnacht*), a name that derived from the number of windows that were broken during the two days of violence. On the evening of November 9, Joseph Goebbels delivered a furious anti-Semitic tirade to Nazi Party and government leaders assembled in Munich for the annual commemoration of the unsuccessful 1923 Beer Hall putsch. Immediately after the speech, orders went out to Stormtroopers and other party units to begin attacks against Jews, their homes, businesses, and synagogues. At the same time, the police were specifically instructed not to interfere as the pogrom took its course during the next two days.

By the time the violence ended, almost all of Germany's synagogues and some seven thousand Jewish homes and stores had been destroyed, mostly through fires set by the Nazi thugs. In addition, thousands of Jews were taken into "protective custody." Many were physically maltreated, and scores died as a result of their injuries. To increase the economic impact of the pogrom on the Jewish community, the government ordered the insurance companies in the Reich to refuse any claims for damages incurred during the Reichskristallnacht. Finally, a 1 billion mark fine was levied on the Jewish community as punishment for having "provoked" the pogrom.

In the first years of the Third Reich, much of the violence against Jews was committed by the Stormtroopers, but the "Night of Crystal" was their last major operation. The responsibility for the systematic killing during the actual Holocaust was in the hands of another party formation, the SS. In addition to Hitler, three men—Heinrich Himmler, Reinhard Heydrich, and Heydrich's successor, Ernst Kaltenbrunner—were primarily responsible for carrying out the Holocaust. Heydrich, a former naval officer who was dismissed from the German navy for violating the service's honor code, joined the SS in 1932.

Himmler, who was already head of the SS at the time, quickly recognized Heydrich's cold-blooded administrative efficiency and placed the young ex-officer in charge of the SS's system of political espionage. After the Nazis' seizure of power, Heydrich's responsibilities expanded to include the whole range of the Nazis' terror activities. Kaltenbrunner, who headed the Austrian SS until the Anschluss, replaced Heydrich when Czech resistance fighters assassinated the chief of the RSHA in 1942.

Like Hitler, Heydrich, Himmler, and Kaltenbrunner were fanatic anti-Semites who believed firmly that World War II was a battle for global control between Jews and "Aryans." The physical extermination of Europe's Jews was an integral part of this Weltanschauungskrieg. Himmler took particular pride in the role of the SS in the extermination process. A few months before the end of the war, in August 1944, the head of the SS called the murder of millions of Jewish men, women, and children the group's "most historic deed."

Systematic planning for the Holocaust began in February 1939. Heydrich ordered the "Reich Central Office for Jewish Emigration," headed by another Austrian SS officer, Adolf Eichmann, to cease its concern with encouraging Jewish emigration and begin instead drawing up plans for the concentration and ghettoization of Europe's Jews. The Nazi attack on Poland inaugurated the extermination of that country's Jews. Behind the German lines roving SS execution squads killed thousands of Jews, mostly intellectuals and individuals of some standing in the community. In addition, the Germans forced those of Poland's Jews who were not immediately killed to live in abominably overcrowded, sealed-off, and easily controlled ghettoes located in the Generalgouvernement, the German-occupied section of Poland.

Between July 1941 and January of the following year, the machinery for the Holocaust was set in motion. On July 31, 1941, Göring in his capacity as chief of administration for the economic war effort instructed Heydrich to submit a coordinated plan for the "final solution" of the Jewish question, as the extermination of Jews and other undesirables living in all areas of Europe under German control was officially termed. Heydrich in turn assigned the tactical job of planning the deportation and concentration of Europe's Jews to Adolf Eichmann. Six months later, the chief of the RSHA presided over the Wannsee Conference, a meeting of representatives of various party and state agencies. The delegates to the conference agreed on the final modalities of the Holocaust: All of Europe's Jews were to be deported to areas of occupied Poland where their actual extermination would take place.

Between the beginning of 1942 and November 1944, when the advancing Red Army forced the closing of the killing centers, the Nazis sent millions of people to their deaths. The Holocaust began with the Jews of western and southeastern Europe. Here the collaborationist regimes had the responsibility for sending their Jewish citizens to concentration camps before the Germans transported the victims to Poland.

A variety of execution methods were used during the Holocaust, ranging from mass shootings to the use of poison gas. Many of the mass executions were carried out by the Einsatzgruppen of the SS, but recent research by Christopher Browning and others has shown that regular police battalions were also active in the slaughter. It is now estimated that more than 500,000 individuals were killed by these regular police units. Eventually, the Nazis decided on specifically designed extermination camps, the largest of which were Auschwitz and Treblinka. After some trial and error, they also determined that an insecticide, the gas Zyklon B, was the most "efficient" means of killing large numbers of people. In Auschwitz alone, some 2 million Jews lost their lives. The Red Army liberated Auschwitz and the other extermination centers in November 1944, but the Nazis had every intention of continuing the killings. As the Soviets advanced on the camps, Himmler ordered the gas chambers and crematoria dismantled but not destroyed.

They were to be reinstalled at the Austrian concentration camp of Mauthausen, just outside of Linz. Fortunately, the swift end of the war prevented such plans from becoming reality.

Of the 6 million Jews killed during the Holocaust, by far the largest number—some 4 million—came from Russia and Poland. Nevertheless, the Jewish communities of virtually every country under Nazi occupation (with the exception of the small number of Danish Jews and the bulk of Bulgaria's Jewish population) were decimated. Roughly half of the 500,000 Jews living in Germany before Hitler came to power lost their lives in the Holocaust. Most of the others had emigrated, the bulk to the United States and what is now the state of Israel, before the systematic exterminations began. About twenty thousand survived the war in hiding in Germany.

The Holocaust left not only millions dead but also numerous unanswered questions. The most basic and important of course was, How could it happen? The answer lies in a combination of factors: the long history of German anti-Semitism, the racial fanaticism of the SS, and the available twentieth-century technology for mass killings are some of them. Did the German people know and approve of the Holocaust? A very controversial book by Daniel Goldhagen argues that most Germans enthusiastically supported the Holocaust, but the Nazis' own actions throw considerable doubt on this thesis. The exterminations were classified "top secret," and the Nazis took great care to hide their gruesome activities. In addition, the killing centers were located in remote areas of the occupied East. Thousands of Germans knew of the Holocaust, nevertheless, and millions more probably guessed the truth. Why then was there no protest by the German people? It was wartime, and people were concerned with their own problems; the terror of the Gestapo did not abate until the end of the war; and, above all, it was easier to ignore the horror than take action against it.

Although the "large" questions involve primarily issues of individual morality and group guilt, three factual queries have increasingly concerned historians in recent years. One is Hitler's personal involvement in the planning and implementation of the Holocaust, the second concerns the timing of the Holocaust, and the third involves the question of Jewish resistance. As we saw, the planning apparatus was formally set in motion by an order from Göring to Heydrich. The absence of written documentation with Hitler's signature on it has led some historians to question whether the Führer actually ordered the Holocaust. The "revisionists" claim that the exterminations were, so to speak, implemented by Himmler and Heydrich behind Hitler's back.

The attempt to relieve Hitler of responsibility for the Holocaust is misguided and futile. As Gerald Fleming has convincingly demonstrated, Hitler's personal responsibility for the exterminations is well established even in the absence of written orders. The dictator often issued oral orders to his subordinates, and the men in charge of implementing the Holocaust left no doubt that their orders had come directly from the Nazi leader. In addition, Hitler repeatedly referred to the Holocaust during his wartime "table talks," indicating that he was kept fully informed of the operations.

A related issue is the question when Hitler and his henchmen decided on systematic killing operations as the "solution" to the "Jewish problem." Some historians argue that in Hitler's mind launching World War II and ordering the physical extermination of Europe's Jews were always linked. Others contend the Holocaust was not the result of such straightforward decision making. Rather, it came about through a combination of factors: Hitler's determination to force the Jews out of Europe, opportunity to implement a "solution" to the "Jewish problem" (some two-thirds of the continent's Jews lived in Poland), and the desire by local Nazi officials in occupied Poland to rid themselves of the problems of overcrowding and ghettoization that their own policies had created.

As for the question of why 6 million Jews permitted a few thousand SS troops to lead them to slaughter, there are two answers. First, the bulk of the victims were East European Jews, a people that traditionally coped with

Im Mittelpunkt   Viktor Klemperer (1881–1960)

Although Klemperer was a noted scholar of eighteenth-century French literature, his real fame rests on the posthumous publication of the voluminous diaries that he kept while living in Germany during the Nazi era. Klemperer was a Jew living in what the Nazis termed a "mixed marriage," which meant that his wife was not Jewish but "Aryan." This circumstance did not prevent Klemperer and his wife from being exposed to numerous forms of hardship and humiliation, but it did prevent him from being killed in the Holocaust.

Klemperer was born as the son of a rabbi in Landsberg a.d. Warthe, an area of eastern Prussia that is now part of Poland. In 1890 Klemperer's father was appointed associate rabbi at Berlin's reformist synagogue, and the family moved to the capital. Klemperer came from a distinguished family whose most famous scion was probably Viktor's nephew, the conductor Otto Klemperer. Klemperer's father wanted him to go into medicine or law, as his brothers did, but Klemperer insisted on pursuing an academic career. He received his Ph.D. in romance literature in 1913 and after military service in World War I joined the faculty of the Technical University in Dresden. This was not the ideal position for a specialist in literature, but the prevailing anti-Semitism in the German academic establishment prevented him from receiving an appointment at one of the "major" universities. Klemperer remained on the faculty in Dresden until 1935 when the Nazis forced him into early retirement.

In 1921 Klemperer had married his first wife, who gave up her budding career as a pianist to join him in Dresden. The Klemperers had an exceedingly happy marriage, although Eva Klemperer suffered from a variety of debilitating ailments that often impaired her physical movements.

Klemperer had kept a diary for most of his adult life, and his enforced idleness during the Third Reich only increased his determination to detail his daily experiences as accurately as possible. As a result, the diaries (which were published in an abridged two-volume version in the 1990s) provide us with an extremely detailed record of the life of a German Jew during the Third Reich. With almost superhuman objectivity Klemperer describes the daily harassments and indignities to

pogroms and other forms of anti-Semitism by bending with the wind. Most did not realize until it was too late that the Nazi Holocaust was not a pogrom, much less a relocation program, but a systematic genocide. And second, there was considerably more Jewish resistance than the Nazis had anticipated or acknowledged. There were periodic revolts in the death camps, the largest taking place at Treblinka in the fall of 1943. But the most noteworthy instance of resistance was the uprising in April and May 1943 of the Warsaw ghetto. For two weeks the Jews of Warsaw, without heavy weapons or outside help, held out against superior German forces. The uprising could not save the Jews—of Warsaw

or of Europe—but it lays to rest the myth that there was no Jewish resistance against the Holocaust.

ECONOMY AND SOCIETY

As the regime moved into the aggressive phase of its plan of conquest, there were some important changes in the management of the German economy. After Hjalmar Schacht's dismissal as Reich economics minister in 1936, military officers increasingly occupied high-level positions in the organization of the Four Year Plan, pushing aside the civilian bureaucrats from the Reich ministry of economics.

which he and his wife were subjected, until in 1941 the Nazis even took away the Klemperers and forced them, along with Dresden's other remaining Jews, to live under extremely trying conditions in a single dwelling, which the Nazis dubbed the *Judenhaus*.

At the same time, Klemperer also records acts of kindness by ordinary Germans throughout the years of his progressive humiliation. (The diaries themselves, for example, were hidden in the house of a German friend.) While keeping his diary of daily life in the Third Reich, Klemperer also made meticulous notes for what was to become his first postwar book. Published in 1947, *Lingua Tertii Imperii* ("The Language of the Third Reich") is a brilliant study of the Nazis' perversion of the German language.

Klemperer was repeatedly urged to emigrate while it was still possible (his brothers went on to distinguished careers in America), but he feared he would have no professional future in a strange land whose language he spoke very inadequately. Klemperer's ordeal came to an end in the chaos that followed the Allied bombing of Dresden in April 1945. Both of the Klemperers survived the bombing, and in the general confusion that followed the attack, Klemperer at the urging of his wife removed the Star of David that he had been forced to wear since 1940. The couple then made their way to Bavaria, where they were liberated by American troops.

After the war ended, the Klemperers returned to Dresden and moved back into their house, which, after some bureaucratic delays, had been restored to them. Despite long-standing concerns about the Communists as left-wing counterparts of the Nazis (a sentiment he often expressed in his diaries), by the end of the war Klemperer felt that only the Communists had formed an effective resistance against the Nazis. He joined the Communist Party in November 1945, and for a few years even served as a delegate to the East German parliament. His postwar academic career took him to the Universities of Greifswald and Halle, and he ended his career at the prestigious Humboldt University in East Berlin. He received numerous academic honors, including membership in the East German Academy of Sciences. Eva Klemperer died in 1951, and a year later Klemperer married a former student. It is thanks to the perseverance of his second wife, Hadewig, that we owe the preservation and publication of the diaries.

Nevertheless, even with the outbreak of hostilities, by no means all of Germany's economic resources were allocated to the war effort. That decision was motivated primarily by political considerations. Hitler was convinced shortages at home had led to declining morale and eventually revolution during World War I. For this reason he was determined to prevent another "turnip winter" in Germany. In consequence, although there were certainly shortages on the home front during World War II, they were never as severe as they had been in the earlier conflict. Especially during the first two years of the war, the regime was also careful to cultivate the goodwill of industrial laborers with extra rations.

In strategic terms, the decision to improvise for a series of short conflicts fundamentally misjudged the nature of World War II. As we have seen, Hitler's scenario of a global blitzkrieg failed completely; by the beginning of 1942 (after the entry of the United States into the conflict), it was clear to competent observers that the Reich faced another war of attrition.

The Nazis for a time dealt effectively with the problems that had plagued Germany's home front in World War I, but they failed to give adequate attention to a new element in warfare, aerial bombardment of civilian populations. The Nazis had used massive bombings with devastating effect on

After the brutal suppression of the Warsaw ghetto uprising, SS troops rounded up the surviving inhabitants for transportation to the extermination camps. (Source: Courtesy of National Archives and Records Administration.)

Rotterdam and later on English cities in the Battle of Britain, but by 1942, partly because Hitler underestimated the Allies' capabilities and refused to accelerate Germany's fighter plane program, the Allies achieved air superiority and turned the new strategy against the Germans. At first daytime and by mid-1943 nighttime bombings of German cities became daily occurrences. World War II, until the Allied invasion, was brought home to the Germans primarily in the form of increasingly destructive aerial bombardments. By the time the war ended, major urban centers like Cologne, Berlin, and Hamburg consisted of little more than rubble and hundreds of thousands of lives had been lost in the air raids.

The Allied air raids of the German cities, which greatly intensified as the war went on, has recently led to a major debate among the practitioners of a relatively new genre of historical writing called the politics of memory. In 2002 a new book on the bombings entitled *Der Brand* ("The Fire") appeared. Its author, the journalist Jörg Friedrich, based his work on contemporary records and interviews with survivors of the raids. The result was a decidedly bottom-up account that focused on the civilian populations and their suffering. The author concluded that the Germans and their counterparts in Rotterdam and London were victims of an immoral and cruel military strategy that was used by both sides in the war.

The book raised a flurry of controversy, with some critics contending that by focusing on the Germans as victims, Friedrich was attempting to relativize the Germans' role as perpetrators of horror. Others defended Friedrich's vivid account of the consequences of the air raids. Like the author they argued it was legitimate to describe those who suffered and died in the Allied bombing attacks—and they were mostly women and children—as victims of forces they could not control. As is true of most historiographic controversies, no consensus could be reached. In a retrospective on the debate, Mary Nolan came to the somewhat contradictory conclusion that "The [Allied] intent was surely moral and legal…. Yet the execution of the air war did contravene morality and legality."

After the German defeat in the Battle of Stalingrad (January–February 1943), it was clear even to insiders in the Nazi regime that the German economy and home front were not prepared for a drawn-out conflict. Consequently, the Nazis introduced major organizational and lifestyle changes. In February 1942, the administrators of the Four Year Plan lost their dominant position in the management of the economy. A new Ministry for War Production, headed by Hitler's architect Albert Speer, was established and given vast powers to coordinate all war-related economic production. Speer and his associates succeeded in increasing the production of war matériel to a remarkable extent. Aided by the fact that the Allies (like the Germans earlier) had for much of the war concentrated their attacks on civilian housing and had limited their bombings of specific industrial targets to onetime raids, Germany's industry achieved its highest output in September 1944, only a few months before the end of the war. In fact, the Reich's economic collapse began only in the late fall of 1944 when the Allies concentrated their attacks on industrial production facilities and Germany's infrastructure as well as civilian targets. In the spring of 1945, the lack of fuel and Allied bombings of the German railroad network brought the Reich's war machinery to a final halt.

Speer accomplished his feat of increasing industrial production partly by returning authority for economic decision making to the private sector, thereby eliminating much of the political interference by party and military officials. Equally important, however, was the regime's decision to use German female workers and forced labor from the occupied areas of Eastern and Western Europe. At the beginning of World War II at least some foreign workers had been attracted by the relatively high German wages, but as the tide of war turned, Sauckel, the Reich commissioner for foreign labor, increasingly relied on terror to fill his and Speer's quotas for laborers. Concentration

Bombed-out refugees in Berlin, July, 1945. (Source: LAPI/Roger-Viollet/ The Image Works.)

camp inmates, too, were forced in ever-larger numbers to work in war-related industries. By the end of the war, foreign laborers were working in German factories, on farms, and even in households.

The concept of "total war" on the home front was formally launched in February 1943. Goebbels addressed an audience hand-selected by the propaganda ministry in the Berlin *Sportpalast,* the scene of many of the minister's propaganda triumphs in the political campaigns before 1933. His speech culminated in the question, "Do you want total war?"—to which the audience screamed a predictable "Yes!" The German populace saw this performance as part of the newsreels shown in movie theaters, complete with close-ups of recognizable media personalities.

The campaign of total war meant that guns now took definite precedence over butter. The civilian population had to get used to growing shortages of virtually all commodities. In addition, total war brought a massive buildup of the regime's terror presence. Anonymous denunciations were encouraged even more than before, and the Nazis introduced the death penalty for a whole series of minor infractions, including the crime of being a "defeatist." By the end of the war, it is clear that whatever sympathies the regime had enjoyed among the Germans had largely dissipated. Life had become a daily struggle in the face of constant bombings, shortages, and fear of the regime's terror.

Still, the Nazi propagandists did not abandon their efforts to replace lack of resources with fanaticism. In the fall of 1944, they ordered the creation of the "People's Storm" (*Volkssturm*), a paramilitary organization composed of all male Germans between the ages of sixteen and sixty who were not serving in the armed forces. In the minds of the writers of propaganda brochures, these units would become the *levée en masse* that would finally destroy the Allied armies as they crossed the German borders. The Volkssturm existed mostly in the minds of its creators. Few units were actually set up, and those that were organized tended to melt away before making contact with the enemy. They did not flee alone; most NSDAP leaders, including the Gauleiters, also took flight, often when the Allied armies were still hundreds of miles away.

In macabre scenes worthy of a greater cause, Hitler spent the last weeks of the Third Reich in the bunker underneath the Reich chancellery in Berlin drafting phantom plans for the future. Hitler was particularly concerned with the architectural reconstruction of the three cities that he saw as the epitome of his regime: Berlin, the capital of the Greater German Reich; Munich, the home of the Nazi Party; and Linz in Upper Austria, the city in which Hitler had spent much of his youth and that he regarded as his hometown. On the dictator's orders, Speer and other architects throughout the years of the Third Reich fashioned drawings and constructed scale models of mammoth pseudo-classical structures that were intended to demonstrate the grandeur of Hitler's vision. Until the end, the Führer took a regular and active interest in all this. He even insisted on seeing how the buildings would look in ruins; he wanted the remains to compare favorably with the pyramids.

THE END OF THE THIRD REICH

Since the 1938 decision to "obliterate" Czechoslovakia, each stage of the Nazi march of conquest across Europe had begun with a "Führer directive," a document drafted by Hitler outlining the basic aim and strategy of the next campaign. The last of these directives came in November 1943. The contents involuntarily revealed how the tide had turned against Hitler and the Nazis. Whereas the earlier directives demonstrated the acumen of Hitler's intuitive approach to balance-of-power politics and military strategy, the November 1943 document was based on little more than illusion and wishful thinking. Hitler was fanatically determined to accomplish his goal of Lebensraum in the East. To this end, he ordered preparations for new land offensives against Russia, and a new air offensive against Great Britain through the use of the rocket-propelled "V-weapons."

Hitler's directive was based on a completely unrealistic assessment of Allied and German resources. The Wehrmacht could not stop the Allied invasion of France in June 1944, the V-weapons were more of an irritant than a threat to England, and on the eastern front the Nazis were unable to prevent the Russian drive westward, much less launch new offensive operations of their own.

After the failure of the Battle of the Bulge, Hitler's essential nihilism broke through entirely. In one of his last orders to his troops, the so-called Nero order of March 1945, he insisted that as the Allies entered Germany they should find only scorched earth, much as the Germans had left behind when they were forced to withdraw from the Soviet Union.

Actually, by the spring of 1945, Hitler's orders were obeyed only in his suite of rooms in the bunker underneath the Reich chancellery. Not only did the Allies advance far too swiftly for the Germans to effect an orderly retreat, but the forces in German society that had been willing to support the Nazis for so long had finally begun to disengage themselves from the regime's headlong dash toward self-destruction. The leaders of Germany's industry, especially, had as early as the summer of 1943 started to make plans for Germany's postwar and post-Nazi future. As the outcome of the war became increasingly obvious, Hitler's senseless orders for destruction were quietly sabotaged by Speer and other government ministers. Just before the end, even some of the Nazi Gauleiters refused to carry out Hitler's scorched earth orders. As a result, when the war ended, Germany's industrial and economic potential was far less completely destroyed than either Hitler or the Allies believed. It was revealed after the war, for example, that only 10–15 percent of the productive capacity of the Ruhr had been eliminated by either wartime bombing or by the destruction of the retreating German forces.

With Germany's unconditional surrender in May 1945, the Reich as a political entity ceased to exist. All levels of government and all administrative decisions were the responsibility of the Allied occupation forces. Hitler's designated successor, Admiral Dönitz, had retreated to Murwik, the naval base outside of Flensburg, where he maintained a shadowy existence as "Reich president" for about two weeks. But the Allies never recognized this "government," and at the end of May the entire "cabinet" was unceremoniously arrested by British forces.

Hitler and the Nazis left Germany a heavy and wholly negative legacy. Millions of Germans had died either at the front or during the air raids; millions more had become refugees when the Russian armies reached the eastern borders and pressed on westward. The country's infrastructure was in shambles; Germany's cities were smoking ruins. More important (for the physical damage turned out to be less devastating than it appeared), the Holocaust attached a permanent weight of moral guilt to the German name. Finally, as Andreas Hillgruber has pointed out, Adolf Hitler's most lasting legacy to Germany was the destruction of the national unity for which Germans had strived since the beginning of the nineteenth century. Hitler had undone Bismarck's historic achievement. The "Germanies" were quite literally once again a geographic expression rather than a nation.

CHAPTER EIGHT

"Condominium of the Allied Powers"

1945–1949

Hans Kelsen, one of the many academics whom the Nazis forced to leave Germany, coined the title phrase of this chapter when he taught at the University of California, Berkeley, during World War II. He sought to describe Germany's unique societal structure after the collapse of the Third Reich. The country was like a condominium. Each of the four occupying powers had separate apartments—their individual zones of occupation—but as owners they were also jointly responsible for maintaining the building as a whole. The original owners, however, had lost their proprietary rights.

As we will see, in its pure form the Allied condominium phase of German history did not last long. Both the Allies and the Germans soon recognized that they were dealing with postwar realities far different from what they had expected. Only four years after the Reich's unconditional surrender, the former landlords began to take charge of their building again, although the Allies retained many rights. Especially surprising

was the rapid economic recovery and political transformation of what was to become West Germany. In 1945 one American observer noted that West Germany looked like "the face of the moon," yet four years later the Western occupation zones experienced the beginnings of an "economic miracle" while laying the foundations for what was to become a highly successful parliamentary democracy.

THE GERMAN RESISTANCE: STRENGTHS AND DELUSIONS

At first glance discussing the anti-Nazi resistance in a chapter devoted to the period after the Nazis had been defeated may seem out of place. But there is a good reason for doing this. The opponents of the Third Reich were not successful in overthrowing the regime, but their failed efforts became a significant part of the politics of memory in the later East and West Germanys.

Relative to the size of the population there were fewer resistance fighters in Germany than in other European countries, although both the Nazis and the Allies, for different reasons, tended to belittle what resistance there was in the Reich. The German resistance, of course, had some peculiar handicaps. Whereas the resistance movements in other countries worked to liberate their nations from foreign domination, the German resistance had to work against its own national government. In addition, after 1939 German resistance fighters had to be active while the country was at war, so their activities risked arousing another stab-in-the-back legend. Nevertheless, in the thirty months between the beginning of 1943 and the end of the war, more than 11,000 Germans were executed for anti-Nazi activities, 5,000 in 1944 alone.

Members of the resistance came from all segments of society and all political camps, although the bulk of the resisters came from the bottom and top layers of the social strata. The earliest—and also least effective—resistance was identified with the political left. Nazi terror turned first against Communists and Social Democrats. Especially the Communists were the targets of the SA, the SS, and the Gestapo. The party's national leader, Ernst Thälmann, was arrested almost immediately after the Nazis came to power and later killed in a concentration camp. In fact, by the time the Nazis broke up the largest communist underground resistance organization—the "Red Orchestra" (*Rote Kapelle*)—in 1943, thousands of German Communists had been put into jails and concentration camps. The leaders of the German communist movement after World War II, however, for the most part came from the ranks of those who had spent the Nazi years in exile in the Soviet Union, although, ironically, many of the exiles there became victims of the Stalinist purges.

In cooperation with the Russians, the German Communists in exile were also instrumental in organizing the *Nationalkomitee Freies Deutschland* (National Committee for a Free Germany, NKFD) among German prisoners

of war (POWs) captured on the eastern front. The group's wartime success in persuading German soldiers on the Russian front to desert was minimal, but the NKFD became a useful training ground for future Communist cadres. In addition, the NKFD provided the Communists with a nationalist veneer.

Many Social Democrat leaders also fled Germany. Unlike the Communists, they chose to spend their years of exile in Western countries—especially Great Britain, the Scandinavian countries, and the United States. Proportionately far more Social Democrats than Communists, however, stayed in Germany. Most Social Democratic activists returned to private life and ceased all political activities. A minority became active resistors, but almost all of them were quickly arrested and spent the years of the Third Reich in Nazi prisons and concentration camps.

The bourgeois groups of the political center and right played a contradictory role in the German resistance story. In contrast to the Communists and Social Democrats, most politically right-wing Germans collaborated with the Nazis both before and after 1933. But although resistance on the right was much less widespread, some members of the old elite who were opposed to Nazism occupied key positions in the government, the military, and the economy even after the *Gleichschaltung*. Those who did join the resistance were therefore in a much better position to make their anti-Nazi activities count.

Given their limited objectives, opposition by the organized religions was particularly effective. The churches faced a dilemma. The Catholic Church had signed a formal treaty with the Nazis, the Concordat, which church leaders were determined to uphold. The Nazis violated the treaty with impunity, but it was not until Pope Pius XI's 1937 encyclical *Mit brennender Sorge* ("With Burning Concern") that Catholic opposition to the Nazis' immoral activities received widespread support from the clergy.

The Protestant churches were institutionally and ideologically even less well prepared to resist governmental actions. German

Protestantism had long been associated with Prussian authoritarianism and German nationalism. Here resistance originally arose not against Nazism as such but as a reaction to the regime's attempt to interfere with the churches' theological teachings and administrative autonomy. Many church leaders' first experience with resistance came in 1933–1934. The Nazis attempted to destroy the independence of the individual state churches and impose a Nazi fellow traveler as "Reich bishop" on a centralized, national Protestant Church, but massive opposition from the ranks of the Protestant clergy forced the Nazis to abandon their efforts. A number of Protestant pastors also rejected the adoption of the "Aryan paragraph," which prohibited pastors of Jewish descent from serving as ministers in the churches. Led by a Berlin minister, Martin Niemöller, several thousand pastors and laity seceded from the established Protestantism and formed the "Confessing Church." In addition, a number of courageous Protestant theologians, like Dietrich Bonhoeffer, joined actively in the plot to overthrow the Nazis. The decision cost Bonhoeffer his life; he was executed in April 1945. Niemöller spent long years in a concentration camp.

High government officials and especially the military had the best opportunities to thwart Nazi aims and policies. But members of these groups also had a long tradition of opposition to democracy, and the leaders of the military enthusiastically applauded Hitler's rearmament program and his early foreign policy successes. Still, some of the most effective and spectacular resistance activities came from a small number of Germany's old elite. In addition to using their offices to save some victims of Nazi terror, government officials and military officers planned and implemented the plot against the regime that culminated in the July 1944 attempt to assassinate the dictator.

There were numerous "private" conspiratorial groups (including the White Rose, an anti-Nazi cell led by two students at the University of Munich, Hans and Sophie Scholl), but one, the "Kreisauer Circle," deserves particular mention. (The name derives from the estate of the Moltke family at Kreisau in Silesia that served as an out-of-the-way meeting place for the group's activists. Several members of the Moltke family were very active in the anti-Nazi resistance.) The Kreisauer Circle consisted of a number of relatively young men, from left-wing Social Democrats like Julius Leber to dyed-in-the-wool conservatives, but the members of the circle were not representative of their social and political groups. On the contrary, they tended to be intellectuals who became resisters precisely because they were outsiders. Virtually all leading members of the Kreisauer Circle were executed in the wake of the July 1944 plot against Hitler.

There was little opposition to Hitler among the military while the dictator seemed to be redrawing the map of Europe without risking war. After the Blomberg-Fritsch crisis and especially after the Munich crisis, however, a few leading officers, like General Ludwig Beck, realized that Hitler's path would inevitably lead Germany into another world war. The German defeat at the Battle of Moscow convinced additional members of the officer corps that only the elimination of Hitler and the Nazi regime would save Germany from complete destruction.

The history of the German military and governmental resistance is punctuated with failed plans to overthrow the Nazi dictatorship. The conspirators—many of whom worked in the *Abwehr*, the Wehrmacht's espionage and counterintelligence unit—were ready to move in late September 1938 when Neville Chamberlain's offer to take the lead in ending the Munich crisis thwarted their intentions. Later, as various plans for a bloodless coup proved unworkable, the conspirators increasingly recognized that only Hitler's death would paralyze the Nazi power structure.

Instrumental in persuading the conspirators that it would be necessary to kill Hitler was a young colonel, Claus Count von Stauffenberg, one of those involved in the Kreisauer Circle. Several attempts to assassinate the dictator failed, but on July 20, 1944, Stauffenberg was able to place a bomb under the table in the conference room at Hitler's East Prussian headquarters. (The explosives were supplied by another young officer, Philipp von Boeselager. He survived the war and in May 2008, at age ninety, he was the last of the conspirators to die.) The conspirators intended that immediately after Hitler's death, units of the reserve army would arrest leading party and SS functionaries while a cabinet composed of members of the resistance, headed by General Ludwig Beck as temporary chief of state, would keep law and order and negotiate an end to the war. The plot failed completely. Hitler was only slightly wounded by the explosion, and the conspiracy quickly collapsed.

The Nazi regime took terrible revenge on its enemies. Stauffenberg, Beck, and their closest associates were killed immediately, and rigged trials before a "People's Court" handed out a steady stream of death sentences in the weeks following the attempt on Hitler's life. Thousands of less prominent members of the resistance were simply seized by the Gestapo. A so-called kith-and-kin directive ordered that members of the extended families of the major conspirators—from second cousins to infant grandchildren—be put into concentration camps.

The failure of the July 1944 plot ended any real chance of overthrowing the Nazis from within, but in retrospect this may not have been altogether bad. Quite aside from the danger of a new "stab-in-the-back" legend, for all their undoubted hatred of the Nazi dictatorship, many leading members of the German resistance were singularly naive about the country's past and future. It was not that they had no plans. On the contrary, if anything there was a surfeit of plans and constitutional schemes. The difficulty, rather, was that many leaders of the resistance assumed that the "excessively" democratic Weimar constitution had permitted the Nazis to come to power. Although some, including Stauffenberg, recognized that Germany's future needed to be built on a democratic basis involving all segments of the population,

several prominent leaders of the German resistance were convinced the country took the wrong path in 1918. For them the answer to Hitler was not a return to the parliamentary democracy of Weimar, but to "authoritarian democracy," a form of government that many in the military conspiracy and even some in the Kreisauer Circle naively associated with the enlightened despotism of the Hohenzollern kings and what Oswald Spengler had called "Prussian socialism."

The naiveté about constitutional reconstruction was matched by illusion about the Reich's international standing after the defeat of the Nazis. Most planners in the resistance assumed that Germany would remain a major European power, and some even insisted that Austria should remain part of Germany. They did recognize that the countries of Eastern Europe (not to mention Western Europe) would become independent again, but many among the military opposition, who were scions of old noble families of eastern Germany, remained convinced that the Reich should continue its "civilizing mission" in Poland and Russia in some form or other.

Many prominent members of the German resistance, then, did not recognize that the Allies refused to respect Germany's status as a Great Power in the future. Moreover the Allies, as we will see, tended to identify—wrongly—Prussianism and Nazism, so they were unlikely to support the resistance's effort to return Germany to the days of Frederick the Great. Instead, the country's postwar future, insofar as it involved the Germans at all, would lie in the hands of the Weimar democratic leaders, most of whom had spent the years of the Third Reich either in concentration camps or as part of the "inner emigration." The term *inner emigration* was coined after the war to designate an attitude of opposition to the Nazis that involved neither exile nor active resistance. The "inner emigrants" essentially dropped out of public life and devoted themselves to awaiting the downfall of the regime and planning for Germany's future after the end of the Third Reich.

ALLIED VISIONS AND PLANS, 1941–1945

In February 1943 the Allies announced that they would not negotiate with any Reich government but would accept only a declaration of "unconditional surrender." The policy of unconditional surrender deprived the Germans of any recognized role in the country's immediate future, but it left unanswered a host of questions about the Allies' own ideas and approaches. Generally speaking, the Russians were most anxious to reach concrete decisions before the hostilities had ended. As early as July 1941, the Soviets demanded the dismemberment of Germany. In principle, American and British planners, too, accepted dividing the Reich into three or more independent states as the most effective means of preventing a German colossus in Central Europe. At the same time, the U.S. president Franklin Delano Roosevelt was particularly reluctant to draw up concrete plans for the future of a country that, as he put it, "we have not yet conquered."

As the tide of the war turned, however, the Americans and the British, too, began to be concerned over the lack of concrete agreements for Germany's postwar future. The Big Three agreed on the eradication of Nazism and were resolved that the Reich should not again be in a position to wage war on its neighbors. But the Western powers had to recognize that the total defeat of Germany would create a power vacuum in Central Europe that would bring with it far-reaching consequences. Almost by definition, a powerless and dismembered Germany would mean Russian hegemonic control of Central Europe. Indeed, some Western analysts expected that at the time of Germany's surrender the Red Army would have reached the Rhine in its westward push. The prospect of Russian domination in Germany was not particularly disturbing to those in the West who expected the wartime alliance of the Big Three to continue as a peacetime partnership, but others were less sanguine. As the Russians made their heavy-handed presence felt in Eastern Europe, installing communist regimes that were clearly not democratically elected, especially Winston Churchill and the British grew increasingly reluctant to tolerate the expansion of Soviet power.

The Americans remained divided. Henry Morgenthau Jr., the U.S. secretary of the treasury and the president's personal friend, argued that a complete power vacuum in Central Europe was the only answer to the "German problem." In contrast, Morgenthau's colleague in the U.S. cabinet, secretary of war Henry Stimson (the War and Navy Departments were not joined and reorganized into the Department of Defense until 1947), and officials in the State Department insisted an economically strong Germany was needed if Europe as a whole was to recover and stand on its own feet.

By the end of 1944, when the Allied armies stood poised to carry the war into Germany proper, the Big Three had not yet made a determination of Germany's territorial and societal future. In response to a British suggestion, the Big Three had agreed in September 1943 that after the Third Reich had capitulated each of the Big Three would administer a zone of occupation. Largely to dilute Russian influence in Germany, the British proposed that France should also be assigned a zone of occupation. Neither the Americans nor the Russians were enthusiastic, but it was eventually agreed to carve out a French territory from the previously established British and American zones. The boundaries of the Soviet, British, and U.S. zones would follow established provincial and Land boundaries. As latecomers, the French had to be content with disjointed parts of four Länder and no contiguous administrative borders.

The basis of the zonal division was Germany's territorial status as of 1937. This meant that Austria and Czechoslovakia would regain their independence, but East Prussia, for example, remained technically part of Germany. Actually, the Allied leaders had already agreed to far-reaching territorial changes in Eastern Europe. In accord with this de facto agreement, the Soviets at the beginning of 1945 had annexed the northern half of East Prussia, including the city of Königsberg. (It was renamed Kaliningrad.) The Russians also held on to eastern Poland (the parts of the country that the Soviet Union had claimed in the Nazi-Soviet Pact) while agreeing that Poland was to be compensated for its losses by German territories lying east of the Oder and Neisse Rivers and the southern parts of East Prussia.

At least on the surface, there seemed to be considerable consensus among the Allies about the need to restructure German society. The Big Three and France agreed that after the war Germany needed to be subjected to the "four D's": demilitarization, decartelization, de-Nazification, and democratization. To be sure, here, too, agreement was more theoretical than substantive. Except for democratization, the "four D's" were essentially negative goals, not a positive blueprint for Germany's political, economic, and social future. And democratization obviously meant something entirely different to the Russians than it did to the Americans.

On the western side, the most comprehensive and—given its basic premise—also the most logical scheme for a fundamental reconstruction of German society was the one proposed in the fall of 1944 by Henry Morgenthau. The Morgenthau Plan, which its author entitled "Program to Prevent Germany from Starting a World War III," postulated that Hitler's rise to power was the logical consequence of the German national character that had earlier produced Prussian authoritarianism and militarism. The U.S. secretary of the treasury argued that a powerful, industrialized Germany would inevitably attempt to wage war on its neighbors and the world. Only the country's territorial dismemberment and political and economic impotence would assure future peace. Concretely, the secretary proposed Germany's permanent occupation by Russia and other European countries (but not the United States) and the "industrial disarmament" of Germany. The Reich's natural resources, such as the Ruhr coal mines, should be placed under permanent international control. Germany was to become

"a country primarily agricultural and pastoral in character." To compensate for Germany's traditional role in the international economic order, Morgenthau proposed that the United States should underwrite the recovery of the Soviet Union and Great Britain with large loans.

The Morgenthau Plan was a radical solution to the "German problem"—assuming one agreed there was a "German" as opposed to a "Nazi" problem. For a brief time, the secretary of the treasury convinced Roosevelt and even Churchill of the effectiveness of his approach. The American president agreed instinctively with many of Morgenthau's assumptions, and he welcomed that under the Morgenthau Plan American troops would be able to come home soon after the war ended, leaving European affairs in the hands of the Europeans. The British prime minister was lured by the expectation that Germany's "industrial disarmament" would eliminate Great Britain's traditional economic rival, and by the prospect of a large American loan for Great Britain's postwar reconstruction.

Churchill and Roosevelt gave tentative approval to Morgenthau's proposals when they met in Quebec in October 1944 but, almost immediately, vigorous opposition to the plan arose among American and British officials. The U.S. secretary of state Cordell Hull (whom Roosevelt had not taken along to Quebec) pointed out that the Morgenthau Plan would give the Russians continental hegemony while Germany's "pastoralization" would permanently disrupt the international economic system. Churchill's advisers used similar arguments against such "planned chaos." A short time later, both Roosevelt and Churchill withdrew their approval of Morgenthau's proposals. As a result, when the first American and British troops crossed into Germany, neither occupying power had a comprehensive plan for dealing with its new responsibilities.

Compared with American and British ideas, Russian and French plans on how to treat Germany at the end of World War II were considerably more concrete. In addition

Im Mittelpunkt Claus von Stauffenberg (1907–1944)

Although he was quite young (thirty-seven years old at the time), and only held the rank of a colonel, Claus von Stauffenberg was the key figure in the 1944 "generals' plot," the unsuccessful effort to kill Hitler and end the Nazi regime. He owed his leadership role to his charismatic personality and his organizational skills.

Stauffenberg came from an ancient Catholic noble family. He was born in 1907 in Jettingen, Swabia, appropriately enough, in one of the family's castles. Stauffenberg initially wanted to pursue a career in literature. Like his brother Berthold, who was also executed for his role in the 1944 plot, Claus von Stauffenberg was a member of the circle around the mystic poet Stefan George. But Stauffenberg gave up his literary ambitions in favor of a military career. In 1926 he joined the 17th cavalry regiment of the Reichswehr; he was promoted to second lieutenant in 1930.

Like most professional German soldiers, Stauffenberg was initially ambivalent about Hitler. He approved of the Nazi leader's rearmament plans and of the dictator's goal to restore Germany to the status of a great power, but Stauffenberg's belief in the principles of Catholic morality led him to reject the state-sponsored terror policies of the regime. Still, he had no objection to Germany's conquest of Poland, and he admired Hitler's military skills in the French campaign. Stauffenberg turned against Hitler and the Nazi regime after Germany attacked the Soviet Union. Although fiercely opposed to Communism, Stauffenberg saw the Holocaust and the treatment of Soviet soldiers by the SS and the German army as evidence that the Nazi regime was a moral evil that had to be stopped.

In 1943 Stauffenberg was posted to the North African campaign. In April he was severely wounded, losing his left eye, right hand, and two fingers on his left hand. During his long convalescence he became increasingly active in the military resistance movement, and by the middle of 1944 Stauffenberg decided that only Hitler's death could topple the regime. The conspirators determined that Stauffenberg, who had been reassigned to Hitler's headquarters, would place a bomb next to the dictator during Hitler's daily military briefing. Stauffenberg would then detonate

---

to territorial changes, the Soviet Union was determined to extract from Germany reparations—in the form of goods and labor, not money—to rebuild the areas of Russia devastated by the Nazis' unprovoked attack. In addition, the Soviets insisted there was a causal link between capitalism and Nazism. Only structural reforms that deprived the big capitalists and landowners of their economic and political power would guarantee that Nazism would not return to Germany.

Like the Russians, the French gave top priority to making the Germans pay for the damage they had inflicted during the war. To this end, the French were determined to use the resources of their zone for France's ben-

efit. In addition, the French, too, demanded far-reaching territorial changes in Germany; both the Saar and the entire Rhineland were to be separated from Germany and put under at least indirect French control. As for the problem of Nazism, French thinking linked this to German nationalism. France argued against the reestablishment of any central German governmental authority. In the words of the leader of the French Resistance, General Charles de Gaulle, there should be "no Reich [but] a return to the Germanies."

In February 1945 the leaders of the wartime alliance—Roosevelt, Churchill, and Stalin (de Gaulle was not invited)—met at Yalta on the Black Sea for their last summit the bomb by delayed action, fly back from Rastenburg (Hitler's headquarters in East Prussia) to Berlin, and declare a state of emergency. Members of the reserve army would arrest major Nazi leaders and appoint a temporary military government.

As we know, the plot failed completely. Hitler was only slightly wounded and he took terrible revenge on the conspirators. Stauffenberg himself was executed on the evening of July 20 on orders of General Fromm, one of the conspirators who was trying to save his own skin but was not able to. Stauffenberg's family, including his young children, were put into a concentration camp and prohibited from using the name Stauffenberg.

Since the failed attempt on Hitler's life, scholars and pundits have debated endlessly about Stauffenberg's motivation. Was he an idealist, or, having realized the war was lost (the July, 1944 plot took place five weeks after D-Day), was he trying to save his career and Germany's status as a great power?

There is evidence on both sides. There is no doubt that Stauffenberg felt a moral revulsion at the Nazis' policies and that he regarded Hitler as the personification of absolute evil. But Stauffenberg, like many of the conspirators, was also incredibly naive about Germany's status after the fall of the Nazis. In late 1943 he wrote a paper outlining the conditions that he felt the Western Allies would have to accept before the new Germany would agree to peace terms. These included restoring Germany's 1914 borders, recognition of the 1938 annexation of Austria, and the extension of Germany's borders southward to include the present-day parts of Italy around the city of Bozen-Bolzano. And if this were not enough, Stauffenberg also expected that the Western Allies would agree to join the new Germany in continuing military operations against the Soviet Union. Needless to say, in 1944 the Americans and British had no intention of agreeing to any of these demands. They were already committed to the policy of unconditional surrender. Stauffenberg, then, was an idealist, a moral force, a martyr, but certainly not someone with a realistic vision for Germany after the Nazis.

---

meeting before the unconditional surrender of the Third Reich. The Big Three refined their zonal arrangements by agreeing on the division of Berlin into four sectors of occupation, with the Russians guaranteeing Western access to the city. (The city of Berlin, of course, was located in the middle of the Soviet zone of occupation.) Specifically, three air corridors from the Western zones to the former Reich capital were established. Stalin raised the reparations issue, and although there was no formal agreement, the Western Allies accepted as the basis for further discussions the Russian proposal that Germany should pay a total of $20 billion in reparations. The Soviets insisted they were entitled to half, or $10 billion, of this sum. The Russians wanted their reparations to be in the form of capital goods, current agricultural and industrial production, and forced labor. Roosevelt and Churchill also took note of the de facto territorial changes in eastern Germany, although final disposition of this issue was left for a later peace treaty. In reality, what in 1990 were to become Germany's permanent boundaries had already been established. The Communist-dominated Polish government had seized the former German territories east of the Oder-Neisse Rivers and was in the process of expelling the ethnic Germans still remaining in the area.

Map 8.1   East and West Germany, 1945–1990

As for Germany itself, the Big Three reiterated their determination to enforce the "four D's." They also clarified the nature of military government in the occupied country. Issues involving Germany as a whole would be decided by the Allied Control Council meeting in Berlin and composed of representatives from the zonal commands, but the military governors in the four zones retained virtually complete autonomy. Not only were they free to make whatever decisions they deemed necessary in their own zones, but each occupying power had the ability to paralyze the Allied Control Council because all decisions of this body had to be unanimous.

THE IMMEDIATE LEGACY OF THE THIRD REICH: THE REALITY OF "ZERO HOUR"

On June 5, 1945, the Allied military commanders took charge of a country that for all practical purposes had ceased to function as a viable society. Five years of bombing had left the German cities, in the words of one American observer, "endless rows of empty, burnt-out structural shells which reached into the sky like twisted fingers of a leper's hand." The housing shortage was especially acute in the larger cities: 50 percent of the housing in Hamburg and 80 percent of that in Cologne had been destroyed. The novelist Heinrich Böll, who was awarded the Nobel Prize for Literature in 1972, described his native city in 1945 as "the gigantic dust cloud that once had been Cologne." An equally serious problem was the breakdown of the transportation system. Concentrated tactical air attacks on the German rail system in the last months of the war destroyed some 10,000 locomotives and 112,000 freight cars and finally broke the back of Nazi resistance, but the bombings also left the country without a distribution system for its immediate civilian needs.

Ironically, the devastated country had to feed and house a population that was far larger than before the war. At the end of the war, 7 million refugees had found their way to the three Western zones; despite wartime losses, the population of what was to become West Germany was 20 percent larger in 1945 than it had been in 1938. At the same time Germany had lost territory that before the war produced 25 percent of the country's food supply.

It was not a good omen for their future cooperation that the Allies began their joint responsibility for Germany with haggling over territory. There were no excessive delays in removing American forces from the parts of eastern Germany that they had occupied in the last days of the war, and the Russians withdrew from the western sectors of Berlin without difficulty; but a serious dispute arose between the Americans and the French over the final delineation of their respective zones.

The French insisted on controlling Karlsruhe and Stuttgart, but the Americans remained adamant. It was not until July that these various territorial disputes had been settled and the military commanders took formal charge of their zones.

At the same time, the leaders of the Big Three (once again France was not invited) assembled at Potsdam, outside of Berlin, for another summit conference. There were several reasons for another exchange of views only six months after the Yalta Conference. Yalta had left a number of issues unresolved. There had also been a change of leaders for two of the Big Three: Vice President Harry S. Truman succeeded Franklin D. Roosevelt when the American president died on April 12, 1945, and in Great Britain, Clement Attlee headed a new Labour government after Winston Churchill's cabinet suffered a defeat at the polls while the Potsdam Conference was in session.

Some agenda items at the Potsdam Conference aroused little controversy. The Allies gave retroactive sanction to the de facto boundary changes in Eastern Europe and the expulsion of the ethnic Germans from this area. (The conference's admonition that the population transfers be affected "under humane conditions" had no practical effect.) The Big Three also reiterated their support for the "four D's" and emphasized the need for educational reforms in Germany with the goal that "German education shall be so controlled as completely to eliminate Nazi and militarist doctrines and to make possible the successful development of democratic ideas."

It was a different story, however, when the Big Three turned to the reparations issue. The Russians reiterated their demand that they should receive half of the $20 billion in reparations that should be imposed on the Germans. The remainder of the sum would be divided among the Nazis' other European victims. In addition, the Soviets demanded that reparations be the "first charge" on any German industrial or agricultural production. The Western Allies were concerned above all that the country should not become

"Berlin at the end of World War II: The building is the heavily damaged Reichstag. (Source: National Archives and Records Administration.)"

a financial burden on their own economies. As a result, they argued that the "first charge" on German production had to be relieving the Allies of the necessity of feeding and housing the German population.

In the end the Big Three, although agreeing that at least for the time being Germany was to be treated as an "economic unit," allowed the zonal commanders to set their own reparations policies: Each occupying power was free to remove or utilize for its own needs whatever production facilities the military administrators deemed not necessary for Germany's future peacetime needs, crediting the value against the eventual reparations bill to be presented as part of a peace treaty. The Western Allies also acknowledged that the Soviets were entitled to receive 10 percent of

the manufactured goods or industrial facilities that the Western commanders determined were not needed for the peacetime needs of their zones. Finally, in return for agricultural products sent from the Russian zone to West Germany, the Soviets could expect another 15 percent of the current production from the Western zones.

Unlike the British and the Americans, the Soviets went into Germany with a specific plan of action. Even before hostilities had ceased, the Russians established the Soviet Military Administration for Germany (usually known by its German acronym SMAD), headed first by Marshal Georgi K. Zhukov and later Marshal Vassily Sokolowsky. Immediately after the German surrender, SMAD authorized what were essentially functional cabinet-level

German ministries for the Soviet zone. Each was headed by a non-Nazi civil servant, with a German exile-Communist as the number-two man (and real power behind the scenes). One month after the end of the war, SMAD permitted the reorganization of German political life on a zonewide basis. Four non-Nazi parties were allowed to set up organizations: the Communists, the Social Democrats, the left-wing Liberals (successors of the Weimar DDP), and the Christian Democrats.

In the area of economic policies, the Russians immediately began a vigorous program of extracting reparations, although, as Norman Naimark has shown, in implementing the reparations policy, the much-vaunted centralized Soviet decision-making process broke down rapidly. Working from lists prepared in Moscow by a variety of agencies and ministries, Russian reparation teams roamed over the Soviet zone dismantling (and shipping to the Soviet Union) everything from scores of factories (such as the Zeiss optical works and an Opel car assembly plant) to thousands of bathtubs. The Russians also transferred large numbers of livestock and agricultural implements to the Soviet Union to replenish their depleted stocks. However, the teams often worked at cross purposes and frequently ignored SMAD and its regional offices. As a result, the benefits to the Soviet Union were questionable. Aside from bureaucratic infighting, the program vastly overestimated the capacity of the Soviet economy to absorb the dismantled German material. Much valuable equipment rusted in open railroad cars that remained standing for months on sidings either in Germany or in the Soviet Union.

In contrast to the purposeful Soviet moves, the early occupation policies of the British and Americans appeared hesitant and even contradictory. The British did establish two central administrative offices, one for economic affairs and one for agriculture; both were headed by leading German anti-Nazis. They also instituted wide-ranging administrative reforms in their zone. In the place of the defunct Prussian administration (the state of Prussia was formally abolished by the Allied Control Council in 1947), the British established three new territorial units—the present German Länder of Schleswig-Holstein, Lower Saxony, and North Rhine-Westphalia. It was not until the beginning of 1946, however, that zonewide German legislative institutions and political parties were again permitted.

Initially, American occupation policies were perhaps the most confusing. Part of the problem had to do with personalities. The Office of Military Government for the U.S. Zone (OMGUS) initially was headed by General Joseph T. McNarney, who had been Eisenhower's deputy. McNarney, however, had little interest in the job, and the key man in the OMGUS administration became General Lucius Clay, McNarney's deputy until 1947 and his successor after that date. Clay was a professional soldier whose military career had been spent in the Army Corps of Engineers; he was sent to Germany because Roosevelt and later Truman felt his construction expertise would be useful in getting the U.S. zone functioning again.

The American administrators in Germany were also hampered by unclear policy directives from Washington. As American troops began their occupation duties, they were issued what were essentially contradictory sets of guidelines. One was the *Handbook for Military Government in Germany,* which showed the influence of planners at the State Department. It assigned first priority—aside from the "four D's"—to economic recovery so as to make the U.S. zone self-sufficient as rapidly as possible. But the handbook was partially superseded by additional guidelines, JCS-1067, drafted under the auspices of the Joint Chiefs of Staff. JCS-1067 followed the basic line of the Morgenthau Plan and emphasized the negative goals of U.S. occupation policies. JCS-1067, for example, contained an absolute (and quickly ignored) ban on "fraternization" between Americans and Germans. (It was not until November 1945 that fraternization with "very small children" was officially permitted.) There was no mention of economic recovery or political activity. Instead, JCS-1067 stressed the need for structural changes that would deprive the wealthy bourgeoisie and large landowners of economic and political power. In this sense, JCS-1067 paralleled some of the Russian directives.

For the first few months of the occupation, then, American commanders could essentially choose between a "soft" and a "hard" line. Some, like General George Patton, who served briefly as military governor in Bavaria, preferred the "soft" approach. He simply returned the pre-Nazi elite in Bavaria to power. Others attempted to apply the spirit and letter of JCS-1067.

In most areas of occupation policy, the French were the odd man out among the Allies. They were even more enthusiastic about political decentralization than the Americans but agreed with the Russians that extracting reparations from their zone had first priority. The French rejected particularly treating the country as an economic unit. Instead, the French military commander, General Pierre Koenig, like the leader of the French Resistance, Charles de Gaulle, was determined that France should retain full control over "her" German territories. For this reason, the French jealously guarded the veto power of each zonal commander on the Allied Control Council.

Early French occupation policies were a curious mixture of economic exploitation, the "four D's," and missionary zeal to bring the blessings of French civilization to the Germans. The zone was hermetically sealed off from the rest of Germany, but even within the French territories German officials had to use the military government as an intermediary when corresponding with each other. This was less counterproductive than it might appear at first glance because many of the French midlevel administrators were Alsatians, who spoke fluent German. French economic policies reminded many Germans of Poincaré's goals in the 1920s. The Saar became economically part of France, and in the first months after the war as much as 80 percent of the industrial production in the French zone was exported to France.

The French took the task of reeducating the Germans very seriously. Censorship in the French zone was stricter than in the U.S. and British zones, but the French also sent dozens of teachers into their zone to rebuild the German school system while touring French theatrical companies brought glimpses of French culture into Germany's bombed-out cities. One of the lasting and salutary legacies of the French occupation was the founding in 1947 of the University of Mainz. (The French looked on it as a reopening because the institution had operated briefly during the Napoleonic occupation of the Rhineland.)

The positive influence the French attached to French culture and civilization was also apparent in their early German personnel appointments. The military government, for example, named Professor Carlo Schmid as the first postwar minister of justice in Württemberg. To be sure, Schmid was a staunch anti-Nazi and Social Democrat, but more important was his French mother, his ability to speak flawless French, and his reputation as a friend of France—which ironically he had earned when he served as a civilian employee with the German army of occupation in France after 1940.

It soon became apparent, then, that the Big Four had quite different ideas about their role as occupying powers in Germany. George Kennan, an especially perceptive American diplomat who had served in the U.S. embassy in Moscow during the war, noted as early as the summer of 1945 that it was "madness" to think that Germany could be governed in unison with the Soviet Union. In the following spring, Winston Churchill had come to the same conclusion; in a March 1946 address delivered in Fulton, Missouri, Churchill spoke of the "Iron Curtain" with which the Soviet Union had divided Europe from the Baltic to the Mediterranean. As we saw, the French were determined to go their own way without much regard for what the other Allies were doing in Germany. Many questions about the former Reich's future remained unanswered, but one fact was clear; only a few months after their united efforts had defeated the Third Reich, the members of the Grand Alliance were unable to agree on a unified policy for the country that was now their joint responsibility.

REPARATIONS AND ECONOMIC RECOVERY

It was perhaps inevitable that discussions about reparations both during and after World War II had a sense of déjà vu about them. Once again, the European countries that had been devastated and exploited wanted the Germans to make good the damage the Nazis had caused. The devastation was heavy in both Eastern and Western Europe, but there was little doubt that the Soviet Union had suffered most from the Nazis. Russia's wartime casualties were estimated at 20 million people, and the Nazis' scorched earth policies had left much of the western Soviet Union an economic wasteland.

Most U.S. and British planners soon recognized, however, that the Russian approach to reparations would in effect force the Western Allies to subsidize the Russian zone. Because the American zone and particularly the British zone did not produce sufficient agricultural goods to feed their populations, agricultural goods would have to be imported, and exports of manufactured goods were the only available means by which the Germans could pay for such imports. With this in mind, another Allied goal—the destruction of much of Germany's industrial base because it could be used in waging war—was counterproductive because there would clearly not be enough manufacturing facilities to pay for both reparations and food imports.

The Potsdam agreements, such as they were, were made in the face of a major unknown: the real condition of the German economy. Its state of health turned out to be a paradox. In the short run, the German economy was worse off than had been anticipated, but in the long run the devastation was less severe than originally thought.

At the moment, of course, it was the immediate future that counted. And it looked

bleak. Germany in late spring of 1945, bore little resemblance to a functioning economy. There was no currency. With the collapse of the government, the Reichsmark had lost its value and credibility. The Allies printed their own "occupation marks," but these had no backing either. American cigarettes quickly became the preferred medium of exchange, severely distorting the incentive to earn money. A typical example of the warped economy was the case of a coal miner who in 1946 earned a weekly wage of 60 marks. He also owned a chicken, which laid five eggs during the week. He ate one egg and traded the other four for twenty American cigarettes, which he sold for 160 marks on the black market. As a result, the chicken produced almost three times as much income as a week's work in the coal mines.

In addition, the transportation system had broken down almost completely. Millions of refugees, expellees, and Displaced Persons (including some 200,000 Jews who survived the death camps) aggravated the already catastrophic housing shortage. A number of reputable economists predicted that it would take a minimum of thirty years to rebuild Germany's cities. The final military operations of the war had prevented spring planting in many areas of the country, and the German diet was often below subsistence levels in the cities. In the summer of 1945, the total amount of foodstuffs obtainable on ration coupons for each inhabitant of Hamburg (which was part of the British zone) amounted to a little more than 1,000 calories per day. (Present-day dietary guidelines in the United States are based on a daily food intake of 2,000 calories for an "average" adult.) The consequences were predictable: As Elizabeth Heinemann has noted, in November 1947 the average weight for German women was 93.5 pounds, for men 92.3 pounds. In addition, as might be expected, petty and organized crime flourished. Despite severe penalties, black markets existed for every imaginable good, particularly food stuffs.

At the same time, especially with the benefit of hindsight, the years immediately after the war acquired a patina of nostalgia. As Arnold Sywottek put it, these were the "times of lovely want" that became the stuff of increasingly embellished stories of how "we survived and coped." The never-existing "zero hour" and its aftermath would form a major part of the politics of memory in the future Germanys.

The state of the economy presented the Germans and the occupying forces with massive problems, but the collapse also provided opportunities for structural modifications. Both the Allies and many in the German resistance were convinced the traditionally close link between business and the political elite in Germany had not been a healthy development. Non-Nazi Germans of all political persuasions wanted to implement massive structural changes in the economy. Concretely, many in the resistance groups envisioned the breakup of the cartels and their replacement by some form of nationalization, particularly in the areas of heavy industry and natural resources. As we saw, the Allies, too, had plans for the "decartelization" of German industry. However, in the face of the devastated condition of the German economy, the Americans, the British, and many Germans in the Western zones rapidly abandoned any structural reform plans.

Only the Russians pursued their structural goals with unrelenting vigor. In line with the tenets of what was then called Marxism-Leninism-Stalinism, the Soviets were convinced that Nazism was essentially a political manifestation of "monopoly capitalism," and they set out systematically to destroy the economic power of "major capitalists" in the Russian zone. SMAD took over immediate control of all banks and their assets, which in Germany traditionally included large stock portfolios. Simultaneously, individual bank accounts with a balance of more than 3,000 marks were confiscated and all private and public debts declared invalid. Much as the Bolsheviks had done in Russia in 1917, Soviet rule in East Germany started with a clean financial slate.

Beginning in the fall of 1945, the Soviets inaugurated a systematic land reform program. Starting with the province of Saxony, SMAD ordered a plebiscite on the breakup and expropriation of all farms larger than 300 acres. The Soviets and German Communists categorized the owners of such properties as Junkers or agrarian capitalists. These lands were to be divided and turned over to smallholders or landless peasants. The plebiscite campaign had the catchy slogan of "Junkers' lands into farmers' hands." (The Russians tended to hold plebiscites first in the province of Saxony because it had the best organized Communist Party.)

Next SMAD turned to the industrial sector of the economy. All manufacturing facilities were classified into one of three categories. List A consisted of "economically important" enterprises, in Marxist terms the "commanding heights" of the economy. These were immediately placed under SMAD's direct control and eventually became the backbone of collectivized industry in what would become East Germany. List B consisted of "small and unimportant enterprises," and most of these were left in private hands. List C was composed of "ownerless" properties, which meant firms whose "Nazi" owners were deprived of their businesses for political reasons. In practice, the third category included all large-scale enterprises because the Russians saw no distinction between leading capitalists and leading Nazis. Enterprises in category C either were dismantled outright or became SAGs—the abbreviation stood for *Sowjetische Aktiengesellschaft*, or Soviet corporation—which meant that they produced solely for export to the Soviet Union. By 1946 there were 213 SAGs in the Russian zone.

The economic effects of the Russian policies were mixed. The takeover of the banks and the cancellation of debts eliminated the inflation and doubts about currency revaluation that for a time hampered economic recovery in the West. More important, however, were the political consequences and severe economic dislocations that followed the structural reforms in the Russian zone. Almost overnight the traditional German economic elite was deprived of its power and property. By the beginning of 1946, the state controlled the "commanding heights" of the economy; free enterprise was restricted to relatively unimportant sectors. In June 1946 another Communist-sponsored plebiscite in Saxony retroactively approved the expropriation without compensation of properties owned by "war criminals and active Nazis."

After being characterized by initial confusion, American economic policies were marked by growing pragmatism coupled with clear political goals. Like the Russians, U.S. economic planners were initially determined to eliminate Germany's war-making potential. American officials drew up a list of 1,210 plants that were to be dismantled. Some American planners, notably those sympathizing with the spirit of the Morgenthau Plan, wanted to reduce German industrial production permanently to between 70 and 75 percent of the 1936 level. But there was a problem. Eliminating all 1,210 plants on the list would have been a major step toward reaching this goal, but it was also a stated American aim to make the U.S. zone as economically self-sufficient as possible, and that raised questions about the future of the dismantling program. Should a ball-bearing factory be dismantled because its products had been used in tanks, or permitted to start up again because its products could now be used in farm tractors?

Despite these questions in May 1946 a so-called Level of Industry Plan endorsed the hard line. This document accepted the goal of maintaining Germany's future industrial production at very low levels. Almost immediately the Level of Industry Plan was severely criticized both by the nascent German economic administration and by American planners. The critics pointed out that in 1946 exports from the American zone were valued at $28 million, but imports, mostly in the form of food, fertilizer, and seeds, had a value of $300 million. In effect, the privilege of occupying a part of Germany cost the American taxpayers $272 million. The experience of the winter of 1946–1947 aggravated the problem. It was one of the coldest in decades. There was widespread suffering and malnutrition, and there would have been more except for massive aid from the Western Allies, especially the Americans. There was clearly no alternative to enlarging German industrial production if the Western zones were to avoid becoming a permanent ward of the United States and Great Britain.

The emerging Cold War and the decline in agricultural productivity in eastern Germany made the goal of treating the four zones as an "economic unit" increasingly unrealistic. As a result, the Level of Industry Plan was essentially shelved and the dismantling program quietly abandoned. Of the 1,210 plants originally tagged for dismantling, only 24 had been disassembled by May 1946. At the same time, reacting to what OMGUS felt was French intransigence, Russian obstinacy, and British inefficiency in running their zones, the United States halted reparation transfers from the American zone. In 1947 a new review removed 523 plants from the list, and virtually no facilities were actually dismantled after that date. In 1949 the entire dismantling program was formally abandoned.

Long before then, American economic policy had undergone a fundamental change. By the spring of 1946, the Americans felt that without West Germany's economic resources the Western zones as well as the countries of Western Europe would become easy prey for communist subversion and eventually Soviet control. Consequently, the United States assigned a low priority to the goals of maintaining a united Germany and good relations with the Soviet Union. The Americans' primary aim now was the creation of a functioning market economy in Western Germany that would be integrated into the economies of Western Europe.

The new direction was publicly signaled in September 1946 in an address by the U.S. secretary of state James F. Byrnes. Speaking in Stuttgart, the secretary announced that in the face of Soviet intransigence the United States would not only retain its military presence in Germany but would also help the Germans in the Western zones get back on their feet. But it would have to be done the American way. The United States now moved to put up barriers against major structural changes in the German economy of the American zone. Economic recovery would essentially mean the preservation of a free-market economy. When the voters of Hessen by a

70 percent majority ratified a state constitution providing for state control of major sectors in the economy, the American military governor ordered the offending parts of the constitution suspended indefinitely. Similarly, the prime ministers of the four Länder in the American zone endorsed the principle of union representatives serving as ex officio members on the boards of directors of major enterprises (the technical term is "codetermination," or *Mitbestimmung*), but General Clay prohibited its implementation.

British economic policies for the most part followed the American lead. Initially, the British had also drawn up an ambitious dismantling program, concentrating on the heavy industry of the Ruhr (part of the British zone), but economic realities soon forced changes. The British zone produced even fewer agricultural goods than the American, and it consequently became a heavy burden for the home government; between 1945 and 1948, the British had to pour £200 million into their zone to pay for needed imports of foodstuffs and raw materials. Because England was experiencing severe economic problems of its own, the British had little choice except to join the Americans in the decision to help German recovery. U.S. aid was crucial not only for economic recovery in England but also for maintaining the British zone in Germany. Until the summer of 1948, the French stubbornly pursued their own single-minded course of action. Despite a lack of economic cohesion in the territories they controlled, the French were determined to treat their zone as a separate unit not linked to the rest of Germany.

By the summer of 1946, the economic unity envisioned for Germany at Potsdam was illusionary. In the face of Russian and French refusals to cooperate in treating Germany as a single economic unit, the Americans and the British charted their own path. On January 1, 1947, the British and the Americans established the "Bizone," essentially creating an economic merger of the American and British zones. The new structure had administrative offices that closely resembled ministries, headed by a "director-in-chief." The latter office was occupied by Hermann Pünder, who

had been chief of staff in the Reich chancellery when Heinrich Brüning was chancellor.

The decision to establish the Bizone was a response to the economic difficulties encountered in the British and American zones in 1945 and 1946, but the decision was politically confirmed, as it were, by the results of the Moscow Four Power Conference on Germany in March 1947. This foreign ministers' meeting revealed the chasm that divided the Allies' economic policies in Germany. The Russians accused the West of violating the Yalta Agreement on reparations. The West countered by disputing that such an agreement had been reached and accused the Russians of failing to supply the promised shipments of agricultural goods to the Western zones.

The Moscow Conference confirmed American policy makers in their belief that the Soviet Union's economic policies were part of a larger plan to subject all of Germany, and indeed all of Europe, to Russian control. In response to this perceived threat to the West, the Americans announced two new policies. First they put forth the Truman Doctrine, which allocated U.S. economic and military aid to Greece and Turkey to help these countries prevail against the communist danger. Second, and even more important, they introduced the Marshall Plan, a bold scheme launched in June 1947 under which the Americans offered to underwrite the economic recovery of Europe, including that of Germany. Under the European Recovery Program, as the Marshall Plan was formally known, the United States between 1948 and 1952 gave some $14 billion (108 billion in 2010 dollars) economic aid to the countries of Western Europe. The Marshall Plan was instrumental in the recovery of Western Europe and West Germany, but American aid did not come without visible and invisible strings. The United States clearly wanted to support free enterprise in Europe. Moreover, given the strength of the American economy, the Marshall Plan would establish the U.S. dollar as the dominant currency. Above all, as far as the Germans were concerned, the Marshall Plan meant that the economies of the three Western zones would become an integral part of the Western economic system. (Inclusion of the French zone was part of the price France had to pay for getting American aid.)

The aid program was officially offered to all European countries, including the Soviet Union, but in view of the political and economic strings attached, the Russian refusal to participate in the European Recovery Program was a foregone conclusion. Under pressure from the Soviets, the countries of Eastern Europe and the Soviet zone of occupation in Germany also rejected the American aid. Although the U.S. program had the effect of hastening the division of Germany into separate eastern and western entities, sentiment for accepting the terms of the Marshall Plan both in West Germany and in Western Europe was overwhelmingly positive. The Soviets and East German Communists countered the Marshall Plan with a propaganda campaign claiming the East German workers did not want American aid, they could rebuild Germany on their own, but such political efforts could not change the fact that without American aid the economic recovery in the Soviet zone would rapidly fall behind developments in the western part of the country.

The Achilles' heel of any recovery plan in the western zones was the absence of a stable currency. The controlled and centrally planned economy in the Russian zone could function with a currency that had neither metallic- nor hard-currency backing, but a resurgent free-market economy would not flourish without a new and trustworthy currency. The Americans had reached this conclusion at the end of 1947, but it took another six months before a new currency, the *Deutsche Mark*, made its appearance in all three Western zones in June 1948. The new currency was valued at one deutsche mark to ten of the old Reichsmark and was exchangeable on international currency markets at 4.2 deutsche marks to one U.S. dollar.

The Marshall Plan, along with the currency reform, set the stage for the West German "economic miracle," although in 1948 the prospects for an economic boom seemed rather more modest. The German economy was still an economy of shortages; everything

from food to furniture was rationed; empty shelves had been the rule for years. The picture changed literally overnight, in large part as a result of an audacious decision by the man in charge of the economic administration for the Bizone since April 1948, Ludwig Erhard. Without consulting the occupation authorities, Erhard combined the announcement of the currency reform on June 20, 1948, with the virtual elimination of all economic controls and forms of rationing. He realized that the certainty of American support for West German recovery and persistent rumors that the currency reform was imminent had already awakened the dormant productive capacities of the German economy. As a result, in June 1948 consumers who now had "real" money in their hands saw stores stocked full of goods that had not been seen since before the war. West Germany became, as one British observer put it, "an economy in search of a state."

"EXORCISING THE EVIL": DE-NAZIFICATION AND REEDUCATION

There was never any doubt among the Allies that de-Nazification—and its corollary, reeducation—was the most important of the "four D's." Demilitarization, decartelization, and democratization remained illusionary as long as Nazism had not been eradicated from German society. Both the Allies and most anti-Nazi Germans also agreed that there were two aspects to de-Nazification: the punishment of individual Nazis for the crimes they had committed during the Third Reich, and the exorcising of fascist and protofascist attitudes from the German population and the country's institutions. The latter process had to involve a critical self-examination among the Germans themselves, including an in-depth look at the country's authoritarian heritage as a seedbed for Nazism. Signs of honest self-criticism came early. For example, the leaders of the Protestant churches publicly acknowledged in the summer of 1945 that their rejection of democratic traditions had indirectly helped Nazism come to power.

A poster extolling the benefits of the Marshall Plan. Against the backdrop calling attention to a construction site, the caption reads, "We're making progress thanks to the Marshall Plan." (Source: Oasis/Photos 12/Alamy.)

The Allies decided as early as September 1943 that the punishment of the Nazi regime's major leaders would be their joint responsibility, whereas the de-Nazification of German society would be handled by each zonal commander implementing instructions from his home government. In addition, Nazi officials who had committed crimes outside of Germany would be extradited and tried in the country in which they had committed their criminal acts.

There was little difficulty with the first part of this scenario. Beginning in November 1945 twenty-four civilian and military officials of the Nazi regime, including Göring, Ribbentrop, Hess, Speer, Keitel, and Streicher, were tried by the International Military Tribunal (IMT) in Nuremberg. (Hitler, Himmler, and Goebbels had committed suicide before they could be tried. Robert Ley, the head of the DAF, killed himself in Nuremberg before the trial began. Martin Bormann, the NSDAP's general secretary after 1941, was tried and convicted in absentia. The IMT did not know that he died while trying to escape from Berlin in May 1945.) The accused were indicted for crimes against peace, war crimes, unleashing aggressive war, and crimes against humanity. The Allied powers provided both judges and prosecuting staffs; the defendants were represented by German non-Nazi lawyers. The trial lasted until the fall of 1946. At its conclusion, eleven of the remaining twenty-two accused (including Göring, Ribbentrop, Keitel, and Streicher) were sentenced to death and executed (Göring committed suicide before he was scheduled to be hanged); eight received long prison sentences; and three were acquitted. The last group included Franz von Papen and Hjalmar Schacht.

Both the premise and the verdicts of the IMT provoked heated debates. The tribunal was accused of practicing "victors' justice." The critics also claimed that the court's moral authority was irrevocably compromised by the presence of Soviet judges on the bench. There were also some problems with the terms of the indictment, especially if the IMT was to serve a didactic function

as part of the larger de-Nazification effort. The tribunal limited itself to trying the Nazi leaders for "international" crimes, so that political treason in Germany itself was left unpunished. This was the reason that someone like Papen, who had been instrumental in destroying democracy in the Weimar Republic, was acquitted.

Some of the criticism is valid, but it is difficult to fault the tribunal for either its procedures or its verdicts. Particularly the British chief justice attempted to be scrupulously fair to the defendants. Most important, however, those accused had really condemned themselves; the trial at Nuremberg for the first time revealed the full horror of the Nazis' reign of terror in Germany and Europe.

The IMT ended the Allies' joint de-Nazification efforts. The remainder of the task was now in the hands of the zonal commanders. The Russian de-Nazification campaign was swift, radical, but, at least from a Western point of view, also unfair and simplistic. As we saw, the Soviets insisted on linking capitalism and Nazism. As a result, they concentrated their de-Nazification efforts on individuals who had occupied positions of economic or political influence in pre-1945 Germany. Under the Russian de-Nazification criteria, some 45,000 leading industrialists, landowners, military officers, civil servants, and Nazi Party officials were identified as active Nazis and punished. About a third of those accused were sent to labor camps in the Soviet Union; all lost their property and positions. The Soviet de-Nazification effort had the virtue of speed—the entire process was concluded by the beginning of 1948—and some obvious criminals were punished, but the Russians were also quick to brand as "fascist" anyone who opposed the Russian-sponsored transformation of the Soviet zone into a "people's democracy"(see below, p. 251, and as result, many Social Democrats, who had just been released from Nazi concentration camps, found themselves back in what were now Soviet concentration camps.) On Stalin's specific orders the Soviets created a new party, the *Nationaldemokratische Partei Deutschlands* (National Democratic Party of Germany—NDPD), to attract former "little

A view of the defendants at the International Military Tribunal in Nuremberg. (Source: Courtesy of Library of Congress.)

Nazis" and convert them into supporters of what was to become the East German Communist regime. Moreover, the Russian de-Nazification procedures could be easily exploited by opportunists. Former members of the Nazi Party or its affiliates who came from a working-class or lower-middle-class background could escape punishment with a simple declaration that false class consciousness had led them to join the Nazis. Cooperation with the Soviet authorities was also seen as evidence that the individual had been cleansed of Nazism.

The Western powers, in contrast, erred on the side of excessive deliberation and overestimating the number of Nazis in Germany. Moreover, their procedures, too, were not free of opportunistic and quixotic considerations. For example, the French often overlooked the "brown past" of individuals who were willing to cooperate with the French occupation authorities, but at the same time they regarded all Germans over the age of twelve as a "lost generation" whose immersion in Nazism was so complete that it would take years of reeducation to eradicate it.

For this reason, the French concentrated their de-Nazification campaign on the teaching profession. Half of all teachers in the French zone were dismissed by the military government.

The Americans launched not only the most conscientious, but in some ways also the most inconsistent, de-Nazification campaign. American military courts tried groups of defendants including major SS officials, leading business persons, Wehrmacht generals, government officials, and members of the diplomatic establishment who had been involved in the Holocaust or the use of slave labor. However, the elimination of "average" Nazis from German society proved much more controversial. Stung by charges that the American army was coddling Nazis, in September 1945 OMGUS took a hard line. Law No. 8 ordered the internment of thousands of former Nazis. In addition, anyone who had been a member of the Nazi Party or one of its affiliates before 1937 was prohibited from continuing in his or her regular line of work. The new policy created an immediate crisis in professional and governmental services. The Nazi Gleich-schaltung had forced not only civil servants but also professionals like doctors and dentists to join a Nazi Party affiliate in order to continue practicing. Under Law No. 8, these professionals were sent out to clear rubble from the streets.

The policy of "guilt by office holding and membership" was obviously unsatisfactory. In an effort to speed up the de-Nazification process and also return to the principle of individual guilt or innocence, the Americans in February 1946 inaugurated the "questionnaire phase" of the de-Nazification campaign. In a massive effort worthy of a greater cause, 12 million questionnaires were issued to all adults in the American zone asking for information on everything from noble titles of the individuals' grandparents to membership in political organizations. The answers on the questionnaire were used to classify the respondents into one of five categories: major offender, offender, lesser offender, fellow traveler, and untainted. Only the last verdict meant there would be no penalties. After the questionnaires were processed, some 3 million persons would have to be tried before "hearing committees" staffed by anti-Nazi Germans but supervised by American officials. In contrast to the "guilt-by-membership" phase, this time the accused was allowed to present exonerating evidence. Such evidence came primarily in the form of affidavits from associates and friends of the defendant that he or she had not been guilty of crimes during the Third Reich. These affidavits were quickly dubbed *Persilscheine* (Persil certificates). Persil, then and now a popular German laundry detergent, used as its advertising slogan that it "washed whiter than white."

The American effort was a well-meant attempt to eliminate Nazism from the American zone "root and branch," but in practice the campaign soon ran into massive difficulties. To begin with, processing millions of questionnaires was too formidable a task for the available personnel. In addition, the Americans complained that German de-Nazification tribunals were too lenient while the Germans contended that the

U.S. authorities failed to understand the nature of living and working under Nazi totalitarianism. More important, changes in the international climate distorted the original intent of the de-Nazification effort. While the hearing committees concentrated on processing first the "lesser offender" and "untainted" categories, leaving the more serious classifications for more detailed examination at a later date, policy changes in 1947 and 1948 reduced the priority value of the de-Nazification effort. Many presumed major offenders and war profiteers did not have to go through the gauntlet of the de-Nazification procedures because they were suddenly needed as senior executives in the revitalized economy. There were bitter comments that whereas it was important in 1945 to have been a member of the VVN (the German letters standing for the "Association of Victims of Nazism"), it was far better in 1947 to be a WWN, a *wirtschaftlich wichtiger Nazi*—that is, an economically important Nazi.

In principle, British de-Nazification practices followed the American lead, although in practice the British military authorities generally showed more astuteness in recognizing that local officials and educators in particular had often held only nominal membership in one or more of the various Nazi organizations. Consequently, this category of officials was de-Nazified and restored to office rather early in the British zone. Still, there were some glaring errors. When the formal de-Nazification program was ended in 1950, the statistical results were not impressive. Of the 3.66 million persons processed in the western zones, only 1,667 were categorized as major offenders, 23,060 were offenders, and 150,425 were lesser offenders. There were 1 million fellow travelers, and almost 2 million were labeled "untainted." The remainder was amnestied before being categorized. On the basis of these numbers, the Nazi era seemed to have had remarkably little impact on Germany.

The reality was more complex, of course. Certainly before the outbreak of World War II millions of Germans supported Hitler and his regime. It is also true, however, that especially after the defeat at Stalingrad, support for the

Nazis steadily eroded; by the end of the war very few true believers were left. In addition, de-Nazification raised practical problems. If all of those who had at one point supported the Nazis were excluded from playing a role in the postwar society, there would be few persons left to rebuild the country. It was this consideration that led the first chancellor of the new West German republic, Konrad Adenauer (who was certainly no sympathizer of Nazism), to call for an end to "sniffing out Nazis" (*Naziriecherei*) soon after he took office in 1949.

De-Nazification was designed to eliminate an evil from German society; the measures grouped under the label "reeducation" were meant to put something positive in its place. Reforms in education and the media would ensure that in the future the German people would be saturated with "antifascist" values. The effort to rebuild the German education system faced formidable obstacles. Physical facilities were woefully inadequate. In major urban centers like Cologne, 92 percent of all elementary schools had been destroyed by bombing. In rural areas, damage was less severe, but here the influx of refugees had led to staggering increases in the school population. There were also problems with textbooks and teaching personnel. Virtually all teachers had been members of the Nazi Party or one of its affiliates, and many had held local offices in the party. Textbooks were largely unusable because the Nazis had inculcated their racist ideas into all subjects.

There was no shortage of reform ideas, either from the Germans or the Allies, but the two sides started from rather different premises. In fact, differences of opinion over educational reforms became one of the first tests of wills between the occupying powers and the Germans' resurgent sense of autonomy. The Germans tended to regard the Nazi influence over the educational system as a perversion of the traditional ideals of German education, which they saw as either Catholic Christian humanism or the progressive ideas of secular reformism that were in vogue during the 1920s. As might be expected,

educational conservatives dominated in the Catholic areas of the south; in the north the reformers turned to ideas associated with the pre-1933 Prussian ministry of education. In fact, the last pre-Nazi Prussian minister of education, Adolf Grimme, became the first minister of education of the new Land, Lower Saxony.

With the exception of the British, the Allies looked on their own educational systems as models for the reforms needed in Germany. The British, to their credit, almost immediately cooperated with the German reformers. The question of textbooks was handled effectively by joint British-German committees, and the person responsible for education policy in the British military government, Sir Robert Birley, assured the German authorities as early as 1946 that the British would make no decisions that had not been approved by the responsible German officials. The French concentrated their reform efforts on bringing a significant number of German teachers to France for intensive retraining courses.

The Americans were originally determined to take a much more direct hand in implementing structural reforms of the German school system. In 1946 a commission of U.S. experts, headed by the then president of the U.S. Council of Education, George F. Zook, recommended several fundamental changes. In essence, the Zook Report concluded that Germany would be better off with an American-type system of education. Specifically, the American experts wanted to abolish the *Gymnasium* and replace it with twelve years of comprehensive schooling for all children. The Americans also advocated eliminating the segregation by religious affiliation in the German public elementary schools. As for textbooks, the Americans wrote their own. Unfortunately, the results, to quote Sir Robert Birley, were "hardly readable."

In the U.S. zone the Zook Report ran into formidable and passionate opposition. Criticism centered on the proposals for a comprehensive twelve-year school system and the "secularization" of elementary schools. German anti-Nazi scholars pointed out that the American comprehensive school system was not the rule in such established European democracies as France and Great Britain. Fierce opposition to abolishing the religion-segregated elementary school came from the Catholic Church and the minister of education in Bavaria, Alois Hundhammer.

The American frontal assault on the traditional German education system was a failure. The major recommendations of the Zook Report were not implemented; the U.S. zone kept the German three-tiered school system, with textbooks and curricula reflecting the ideas of Christian Catholic humanism. The elementary schools were not secularized, although in practice the postwar population changes destroyed the religious homogeneity of southern Germany and transformed the public schools into multiconfessional institutions.

As had been true of their de-Nazification efforts, the Russians did not allow obstacles to stand in the way of implementing the educational reforms they felt were needed. In 1946 SMAD ordered the abolition of the three-tiered school system. In its place a comprehensive twelve-year school program was established throughout the Soviet zone. The Russians also decreed changes in teacher education and textbooks, putting reliable German Communists in charge of implementing these reforms.

Like de-Nazification, reeducation succeeded in spite of itself. Except for the Soviet zone where cooperation between SMAD and the Communist-dominated German educational administration was intense and purposeful, the Allies had little success in transforming German education to bring it in line with their own national systems. The Allied pressures rather became catalysts that allowed the reform ideas of the Weimar era to be resurrected and finally implemented.

Immediately after the war, control of the mass media was important for both practical and political reasons. With a shortage of newsprint and transportation facilities, the radio became the military governments' primary means of communicating with the German population. As life returned to a semblance of normalcy, newspapers served as major vehicles for reeducation in the widest sense, that is, dissemination of the truth about the Nazis and the propagation of antifascist values.

Initially the Allied military governments took direct charge of the mass media. Radio stations were run by Allied personnel, and each of the four occupying powers founded German-language newspapers. Of particular interest was the paper in the American zone, *Neue Zeitung* ("New Newspaper"). The paper was well edited by Hans Habe, a Hungarian refugee who had lived for some years in Austria prior to the Anschluss.

Not surprisingly, in media affairs, too, each of the Allies was convinced its own national system was best. As far as the radio was concerned, the British proposed a German equivalent of the BBC, in other words, a politically autonomous public radio organization. The Americans preferred a decentralized, privately owned, and commercially financed radio system, whereas the French insisted on a centralized but politically balanced system. The Russians set up a state-controlled monopoly. The Germans, for their part, wanted to go back to the Weimar model, a centralized but apolitical system financed by compulsory fees from listeners.

What emerged in the end was an amalgam of German and Allied ideas—at least in the west. The Germans rejected commercialization of their airwaves but accepted decentralization of the radio network. As for control of program content, the Germans adopted the BBC model of an autonomous board of governors, but, like the French, they insisted on including political parties among the "balance of interests" that controlled the public radio stations.

In permitting the German press to start up again, the four Allies also went their own ways. Initially the Russians appeared to take the most liberal and permissive approach. Almost simultaneously with the publication of SMAD's own newspaper, the *Neue Rundschau* ("New Observer"), the Russians allowed "antifascist progressive forces" to publish newspapers. All of the newly legalized political parties took up the Russian offer, although for most the experience soon became frustrating. SMAD's allocation of newsprint favored the communist press and views critical of the Soviets and, ironically, the Western allies were routinely censored.

The Western Allies were less insistent on political conformity. The French permitted the newly legalized political parties to maintain their own press organs, whereas the Americans and British preferred a nonpartisan press with editorials clearly separated from news stories. All of the Western Allies gave permission to publish newspapers on a case-by-case basis. "Licenses" were granted only to potential publishers who could demonstrate their democratic credentials to the military authorities.

The postwar German newspaper scene showed the least continuity with the Weimar years. Some of the editors and reporters returned to their desks, but the leading West German dailies after 1945—such as *Die Welt* ("The World"), the *Frankfurter Allgemeine Zeitung* ("The Frankfurt General Newspaper"), and the *Süddeutsche Zeitung* ("The South German Newspaper")—were all newly founded, often by journalistic novices like West Germany's later longtime press czar, Axel Springer. This was an area in which the Allies' direct influence was most noticeable. Sixteen publishers who eventually obtained newspaper licenses in the American zone had earlier worked on the editorial staff of the *Neue Zeitung*. The format of German papers also changed. After 1945 the press in the West was far less politicized and, in particular, the earlier habit of permeating news stories with a particular political slant disappeared. Owing largely to French influence, the *feuilleton* ("art and culture") sections of the German provincial press became a more important part of the papers.

De-Nazification and reeducation were important factors in the reconstruction of the German society, but the actual results were hardly what the Allies originally set out to accomplish. In the west the Allied practices had the effect of resurrecting and strengthening the liberal and democratic traditions of the Weimar Republic, rather than creating a society modeled more decisively on Western examples. In the Soviet zone, Russian policies were part of the Russians' effort to transform this part of the country into a "people's democracy," an entity that Soviet theorists at the time defined as a society in which "the commanding heights of decision making" would be under the direct or indirect control of the Communists and SMAD, although ostensibly the society retained its pluralistic character and mixed economy.

REVIVAL OF ADMINISTRATIVE, POLITICAL, AND CULTURAL LIFE

Immediately after the war, much of Germany may have reminded observers of the surface of the moon, but the country was hardly devoid of life. As we saw, although an estimated 6 million Germans died from war-related causes, by 1950, as a result of the influx of millions of refugees, Germany's population was larger than it had been before the war. The population transfers created not only major immediate problems but had important long-range effects on the structure of German society as well. Population density increased markedly, especially in western Germany. The population also became more heterogeneous. In 1950 one out of every four inhabitants in the western zones had been born east of the Elbe. The refugees transformed the religious mix of Germany. Although the Soviet zone remained predominantly Protestant, in the west Catholics for the first time since the Reformation were no longer a minority. The population of the western zones became almost evenly divided between Catholics and Protestants.

At the time of "zero hour" both the Allied authorities and the Germans were primarily concerned with restoring a rudimentary level of service to the society. But the feeling was also widespread that there was in 1945 an unparalleled opportunity to "start over again" and create a new and better society.

Much earlier than their transatlantic cousins, the British gave the Germans considerable autonomy in rebuilding their society. They recognized that there were many Germans who were as anxious to create a new democratic society as their conquerors. As a senior British official pointed out, it was hardly necessary to give elementary lessons in democracy to a man who had just spent the last ten years in a Nazi concentration camp for his democratic beliefs.

The French and the Russians undertook the most radical restructuring of their zones. The French program was simple: to maximize French control over all affairs of their zone and to delay the rebirth of autonomous German societal institutions as long as possible. The Russians had no hesitation in putting Germans in charge of their zone, but they had to be "their" Germans. Unlike the Western Allies, who appointed German administrative officials on a case-by-case basis, the Soviets brought administrative and indoctrination teams with them. In April and May 1945, three groups of German Communists who had spent the war years in Russia were brought back to Germany by the Soviet Air Force. The most important of the three was headed by Walter Ulbricht, the prewar Communist leader of Berlin; it began its work on April 30.

The Russians and the Communists repeatedly assured the inhabitants of their zone that they did not intend to create a Soviet-style Germany. The KPD's first postwar proclamation, issued on June 15, 1945, promised the party would work to establish a full-scale parliamentary democracy. A quote from Stalin also made the rounds: "Socialism fits Germany like a saddle fits a cow." Despite the KPD's lofty proclamations, the Communists worked systematically to shape the contours of societal life in the Soviet zone. In remarks to a Communist Party meeting in 1946, Ulbricht expressed these goals in blunt terms: "Everything has to look democratic, but everything has to be controlled by us." The

Communists succeeded; by the summer of 1946, the Russian zone was a people's democracy in all but name.

Most postwar German leaders—with the obvious exception of the Communists—did not advocate a root-and-branch approach to societal rebuilding, but, to stay with the metaphor for a moment, advocated pruning the tree to remove dead branches and alien growth. For the most part their ideal of a "new" society was an improved and corrected version of the Weimar Republic. In concrete terms, this meant that the basic principles on which the Weimar Republic had been founded would be accentuated in any post–World War II German society. Subject to varying degrees of control by the occupation powers, the Germans began rebuilding their political organizations in the summer and fall of 1945. Except for the discredited extreme right, whose renewed activity all of the Allies prohibited, the ideological spectrum was essentially the same as during the Weimar years.

Aided by a clear vision of Germany's postwar future and prodded by the Soviets, the Communists took the initiative in rearranging political life in East Germany. In the spring of 1946, they proposed the union (or better, *re*union) of the Social Democrats and Communists. It is, of course, one thing to propose a political alliance and quite another to obtain the partner's agreement. Most Social Democrats rejected a merger of the two parties. They regarded the KPD as an undemocratic front organization for SMAD, and they feared—quite correctly—that the Communists would dominate the new party. SMAD and the Communists ignored the Socialists' objections. In April 1946 massive pressure from SMAD resulted in the creation of the Socialist Unity Party of Germany (*Sozialistische Einheitspartei Deutschlands*—SED) as a single successor organization to the SPD and the KPD. The forced union was restricted to Soviet-occupied territory. In West Berlin, 82 percent of the SPD's membership turned down the merger proposal when it was put to a vote. (The Russian authorities prohibited a polling of SPD members in East Berlin and the Soviet zone.) With the backing of the Western Allied authorities, the Social Democrats in the Western zones also rejected the merger.

The shotgun marriage of Social Democrats and Communists in the Russian zone put an end to the SPD's existence as an independent political party east of the Elbe, but in the western zones the SPD was the first party to be reorganized. On April 18, 1945, eight days after British troops occupied the city of Hanover, Kurt Schumacher, a regional party leader in Württemberg and member of the Reichstag before 1933 who lived in Hanover at the end of the war, presided over the SPD's first postwar meeting. Schumacher, who had spent ten years during the Third Reich in a concentration camp, quickly emerged as the SPD's unchallenged and charismatic leader in all three Western zones. The SPD reiterated its belief in parliamentary democracy and democratic socialism. Schumacher was also adamant that the Reich's unity needed to be preserved, although his eventual goal was the integration of a socialist Germany in a democratic-socialist Europe.

Under Schumacher's direction, the SPD became again what it had been in the later 1920s: a Marxist, democratic, nationalist, working-class party. The SPD rejected the communist doctrine of the dictatorship of the proletariat, but the party's essentially Marxist program did not facilitate cooperation with the middle-class parties. The SPD's dealings with the occupation authorities were not much better. Schumacher was convinced that Germany's capitalists, aided and abetted by their compatriots in the Allied countries, had been responsible for the rise of Hitler. He liked to remind officials in the military governments that he and many of his fellow Social Democrats had been incarcerated in concentration camps at a time when the Allied leaders were still negotiating treaties with Hitler.

In contrast to Schumacher, whose leadership of the SPD remained unchallenged until his death in 1952, the dominant figure in the largest middle-class party had to overcome considerable obstacles before his position was generally recognized. The Christian Democratic Union (*Christlich-Demokratische Union*, CDU) was a new organization that united parts of the old Catholic Center Party with elements of anti-Nazi Protestant conservatism. The new party was founded in the Soviet zone in June 1945 and in the western zones in the fall of that year. Almost immediately, two leaders and two strategies battled for supremacy in the CDU.

In the Soviet zone Jakob Kaiser, a former official in the Catholic Union movement, emerged as the CDU's leader. Kaiser did not sympathize with communism, but like the Communists, he did agree that the democratic parties should cooperate to form an antifascist bloc. Kaiser was convinced only the preservation of the Grand Alliance would preserve Germany's national unity, and the country had to play a vital part in achieving this goal. A united, democratic Germany would function as a "bridge" between the Russians and the Western Allies, preventing the breakup of the Allies. To this end, Kaiser was willing to go to a considerable distance in cooperating with the Russians.

These views were vigorously opposed by the man who was to become the leader of the CDU in the western zones, Konrad Adenauer. The mayor of Cologne, seventy years old when he was elected chairman of the CDU in the British zone, had already been a major figure in Weimar politics in the 1920s. Adenauer argued that Kaiser's "bridge function" was an illusion because the Soviets had already decided against genuine democracy in their zone and planned to incorporate East Germany into the Soviet orbit. According to Adenauer, then, the CDU's task was to build democracy in the western zones and to forge a strong link between western Germany, Western Europe, and the United States. Programmatically, the CDU stood for federalism, individual freedoms, and free enterprise.

As had happened after World War I, middle-class politics in Bavaria went their own way. After an attempt to revive the Bavarian People's Party as the Bavarian Party

(*Bayernpartei*—BP) failed; the dominant political force in the state became the Bavarian branch of the CDU, the Christian Social Union (*Christlich-Soziale Union*—CSU). In national politics, the CSU formed a partnership with the CDU that has continued to this day, but organizationally the Bavarian group has remained separate from the parent body. The CSU's activity is restricted to Bavaria; by agreement with the CDU the party does not attempt to organize supporters outside of the state.

The liberals, too, established themselves first in the Soviet zone. The party called itself the Liberal Democratic Party of Germany (*Liberaldemokratische Partei Deutschlands*—LDPD). The leaders had no choice but to steer the LDPD in the tradition of the Progressives and the DDP because the Russians regarded right-wing liberalism as a fascist ally of monopoly capitalism. Nevertheless, the LDPD quickly ran into difficulties with SMAD. Its founders were forced to resign, and it was not until Otto Nuschke, a left-wing DDP delegate in the Prussian Landtag during the Weimar years, became the party's chairman that the Soviets judged the LDPD suitably "progressive." Nuschke led the LDPD to a position as bourgeois fellow traveler of the SED.

In the western zones, liberalism did not follow Nuschke's lead. Instead, the West German liberals succeeded in uniting their traditionally feuding left and right wings into a single party, the Free Democratic Party of Germany (*Freie Demokratische Partei Deutschlands*—FDP). Still, the FDP had considerable difficulty agreeing on a consistent program. The national liberal priorities of nationalism and unfettered free enterprise vied for supremacy with the civil libertarian, anticlerical, and social welfare traditions of progressivism. There were also some practical organizational difficulties. In the west, liberalism was traditionally strongest in southwestern Germany. These areas, however, were mostly located in the French zone, and until the middle of 1948 the French authorities severely restricted travel between their zone and the rest of Germany.

After parties were permitted to organize again in the summer and fall of 1945, political life in the Soviet and Western zones proceeded along increasingly divergent paths. Although the Soviets allowed zonewide elections for a "German People's Congress for Unity and a Just Peace" as early as the fall of 1946, they also insisted that all "democratic" parties cooperate under the leadership of the SED. Candidates nominated for the Congress had to promise support for an antifascist-bloc strategy before they could be certified by SMAD. The actual elections were relatively free of direct Soviet interference, but by a variety of tactics SMAD assured that the Congress would be dominated by the SED.

The Western Allies followed a more cautious approach in allowing the resumption of organized political activity, but after political parties were allowed, the Western Allies made no effort to control the emerging party spectrum, except for the obvious prohibition of the Nazis and their fellow travelers. No restrictions were put on the KPD.

In line with their more cautious approach the Western Allies initially sought to make local and state affairs the focal point of political activity. In 1946 the voters in each Land elected state legislatures which then drafted new state constitutions. To coordinate decisions at the zonal level the British and Americans institutionalized meetings of the states' prime ministers in the two zones under the name of States' Councils (*Länderräte*) in the American zone and *Zonenbeirat* (Zonal Advisory Council) in the British zone. With the establishment of the Bizone, a quasi-parliamentary body, called the *Wirtschaftsrat* (Economic Council), was established. The Americans wanted to extend this confederative arrangement to all four zones. Secretary Byrnes in his September 1946 Stuttgart speech proposed that the prime ministers of the Länder meet as a "national council" to work out a German federal constitution. The proposal was rejected by the Russians, who argued that this was the proper task of the Soviet-sponsored People's Congress, and by the French, who at this time still wanted to restrict German political activity to the local and state levels.

Along with renewed political life, there was also a rebirth of art and literature. But whereas post-1945 politics was grounded in the experiences (and missed opportunities) of the revolution of 1918–1919 and the Weimar years, German writers and artists turned to new forms. For the past twelve years, German cultural life had stagnated under the iron hand of the Nazis' blood-and-soil ideology, and artists and audiences alike after the war rejected taking up again the stale debates of the 1920s and 1930s.

There was an explosion of new literary magazines and sophisticated journals of opinion. Between 1945 and 1950 more than 150 periodicals began publication, and although most folded after a few issues, some, like the *Frankfurter Hefte* ("Frankfurt Notebooks") and *Der Monat* ("The Month"), continue to enliven the literary scene. Audiences eagerly discovered the literature of the occupying powers; immediately after the war Thornton Wilder's *Our Town* was the most popular stage production in Germany.

New German dramas and novels were less predominant, but two stage productions—Carl Zuckmayer's *Des Teufels General* ("The Devil's General," 1946) and Wolfgang Borchert's *Draussen vor der Tür* ("On the Outside," 1947)— played to packed audiences. Zuckmayer had spent the Nazi years in exile in Vermont, and his play dealt with the problem of "inner emigration" and resistance among the German military. Borchert, a young veteran, attempted to address the emptiness and alienation felt by those who returned home to lost ideals and bombed-out cities.

Borchert's play illustrated one of the dominant themes of the post-1945 cultural revival: a profound pessimism about the future of civilization. World War II, "the picture of hell on earth," had ended the age of humanism. Modern people, most artists suggested, could only seek refuge in religious revival, absurdity, nihilism, or a private world

unconnected with larger events. Totally absent was the celebration of the "front experience" that had characterized so much of the literature after World War I. There were war novels, like Theodor Plievier's *Stalingrad* (1945), but their emphasis was on the senseless horror of war, not its supposed heroism. Even Ernst Jünger, whose books had been instrumental in creating the myth of the "front experience" after World War I, abandoned his belief that war forged a "new man." His diary of World War II, *Strahlungen* ("Rays"), is a powerful statement of the author's recognition that his earlier ideals had become perverted and useless.

Except for the British, all of the Allies took active steps on their own to encourage the permeation of democratic values in German cultural life. (The British tended to rely more on Germany's own regenerative processes.) The Americans did not even wait for the war to end. Talented writers among the German prisoners of war in the United States were encouraged to contribute literary pieces to a camp magazine called *Der Ruf* ("The Call"), which the U.S. authorities distributed among the German POWs. Many of these authors would later become leaders of the West German literary establishment.

The Russians, too, made an effort to encourage "progressive" traditions among the writers and artists in their zone. In early July 1945 the *Kulturbund zur demokratischen Erneuerung Deutschlands* ("Cultural Association for the Democratic Renewal of Germany") was founded as the umbrella organization for "cultural producers" in the Soviet zone. Although the guiding forces behind the Kulturbund were a group of communist fellow-traveling authors, many of whom had belonged to the "Association of German Proletarian and Revolutionary Writers" during the 1920s, at first SMAD made no effort to politicize the association. Indeed, the group's journal *Aufbau* ("Construction") for a time became one of the liveliest literary journals in Germany. Its pages were open to a wide variety of authors and literary forms.

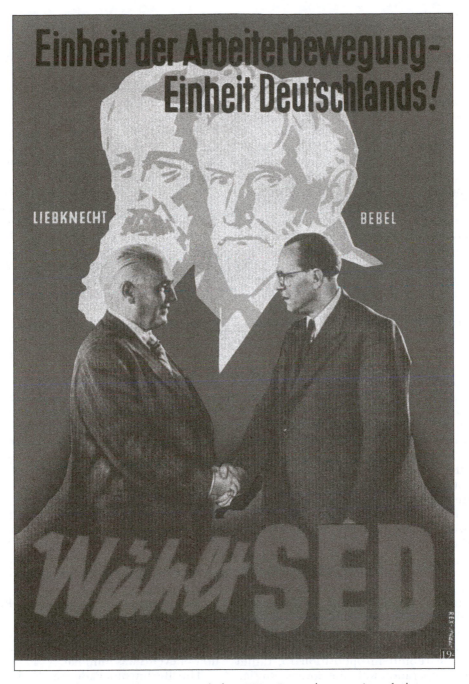

An early campaign poster of the SED. Beneath portraits of the nineteenth-century SPD leaders Wilhelm Liebknecht and August Bebel, Otto Grotewohl (SPD) and Wilhelm Pieck (KPD) are reuniting the German working class. The text reads, "Unity of the workers' movement—unity of Germany." (Source: akg-images.)

THE COLD WAR AND THE DIVISION OF GERMANY

The wartime agreements among the Allies were based on the assumption that joint and cooperative control by the Big Four of the defeated Reich would extend into the peacetime future. Within a year after Germany's unconditional surrender, however, the Cold War had destroyed the anti-Hitler alliance and pitted West against East. In Germany the Cold War led first to the breakdown of four-power cooperation and later to the establishment of separate East and West German states.

The Cold War was not planned. As far as Germany was concerned, it came about because the Big Four increasingly recognized that their policy goals and priorities for the country were incompatible. The Russians insisted that reparations be given absolute priority in any Allied "German policy" and that "democratization" and capitalism were incompatible. The West was equally adamant that reparations should not take precedence over current production or economic recovery and that "democratization" should not be a synonym for Communist control and the destruction of political and cultural pluralism.

In the Russian zone, the establishment of SAGs and the Saxon land reforms in 1946 signaled the Soviets' determination to go their own way. In the west the founding of the Bizone at the beginning of 1947 indicated that the British and the Americans intended to assign German economic recovery a higher priority than reparations and structural reforms.

As recent research by Carolyn Eisenberg and others has demonstrated, these decisions reflected feelings by American planners as early as 1945 that the West German economy should be rebuilt in opposition to, rather than in cooperation with, the Soviets. Russian aggression in southeastern Europe and the U.S. responses in the form of the Marshall Plan and the Truman Doctrine further worsened the climate for four-power cooperation.

The London Conference of Big Four foreign ministers in December 1947 was a watershed in the developing East–West split over Germany. As a result of this meeting, each side became convinced that the other was unwilling to compromise on Germany. Immediately after the failure of the London Conference, the Russians moved to solidify control of their zone and their general sphere of influence in Eastern Europe. SMAD dismissed Jakob Kaiser, the chairman of the CDU in the Soviet zone, and under Kaiser's successors the party abandoned its quest for an independent policy and became instead one of the SED's junior partners. Two months later, a bloodless coup in Czechoslovakia brought the Communists to power in this Central European country. In April 1948 the Soviet authorities began harassing Allied and German traffic in and out of Berlin. True, simultaneously the Russians offered a comprehensive proposal for maintaining four-power cooperation in Germany, but the West treated such gestures as mere propaganda.

Instead of chasing after the chimera of inter-Allied cooperation, the Western powers set about integrating their zones into the Western political and economic orbit. From February to June 1948, the Big Three Western Allies and the Benelux states of Belgium, Luxembourg, and The Netherlands met again in London. Prodded by the Americans, the delegates agreed that the three Western zones would be joined into a single economic unit and would participate fully in the European Recovery Program under the Marshall Plan. Most Germans regretted the deepening division among the Allies because they were anxious to preserve the unity of the Reich, but despite a wealth of conflicting ideas on how to prevent a falling out of the Grand Alliance, the practical influence of the Germans on the flow of events was minimal.

The Berlin blockade was both the most dramatic development in the growing division of Germany and the event that convinced most Germans in the western zones and West Berlin that they had no real alternative to becoming part of the Western camp. As with most conflicts in the accelerating Cold War,

West and East attributed aggressive motives to each other. The Russians accused the West of violating the wartime agreements by creating a separate West German state and using economic pressure to subvert Soviet control of the Russian zone; the West was convinced that the Soviets were attempting to drive the Western Allies out of the former capital and incorporate all of Berlin into the Soviet zone.

The Berlin blockade was triggered by a dispute over the type of currency to be used in the city. Until June 1948 the legal tender used in the Soviet zone and all sectors of Berlin was the occupation money issued under the authority of SMAD. Because the city's economic hinterland was the Soviet zone, this arrangement made economic sense. But with the West German currency reform, an entirely new situation arose. The introduction of the deutsche mark signaled the creation of two separate economic systems. The Western Allies had not originally intended to introduce the new currency in Berlin, but German economic administrators in the city and the western zones pointed out that not distributing the deutsche mark in Berlin condemned the city to economic isolation and eventual incorporation into the Soviet zone. As a result, the Western Allies agreed to introduce the new mark in the parts of Berlin under their control. It became legal tender alongside the occupation currency of the Soviet zone.

Aware of the old adage that a hard currency would drive out soft money, the Russians saw the Western decision as a direct challenge to their control of East Germany and East Berlin. They also argued that by distributing the new currency in the western

"West Berlin children watch an American supply plane land at Tempelhof Airport during the Berlin Airlift. (Source: Iberfoto/The Image Works)

Im Mittelpunkt   Konrad Adenauer (1876–1967)

The first chancellor of the Federal Republic was certainly no newcomer to either politics or public affairs when he took his oath of office in September 1949. He was also no youngster. In fact, at age seventy-three he was well past retirement age. He remained in office until October 1963, when he left the chancellorship, not very gracefully, at age eighty-seven. (During his last years in office there were increasing suggestions that it was time for him to retire, but Adenauer always countered such ideas by noting that he already had his retirement: the twelve years of the Third Reich when the Nazis forced him to remain idle.)

Adenauer was born in 1876 in Cologne, and he remained attached to this city and the Rhineland all of his life. He studied law, and in 1906 began his political career. A lifelong devout Catholic, there was never any doubt that he would make the Center Party his political home. He was elected a member of the Cologne City Council in 1909 and became mayor of the city in 1917. Adenauer remained Cologne's chief executive until 1933 when the Nazis forced him out of office.

During the Weimar Republic Adenauer was also active in state and national politics. He was a member of the Prussian State Council (an institution that represented the state's cities and provinces) from 1922 to 1933, and on several occasions his name appeared on a short list of candidates for chancellor. That he was never chosen was in large part the result of opposition to Adenauer's candidacy by the longtime prime minister of Prussia, Otto Braun. Adenauer consistently favored breaking up the Prussian superstate into several smaller Länder, including a Rhineland state. Braun, understandably, did not wish to lose his base of political power.

Adenauer was a fervent opponent of Nazism, although he was not active in any resistance group. The future West German chancellor disliked the Nazis' political violence, their anti-Semitism, and above all their opposition to Christianity. For Adenauer the Nazis, like the Communists, were un-Godly materialists who denied the importance of divinely ordained morality. The Nazis in turn distrusted Adenauer. He was interrogated several times by the Gestapo, the last time after the failed 1944 plot. To keep out of sight, Adenauer took up residence at the abbey of Maria Laach during part of the war years.

The Americans were the first Allied troops to reach Cologne in 1945, and they promptly reinstalled Adenauer as mayor. That decision was—briefly—rescinded by the first British commander in the city (by inter-Allied agreement Cologne was part of the British zone of occupation), who regarded Adenauer as "authoritarian and incompetent." But the brigadier was soon overruled by his superiors and Adenauer became mayor once again.

When political parties were allowed to organize again in the Western zones, Adenauer naturally enough became active in the successor organization of the Center Party, the Christian

sectors of the city, the Western Allies would effectively undermine four-power control of the former capital. On June 22 SMAD prohibited the distribution of the deutsche mark in all sectors of Berlin. The West, in turn, protested the Soviets' action and went ahead with the distribution of the new currency in the Western sectors. One day later, the Russians, citing the pretext of needed repairs to road, rail, and water networks, closed all land access to West Berlin from the Soviet zone and western Germany. They also attempted to prevent the shipment of all supplies from their zone to the city; the western part of Germany's former capital was subjected to a full-scale blockade.

Democratic Union (CDU). Early on he took a firm position on two of the major controversies facing the nascent CDU: the religious orientation of the party and its foreign policy. Unlike many of the traditionalists in the party, Adenauer did not want the CDU to be a purely Catholic organization; he argued it should be open to conservative Protestants as well. Adenauer also rejected the idea that the CDU (and Germany) should act as a sort of mediator between the Soviets and the Western Allies. Instead, Adenauer insisted the CDU's and Germany's place was firmly in the Western camp.

As chancellor Adenauer consistently pursued several goals. One was to create a firm foundation for parliamentary democracy in West Germany. This meant, as far as the chancellor was concerned, a strong executive and an emphasis upon the future rather than the past. Adenauer argued most of the former Nazis needed to be integrated into the new Germany and for that reason he opposed long-winded de-Nazification campaigns. Another priority for Adenauer was West Germany's place in the Western alliance. He worked hard at reconciliation with Germany's former enemies in the West, especially the United States and France.

The chancellor's critics always contended that his Western orientation meant that German reunification was not a major goal for him. According to this view for Adenauer the regions east of the Elbe were not part of the true, Western, European, Christian (Catholic) Germany. He is supposed to have said that whenever he crossed the Elbe River in an eastward direction he could "smell Asia." On a more positive note, Adenauer was instrumental in improving the relations between Germans and Jews. Under the guidance of the chancellor and the Israeli prime minister David Ben Gurion, German and Israeli diplomats in the early 1950s negotiated a treaty that provided billions of dollars in restitution payments to Jewish survivors of Nazi persecution.

In his last years in office, Adenauer became increasingly authoritarian, irascible, and convinced he was indispensable. On several occasions he was overheard to mutter, "Oh my God, what will happen to Germany when I am not around anymore?" These tendencies culminated in the 1962 *Spiegel* affair, when the Adenauer government ordered the arbitrary arrest of the magazine's editors. This wanton disregard of the law and the constitution led the Liberals in the coalition government to insist that the chancellor leave office before the end of the legislative term in 1965.

Adenauer resigned in 1963, and died four years later at the age of 91. At his death he was a highly respected statesman who had transformed West Germany from an international pariah to an accepted member of the family of Western nations. His funeral mass was attended by a large contingent of world leaders, including President Lyndon B. Johnson of the United States and President Charles de Gaulle of France.

In 1948 the city of Berlin had a population of roughly 4 million, of which 2.5 million lived in the western sectors. Almost all of the supplies of food, fuel, and other necessities for the inhabitants of all four sectors came from the surrounding Soviet zone. Because it was well known that the leaders of the Western Allies were anxious to avoid a direct military confrontation, the Soviets felt they were in a position to dictate terms to the West. The Western Allies, however, again led by the Americans, used the inter-Allied agreements on access routes to practice a form of brinkmanship that would call the Russian bluff without resorting to military force. In November 1945 the Four Powers had agreed that the

Western Allies could use their air corridors, one from each of the western zones, to supply their forces in Berlin. The Western Allies now decided to use these corridors to airlift supplies not just to their troops but to the entire population of the three western sectors in the city.

The Russians, like the Western powers, were unwilling to mount a direct military challenge to their opponents, and the Berlin Airlift remains one of the most impressive examples of logistical support in modern times. Landing virtually nonstop in West Berlin, planes of the Western Allies by December 1948 were able to bring 4,500 tons of supplies to the city each day, and by the spring of the following year that figure had been increased to 8,000 tons. It became clear that despite tremendous hardships— electricity could be turned on only four hours each day—West Berlin could be supplied from the air indefinitely. The Russians also recognized their defeat, and during the winter began signaling that they were anxious to end the blockade without losing diplomatic face. After months of behind-the-scenes negotiations, the Soviets—in May 1949— lifted the blockade (officially, the needed repairs to the transport networks had been completed) without having achieved any of their objectives. In terms of the Cold War, the Berlin blockade was a clear Western victory.

The year-long confrontation over Berlin sealed the decades-long economic and political division of Germany and the city itself. Berlin developed into two separate administrative entities. The city was not yet physically divided, as it would be later, and in all four sectors the Allied commanders retained far-reaching control rights, but by June 1949 Germany's former capital had two separate municipal governments. In the three western sectors, the mayor and city council were freely elected; in the Soviet sector, a communist city government was installed by SMAD. Even more important, the introduction of the deutsche mark as the only legal currency in the western sectors at the end of the blockade meant that West Berlin would become an integral part of the West German and Western European economic systems.

The ongoing Berlin blockade also provided the final catalyst needed to push the Western Allies and the Germans in the west to the realization that there would have to be separate political entities in East and West Germany. In view of the Russian attempt literally to starve out West Berlin, no major political group in the western zones—with the exception of the Communists— held fast to the conviction that national unity was worth the price of Russian domination. Some political leaders continued to drag their feet, but by July 1948 most German leaders in the western zones had accepted the position of the Allied military governors: that there was no alternative to a separate state in the western zones. As Ernst Reuter, the Social Democratic mayor of West Berlin, reminded his colleagues, "Germany is not being divided; it is already divided." It is also noteworthy that the fortitude of the West Berliners during the blockade did much to change the image of the Germans among the Western Allies. The Berliners' willingness to endure months of hardship to preserve their freedom in the face of communist threats did much to wipe away the image of the "ugly Germans" and to replace it with the beginnings of a picture of "good, democratic Germans."

In July 1948 the state legislatures of the three Western zones elected delegates to a Parliamentary Council. Beginning in September 1948, to the accompaniment of the continuing blockade, the Parliamentary Council met in the Rhenish university town of Bonn and debated the terms of a West German constitution. It was completed and submitted for ratification to the state legislatures in the spring of the following year. The Russians and their communist allies watched developments in West Germany with great interest. All along, the Soviets were anxious to prevent the formation of a separate noncommunist West German state; indeed it seems clear that one reason for the blockade had been a last-ditch effort by the Soviets to prevent the creation of such an entity. Even when this strategy failed, the Russians did everything possible to put the onus for dividing Germany on the Western Allies and the West Germans. Only after the West German constitution had been ratified was a newly elected (Third) Congress for Unity and a Just Peace charged with drafting an East German alternative constitution. Unlike the Parliamentary Council, the Third Congress was formally elected directly by the voters of the Soviet zone, but in reality the people had little choice in the matter. The ballots permitted only a "yes" or "no" vote on a list of antifascist-bloc candidates selected by SMAD and the SED.

CONCLUSION

By the middle of 1949, then, only four years after the "condominium of the Allies" had been established, the owners of the building had developed irreconcilable differences and divided their property. In both East and West,

the new German societies attempted to revive and fulfill the promise of the post-1918 era. In the Soviet zone, SMAD and the SED intended to complete the socialist revolution that had failed in 1919. The new leaders of the West were also determined to avoid the mistakes of Weimar while holding fast to the ideals of the first republic: cultural pluralism, a socially responsible free-market economy, and parliamentary democracy.

The Germans' selective dipping into their past was, of course, only part of the story of the country's division—and the lesser part at that. More important, as long as the Cold War lasted, both German states were part of the East–West confrontation—and subject to control and guidance by the Big Four. East and West Germany were founded as—and would remain for many years—objects of Cold War politics.

CHAPTER NINE

The Federal Republic of Germany

1949–1990

Two states emerged from the rubble of the Third Reich, and whereas the East German Democratic Republic (GDR) would eventually collapse under the weight of its economic and political problems, the West German Federal Republic of Germany (FRG) would be recognized as the most successful society in modern German history. Germans on the western side of the Elbe have enjoyed democratic freedoms, unprecedented political stability, economic prosperity, and genuine international respect.

THE ADENAUER ERA, 1949–1963

Political Stability

In 1949 few West Germans would have predicted that the state they were reluctantly creating was in fact the beginning of a West German nation. The framers of the constitution constantly emphasized the provisional nature of their work. Nevertheless, they

succeeded in writing a remarkably effective document. Moreover, the "Basic Law," as the Germans insisted on labeling the constitution to underscore its provisional character, became the constitution for all of Germany after the country was reunited in 1990. So the analysis that follows now applies to the former East German areas as well. In constitutional terms, then, after 1990 "West Germany" and "Germany" are identical.

West Germany's leaders faced a difficult task. They wanted to write a constitution that was in accord with Germany's own political traditions, but they also had to construct a document that could obtain the approval of the Allied military governors. Fortunately the two sets of criteria were not incompatible, although the priorities of the Allies and the Germans differed. Both sides agreed that the new West German state should be a parliamentary democracy and that the new constitution should draw on Germany's only other experience with parliamentary democracy, the Weimar constitution. The Allies assigned a high priority to redrawing the German state boundaries, but territorial reform ranked much lower on the German agenda. Understandably, the disagreements were sharpest on the sovereignty issue. The Allies wanted to retain far-reaching rights even after the constitution had gone into effect; the Germans were anxious to reduce as much as possible the residual powers of the occupation forces.

The Basic Law was drafted by the Parliamentary Council, an assembly of sixty-six delegates selected by the state legislatures. In this body the SPD and the CDU/CSU were each represented by twenty-seven delegates; the remaining twelve delegates were divided among five smaller parties, including the Liberals and the Communists. Eleven of the sixty-six delegates had sat in the state legislatures or the Reichstag during the Weimar years. The chairman of the CDU, Konrad Adenauer, was elected president of the Parliamentary Council; Carlo Schmid, a recognized constitutional expert and leader of the SPD in southwest Germany, became chairman of the council's most important committee, the main or drafting committee.

The Parliamentary Council began its deliberations at the beginning of September 1948 when the Berlin blockade was nearing its climax. Eight months later, in May 1949, coincidentally as the Soviets abandoned their blockade, the council submitted the Basic Law for ratification to the state legislatures. The final document was in many ways an improved version of the Weimar constitution. Particularly apparent were three major changes. One concerned the election and powers of the head of state, the federal president. (Partly in response to Allied sensitivities, the Basic Law avoided using the word *Reich*. Instead, the delegates went back to the pre-1871 term *Bund*, or federation.) Second, the framers of the Basic Law attempted to reduce the large number of cabinet crises that had been characteristic of the Weimar years. Finally, there was the problem of the second chamber of the national legislature. During the Weimar Republic the power of this Länder-controlled body had resulted in constant friction between the states and the federal government.

The Basic Law sought to provide correctives for all of these weaknesses in the Weimar constitution. The powers and stature of the federal president were significantly reduced. In contrast to the Weimar practice the West German counterpart is not elected by direct popular vote and his or her functions are largely limited to representative and ceremonial duties. The West German federal president has no emergency powers analogous to Article 48 of the Weimar constitution.

Undoubtedly the most important features of the new constitution concerned the nature of relations between the federal executive and the legislature, as well as the election of the federal parliament. Like the Weimar Reichstag, the West German national parliament is elected at least every four years. However, unlike the system of extreme proportional representation under which the Weimar Reichstag was elected, the West German national parliament, or *Bundestag*, has members elected both by a system of proportional representation and by delegates chosen in single-member districts. Half of the Bundestag members are elected in single-member districts (originally it was three-fifths), and the remainder are selected from "party lists" allocated on the basis of proportional representation. Equally important, subsequent election laws enacted effective provisions making it more difficult for splinter parties to gain representation in the national parliament. To gain a seat in the Bundestag, a party had to obtain at least 5 percent of the popular vote in a state or a majority in at least one single-member district. (Since 1949 these hurdles have been raised, increasing the votes required to 5 percent of the national total or a majority in three single-member districts.)

The delegates to the Parliamentary Council also attempted to reduce the likelihood of cabinet crises. In a parliamentary democracy, the legislature has both the power to elect and—through a vote of no confidence—to dismiss the cabinet. In the last years of the Weimar Republic, cabinet crises had been frequent and long as Communists and Nazis combined their strength to overthrow one government after another. To prevent a repetition of this state of affairs, the Basic Law provides for a "constructive vote of no confidence." In practice this means that a vote of "no confidence" is not valid unless the opposition can demonstrate beforehand that it has agreed on the composition of a new cabinet to take the place of the one it seeks to dismiss.

The guarantees of civil liberties and individual rights in the Basic Law were also a modified version of the Weimar model. The new constitution lists the classic civil rights—such as freedom of speech and assembly—but remembering the Nazis' abuse of these rights, the Parliamentary Council coupled them with a specific prohibition against their use by any individual or organization to advocate anti-Semitism, racism, or the overthrow of the democratic form of government. The delegates rejected Social Democratic proposals to include a list of "socioeconomic rights"—such as the right to employment and joint labor–management control of major corporations—in the Basic Law. They did, however, reaffirm the constitutional duty of public support for institutions like family and church. An important symbolic link to Germany's first attempt at democracy was the reinstitution of the colors black, red, and gold as the FRG's flag.

In line with German particularist traditions, but also at the insistence of the Allies, the Basic Law is quite solicitous of states' rights. As they had during the empire and the First Republic, the Länder retain a number of specific residual powers, especially control over public education at all levels. In addition, the state governments control the second chamber of the national legislature, the Federal Council (*Bundesrat*), whose members are not elected directly by popular vote but selected by the state legislatures. The second chamber has less direct influence over national legislation than the Bundestag, but the states can use this body to at least delay measures that they see as inimical to their interests.

An interesting innovation in German constitutional practice was the establishment of a Federal Constitutional Court (*Bundesverfassungsgericht*). This tribunal, modeled on the U.S. Supreme Court, has original and final jurisdiction on all questions affecting the constitutionality of federal, state, and local legislation as well as administrative acts and international treaties. The judges on the court do not serve for life but are selected for a term of twelve years by a committee composed of delegates from the federal and state parliaments. To facilitate quick decisions on constitutional questions, cases involving the constitution are brought directly to the court rather than through the appeals process. To prevent an excessive backlog of cases, the court has two chambers that hear cases separately.

By a vote of 50–12 the Parliamentary Council approved the Basic Law on May 8, 1949. The negative ballots came from some of the smaller parties, including the KPD, and all members of the Bavarian delegation. Bavaria rejected the Basic Law because, in its view, the document did not go far enough in guaranteeing states' rights. Four days later, after a brief battle over the financial powers of the federal government, the three military governors gave their approval. The draft was then submitted to the state legislatures for ratification. With the exception of Bavaria, all of the German states voted for the Basic Law. In September 1949 the new Federal Republic of Germany elected its first national parliament.

At the same time, the Allies transformed their offices of military government into civilian high commissions. Both the Americans and the French replaced their military chiefs of administration with civilian officials. John J. McCloy, a New York banker and close associate of presidents Roosevelt and Truman, took the place of General Lucius Clay, the head of OMGUS. The French high commissioner was André François-Poncet, a career diplomat who had been France's ambassador to Berlin in the 1930s. The British retained General Robertson as high commissioner, but to underscore his new status the general retired from active army service.

The early West German political scene maintained its "traditional" multiparty appearance—in the first federal elections thirteen parties were represented on the ballot—but it soon acquired a decidedly more "American" feel. Increasingly, two parties, the CDU/CSU and the SPD, appealed to a wide spectrum of voters across class and geographic divisions. By the end of the 1950s, West Germany had developed into a two-and-a-half-party system, with the Liberals running a distant third to the two major groups. Essentially, the CDU/CSU represents the center right and the SPD the left of center; the Liberals (FDP) act as a smaller swing party in the center that has shifted alliances several times between the CDU/CSU and the SPD.

One man, Konrad Adenauer, the leader of the CDU/CSU, was largely responsible for the transformation of the West German party scene. Aided by undaunted self-confidence, considerable charisma, and the "economic miracle" of the 1950s (see pp. 270–73), Adenauer succeeded in transforming the Christian Democrats into West Germany's dominant party. In fact, in the 1957 federal election they became the first party in German history to win more than 50 percent of the popular vote in a free election.

The Christian Democrats' success had two major consequences for West German politics. One was the disappearance of the smaller parties; the CDU absorbed most of them. Even more importantly, the CDU's strategy forced the other major parties to make programmatic and stylistic changes as well. The Liberals were the least successful in adapting to the new era. The Christian Democrats succeeded in making major inroads into the Liberals' traditional voter reservoir, and the FDP became a party chronically fearful of not clearing the 5 percent hurdle.

During the 1950s the FDP tried to escape its dilemma by seeking refuge in the shadow of the CDU. The Liberals served in a succession of cabinets headed by Konrad Adenauer, acting as the self-proclaimed voice of Germany's upper-middle class and professionals. By the end of the decade, however, that strategy meant that the voters increasingly saw little difference between the FDP and the CDU. The Liberals' left wing demanded that the party take steps to preserve a political identity of its own.

The result was a drawing together of FDP and SPD, a development that was made possible because the success of the CDU also forced the Social Democrats to change their traditional profile. Kurt Schumacher, the SPD's first leader after the war, believed that the magnitude of West Germany's economic difficulties and social dislocation after World War II would "proletarianize" a large majority of the population, who would then be receptive to the idea that democratic socialism alone could rebuild the country. But this theory did not work out. In the national contests of the 1950s the party's share of the popular vote grew only slowly above the 30 percent level while the CDU eventually exceeded the 50 percent mark. Schumacher's strategy seemed to doom the SPD to the status of a permanent opposition in the federal legislature.

Schumacher died in 1952. His successor, Erich Ollenhauer, a "comfortably rotund, innately decent, and averagely competent" party bureaucrat, as the British journalist Terence Prittie described him, recognized the SPD's dilemma. The SPD had to transcend its traditional image as a working-class party. Ollenhauer quietly encouraged the rise of younger, more dynamic people to leadership positions in the party. Significantly, the newcomers, for the most part, had made their mark not as party functionaries but as members of the Bundestag and as municipal and state government officials. (The SPD tended to do much better in state elections than at the federal level.) The parliamentarians included Fritz Erler and Herbert Wehner, in the 1950s and 1960s chairman and vice chairman, respectively, of the SPD's Bundestag delegation. Especially Wehner, a former Communist who broke with Stalin in the 1940s, turned out to be a highly skilled parliamentary strategist and tactician. Among the Länder leaders, Ernst Reuter, the mayor of West Berlin during the 1948 blockade, Willy Brandt, Reuter's protégé and successor, and Carlo Schmid, the minister of justice of Baden-Württemberg and the principal architect of the Basic Law, rose to positions of prominence.

In 1959 the SPD's national convention met in Bad Godesberg (now a suburb of Bonn) and adopted a new party program. It was the first fundamental revision of the SPD's ideology and platform since the Erfurt Program of 1891. The changes embodied in the Bad Godesberg Program were profound. In essence, the SPD cast off its Marxist mantle and became a pragmatic, issue-oriented, catch-all party that attempted to appeal to a wide spectrum of voters. The SPD emphasized reform instead of revolution. The SPD no longer insisted on centralized planning and socialization of the means of production. Instead it promised to work for "as much economic freedom as possible, as much economic planning as necessary."

The self-transformation of the major parties was instrumental in bringing about one of the most surprising developments in West German politics—the rapid disappearance of the splinter-party problem. In the 1949 federal election, the splinter parties still attracted 28 percent of the popular vote, but by 1965 their combined total was only 3.6 percent. The trend was a surprise because the political and especially the economic situation in the early years of the FRG seemed ready-made for radical politics. Indeed, the occupation authorities were so fearful of the potential for radical politics among refugees that they refused to "license" a refugee party.

For this reason, the Union of Expellees and Dispossessed (*Bund der Heimatlosen und Entrechteten*—BHE) was not organized until 1950, when the Allied controls on party formation had been dropped. The history of the BHE quickly demonstrated, however, that fears of refugee radicalism were vastly exaggerated. The party, whose program included demands for the return of Germany's eastern territories and special benefits for refugees living in West Germany, captured more than 5 percent of the popular vote in 1953, but this figure represented less than 20 percent of those refugees who cast ballots. The party's initial success, moreover, was also the high point of its appeal. Within four years, most of the refugee vote had been absorbed by the mainstream parties, primarily the CDU. In the 1957 election, the BHE was unable to clear the 5 percent hurdle, and thereafter the party rapidly disappeared from the political landscape.

Weimar democracy had been weakened by political extremism. The FRG escaped this problem as well. Communist and neo-Nazi parties did attempt to gain a foothold, but neither developed into a serious political force. The failure of West German communism was closely related to the Cold War and Stalin's control of East Germany and the West German Communist Party. Between 1947 and 1951 the KPD's internal organization was seriously weakened by a purge of *Titoists,* a term the party leadership used to characterize members whom the Soviets accused of deviating from Moscow's Stalinist line. During the first federal election campaign in 1949, the Communists, who resolutely defended the SED's and SMAD's policies, were very much on the defensive trying to justify the Soviet blockade of West Berlin.

The KPD managed to obtain 5.7 percent of the popular vote in 1949, but thereafter its appeal declined rapidly. The party's membership dropped from 300,000 in 1945 to 60,000 in 1956. In the 1953 Bundestag election, the KPD's popular vote fell to 2.2 percent. This was the party's last national campaign effort. In view of the party's precipitous political decline, prohibiting the KPD hardly seemed necessary, but as part of the anticommunist hysteria that swept through West German society in the 1950s, the government was determined to dissolve the Communist Party as a threat to democracy. In 1956 the Federal Constitutional Court agreed—the KPD was attempting to destroy parliamentary democracy in West Germany and as a result the government had the right to prohibit the party.

Both the Allies and the leaders of West Germany's new democracy were also concerned about the rise of neo-Nazism. The Nazi Party, of course, was prohibited, but there were legitimate fears that rightist extremism would attempt to rise under a variety of subterfuges. In fact, neo-Nazis did become active again very quickly. The German Reich Party (*Deutsche Reichspartei*—DRP), which had been established as a conservative group in late 1945, became increasingly extremist as ex-Nazis gained the upper hand in this organization. Fortunately, its voter appeal remained small. In the 1949 election the DRP gained only 1.8 percent of the vote nationwide, although it rose above 5 percent in the state of Lower Saxony, where many refugees and ex-Nazis lived.

Like the Communists, the neo-Nazis were unable to hold on to a place on the West German political landscape. In 1950 the DRP split. Its conservative elements eventually became part of the FDP and the CDU while the radicals went on to found a new group, the Socialist Reich Party (*Sozialistische Reichspartei—SRP*). The leaders of the SRP were easily recognizable as prominent ex-Nazis (including Werner Naumann, a former state secretary in Goebbels's propaganda ministry), and the program left no doubt about the party's fascist aims. As a result, the Federal Constitutional Court outlawed the SRP before it could participate in the 1953 election. After 1953 the neo-Nazis remained an unorganized force until they reappeared in a different guise in the 1960s.

With both the splinter parties and the extremists unable to gain a significant portion of the vote, elections during the Adenauer era were dominated by shifts in popularity among the "big three": the Christian Democrats, the Social Democrats, and the Liberals. The first Bundestag election seemed to indicate that the forces would remain somewhat balanced. The CDU/CSU (31 percent) and the SPD (29.2 percent) stood at almost equal strength while the Liberals came in a respectable third (11.9 percent). Because no party had a parliamentary majority, Konrad Adenauer put together a coalition composed of the CDU/CSU, the Liberals, and some smaller parties.

In the 1953 election the voters gave the coalition a strong mandate to continue governing West Germany. The government was credited with the economic recovery (see pp. 270–273), while the Russians' suppression of freedom in East Germany (p. 303ff) and the outbreak of the Korean War seemed to show that there was no realistic alternative to Adenauer's program of anchoring West Germany firmly in the Western alliance. In 1953 the CDU/CSU's share of the popular vote exploded to 45.2 percent, the FDP dropped to 9.5 percent, and the SPD fell to 28.8 percent.

In the "stomach election" of 1957, the CDU/CSU did even better. As already noted, for the first time in German history a single party gained a majority of the popular vote (50.2 percent) in a free election. The SPD's share also rose slightly. In fact, the 1957 contest seemed to provide evidence that the FRG was evolving into a two-party state. The Liberals' meager 7.7 percent vote share brought them dangerously close to the 5 percent barrier.

But Adenauer's 1957 triumph also began the long and, in some ways, sad political decline of the CDU's leader. The chancellor was now eighty-one years old, and he had been the unchallenged, dominant figure in West German politics for almost a decade. Adenauer remained physically and mentally fit, but he was also becoming increasingly irascible and suspicious of potential rivals. For some years now, the chancellor's heir apparent had been Ludwig Erhard, the minister of economics since 1949 and the man credited with engineering West Germany's "economic miracle." Erhard was one of the CDU's most popular figures, and both he and many of the party's leaders felt that the time had come for him to take Adenauer's place. Unfortunately for Erhard, Adenauer was convinced his heir apparent would be a disaster as head of the government.

At the beginning of 1959, an opportunity seemed to present itself for a politic solution to the impasse. Since 1949 the federal president had been Theodor Heuss, a respected scholar and urbane Liberal. His second term was coming to an end, and a number of CDU leaders proposed to Adenauer that he should become federal president. After some consideration, the chancellor refused the largely honorific office. He proposed Erhard instead for the job, an offer that the economics minister regarded as an insult.

The 1959 "presidential crisis" ended with ill feeling on all sides, and the results of the 1961 federal elections provided further evidence that the voters, too, were becoming disillusioned with the Adenauer era. The campaign itself was characterized by a series of blunders and setbacks for the government. Even before the election, the Liberals had announced that they would demand a date for Adenauer's resignation as chancellor as a precondition for reestablishing a coalition with the CDU/CSU. Adenauer's lame response to the Berlin Wall (see pp. 310–11) antagonized many voters. The chancellor himself seemed to campaign almost as much against his heir presumptive, Ludwig Erhard, as he did against the SPD opposition. In contrast to the CDU's squabbles, the SPD presented a fresh platform in the Bad Godesberg Program, and its candidate for chancellor—the forty-seven-year-old photogenic and charismatic mayor of Berlin, Willy Brandt—personified a generational change in political leadership.

The 1961 election results were a severe disappointment to the chancellor and the CDU. The Christian Democrats' share of the popular vote dropped to 45.3 percent while the SPD's broke the 35 percent barrier, rising to 36.2 percent. Equally significant, the Liberals' campaign for a CDU/FDP coalition without Adenauer seemed to rescue them from political oblivion; their popular vote this time was 12.8 percent. As a condition for rejoining the coalition, the Liberals extracted a promise from Adenauer that he would resign as chancellor before the next scheduled federal elections.

It was unfortunate that scandals marred Adenauer's last months in office. The most damaging of these was the Spiegel affair in October 1962. *Der Spiegel* ("The Mirror"), then, as now, the leading newsmagazine of Germany and Europe, had a well-deserved reputation for irreverence, iconoclasm, and, on occasion, sensationalism. In the fall of 1962, the magazine published leaked documents demonstrating the lack of defense readiness of some West German army units. Claiming *Der Spiegel* had endangered national security, the minister of defense, Franz Josef Strauss (CSU), with Adenauer's approval, ordered the arrest of the magazine's editors and a police search of the publication's offices in Bonn and Hamburg. The reaction to this high-handed action was a storm of indignation from the press and public opinion over what appeared to be a clear attack on the freedom of the press. The Liberals threatened to quit the coalition (which would have brought down the government) unless Strauss resigned. The defense minister did so immediately, and in October 1963 Adenauer, keeping his promise to the FDP, also retired; he died four years later at the age of ninety-one.

Economic Prosperity

Ludwig Erhard became chancellor of the Federal Republic in October 1963; he was one of the most popular figures in Germany. More than any other individual, he personified the most dramatic success story in the FRG, the country's postwar "economic miracle." The prospects for rapid and sustained economic recovery were certainly not promising in 1949. The list of the country's economic and social needs was staggering: reconstruction of houses, apartments, and industrial plants; repair of the transportation system; resumption of industrial production; reopening of export markets; and integration of the millions of refugees and homeless into the fabric of society. These were tasks formidable enough to daunt most decision makers, but Ludwig Erhard recognized that, hidden beneath the prevailing picture of physical destruction and social misery, West Germany possessed some major assets.

The influx of people brought overcrowding in many areas but also a ready supply of labor so that economic recovery was not be held back by a shortage of labor workers labor–management relations had also been put on a new footing. The German workers were now organized in a single union, the German Labor Association (*Deutscher Gewerkschaftsbund*—DGB). The new umbrella organization embraced Socialist, Liberal, and Catholic unions and facilitated collective bargaining on a national level. Labor was also accorded a much larger role in the process of economic decision making. A federal codetermination law—the precise law which OMGUS had vetoed in 1947—mandated that the employees of all major corporations had the right to elect at least one member of the board of directors. (The law has since been amended so that labor representatives now make up half of the membership on the board of directors of major enterprises.) The result was a form of democratic corporatism that inaugurated a long period of generally harmonious labor–management relations. West Germany has experienced far fewer strikes and other forms of labor unrest than most leading industrial nations.

One of the most famous and controversial campaign posters of the post-1945 era. In the 1953 Bundestag election, the CDU, campaigning against a still officially Marxist SPD, argued, "All Marxist roads lead to Moscow. For that reason [vote] CDU." (Source: akg-images.)

In addition, the very magnitude of the rebuilding effort meant that for many years there would be a virtually limitless market for civilian goods and, provided production was sufficiently high, an almost total absence of inflationary pressures. It was, in other words, a golden opportunity for daring and innovative entrepreneurs, although, as Arnold Sywottek has pointed out, the boom was also facilitated by massive investments to modernize what in the 1950s and 1960s were still publicly owned enterprises, such as the post office, the national airline, Lufthansa, and the railroads. Especially important was the steady electrification of the federal railroad system, an improvement that increased train speed and had a positive impact on Germany's air quality.

The international scene looked equally good; after long years of war-related shortages, there was an international sellers' market for civilian goods. The Korean War, which forced the United States to shift much of its industrial production capacity to meet the needs of the military, brought additional opportunities for German exports. For a time, West Germany had a serious capital problem, but the growing strength of the deutsche mark, which was backed by the U.S. dollar, soon made West Germany an attractive place for foreign and domestic investors.

In recent years, the significance of the Marshall Plan and its aid has been questioned as a factor in the recovery of Western Europe. New research has pointed out that American help acted more as a catalyst than as a causal agent. One researcher has estimated that only about 7 percent of the capital and materials needed for recovery was provided from U.S. sources; the remainder was generated by the Europeans themselves. At the same time, the psychological impact of U.S. aid for the war-ravaged continent should not be underestimated. In contrast to the situation after World War I, the Marshall Plan signified that America would not turn its back on Europe.

All of these positive factors could not answer two fundamental questions. One involved the best method for stimulating the productive forces of the country, and the other concerned the social implications of any economic policy adopted. In 1949 the social misery index in West Germany was very high, but it was rather evenly distributed. If the forces of a free-market economy were unleashed, was there not a very real danger that prosperity would come to a few while most remained destitute? Such a scenario—and the many poor were likely to include the 13.2 million refugees who were already bitter about their fate—raised real fears of political destabilization and a return to the conditions of Weimar.

Erhard and the Social Democrats proposed radically different plans for West Germany's economic recovery. Both as chief administrator for economic affairs in the Bizone and later as economics minister in a succession of federal cabinets, Erhard argued that relatively unfettered market forces would provide the greatest amount of prosperity for the largest number of West Germans. The minister recognized that the free enterprise system would increase the gap between rich and poor, but he was also convinced that the rapid increase in the country's GNP, made possible by freewheeling opportunities, would generate sufficient resources to reduce the misery index for all. In effect, the benefits would be highly differentiated in relative terms, but in absolute terms all would be better off.

The SPD vigorously opposed Erhard's plan for recovery, which it saw as perpetuating the rule of capitalism in West Germany and widening the gap between rich and poor. Until the mid-1950s the Social Democrats advocated a democratically controlled, centrally planned economy with public ownership of basic industries and natural resources. Small and medium-size businesses as well as family-owned farms would remain in private hands. In addition, prohibitive taxation of large incomes would ensure there was an equitable system of income distribution.

As we saw, the election returns of the 1950s demonstrated that the voters in increasing numbers sided with Erhard. As the minister had anticipated, after some initial pump priming by the European Recovery Program (ERP), the economy became self-propelling.

What Erhard called a "social market economy" provided the West Germans with a level of prosperity unprecedented in German history. Pockets of poverty remained, but virtually all West Germans benefited from the spectacular expansion of most sectors of the economy.

The figures were truly impressive. Between 1951 and 1963 the West German economy expanded at an average annual rate of 7.1 percent. Disposable income of the average German household grew by 400 percent between 1950 and 1970. In 1950, 16.4 million families had to live in 10.1 million houses and apartments. Eight years later, the housing shortage had been significantly eased by the construction of 4.5 million units. Unemployment dropped from 8.1 percent in 1950 to an extraordinary 0.5 percent in 1965. In economic and political terms, the Erhard program was so successful that in 1959 the SPD dropped its proposals for state-directed planning and endorsed the concept of free, but socially responsible, market economics.

Translating economic growth into social policy required political decisions and compromises. In part, the goal of social responsibility was realized by earmarking large amounts of public money for social welfare projects. Much of the housing construction, for example, was made possible with government subsidies. In addition, two major laws were instrumental in making the fruits of economic expansion available to all segments of the society. Both came in the early 1950s, that is to say, at a time when the West German economy was clearly taking off. In May 1952 the Bundestag passed the Law for the Equalization of Burdens (*Lastenausgleichsgesetz*). Under the provisions of this legislation, the government provided payments stretching over a number of years as partial compensation for war-related losses of either real property or liquid assets. By the end of 1986, more than 130 billion deutsche marks ($68.4 billion) had been distributed to 57 million applicants.

The same principle of compensation was also extended to Jewish victims of Nazi persecution. The West German government negotiated an agreement with the Israel to give money payments to German Jews and their descendants.

Between 1952 and 1966, 3.5 billion deutsche marks ($820 million) was appropriated for this purpose. In another important acknowledgment of the former Reich's obligations, the Federal Republic accepted liability for the Weimar Republic's external debt. Under an agreement with the creditors, the Western Allies eventually cancelled two-thirds of the debt while West Germany paid the remainder in annual installments. The last payment was made in October 2010.

Equally important was the second piece of legislation, the Refugee Law (*Vertriebenengesetz*) of February 1953. Germany's refugee population was very unevenly distributed. Disproportionate numbers resided in the rural areas closest to the Soviet zone—Schleswig-Holstein, Lower Saxony, Hessen, Bavaria—causing severe problems for state and municipal governments and resentment among the local population. The Refugee Law determined a quota for proportional and equitable resettlement of the refugees throughout the West German Länder and provided federal funds for new housing and job training.

The sums involved in these two major social policy efforts were quite large. Between 1952 and 1962, 47 billion deutsche marks ($11.2 billion) were distributed under the auspices of the two laws; individual payments averaged 6,000 deutsche marks per person. But the effort was well worth it. The income redistribution policy undoubtedly removed what might have become a serious source of political radicalism—it certainly helped undermine the strength of such groups as the BHE—while the overall rise in the standard of living mitigated resentments against the wealth of the old and new rich that was a definite by-product of the "economic miracle."

Still, for all its undoubted benefits, Erhard's "social market economy" was essentially a trickle-down economy, one that in absolute terms widened the rift between rich and poor. It became acceptable and indeed was enthusiastically endorsed by most West Germans because the trickle came fast enough and in sufficient amounts to provide major increases in the standard of living for virtually all. But these results could be achieved only by economic growth rates that have not been possible since the early 1970s.

In addition to phenomenal growth rates, the economic miracle also began the shift of Germany's economic fulcrum from the north to the south and southwest. As coal mining, ship-building, and steel manufacturing declined in importance, many areas of northern Germany and the Ruhr became a "rust belt." In contrast, the regions of Bavaria, Baden-Württemberg, and Hessen that were home to Germany's primary export industries—chemicals, automotive products, electronics—experienced times of sustained prosperity.

International Recognition

Ludwig Erhard personified the economic miracle, but there was never any doubt that Adenauer himself directed West Germany's foreign policy. Especially for the early years of the Adenauer era, it is actually a misnomer to speak of West Germany's foreign policy. Under the Occupation Statute of 1949, the Allied high commissioners reserved for themselves the power to conduct West Germany's foreign relations. Not until 1954 did the FRG regain the right to conduct its own foreign affairs.

In his quest to have the Federal Republic rejoin the family of nations on a near-equal basis, Adenauer identified three issues as pivotal for West Germany's international standing. First, priority was given to continuing good relations with the Western Big Three, with West Germany's ties to the United States of paramount importance. Closely related was the area of political, military, and economic cooperation with the countries of Western Europe, especially France. Finally, there was the problem of West Germany's relationship to the Soviet Union and the countries of Eastern Europe. (Relations with the German Democratic Republic were not a foreign policy concern for the Federal Republic at this time. The GDR was still routinely referred to as the Soviet Zone of Occupation, and East German matters were handled by the ministry for all-German affairs, not the foreign office.)

As far as relations with the Western Big Three were concerned, Adenauer single-mindedly set out to demonstrate to West Germany's former enemies that the Federal Republic would become and remain their loyal friend. The chancellor's critics denounced his efforts to obtain the trust of the Western Allies as excessively obsequious (Kurt Schumacher called him "chancellor of the Allies" during a foreign policy debate in the Bundestag in November 1949), but Adenauer was convinced that as the occupying powers recognized West Germany's unflinching support for the Western position in the Cold War, they would relinquish their remaining controls piece by piece.

In essence Adenauer was right, although the process was slow and the price high. A major breakthrough came with the General Treaty (*Generalvertrag*) of 1952. Under this arrangement, the Western Allies agreed formally to abolish major parts of the Occupation Statute of 1949, although they still retained "supreme power" in Germany. They also promised to defend West Germany and West Berlin if attacked. But, in return for West Germany's inclusion in the Western defense perimeter, the Adenauer government yielded to American pressure and agreed to reestablish armed forces in West Germany. The Social Democrats severely criticized the General Treaty, objecting particularly to the remilitarization of the Federal Republic.

The fierce battles between government and opposition over West Germany's foreign policy in the early Adenauer years were reminiscent of the lack of national consensus during the Weimar years, but by the mid-1950s the apparent success of Adenauer's strategy had taken much of the steam out of the opposition. Disagreements on details remained, of course, but since about 1954, West Germany has enjoyed a large measure of bipartisan consensus on major foreign policy goals.

Another milestone in the Federal Republic's quest for recognition as an equal in the Western concert of powers was the 1954 Germany Treaty (*Deutschlandvertrag*). Under this agreement, West Germany became a formally sovereign nation, able to conduct its own foreign policy. The Western Allies also recognized the Federal Republic as the sole representative of the German people, thereby supporting the FRG's contention that there was only one legitimate German state. Allied troops remained stationed on German soil, but as allies and friends, not occupiers.

Adenauer and his supporters looked on the Germany Treaty as a major setback to Russian efforts toward gaining international recognition for the GDR and luring West Germany to accept unification under Russian hegemony. Throughout the Adenauer years, the Russians consistently argued that the only way to restore German unity was through the demilitarization of the country and mutual recognition of both German states. Adenauer as well as the two U.S. secretaries of state in the 1950s, Dean Acheson and John Foster Dulles, rejected this scenario out of hand. For a time, the Social Democrats seemed willing to consider the Russian proposals. They offered to accept Germany's permanent demilitarization if the Soviets consented to free elections in East and West Germany. The Russians, however, sent conflicting messages. On the one hand, in 1951 and 1952 they launched a series of diplomatic initiatives that seemed to hold out the prospect of free all-German elections, and in 1955 the Soviets set a precedent by agreeing to remove all foreign troops from Austria provided that this country remained permanently neutral and demilitarized. On the other hand, the Russians also forced the pace of Stalinization in East Germany, thereby making a united, democratic Germany less likely.

In 1955, after the Western Allies and Adenauer had repeatedly rejected Soviet overtures, and the Germany Treaty had been signed, the Soviets asserted their "two-Germanies" doctrine. They forced the West German government to open diplomatic relations with the Soviet Union, largely by threatening to refuse to release the thousands of German POWs who were still held in Russia. The Soviets became the first power to send ambassadors to East Berlin and Bonn, thereby underscoring their contention that there were two legitimate German states.

The West Germans were clearly fearful of the diplomatic precedent created by the exchange of Soviet and West German ambassadors. The Adenauer government attempted to counter any spread of the dual-state theory with the Hallstein Doctrine. (Walter Hallstein was the state secretary of the West German foreign ministry from 1951 to 1958 and later president of the European Common Market.) Under this policy, West Germany announced that it would refuse to establish or break off diplomatic relations with any nation, except for the Soviet Union, that simultaneously recognized East and West Germany. With the support of the United States, and by using its impressive economic strength to pressure developing countries, West Germany for some years succeeded in enforcing the Hallstein Doctrine. The GDR's diplomatic ties were limited to the communist regimes of Eastern Europe and Asia.

While the Adenauer cabinets were erecting diplomatic barriers against the east, they sought by every means possible to hasten the integration of the Federal Republic into the fabric of the Western Alliance. An important part of this effort was West Germany's willingness to supply military forces for the defense of Western Europe. Such plans were not uncontroversial. In Germany a grassroots campaign against rearmament (it adopted as its slogan *Ohne Mich!* ["Not with me!"]) attracted thousands to its rallies. Among Germany's neighbors especially the French remained understandably suspicious of a German military establishment only a few years after the end of World War II.

In the face of these objections, the European Defense Community (EDC) seemed ideally suited to meet the dual objectives of rebuilding the German army while laying to rest French fears of independent German military action. The terms of the EDC, negotiated at the same time as the General Treaty of 1952, provided for an integrated Western European army. Troops from six Western European countries—France, Italy, West

Germany, and the three Benelux countries—would be removed from the control of their national general staffs and deployed under an international command composed of officers from the six countries. In effect, then, any West German army would become a military force under international control.

The EDC was politically controversial in Germany, but the Bundestag eventually ratified the treaty and passed the necessary amendments to the Basic Law, removing the constitutional prohibitions against a West German military establishment. In August 1954, however, the French National Assembly defeated the EDC concept, ending the effort to create an integrated European military force. With the EDC jettisoned, in 1955 West Germany became a full member of the North Atlantic Treaty Organization (NATO), the option which the United States had always preferred. Two years later, conscription was reintroduced in West Germany, and by the early 1960s Germany's full contingent of 500,000 men, divided into twelve divisions, had been turned over to the NATO command.

Paralleling their talks on the abortive EDC treaty, the six countries also negotiated a series of agreements that would eventually lead to the European Economic Community (EEC). Spearheaded by the French foreign minister, Robert Schuman, "the Six" agreed to establish the European Coal and Steel Community (ECSC). (Schuman, an Alsatian, had very personal reasons for wishing to reduce Franco-German animosity: He fought on the German side during World War I, when Alsace was part of the German Reich, and for the Free French during World War II.) The ECSC abolished tariffs and created a common market for coal and steel products among the six countries. Even more important, control of trade and manufacturing levels of these products was turned over to an international High Authority whose judgment superseded national decision-making bodies.

The ECSC was the forerunner of the Treaty of Rome, which in 1957 established the EEC. This time "the Six" agreed to a whole series of cooperative agreements, ranging from tariff reductions to conducting joint research into the peaceful uses of atomic energy. At the heart of the Treaty of Rome was a commitment to a timetable for tariff reductions until all levies among the six countries were abolished. In addition, the partners established a Common Agricultural Policy (CAP) providing for massive subsidies to Europe's farmers. As in the case of the ECSC, the administration of the Common Market was vested in a multinational European Commission, headquartered in Brussels, Belgium.

The Treaty of Rome was a genuine compromise. West Germany benefited politically by being reaccepted as an equal in the European family of nations and economically because Germany's industry, the strongest and most advanced among the six countries, was the primary beneficiary of the agreement to abolish tariffs among the six partners. The CAP, however, was most beneficial to France with its large number of small farms. The FRG contributed the largest share of the EEC's fund for farm subsidies.

West Germany's accommodation on the CAP as well as its general "good citizenship" in Europe were instrumental in putting Franco-German relations on a new footing. A major symbol of the new era of good feelings was the return of the Saar to German control. Recall that in 1945 France had severed this territory, German in population and culture, from Germany and placed it under French economic and political control. As they had after World War I, the French endorsed a plan to "Europeanize" the Saar by placing it under the administration of the Council of Europe in 1955. Adenauer accepted the scheme as part of the price Germany had to pay for better Franco-German relations, but the people of the Saar overwhelmingly defeated the proposal in a plebiscite. France in turn proved a gracious loser. The French obtained some economic concessions in the Saar, but politically the territory again became part of Germany.

The treaties leading to Western European integration as well as the return of the Saar were negotiated with the leaders of the

French Fourth Republic. An entirely new situation arose in 1958 with Charles de Gaulle's return to power in France as president of the Fifth Republic. It was a pleasant surprise to the Germans that de Gaulle was no longer the vindictive Free French leader but anxious to continue along the road to Franco-German rapprochement. De Gaulle and Adenauer got along particularly well.

The French president made a triumphant tour of West Germany, and the picture of the two leaders praying side by side in France at the Reims cathedral symbolized the new era of Franco-German friendship around the world. The relationship culminated in 1963 with the signing of a mutual consultation treaty. Since then the leaders of West Germany and France have held

A photo from the 1963 visit of the French president Charles de Gaulle to Germany. The picture shows de Gaulle in the foreground on the left and Konrad Adenauer on the right. De Gaulle was received by enthusiastic crowds everywhere he went. The signs held aloft read (from left to right): "Long live France, long live the united Europe" [in French], "We want the European federal state" [in German], "Long live de Gaulle" [in French]. (Source: Courtesy of De Agostini Editore Picture Library.)

regular summit meetings twice a year to discuss questions of mutual interest.

The balance sheet of the foreign relations during the Adenauer era is mixed. Franco-German rapprochement, the economic and political integration of Western Europe, and the Federal Republic's return as a respected member of the family of nations were obviously positive items on the ledger. These were goals that had eluded the leaders of the Weimar Republic. But there were also some significant setbacks. Most important was the failure of the strategy for German reunification. Relying on the West's strength and determination to force the Soviets out of East Germany clearly did not work. It remains an open question if at this time the Russians would have permitted a democratic and united, although neutral and demilitarized, Germany, but neither the West Germans nor the Western Allies seriously explored this possibility.

In 1963 it had also become obvious that Adenauer's policy of attempting to deny the GDR's existence was a failure. In fact, the inherent dangers of that policy became obvious when at the end of 1958 the Russian leader Nikita Khrushchev initiated the Berlin crisis that was to culminate in the building of the Berlin Wall (see pp. 310–11). By the end of the Adenauer era, the existence of the GDR seemed secure while the Hallstein Doctrine was becoming threadbare. The countries of Western Europe and the United States still supported West Germany's effort to isolate the GDR, but the rapidly multiplying number of governments of developing countries had little interest in these intra-German quarrels, and they saw no reason why they should not have diplomatic relations with both Germanies. In 1957 Yugoslavia became the first nonaligned country to recognize East Germany. The Federal Republic immediately invoked the Hallstein Doctrine and severed diplomatic relations with Yugoslavia, but it was clear even then that the Hallstein Doctrine would not for long prevent other countries from following Yugoslavia's example.

Even rapprochement with France had its negative side. The price for de Gaulle's friendship was high. To be sure, the French leader had a sincere interest in better Franco-German relations, but he was also seeking German support for his policy of freeing Western Europe from what he regarded as the excessive control by the Americans and the British. The West Germans, for whom friendship with the United States was the bedrock of any foreign policy, had considerable difficulty reconciling the goal of Franco-German friendship with maintaining a special relationship to the Anglo-Saxon powers. West Germany could not, for example, prevent de Gaulle's unilateral veto in January 1963, which blocked Great Britain's application for membership in the Common Market. By the time Adenauer reluctantly resigned from office, the solidarity of the Western Alliance on which he had built his foreign policies was showing serious cracks.

THE CHANGING OF THE GUARD, 1963–1974

When Ludwig Erhard became chancellor in October 1963, he did not anticipate troubled times ahead, although in fact Adenauer had bequeathed him a difficult legacy. The departure of the old chancellor left the CDU/CSU with a number of problems that would become magnified in the years ahead. The Christian Democrats were composed of many wings and factions. A strong leader like Adenauer had been able to prevent dissension and factionalism from getting out of hand, but Erhard did not possess these qualities. He had little interest in day-to-day party affairs, believing his personal popularity with the voters would enable him to remain aloof from partisan politics.

Without the integrative force of a strong national leader, the Christian Democrats became a coalition of "feudal fiefs" headed by territorial chieftains and leaders of various interest groups. This development in turn strengthened particularly the position of the Bavarian CSU in the Christian Democratic camp. In the course of the 1960s, the Bavarian CSU became the unchallenged political force in the state, regularly obtaining more than 50 percent of the popular vote cast in state and national elections. Unlike the decentralized CDU, however, the Bavarian CSU was firmly controlled by its chairman, Franz Joseph Strauss. The Bavarian leader gained a strong favorite-son position, which he used effectively to influence the outcome of the power struggles in the CDU by backing one or another of the CDU's factional leaders.

Erhard's strength was also undermined by the growing power of the Social Democratic opposition. The SPD gathered the political fruits of the personnel and ideological changes that the party had introduced since the mid-1950s. The party was now led by a group of younger and more dynamic leaders who presented a marked contrast to the aging chiefs of the CDU. Figures like Willy Brandt, who became party chairman after Erich Ollenhauer's death in 1963, and Helmut Schmidt, the party's dynamic parliamentary leader after 1966, were attractive spokespersons for the concerns of the postwar generation of German voters. For the first time in its century-long history, the SPD, too, developed into a genuine *Volkspartei*. The social profile of the party's membership also changed. In 1960, 55.7 percent of the SPD's members were blue-collar workers and only 21.2 percent were salaried employees or civil servants, but at the end of the decade the blue-collar share had dropped to 39.6 percent while the white-collar proportion had risen to 33.6 percent.

True, younger and more educated members and voters presented the SPD with problems as well as votes. Many in the new generation of Social Democrats demanded far-reaching social reforms that would lead to a new "quality of life." Especially among the university-educated members, most of whom joined the party after the collapse of the student movements in 1968–1969 (see pp. 281–82), there was also a resurgence of interest in Marxist ideological positions. By 1973 some 25 percent of the party's executive committee described themselves as "leftists."

The Liberals undoubtedly experienced the most radical changes among the major parties. In fact, the FDP almost became a new party. Increasingly frustrated by their inability to secure a stable bloc of voters on the right side of the political spectrum, the Liberals sought an opening to the left. The shift began in 1966 with an agreement between the FDP and the SPD to form a coalition in Germany's largest state, North Rhine-Westphalia. Two years later, there was a change in the party's leadership. Delegates at the FDP's annual convention elected Walter Scheel as the party's national chairman. Scheel, who had strongly supported an FDP-SPD coalition in North Rhine-Westphalia, replaced Erich Mende, a staunch right-wing Liberal and nationalist. (Mende liked to remind listeners that in World War II he had been awarded the Knight's Cross, the Wehrmacht's highest decoration for valor.)

The political consequences of the Liberals' experiment were mixed. The party did gain a portion of the new Mittelstand vote, especially among middle-level executives and professionals. But there was a price to pay. The FDP lost most of its traditional support among the old Mittelstand strata, and its farm vote all but disappeared. In 1953, 15 percent of Germany's farmers voted Liberal; in 1972 that figure had sunk to 2 percent. In general, the party's own polls concluded only 25 percent of those who had voted FDP in 1965 (when the party was still allied to the CDU) cast their ballots for the Liberals in 1969. The FDP's political shift had essentially succeeded in exchanging one set of supporters for another, rather than gaining new members and voters.

The fear of falling below the 5 percent mark remained acute. In 1970, a year after the Liberals had become the SPD's partner in a national coalition (see pp. 283–84), the FDP's popular vote dropped to less than 5 percent in state elections in Lower Saxony and the Saar. In North Rhine-Westphalia the FDP cleared the barrier only with the help of voters "borrowed" from its new ally, the SPD. The practice of borrowing and lending votes, which is really a form of ticket splitting, became increasingly common in elections of the 1960s and 1970s. Because delegates to the national and state legislatures are elected both from single-member districts and on the basis of proportional representation, German voters always cast two ballots: one to indicate the choice for representative in the single-member district and a second to designate the party list from which the other half of the members of the legislatures will be chosen. In close national contests, some voters developed the habit of casting their first ballot for the direct candidate of their own party and their second ballot for the party that had indicated it would form a coalition with their "home" party. The political significance of "borrowing" was well illustrated in the 1972 federal elections. The FDP's share of the popular vote rose from 5.8 to 8.4 percent, and later analyses showed that many SPD voters had "lent" their second ballots to the Liberals.

The 1960s brought not only changes for the major parties but also a seeming rebirth of political extremism. After the government quietly dropped its prohibition against communist organizations, the German Communist Party (*Deutsche Kommunistische Partei*—DKP) was founded in September 1968. The DKP paid lip service to parliamentary democracy to stay within the bounds prescribed by the Basic Law, but the party was really a West German branch of the East German SED from whom it received its political directives and almost all of its financial support. Largely because of this tie, the DKP was not very successful. In 1969 it had only twenty thousand members, and its share of the national vote was 0.6 percent.

Although the Communists remained an unimportant splinter group, the extreme right for a time appeared to present a graver threat. By 1961 neo-Nazism had sunk into political oblivion. However, in 1964 a leader emerged to breathe new life into the movement. Adolf von Thadden was a member of the DRP, but instead of attempting to resurrect the moribund DRP, Thadden and his allies dissolved the group and founded a new political organization, the National Democratic Party (*Nationaldemokratische Partei Deutschlands*—NPD).

The party was (and is) careful not to advocate the overthrow of West Germany's constitutional system, but both the NPD's program and its tactics leave little doubt that the party continues the traditions of the German extreme right. Chauvinism ("We have a right to all of Germany [including the areas east of the Oder-Neisse line]!"), xenophobia ("Throw out all foreigners!"), and attempts to whitewash Nazi crimes and criminals justify labeling the NPD as "neo-Nazi." (More on the activities and problems of this party in the 1990s in Chapter 11.)

Political extremism in Germany has always benefited from adverse economic conditions, and the NPD had the good fortune to make its appearance just as West Germany experienced its first serious postwar recession. The NPD quickly gained representation in a number of state legislatures, receiving 8 percent of the popular vote in the 1966 state elections in Hessen and Bavaria. Two years later, it reached 10 percent in Baden-Württemberg. A number of analysts were uncomfortably reminded of the earlier rise of the Nazis, particularly because the NPD's support was strongest in areas that had also been early pockets of strength for the old Nazis. At the height of its popularity, more than a million voters cast their ballots for the NPD in state and local elections. Thadden confidently predicted that fifty NPD delegates would sit in the Bundestag after the 1969 federal elections.

Fortunately, the NPD's leader turned out to be a poor political prophet. The party did not clear the 5 percent hurdle in 1969; it received only 4.3 percent of the national vote. The setback, along with the rapid economic recovery, deflated the acute threat of rightist extremism. The NPD fell victim to factional infighting and disintegrated rapidly. In the Bundestag election of 1983, its share of the popular vote was only 0.2 percent.

The challenges to parliamentary democracy and the recession of 1966–1967 (see p. 284) formed the background for the creation of the Federal Republic's first bipartisan government, a "grand coalition" composed of the

CDU/CSU and the SPD. Because of the chancellor's inability to lead the CDU effectively, the Erhard government was in trouble almost from the start. Its fate was sealed when the "father of the economic miracle" was unable to cope with the recession. As Erhard struggled unsuccessfully to gain control of the situation, behind the scenes leaders of the CDU/CSU and the SPD were discussing the formation of a bipartisan government. The new cabinet took office at the end of November 1966. Each partner had its own reasons for forming the unusual coalition. The CDU/CSU was anxious to saddle the SPD with part of the responsibility for dealing with the recession; the SPD, which had not been part of a federal government since March 1930, wanted to show that it could govern responsibly before facing the voters in the next election.

As the stronger party, the CDU/CSU was to provide the chancellor in the bipartisan government. Two men were seriously considered: Gerhard Schröder, one of the leaders of the CDU's Protestant wing and West Germany's foreign minister since 1961, and Kurt-Georg Kiesinger, the prime minister of the state of Baden-Württemberg. The choice between the two candidates was determined to a large extent by Franz Josef Strauss, and the Bavarian leader favored Kiesinger. The post of vice-chancellor and foreign minister fell to Willy Brandt as the leader of the SPD. The Social Democrats also provided the economics minister—at least in the short run the most important member of the cabinet— Karl Schiller, a young economics professor.

The "grand coalition" was in many ways a watershed in the postwar development of West Germany. Its leaders personified a nation divided that had come together again. Kiesinger, as a young and ambitious career diplomat, had joined the Nazi Party in 1933. During the Third Reich, he remained a nominal party member while working in the propaganda section of the foreign ministry. Willy Brandt, in contrast, had had to flee Nazi Germany as a teenager, and during World War II he had been active against Nazism while in exile in Norway and Sweden.

The new government succeeded in bringing West Germany out of the recession, but it was by no means all smooth sailing for the grand coalition. The two leaders, Kiesinger and Brandt, did not work well together. They had quite different personalities, and Brandt resented what he regarded as Kiesinger's attempt to run the foreign ministry from the chancellor's office. More important, the formation of the grand coalition essentially suspended the normal processes of parliamentary democracy, which depend on the give-and-take between government and a constructive but vigorous opposition. With both SPD and CDU/CSU backing the cabinet, the FDP, which had obtained less than 10 percent of the vote in 1965, was not able to act as an effective opposition in the Bundestag. It was particularly unfortunate that this development came at a time when a new generation of Germans born in the years immediately after World War II reached political maturity. Some of them formed what they called the "extraparliamentary opposition" (APO), a concept that had no constitutional basis in a parliamentary democracy.

It must be remembered that the 1960s were a time of worldwide turmoil. The American protest movement against the Vietnam War, French student revolts, and the activities of the West German APO were all symptoms of a vague, but passionate, search for a new lifestyle and a fundamental change of consciousness. The age of materialism, which in the eyes of young Europeans and Americans had characterized the decade of the 1950s, was to end as a new generation of leaders took charge. One author claims that 1968 marked Germany's transition from modernity to postmodernity.

The APO—in reality a few thousand activist university students—exploded on the German scene on June 2, 1967. Students from the Free University in West Berlin had organized a large demonstration to protest a visit by the then shah of Iran to the city. The demonstration erupted into violence and, as a result of clashes between demonstrators and police, one student, Benno Ohnesorg, was killed. (In 2009 it was revealed that the policeman who killed Ohnesorg, Karl Heinz Kurras, was a secret member of the East German SED and an informant for the GDR's security service, although there is no evidence that the Stasi had a hand in the shooting of Ohnesorg). The tragedy polarized the country. In the next few weeks, demonstrations in virtually all university towns protested against "police brutality" at home and the "fascist" American war in Vietnam. At the same time the right wing of the CDU/CSU called for effective measures to deal with the "young hoodlums."

The newspapers owned by West Germany's largest publisher, Axel Springer, were particularly vociferous in their editorial support of demands for the effective suppression of student protest. Springer's papers were read by millions daily. The tabloid *Bild* ["Picture"] alone had (and has) a circulation of more than 6 million. Day after day Springer's papers portrayed the student activists as agents of international communism whose real aim was to extend Moscow's rule to West Germany. This was certainly not true for most of the APO, although the East Germans did subsidize some antigovernment publications. The monthly *konkret* ("concrete"), for example, a successful mixture of soft pornography and leftist politics with a large circulation among high school and university students, received some 2 million deutsche marks in laundered funds from East German sources between 1965 and 1968. Not surprisingly, the East Germans' financial aid came with constraining strings: The Communists controlled *konkret*'s editorial content from East Berlin.

The polarization of the country escalated. In April 1968 the most popular APO leader, Rudi Dutschke, was shot and severely wounded by Josef Bachmann, a self-proclaimed nationalist and anticommunist. Bachmann had clear ties to the neo-Nazi scene, although this connection did not become known until 2009. The immediate reaction was a new wave of demonstrations all over Germany. Some of those demonstrating attacked and burned some printing plants and editorial offices of the Springer press. Fringe groups in the APO went still further.

The firebombing of a Frankfurt department store was a prelude to the terrorist activities that were to plague West Germany in the mid-1970s (see pp. 292–93).

The cabinet of the grand coalition was remarkably ineffective in dealing with the signs of unrest. Kiesinger had trouble finding the right words to communicate with the young generation of Germans, and Strauss was one of the leaders in the camp of hard-liners. In May 1968 the Bundestag passed a package of Emergency Laws that enlarged the powers of the police in dealing with demonstrations and significantly increased the speed with which leaders of violent demonstrations could be brought to justice.

The Emergency Laws, which were under consideration for more than a decade and not directly related to the APO's activities, pleased the hard-liners, but they did little to alleviate the malaise that had led to the demonstrations in the first place. However, the scheduled election of a new federal president in May 1969 provided an opportunity to show the APO that the establishment was mindful of the changing times. The West German federal president is elected every five years; since 1949 all of West Germany's presidents had been either Liberals or Christian Democrats. In 1969 the *Bundesversammlung*—the assembly that elects the president is composed of all members of the Bundestag, and an equal number of delegates from the state legislatures—had the same political makeup as the Bundestag. The largest bloc of delegates came from the CDU/CSU, but the Social Democrats and Liberals together formed a majority.

The two candidates in 1969 were Gerhard Schröder (CDU) and Gustav Heinemann (SPD). Schröder was well known, respected, and conservative; Heinemann was a political maverick. Originally a Christian Democrat, he had served in the first Adenauer cabinet as minister of the interior. He resigned in 1950 to protest Adenauer's rearmament plans. Eventually Heinemann joined the SPD. In the grand coalition cabinet he was minister of justice, a position from which he repeatedly expressed his understanding of the APO's concerns. The election of Gustav Heinemann, then, would be seen as a breath of fresh air in the rather frozen tableau of West German politics. Walter Scheel, the FDP's new leader, persuaded his party to cast its votes for Heinemann as part of the Liberals' opening to the left, and the Social Democratic candidate was elected.

As it happened, the 1969 Bundestag campaign was scheduled for September, only a few months after the presidential election. The Christian Democrats' attempted to "pass the NPD on the right," portraying themselves as the guardian of national unity and law and order. The SPD appealed to the voters as a progressive, reform-minded party whose dynamic minister of economics had been primarily responsible for bringing Germany out of the recession. The FDP, finally, sought to gain the benefits of not having participated in the government. It pictured itself as a new young party unencumbered with the failures of the grand coalition.

The results were yet more "massing at the center," although in practice the relatively minor shifts in voter sentiment had a profound impact. The CDU/CSU's share of the popular vote dropped slightly, from 47.6 to 46.1 percent. The SPD did somewhat better, increasing its share from 39.3 to 42.7 percent. The pollsters attributed the Social Democrats' success to the charismatic image of Karl Schiller and the effect of "comrade momentum," that is to say, the snowballing effect of the voters' continued enchantment with the SPD's new image. The FDP vote was a severe disappointment to its new leaders. The Liberals' share of the popular vote went from 9.5 to 5.8 percent.

Because the CDU/CSU remained the strongest party in the legislature, Kurt Georg Kiesinger confidently expected that he would lead a new government with the now-contrite Liberals as junior partners. As soon as it became clear, however, that Social Democrats and Free Democrats together would have a very small majority in the new Bundestag (it turned out to be a margin of 6 out of 529), Brandt called Scheel with an offer to form a coalition agreement. The Liberal leader accepted immediately.

The FDP-SPD coalition was less of a marriage of political opposites than it might appear at first. True, the two parties were far apart on most economic issues. The Liberals had traditionally taken positions in favor of free enterprise and against powerful unions, whereas the Social Democrats were historically the party of labor. But the new partners agreed on the need for new foreign policy initiatives, and on the domestic scene they favored judicial and educational reforms.

On October 21, 1969, Willy Brandt became federal chancellor—the first freely elected Social Democrat head of government since March 1930. The members of the Social-Liberal cabinet, as it was called, included some quite distinguished figures. Walter Scheel turned out to be an effective foreign minister. Karl Schiller continued as economics minister. Helmut Schmidt, another of the rising young Social Democrats, switched from chairing the SPD's Bundestag caucus to serving as the first Social Democratic minister of defense since 1920. Hans-Dietrich Genscher, the deputy chairman of the FDP, headed the interior ministry.

The impact of the Social-Liberal coalition on West Germany's political and social life was profound. Determined to "dare more democracy," as Willy Brandt put it, the cabinet pushed through a reform program that helped create a more open, less tradition-bound society, and in the area of foreign policy the *Ostpolitik* succeeded in putting West Germany's relations with the Soviet Union and Eastern Europe on a new footing (see p. 285ff).

In the 1972 election the voters gave the FDP-SPD coalition an overwhelming victory. For the first time since 1949, SPD and CDU/CSU ran almost neck to neck: 45.8 percent for the CDU/CSU, 44.8 percent for the SPD. The Liberals' gamble also paid off; their share of the popular vote rose to 8.4 percent.

The triumph came just before the fall. Less than two years later, Willy Brandt left office. In April 1974 West German counterintelligence exposed one of Brandt's personal assistants,

Günter Guillaume, as an East German spy. GDR agents in West Germany had long been a serious problem. It was inevitable that East Germany's State Security Service would be able to hide a number of spies and communist agents among the 3 million refugees who had fled communist East Germany since 1949. Guillaume was a "mole" of this type. The agent and his wife came to West Germany as ostensible refugees in 1956. Guillaume soon became active in Social Democratic politics, and in 1970 he joined the chancellor's office. When Guillaume's role as a longtime agent was revealed, Brandt felt that his own position was so compromised that he could not continue as head of the government. In May 1974 he resigned as chancellor; Helmut Schmidt became his successor.

The Weakening "Economic Miracle"

In the second half of the 1960s, West Germany's economy would be buffeted by challenges and problems. In 1964, Erhard's first full year in office, all signs pointed to continued growth and prosperity. Industrial production was up by 8 percent; wages and salaries increased by 8.5 percent. Inflation and unemployment were virtually nonexistent. A year later, the Federal Republic went into a serious recession.

There were a number of reasons for the downturn of 1965, not all of them German made. The mid-1960s saw the beginnings of a worldwide inflationary wave, and the West German economy, with its high dependence on exports, was particularly sensitive to inflationary pressures in the world market. Still, some of the difficulties were undoubtedly the Germans' own responsibility. The earlier boom had stimulated overinvestment while hiding structural dislocations such as unemployment among coal miners, demographic changes, and the chronic inefficiency of West German agriculture. The sustained growth rates had enabled the country to institute massive retraining and subsidy programs in the 1950s and early 1960s, but the costs were high. In fact, increasingly large expenditures

for social services and government subsidies to various interest groups were a primary cause of the recession in the mid-1960s.

When the economy began to slow down, the Erhard government was faced with a dilemma. Ever since the runaway inflation of the 1920s, Germans have been particularly sensitive about uncontrolled government spending. In an attempt to head off the political and economic consequences of this psychology, the government took immediate steps to slash the federal budget, but the short-term effect was to deepen the recession. For the first time since 1955, unemployment became a significant problem.

Led by the economics minister, Karl Schiller, the grand coalition attacked the recession with a bevy of neo-Keynesian measures. The 1967 budget was balanced partly by tapping the balance-of-payment reserves accumulated in the boom years of the 1950s by the German Federal Bank but also by raising taxes. Some of these taxes came in the form of surcharges on higher incomes, but in order not to cut off private investment, the bulk of the new taxes fell on consumers. Specifically, the value-added tax (VAT), a national sales tax whose proceeds are divided between the federal government and the states, was raised to 11 percent. Continuing the practices of "democratic corporatism," Schiller organized the "concerted action," a series of summit meetings between the leaders of labor and management, presided over by Schiller himself. The government's crisis management was successful. By the fall of 1968 the unemployment rate had fallen to 1 percent, and the economy was again growing at an annual rate of 7.3 percent.

Except for the 1966–1967 recession, the economy, until 1974, faced more potential than actual dangers. Some of these would cause serious difficulties for the Social-Liberal coalition in the latter 1970s and 1980s, but until then both money and resources seemed plentiful. There was a chronic labor shortage, especially after the building of the Berlin Wall cut off the stream of refugees from the GDR, but millions of foreign "guest workers," with Turkey supplying the largest contingent, eased the problem. The massive influx of foreigners, in turn, caused some major social problems (see pp. 296–97), but these lay in the future. For the moment, West Germany's booming export industry enabled the government to continue a broadly based social welfare program. The principle of "dynamicized pensions," which had been established in the 1950s, meant that increases in social security payments continued to match the average wage increases of the active workforce. Farm subsidies, in part mandated by the Common Market's CAP, continued to take up a large portion of the federal budget.

The Brandt-Scheel government also spent massive sums on efforts to improve the infrastructure of the society. These included a vast expansion of the network of Autobahnen, labor retraining programs (many earmarked for the by-now chronically depressed coal-mining industry), and federal help to construct a whole series of new universities and other institutions of higher learning. Many of these projects would later be criticized as too expensive, but given the continuing growth rates and the obvious need for preparing for structural changes in the West German economy, there was some logic behind the government's decisions. The neo-Keynesians who made economic decisions in the years 1963–1974 were convinced that as the tertiary sector of the economy became increasingly important, the country's physical and especially its educational infrastructure had to keep pace.

Ostpolitik

The decade between Erhard and Schmidt also saw some dramatic developments in the area of foreign relations. Instead of concentrating almost exclusively on relations with the United States and Western Europe, the FRG's new leaders inaugurated the *Ostpolitik* ("Eastern policy") in an effort to improve West Germany's dealings with the Soviet Union and its European satellites, including the GDR.

The contours of the Cold War confrontation softened as times and leaders changed. In the United States, a new generation of leaders headed by John F. Kennedy saw Asia, and specifically Vietnam, rather than Europe and the GDR, as the pivot of East–West relations. On the other side of the Iron Curtain, the post-Stalin leaders of the Soviet Union made it clear that they would not sit idly by while the United States and West Germany continued to refuse to acknowledge the "postwar realities" in Europe. Nikita Khrushchev and his successor, Leonid Brezhnev, were determined to see that West Germany acknowledged it had no claim to the areas east of the Oder-Neisse Line, and that there were now two separate and independent states on German soil. The lever was not difficult to find. Ever since 1958, the Soviet Union had periodically reminded the West Germans that Russia held a trump card in this test of wills: The Soviet Union could create a Berlin crisis any time it wished.

This background of a world in flux led to a division of views in the West German foreign policy establishment. Since the founding of the FRG, all responsible leaders in West Germany had agreed that the country was not and did not wish to be a Great Power pursuing a foreign policy independent of its allies. This consensus did not, however, prevent considerable differences of opinion over the arranging of priorities, particularly in the 1960s. To begin with there were the "Atlanticists" who, much like Adenauer, felt German–American relations were the bedrock of West Germany's security. They argued for close support of the American positions even if this meant some cooling in Franco-German relations. A second group, the "German Gaullists," whose most prominent spokesman was Franz Josef Strauss, sharply disagreed. They argued that de Gaulle was right: European (and hence German) interests were not necessarily the same as those of the United States; Europe needed to follow its own priorities, including the development of a nuclear strike force that would be under European rather than American control.

Both the "Atlanticists" and the "German Gaullists" were minorities in the German foreign policy establishment. Most decision makers counted themselves among the "new realists." This third group, which certainly included Brandt and Scheel, the leaders of the Social-Liberal coalition, did not reject the FRG's Western orientation. On the contrary, they felt it was precisely West Germany's unquestioned allegiance to the Western camp that would enable it to test the possibility of détente with the Soviet Union and the countries of Eastern Europe. The overall objective of the Ostpolitik was to achieve improved East–West relations, create politico-economic stability for West Berlin, and increase "humanitarian" contacts between East and West Germans. In return, the West Germans would be willing to give up the Hallstein Doctrine and accept Russia's position that the post-1945 boundary changes in Eastern Europe could not be altered without the Soviet Union's agreement.

The Ostpolitik did not come into being overnight. In the Erhard cabinet, Foreign Minister Gerhard Schröder had followed a policy of "small steps" to bring about a thaw in relations between the Soviet bloc and West Germany. Schröder's initiatives were severely limited, however, because the right wing of the CDU/CSU regarded all such efforts with deep suspicion. In the FDP-SPD government, these hindrances did not exist. Willy Brandt and Walter Scheel worked closely together to advance the cause of the Ostpolitik. In addition, a major force behind the scenes was Egon Bahr, a former Thuringian who had been Brandt's confidential adviser since the chancellor's days as mayor of West Berlin.

Bahr had been "thinking the unthinkable" for some years. He recognized the Soviet Union's deep-seated fears of a reunited and remilitarized Germany. He felt that Russia's legitimate security demands could be met by acknowledging the existence of Russian control over Eastern Europe and East Germany. In a little-noticed speech in 1963, he suggested it was futile to expect the GDR or the Soviet Union to change their repres-

sive character as a result of pressure from the West. "Change resulting from East and West drawing together" (*Wandel durch Annäherung*) was far more likely.

When the Social-Liberal coalition assumed office, the evidence that the Soviet Union was not about to be dislodged from Central Europe had just been strengthened. In August 1968 Warsaw Pact troops had invaded Czechoslovakia to oust the communist, but independently minded, Dubšek government. American inaction confirmed once again, as had the similar attitude of the United States at the time of the building of the Berlin Wall, that the leader of the West was not prepared to use force to push back the Soviet empire in Europe.

The Ostpolitik was a process and a goal whose concrete results were a series of bilateral agreements between West Germany, the Soviet Union, the communist regimes of Eastern Europe, and finally the GDR. For both prestige and practical reasons, the negotiations began with the Soviet Union. In January 1970 Egon Bahr began meeting with the Russian foreign minister Andrei Gromyko. Eight months later, a treaty was signed. The actual terms were not very dramatic. West Germany recognized the "map of Europe," which meant it acknowledged the German losses in World War II, including, of course, the annexation of part of East Prussia by the Soviet Union. The West Germans also agreed to support Moscow's call for an international conference, with both Germanies participating, to legitimize the status quo in Europe. More important from West Germany's point of view, the Soviet Union agreed to put pressure on the GDR to negotiate a modus vivendi with the Federal Republic.

In 1970 and 1971 analogous treaties were signed with Poland and what was then Czechoslovakia. Again, the FRG recognized the legitimacy of these countries' 1945 frontiers. In the case of Poland particularly, Brandt felt a dramatic symbolic gesture was needed to underscore the importance of the new relationship. He traveled to Warsaw to sign the treaty and while there knelt publicly before the Warsaw ghetto memorial.

The *Grundlagenvertrag* (Basic Treaty) with the GDR was the most difficult part of the Ostpolitik because the German–German agreement faced special difficulties. The East Germans wanted full and unequivocal recognition; the FRG was willing to acknowledge the GDR as a sovereign state with recognized boundaries but not as a foreign nation. To press their point, the West Germans insisted that part of the instruments of ratification for the Basic Treaty include a statement issued by the Bonn government that reiterated the right of all Germans to self-determination through free elections.

The problem of West Berlin was also a vexing aspect of the Ostpolitik. It came up in every one of the negotiations between West Germany and the East European countries, but because the Western Allies retained rights of sovereignty over the western sectors of the former German capital, any settlement of the Berlin problem required Four-Power talks. In 1972, after months of tough negotiations, the Big Four initialed an agreement. The Western Big Three recognized East Germany, in return for which the Russians and the GDR agreed to respect West Berlin's political, economic, and social ties to West Germany. In exchange for a diminished West German political presence in Berlin, the GDR agreed not to interfere with the land, water, and air access routes to West Berlin.

Was the Ostpolitik a success? World opinion certainly thought so. In 1971 Willy Brandt received the Nobel Peace Prize largely for his efforts to advance the cause of East–West détente. Brandt was the first German statesman since Stresemann to receive the prize. But the policy was also controversial. The opposition, led by the "German Gaullists," accused Brandt and Scheel of "giving away" German rights and lands while neglecting the Western alliance in favor of chasing after *ostpolitische* illusions. The CDU/CSU brought a case before the Federal Constitutional Court to test the constitutionality of the treaty with the GDR. The suit claimed recognition of the GDR violated the Basic Law, which postulated a single German Nation. Ruling on very narrow grounds, the court decided that the specific terms of the treaty between the FRG and the GDR did not violate the constitution.

Brandt and Scheel countered the criticism by pointing out that Adolf Hitler, not the Social-Liberal coalition, had lost the territories east of the Oder-Neisse Line and divided the German nation. The Ostpolitik merely ended a sterile policy that had attempted to deny the consequences of Hitler's aggression. As for neglecting the FRG's relations with Western Europe, the Liberals and Social Democrats noted that the coalition had been instrumental in inviting new members to join the EEC, and that the Ostpolitik had been successful precisely because the FRG remained firmly anchored in the Western alliance.

Today, almost four decades after the Ostpolitik treaties were signed, it is perhaps possible to assess the impact of the opening to the East without the emotional overtones of the 1960s and early 1970s. Certainly, West Germany gave up no territories as a result of the Ostpolitik. World War II permanently changed the map of Europe, whether the Federal Republic acknowledged this or not. As for the Hallstein Doctrine and the policy of isolating the GDR, by 1970 that strategy had clearly failed. However, West Germany's economy benefited from the Ostpolitik as the Federal Republic's trade with Eastern Europe and the Soviet Union increased in the wake of the treaties with these countries. (In fact, economics played a part in the Ostpolitik right from the start: The path to the successful treaty with the Soviets was smoothed by a 1.2 billion deutsche marks credit package that a consortium of West German banks extended to the Soviet Union.) The absence of recurrent Berlin crises helped that city and contributed to a lessening of Great Power tensions in Central Europe.

There remains, however, the question that particularly Timothy Garton Ash has raised: Did the Ostpolitik, by recognizing the legitimacy of the East German regime, delay the collapse of communism in the GDR? More specifically, Ash criticizes the West German political establishment and especially the Social Democrats, for neglecting the emerging dissident movements in the GDR and Eastern Europe in favor of better relations with the Communist rulers. Even with the benefit of hindsight, Ash's analysis is not entirely convincing. The various agreements made possible significantly increased people-to-people contacts between East and West Germans that undermined the SED's domestic legitimacy, even while the regime basked in the glow of enhanced international recognition.

CULTURE AND SOCIETY

As one would expect, West Germany's social and cultural history evolved in tandem with the profound changes in the country's political and economic life. In 1980 the Federal Republic's population profile was considerably different than it had been thirty years earlier when the FRG was founded. Not only had the population increased rapidly (from roughly 50 to 61.5 million), but the West Germans were also getting younger. Part of the reason was a baby boom that accompanied the return of prosperity. Then, too, many of the more than 3 million East Germans who fled to the West between 1949 and 1961 were under twenty-five years of age. Finally, toward the end of the 1960s when the labor shortage again became acute, West Germany actively recruited foreign guest workers, and many of these (some 3.4 million persons by 1974) were also young.

When the FRG's history began, these developments still lay in the future. During the Adenauer years, sociologists were more impressed with the evidence that in many ways little had changed in German society; signs of social and cultural continuity seemed to abound. Elite continuity was strong in many areas, including the leadership of both Catholic and Protestant churches, union officials, business executives, and university professors. Critics would later complain that after the abrupt end of de-Nazification, many high-ranking Nazi officials quickly found comfortable positions, a few in the government but most in private industry. Social mobility remained low because the educational system restricted upward mobility to a narrow stratum of the population. Throughout the decade of the 1950s, only 2 percent of the eighteen-year-olds went on to institutions of higher learning, and virtually all of them came from families in which the father (but not the mother) had graduated from a university. Until 1957 husbands still had control of their wives' checking accounts.

To be sure, this was not the whole story. As we saw earlier, young professionals who had learned their craft in Allied reeducation programs moved early into leadership positions in both the print and electronic media. Equally significant was the striking absence of some traditional sociopolitical elites from the West German scene. For the first time in modern German history, the Prussian landed aristocracy did not dominate the high ranks of the civil service or the military.

Socioeconomic developments during the Adenauer years created what the sociologist Helmut Schelsky has called a "leveled-off middle-class society." Portions of the traditional upper classes and underclasses were merged into a large middle class consisting of skilled blue- and white-collar workers and technicians. The rural population—and especially the number of independent farmers—declined precipitously. Along with urbanization (and "suburbanization") came secularization and increased leisure time. The average workweek declined from forty-eight hours and a six-day week in the 1950–1957 period to forty hours and a five-day week by the end of the decade. At the same time, the increasing number of women employed outside the home (this development was, in part, a result of the war-related absence of men) affected the traditional patterns of family relations.

Cultural life during the first part of the Adenauer era was still dominated by traditional forms—the print media, radio broadcasting, live theater, concerts, and movies. Especially the last three modes of entertainment tended toward the traditional and established classics rather than avant-garde productions. Average

Germans spent much of their leisure time as they always had, in organized club activities ranging from sports to "colonies" of weekend gardeners. As prosperity and leisure time increased, vacations and travel became a West German obsession. Growing numbers wanted to spend "the best weeks of the year" in foreign parts, notably the sun-drenched countries around the Mediterranean. The rapidly growing number of privately owned cars (by 1974 West Germany was close to the American level of "motorization") facilitated the mania for travel still further.

German mass tourism to the Mediterranean was criticized in numerous scholarly analyses for its superficiality and lack of real interaction with the foreign cultures. The picture of Lieschen from Wanne-Eickel's (a town in the Ruhr), the German equivalent of the "hick from Peoria," acting the boor on the beaches of Mallorca or in the Sistine Chapel in Rome became the butt of many jokes on the stand-up comedian circuit. Much of this criticism and derision had a point. German tourists, especially those on a two-week all-expense-paid group tour behaved pretty much as tourists in these circumstances do. But it is not true that vacation travel had no effect on postwar German society. It did, and nowhere was this more noticeable than Germany's culinary habits. The traditionally heavy and monotonous German cuisine was lightened and enlivened by Mediterranean spices and flavors. "Pasta asciutta" quickly became a children's favorite, and the saying often heard in Germany, "Let's go to the Italian around the corner" had a ring of literal truth. The landscape became (and remains) dotted with Italian restaurants. There was (and is) one on almost every corner.

Television became a mass medium at the end of the 1950s. The first German TV station began broadcasting in 1952, but as late as 1958 only some 2 million West German households had TV sets. Television programming and administration remained in the hands of the existing radio broadcasting networks. In 1957 the Adenauer government attempted to create a second, commercially financed television network alongside the ARD (*Arbeitsgemeinschaft der Rundfunkgesellschaften Deutschlands*—network of broadcasting stations of Germany), but the prime ministers of the Länder frustrated these efforts. The second channel finally established in 1961— it bears the pedestrian name *Zweites Deutsches Fernsehen* ("Second German Television"— ZDF)—is also a publicly financed network run by a politically "balanced" board of directors. It was only in the 1980s, with the availability of cable television, that a number of commercial channels began operating.

Much of West German mass culture reflected a desire for material comfort and value stability. There was little concern for searching questions about either the past or the present in the 1950s. Concern about "conquering the past" was, for the most part, limited to intellectual circles. A particularly noteworthy and successful effort was the establishment, in 1953, of the Institute for Contemporary History in Munich. Largely financed by public funds from the state of Bavaria, the institute has become a leading clearinghouse for research into the causes and consequences of modern German history, especially the Weimar and Nazi eras.

Most West Germans in the Adenauer era, however, wanted the symbols and symptoms of the *heile Welt* ("intact world")—that is, scenes of harmonious family life and uncomplicated narratives. The films of the 1950s abound with what one angry critic has called *süsser Kitsch* (sweet kitsch). Comedies starring established stars from the 1930s and 1940s like Heinz Rühmann and Hans Moser were very popular. *Heimatfilme* (homeland films) played to packed audiences. Usually set in bucolic villages in the Alps or the Black Forest as well as royal palaces, these films had beautiful scenes and rudimentary plots invariably centered on the perils of young love. A happy end was always part of the script. The largest number of films shown in West Germany, however, were American imports. In fact, the Adenauer years also saw a pronounced, if superficial, "Americanization" of German society. It was then that American popular music (especially jazz), films, and fast-food outlets began to proliferate in West Germany.

There is little doubt that most Germans were facile and materialistic, but there was already evidence of a growing generation gap. This was a period of widespread, if naive, idealism among the generation born after 1930. Enthusiasm for European unification ran high, and thousands spent at least some time in youth camps with compatriots from these developments were symptoms of a sincere effort to deal with a troubled past. The youthful initiatives are all the more remarkable in that they were undertaken with little guidance from the educational establishment. It was not really until the 1960s that attempts to deal honestly with the Nazi era became part of the regular school curriculum. Until then the "time of troubles" was largely ignored. The "generation of 1968" would accuse its parents of perpetuating a "conspiracy of silence" about the Nazi crimes that amounted to a "second guilt," as the essayist Ralph Giordano put it. There was considerable truth in this, although this particular statement was an exaggeration.

The 1960s and 1970s were a period of transition and conflict. The "rock-and-roll generation" that came of age in the 1960s was disdainful of the materialism and self-satisfaction of their elders. Within and outside the APO, young West Germans demanded increased chances for social mobility, concern for the ecology, and a greater emphasis on the "quality of life."

Gender relations were also put on a new footing; this was the beginning of a viable feminist movement in West Germany. Women demanded especially reforms of the country's restrictive abortion laws and educational and occupational quality. Some left-of-center political organizations, like the Greens (see later, pp. 293–94) adopted rules that instituted gender parity for all executive positions.

The "revolt of the young" did not bring about a cultural revolution as some of the leaders had hoped, but especially in the area of education important and permanent changes were introduced. Against the bitter opposition of the conservative establishment, twelve-year comprehensive schools (*Gesamtschulen*) were established in significant numbers to compete with the three-tiered system dominated by the *Gymnasien* and elite universities.

Student revolts and the vast expansion of the university system undermined the pattern of privilege that tenured professors had traditionally enjoyed in German higher education. Instead, more democratic—often hyperdemocratic—structures of collegial government were instituted. More important in the long run, the self-perpetuation of the educated elite was broken. The number of eighteen-year-olds who went on to institutions of higher learning rose from 2 percent in the 1950s to around 20 percent in the mid-1980s. In 1964 there were twenty-six universities and polytechnic schools in Germany; ten years later that number had increased to forty-nine. But here, too, progress was not without its price. Job opportunities have not kept pace with the expectations of social mobility among increasing numbers of university-educated West Germans, and a volatile academic proletariat has been the result.

Literature is perhaps the best mirror of a society's values and problems. In their novels, plays, and films, German intellectuals commented on, often critically, the values of their society and molded them as well. In the first part of the Adenauer era the trends we observed for the occupation years continued. Foreign authors, particularly American, French, and British, remained very popular. In the 1950–1951 West German theater season, almost as many productions by non-German authors were mounted as by German playwrights. It was also symptomatic that the most popular contemporary German-speaking authors were not German but Swiss: Max Frisch and Friedrich Dürrenmatt. Among writers of fiction and poetry, there was a return to the pre-Nazi era. A survey among Munich university students in 1950 listed Hermann Hesse, Gerhard Hauptmann, and Rainer Maria Rilke as the three most popular German authors. Ernst Jünger and Gottfried Benn, both of whom had established their reputation as right-wing authors in the 1920s, experienced comebacks with prose works dealing self-critically with their earlier views. But for the decade as a whole, Ernest Hemingway was far and away the best-selling author; Thomas Mann ranked only ninth.

A genuine postwar literature did not really emerge until the second half of the 1950s. A group of younger writers (i.e., of the generation born after World War I) scored major successes in 1959. Virtually all were associated with a literary organization called Group 47, one of the more remarkable intellectual peer groups in German history. The Group 47 was organized in 1947, hence the name, by a number of young authors for the purpose of mutual criticism and encouragement. In 1959 three members of the organization, all previous winners of the annual prize the Group 47 awarded to the most promising authors, published works that became international best sellers.

Heinrich Böll's *Billiard um halbzehn* ("Billiards at Half Past Nine") introduced a laconic, sarcastic look at the Establishment's foibles before and during the Adenauer years. Günter Grass's *Die Blechtrommel* ("The Tin Drum") portrayed the horror and surrealism of the Nazi and early postwar years through the eyes of a child (and later man) who refuses to grow. Finally, Uwe Johnson's *Mutmassungen über Jakob* ("Speculations about Jacob") was an understated novel about the life and death of an East German railway dispatcher. The three authors illustrate well the thematic and stylistic eclecticism of the new German literature. The topics ranged from Böll's concern with the Adenauer years to Grass's obsession with the Nazi era and Johnson's attempt to portray the dilemma of life in East Germany. Stylistically, Böll's "neoverismo" contrasted with Grass's surrealism and Johnson's minimalist, Fontane-like approach.

In the 1960s and 1970s, these authors continued to be recognized as major literary talents; in 1972 Heinrich Böll was awarded the Nobel Prize for Literature. Günter Grass had to wait a little longer; his turn did not come until 2000. A common theme in the writings of all these emerging new talents was their attempt to "conquer the past," which in Germany refers to dealing both with the horrors of Nazism and the effort by the Adenauer establishment to keep silence about the whole experience. As Grass's *The Tin Drum* had done earlier, Heinrich Böll's *Gruppenbild mit Dame* ("Group Portrait with Lady," 1971) and Siegfried Lenz's *Die Deutschstunde* ("The German Lesson," 1968) contain central figures who cannot lead "normal" lives because Nazism has destroyed their moral equilibrium. Rolf Hochhuth's *Der Stellvertreter* ("The Deputy," 1963) makes the same point in dramatic form and also accuses Pope Pius XII of moral indifference in the face of his knowledge of Nazi crimes.

The leitmotiv of the intellectuals' criticism of the Adenauer era was that West German political leaders had missed the opportunity to establish a new and better society, and instead chosen the road of exploitative capitalism, egocentrism, and materialism. Some more radical APO leaders went even further. Following the ideas of Herbert Marcuse's very influential *Der eindimensionale Mensch* ("One Dimensional Man"), whose German edition appeared in 1967, argued that real freedom was impossible under conditions of capitalist democracy. Typical of this sort of view of contemporary society was Bernward Vesper's description of the process of buying a pack of cigarettes:

> [T]the anonymous automaton, which makes our subjugation obvious. Sitting there like a trap.... The coins that I insert connect me to a circulatory system: An unknown corporation increases its profits, a huge bureaucracy is financed by my purchase.... I, myself an automaton, stand before the machine carrying out orders drafted by advertising executives.

This sense of alienation was by no means devoid of artistic merits. Critics have been particularly impressed with the series of films directed and produced in the 1970s and 1980s by Rainer Werner Fassbinder. In films like *Effi Briest* and *Die Ehe der Maria Braun* ("The

Marriage of Maria Braun") Fassbinder, who died in 1982, mounted attacks on the establishment that were also consummate works of art. The intellectuals' effort to confront West Germans with their past has also borne some fruit. The U.S. television production *Holocaust* was seen by 20 million people when it was shown on West German television in January 1979; almost a third of the nation saw one or more of the episodes.

West German cultural developments in the post–World War II era, then, were and are dominated by two somewhat contradictory characteristics. On the one hand, West German culture is an integral part of the larger Western scene. This is particularly true for visual art, music, and architecture. Postwar German art was until fairly recently for the most part abstract—just like its American, French, or Dutch counterparts. In the last ten years, however, there has been a return to figurative art in the West. This development was to some extent spearheaded by the New Expressionism that emerged in West Germany in the late 1970s. In rebuilding Germany's cities, architects turned to a sort of a neo-Bauhaus style that German refugee architects had already popularized in the United States. However, in the field of literature something of a "Pan-German tradition," to use the critic Marcel Reich-Ranicki's phrase, has continued. As we will see, East German authors were concerned with many of the same themes as their West German colleagues.

TROUBLED 1970s AND 1980s

Willy Brandt's resignation as chancellor changed the personnel but not the political makeup of the Social-Liberal coalition. The new chancellor was Helmut Schmidt, like Brandt a Social Democrat from northern Germany. (Brandt continued as the SPD's party chairman after he left the government.) Schmidt had earned a reputation as a tough administrator when he served as minister of the interior in his native city-state of Hamburg during the early 1960s. Subsequently, he became

an effective leader of the SPD's Bundestag caucus and, after 1969—to use the words of one British observer—an "outstandingly successful" minister of defense in the Brandt-Scheel cabinet. A few months after Brandt left office, Scheel succeeded Heinemann as federal president. His place in the cabinet was taken by Hans-Dietrich Genscher, who also became the new national chairman of the FDP.

The most serious domestic challenge in the mid-1970s was a wave of political terror that swept through the country. The domestic reform program enacted by the Brandt-Scheel government (especially the expansion and structural changes in the universities) persuaded most of those active in the APO to abandon the quest for "the revolution," but such "appeasement" of the establishment infuriated a small but volatile radical fringe.

Especially dangerous were the activities of some self-styled anarchist groups, notably the *Rote Armee Fraktion* (Red Army Faction—RAF) and its spin-offs. The RAF, also known as the Baader-Meinhof gang, was led by an eclectic group of misfits. They included Andreas Baader, a high school dropout; Ulrike Meinhof, the former wife of the publisher of the magazine *konkret;* and Gudrun Ensslin, a sociology student. In the early 1970s these radicals determined that only acts of individual terror would succeed in destabilizing West German society to the extent that it would be ripe for "the revolution." Between 1974 and 1977 the RAF and its allies were responsible for a series of murders, kidnappings, and bombing attacks. Among the victims of assassination were a West Berlin judge, the head of the FRG's employers' association, and West Germany's solicitor general.

RAF terror did not succeed in destroying the political and social stability of West German society. Despite their numerous contacts with various Middle Eastern and Western European terrorist groups (as well as the East German security apparatus), Baader, Meinhof, Ensslin, and most of their associates were eventually captured, tried, and sentenced to long prison terms. (There is no death penalty in West Germany.) Ulrike Meinhof committed suicide while in prison in 1976. A year later, an attempt by some Middle Eastern associates to free Baader, Ensslin, and some others by hijacking a Lufthansa passenger plane failed when a special antiterrorist unit of the Federal Republic's Border Protection Police successfully liberated both plane and passengers in Somalia. When the failure of the hijacking attempt became known, the major imprisoned RAF leaders, including Baader and Ensslin, committed suicide.

Terrorism challenged West Germany's ability to defeat internal subversion without resorting to measures that were not sanctioned by the democratic constitution. By and large, the Federal Republic met the test well. After he retired from politics Helmut Schmidt remembered that the government's crisis management team never met without the presence of an expert on constitutional law, and that "Does this violate the Basic Law?" was the first question asked about any proposed counterterrorist measures.

Nevertheless, some of the antiterrorist legislation was controversial. Civil rights activists objected particularly to a 1972 law mandating a political litmus test for civil servants. The law attempted to exclude opponents of parliamentary democracy from entering the civil service. Some critics in Germany and abroad labeled the law a "*Berufsverbot*" (prohibition to enter a profession), a term the Nazis had used when they excluded Jews and political opponents from public employment. It is certainly true that this sort of political-conscience examination violated at least the spirit of democracy, but it should also be noted that in practice the law was applied very sparingly. Of the 745,000 applicants for civil service jobs between 1977 and 1979, 287 were refused employment for political reasons. Since 1979 the practice of making routine inquiries about prospective civil servants has been abandoned.

The 1976 election confirmed the Schmidt-Genscher coalition in office, but its majority in parliament was cut considerably. The Social Democrats' share declined from 44.9 to 42.6 percent and that of the FDP from 8.4 to 7.9 percent, although Schmidt's personal popularity remained very high. The CDU/CSU opposition increased its popular vote from 45.8 to 48.6 percent, but the CDU had problems of its own. The opposition lacked an effective leader to compete with Helmut Schmidt's increasing popularity. The CDU/CSU's shadow chancellor in 1976 was Helmut Kohl, the prime minister of the state of Rhineland-Palatinate. Shortly after the 1976 election, a major scandal surfaced around Hans Filbinger, the right-wing CDU prime minister of Baden-Württemberg. Published documents revealed that Filbinger, in his capacity as a Wehrmacht judge in Norway, had imposed wholly unnecessary death sentences in the last days of World War II. The Filbinger affair and the CDU/CSU's equivocal attitude in 1979 toward extending the statute of limitations for Nazi war crimes (it was eventually extended by a vote of the Bundestag) gave the CDU/CSU a reputation for attempting to hide Germany's Nazi past.

Frustrated by ten years out of power, the CDU/CSU turned to Franz-Josef Strauss and named him shadow chancellor for the 1980 campaign. It was a politically disastrous decision. The CDU/CSU's popular vote fell to 44.5 percent while the SPD, helped by the personal popularity of Helmut Schmidt, marginally increased its vote to 42.9 percent. On paper the Liberals were the big winners; their vote share rose to 10.6 percent. However, the figures were somewhat misleading. Closer analysis showed that a significant number of FDP ballots had been "lent" by SPD voters.

Economic problems, concern over acid rain and other ecological matters, and opposition to the nuclear arms race, but also Strauss's stridently right-wing campaign facilitated the growth of a new political phenomenon, the Green Party. Founded in 1978, the new group was less a party than an amalgam of local and regional organizations. The "Greens" were convinced that the mainstream parties were not addressing West Germany's most pressing problems, which the newcomers identified as the ecology and the arms race. The members of the new organization came from a wide variety of backgrounds, ranging from former

Communists to adherents of macrobiotic food sects and extreme pacifist organizations. Although they already had representation in a number of city councils and state legislatures, in 1980 the Greens' share of the national vote was only 1.5 percent.

Despite its good showing in the election, the days of the Social-Liberal coalition were numbered. Chronic economic problems and the end of détente eroded the grounds of cooperation that had supported the coalition since 1969. In 1982 Genscher and a majority of the Liberals decided to end their cooperation with the SPD and instead form a coalition with the CDU/CSU. (Ironically, Schmidt's personal popularity increased after he left office. He became copublisher of *Die Zeit* ["The Time"], an influential Liberal weekly. Here he wrote a regular column giving thinly veiled

Im Mittelpunkt Günter Grass (1927–)

Günter Grass continues two long-standing traditions among German artists and novelists: political engagement and the writing of *Bildungsromane*—albeit in Grass's case the latter often have a surrealist twist.

Grass was born in what was then the free city of Danzig (now Gdansk in Poland). At the time of Grass's birth, the city had a largely German population, although there was also a sizable Polish minority. Grass himself added to the mix with a third ethnic minority, the *Kaschuben,* a group of farmers and fishermen on the shores of the Baltic that claimed a unique cultural heritage of its own. Grass used the ethno-cultural mix in which he grew up to good effect in his novels.

After World War II, Grass settled in West Germany and began writing fiction. As in the case of Thomas Mann's *Buddenbrooks,* Grass's first novel *Die Blechtrommel* (*The Tin Drum*) was also destined to become his most famous and influential work. Using surrealistic images, Grass describes in the novel not only the tensions, but also the easy familiarity of Germans and Poles in Danzig in the 1920s and 1930s. This was the time when the Nazis were becoming increasingly prominent in the city. In the second part of the book, the scene shifts to West Germany, and the central theme becomes the emergence of postwar West German society and its (largely unsuccessful) attempt to cope with Germany's Nazi heritage. Tying the two parts together is the novel's central character, Oskar. As a boy in Danzig, he wills himself to remain physically stunted, and although he grows somewhat taller after World War II, he remains undersized and mischievous. The novel was later made into an award-winning film directed by Volker Schlöndorff.

In *The Tin Drum,* as in a number of subsequent writings, Grass deals with the large themes that confronted the entire generation of German writers after World War II: the simultaneous moral abhorrence and banality of Nazism and the variety of efforts by the Germans after World War II to cope with this phenomenon. More recently, Grass's novels have dealt with contemporary issues, including the environment and the problems of German reunification.

Günter Grass has always been a very contemporary writer willing and anxious to become engaged in present-day politics. A good friend of Willy Brandt's, Grass actively campaigned in the 1960s for the SPD ticket and Brandt personally as the Social Democrats' candidate for chancellor. Such efforts put Grass squarely in the moderate, left-of-center part of the German political spectrum, but more recently he has taken positions that put him outside any of the major political camps. To the consternation of his Social Democratic friends (not to mention the Christian Democrats), Grass became an outspoken opponent of German reunification. He contends that after Auschwitz the Germans had no right to a reunited country. This position did not enhance Grass's popularity advice to his successor. In an August 2010 poll conduction by the *Spiegel*, the former chancellor, now ninety-two years old, had an approval rating of 83 percent. In contrast, Angela Merkel, the present chancellor, managed 59 percent and the "German" Pope 35 percent.) Helmut Kohl became the new chancellor. In the new cabinet Genscher retained his position as foreign minister. Other major figures included Gerhard Stoltenberg (CDU), a former prime minister of Schleswig-Holstein, as finance minister; Count Otto Lambsdorff (another holdover from the old cabinet) as economics minister; and Friedrich Zimmerman, the head of the CSU caucus in the Bundestag, as minister of the interior.

The 1983 elections revealed a growing polarization among the voters. The CDU/CSU increased its popular vote to 48.8 percent, but

---

among the German political establishment, and it is perhaps not entirely surprising that nowadays he spends most of his time in his second home in Portugal.

Despite the controversy surrounding Grass's political pronouncements, he remains the most popular of Germany's postwar authors. He is the only one whose major works have all been translated into English, and one of only three contemporary German authors (the others are Heinrich Böll and Herta Müller) to receive the Nobel Prize for Literature. Grass was awarded the prize in the year 2000, a long time after the publication of the *The Tin Drum* but a much-deserved honor nonetheless.

Since receiving the Nobel Prize for Literature, Grass has repeatedly devoted his literary talents to dealing with the politics of memory. Particularly controversial was the novel *Im Krebsgang* (which appeared in English as "Crabwalk"), published in 2002. The work dealt with the sinking of the *Wilhelm Gustloff* in the Baltic Sea by a Russian submarine in January 1945. The ship was built as a cruise liner for the Nazi Strength Through Joy organization; it was named for the leader of the minuscule Swiss Nazi movement, who was assassinated in February 1936. During World War II the *Wilhelm Gustloff* was commandeered by the German navy, and on its last voyage it was attempting to transport German civilian refugees, who were fleeing the advancing Red Army, and wounded soldiers to the relative safety of the western shores of the Baltic Sea. After the ship was hit by a torpedo, it sank rapidly with a loss of some eight to nine thousand lives.

The controversy over Grass's book resulted from the focus of his subject matter. Using his usual surrealistic, multilayered narrative style, Grass concentrated the reader's attention on the suffering of the passengers. They were openly described as victims, and *Crabwalk* was one of the first books to treat some Germans in World War II not as perpetrators but as victims. For Grass this was something of an ironic twist. After all, only a dozen years before he had opposed German reunification as unmerited because the division of the country was the just punishment for the Holocaust.

More recently Grass has dealt with his own personal politics of memory. In his autobiography *Beim Häuten der Zwiebel* ("On Peeling the Onion"), published in 2006, Grass peeled away the layers of his early life to reveal a secret that he had hidden since 1945. In the last weeks of World War II he served as a draftee in the Waffen SS. It did not take long for the critics to note the contradiction between Grass's long silence about his own Nazi past and his constant admonition to his fellow Germans to come clean about their own involvement with the Nazis. Hypocrisy was one of the milder accusations hurled at the best-selling author. Grass himself admitted that this part of his life "will stain me forever."

the Liberals suffered from their reputation as political turncoats. The FDP's vote dropped sharply from 10.6 to 7.0 percent. Nevertheless, with a combined total of 55.8 percent of the popular vote, the Christian Democrats and the Liberals had a clear majority in the new Bundestag. The SPD seemed to suffer from political burnout. Intraparty quarrels and highhanded treatment of the party's left wing lost the SPD votes. Its share of the popular vote fell to 38.2 percent. Many disgruntled younger SPD voters had given their ballots to the Greens, enabling them to obtain 5.6 percent of the vote to become the first new party since 1953 to clear the 5 percent hurdle.

The 1983 election, like the 1957 contest, was a "stomach election"; this time, however, the issue was not continued prosperity but finding solutions to nagging structural problems. By the 1980s the bloom was off the "economic miracle"; for the first time since the 1950s, West Germany's economy experienced not a brief "growth recession" but a long-term leveling off. Two "oil shocks" in 1973 and 1979 fueled inflation (6 percent annually in 1983) and disrupted world trade patterns on which Germany's export-oriented economy depended. The German economy actually began to show "negative growth rates"; that is, it was contracting. At the same time the high cost of the reforms of the 1960s and early 1970s had significantly increased the West German national debt; in 1983 it was approaching 55 billion deutsche marks. Compared to other industrialized countries the Federal Republic was still doing well, but for a country that was used to stable prices, rapid growth, and budget surpluses, these were disturbing developments. The climate of cooperation between management and labor cooled; the number of strikes increased.

The Schmidt-Genscher cabinet had compounded the problems by inaction and paralysis. The Liberals and Social Democrats disagreed on fundamental policy questions. The economics minister Lambsdorff gave top priority to budgetary belt tightening, and although Schmidt sympathized with this approach, the bulk of the Social Democrats

felt achieving full employment was more important. The government took a series of half measures that satisfied neither side.

The Kohl-Genscher government concentrated its efforts on deficit reduction, controlling inflation, tax reform, and stimulating private investment. Some of the results were impressive. The federal deficit was cut in half to 24 billion deutsche marks and inflation to around 2 percent annually. But growth rates remained sluggish in the mid-1980s (2.5 percent for 1984) and only increased toward the end of the decade. Moreover, despite the increased growth rates, unemployment became a chronic problem, with the jobless rate remaining fairly constant at between 7.5 and 10 percent. That in turn raised some major social issues, including the future of the millions of foreign guest workers, whom the country had eagerly sought in the 1960s and 1970s.

What was to become the "guest worker problem" began as a modest program in the 1950s. In December 1955 the Federal Republic and Italy signed an agreement regulating the terms and conditions of Italian citizens working in Germany. The expectation was that Italian guest workers would stay in Germany for a few months and then return home. In general, the initial program worked out as planned, but as Italy's own economic situation improved, that source of guest workers largely dried up.

Germany's need for additional workers did not abate, however, especially after the Berlin Wall abruptly ended the flow of refugees from East Germany. In the early 1960s German industry began recruiting guest workers from a range of countries. By 1966 there were some 1.3 million guest workers, constituting 6.1 percent of the workforce. By far the largest contingent came from Turkey. However, unlike the Italians in the 1950s, the Turks did not, for the most part, go home after a few months; they stayed and eventually brought their families. In effect the workers became immigrants rather than guest workers. But the designers of the guest worker program had given little thought to the difficulties that immigrants would confront in adjusting to life in a strange environment.

Soon guest worker ghettoes with all their attendant problems became commonplace in many German cities. The district of Kreuzberg in West Berlin, for example, has had a majority of Turkish inhabitants for a number of years. In some inner-city schools, a large percentage of students did not speak German as their first language. The difficulties of adjusting to life in Germany are most severe in the case of Turkish guest workers. Not only their linguistic and cultural, but also their religious traditions are far different from those of the Germans.

As the 1966–1967 recession and the structural problems of the 1970s led to an increase in unemployment, right-wing demagogues tried to blame the guest workers ("they are taking away German jobs"), fortunately with limited success. So far the problems have defied solutions. The Social-Liberal coalition worked hard to facilitate the eventual integration of most foreign workers into German society, but as unemployment became a major problem in West Germany that course of action became increasingly unpopular. The Kohl government, prodded by the energetic but controversial minister of the interior, Friedrich Zimmermann, relied instead on a variety of monetary incentives to persuade guest workers to return home, but relatively few took advantage of the offer.

The victory of the Liberals and Conservatives in 1983 also made possible the 1984 election of a new federal president from the ranks of the CDU, Richard von Weizsäcker. In retrospect, Weizsäcker's election was a piece of singularly good fortune for West Germany. He became not only the most popular officeholder in the country but also an internationally respected statesman. The president used his largely ceremonial office very effectively to articulate democratic sentiments and the need for consensual politics. In May 1989 Weizsäcker was reelected for a second five-year term; this time he was unopposed.

The 1987 elections brought severe setbacks for the coalition parties. Despite a generally favorable economic climate, the CDU/CSU's vote fell to 44.3 percent, its worst showing since 1949. The FDP picked up some of the votes lost by its conservative partner (they received 9.1 percent in 1987, as compared to 7 percent in 1983), a circumstance that most observers attributed to the popularity of West Germany's longtime Liberal foreign minister, Hans-Dietrich Genscher, and the corresponding lack of charisma exhibited by the Christian Democratic chancellor, Helmut Kohl.

The most important result of the 1987 election, however, was not the relatively poor showing of the coalition (with a combined vote of 53.4 percent the government remained in office), but the indications of major shifts in the overall political landscape of West Germany. The big winner in 1987 was not the largest opposition party, the SPD (its vote actually fell from 38.2 to 37 percent), but the new force in politics, the Green Party. The Greens were able to increase their popular vote from 5.6 percent in 1983 to 8.3 percent in 1987.

This trend of loosened political contours has continued since 1987, forcing the established parties to scramble for new programs and new leaders. Under attack on their left flank, the Social Democrats have attempted to steal the Greens' issues by emphasizing the SPD's concern for ecological matters and the role of labor in the "postmodern" age. At the same time, talks of a possible federal "Red-Green" coalition were in the air. There were even "practice coalitions" at the state level: At various times after 1989 the SPD and the Greens formed coalition governments in the states of West Berlin, Lower Saxony, and Hessen.

The Christian Democrats faced similar challenges on the right. In 1988 a new extreme right-wing group, the *Republikaner* (Republicans), made its appearance. The party was led by Franz Schönhuber, a former soldier in the Nazi Waffen-SS, an actor, and sometime journalist, whom one pundit described as a combination of "Mr. Average and political arsonist." Like similar groups in other West European countries, the Republicans appealed to voters with real or

A picture illustrating the vibrancy of Turkish life in the Kreuzberg district of Berlin. (Source: Courtesy of Corbis/Bettmann.)

perceived resentments: workers displaced by structural changes, farmers dissatisfied with the Common Market's agricultural policies, and anybody who disliked the "postmodern" world.

In 1988 Franz-Josef Strauss, for many years the unchallenged champion of the moderate German right, died. With his powerful presence removed from the political scene, the Republicans were able to gain 7.5 percent of the vote in the February 1989 West Berlin election. (For comparisons, the CDU obtained 37.8 percent, the FDP 3.9 percent, the SPD 37.3 percent, and the Greens 11.8 percent in the same contest.) A few months later Schönhuber's group repeated its Berlin triumph in the elections for the European Parliament. Here the Republicans were able to obtain 7 percent of the vote, mostly at the expense of the CDU/CSU.

The CDU's and especially the chancellor's primary reaction to his party's declining fortunes was to make personnel changes. Insisting that his policies were correct, Kohl reshuffled his cabinet in the

spring of 1989. He dismissed the unpopular minister of defense, Rupert Scholz, and placed a number of trusted "Kohl men" in key ministries. Even more dramatic was the dismissal of Heiner Geissler, the CDU's longtime secretary-general. Widely regarded as the architect of the CDU's good showing in the 1983 election, Geisler made no secret of his conviction that Kohl was increasingly becoming a liability for the Christian Democrats.

One reason for the government's complacency in the face of electoral setbacks was the belief that the recent good news on the economic front, as well as the dramatic changes in the GDR (see p. 330ff for a discussion of these events), would be reflected in voter support in upcoming elections. For much of the decade the West German economy exhibited a lackluster performance. The Kohl-Genscher cabinet could (and did) take pride that its supply-side economic policies had halted the danger of inflation, but in many other areas the record was far less impressive. West Germany's version of the American "rust belt"—the iron- and steel-producing regions in the Saar and Ruhr valleys—languished in need of restructuring. For the nation as a whole, until 1984 the disposable income of the average German worker actually fell from a high point in the 1970s. Incomes began climbing again in 1984, but as late as 1986 they had reached only the levels of 1977. Above all, unemployment remained high—above 2 million, some 9 percent of the workforce.

Beginning in 1987, however, things began to look up. Supply-side economics produced high business profits (after adjustment for inflation, in 1985 wages and salaries rose by 2.5 percent, but capital gains and corporate profits by 7 percent), which in turn led to increased investments, especially in export-oriented industries. And exports had always been the "locomotive" that pulled the West German economy. Recession-free economies in the Federal Republic's largest trading partners—members of the European Community and the United States—helped West Germany to amass huge favorable trade balances. Accelerated growth of the economy (almost 4 percent in 1988) finally made a dent in the unemployment figures as well. Unemployment fell to 2.2 million (8.4 percent of the workforce) in August 1988, and a year later it dropped to 1.9 million (7.5 percent of the workforce), its lowest level since 1982.

Foreign relations grew more complicated, although both the Schmidt-Genscher cabinet and its successor stressed the continuity of West Germany's foreign policy aims: ongoing close cooperation with the United States and the EEC and simultaneous pursuit of improved relations with the Soviet bloc, especially the GDR. The difficulties were in the area of implementation. Relations between Bonn and Washington especially in the early years of the Reagan era, which began in 1981, were subject to some strains. Most serious was the rift over East–West détente. In the latter 1970s the Soviets began a massive buildup of their nuclear strike

force in Europe. Responding to this threat, the members of NATO in 1979 decided on countermeasures in the form of a dual-track response. On the one hand, NATO would strengthen its nuclear capabilities; the United States would station Pershing II and cruise missiles in West Germany and other European countries. At the same time, the members of the alliance voted to pursue intensive negotiations with the Soviets on arms control in the hope that an agreement would make the planned military countermeasures unnecessary.

The Schmidt-Genscher government and the Reagan administration attached different degrees of importance to the two parts of NATO's "dual track decision." The West German policy makers, taking into account the strength of public opposition to new nuclear arms on German soil, emphasized negotiations, whereas the Reagan administration felt that until the Western defenses had been strengthened and the missiles deployed, the Russians would not begin serious bargaining. Disagreement over the deployment of U.S. missiles also weakened Schmidt's position. The chancellor favored the stationing of new American missiles to counter the Soviets' nuclear buildup, but a majority of his party was convinced the deployment of additional weapons in West Germany would increase rather than decrease the danger of nuclear war in Europe.

The relaxation of tensions between the superpowers, which made possible the 1987 treaty on the elimination of medium-range ballistic missiles in Europe, inaugurated something of a new era in West Germany's foreign relations. The Federal Republic's longtime foreign minister, Hans-Dietrich Genscher, was in the forefront of those leaders who argued that the West should actively support the efforts of the new Soviet leader, Mikhail Gorbachev, to institute far-reaching political and economic reforms in the Soviet Union.

As a result, German-Soviet relations improved rapidly. In June 1989 Gorbachev visited the Federal Republic. He was welcomed by enthusiastic crowds wherever he traveled, and his talks with the country's leaders went extremely well. Reaction to these moves was not uniformly positive. In the United States some commentators feared that West Germany's continued pursuit of détente would lead to its "Finlandization"; that is to say, it would opt out of the Western camp in favor of neutralism.

Distrust and acrimony between West Germany and East Germany also increasingly gave way to cooperation. In 1978 the two governments signed an agreement for the construction of an Autobahn between Berlin and Hamburg, and five years later the Kohl government guaranteed a 1 billion deutsche marks commercial credit for the GDR in return for the prospect of further "humanitarian" concessions for the East German people. In 1987, ironically only two years before the collapse of the GDR, Erich Honecker made a state visit to the Federal Republic, where he was received with all of the ceremonial honors due a head of state. The visit had originally been scheduled for 1984, but at that time the Soviet leadership had forced Honecker to cancel his trip. Three years later Gorbachev and the new leaders in Moscow put no obstacles in Honecker's path.

In 1989 relations between the two countries briefly became acrimonious again. In the summer and fall, tens of thousands of young East Germans took advantage of the more liberal policies in some of the East European countries to escape to West Germany. By the end of the year, more than 200,000 persons had fled the German Democratic Republic and settled in West Germany. The East German government angrily protested what it called a concerted media effort by the West Germans to "lure" East German citizens to the West as an unacceptable "interference in the internal affairs of the GDR." But then the collapse of the GDR's communist regime in the fall of 1989 virtually overnight dramatically altered the relationship between the two German states.

CONCLUSION

Uncertainties characterized the situation of the Federal Republic on the eve of reunification. In 1989 the Federal Republic celebrated its fortieth anniversary with a flood of self-congratulatory articles and books. As one government publication put it, the last forty years had been "a mandate for democracy." Consensus remained high, and political extremism was not a serious problem. The overwhelming majority of West Germans endorsed close cooperation with the United States and the countries of Western Europe. The economy remained solid, especially in comparison with the lackluster performance of some of the FRG's West European trading partners.

Yet in the midst of the celebration of success it was difficult to overlook a note of creeping anxiety. One major West German newspaper caught this mood well when it described the FRG as a forty-year-old "provisional entity." The country's capital, Bonn, was an urban embodiment of this sense of hovering between past and present that characterized much of West German life. Despite some modern-day pretensions to international sophistication, Bonn retained much of the flavor of a sleepy university town on the Rhine.

Moreover, a mood of pessimism or at least uncertainty about the future was spreading. Public opinion polls in the early 1980s revealed that some 8 million West Germans felt angst about the future, and about a third of those under twenty-five were convinced the future would not be better than the past. This phenomenon of youthful alienation was undoubtedly linked to the immediate economic problems, but there was also widespread concern about less tangible issues, like the threat of ecological disaster. Like much of Western Europe, the Federal Republic stood at a crossroads, but West Germans faced some peculiar problems of their own. The future remained shrouded, but it was clear that the simplistic answers of the 1950s and 1960s provide inadequate guideposts for the 1990s and beyond.

CHAPTER TEN

~~~~~~~~~~~~~

The German Democratic Republic

1949–1990

The German Democratic Republic (GDR) was always a house divided against itself. In the politics of memory the East German people for the most part saw themselves as perpetual victims. Misguided by the Nazis, maltreated by the Red Army, and oppressed by their own communist leaders, they had neither the freedom nor the prosperity that the West Germans enjoyed. The East German leaders, however, regarded themselves as history's winners. Having kept the faith in the Nazi resistance, they were liberated by the Red Army, and now, with the Soviet Union at their side, they would build socialism in Germany. For them, the slogan that sustained them during the nightmare of the Third Reich, "After Hitler it's our turn," had literally come true.

Until the late 1950s the GDR's communist leaders insisted socialism would encompass all of Germany. During these years, the East German regime claimed only the West German government and its American backers prevented Germany's reunification and evolution toward socialism. As it became clear that the West Germans had no intention of accepting communist rule, the official East German version of Germany's past and future changed. The adoption of a new national flag in 1959 (until then both East Germany and West Germany had the same red-black-gold flag; the GDR now added a hammer-and-protractor emblem to its banner) signaled the beginnings of a new era. After the building of the Berlin Wall in August 1961, the regime increasingly stressed *Abgrenzung* (demarcation) between East and West Germany. In 1972 Albert Norden, the chief propagandist of East Germany's ruling Communist Party, proclaimed that Germany had always been two nations—one bourgeois, the other proletarian—with no common ground between them. This view was officially sanctioned by a new East German constitution in 1974, which dropped all of the references to a single German Nation that had been part of the GDR's earlier constitutional documents. Simultaneously, the regime mounted vigorous propaganda campaigns stressing patriotic pride among its citizens with the slogan "my fatherland is the GDR."

The official line never enjoyed much support among the East German people. As the events since 1989 have demonstrated, most East Germans did not look on West Germany as a "foreign" country or feel that Germany's common history had no meaning for them. It was in part to accommodate such sentiments that in the last years of the GDR's existence, the state's leaders attempted to appropriate such "all-German" historical personages as Bismarck, Frederick the Great, and Luther, who, at first glance, hardly seemed "progressive" in a Marxist-Leninist sense. In 1981 Erich Honecker, East Germany's last communist leader, all but returned to the GDR's original position. He proclaimed that "one day" the "workers of the Federal Republic would begin the socialist reconstruction of the FRG," thereby creating the basis for a reunification of the country. In the meantime, Honecker acknowledged that although there were two German states, there remained a common German nationality.

There is finally the irony that East Germany, for all its pretensions to representing Germany's socialist future, had always been more like the "old" Germany than the "new" Federal Republic. The GDR's drab physical appearance and its authoritarian political system contained vivid reminders of life in Germany before 1945.

THE QUEST FOR VIABILITY

Although many of the concepts and terms used in East German official parlance—elections, democracy, progress, prosperity, people, and parliament—sounded like their Western equivalents, in practice the GDR throughout its forty-year existence was a dictatorship controlled by the Communist Party and its affiliated organizations. Walter Ulbricht, the longtime general secretary of the GDR's governing party, had expressed the principle early on. In July 1945, just after his return from exile in the Soviet Union, he told

a group of Communist Party functionaries, "Everything has to look democratic, but we have to be in control of everything."

In October 1949 the Third People's Congress for Unity and a Just Peace adopted the GDR's first constitution, and the contradictions between propagandistic catchphrases and actual political practice were already apparent. On the surface, this document seemed to enshrine the principles of federalism and parliamentary democracy. The country was divided into five Länder—Brandenburg, Mecklenburg-Vorpommern, Saxony, Saxony-Anhalt, and Thuringia—all five had either been separate states or Prussian provinces in the Weimar era. Whole passages, especially in the section dealing with civil liberties, were lifted verbatim from the earlier Weimar constitution. The document permitted a multiparty system and free elections. The constitution also gave workers the right to organize unions and to strike.

The reality of political practice in the GDR, however, was determined not by the words of the constitution but by the ideology of Marxism-Leninism as interpreted by the East German Communists and their allies in Moscow. This lack of real reliance on the constitution also explained the lack of permanence for what should have been the basis of the GDR's political and social system. As the party line changed, so did the constitution. Between 1949 and 1990 there were four separate constitutions in the GDR.

The key to understanding the 1949 constitution was the concept of a people's democracy as enunciated by the Soviet and East German Communists. According to Soviet ideologists, by 1949 the countries of Eastern Europe, including East Germany, had reached this level of societal development—"people's democracy"—that put them one historical step behind the Soviet Union, the only country that had already achieved socialism. In a people's democracy, elements of society's bourgeois-capitalist structure remained in existence, but real power was in the hands of the workers and farmers, led by their political vanguard, the Communist Party.

The East German Communist Party, called the *Sozialistische Einheitspartei Deutschlands* (Socialist Unity Party of Germany, SED), in cooperation with the Communist Party of the Soviet Union, claimed the historic right and duty to "create socialism on German soil." For this reason the role of the SED is pivotal for understanding the history of the GDR, even though the party was not even mentioned in the country's constitutions until 1968.

The principle of the SED's societal leadership was well illustrated by elections in the GDR. The members of the *Volkskammer* (People's Chamber), the East German legislature, were elected regularly every four years, but the voters had no genuine choices in selecting their representatives. Rather, voters "elected" or rejected the entire list of candidates presented on the ballot by dropping a ballot marked "yes" or "no" into a box. A "no" vote or not voting at all was considered a sign of asocial behavior. GDR statistics invariably reported "yes" votes above 99 percent for the official list of candidates. The SED controlled the legislature because more than half of the official candidates were members of the Communist Party or its affiliates.

As we saw earlier the SED was the result of a forced merger between the SPD and the KPD in the Soviet zone. By 1949 what had ostensibly started out as a marriage of political equals had been transformed into a Soviet-style Communist Party, a "party of the new type." Thereafter, almost until the end of the GDR, the SED slavishly followed the Communist Party of the Soviet Union in its structure and ideology. In theory, policy and programmatic decisions were made by the SED's party congress, which met every four years. The delegates were ostensibly elected by the membership at large. The congress in turn elected a Central Committee (CC), consisting of between 150 and 200 members and "candidates." (As in the former Soviet Union, candidate members had a voice but no vote on the committee.) The Central Committee acted in the name of the congress when the latter was not in session. The CC in turn elected the Politburo, a body consisting of

between fifteen and twenty-five members and candidates, whose members staffed a variety of commissions that paralleled the major government ministries and offices.

All of this sounds reasonably democratic in a Western sense, but again the appearance was deceptive. In reality, the principle of democratic centralism transformed the appearance of making policy and personnel decisions from the bottom up into the reality of control from the top down. Although information did filter upward through the ranks of the membership at large, all substantive decisions were determined by the Politburo and rubber-stamped by the Central Committee and the periodic congresses. The members of the Politburo had a final say on all appointments in the *nomenklatura* (the East Germans used the Russian term), the list of major positions in the party, the government, and the economy. The Politburo also selected delegates to the congresses.

The SED's congresses permitted neither free debate nor democratic decision making, although the meetings were important as indicators of major shifts in policy, ideology, or personnel. The July 1950 congress, for example, signaled the increasingly close alignment between the SED and the Communist Party of the Soviet Union, and the victory of the "exile" Communists over the KPD and SPD members who had remained in Germany during the Nazi era. Shortly after the congress, the newly elected Politburo launched a massive purge of the SED's membership. Some 150,000 party members were expelled as sympathizers of the "Tito clique." (In 1948 Moscow broke with the Yugoslav communist leader Josip Broz Tito. "Titoism" was therefore a form of "anti-Soviet deviationism.")

The SED, of course, did not limit its role in East German society to resolutions and doctrinal announcements. Numerous officials held party and government jobs simultaneously, providing critical links between party and government at all levels of administration. Most members of the Politburo were also ministers in the GDR's cabinet. In 1952 the federal structure of the

GDR, provided for in the 1949 constitution, was abolished, and the five Länder were replaced by fourteen districts. All of the chiefs of district administration were SED functionaries. The Politburo was also directly involved in the system of political repression in the GDR. In 1950 the ministry for state security (*Ministerium für Staatssicherheit*), known in the GDR as *Stasi*, was established. Following the Soviet model, the East German secret police was organized along military lines; all full-time functionaries had military ranks. The first minister, Wilhelm Zaisser, was a member of the Politburo. The tradition was continued with the GDR's longest-serving Stasi chief, Erich Mielke. In charge of the Stasi from 1957 until the collapse of the SED regime in 1989, Mielke became a candidate member of the Politburo in 1971 and a full member in 1976.

The SED's control of the major mass organizations also constituted an important aspect of its system of political and social manipulation. The concept of the people's democracy assigned mass organizations a specific role as "transmission belts" in creating and maintaining a "socialist mentality," particularly among segments of the society that had not yet achieved a "proletarian consciousness." Members of the SED, as the most "advanced" segment of society, always occupied leading positions in the mass organizations. Among the most important of these groups were the labor unions (*Freier Deutscher Gewerkschaftsbund—FDGB*), the GDR's youth organization (*Freie*

Im Mittelpunkt Erich Mielke (1907–2000)

No one personified the system of political oppression in the GDR better than Erich Mielke, the longtime head of the Stasi. He liked to call himself East Germany's first *chekhist* because his model for the Stasi was the Bolsheviks' original secret police, the *Chekha*. As was true of his counterparts in the former Soviet Union, Mielke was a firm believer in the dictum, "Trust is good, control is better."

Mielke was born in 1907 in Berlin, the son of a carpenter. He learned the trade of a dispatcher, but, after joining the KPD in 1925, soon became a full-time Communist Party functionary. Among the tasks the party assigned him was that of a reporter for the KPD's newspaper, *Red Flag*. Mielke also actively participated in the political violence that increasingly characterized the last years of the Weimar Republic, and in 1931 he was involved in the killing of two Berlin policemen. To escape prosecution for this crime, he fled to Belgium.

When the Nazis came to power in 1933, Mielke, understandably, did not return to Germany but went into exile in Moscow instead. From 1934 to 1936 he received training at the Comintern's school for subversives, and subsequently the Comintern sent him as a secret police agent on a variety of assignments; like many German Communists, Mielke operated on the Loyalist side in the Spanish Civil War.

During World War II, Mielke, who by now was thoroughly fluent in Russian, was a full-time agent for the Soviet secret police. After the war, he returned to Germany with the group of communist exiles led by Walter Ulbricht and immediately began working for SMAD. In 1946 he became the vice president of SMAD's Internal Administration, with responsibility for police training.

When the GDR was formally established, the regime created a Ministry for State Security, usually known by its acronym, Stasi. Initially headed by Wilhelm Zaisser with Mielke as the number-two man, Mielke succeeded Zaisser in 1957 when the latter was purged for his role in the 1953 uprisings. Mielke remained minister for state security until the collapse of the GDR in 1989.

Deutsche Jugend—FDJ), the German Women's Association (*Deutscher Frauenbund*—DFB), and the Association for German-Soviet Friendship (*Gesellschaft für Deutsch-Sowjetische Freundschaft*—DSF). The theoretical functions of these mass organizations changed somewhat as the GDR proclaimed it had advanced from the status of a people's democracy to that of "developed socialism," but their main task remained the instillation of a "socialist mentality" among all segments of East German society.

Paralleling the "positive" controls of the mass organizations was a system of political repression. Freedom of expression in the Western sense did not exist in the GDR. Press, radio, and all other media were tightly censored to prevent the airing of views "contrary to the interests of the people." Full- and part-time Stasi officials—271,000 by 1988—kept their eyes on every sphere of societal activity. Beginning in 1950 Western countries, particularly the Federal Republic and the United States, were classified as "warmongering" states. Expressing views favorable to these "warmongers" became a criminal offense.

The leaders of the GDR regarded the development of a sophisticated industrialized economy in East Germany as the key to building socialism in the GDR and later all of Germany. It was a formidable task. Except for some deposits of soft coal and potash, the GDR had few natural resources. On the whole, agricultural land has always been poorer east

During his tenure, his party career advanced as well, especially under Erich Honecker. He became a candidate member of the Politburo in 1971 and a full-time member in 1976.

As head of the Stasi, Mielke developed a mania for accumulating as much information as possible about the GDR's citizens. The Stasi also ran a quite efficient foreign espionage department, headed by another long-term Communist functionary, Markus Wolf. This Stasi division was especially successful in planting moles in a variety of West German government and party offices. By the time the Stasi was dissolved, Mielke's organization employed some 85,000 full-time functionaries and 110,000 part-time "informal collaborators." This army of informers created literally mile-long corridors of paper files, and it may well be true that in the end the Stasi collapsed under its own weight, unable to make effective use of the information it gathered.

With his passion for secret police work, Mielke had very little time left for private life, but he did have two well-known private indulgences. One was the wearing of military uniforms. As head of the Stasi, Mielke held the GDR's highest military rank—general of the army—and he loved wearing the appropriate dress uniform complete with a chestful of medals that covered most of his diminutive front. Mielke was also a great fan of the Berlin soccer club, Dynamo Berlin, and he used his official position to secure the best players for the club. Not surprisingly, Dynamo Berlin was the perennial champion of the East German soccer league. However, despite Mielke's best efforts, neither Dynamo Berlin nor any of the other East German clubs did well in international competition.

Mielke was arrested at the end of 1989 but soon released for health reasons. He was rearrested in 1991 and tried two years later—not for his role as head of the Stasi but for the 1931 murders of the two policemen. (Under German law, there is no statute of limitation for murder.) Mielke was sentenced to six years in prison but released in 1995 as a result of his failing health. He died in May 2000, an unrepentant Communist to the end.

of the Elbe than on the western side. Human decisions added to the natural difficulties. The Soviets' policy of "first charge" for reparations, which they did not abandon until 1952, meant that much of East Germany's productive capacity benefited the Soviet Union, not the GDR. Until 1952 some two hundred industrial enterprises, the SAGs (see earlier, p. 241), which included many of the country's largest industrial firms, produced exclusively for export to the Soviet Union.

Above all, however, the communist regime in East Germany imposed on the country a system of economic planning and production that maximized politicization and centralized control while minimizing individual initiative and responsibility. Following the path charted by Stalin for the Soviet Union in the 1930s, the decade of the 1950s marked the systematic advance of collective—that is to say, state and party—control of the major sectors of the economy. A key milestone in the nationalization of the GDR's economy was the restoration of the SAGs to East German control in 1952. These production facilities were not returned to their former owners but were converted immediately into *Volkseigene Betriebe*—VEB ("people-owned enterprises")—and placed under the direct control of the state. By the end of the decade, privately owned companies constituted only a minor part of the East German economy. (In 1949 almost 40 percent of East Germany's productive capacity was in private hands; by 1960 that figure had sunk to 3.8 percent.) Another plateau in the takeover of the economy came in 1959–1960 when the regime, ignoring the farmers' objections, decided to collectivize East Germany's agriculture. By 1963 more than 90 percent of the GDR's farmers worked on Agricultural Production Cooperatives (*Landwirtschaftliche Produktionsgenossenschaften*—LPG), or collective farms.

The East German leaders considered an accelerated pace of industrialization and the rapid growth of the state-controlled parts of the economy as the twin foundations for the construction of socialism. The first Five Year Plan adopted by the SED's 1950 congress targeted a 100 percent increase in the GDP over the levels of 1936 and a 72 percent increase in productivity. The party also assigned absolute priority to the heavy industry sector (steel, electrification, machinery). The manufacture of consumer products was considered relatively unimportant.

Nationalization meant not only the elimination of private enterprise but also massive centralization of decision-making authority in the economy. Individual VEBs received their orders from one of eight economic ministries (heavy industry, light industry, and so on). The government directives in turn were implementations of the multiyear plans worked out by the state planning commission. Following the Soviet example, these documents were extremely detailed, determining not only what and how much was to be produced, but also wages, hours, and prices. Until 1958, when the system was changed (see p. 314), the individual manager of a VEB had very little autonomy to make executive decisions. But the SED's leadership was satisfied. A propaganda ditty proclaimed, "As I walk along the street, seeing something new and beautiful, I know what made it possible: my friend the Plan."

In the 1950s, as the West German boom was beginning its long run, the centralized economic system produced stagnation in East Germany. The lack of resources, coupled with politically determined production goals and an unwillingness to give economic managers (not to mention labor) the freedom to make decisions, led to chronic shortages and widespread public dissatisfaction. The plan fell particularly short in meeting its goals in areas not accorded top priority, that is, consumer-oriented industries. Agricultural production was similarly treated as an economic stepchild. The regime tried to make up for a serious shortage in investment capital by increasing work norms and sponsoring "socialist competitions" in the manner of the Stalinist *stakhanovite* campaigns of the 1930s, but ideological incentives were no compensation for a miserably low standard of living and lack of political freedoms.

(The term *stakhanovite* derives from Aleksei Stakhanov, a Soviet worker who in the 1930s was held up as a model proletarian for vastly exceeding his assigned production quotas.)

The most visible result of the GDR's misguided economic policy was a development that in itself further worsened the situation in East Germany: The GDR's citizens "voted with their feet." Taking advantage of the open frontier in the city of Berlin, between 1949 and 1961, 2.5 million East Germans moved permanently to the Federal Republic. (By 1953 the GDR had essentially closed the rest of the border between East and West Germany.) Moreover, to the consternation of the regime's leaders, almost half of the refugees were under twenty-five years of age, so the country was steadily losing a major part of the economically most productive segment of its population.

The SED's reaction to the massive signs of dissatisfaction (between 1950 and 1952 alone there were more than 500,000 refugees) was not to reconsider its economic course but to intensify the pace of development and tighten the screws still further. In July 1952 the party's Central Committee voted to "accelerate the construction of socialism." There was to be even more emphasis on heavy industry at the expense of consumer goods. To achieve the new plan objectives, production norms and work hours were increased. Food rations, however, would remain low and unchanged.

Stalin had given his approval both to the GDR's original Five Year Plan and to the mid-1952 changes, but in March 1953 the Russian dictator died. The new Soviet leadership, confused and unstable, sent a different message to East Berlin. As early as April 1953 the Russians urged the East German authorities to reduce economic pressures and appease popular discontent. In response, on June 9, the SED's Politburo adopted a new line: the "New Course." This policy provided for an increase in the production of consumer goods, a halt to further nationalizations, and some incentives for those who had fled to the West to return to the GDR. However, like Stalin's successors in the Soviet Union, the SED's leadership was divided. Walter Ulbricht, the secretary-general

of the party since July 1950, and his supporters followed the new Soviet line only reluctantly. Others, like Rudolf Herrnstadt, the editor of the SED's official newspaper, *Neues Deutschland* ("New Germany"), and Wilhelm Zaisser, the head of the Stasi, argued that the regime's real problem was Ulbricht himself; they urged that the SED's general secretary be removed from office.

The New Course failed to ease tensions in East Germany because it did not address the one feature of the old plan most resented by many East German workers: an additional arbitrary increase in work norms decreed at the end of May 1953. On June 16, 1953, spontaneous demonstrations and strikes erupted among East Berlin's construction workers. Ironically, the first workers to put down their tools were those constructing the GDR's most prestigious building project, the *Stalinallee*. Here the regime was erecting a mammoth complex of buildings in the architectural style of what was then the Soviet republic of Georgia. This was to honor Stalin, who was born in Georgia.

The workers in Berlin were soon joined by others in all parts of the GDR. Recent research has shown that from the beginning the demonstrators voiced economic and political goals: They demanded immediate rescinding of the increased norms and insisted on Ulbricht's dismissal, free elections, parliamentary democracy, and reunification with West Germany. On June 17 the demonstrations turned violent. Angry demonstrators set fire to SED offices and hauled down red flags. By the afternoon of June 18, the regime had lost control of the situation; units of the *Volkspolizei* (People's Police—VP) sent out to contain the crowds often fraternized with the demonstrators. It was not until the Soviets intervened with tanks and troops that order was restored.

The reaction of the East German leadership to the June uprisings was an inconsistent mix of propaganda offenses, purges, and tactical concessions. The official line was that the strikes and demonstrations were an attempt by neo-fascists to topple the government of the GDR. Organized by

A West German comment on East German elections. Walter Ulbricht, the GDR's strongman orders the number of voters to be counted. That number will be equal to the number of "yes" votes for the Communist-dominated official list of candidates. (Source: akg-images/ullstein bild)

American and West German intelligence services, the strikes and demonstrations had been fomented by outside agitators from West Berlin ("Texas cowboys" in the SED's parlance), who were given their orders by the West Berlin radio station RIAS. (RIAS stands for Radio in the American Sector.) The intervention of Soviet troops, then, had prevented the return of fascism to power in Germany. Within the GDR, Ulbricht and his supporters moved quickly against the reformers in the Politburo. Both Zaisser and Herrnstadt were accused of antiparty activity and expelled from the SED. And the purge was not restricted to the top echelons. A number of lesser functionaries were executed for their failure to contain the uprising. More than half of the SED's district party secretaries and almost two-thirds of the county

secretaries were dismissed. Among rank-and-file members a large-scale purge took place as well.

The collapse of the June 1953 uprising marked the end of the first phase of the GDR's history. The unrest had demonstrated not only the regime's lack of popularity but also the Soviets' determination to maintain communist control in East Germany. Beginning in the summer of 1953, the GDR's rulers set out to repair their shaken power position. For a time the East Germans experienced relief from the pressures of "accelerated construction of socialism." In July 1953 priorities for the Five Year Plan were permanently readjusted. The projected annual growth rate for heavy industry dropped from 13 to 5.6 percent while the output of consumer goods was to be increased by 30 percent. The regime announced an end to arbitrary arrests, and intellectuals were promised greater artistic freedom. These changes did have some effect. The stream of refugees, until 1961 always a good barometer of public opinion in the GDR, decreased from 331,330 in 1953 to 184,198 a year later.

In retrospect, it is clear that Ulbricht and his allies never regarded the New Course or the reforms that followed the June 1953 uprising as anything but a tactical and temporary maneuver. However, others among the SED's leaders did advocate fundamental policy changes. Encouraged by Nikita Khrushchev's denunciation of Stalin's errors and crimes at the 1956 Twentieth Congress of the Soviet Communist Party, they argued that the GDR needed to become a more decentralized and open society. The SED should permit greater freedom for intellectuals and more autonomy for economic managers. The reformers also advocated better relations between East and West Germany. The group included Wolfgang Harich, East Germany's leading Marxist philosopher; Fred Oelssner, the secretary for propaganda of the party's Central Committee; and Fritz Selbmann, the chairman of the Commission for Industry and Transportation.

For a time, Ulbricht and the old guard were put on the defensive, but in the spring and fall of 1956 the Hungarian revolution and widespread unrest in Poland inadvertently strengthened the position of Ulbricht and the SED's conservatives. The Russians feared for the cohesion of their satellite system and hastily withdrew their support of further liberalizations. This left the East German reformers isolated and vulnerable. In November 1956 Harich was arrested on a charge of conspiracy and "revisionism." He was subsequently sentenced to ten years in prison. Selbmann and Oelssner lost their positions and were purged from the party. The SED's July 1958 congress gave official party sanction to the restored hard-line. The congress confirmed that the GDR had now achieved "the foundations of socialism."

A superficial glance revealed some striking parallels in the foreign relations of the Federal Republic and the GDR during the decade of the 1950s. Both countries wanted to establish their international viability, which required recognition from their sponsoring superpower and its allies. For West Germany support from the United States was of paramount importance, whereas the GDR needed approval from the Soviet Union. At the same time, these surface parallels should not obscure some fundamental differences in the relations of the FRG to its allies and those of the GDR to the Soviet Union and the countries of Eastern Europe. The new West German republic was an open society whose political system was supported by the overwhelming majority of the people. In sharp contrast, the GDR's leaders depended on the physical presence of Russian troops to maintain themselves in power. As a result the relationship of the GDR and the Soviet Union, at least until the 1960s, was not an alliance of partners; East Germany remained a Russian satellite.

Still, the formal steps that led to the GDR's integration into the Eastern bloc in large part paralleled the process by which the FRG joined the Western alliance. As was true for West Germany, economic ties preceded political ones. East Germany was accepted into membership in the East European Council for Mutual Economic Aid (Comecon) in 1950. Five years later the GDR became a formally sovereign state. Under the terms of the friendship treaty between the GDR and the Soviet Union signed that year, Soviet troops remained stationed in East Germany, but officially now at the invitation of the East German regime. In the same year, the East German state joined the Warsaw Pact, the Soviet bloc's equivalent of NATO.

Along with East Germany's technical sovereignty came diplomatic recognition by all of the countries of the Soviet bloc. In contrast to West Germany, the GDR did not insist that the fate of Germany's former territories that lay east of the Oder-Neisse Rivers was an open question, to be decided only in a future peace treaty. Rather, as part of the agreements between East Germany and the other Soviet satellites, the GDR recognized the de jure legitimacy of the de facto annexations of the territories east of the Oder-Neisse Line by Poland and the Soviet Union.

Before 1961 the GDR was unsuccessful in breaking through the barrier of the Hallstein Doctrine. The West Germans, their Western allies, and most of the developing countries did not recognize East Germany. To end this isolation, the Soviets and the East German regime repeatedly proposed official talks between the East and West German governments as a prelude to a Confederation of East and West Germany. What appears to have been the most serious offer came in March 1952. The Soviet Union and the GDR suggested that after a period of Confederation between the GDR and the FRG, there would be free elections for an all-German government. Scholars are still divided about the real aim of Stalin's initiative. Some regard it as an obvious propaganda ploy to prevent West German rearmament (this was the time of the debate over the European Defense Community [EDC] in West Germany); others, without denying this motive, claim that the Russians were also sincerely interested in exploring the possibility of coupling German reunification with permanent demilitarization of the entire country. In the end it did not matter because both Adenauer and the Americans rejected the Russian proposal out of hand.

Toward the end of the decade, signs indicated that the GDR's rulers were abandoning the dream of a united Germany under communist control. Instead, increasingly the GDR was determined to seal itself off from the West. In December 1957 a new law made *Republikflucht* ("flight from the republic") a criminal offense. A year later, Khrushchev, whose position had been weakened by the Hungarian and Polish upheavals in 1956, heeded the pleas of the GDR's leaders to adopt measures that would put an end to the flow of refugees through West Berlin. In November 1958 the Russians unilaterally abrogated the Four-Power agreement on Berlin and issued an ultimatum to the Western Big Three. The Soviets set a deadline of six months for negotiations that would lead to an agreement recognizing West Berlin as a "free and independent political entity." Western troops were to be removed from the city. If the Western Allies did not agree to the proposal, the Russians threatened to turn the fate of West Berlin over to the GDR.

In their reply to the Soviet ultimatum, the Western powers enunciated three "essentials" of their Berlin policy: guaranteed access from West Germany to West Berlin, continued presence of Western troops in the city with undisturbed use of the air corridors, and guarantees for the viability of the Western sectors. The "essentials" did not involve East Berlin, and they did not include a demand for continued unrestricted travel between East and West Berlin. Because it was this last issue that was of major concern to the Russians and the GDR, the Western reply was, from their point of view, an encouraging development.

Shortly after midnight on August 13, 1961, East Germany began the construction of the Berlin Wall. The Wall was quite literally that, a concrete barrier preventing uncontrolled travel between East and West Berlin. Travel between the two halves of the city became possible only by passing through one of four checkpoints manned by East German guards. In addition to erecting a new barrier in Berlin, in the next few months the already closed boundary between East and West Germany was further fortified. The physical barrier was reinforced by sophisticated electronic detection devices and heavily armed guards.

The Western Allies protested vigorously against the Wall as a violation of the Potsdam Agreements providing for Four-Power control over all of Berlin, and there were some tense scenes as American tanks rumbled close to the Eastern sector. But, as the Russians had anticipated, the West took no concrete measures to force a dismantling of the barrier between East and West Germany.

The Wall was simultaneously the GDR's greatest success and its most abject failure. On the one hand, the barrier made it obvious that the East German regime had been unable to win the consent of its own people. At the same time, the Wall demonstrated that the GDR's

In June 1963, almost two years after the Berlin Wall was built, President Kennedy visited Berlin to demonstrate American concern for the security of West Berlin. In time it became a ritual especially for prominent foreign visitors to West Berlin to include as part of their program a photo opportunity of their visit to the Wall. Note that the barbed wire fortifications point toward East Berlin, clearly demonstrating that the Wall was meant to prevent East Germans from getting out rather than hinder so-called West German fascists from invading the GDR. (Source: Courtesy of National Archives and Records Administration.)

existence could no longer be ignored. At least for the foreseeable future the West Germans, the Western Allies, and, above all, the East German people could not wish the SED's regime away. The flow of refugees stopped abruptly. In all of 1962, 21,356 persons succeeded in reaching West Berlin and West Germany; this was less than half of the figure for the first twelve days of August 1961 (47,433).

EAST GERMANY IN THE 1960s

The building of the Berlin Wall climaxed the rise to undisputed power of the SED's general secretary, Walter Ulbricht. He had already triumphed over the reformers at the party's 1958 congress, but it was the

Wall that became the real foundation for Ulbricht's unchallenged rule and ambitious plans. Although Ulbricht increasingly became the object of organized public displays of adulation, the GDR's powerful and hated leader was a personally unprepossessing individual. Walter Ulbricht was the epitome of a party functionary. Born in 1893 in Leipzig as the son of a tailor, he learned a trade as a carpenter but soon became a full-time political functionary. In 1919 Ulbricht joined the newly founded KPD, and by 1921 he was the party's district leader in Thuringia. Two years later, he was elected to the KPD's Central Committee, and in the last years of the Weimar Republic Ulbricht headed the party organization in Berlin. After the Nazis came to power, Ulbricht went into exile, spending the years of the Third Reich in the Soviet Union. Throughout the Stalinist purges, he never wavered in his support of the Soviet dictator's policies. (Ulbricht, for example, heaped fulsome praise on the Nazi-Soviet Pact in the years 1939–1941.) As we saw, in April 1945 the Red Army brought him back to Germany.

For the Marxist-Leninist ideologists in the SED, achieving socialism in the GDR was of more than semantic significance. The process had important implications for the role of the Communist Party in East German society. The SED was no longer just the organization speaking for the interests of the dominant class in East Germany; it was the institution charged with the "scientific management of society." In other words, as the GDR made its leap toward socialism, the party would take an even greater direct role in influencing all aspects of societal life. A new constitution adopted in 1968 gave legal sanction to the SED's role. Article 1 of the new constitution described the GDR as "a socialist state which under the leadership of... its Marxist-Leninist party is building socialism." At the end of the 1960s, Ulbricht proclaimed that the GDR had reached the stage of "developed socialism."

As the SED increased its power in East German society, Ulbricht's personal stature grew as well. In September 1960 Wilhelm Pieck, the jovial president of the GDR and cochairman of the SED, died. Instead of naming a successor, the regime replaced the office of president with a twenty-eight-member State Council; Ulbricht became its chairman. Four years later, Otto Grotewohl, East Germany's prime minister since 1949 and the GDR's most prominent former Social Democrat, also died. He was succeeded by Willy Stoph, another old-line Communist, who had been minister of defense since 1956.

During the 1950s the SED was dominated by veteran Communists of the Weimar and Nazi era and characterized by frequent factional strife. In contrast, the 1960s were a period of orderly transition and rejuvenation. In 1963 the Politburo consisted of fourteen members and nine candidates. All of the full members had served on the highest party body since 1958 (ten since 1954), but the entire group of candidates was newly elected in 1963. The trend was even more noticeable in the numerically larger Central Committee. By 1963 the majority of its members were functionaries who became politically active only after World War II. The social composition of the party's rank-and-file membership was also changing rapidly. The SED was successful in attracting large numbers of blue-collar workers to the party. Between 1961 and 1971 the percentage of those who listed their occupation as "workers" increased from 33.8 to 56.6 percent. Perhaps most significant, however, the party was increasingly seen as the vehicle to power and success by groups outside the working class. The percentage of members from the "intelligentsia" almost doubled in the same period, from 8.7 to 17.1 percent.

Ulbricht's rising personal stature ironically coincided with Khrushchev's repeated denunciations of Stalin's cult of personality. In 1956 and again in 1961, the Russian leader attacked Stalin's excessive vanity and praised Lenin's supposed adherence to the principles of collective leadership. Ulbricht paid lip service to the new era, but in the process he subtly enhanced his own stature. In the 1960s he felt it was no longer necessary to deny the significance of the German socialist tradition in favor of praising the Russians. Ulbricht and his sycophants portrayed him as the culmination of an ongoing line of leaders that included Marx, Lenin, and Thälmann before him. At the end of the decade, Ulbricht boldly put the GDR's status as a developed socialist state on the same level as that of the Soviet Union. He also suggested the two societies would remain parallel for some time to come—implying that the Russians would not soon push ahead to reach true communism.

The SED's enhanced role in East German society became apparent as well in the

"Walter Ulbricht, on the right, and Nikita S. Khrushchev at the height of their power in the 1960s. (Source: Interfoto/Alamy)"

reallocation of Volkskammer seats. In 1963 the composition of the GDR's legislature was changed to give the Communists an even greater majority among the delegates. Until then, the SED had been allotted 100 seats in the Volkskammer, and the noncommunist parties (Liberals, Christian Democrats, and Farmers) 45 each. The remaining 110 seats went to representatives of the mass organizations; virtually all of these were also SED members. Now the number of SED and mass organization delegates was increased to 110 and 144, respectively, while the other parties remained at 45 each. In reality, of course, these changes were largely symbolic. All votes in the Volkskammer were unanimous in support of decisions taken earlier by the SED's leadership.

At the same time the "official" function of the noncommunist parties of the GDR was redefined. Instead of acting as voices for the interests of their voters and members, they were now only "transmission belts," explaining the reasons for the SED's policies to their supporters. Their role, in other words, was not essentially different from that of the mass organizations.

The attainment of "socialism" and with it the regime's ability to stay in power ultimately depended on the performance of the GDR's economy. We have already seen that the failure of the system to satisfy the minimum needs of its people had led to the uprisings of June 1953. Since then the situation had definitely improved, largely because the GDR's leaders rearranged the planning priorities to increase the supply of consumer goods. The growth figures for the economy toward the end of the 1950s were impressive; in 1957, for example, the economy grew by 7.9 percent. Emboldened by such figures, at the SED's July 1958 congress, Ulbricht announced that within three years the GDR would have reached and surpassed West Germany's standard of living. In 1960 Ulbricht prophesied that within ten years the GDR would be completely independent of Western imports.

At the time labor productivity in the GDR was 25 percent below that of the FRG, and East Germany had a standard of living that was 40 percent lower than West Germany's. So where did the general secretary and his supporters find the basis for their vastly inflated expectations for the future performance of the East German economy? In part the reason was misplaced faith in the structural transformation that had been completed by the end of the 1950s. All sectors of the economy with the exception of some small businesses (mostly craftspeople doing repair work) had now been nationalized. Overall, almost 90 percent of all industrial goods were produced by VEBs, more than 90 percent of the GDR's food production came from collectivized farms, and almost 80 percent of all retail operations were transacted by state-owned stores. In addition, the GDR benefited indirectly from the West European Common Market. To emphasize its position that there was only one German nation, the FRG had insisted that the GDR be treated as part of the West German tariff area. This meant essentially that East Germany was part of an expanding free market in Western Europe.

Most important, however, the East German leaders felt they had found the solution to the problems created by the economy's cumbersome decision-making apparatus. Under the catchy label of the New Economic System (NES), Erich Apel, who in 1963 became chairman of the State Planning Commission, attempted to apply some of the ideas of the Soviet economist Evsei Liberman to the East German situation. Liberman, who enjoyed great favor with Khrushchev, argued that real costs, profitability, and plans calculated on the basis of real productivity had a legitimate place in socialist economy.

Using these ideas, the East Germans hoped to increase the freedom of economic decision making for individual plant managers, without abandoning effective political control. In an effort to reduce the multiple layers of decision-making authority, the eight separate economic ministries in East Germany were abolished. The State Planning Commission took over most of their functions. The sphere of decision making of individual VEB managers was increased, and they now dealt directly with the State Planning Commission. For production-line workers "socialist competition" provided both material and ideological incentives to increase productivity. Simultaneously, a major curriculum reform in the public schools stressed polytechnic education and vocational training to smooth the transition from school to factory.

For some years after it was introduced in 1963, the NES appeared to be successful. The standard of living for the average East German increased significantly. The regime continued its traditional policy of heavily subsidizing the cost of housing and basic foodstuffs while the NES for the first time made sophisticated consumer goods—washing machines, cars, television sets—available on a larger scale. Equally important, party officials reduced the emphasis on the "primacy of politics," and in some cases they even facilitated rather than hindered the production process.

But there were problems as well. It required vast levels of capital investment to bring the East German economy to the level of West Germany. Because the GDR did not interact with the international investment market, the funds would have to come from the East German people. Yet massive levels of investment (estimated at around 66 billion East German marks between 1961 and 1964) could only be maintained if the economy enjoyed steady and phenomenal growth rates. That economic surge, however, was hampered by the structural problems that continued to plague major sectors of the East German economy.

Agricultural production on the collectivized farms consistently lagged behind planned projections, and the GDR had to import large amounts of foodstuffs. In addition, despite efforts at decentralization, the system of economic decision making remained cumbersome. Projected goals for future plans were routinely based on the anticipated accomplishments of previous plans, even when it was obvious that the earlier plans had fallen short of their goals. Decision makers continued

to ignore production costs and the quality of products; quantity alone counted. The massive subsidies for "basic" goods and services—food, housing, and transportation—meant that "luxury goods" remained disproportionately expensive. This was glaringly apparent because most East Germans had access to West German television and its advertisements. (At the time West German TV was publicly owned, but it allowed brief blocks of time for ads each day.) Symptomatic of the situation was the question by a "common worker" at an SED indoctrination meeting in 1966. He asked why a nylon shirt cost 12 deutsche marks in the West and 78 [East German] marks in the GDR? The SED propagandist had no answer, but he said he would report the incident to his superiors. We don't know what their answer was. Finally, when in the mid-1960s it became clear that economic liberalization was also leading to demands for more artistic and political freedom, some party functionaries had second thoughts about the benefits of economic reforms.

The GDR also experienced firsthand the negative consequences of socialist internationalism. When the Soviet economy began to develop massive difficulties (one of the reasons leading to Khrushchev's downfall in 1964), the Soviets turned to help from the satellites. In December 1965 East Germany was forced to sign a new trade treaty with the Russians that contained extremely favorable terms for the Soviet Union. There were even rumors that Erich Apel's suicide at the end of the year was a form of protest against Russia's exploitation of East Germany's economy.

In April 1967 the Seventh Congress of the SED voted to modify substantially the NES and replace it with the Economic System of Socialism (ESS). Like the Soviets after the fall of Khrushchev, the GDR, too, reinstituted a centralized production system. A technologically advanced society remained the ultimate goal, but instead of emphasizing individual material incentives and decentralized decision making, the East German leaders now attempted to combine the concepts of developed socialism and the theory of cybernetics to create a new form of self-regulating economic structure in the GDR.

Cybernetics as a theory of systemic control and information aroused much interest on both sides of the Iron Curtain, but in the GDR it did not become respectable until 1961, when Khrushchev described it as the "fundamental science of the coming age." For East German theoreticians, notably the philosopher Georg Klaus, cybernetics promised to create the "man–machine symbiosis" that they saw as the essence of socialism. The East German proponents of cybernetics claimed that in the era of developed socialism alienation between worker and machine had been eliminated, so by applying the theoretical precepts of cybernetics to the work process it could be made completely controllable. It followed, then, that combining the knowledge of cybernetics and dialectical materialism would enable East Germany's leaders to create an economy that was simultaneously dynamic and ultra-stable because it would not be subject to any inherent contradictions.

All this sounded very appealing to the GDR's economic planners disappointed by the performance of the NES, but the promises of the ESS remained equally unfulfilled. Recognizing the futility of modernizing all aspects of the economy, the ESS gave priority to those sectors that promised to be competitive on the international market, primarily chemicals, precision machinery, and eventually high-technology products. The East German leaders were particularly hopeful that exports in these areas would bring in enough hard currency to pay for needed food imports (agricultural productivity increased by only 1.7 percent per annum between 1967 and 1971) and for computerized machinery from the West. The hopes proved illusionary. Concentrating on specific economic sectors meant a general neglect of those parts of the East German economic infrastructure that were not high-priority items, with the result that the hidden

costs of all East German products increased substantially.

Still, as the decade ended, the East German economy had experienced some impressive growth rates, and the standard of living had increased substantially. In the 1960s there was really something of an East German "economic miracle." In both productivity and standard of living, East Germany far outstripped its communist allies in Eastern Europe, including the Soviet Union. But productivity and the standard of living remained substantially below that of West Germany and other Western countries, and it was this comparison that mattered to the East German people. Despite its boast that the GDR had reached the stage of "developed socialism," East Germany had not found a way that enabled the regime simultaneously to maintain total political control while creating an economy that could match the productivity and prosperity of the West.

An additional liability on the GDR's economy was the disproportionately large amount of resources earmarked for the armed forces. In the 1980s the GDR's military budget (including the cost of the *Nationale Volksarmee* (National People's Army—NVA), the Stasi, and the Soviet troops stationed in East Germany made up 11 percent of the country's GDP. The beginnings of the East German armed forces went back to the early 1950s, but the NVA was not officially established until 1956. The GDR introduced conscription in 1962, and the NVA grew into an impressive military force of some 170,000 soldiers. To an even greater extent than the West German *Bundeswehr,* all NVA units were integrated into the multinational Eastern alliance and remained under the control of the commander in chief of the Warsaw Pact forces, who was always a Soviet general. The GDR's armed forces were equipped with sophisticated conventional weapons, but, again like the West German *Bundeswehr,* they did not have control over any nuclear arms. This did not prevent the NVA from developing ambitious plans for conquering West Germany. Since the 1960s the NVA had been working on detailed scenarios for securing Communist control of West Berlin and West Germany, including lists of persons to be arrested and draft proclamations as the NVA took control of the conquered territories.

The construction of the Berlin Wall in 1961 inaugurated a new era in the country's foreign relations. Emerging from the isolation of the 1950s, the GDR went on the diplomatic offensive. In the 1960s the GDR established diplomatic relations with most of the new nations of Africa and Asia. These ties benefited both sides. The newly independent nations of Africa and Asia were as anxious for international recognition as the GDR, and they had no preconceived ideas about the "German problem." At the same time their relationship to the former Western colonial powers and the United States was often strained. In addition, the GDR's seeming ability to build a "socialist" economy in a country with few natural resources impressed many developing nations that faced similar problems. East Germany, for its part, gained international respectability and the good-will of the Soviets; in the developing world the GDR often acted as the surrogate of the Soviet Union.

Although international recognition was gratifying to the East German regime, success also brought problems. In the 1960s the rigid contours of the bipolar bloc system were becoming more fluid. The Sino-Soviet split destroyed the myth of the communist monolith, and East–West détente brought further uncertainties. In the Sino-Soviet dispute the GDR officially never wavered in its support of the Soviet Union, although it is now clear that Ulbricht toyed with the idea of establishing better relations with the People's Republic of China as a way of lessening the GDR's dependence on the Soviets.

The SED's leaders were highly skeptical about East–West détente. They argued that painting the capitalist enemy in less stark colors was dangerous for the cohesion of the

Soviet bloc. Such fears were given unwitting credence by the 1968 crisis in what was then still Czechoslovakia. In the spring of that year Alexander Dubšek, the chairman of the Slovak Communist Party, replaced a holdover from the Stalinist era, Antonin Novotny, as leader of Czechoslovakia. Dubšek was willing to allow substantial reforms in the Czechoslovak economic system, and his promise of "socialism with a human face" was enthusiastically welcomed by the people of Czechoslovakia. However, as spring turned to summer there were signs that the Communist Party's monopoly of political power was being threatened. Meeting at Karlovy Vary in mid-August, the leaders of the Warsaw Pact attempted to persuade Dubšek that he needed to take firm measures to restore communist control. If he failed to do so, the Russians and their allies would invade the country and restore order.

When the Czechoslovak situation seemed to deteriorate further, Soviet troops, aided by units from other Warsaw Pact nations, invaded Czechoslovakia on August 21. (East German forces were mobilized, but they did not actually enter Czechoslovakia. The communist leaders clearly feared that the presence of East German troops on Czechoslovak soil would evoke bitter reminders of the Nazi takeover of that country in March 1939.) Dubšek was taken to Moscow, forced out of office, and replaced by the hard-liner Gustav Husak. The invasion of Czechoslovakia was justified under what became known as the Brezhnev Doctrine (Leonid Brezhnev had in the meantime replaced Khrushchev as Soviet leader). This policy stated it was the duty of all Socialist nations to come to the aid of any country in which socialism appeared threatened. Although earlier accounts portrayed Ulbricht as an enthusiastic supporter of the Brezhnev Doctrine, more recent works show the East German leader to have been ambivalent. Ulbricht certainly disapproved of Dubšek's reformism, and he welcomed the Brezhnev Doctrine as a guarantee of Russian help for the East German regime in case the

East German people again revolted against the communist dictatorship. But there is also evidence that Ulbricht was smarting under the tight constraints that the Soviets imposed on the freedom of action of their satellites.

The Soviets' initial reaction to the overtures of the West German Social-Liberal government was decidedly negative. Russian propaganda portrayed Willy Brandt as a lackey of capitalism and the *Ostpolitik* as an effort to undermine the solidarity of the Socialist camp. The SED's leaders seconded such sentiments. Oskar Fischer, the GDR's foreign minister, called Egon Bahr's concept of change resulting from East and West drawing together "aggression on cat's paws" (*Aggression auf Filzpantoffeln*). And it is true that the Ostpolitik presented the GDR with special problems. For the Russians the policy of intra-European détente promised long-sought recognition of the Soviet Union's preeminent position in Eastern Europe, but for the GDR it posed the danger of isolation as West Germany, the Soviet Union, and the communist countries of Eastern Europe dealt directly with each other.

In an effort to counter the danger of isolation in the communist camp, the GDR—just at the time West Germany was abandoning the Hallstein Doctrine—invented the "Ulbricht Doctrine." Its aim was to force communist nations to refuse recognition to West Germany as long as the FRG did not treat the GDR as an equal. It is now clear that the SED's Politburo was divided on the best approach toward the West German Social-Liberal cabinet. Although a majority of the Politburo wanted to reject the overtures from Bonn, Ulbricht, until now the quintessential Moscow man, planned to take up initiatives toward West Germany on his own. To do so he simultaneously pursued a hard and a soft line.

To underscore the "equality" of the two Germanies, the East German regime insisted on personal meetings of the two governments' leaders, but the two meetings between Willy Brandt and his East German counterpart, Willy Stoph, were near disasters.

As we have seen, during the first meeting in Erfurt, cold formality on the part of the East German officials contrasted with the embarrassing and spontaneous acclaim by the people of Erfurt for Willy Brandt. Stoph's return visit to Kassel in May 1970 did not improve matters. The East German prime minister began the discussions by demanding that West Germany pay the GDR 100 billion deutsche marks to compensate East Germany for "luring away its people" between 1949 and 1970. Ulbricht also held fast to the position that West Berlin had to become an "independent political entity," with the Western sectors of the city existing at the sufferance of the GDR.

At the same time the general secretary signaled his interest in improved relations with the Brandt-Scheel government. Ulbricht held out hope for greater economic cooperation and political détente. He seems to have envisioned eventual Confederation and even reunification of the two Germanys. Repeatedly Ulbricht expressed the wish that the Social-Liberal government stay in office, and he went so far as to suggest the GDR should help the SPD to win elections in West Germany. That degree of potential goodwill toward the "class enemy" was too much for Ulbricht's comrades on the Politburo. Led by Erich Honecker, Ulbricht's longtime presumptive successor, a majority of the SED's policy-making body petitioned the Soviet Communist Party leader, Leonid Brezhnev, to put pressure on Ulbricht to resign as the SED's general secretary. Brezhnev agreed, but not without reminding Honecker, "Remember, Erich, without us you are nothing."

In May 1971 Walter Ulbricht was forced from power and succeeded by Erich Honecker. It was not a graceful exit. Ulbricht bitterly resented that Honecker ordered the East German media to make his predecessor's name and face disappear from public view. The former strongman of East Germany continued as chairman of the State Council until his death in August 1973, but the State Council was stripped of all real power.

CULTURE AND SOCIETY

When discussing art, literature, and education in the GDR, it is important to keep in mind the special position that Marxism-Leninism assigned to all cultural endeavors. Artists, educators, and writers had the task of acting as "engineers of the soul." It was their duty to help create a "socialist mentality" among the East German people. They were also to serve the SED. "Truth is what benefits the party politically," proclaimed a leading GDR historian. The regime over the years took this self-defined goal quite seriously. To set the stage for a new era in interpersonal relations, the SED's 1958 congress voted a set of "Ten Commandments of Socialist Morality," which stressed that the interests of the working class, rather than the biblical admonitions, should guide all individual behavior.

For the East German Communists *Kulturpolitik* ("cultural policy") involved control of everything from literature to newspapers and films. The GDR's educational system was an integral part of the country's Kulturpolitik. As we saw, the structure of education in the Soviet zone had already been fundamentally changed during the years of occupation. In the 1950s, reform of the school curriculum emphasized still further ideological indoctrination; Marxism-Leninism and Russian became required subjects. Religious instruction, traditionally a regular subject in German schools, was eliminated. The regime also attempted to use education to further the social mobility of blue-collar workers. Workers and children of workers were given preference for admission to institutions of higher learning. By 1954, 13 percent of all East German university students came from a blue-collar family background. The comparable figure for West Germany was less than 2 percent.

In the 1960s the curricular focus shifted toward "polytechnical" education, with an emphasis on science and technology at the expense of the humanities. A third of the curriculum after the primary grades was devoted to science courses and prevocational training. To prepare children for their role in the production process, pupils spent considerable time outside the school; at least one day a week was to be spent in a factory or on a collective farm. Grade school and junior high school classes "adopted" as models of behavior individual "heroes of labor." (As in Russia, this title was awarded to workers who had significantly exceeded their production norms, as well as to party functionaries.) Increasing amounts of time both in school and during extracurricular activities were given over to sports and premilitary training. School classes also developed "special relations" with selected regiments of the NVA. The GDR's nationwide search for talented athletes yielded spectacular results, at least as measured by the success of GDR athletes in international competition. (After the collapse of the GDR it became clear that much of the athletes' success was the result of the systematic and widespread use of illegal doping practices.)

These trends continued under Honecker, although the emphasis on polytechnic education brought its own problems. Predictably, the regime found that science teachers had little interest in political indoctrination. Party functionaries complained that in some schools not one teacher subscribed to the SED's official newspaper. More important, the transformation of the economy did not keep pace with the changes in education. Specifically, the number of jobs requiring sophisticated skills was not large enough to absorb the increasing number of university and technical-college graduates. As a result, many graduates were forced to perform production-line tasks considerably below their skill levels.

The GDR's attitude toward artists and writers shifted over the years, although the changes were variations of the basic line laid down by the party in 1951. Cultural life during the years of occupation from 1945 to 1949 had been relatively free, but the situation changed abruptly in March 1951. The SED's Central Committee passed a resolution "Against Formalism in Art and Literature—for a Progressive German Culture." The document established socialist realism, the cultural policy that had been in effect in Russia since 1934, as the official guideline for East Germany's "cultural producers." The pure Stalinist form of socialist realism, which insisted on the superiority of all things Russian and Soviet, became diluted after the dictator's death, but the dogma that art and literature must exhibit "party-mindedness, typicality, and optimism" remained in force.

The SED used the concept of socialist realism to control the GDR's artistic life and to convert art into propaganda. Writers were admonished to picture life in the GDR "realistically as it will progress toward the future." This meant that artists were to portray what the party proclaimed would be the "true" life in the future even if the present lagged far behind this idealized picture. "Typicality" also had a specific political meaning. In portraying workers, for example, artists were told that in the GDR the abolition of capitalism had led to the "self-realization of man." The face of a worker in a painting or his or her actions in a novel should mirror that the worker was simultaneously "producer, owner, and holder of political power" in the German Democratic Republic.

The "positive" concept of socialist realism was contrasted with the "negative" term *formalism*. Formalism referred to individual artistic indulgence and introspection, which the regime identified with Western culture and U.S. imperialism. All schools of art and literature other than socialist realism were regarded as reactionary and degenerate. These included expressionism, abstractionism, and naturalism. Even Bertold Brecht, a lifelong sympathizer of Communism, was criticized for his libretto for the 1951 opera *The Trial of Lucullus*. The review in the SED's newspaper, *Neues Deutschland*, complained that Brecht's text was excessively abstract and failed to put the working class at the center of the action.

In the iron grip of socialist realism, East German cultural life in the early 1950s quickly became a wasteland of hacks. Endless "production-oriented" narratives ("I love you, but my tractor is more important") saturated the market. Painters and sculptors presented idealized revolutionary and factory scenes with assembly-line monotony. Some distinguished writers, including established figures such as Arnold Zweig and Anna Seghers—both of whom, like Brecht, had returned from exile in the West to live in the GDR—attempted to evade the party's censors by writing about historical topics. Others took to writing poetry, a literary field that, because of its masked content, was less subject to control by the party's censors.

The New Course and the establishment of a ministry of culture in 1954 raised hopes for a cultural thaw. Spearheaded by internationally known Communists like Anna Seghers, delegates to the Fourth Writers' Congress in January 1956 demanded a return to the freedom and experimentation of the early Bolshevik years before Stalin imposed socialist realism in the Soviet Union.

The SED's culture czars remained noncommittal for a time, but when the 1956 Hungarian revolution revealed what they perceived as the consequences of liberalization, they returned to a hard-line. In 1959 a sort of modified version of socialist realism called the Bitterfeld Movement became official literary policy. A conference of writers, functionaries, and industrial workers assembled at the Bitterfeld chemical works and proclaimed the need for close contact between East German writers and the country's industrial workers. Writers were encouraged to visit factories to learn how workers lived their lives of "optimistic typicality." At the same time, encouraged by the slogan "*Greif zur Feder, Kumpel*" ("Pick up a pen, buddy"), industrial workers were to become authors in addition to serving as literary models. This aspect of the Bitterfeld Movement was spearheaded by Alfred Kurella, a communist writer who had been active in a similar venture during the 1920s.

The Bitterfeld Movement and other efforts to breathe life into "production-oriented" literature and art did not meet with great success. Few of the worker-authors turned out to be hidden literary talents; living a proletarian life did not, it appeared, mean that one could produce great proletarian literature.

The intellectuals who went into the factories were profoundly affected by their experience but not always in the way the party had hoped. Many came away from their factory experiences impressed not with the new "socialist mentality" of the workers, but with the emptiness of their lives and the conflicts between individual self-realization and the enforced ideal of artificial collectivity. "Developed socialism" had not eliminated alienation.

Along with building the Berlin Wall, the SED intensified its efforts to seal off the GDR from Western, and particularly West German, cultural influences and contacts. In December 1961 Alexander Abusch, the GDR's minister for culture, proclaimed the "two-culture" doctrine: East and West Germany belonged to two separate cultural spheres, one progressive and humanistic, the other reactionary and imperialistic. For East German writers and artists, only the experiences of life in the GDR and other socialist countries formed valid bases for cultural productions. East German journals, like the leading literary forum *Sinn und Form* ("Meaning and Form"), which until 1962 frequently published contributions by West German authors, abruptly stopped the practice. To be sure, these efforts at cultural isolation failed. The common language and ready availability of West German radio and television in most parts of the GDR assured that news from the West would continue to reach East Germany.

Even without "interference" from the West, the GDR was having problems in its own camp. Marxist philosophers like Robert Havemann argued that armed with the scientific insights gained from cybernetics and Marxist dialectical materialism, neither economic planners nor artists needed the constant interpretive guidance of party functionaries and ideologues. The party took swift action against such heretical views. In 1964 Havemann was expelled from the party, although he was an old-line Communist and antifascist activist. (During the Third Reich the Nazis had imprisoned Havemann in the same jail as Honecker.) From 1976 until his death in 1982 Havemann was placed under house arrest. He was rehabilitated posthumously in 1989.

Havemann's writings (and the regime's criticism of them) caused a major stir among the GDR's intellectuals and Marxist theorists, but the SED was even more concerned about the impact on the public at large of critical views expressed by the country's best-selling authors. A favorite theme of East German literature during the 1960s was the conflict between the individual's desire for self-realization and society's pressure for conformity. Wolf Biermann's very popular poetry accused the party functionaries of "preaching Communism by destroying men's souls." In the novel *Gedanken über Christa T.* ("Thoughts about Christa T."), Christa Wolf, an internationally respected author and member of the SED's Central Committee, told the story of a young woman who commits suicide because she cannot resolve the conflicts between maintaining her individuality and yielding to the pressures of collectivity.

The most popular novel in the 1960s was Erwin Strittmatter's *Ole Bienkopp* ("Old Beehead"), published in 1963. Ole Bienkopp is a wily peasant who establishes his own small-scale cooperative farm, only to see it destroyed by party functionaries who insist on his joining a much larger agricultural commune. And these were only the works that got past the censor. A book like Stefan Heym's *Tag X* ("Day X"), a novel about the June 1953 uprisings, could not be published in the GDR "because it contained obvious errors." (It was published in West Germany.) Incidentally, until his death in 2001, Heym remained a curmudgeon. After the reunification of Germany, he regularly denounced the Bonn government for what he saw as its unfair treatment of the former East Germany.

A central concern of all these writers was the problem of alienation in the German Democratic Republic. The party's functionaries claimed they did not object to treating alienation per se, but they would not tolerate narratives in which the party was portrayed as part of the problem rather than the solution. The party functionaries objected particularly to portrayals of party officials as unfeeling bureaucrats, rather than as friends who would resolve the conflict between the individual and society. In addition, the party criticized the tragic outcome of many stories. Pessimism, after all, was not in accord with socialist realism.

Youthful dissatisfaction with life in the GDR was another constant problem for the country's political leaders. In the early 1960s the party made an effort to accommodate youthful iconoclasm. The chairman of the East German youth organization (the FDJ), Horst Schumann, announced in 1963 that the party was not trying to raise a generation of "little Lord Fauntleroys." The FDJ's official organ even printed some early Biermann poems. In the mid-1960s, however, as Brezhnev turned against dissidents in the Soviet Union, the SED also cracked down again on youthful freedom in East Germany. Especially the freer treatment of sex by some East German authors aroused the ire of the SED's puritanical censors.

Led by Erich Honecker, the former head of the FDJ and already Ulbricht's heir apparent, the Central Committee at the end of 1965 launched a broad attack on cultural revisionism. Incipient signs of rowdyism, aping of Western dress and mannerisms, and listening to "unaesthetic beat music" were condemned as evidence of the influence of Western television and radio. The regime's attitude toward the home-grown pop music called *Ostrock* (Eastern rock) was always ambivalent. Performers might be tolerated for a time, but a single "offensive" lyric could end a career. What the party really wanted was clear from its treatment of Christa Wolf. That author's *Gedanken über Christa T* ("Thoughts About Christa T.") was condemned as too pessimistic, but her 1963 work *Der geteilte Himmel* ("Divided Heaven") received high praise. *Der geteilte Himmel* dealt with the decision by a young East German woman to return to East Berlin after having lived for some time in the Western part of the city; despite the material advantages there, she finds life in the West empty. Strittmatter's *Ole Bienkopp*, too, fell afoul of the party's critics. The functionaries would have preferred a happy end, complaining that the party should have been portrayed as helping Ole Bienkopp win his case for smaller collective farms. (In the novel the party functionaries recognize the value of Bienkopp's endeavors only after his death.)

Intellectuals, artists, and the party coexisted uneasily in the last years of the decade. The party continued to insist that artists and writers conform to its political dictates. To that end, the State Security Service (*Staatssicherheitsdienst,* or *Stasi*) saturated artistic ensembles like theater and ballet companies with a small army of "informal collaborators" (*Informelle Mitarbeiter,* or *IM*), who spied on their colleagues and reported to the Stasi.

Despite some distinguished works, especially in literature, the artistic results of East Germany's Kulturpolitik were disappointing. Painters and architects, for example, produced few works of real distinction. The GDR journal *Deutsche Architektur* ("German Architecture") editorialized in 1964 that since 1945 East German architects had produced absolutely nothing of note. The author of the article was denounced for his attempt "to escape party discipline."

CONFLICTING SIGNALS: EAST GERMANY UNDER ERICH HONECKER, 1971–1989

Erich Honecker, East Germany's leader from 1971 to 1989, was born on August 25, 1912, in Neunkirchen, a small industrial town in the Saar region of West Germany. He came from a family of coal miners and left-wing political activists. Honecker's father was a local leader of the Communist Party during the 1920s, and Honecker himself joined the KPD's youth organization when he was only ten. As an official of the communist youth movement, Honecker was on the Nazis' list of dangerous political opponents; he spent the years from 1935 until the end of World War II in Nazi jails.

After the war, Honecker remained in East Germany, serving as chairman of the official East German youth organization, the FDJ, from March 1946 to May 1955. In 1950, at the relatively young age of thirty-eight, Honecker became a full member of the SED's Central

Committee and a candidate member of the Politburo. In the CC, he was responsible for youth and security affairs. In 1956 and 1957 Honecker was in the Soviet Union, apparently for advanced training, and at the SED's Fifth Congress in 1958 he was elected a full member of the Politburo.

Honecker personified the type of pragmatic apparatchik whose major aim was to preserve the Communist Party's monopoly of political power. At the same time, he was far more "GDR oriented" than his predecessor. To the end of his life, Ulbricht apparently continued to hope that he would see the victory of "developed socialism" in all of Germany. Honecker was content to safeguard communist control in the GDR; the new 1974 constitution ("Honecker's constitution") was the first to contain no mention of a German Nation. Honecker liked to use the phrase "real existing socialism" to characterize East German society rather than the more ambitious and finished-sounding "developed socialism."

Much as Ulbricht did, Honecker surrounded himself with personnel of his own choosing. This process involved both a generational and a functional shift among the top ranks of the GDR's leaders. Of the twenty-nine full and candidate members of the Politburo elected in 1976, nine were former FDJ functionaries. These men—the only woman to occupy a major position was Honecker's wife, Margot, who was minister of education—generally belonged to a generation of communist leaders who became politically active at a time when both a united Germany and the old communist movement had disappeared.

At the same time, there was evidence of growing professionalization among the party bureaucracy at the middle-management level: the ranks of county, city, and district secretaries. Increasingly under Honecker, these officials came from the ranks of the intelligentsia and the professions, rather than the working classes—in other words, people who had deliberately chosen the party as a management career. The dominance of the professional political managers gave the GDR in its last years

a more pragmatic, less ideologically fixed image than it had under Ulbricht. The East Germans and their self-appointed leaders seemed to have grown accustomed to each other. The SED still ruthlessly suppressed organized opposition and dissent, but it tolerated unfocused grumbling and withdrawal into private life.

The early 1970s were also a time of rapid rejuvenation of the SED's cadres. After that the doors closed. The communist systems had no provision for orderly retirement at the top ranks of the *nomenklatura*. Members of the SED's Central Committee and the Politburo stayed in their positions unless they left for reasons of poor health or were purged. As a result, the top decision makers became a group of overaged veterans who refused to see or deal with the new challenges of the 1980s. A popular joke making the rounds went as follows: "What are the first three agenda points for every Politburo meeting? 1. the members are carried into the meeting room. 2. their pacemakers are turned on. 3. the members sing the anthem, 'We are the young élite of the proletariat.'"

The new leaders were aware, of course, that economic difficulties at the end of the 1960s had been one of the factors leading to Ulbricht's fall. For this reason Honecker and his men worked hard to raise the East German standard of living, although they did not depart from the established principles of communist economic planning and thinking. Structurally, Honecker intensified the drive for nationalization. The sectors of the economy that had retained a sizable percentage of privately owned businesses, notably independent artisans and small-scale building contractors, became part of the network of VEBs. By the end of 1972, 99.4 percent of all industrial workers in the GDR worked for a state-owned enterprise. After 1980 the industrial production was further centralized by putting groups of related VEBs into *Kombinate* (literally, "combinations"). The new organizational forms were really vertical or horizontal cartels, although, of course, they did not have the economic power

Im Mittelpunkt Wolf Biermann (1936–)

Wolf Biermann is a traveler between two worlds, East and West Germany. He was born in November 1936 in the port city of Hamburg in northwestern Germany. His father was a dockworker and Communist Party activist. (The dockworkers of Hamburg were traditionally strong supporters of the KPD. The party's national leader during the Weimar years, Ernst Thälmann, had also been a dockworker in Hamburg.) Biermann obtained his *Abitur* (high school graduation certificate) in Hamburg, but remaining true to his family's political convictions (he was already a member of the Communist Party's youth organization) he was unhappy with West Germany's rapidly emerging free-enterprise economic system and its parliamentary democracy.

In 1953, at age seventeen, Biermann moved to East Germany where he thought his communist ideals were being realized. Here he followed a somewhat idiosyncratic career path. He studied political economics, philosophy, and mathematics at East Berlin's Humboldt University, but he was also drawn to the world of theater and entertainment. He was an assistant director at Berthold Brecht's Berliner Ensemble theater from 1957 to 1959, and in 1961 struck out on his own. With the support of Hanns Eisler, then the head of the GDR's radio operations, he formed the Workers' and Students' Theater, but the group's productions soon ran afoul of the Communist authorities. They regarded the shows as too nonconformist and formalistic—the SED's code words for artistic individualism and freedom.

In the 1960s Biermann began a solo career as singer-songwriter. Riding the worldwide wave of the folksong revival, he soon became one of the most popular East German performing artists, especially among high school and university students. He also became increasingly critical of the SED's stifling of artistic freedom. (In 1965 the SED's Central Committee had issued new guidelines for authors and artists that prohibited any deviation from the officially sanctioned "socialist realism" line.) Biermann's music was easily accessible, but the lyrics of his songs were often iconoclastic and bitterly sarcastic.

The regime's retaliation was not long in coming. In the pivotal year of 1965 Biermann was declared a "class enemy," and forbidden to perform his songs in public. He was also put under Stasi surveillance. Ten years later, while Biermann was on an officially approved concert tour in West Germany, the East German government used the excuse that Biermann had performed some songs critical of the Communist regime to strip him of his East German citizenship and prohibited him from returning to the GDR.

This decision, which was reminiscent of the Nazis' policy of depriving Germany's Jews of their citizenship, evoked a storm of protest inside and outside of the GDR. In East Germany more than one hundred authors and artists, including Christa Wolf and the rock star Nina Hagen, signed a letter protesting the SED's decision to expel Biermann. At the time, the SED did not relent, but many historians see the Biermann affair as the beginning of the regime's implosion fifteen years later.

Biermann himself embarked upon a second and equally successful career in West Germany. Politically, to the consternation of his left-leaning friends, he abandoned his communist views and embraced a more centrist line. He was not able to perform publicly in East Germany until the fall of Erich Honecker in late 1989. Under Honecker's successor, Egon Krenz, the SED was anxious to show that it had abandoned its cultural strangulation policies, and Biermann was invited to resume his East German career. He did, once again to great popular acclaim. Today, at age seventy-four he continues to be one of the most successful entertainers throughout Germany.

that the term implies in the West. Each of the Kombinate employed between 20,000 and 40,000 workers.

Honecker's regime modified some of the economic decision-making apparatus it inherited. Ulbricht's successor did not share his predecessor's fascination with cybernetics, and Honecker reintroduced some centralization in economic decision making. (The economics ministries abolished in 1963 were all reestablished.) But after 1971 the GDR's planning priorities emphasized the production of consumer goods while continuing efforts to bring certain sectors of the economy—notably chemicals, precision machinery, and electronics—to the level where East German products could compete on the world market.

Despite some notable gains in these export-oriented sectors during the 1970s, the GDR never earned enough hard currency to pay for food imports and sustain a rising standard of living. The problems were not all the responsibility of the GDR's planners. As a country that had to import virtually all of its raw materials, East Germany was particularly adversely affected by the rapid rise in the cost of raw materials and energy during the 1970s and 1980s. Until 1980 the Soviets cushioned the effect of the oil shock for their satellites. The price of Russian oil—the GDR obtained virtually all of its oil from the Soviet Union—increased by 22 percent, but this increase was modest in comparison to the staggering price increases on the free market. After 1980, however, the Soviets, who had their own economic problems, ceased subsidies to their allies and raised prices for Russian oil to world levels.

Nevertheless, some of the problems were clearly the responsibility of the GDR's economic planners. The continued absence of political freedom and the overly centralized economic decision-making apparatus stifled the economy. Labor productivity in East Germany remained some 60 percent lower than in West Germany. The productivity problem in the GDR was compounded by its rapidly aging population, a problem that was intensified in the late 1980s by the flight of

tens of thousands of refugees—most of them under twenty-five years of age—from the GDR to West Germany (see later, p. 330ff).

In the late 1970s the GDR for the first time experienced the consequences of significant, albeit hidden, inflation. In the West increased costs are routinely passed on to the consumer, but in East Germany political and social reasons precluded this course of action. Basic foodstuffs, housing, and local transportation remained heavily subsidized. To close the gaping cost–price chasm, East Germany used a variety of strategies. In part, the GDR cut back on the production of nonbasic consumer goods. (As a result, used private automobiles were twice as expensive as new ones because there was a two- to three-year waiting period for a new car.) A second strategy was to go into debt. Unable to finance technological advances from its own resources, East Germany, like other East European countries, accumulated sizable obligations to Western banks. The East German foreign debt, which had been negligible during the Ulbricht years ($1 billion in 1970), was estimated at some $11.4 billion at the end of 1981, and $26.6 billion in 1989. Moreover, half of the debt was literally eaten up; it represented the cost of needed food imports from Western countries. When the GDR collapsed in 1989, its hard currency income from exports to Western countries covered only about two-thirds of the interest the country owed Western banks.

Nevertheless, the political leaders found ways of delaying the reckoning. The complicated financial ties between East and West Germany played a major role in the GDR's strategy for coping with its economic problems. In its trade relations with the FRG, East Germany could draw on a sizable interest-free credit line. In addition, millions of deutsche marks were paid annually by West Germany in the form of user fees for postal, railroad, and road services in connection with travel by West Germans to and from West Berlin and as "compensation" for the release of political prisoners from East German jails to West Germany. (Between 1964 and 1989 the Federal Republic "bought" 33,755 prisoners at a total cost of 3.44 billion deutsche mark.)

The regime collected additional millions after private West German travel in East Germany was liberalized in 1972; in 1985, 6.7 million West Germans and West Berliners made trips to the GDR. East Germany benefited directly from these visits because visitors had to exchange 25 deutsche marks—at the official exchange rate of one to one for East German marks—for each day spent in the GDR. In addition, individual East Germans were permitted to receive up to 500 deutsche marks per visit from West German friends and relatives.

The consequence of this influx of hard currency was the establishment of a dual system of marketing consumer goods in the GDR. To prevent the hard currency in private hands from generating a black market, the state created special hard currency stores called *Intershops.* Run by the state retail trade organization, they offered a variety of goods unobtainable in regular stores. Payment, however, had to be made in Western currencies. The regime also set up another string of stores, the *Exquisitshops,* which sold scarce consumer goods for East German marks but at much higher prices than those officially set. These strategies were effective in containing popular discontent with the lack of availability of consumer products at the officially set prices, but they were hardly the hallmarks of a well-functioning socialist economy.

Still, it is true that East Germany's GDP was higher by a third than that of any other Soviet bloc country. Technologically, the economy was the most advanced among the Comecon nations, and for a time the GDR even exported some high-technology products, such as small computers, to the West. However, Honecker's hope that exports would propel the economy permanently forward proved illusionary. The East German economy was increasingly dependent on West German imports and financial subsidies. After the fall of the GDR it became clear that the true facts of the GDR's growing bankruptcy were hidden from the people and even most members of the Politburo by false reports of economic growth and illusionary levels of productivity regularly issued by the office of Günter Mittag, the member of the Politburo responsible for the economy. Honecker seems to have known the truth, but, like Mittag, he was convinced that in time the economy would "grow itself" out of its problems.

Under Honecker, while the economy languished, the GDR scored some remarkable foreign policy successes. The Hallstein Doctrine was a memory of the past, and the GDR became a recognized member of the family of nations. East Germany maintained full diplomatic relations with most countries in the world, including the United States and other NATO members. For both East Germany and West Germany, diplomatic milestones in the achievement of international respectability were their simultaneous acceptances as members of the United Nations in 1973, and their participation as sovereign nations in the 1975 Helsinki Conference on European Security and Cooperation. No one enjoyed the GDR's international visibility more than Erich Honecker. In the 1980s the SED's general secretary went on thirty-eight official state visits to foreign countries. The culmination of the GDR's quest for prestige was, of course, Honecker's state visit to West Germany in 1987.

Despite the GDR's growing international recognition, Honecker never lost sight of the real foundations of his power. Except for taking a somewhat softer line on the deployment of American missiles in West Germany in the mid-1980s, the East German leader was a loyal and consistent supporter of the Soviets' foreign policy line. Among the USSR's East European satellites, only Bulgaria and Czechoslovakia aligned themselves more closely with the Soviet Union. The GDR and the Soviet Union were particularly close in their views of the developments in Poland that began in 1981 with the formation of the Solidarity free labor-union movement. Like the USSR, East Germany showed no sympathy with the aims of the reformers inside and outside the Polish government. In developing countries East Germany continued its role as Soviet surrogate. The GDR established sizable economic and military aid programs and sent several hundred military advisers to African, Asian, and Latin American countries, notably Angola, Ethiopia, Cuba, and Vietnam.

In the 1980s the relationship between the GDR and the USSR became less harmonious. As the world's two superpowers at the time, the United States and the Soviet Union, were abandoning détente and returning to the politics of confrontation, both the GDR and the FRG for a time attempted to continue something like a "little entente" in their bilateral relations, but that effort aroused the Soviets' ire. They portrayed the West Germans as the chief warmongers among the U.S.–led imperialist camp, and Honecker's accommodating stance ran counter to the Soviets' line. In the fall of 1984 Honecker was ordered to Moscow and told in unusually undiplomatic and blunt terms that his Russian mentors "advised" against undertaking his long-planned and (by Honecker) eagerly awaited visit to West Germany. The secretary general accepted the "advice," realizing, as he told a reporter in November 1984, "Small nations can't do much without the approval of great powers."

Despite continuing economic problems and some foreign policy constraints, the GDR under Honecker almost until the end appeared to be a "normal" and stable society. Totally misreading the signs of the looming crisis, the regime insisted it had the enthusiastic support of the people. In May 1986 Honecker told a visiting West German dignitary that the recent (carefully staged) May Day demonstrations were clear evidence of the regime's popularity in all parts of the GDR. The SED held out to its citizens no promises of major political reforms, but it had also abandoned any attempt to force the East Germans to sacrifice material benefits in the name of a future socialist utopia. In fact, rather the reverse was true. East Germany became a somewhat drab and unexciting but "real, existing"—to use favorite adjectives of the SED's propaganda machine—welfare state.

Very early on, the GDR developed into a cradle-to-grave welfare state with clear,

ideologically determined social-policy priorities. The system was designed to benefit particularly the industrial working class. Such necessities of life as basic foodstuffs—particularly bread and potatoes—housing, and local transportation were heavily subsidized by the state. For example, a mass-transit ride in any East German city, including East Berlin, cost 20 East German pfennigs, less than 7 U.S. cents at the official rate of exchange. Housing, too, was very cheap in East Germany, but the enforced low rents also meant that there was little income to pay for repairs or finance new construction. Moreover, during the Ulbricht years, housing ranked low in the planning priorities. The result was a chronic housing shortage and constant complaints about poor living conditions. Honecker gained immediate popularity with his people when he pushed through a massive program of housing construction. Between 1971 and 1980 more than 1.3 million apartment units were newly constructed or renovated, making housing construction one of the few parts of the 1976–1980 Five Year Plan whose targets were actually exceeded.

But the building program also had a tremendous negative impact on the GDR's internal indebtedness. Lothar Mertens has calculated that on average each new apartment cost 120,000 East German marks. The annual rent for the average unit was 600 marks. (Rents in the GDR were massively subsidized.) This meant that the apartment would be paid for in 200 years provided there were no maintenance or repair costs. But, of course, there were; on average 4,173 marks per year. In effect, then, the annual rent paid for about one-seventh of the maintenance and repair costs and none of the original construction outlays.

In contrast to the basic necessities of life, items that the regime identified with a middle-class or "capitalist" lifestyle remained very expensive and in short supply. There were never enough cars, color televisions, refrigerators, and washing machines to meet consumer demands. Average East Germans had to wait months and often years before being able to buy such big-ticket items, and even then they paid five or six times the comparable Western price for a lower-quality product. Under Honecker the regime assumed that if the GDR's citizens had a roof over their head, a full stomach, and an assured workplace they would not be concerned about the continuing lack of political freedoms. That assumption was false, but there was also another problem. While the regime pointed out how much better things were than they had been during the Weimar years, the East German people saw how much worse off their were in comparison to their West German compatriots. As another popular joke had it, "In the GDR everything is getting better, but nothing is ever good."

Toward the end of the decade, the GDR's economic and political high-wire act became more and more difficult to maintain. Increasingly, the iron law of oligarchy seized hold of the party organs at all levels of administration. Overcentralized, staffed with aging functionaries (in 1989 the average age of the members of the SED's Politburo was sixty-seven), East Germany more and more stood as odd man out among the countries of Eastern Europe in which *glasnost* (openness) and *perestroika* (restructuring) were becoming the norm.

Two books by SED insiders published in 1977 and 1984 provided excellent analyses of the problems. In his publication *Die Alternative: Zur Kritik des real existierenden Sozialismus* ("The Alternative: A Criticism of Real Existing Socialism"), Rudolf Bahro, who was a young SED functionary at the time he wrote the book, subjected the GDR's party and state bureaucracy to scathing criticism. (East German censors prohibited publication of the work in the GDR; it was published in West Germany.) Bahro accused the East German "Politburocracy" of existing to perpetuate its own power, rather than serving the needs of society. In 1984 another work published in West Germany, *Der Rat der sozialistischen Götter* ("The Council of Socialist

Gods"), made the same observation from an even better vantage point. Before emigrating to the FRG, the author, Franz Loeser, had been the party secretary at East Berlin's prestigious Humboldt University, and he had frequent dealings with the highest officials of the SED's Central Committee and Politburo.

The GDR's leaders failed to "win the hearts and minds" of their people. Each year thousands of East Germans (estimates for 1985 ran as high as 400,000) applied for exit permits to leave the GDR and resettle in West Germany. Virtually all applications were refused without explanation. In fact, until 1989 submitting an application to emigrate was officially deemed a "criminal offense." Another indication of the mutual distrust between the people and their leaders was the growing and ubiquitous presence of the Stasi throughout all levels of society. Since the fall of the GDR it has become clear that the Stasi made use of a veritable army of "informal collaborators" to report on their neighbors, colleagues, and family members.

While thousands were prevented from leaving, others were forced to leave the GDR. The regime's reaction to attacks by insiders like Bahro, Loeser, and others was swift, although restrained, repression. Unlike Ulbricht, Honecker did not resort to massive purges in the party or wholesale terror of the population at large. Rather, the regime attempted to silence criticism by expelling its most prominent critics. Leading opponents of the SED were simply deprived of their East German citizenship and deported to West Germany. Until his death in 1999, Bahro embarked on a second career in the West as a prominent spokesperson for the radical anti-industrial wing of the West German Green Party. Loeser was hired to teach philosophy at the University of Kiel. In some cases, like that of Robert Havemann, the regime resorted to internal repression. As we saw, the famous Marxist philosopher was not deported but placed under house arrest for the rest of his life; he was also prohibited from writing or speaking publicly.

A somewhat dreary and uninspired window display in a shop to celebrate the friendship between the USSR and the GDR. (Source: SZ Photo/Lehnartz, Klaus/The Image Works)

Although the regime reacted strongly to criticism from within the SED, it was even more concerned about the signs of growing alienation among the country's youth. It was this phenomenon that made the case of the popular singer and songwriter Wolf Biermann such a cause célèbre. Biermann had long been a thorn in the side of the party establishment. As early as 1965 Honecker had pointed to Biermann's poems, which were bitingly critical of the regime's inhumanity, as examples of the influence of Western decadence. In November 1976 Biermann, too, was expelled from East Germany.

Biermann was deported at a time when, ironically, there were signs that the SED was relaxing its definition of socialist realism. Although in the 1960s Honecker had acquired a well-deserved reputation as a cultural hard-liner, the party censors after 1971 seemed to work with a less heavy hand. An interesting case of liberalization came in 1980 with the first public production of Heiner Müller's play *Der Bau* ("The Construction Site"). Written in 1965, the play concerns the fate of a party secretary who succeeds in raising the productivity of the construction site for which he is responsible, but who loses his personal integrity in the process. When it originally appeared in print the play was severely criticized by party officials (among them Honecker) and not allowed to be staged.

Such tokens of liberalization could not stifle the growing criticism of the regime's cultural policies by the country's intellectuals. They reacted especially strongly to the process of depriving some East Germans of their citizenship, a practice that was reminiscent of the Nazis' stripping Jews and opposition figures of their rights as German citizens. When Wolf Biermann was expelled from the GDR, more than a hundred prominent East German artists and writers signed a Statement of Protest against the regime's measures. The list included virtually every well-known East German author. The SED reacted swiftly, mounting a massive campaign of criticism against the signatories of the statement. Eventually some thirty members of the writers'

union were expelled from the organization for their "antisocial" activity, a punishment that was tantamount to being blacklisted because authors who were not members of the writers' union had great difficulty being published in the GDR. World-famous writers like Stefan Heym and Christa Wolf were largely silenced in their own country.

The crackdown on intellectuals heightened the significance of the only mass-membership institutions that had succeeded in evading direct control by the SED—the churches. In East Germany, this meant primarily the Protestant churches because about two-thirds of those individuals who maintained a church affiliation were Protestant. In the early years after the founding of the GDR, the regime pushed through a total separation of church and state, and during the Stalinist and Ulbricht phases the churches were actively persecuted as well. The Communists especially tried to discourage younger East Germans from maintaining church membership. (Being a church member was sufficient reason for being barred from attending universities and other advanced training institutes.) The regime also introduced a secular *Jugendweihe* (youth consecration) ceremony to take the place of Christian confirmation. In addition, the churches were forced to cut off all institutional connections to their counterparts in West Germany. Nevertheless, under Honecker the regime not only respected the churches' organizational autonomy, but also permitted them to become the unofficial "sponsors" of the GDR's growing ecology and pacifist movements. In fact, the SED hoped that the churches would control these groups of dissidents and prevent them from becoming an organized political opposition.

The uneasy accommodation between leaders and people in the GDR was shattered in the summer and fall of 1989. Tensions had been building for some time. The East German regime was clearly uncomfortable with Mikhail Gorbachev's reform policies in the Soviet Union, and it sought to reduce their fallout in the GDR as much as possible. East German censors prohibited the dissemination of the suddenly less controlled Soviet periodicals. In 1987 the East German postal authorities prohibited the importation and distribution of the Soviet journal *Sputnik*. This journal, which began publication in 1967, was a sort of cross between the *National Enquirer* and the *Reader's Digest*. The contents ranged from cooking recipes and travel accounts to sightings of Himalayan yetis. Beginning in late 1988 *Sputnik* started publishing a number of articles highly critical of the past history of communism. The authors compared Stalin to Hitler and pointed out that the German Communists were partially responsible for the rise of the Nazis. *Sputnik* had 130,000 subscribers in the GDR. This was the first time the GDR had ever censored a Soviet publication. Again and again, spokesmen reiterated that although changes might be needed in the Soviet Union, reforms in the GDR were not necessary. In a much noted (and quoted) figure of speech, Kurt Hager, the member of the Politburo responsible for propaganda, told a West German magazine, "Just because your neighbor is putting up new wallpaper, doesn't mean you have to."

In the summer of 1989, the GDR and the other Soviet bloc countries seemed to embark on increasingly divergent paths. Freedom of expression was the watchword in the Soviet Union, a noncommunist government took power in Poland, and Hungary permitted noncommunist parties to organize, but in the GDR there were no moves in the direction of greater freedom and pluralism. On the contrary, the regime went out of its way to praise the brutal repression of the Chinese students' movement for more democracy in June. In sharp contrast to developments in Hungary, the East German authorities specifically prohibited the organization of independent political groups. A number of such organizations were now appearing, often working under the protective umbrella of the Protestant churches. Their agendas ranged from environmental concerns to political reforms, but interestingly in the spring and summer of 1989 none of these groups put

reunification between East and West Germany on their agenda.

To persist in a course of action that was at odds with developments among its neighbors and unpopular with its people, the GDR needed strong and firm leadership. But precisely that was lacking. In the spring of 1989, Erich Honecker fell ill. An official announcement spoke of minor gallbladder trouble. Actually he was suffering from cancer of the liver, and his illness—Honecker was not seen in public for weeks—paralyzed the regime's decision-making apparatus since Honecker's associates were unwilling to act in the absence of their leader.

The regime turned to its well-stocked arsenal of propaganda tactics. In May 1989 there were local elections in the GDR. These events normally aroused little interest, since the results were a foregone conclusion: 99 plus percent of the voters always cast their ballots for the official candidates. But this time things were different. In many localities the SED party secretary, anxious to prove the regime's popularity, reported "yes" votes that clearly exceeded the number of registered voters. And, equally important, the newly emerging opposition groups sent observers to the voting places. These monitors immediately publicized voting fraud when they saw it firsthand.

This combination of paralysis and ineptitude at the top and dissatisfaction at the bottom began a process of dramatic change in East Germany. Taking advantage of Hungary's decision to dismantle its border fortifications with Austria, in July and August thousands of East German vacationers in Hungary decided not to return to the GDR, but to flee instead to Austria and from there to West Germany. Several thousand more took refuge in the West German embassies in Prague and Warsaw. The East German authorities eventually permitted them to travel to the West as well. By the end of 1989, some 400,000 East Germans—mostly young families and skilled workers—left the GDR, the largest exodus since the Berlin Wall was built in 1961.

In handling the refugee issue as well as other problems facing the regime in the last months of its existence, the SED's leaders demonstrated a singular lack of understanding of the reality of the rapidly changing times. It should have been obvious to the Politburo that the thousands clamoring to leave the GDR were a public relations embarrassment, and that it was in the GDR's interest to let them resettle in West Germany as quickly and quietly as possible. Once the decision was made, for example, to let the refugees leave the West German embassy in Prague and travel to the Federal Republic, logic and politics would have dictated that the special trains, supplied by the West German Federal Railways, travel directly from Czechoslovakia to West Germany.

Honecker and Mielke, however, insisted that the trains take the long way through East Germany before reaching their destination in the West. There were two reasons for this decision: One was to demonstrate strength. As the trains were traveling through the GDR, East German border guards stamped the papers of the refugees "expelled from the German Democratic Republic" to keep up the fiction that these were expellees, not refugees. But the regime was also trying to preempt further unrest in the GDR. Since the Stasi had no idea who had taken refuge in the West German embassy in Prague, collecting personal data on the trains enabled the secret police to identify close relatives of the refugees and either let them emigrate as well or keep a close watch over them. Needless to say, everywhere the trains stopped in East Germany for technical reasons, there were clashes between police and people trying to board the trains. The public relations disaster continued.

The flight of the refugees was an embarrassment to the East German regime, but the massive antigovernment demonstrations that began in October endangered the regime's very existence. In Leipzig more than 100,000 people took to the streets in what became weekly "Monday night"

demonstrations. The assemblies were either spontaneous get-togethers or organized by the many political reform movements that had evolved out of the earlier ecology and pacifist groups. Their names—*Neues Forum* ("New Forum"), *Demokratischer Aufbruch* ("Democratic Awakening"), *Demokratie Jetzt* ("Democracy Now")—were meant to suggest the coming era of openness and democracy in East Germany. At this time none of the organizations advocated the abolition of the GDR's socialist system; they wanted reforms, and their hero was Mikhail Gorbachev.

From the viewpoint of the SED, the situation was reminiscent of events in June 1953, but this time there was a fundamental difference. The Russians had already made it clear to the East Germans that the GDR was on its own. Soviet troops stationed in East Germany would not intervene in the conflict between the regime and its people. Left to its own devices, the SED proved singularly inept in dealing with the growing crisis. The Stasi attempted to infiltrate the demonstrations with "reliable, class-conscious" workers, but such efforts had little effect. The party leaders also contemplated the time-honored "exchange of party documents," a code phrase for a purge of the party membership, but this too proved to be a blunt instrument, since each day thousands of SED comrades were already turning in their party membership books.

The Politburo lived in a world of its own. Its members later recalled that the first item on the agenda at each weekly meeting was not the growing unrest in the streets but organizing the celebrations for the fortieth anniversary of the GDR's founding in early October. There was some consideration of calling out the army to suppress the demonstrations, and at one point a unit of the NVA was mobilized as a demonstration of force, but in the end the regime recoiled from such violent measures, no doubt in part because the members of the Politburo were not at all sure that the soldiers would obey orders to shoot the demonstrators. Honecker's successor,

The East German leadership on the reviewing stand for what turned out to be the disastrous fortieth anniversary celebration of the GDR. Gorbachev is at the center of the front row; Honecker is the rather forlorn-looking man in the front row second from right. (Source: Courtesy of Corbis/Sygma.)

Egon Krenz, claims that he personally drafted an order prohibiting the use of live ammunition by the NVA and that Honecker signed the order on October 13, 1989.

Actually, as Ilko-Sascha Kowalczuk has shown, the decision not to use force was made at the local level as a result of negotiations between ad hoc elected leaders of the demonstrators and representatives of the SED and the *Stasi*. In Leipzig, where the largest demonstrations took place, Kurt Masur, the music director of the Leipzig *Gewandhaus* orchestra (he later held the same position with the New York Philharmonic), took a leading part in the talks with the party and *Stasi* authorities. These local agreements were then merely ratified by the higher levels of the party and government apparatus.

The event on which Honecker and his associates had pinned their hopes for stabilizing the GDR turned out to be another public relations disaster. The official celebration of the GDR's fortieth anniversary proceeded as planned, complete with a military parade and banner-swinging youth and worker groups, but the official event was upstaged by thousands of demonstrators shouting "Gorbi, Gorbi" within hearing distance of the celebrities' viewing stand. Gorbachev, who was a guest of honor at the celebrations, met with the SED's leaders, but the two sides talked past each other. The Soviet leader reiterated his plea for reforms, and Honecker icily responded that the GDR had no need for reforms. No one contradicted the SED's general secretary. Günter Schabowski, the party's leader in East Berlin, later remembered, "We just sat there like … "

Now the old order in the GDR crumbled fast. Confronted with ever larger popular demonstrations, increasing criticism from the leaders of the usually subservient noncommunist parties, and fast-growing new political groups (which now included a resurrected Social Democratic Party), the SED hastened to throw out old leaders and old policies. In mid-October 1989 the

Politburo forced Erich Honecker and his closest associates to resign.

Honecker was succeeded as head of the party and chief of state by Egon Krenz. When he began his brief stint as the leader of East Germany, Krenz was hardly the embodiment of a new beginning. True, he was relatively young by Politburo standards; Krenz was fifty-two at the time of his selection. But he was also an old-line apparatchik, who had spent his entire career serving the SED in a variety of functions. He was a professional youth organizer and long-term head of the FDJ. On the Central Committee Krenz was responsible for security affairs, and in this capacity he headed the delegation that traveled to China in June 1989 to congratulate the Chinese Communists for their forceful repression of the "counter-revolutionaries" assembled in Beijing's Tiananmen Square. Finally, as head of the national election commission overseeing the fraudulent local elections in May, Krenz had earned the popular title of "chief election manipulator."

In the manner of a Western politician, the "youthful" Krenz moved energetically to convince the East German people he represented a true "turnaround." (He used the word *Wende* in German, the same term Helmut Kohl had used to characterize his new course in 1982.) But the selection of a new leader was not enough, and more profound changes soon followed. In the first week of November 1989, the entire Politburo and all members of the East German cabinet resigned. The new prime minister was Hans Modrow, the SED's district chief in Dresden. Modrow had long advocated economic and political reforms, and it was precisely for that reason that Honecker had kept him out of the Politburo and the corridors of national power.

The regime announced plans to decentralize the economy and, most important, an easing of travel restrictions. But yet again it was a case of too little too late. The Politburo considered a scheme under which citizens of the GDR could apply for permission to travel outside the country.

However, travel was to be limited to thirty days per year, and the East Germans had long experience with applications that languished for years in the Stasi's file cabinets. In view of yet more signs of dissatisfaction with its halfway measures, the Politburo decided to open the borders, although it was not clear when this would happen. That decision was inadvertently made by Günter Schabowski, who could claim his fifteen minutes of fame on November 9, 1989. Schabowski, the SED's chief in East Berlin, and the Central Committee's newly appointed secretary for information and media relations, was asked to explain the Politburo's decision to the press. In response to a reporter's question when the borders would be open, Schabowski, finding nothing specific in the materials he had been given, mumbled "immediately, without delay."

In effect, the regime had opened the Berlin Wall. Thousands rushed to the border-crossing points between East and West Berlin. The guards, left without instruction about how to handle the surging masses, eventually opened the gates. The Berlin Wall had become a porous, if still ugly, concrete structure. (Again, the ironies of history: The 1918 revolution in Berlin began on November 9; exactly five years later in 1923, Hitler launched his abortive Beer Hall putsch; and on the same date in 1938, the anti-Jewish pogrom of the *Reichskristallnacht* took place.)

If the SED had anticipated that these changes would be sufficient to appease the aroused people of East Germany, its hopes were soon shattered. Revelations in the newly free East German press about the elite's life-style led to further personnel and policy changes. Erich Honecker and his associates had for years preached austerity in the name of egalitarian communism, but it now became clear that austerity was meant only for the people, not the party leaders. The members of the Politburo hardly lived lives of luxury by Western standards, but they enjoyed privileges that the average East German could only dream of. The top echelons of the SED occupied a separate housing compound, had hunting preserves at their disposal, shopped in special stores well stocked with Western goods, and some even maintained secret Swiss bank accounts.

The furor over these revelations led to the arrest of the leading members of the old guard (because of his illness Honecker was only placed under house arrest), and it swept Egon Krenz from power after only forty-six days in office. Although there was no evidence that he had personally benefited from the corruption at the top, Krenz's long years as a loyal apparatchik now made him a political liability. He resigned both as party leader and as head of state. In the latter position he was succeeded by Manfred Gerlach, the head of the small Liberal Democratic Party. The East German liberals had long been a mere appendage of the SED, but in the fall of 1989, the party and its leader suddenly became vigorous advocates of further reforms and democratization.

Throwing Egon Krenz to the wolves of popular discontent was only the first step in the SED's desperate attempt to regain a measure of popularity among the people of East Germany. At a hastily called special party congress in mid-December, the delegates voted to rename the SED *Partei des Demokratischen Sozialismus* (Party of Democratic Socialism, PDS). They also agreed to eliminate all of the familiar institutional trappings of a Marxist-Leninist party. The post of general secretary was abolished, and a democratically elected executive committee replaced the dictatorial Central Committee and Politburo. The congress also elected a new leader, Gregor Gysi, someone who really was untainted by the sins of the past.

The PDS's new chairman was a forty-one-year-old lawyer who had never been close to, much less at home in, the corridors of power. However, what he lacked in age and experience, he seemingly made up in moral stature and personal integrity. The son of a Communist resistance fighter who was persecuted by the Nazis both for his political views and his Jewish ancestry, Gregor Gysi joined the SED at age nineteen, but he never became a party functionary. Instead, he remained in private law practice, and many of his clients were dissidents and opponents of the regime. (Incidentally, Gysi's father, Klaus Gysi, did hold a high position in the GDR's government; he was the state secretary for church affairs.)

Would the rejuvenated SED be able to lead the GDR along a path of "socialist democracy," a course that Gysi proclaimed as a "third way" between Stalinism and capitalism in his inaugural address to the party congress that elected him? At the end of 1989, the party's prospects were not promising. Almost a half million members (out of a total of 2.3 million) had resigned their party membership in the course of the year, and in an interview with a West German magazine, Hans Modrow, the GDR's new and last SED prime minister, acknowledged that "our newly active sociologists" predicted the SED would get no more than 20 percent of the vote in a free election.

Modrow was overly optimistic. The people of the GDR remained in ferment. The government had agreed to participate in so-called Round Table discussions with the major opposition groups to chart a democratic future for East Germany, but for the irate masses the pace of reform was too slow. On January 15, 1990, an angry crowd stormed the East Berlin headquarters of the hated Stasi. (After some hesitation the government eventually decided to disband the security apparatus.) Now clearly on the defensive, Modrow in early February agreed to take representatives from the Round Table groups into his cabinet and to schedule free elections for March 18.

The results of that contest, the first genuinely free elections in East Germany in fifty-eight years, were both surprising and decisive. Although the SED's regime had been toppled by indigenous grassroots political groups, the March campaign was dominated by parties that were sister organizations of the major West German parties. The Alliance for

Germany was an amalgam of groups closely affiliated with the West German CDU/CSU, the Social Democratic Party was linked to the SPD, and the Union of Free Democrats had the support of the FDP. Prominent West German politicians also campaigned widely throughout the GDR.

The clear victor was the Alliance for Germany. With 93.3 percent of the eligible voters casting their ballots, the Alliance, vigorously supported by Helmut Kohl, and campaigning on a platform of reunification with West Germany as soon as possible, gained 48 percent of the popular vote. The Social Democrats were second with 21.9 percent, and the former SED (now the Party of Democratic Socialism) came in a poor third with 16 percent. In what might be considered a case of political ingratitude, the voters soundly rejected the grassroots opposition groups which had been so instrumental in leading the peaceful revolution that toppled the SED regime. None of them received more than 3 percent of the popular vote.

Hans Modrow's days as prime minister were clearly numbered. His successor, with a mandate to guide the GDR toward union with the Federal Republic, was Lothar de Maizière, an unprepossessing lawyer and amateur musician who headed the East German CDU. The end of the GDR came more quickly than most observers (and politicians) had anticipated. Political leaders in the West as well as the reformers in the East had envisioned that as East Germany became a genuinely democratic state, relations with the FRG would become increasingly cordial, but that the two states would remain separate entities. Anxious to channel the increasingly turbulent developments in the GDR, West German chancellor Helmut Kohl at the end of November 1989 proposed a multistep plan for a Confederation and eventual unification of the GDR and the FRG. Kohl was careful not to insist on a timetable, but even so his initiative sent up warning flags in Moscow as well as in Paris and London.

Especially Margaret Thatcher, the British prime minister, was adamantly opposed to German reunification. She embarked on a vigorous campaign to persuade both the U.S. president George Bush and President François Mitterand of France that the Western Allies should take steps to prevent the political union of the two Germanies. The French president was sympathetic to Thatcher's position, although he was less vocal. Nevertheless Mitterand, too, made an effort to stop German reunification. In late December 1989 he traveled to East Berlin and met with several East German leaders, including the SED's new chairman, Gregor Gysi. Mitterand assured Gysi of France's continued support for an independent and sovereign GDR. In contrast, President Bush was a leading proponent of reunification, insisting only that if and when reunification came a united Germany needed to retain its membership in NATO. Still, Helmut Kohl and his cabinet were certainly aware that Thatcher and Mitterand were not alone in their fears of a reunited Germany. In October 1989, months before reunification emerged as a likely event, the distinguished Anglo-Irish publicist Conor Cruise O'Brien warned, "Beware, the Reich is Rising" (the title of his article in the London newspaper, *The Times*), and predicted there would soon be a statue of Adolf Hitler in every German town.

West Germany's partners in the European Community (EC) were also initially skeptical. At a hastily called summit conference in Strasbourg in mid-December 1989, the leaders of the EC (including Kohl) issued a statement favoring that "the German people will regain its unity through free self-determination," but the leaders also warned that the process of unification had to take place in the context of better European and superpower relations. As for the Soviet Union and the new leaders of East Germany, they insisted reunification was not "on the agenda." And even if it were to come some day, any united Germany had to be created within the territorial boundaries established in 1945.

In the face of opposition from the East and cautioning statements from the West, the Federal Republic retreated. Government leaders from President von Weiszäcker on down emphasized that "there should be no effort to push it [reunification] to frantic growth." But events outpaced the leaders' cautious blueprints. The decisive catalyst was the rapidly collapsing East German economy. Freed from the restrictions of censorship and the requirement to report "optimistic typicality," the East German press revealed an economy that was saddled with huge debts and outdated and inefficient equipment. The communist system had also left staggering environmental problems in the wake of the drive to increase production at all costs. In 1989 only 3 percent of the streams and rivers and 1 percent of the lakes in the GDR were "ecologically alive." The GDR's government desperately sought help from the West.

Under Hans Modrow, the government began decentralizing the economy and making it responsive to "market forces." The prime minister welcomed investors from the West and encouraged joint ventures with Western companies. But it was not at all clear how such changes could be accommodated in a system that continued to call for "socialism." The de Maizière cabinet essentially abandoned the GDR's fiscal and economic independence. Negotiations between the central banks of East and West Germany on a currency union between the two countries resulted in an agreement that made the deutsche mark the East German currency as of July 1, 1990.

Political union between East and West Germany followed a few months later. After Chancellor Kohl in a triumph of personal diplomacy had secured Mikhail Gorbachev's agreement to a reunited Germany that would remain a member of NATO, the GDR and the FRG negotiated a "second state treaty" (the first was the agreement on economic and social unification), which was signed on August 31. Technically, the lengthy document (over a thousand pages long) represented an agreement between two sovereign states, but actually there was never any doubt that the GDR would be absorbed into West

Germany. At the same time, the Big Four, the GDR, and the Federal Republic in so-called two-plus-four negotiations worked out what amounted to a peace treaty for Germany forty-five years after the end of World War II. The two-plus-four talks were primarily concerned with the rights of the Allies after reunification. One result was a stipulation that the Western Allies would continue to station troops in Germany as part of their NATO obligations. The Russians, however, agreed to remove their forces from German soil. The relocation costs were borne by the German government.

German reunification was to take place under the provisions of Article 23 of the Basic Law. The five (reestablished) Länder in the GDR would become federal states in the same manner that the Saar had joined the FRG in 1957. The date for full-scale political reunification was set for October 3, 1990. Shortly before then, on September 12, the former occupying powers gave their formal assent to German reunification.

CONCLUSION

Much like the Federal Republic, but for entirely different reasons, the German Democratic Republic at the end of the 1980s found itself at a crossroads. In some ways East Germany was a successful society. Starting from a poor base of natural resources and devastated by war and reparations, the GDR had given its people a standard of living that was higher than that of any other Soviet bloc country.

During the Ulbricht years, the regime had a vision of the future that, although it was utopian and unrealistic, did give the society, and especially its leaders, a goal that set the GDR apart from the "other" Germany. The Honecker regime largely abandoned ideological utopianism in favor of pragmatism and short-term economic goals, but it did not relax the political dictatorship.

But the communist dictatorship imposed on the GDR by Stalin and his German partners and successors was never accepted by the

East German people. Neither Ulbricht's nor Honecker's version of "socialism" satisfied the citizens of the GDR, most of whom wanted political and economic freedoms. True, in the absence of any alternative, the citizens of the GDR in time seemed to accept, if not love, their leaders and system.

All of the GDR's accomplishments were thrown into question by the Gorbachev era. While processes of political and economic liberalization were taking place in other East European countries, the GDR remained a neo-Stalinist communist dictatorship. But Honecker and his associates could not hold back the tide of reform. The demand for freedom and the collapse of the East German economy swept away both Honecker and the SED's dictatorial regime.

Before that happened a group of "reformers" desperately attempted to stabilize the situation in the fall and winter of 1989–1990. They moved to expose and punish the rampant corruption among the old leaders, eliminated travel restrictions, lifted press censorship, and abandoned the constitutionally mandated "leading role" of the SED. But their efforts came too late. The regime had forfeited the trust of its people, who, naively as it turned out, expected union with West Germany to solve all of the GDR's problems.

CHAPTER ELEVEN

Germany since Reunification

Euphoria and Disillusionment, 1990–Present

In the evening of October 2, 1990, political leaders from West and East Germany assembled at the restored Reichstag building in Berlin to celebrate a momentous event: At one minute after midnight, Germany would once again become a united nation. Speaking before an enormous and enthusiastic crowd, the politicians stressed some common themes. Unity, not separation, had the logic of history on its side. The leitmotif of the evening had been provided by Willy Brandt, the leader of the Social Democratic Party, in another speech in Berlin a year earlier: "What belongs together is coming together." All of the political leaders also emphasized that reunification was not an expression of renewed German chauvinism, but the result of a desire for freedom and self-determination. At the same time, the speakers at the Reichstag provided what might be called the official interpretation of the course of events since the fall of 1989. The collapse of the GDR was the work of its own citizens, and reunification was the result of joint efforts by East and West Germans, aided and encouraged by the four Allies, especially the Russians and the Americans.

If there was any defensive note about the developments of the recent past, it concerned the nature and speed with which unification had taken place. In answer to the criticism that complete union needed a longer period of preparation, spokespersons for the governing coalition pointed out repeatedly that a million East Germans would have moved to the West if economic and social union had not taken place in July 1990. As for the political dimensions of reunification, the political leaders did their best to play down what was actually true: The old GDR had essentially been annexed by the Federal Republic. Since Hitler's annexation of Austria, the word *Anschluss* has had an unpleasant connotation in German political vocabulary, but German reunification really was a form of peaceful and popular Anschluss by the Federal Republic of the old GDR. The new country consists of sixteen federal states, including a single Land composed of what used to be East and West Berlin.

The Bundestag voted to make Berlin the seat of the national government once again. Despite its heavy symbolic implications, moving the German capital from Bonn to Berlin was a rather low-key affair. In September 1999 the Bundestag held its first official session in the newly restored and redesigned Reichstag building. As a symbol of democratic transparency, the British architect in charge of the Reichstag project, Sir Norman Foster, had added a huge glass cupola to the complex. It is accessible to visitors, enabling them to look right down into the meeting hall; the new feature has quickly become one of Berlin's most visible and recognizable landmarks.

While foreign observers emphasized the checkered past of the new (and old) capital and the Reichstag building itself—after all, both Bismarck and Hitler had spoken in the hall—the speeches by Germany's political leaders during the inaugural session of the Bundestag were deliberately subdued. Representatives from all parties emphasized the democratic traditions that had been established in the last fifty years, and they sought to disassociate the new capital from its Prussian and Nazi past. Here another symbol served to underline the rhetoric. Facing the delegates in the hall is a mounted eagle, the traditional German heraldic animal. After much discussion of designing a new eagle for the restored building, it was in the end decided to transport the eagle that had graced the Bonn Bundestag to Berlin. Because of its rather pudgy and decidedly nonaggressive appearance, it had long been affectionately known as "the fat hen."

In October 1990 the critics of unification constituted a very small minority; both Germany's leaders and its people overwhelmingly favored reunification. They also had completely unrealistic expectations about the future of the united country. Typical of this naiveté was Helmut Kohl's address on German television on the evening of October 2. The chancellor described the economic future of Germany in very optimistic terms. With the system of free enterprise installed in all of Germany, West Germany's financial and economic strength, combined with the skills and eagerness to work of the East Germans and the now wide-open markets of Eastern Europe, would bring greater prosperity for all Germans. True, there were some staggering environmental problems in the old GDR, but they, too, would yield quickly to Western cleanup methods.

In the treaty of union between the ex-GDR and the Federal Republic, there had been an agreement that a special commission would reexamine the Basic Law and recommend any constitutional amendments that might be needed. This provision turned out to be pretty much of a dead letter. In July 1994 the commission issued a report that suggested no major changes in what for forty years had provided a very successful constitutional framework for a democratic state in West Germany. The situation was a little different at the Länder level. All of the five new states elected constitutional conventions to write new and democratic state constitutions. (The last, in Thuringia, was finished in October 1993.) Interestingly, some of the most fiercely debated points were issues that had also divided the West German Parliamentary Council, the body that had drafted the Basic Law in 1949. Once again, some delegates wanted to make so-called social rights, such as the right to work and the right to housing, part of the constitution. Again, there was considerable support for their inclusion. But like their counterparts in Bonn, in the end a majority of the delegates in the East German states rejected including such "social rights" in their state constitutions.

At the beginning of the twenty-first century, new constitutional issues emerged on two fronts. In Germany itself the allocation of powers between the states and the federal government needed to be reexamined. At the same time the European Union proposed a new constitution for its supranational institutions that would have an impact on the national units of the EU.

In the wake of the massive problems associated with the absorption of the new East

German Länder, the states complained that they were asked to administer an increasing number of federal laws without the resources to do so. In addition, after the terrorist attacks on the World Trade Center in September 2001, critics complained that the German police establishment was ill designed to deal with the new threat to public safety. Germany has a Federal Criminal Office (*Bundeskriminalamt*), but, unlike the Federal Bureau of Investigation (FBI) in the United States, it is limited to investigative powers. Only the states' police authorities can arrest a suspect.

In 2004 representatives from the federal government and the Länder met to devise what was termed a new federal contract. There were expressions of goodwill on all sides, but, as is often the case, the devil was in the details. As might be expected, the richer states rejected any scheme that mandated a transfer of funds to poorer states. Similarly, when it came to the question of giving up what they considered to be their constitutionally vested rights, the states, led by Bavaria, refused to budge. There would be no new federal contract.

The other, equally stillborn, attempt at constitutional innovation came at the European level. At the beginning of 2004, five new members—Poland, Hungary, the Czech Republic, Slovakia, and Malta—joined the EU, and more were to come; by 2007 the EU had twenty-seven member states. With the growing number of members, the EU's structures were becoming increasingly cumbersome. For this reason the EU's executive arm, the Commission, determined that the entity needed a formal constitution to streamline its functions and define more precisely the rights and duties of its various components.

In February 2002 the European Commission asked a group of thirty experts, led by a former president of France, Giscard d'Estaing, to present a draft constitution for the EU. Two years later the governments of all of the member states initialed the document. It would go into effect after it had been ratified by the members' parliaments or approved by a national referendum. Almost as soon as the ratification process began, the draft constitution was in political trouble. Some four hundred pages long, the document was too detailed, and the group of experts, who did not hold elected office, had little appreciation for popular sensitivities. Opponents described the draft constitution as an effort to destroy national liberties in favor of giving power to faceless bureaucrats in Brussels.

Although most of the member states, including Germany, submitted the draft constitution for parliamentary approval (the Bundestag ratified it), France and The Netherlands decided to hold a popular referendum on the issue. Not surprisingly, the opposition mobilized its forces in these countries, and the campaign was successful. In June 2005 a plurality of voters in both France and The Netherlands rejected the European constitution.

Since this setback, the Europeans have been working behind the scenes to revise and revive the draft constitution, and in 2009 the negotiators, led by Sweden, which held the rotating European presidency at the time, came up with the Treaty of Lisbon. This document, too, was controversial, but in the end it was ratified by all member states. (Ireland had to vote twice.) The agreement provides for increased powers for the European parliament, a reduction in the number of issues that require a unanimous votes on the Commission, and, for the first time, a permanent president for the European executive office. The first man to hold that post is the former Belgian prime minister Herman van Rompuy. The EU also now has a permanent foreign and security minister, the British politician Lady Catherine Ashton, Baroness of Upholland. One of her first tasks will be to create a European diplomatic service.

POLITICAL DEVELOPMENTS

As noted earlier, the German president serves as titular leader of the nation, but the office carries few significant powers. As a result, the incumbents tended to be elder statesmen who stayed above the divisiveness of partisan politics. Helmut Kohl attempted to break with this tradition. The chancellor's choice to succeed Richard von Weizsäcker was an Easterner, Steffen Heitmann, the CDU minister of justice in Saxony. Since Heitmann's political views placed him on the extreme right wing of the CDU, Kohl's plan met with stiff opposition even in his own party. A number of CDU leaders, including the speaker of parliament, Rita Süssmuth, complained that he was a singularly poor choice to succeed Weizsäcker. In the face of widespread criticism, Heitmann withdrew his candidacy at the end of November 1993, leaving the chancellor without a suitable candidate for the May 1994 election. After some hesitation the CDU/CSU nominated Roman Herzog, the chief judge of the Federal Constitutional Court; on May 23, 1994, he was elected federal president.

Surprising many observers, Herzog continued the line of remarkably successful federal presidents. A peripatetic traveler, especially in the Eastern states, this jovial Bavarian became one of the most popular public figures in the country. He used his office effectively as a bully pulpit to voice his concerns about present and future problems, and most Germans regretted his decision to serve only one five-year term. (It was subsequently revealed that Herzog's wife was suffering from terminal cancer.)

In 1999 the Federal Assembly elected a successor to Roman Herzog. This was Johannes Rau, a former prime minister of Northrhine-Westphalia. He was nominated by the SPD and the Greens. His opponents were two women—Dagmar Schipanski, a professor at the University of Ilmenau in Thuringia, whom the Christian Democrats nominated, and the candidate of the PDS, Ute Ranke-Heinemann, a theology professor and daughter of the former president Gustav Heinemann. Because the Social Democrats and the Greens had a majority in the Federal Assembly, Rau was elected easily. Rau was the first Social Democrat in the president's office since 1974, and he quickly continued the tradition of using his bully pulpit to admonish, scold, and encourage his people. This was a task for which his long experience as a lay leader in the Protestant Church had prepared him well.

Like Herzog, Rau chose to serve only one five-year term. At the end of his first term in 2003, he was seventy-two years old and decided that he wanted to return to private life. That meant that in 2004, there would be another contested election. This time there were two candidates. Horst Köhler, a Christian Democrat, had the backing of the CDU leader, Angela Merkel (see pp. 352ff). Köhler had a distinguished career as a national and international civil servant. A former deputy finance minister in Kohl's cabinet, at the time of his nomination he served as the president of the International Monetary Fund and lived in Washington, D.C. His opponent, Gesine Schwan, a right-wing Social Democrat who was backed by Gerhard Schröder, had a quite different career. She was an academic, and at the time of her nomination she served as president of Viadriana University, in Frankfurt-on-Oder on the Polish-German border. In this position she symbolized Polish-German cooperation; at least a third of Viadriana University's students come from Poland. A majority of Christian Democrats and Liberals in the Federal Assembly assured Köhler's election. The new president used his bully pulpit primarily to exhort his fellow Germans to shake off their pessimism (see p. 371ff) and embrace needed economic and social reforms.

Quite unexpectedly, Köhler's second term was cut short in June 2010. He resigned his office after an infelicitous speech in which he noted that German troops were serving in Afghanistan not only to bring democracy to the country and defeat international terrorism, but also to safeguard Germany's well-founded global economic interests. The president's remarks aroused a storm of protest that led to his resignation. Merkel nominated the then federal minister of labor, Ursula von der Leyden, as Köhler's successor, but the Federal Assembly chose instead Christian Wulff, the CDU prime minister of Lower Saxony.

On December 2, 1990, some 17 million German voters went to the polls to elect a new federal parliament. It was the first all-German election since the end of World War II, and the new Bundestag would also be the first to include representatives from the five new Länder. (The total number of deputies in the Bundestag was increased by 144 to reflect the addition of the former East German territories.)

At first glance, the Kohl government had every reason to be pleased with the results. The ruling coalition of CDU/CSU and FDP won a comfortable majority of 54.8 percent of the popular vote. The CDU remained Germany's strongest party with 36.7 percent of the popular vote overall, and an even larger share (44.3 percent) of the vote in East Germany. The SPD, which had expected to do particularly well in the East, paid a high price for its ambivalent stand on reunification. Its share of the vote fell to 33.5 percent overall, and a very disappointing 24.5 percent in the eastern districts. The Free Democrats (FDP) obtained 11 percent overall, and they did even better in the east (12 percent). Here the popularity of Germany's foreign minister and the party's leader, Hans-Dietrich Genscher (whose hometown is Halle in Saxony), was a major factor.

In contrast, the extreme right-wing party, the *Republikaner*, did very poorly. Its share of the vote was 2.1 percent nationwide, and 0.1 percent in the east. This meant that the Republikaner fell far short of the 5 percent hurdle and there would be no far-right representation in the 1990 Bundestag. On the left side of the political spectrum, the PDS, the successor organization to the SED, did only marginally better. It gained 9.9 percent of the vote in the former East Germany but only 2.4 percent nationwide. (The PDS would be represented in the new Bundestag because the election law provided that for this single election only, the 5 percent barrier would apply in East and West Germany separately.) A major surprise was the poor showing of the Greens, who obtained only 3.9 percent of the popular vote nationwide. Like the SPD, the Greens were hurt by their stand on reunification; the ecology party had

strongly opposed the rapid merger of East and West Germany. However, the Greens would still be represented in the new Bundestag. They negotiated an agreement to form a single caucus with one of the East German reformist groups, *Bündnis '90* (Alliance '90), which cleared the 5 percent hurdle with 6.6 percent of the vote in the eastern districts.

Seemingly, the only indication of future problems was the relatively low voter turnout. Voter participation of 77.8 percent reflected the beginning of what the Germans call *Politikverdrossenheit* ("being tired of politics"). In the 1987 West German Bundestag elections, voter participation had been 84.3 percent. It quickly became apparent, however, that low voter turnout was only the tip of the iceberg. Soon malaise, scandals, and the rise of political extremism tarnished the image of all of the major parties. Perhaps most striking was the rising number of political corruption cases.

Traditionally, Germany was a country in which corrupt politicians were rare, but after 1990 several prominent leaders were hurt by revelations that they mixed public and private interests or engaged in unethical behavior. In January 1993 the FDP minister of economics, Jürgen Möllemann, had to resign from the cabinet; he had used his ministry's letterhead to help the private business interests of a cousin. A few months later, in May, the head of the country's largest labor union, Franz Steinkühler, resigned when it became known that he had benefited from insider stock trading. In the same month, the prime minister of Bavaria, Max Streibl, gave up his job when press reports revealed he had accepted paid vacations from a businessman friend.

The opposition SPD should have been delighted by the coalition's political embarrassments, but the Social Democrats had problems of their own. To begin with, there were leadership difficulties. Oskar Lafontaine, the party's candidate for chancellor in 1990, was blamed for the party's poor showing in the federal elections of that year. The voters had not forgotten that despite pleadings from other Social Democratic leaders, Lafontaine refused to say that he welcomed Germany's reunification. In October 1992 Willy Brandt, the party's grand old man and lifetime honorary chairman, died. The eclipse (temporary, as it turned out) of Lafontaine and the death of Brandt left a double vacuum that the party found difficult to fill. At first the succession seemed to go smoothly. The new party chairman was Björn Engholm, the Social Democratic prime minister of Schleswig-Holstein. A pragmatic and charismatic politician, who had led his party to victory in a traditionally conservative Land, Engholm seemed like the ideal leader for the reunification era. Unfortunately, in that fateful month of May 1993 he, too, resigned his post. Engholm had to admit that he had lied to a parliamentary investigating committee about how much he knew of the dirty tricks campaign his CDU predecessor as prime minister, Uwe Barschel, had waged against him.

Reflecting intraparty disagreements about the future direction of the SPD, the party was divided over a new leader. There were two serious contenders. One was Rudolf Scharping, who had led the SPD to victory in the overwhelmingly Catholic and conservative state of Rhineland-Palatinate, an area in which the party had not won an election since the founding of the Federal Republic. The other was Gerhard Schröder, the prime minister of Lower Saxony, who headed a coalition of Social Democrats and Greens. After polling the party's rank-and-file members, Scharping became the SPD's new chairman in the summer of 1993.

The debate over the party's leadership was part of a larger discussion about the SPD's future direction. (Scharping was seen as a spokesman for the party's right wing.) Since the end of the 1980s, various party commissions and congresses have attempted to develop new ideas to cope with the increasingly difficult structural problems in German and European society. There were no major neo-Marxist factions—all of the party's wings continued to support the essentials of the Bad Godesberg Program—but there were (and remain) major disagreements on such

issues as the prioritization of environmental policies, state intervention in creating and implementing an economic policy, and Germany's role in foreign affairs. Until he broke with the SPD altogether, the leading voice of the party's left was Oskar Lafontaine. He argued that instead of following the supply-side economic models of the United States and Great Britain, Germany should prioritize demand-side policies and keep its generous social welfare system. He proposed to finance the traditional benefits to labor by such measures as a surcharge on the income tax for the wealthy and by eliminating tax benefits for firms that engaged in outsourcing labor to foreign countries.

Rudolf Scharping took the blame for the SPD's poor showing in the 1994 elections (see pp. 355–56), and he resigned as party chairman. Actually, the results demonstrated that Lafontaine's left-of-center views did not appeal to most voters. Somewhat inexplicably under the circumstances, the party once again elected Oskar Lafontaine as chairman. But when Lafontaine announced that he also wanted to be the SPD's candidate for chancellor in 1998, many of the party's leaders balked.

Lafontaine's rival as the SPD's candidate for chancellor in 1998 was Gerhard Schröder. He presented a political profile sharply different from that of Lafontaine. The Lower Saxon prime minister is a right-wing Social Democrat cast in the mold of Tony Blair and Lionel Jospin. The prime minister of Lower Saxony did not hesitate to endorse supply-side economics and was known for his close relationships with several leading industrialists. (In his official position as the prime minister of Lower Saxony, Schröder was actually a top-ranking business manager; the state of Lower Saxony owns 20 percent of the shares of the Volkswagen Company, and as prime minister Schröder was an ex-officio member of the board of directors.) In contrast to Lafontaine, Schröder wanted to make the SPD into a centrist party that would be attractive to middle-class voters as well as the party's traditional core constituency of industrial workers.

Map 11.1 Germany Since 1990

SWEDEN

DENMARK

BALTIC SEA

NORTH SEA

POLAND

NETHERLANDS

Kiel

SCHLESWIG-HOLSTEIN

Rostock

Lübeck

MECKLENBURG-WESTERN POMERANIA

Hamburg

Schwerin

Bremerhaven

Elbe River

Weser R.

Bremen

Oldenbrug

LOWER SAXONY

BRANDENBURG

Oder River

Hanover

Wolfsburg

Potsdam

Berlin

Osnabrück

Hildesheim

Brunswick

Salzgitter

Magdeburg

Bielefeld

Münster

Göttingen

SAXONY-ANHALT

Dessau

Cottbus

Recklinghausen

NORTH RHINE-WESTPHALIA

Gelsenkirchen

Herne

Hamm

Dortmund

Paderborn

Halle

Leipzig

Bottrop

Mulheim

Duisburg

Bochum

Essen

Krefeld

Kassel

Dresden

Neuss

Düsseldorf

Wuppertal

Mönchen-Gladbach

Remscheid

Solingen

Erfurt

SAXONY

Leverkusen

Cologne

Bergisch-Gladbach

Siegen

Jena

Gera

Chemnitz

Aachen

THURINGIA

Zwickau

Bonn

BELGIUM

HESSE

Koblenz

Mosel River

Rhine

Wiesbaden

Frankfurt

Würzburg

Main River

Czech Republic

Mainz

Offenbach

LUX.

RHINELAND-PALATINATE

Darmstadt

Erlangen

SAAR-LAND

Mannheim

Ludwigshafen

Fürth

Nuremberg

Saarbrücken

Heidelberg

FRANCE

River

Heilbronn

BAVARIA

Regensburg

Karlsruhe

Ingolstadt

Pforzheim

Stuttgart

Danube River

Ulm

Inn River

Augsburg

BADEN-WÜRTTEMBERG

Munich

Freiburg

AUSTRIA

■ More than 1,000,000 inhabitants
• More than 100,000 inhabitants
Berlin National capital/Seat of government
Mainz State capital
--- Federal state boundary
— National border

0   100 Miles
0   100 Kilometers

SWITZERLAND

(Source: *Scala*. Deutschland Magazine.)

With a firm eye on the polls, the party activists selected Schröder as their candidate for chancellor. The prime minister underscored his vote-getting power by handily winning reelection in the Lower Saxon state elections a few months before the federal contest, and he led the SPD to victory in the federal elections of 1998. Lafontaine seemingly accepted his setback, and joined Schröder's SPD–Greens coalition government as finance minister. But in March 1999 he suddenly resigned from the cabinet (see pp. 365–66), and temporarily withdrew from political life altogether. In December 1999 a special party convention elected Schröder as the SPD's new chairman. However, Schröder found that the burdens of leading the government and the party were too much for him. In addition, although respected in the party for his prodigious skills as a campaigner, Schröder was never very popular with the SPD's rank-and-file members, and criticism of his government's neoliberal policies (see p. 366) increased as Germany's economic and social problems mounted.

In 2002 Schröder resigned as party chairman. He was succeeded by Franz Müntefering, until then the chairman of the party's Bundestag delegation. As a longtime party functionary, Müntefering was popular with the SPD's rank-and-file membership. Something of a populist, Müntefering stirred a great deal of controversy when in 2005 he compared hedge funds to locusts that were destroying the economy. He also liked to appear in public wearing a long red scarf to symbolize his attachment to the traditional color of the European left.

Although there was every expectation that Müntefering would remain in office for a number of years, rebuilding the party organization that in many areas had become disturbingly weak, his role as chairman lasted less than three years. When the grand coalition took office in 2005 (see pp. 355–57) Müntefering became vice-chancellor and minister of labor. Like Schröder before him, Müntefering felt that he should not be both party chairman and a member of the cabinet. In addition, his wife, too, was suffering

from terminal cancer. In November 2007 Müntefering resigned as chairman.

He was succeeded by Matthias Platzeck, the prime minister of the state of Brandenburg and the first East German to chair the SPD since Germany's reunification. Platzeck was elected chairman in November 2005, but whatever hopes the party members might have had for a long tenure of their new chairman were shattered within a few months. Platzeck became seriously ill, and decided to devote his diminished energies to his position as prime minister of Brandenburg. To replace Platzeck the party again turned to a West German, Kurt Beck, the prime minister of the state of Rhineland Palatinate.

Beck, a jovial, temperamental, thick-set Rhinelander, certainly did not lack initial confidence. He announced, "I am robust enough" to lead the party as chairman and candidate for chancellor in the 2009 federal elections. But Beck's political strategy was controversial from the beginning. Recognizing that the Left Party (see below, p. 349) was making inroads into the SPD's core voter constituency, the new chairman proposed to pass the Left on the left. He wanted to return the SPD to its populist roots and appeal to all voters on the left side of the political spectrum. He was also willing to consider coalitions with the Left Party on the state level, although he rejected a partnership in the federal government.

Beck's scenario was a personal and political failure. A string of election losses in state contests culminated in a high-stakes, failed gamble to form a coalition with the Left in the state of Hessen. The final nail in Beck's political coffin was the disastrous result in the 2009 federal election. The SPD had its worst showing since 1945. Beck took the blame and resigned as chairman. Faced with an unprecedented catastrophe at the polls, the Social Democrats embarked on a novel experiment: a team rather than a single person at the top. The party selected Sigmar Gabriel, a right-wing former prime minister of Lower Saxony (he was regarded as Gerhard Schröder's political godson) and federal minister of the environment, as its chairman. At the same time the feminist and more left-leaning Andrea Nahles (she entitled her recently published autobiography, "Woman, Believing, Left: What is Important to me") became the national executive secretary. The duo professed to work well together as the party tackles a formidable problem: How to preserve the SPD as Germany's major center-left party.

The Greens, too, faced problems. In the fall of 1992, the party was profoundly shocked by the death of two of its most prominent members, Petra Kelly and Gert Bastian. The two, who were living together, seemed to have concluded a murder–suicide pact. Far more serious, however, were ideological and programmatic splits. The party divided along three lines. One group wanted to ally the Greens more closely with the PDS, forming the nucleus of a "socialist left." A second faction, the "Fundis," continued to reject all cooperation with any other political parties in or out of government. The third group, the "Realos," advocated cooperating with the SPD in "red–green" alliances.

The story among the Greens from 1990 until 2005 was the rise of the Realos faction and the corresponding decline of the Fundis. Under the energetic leadership of Joschka Fischer (Germany's foreign minister from 1998 to 2005), the Greens increasingly moved to the center of the political spectrum. In 1998 the Greens joined the SPD to form a federal coalition, and four years later the voters gave that political combination a new mandate. Joschka Fischer became a widely recognized and respected figure on the national and international stages; for some months he was Germany's most popular politician.

At the same time, government responsibilities brought new challenges. The Greens had begun as a quintessential protest party, and some of their supporters wanted to keep it that way. For this group seeing their party leaders sacrifice the party's ideals in political compromises was jarring. In a sense the dissatisfied elements obtained their wish in 2005. The SPD–Greens coalition lost the 2005 elections and with the formation of the grand coalition (see pp. 355–57) the Greens were once again part of the opposition. In addition,

the party lost its longtime chairman and most popular spokesman. After the 2005 electoral defeat, Joschka Fischer left public life and accepted a position as visiting professor at Princeton University.

Fischer's departure left a vacuum that was difficult to fill. As chairman, Fischer was succeeded by Claudia Roth, a fiery but not very charismatic member of the Greens' Bundestag delegation. Returning to their collective roots, the Greens elected two cochairpersons to lead their (much smaller) delegation in the federal parliament: Renate Künast, who had been minister for agriculture in the Schröder cabinet, and Fritz Kuhn, a former national chairman of the Greens and campaign manager for the 2002 election. Then, in November 2008 they made history when they elected a member of Germany's Turkish minority, Cem Özdemir, as cochairman of the party. Özdemir, a social scientist, was born to Turkish parents who came to Germany as guest workers in the 1960s.

Not surprisingly, without Fischer's firm hand, disagreements on policy issues surfaced once again. Fischer had persuaded the Greens to accept such controversial decisions as sending German troops on peacekeeping missions outside the NATO area and pushing for Schröder's agenda of neoliberal economic reforms. After the party's poor showing in 2005 and 2009 the Greens presented a somewhat schizophrenic image. On the one hand some of the Fundis returned, arguing that the party must uncompromisingly oppose atomic energy and military engagements. Claudia Roth at one point contrasted the Greens as a value-based political party with the other mainstream groups, which, she claimed, were only interested in governing at all costs. At the same time the Realos are alive and well. In February 2008 the Greens joined the CDU in a coalition in the city state of Hamburg. In essence, the Greens are facing the dilemma of many one-issue parties: They were organized to articulate concerns about the environment, but some thirty years after their founding much of their program has become the law of the land.

The successor organization to the SED, the PDS, was initially unable to find a reliable voting constituency, despite the personal charisma of its leader, Gregor Gysi. A highly articulate politician, he was much sought after by talk-show hosts, but he was unable to translate his personal popularity into significant political influence for his party. For most Germans, especially in the Western Länder, the PDS remained the old SED under a new name, an association that was underscored by the personnel continuity in the party. (The last SED prime minister of the GDR, Hans Modrow, for example, became a PDS member of the Bundestag.) In February 1993 Gysi, who never enjoyed the day-to-day duties of a party chairman, resigned this post. He was succeeded as party chairman by the head of the PDS in Brandenburg, Lothar Bisky. The new leader saw the PDS of the future "as a socialist party to the left of the SPD."

For the remainder of the decade, the PDS languished as a protest party in Eastern Germany. (In federal elections the party succeeded in passing the 5 percent hurdle in 1998, but it failed to do so in 2002.) In the former GDR the party became the voice of the dissatisfied and disappointed. As a group the party's members and voters were relatively old (predominately over sixty) and well educated. In other words, they were men and women who had occupied a good position on the career ladder in the old GDR, but who were now either unemployed or had jobs they felt were not commensurate with their skills and social prestige. By the end of the last century, the PDS was a well-established party in Eastern Germany (it was represented in all of the state legislatures in the former GDR and joined government coalitions with the SPD in Brandenburg and Berlin), but its prospects for playing a national role appeared dim. In October 2000 the PDS's national convention elected Gabi Zimmer, the party's leader in Thuringia, as its chairperson. As a clear sign of *Ostalgie*, the delegates also elected Sarah Wagenknecht, the charismatic leader of the party's provocatively titled "Communist Platform" faction, as one of the PDS's vice chairpersons.

The PDS's self-isolation changed after its poor showing in the 2002 federal elections. Gabi Zimmer was voted out, and the centrist Lothar Bisky returned. The PDS's prospects in the West also took an unexpected turn for the better when Oskar Lafontaine joined forces with the ex-Communists. In 2004 a small group of disgruntled former SPD members formed a new party, the *Wahlalternative Arbeit und soziale Gerechtigkeit* (Voters' Alternative for Work and Social Justice—WASG). Lafontaine was not a member of the founding clique, but he quickly recognized the WASG as a potential vehicle for returning to political prominence. The SPD's former chairman had by now given up on his quest to turn the Social Democrats toward left-wing populism, and he needed a different forum to return to the national scene. Under Lafontaine's leadership the WASG quickly achieved media recognition. With Lafontaine as its most prominent, media-savvy spokesman, the WASG also attracted the attention of the PDS. In July 2005 the PDS and the WASG merged to form a single, new party, simply called *Die Linkspartei* (the Left Party). With Bisky as chairman and Gysi and Lafontaine as star speakers, the Left Party was able to attain 8.7 percent of the popular vote in the September 2005 federal elections (see later, p. 356).

The Left Party not only has ambitious plans for the future, but it also faces a number of organizational and political problems. The group still has a weak organizational base in the West, and the party's membership patterns in Western and the Eastern Germany are significantly different. The young members of the former WASG in the West distrust the older apparatchiks that dominated the PDS in the East. The party's voting constituencies also remain quite different in East and West Germany. In the West Left Party voters are predominantly young and relatively unskilled and uneducated, while in the East the party attracts older voters who regret the passing of the GDR.

The Left did quite well in the 2009 federal elections (see below, p. 360), but this may have been a pyrrhic victory. Against the background of the worldwide financial crisis some voters reacted positively to the party's populist message of soak-the-rich and bash-the-bankers, but the Left has little of a positive program to offer. It deliberately decided not to adopt a platform until after the election, and for good reason. The Left is seriously divided about its political future. In Western Germany the party is increasingly dominated by far-left sectarians (a picture of a birthday party complete with pictures of Stalin made the rounds on the Internet) who insist the Left should stand for the total abolition of capitalism. In Eastern Germany the activists are busy polishing the image of the GDR as a society of social and economic justice, while downplaying the communists' political dictatorship. And if these problems were not enough, shortly after the 2009 election Lafontaine resigned as chairman; he is also suffering from cancer.

The persistent presence of extreme right-wing groups since reunification (they are usually grouped together under the umbrella term *neo-Nazis*, although this is something of a misnomer) has raised concern among many observers, both inside and outside of Germany. The extreme right has found the former GDR a particularly fertile ground for its political propaganda. Large areas of the former East Germany remain economically blighted, and the extreme right's message of protest and xenophobia has found a positive response among many younger East Germans, especially in rural areas and small towns.

There are dozens of extreme-right organizations, but only three had any significant following. They are the *Republikaner,* the *Deutsche Volksunion* (German People's Union—DVU), and the resurrected and reorganized *Nationaldemokratische Partei Deutschlands* (National Democratic Party of Germany—NPD). The DVU is the organizational brainchild of a long-term fixture of far-right politics, Gerhard Frey. Publisher of the *Deutsche Nationalzeitung* ("German Nationalist Newspaper"), Frey has for years specialized in xenophobic and chauvinistic outbursts. He and the DVU were also bitter rivals of the Republikaner and their leader, Franz Schönhuber.

In recent years the DVU and the Republikaner have faded into the background while the NPD has become the strongest far-right organization in Germany. Under the leadership of Udo Voigt, the son of a former Nazi Stormtrooper and a retired Bundeswehr captain, the NPD absorbed the Republikaner; Franz Schönhuber became an "adviser" to the NPD. Under Voigt the NPD has given itself an image of respectability, claiming it does not endorse the political violence of the skinheads. Such protestations are primarily a public relations ploy. There is considerable evidence of ongoing and clandestine contacts between the NPD and the right-wing paramilitary scene.

Politically the NPD has tried to position itself as the spokesman for the "little man," the "average German" who has been forgotten and neglected by the mainstream parties. The supporters of the NPD certainly see themselves as unfairly disadvantaged. In a September 2004 survey of NPD supporters in Saxony, 54 percent answered "yes" to the question, "I have less than I am entitled to." To redress this situation the NPD claims it will work for better schools, environmental measures, and tax relief for small businesses. It promises to finance such improvements by withdrawing social services and welfare payments from the millions of foreigners living in Germany.

The NPD has found effective ways of organizing its potential supporters. In addition to marches and demonstrations familiar from earlier times, the party also organizes barbecues and rock concerts featuring pounding music with politically inspired lyrics. Anonymous groups produce CDs that substitute texts celebrating political violence and racism for the original lyrics of popular rock tunes. While the party has failed to enter the Bundestag (in the 2009 federal elections it received 1.5 percent of the popular vote), the NPD has been quite successful in Eastern Germany, at the state and especially at the local level. In 2005 there were NPD representatives in the state parliaments of both Saxony and Mecklenburg-Pomerania; in 2009 far-right delegates were present only in the Saxon state legislature. The NPD's real success story, however, has been at the local level. In dozens of East German communities far-right councilmen and women serve alongside delegates from mainstream parties.

The NPD's political fortunes are aided indirectly by sharp disagreements among the major political parties on how to respond to this threat. They agreed that they would refuse any political dealings with the NPD and other extremist groups, but beyond ostracism there was little consensus. In March 2003 the Schröder government brought a case before the Federal Constitutional Court asking the tribunal to prohibit the NPD as an anticonstitutional organization. The court refused when the government had to admit that the Federal Office for the Protection of the Constitution had infiltrated the NPD with a number of its agents. As a result, the court decided, it was impossible to tell what actions were the responsibility of genuine NPD members and which were undertaken by government provocateurs.

Other analysts argued the answer was not prohibition but education. Informational campaigns targeted especially at younger East Germans, a cohort where the former GDR's misguided politics of memory had left a bitter heritage, in the hope that such efforts would immunize them against the NPD's simplistic messages. By the end of the 1960s, the West Germans had implemented broadly based programs to teach junior high school and high school students about Nazism and its consequences, but the communist regime in East Germany claimed this was not necessary in the GDR. East German students were taught that Nazism was simply another manifestation of capitalism, and therefore no problem in the GDR.

Whether retroactive education will be successful in defusing the extreme right is not yet clear. Some analysts have concluded that there will probably remain a small, hardcore reservoir of extreme right-wing support; at least at the local level the extreme right can count on between 4 and 6 percent of the popular vote.

In the long term, economic improvements in the East are probably the only viable answer to this ongoing political problem.

Left-wing terrorist groups have been relatively quiescent, although they have not disappeared. The most spectacular action of what remained of the RAF was the murder at the end of 1989 of Detlev Rohwedder, the head of the agency that took charge of state-owned property in East Germany. In the summer of 1993, a shootout between RAF members and special police forces led to the death of a police officer and one of the leaders of the underground terrorists. Since then, however, the RAF's leadership has apparently abandoned terrorism as a political weapon.

A new political phenomenon that became apparent in the 1990s was the emergence of "nonparty parties." The most notable, albeit short-lived, success story was the group running under the name *Statt-Partei* (literally "instead of party," although the German word *statt* [instead of] is pronounced almost the same as *Stadt* [city]). In the October 1993 election in the city-state of Hamburg, the Statt-Partei, with no program except opposition to the established parties, gained 5.6 percent of the popular vote. The group was led by Roland Schill, a district judge in Hamburg, who had a reputation of being particularly tough on crime; as a magistrate he had earned the nickname "Judge Merciless."

Schill's group did even better in the September 2001 elections. The protest party received 19.4 percent of the popular vote. During the campaign Schill promised that if elected he would cut the crime rate in the city by half and also deal with the "problem" of foreigners. To their later regret the governing Christian Democrats offered to form a coalition with the Schill Party; Schill would become the city's deputy mayor. It soon turned out, however, that Schill had little interest in governing a large city. He became a frequent figure on the party circuit, and there were accusations of cocaine use. In August 2003, in a dramatic move, the mayor of Hamburg, Ole von Beust, fired his deputy for attempted political blackmail. Schill had threatened to expose Beust's homosexual orientation. (Beust subsequently acknowledged that he was gay.) That was the political end of Roland Schill; he vanished into oblivion. In contrast, Ole von Beust won a resounding victory in the next election.

Among the Christian Democrats the rise and fall of Helmut Kohl and the rise of Angela Merkel has been the most dramatic story. The 1994 election was Kohl's personal triumph; the chancellor stood at the apex of his political career. Two years later, he was reelected chairman of the CDU, with 95.5 percent of the delegates at the convention casting their ballots for him. Now the longest-serving chancellor in modern German history, comparisons with Otto von Bismarck and Konrad Adenauer were inevitable. (Joschka Fischer, the leader of the Greens, suggested a new title for Kohl: "His Eternity.") Convinced that he alone could

Helmut Kohl, Germany's longest-serving chancellor, at the height of his prestige and influence. (Source: Courtesy of German Information Center.)

finish the work of German reunification and European unification, Kohl also announced that he would head the CDU ticket for the 1998 Bundestag election.

However, nemesis was on its way. Helmut Kohl lost the 1998 election, but far worse was to come. In the wake of his defeat, Kohl resigned as party leader; he was succeeded by Wolfgang Schäuble, the head of the CDU's Bundestag delegation. What had been expected to be a smooth transition began to unravel in the spring of 2000. The state attorney general in Augsburg (Bavaria) announced that his office was investigating the CDU's national treasurer, Walter Leisler Kiep, for violating the laws on campaign financing. Under German law, donations in any amount to political parties are not illegal, but both the amounts and the names of the donors must be made public.

Kiep staunchly denied that he received unreported donations, and he may well have been right. It was Helmut Kohl himself, who, keeping separate accounts, received large donations which he did not report: some 9 million deutsche marks (ca. $4.5 million) between 1991 and 2000. The chancellor seems to have used these illegal funds to stifle criticism of his increasingly authoritarian ways. Confronted with the evidence (the *Spiegel* was at the top of its investigative reporting mode), Kohl admitted at a Bundestag hearing that he had received the donations, but he refused to make the names of the donors public as required by law. He claimed that he had given his "word of honor" to the donors that he would not reveal their names. As the scandal drew ever-wider circles, the former chancellor fell into disgrace. Helmut Kohl remained unrepentant. He ended the criminal investigation by paying a $140,000 fine, but the former chancellor still refuses to reveal the donors' names. And things did not end there. It soon turned out that the practice of unreported donations was also common among some of the Christian Democrats' state organizations, and that the CDU's new national chairman, Wolfgang Schäuble, had accepted unreported donations as well. Schäuble, too, resigned.

Since 2000 the big story in the Christian Democratic camp has been the rise of Angela Merkel, although her march to the top was not a smooth process. Merkel did represent a radical break with the past. She could claim a number of firsts for herself: She is the CDU's first female party chairperson, the party's first Protestant leader, and the first one who grew to adulthood in East Germany. Born in 1954, Merkel obtained a degree in physics and became a researcher at the East German Academy of Sciences. In 1994 she joined Kohl's cabinet as minister for environmental affairs, and in 1998 she became the executive secretary of the CDU.

The CDU/CSU has always had a number of strong regional personalities, the so-called Länder lords. Often combining the positions of party leader and prime minister in their respective states, these regional bosses tended to resent a forceful national party chairperson. This was particularly true of someone like Angela Merkel, who did not rise through the ranks but was accorded a position in the federal cabinet without having held local or regional office. Such well-established regional leaders as Christian Wulff, the prime minister of Lower Saxony and now the federal president (see p. 342); Roland Koch, the CDU's leader in Hessen; and especially Edmund Stoiber, the undisputed leader of the CSU in Bavaria, made no secret of their doubts about Merkel's ability to wear her many political hats.

As the 2002 federal election drew near, Merkel's rivals seemed to triumph. After months of not very subtle jostling, Merkel agreed that Stoiber should be the CDU/CSU's candidate for chancellor. It was only the second time since 1980 that the leader of the CDU's Bavarian sister party was the Christian Democrats' candidate for chancellor. Some analysts suspected this was a deliberate and rather shrewd ploy on the part of Merkel, who anticipated that Stoiber, like Franz Joseph Strauss before him, would be unable to succeed among voters outside of Bavaria.

If that had been her intention, she won her gamble. Much to his own surprise, Stoiber was narrowly defeated in 2002. Merkel now moved swiftly to consolidate her position in the Christian Democratic camp. After a whirlwind campaign among the party's regional and local organizations, Merkel was overwhelmingly elected chairperson at the CDU's annual convention in April 2007. Merkel also surrounded herself with a team of younger advisers who were neither tainted by the Kohl scandals nor intimates of the Länder lords.

It was less clear what Merkel intended to do with the increasing power she was accumulating. As we shall see later, at times she seemed to advocate radical reforms that would liberalize Germany's economic and social structures, but at other times she seemed equally willing to retreat from her publicly stated positions. Joschka Fischer described Merkel as a soufflé that looks good in the oven but collapses when you take it out.

She may be an enigma, but she is a very successful politician. In 2005 the CDU/CSU selected Merkel as the parties' candidate for chancellor. Subsequently she headed a grand coalition of the CDU/CSU and the Social Democrats, a combination that some described as a fire-and-water mix. Merkel's greatest strength as an administrator is her ability to mediate differing and even opposing points of view. Under her leadership the grand coalition functioned remarkably smoothly, although critics complained that the price of harmony was inaction. According to this view, Germany needed reforms in virtually every sphere of public life, but under Merkel the federal cabinet did little but administer the status quo.

Five years later Merkel triumphed again. In September 2009 she led the CDU/CSU to victory in the federal elections. She stayed on as chancellor, but this time with a new political partner, the FDP. The Liberals have traditionally stood for supply-side economic policies, low taxation, and against "excessive" social services. Merkel's skill as mediator is needed in the new cabinet as well. The FDP's demand for meaningful reforms, especially in the area of taxation, has already clashed with the Christian Democrats' inclination to preserve much of Germany's social net.

The Liberals also experienced leadership problems. After the defeat of the Kohl government in 1998, the FDP's popular chairman, Klaus Kinkel (who was also foreign minister in the last Kohl cabinet), returned to private life. He was succeeded by Wolfgang Gerhardt, an honorable party veteran who lacked charisma, however. At the end of 2000, two new contenders for the party's leadership emerged. One was Jürgen Möllemann, the head of the FDP in Germany's largest state, Northrhine-Westphalia. He led the Free Democrats to a particularly good showing in the state elections of May 2000. His rival was Guido Westerwelle, the FDP's executive secretary. In May 2001 Gerhardt resigned and Westerwelle was elected as his successor.

Although he was defeated in the race for the party's highest position, Möllemann did not retreat quietly into the background. Since Germany's reunification the Liberals' organizational and political problems had increased. The FDP had only a rudimentary organizational framework in Eastern Germany, where it missed clearing the 5 percent hurdle in several state elections. The Liberals were well established in the West, but here, too, they often had difficulty obtaining more than 5 percent of the popular vote. Jürgen Möllemann thought he had a plan that would rescue his party from the danger of political marginalization. He persuaded the FDP's leadership to launch "Project 18." (The figure 18 referred to the goal of obtaining 18 percent of the popular vote for the FDP.) These were seemingly stratospheric and unrealistic numbers for the party, but Möllemann thought he knew where the votes required to reach the 18 percent goal would come from. Taking as his models contemporary right-wing populists in other European countries— Jörg Haider in Austria, Pim Fortuyn in The Netherlands, and Jean-Marie Le Pen in France—Möllemann proposed that the FDP tap into the potential of frustrated voters on the right side of the political spectrum. Under Möllemann's guidance, the FDP in

Northrhine-Westphalia would wage a campaign that attacked "foreigners" and was laced with not very subtle anti-Semitic overtones.

During the campaign Möllemann suggested that the vice president of the Central Council of Jews in Germany, Michel Friedmann, contributed to the renewed rise of anti-Semitism with his flamboyant lifestyle. In the last days of the campaign Möllemann's organization sent a glossy flyer to every household in Northrhine-Westphalia, linking Friedmann and Ariel Sharon, then the prime minister of Israel and for some a symbol of Israeli arrogance in the Middle East. The flyer had not been authorized by the FDP's national office, nor was it paid for by the party. Questions were raised immediately about the financing of this expensive flyer, and these queries were the beginning of Möllemann's downfall.

"Project 18" was a political failure. The FDP obtained only 9.8 percent of the popular vote in the May 2001 Northrhine-Westphalian election. But Möllemann's problems were not limited to the party's poor performance at the polls. The state prosecutor in Düsseldorf began an investigation of Möllemann's finances, which revealed a maze of dummy corporations, tax evasions, and ties to a variety of shady Middle Eastern interests. By mid-2003 it was clear that Möllemann would soon face criminal charges. Rather than confront what would undoubtedly be his personal and political ruin, Möllemann committed suicide, and he did so in a spectacular way. For many years he had been an avid amateur parachutist, and on June 5, 2003, he made his last jump. After stepping out of the plane, he deliberately did not open his parachute and fell to his death.

For the federal campaign of 2002 the party's chairman, Guido Westerwelle, tried his own hand at spectacular campaign stunts. Traveling throughout Germany in a colorful campaign bus dubbed the "Guidomobil," Westerwelle attempted to create an image for the FDP as a fun-loving, optimistic party of the future. The tactic was not a success; obtaining 7.4 percent of the popular vote was hardly a stellar result.

The Liberals still needed to find a secure position on the German party spectrum. One of the party's former general secretaries proposed that the FDP was "the party of those who make more money and those who want to make more money," but that reduced the party's ideals to pure materialism. Westerwelle himself has offered the shorthand response that his party stands for "a willingness to be productive, for global openness, and for toleration" (*Leistungsbereitschaft, Weltoffenheit und Toleranz*), and for the 2005 and 2009 elections the Liberals' chairman abandoned both the party's fun-loving image and the "Guidomobil." The FDP repackaged itself as the "party of know-how" (*Fachkenntnis*). In the meantime the arrival of the grand coalition kept the FDP on the opposition benches, but to his credit Westerwelle used his role as a credible voice of responsible criticism of the half-hearted policies of the grand coalition.

Although the grand coalition started out as a partnership of near equals, politically the Christian Democrats benefitted far more from the combination than the Social Democrats. Angela Merkel had very high approval ratings, while Schröder's successors were regarded as lackluster party functionaries. Still, in state elections scheduled between 2005 and 2009 neither the CDU/CSU nor the SPD did particularly well (the big winners were the FDP and the Left), but the Social Democrats suffered far more dramatic losses than the Christian Democrats. For example, in Schleswig-Holstein the CDU went from 40.2 percent in 2005 to 31.5 percent in 2009, but the SPD declined from 38.7 percent to 25.4 percent in the same period.

All observers agreed that the 2009 federal election campaign was one of the most boring in modern German history. Since both the CDU/CSU and the SPD were responsible for the government policies of the last four years, they ran on what amounted to was the same record; neither could legitimately attack the other. The most excitement was caused by a minor scandal: It turned out that the minister of health Ulla Schmidt (SPD) had used her official car while on vacation in Spain.

The most charismatic candidate was neither a candidate nor a politician. He was a fictional character, Horst Schlämmer, created by a best-selling comedian, Hape Kerkeling. Schlämmer ran on a platform promising to change the German heraldic animal from the eagle to a bunny rabbit, and provide free cosmetic surgery on demand. He proclaimed, "I promise nothing, but I keep my word," and described his own political position as, "conservative, free market [oriented], and left." According to a poll conducted by the magazine *Stern*, at one point Schlämmer would have obtained 18 percent of the vote if he had been on the ballot.

He was not, but even without his actual competition the largest parties did not do very well. The CDU/CSU held its own (33.8 percent in 2009, 35.2 percent in 2005). The biggest loser was the SPD (23.0 percent in 2009, 34.2 percent in 2005), and the winners were the FDP (14.6 percent in 2009, 9.8 percent in 2005) and the Left (11.9 percent in 2009, 8.7 percent in 2005). The Greens also benefitted from being out of the government (10.7 percent in 2009, 8.1 percent in 2005). As we saw, the new government was a coalition of the CDU/CSU and the FDP. The SPD was left to lick its wounds.

ELECTIONS

In the state contests leading up to the September 1998 federal elections, the opposition parties—the SPD and the Greens—had not done particularly well. It therefore came as a considerable surprise to both the pundits and Chancellor Helmut Kohl that his coalition of the CDU/CSU and the FDP was severely trounced in the elections. The SPD gained 40.9 percent (1994: 36.4 percent) of the popular vote, while the CDU/CSU could muster only 35.1 percent (1994: 41.5 percent). The FDP joined its larger partner in defeat. The Liberals fell from 6.9 percent in 1994 to 6.2 percent four years later. In contrast to the SPD, the Greens did not do as well in 1998 as they had in 1994; they obtained

7.3 percent of the popular vote in 1994 and 6.2 percent in 1998.

The federal elections of 1998, which began the seven-year tenure of the SPD–Greens coalition, were a political triumph for the Social Democrats and a personal victory for Gerhard Schröder. The new government was headed by Schröder as chancellor and Joschka Fischer as foreign minister. Oskar Lafontaine, Schröder's erstwhile rival for the chancellorship and the SPD's chairman, became federal finance minister. Initially the SPD and the Greens formed something an awkward coalition which seemed to stumble from one misstep to the next. The coalition was rescued partly by its own improved performance and partly by the CDU's problems in the wake of the Kohl scandal. As the illegal operations of various Christian Democratic Party leaders became public, the CDU was increasingly put on the defensive, spending far more time in damage control than in developing programs of its own.

Because Germany has sixteen states, and no nationally fixed election date (the only rule is that elections are always held on Sunday), there are Land elections almost every year. In effect, then, the voters have the opportunity to provide a running assessment on the performance of both their state governments and the federal coalition. The state elections in 2001 and 2002 were a mixed blessing for the federal coalition. In Hamburg, for example, the CDU took over what had been an SPD stronghold, but in Berlin the coalition of SPD and PDS prevailed. The election in the capital was also a personal triumph for the Social Democratic mayor of Berlin, Kurt Wowereit.

The 2002 federal elections resulted in a narrow SPD-Green victory. Schröder's coalition won 47.1 percent of the popular vote while the CDU/CSU obtained 45.9 percent of the vote. For most analysts the outcome was a surprise; they had expected a defeat for the coalition. In retrospect the pundits identified three major factors that helped the SPD–Greens to stay in power. Especially American commentators portrayed Schröder's America-bashing as the decisive issue in the election. It is certainly true

that the chancellor's promise that no German troops would participate in the American-led war in Iraq was very popular with the electorate. Upon closer examination, however, it appears that the Iraq issue was less than pivotal. After all, the Christian Democrats had no intention of sending German troops to the Middle East either.

Rather than Iraq, two other factors seem to have swayed the outcome of the election: the government's successful relief efforts following major floods in Eastern Germany and the ineffective campaign of Schröder's opponent in the race, Edmund Stoiber. When floods devastated large areas of Eastern Germany in the summer of 2002, the government acted both swiftly and effectively to provide relief. Utilizing all of the resources available to the public authorities, including the armed forces, help arrived quickly where it was needed most. Pictures of the chancellor personally heaving sandbags to repair the levies did not hurt his image either. As for Edmund Stoiber, the Bavarian prime minister had a well-deserved reputation as a staunch conservative, a reputation that was indispensable for winning elections in Bavaria. He sensed, however, that the rest of the country was less conservative, and during the 2002 federal campaign he tried to repackage himself as a moderate. That effort lacked credibility, and many swing voters refused to accept Stoiber's new image as a man of the center.

The SPD/Greens coalition won the federal elections of 2002, but the subsequent state elections showed that its mandate was eroding quickly. In February 2003 the CDU won an absolute majority of the popular vote in Hessen. In Schleswig-Holstein, Germany's northernmost state, the SPD first dismissed its own leader and prime minister, Heide Simonis, and then lost the election to the CDU. Schröder's party won in Bremen, but then it always had. In September 2003 the Bavarian voters gave Stoiber yet another vote of confidence. The CSU obtained 62 percent of the popular vote.

The state elections of 2004 and 2005 were a series of disasters for the federal coalition. It began in February 2004 with Ole von Beust's and the Christian Democrats' triumph in Hamburg; the CDU obtained 47.2 percent of the vote. In Brandenburg the Social Democrats held their own, but the big winner was the PDS with 27.8 percent of the popular vote. The last straw came in May 2005 in the state elections in Northrhine-Westphalia. Here, in Germany's largest and most industrialized state, the SPD had been the governing party with few interruptions since the early 1950s, but in the May 2005 elections the Social Democrats were soundly defeated by the CDU.

Im Mittelpunkt Angela Merkel (1954–)

Angela Merkel is a woman of many firsts. She is the first female chairperson of the CDU, the first Protestant and first East German in that post, and the youngest leader of the Christian Democrats of either sex. Ironically, Merkel was actually born in Hamburg in West Germany. However, when she was still quite young, her family moved to East Germany where her father had accepted an appointment as a Protestant minister. Merkel herself pursued a scientific career, eventually obtaining her Ph.D. in physics. After getting her degree, she worked as a researcher at the East German Academy of Sciences.

Although before 1989 she had not been active in politics, as the GDR collapsed she not only entered political life but quickly developed a high profile. As the SED regime imploded, Merkel joined one of the new noncommunist groups in the GDR, *Demokratischer Umbruch* (Democratic Innovation—DU). The DU was really a front organization for the West German CDU, and Merkel herself soon joined the parent party. Although she certainly had no background in public relations work, she also served as the deputy press secretary of the last GDR government, which was headed by a Christian Democrat, Lothar de Maizière. In the first postreunification elections—December 1990—Merkel was elected to the Bundestag on the CDU ticket as a delegate from Mecklenburg-Vorpommern.

After Germany's reunification, Merkel had a meteoric career, largely because she happened to be the right woman in the right place. Helmut Kohl, who was anxious to have some East Germans in his cabinet, appointed her minister for families and youth. This is traditionally one of the lightweight ministries in the cabinet, but in 1994 she moved to a more prestigious post as minister for environmental affairs. In this position, her East German background was particularly pertinent because Germany's worst environmental problem areas were in the former GDR. Four years later, after the defeat of the Christian Democrats in the 1998 elections forced the CDU's incumbent secretary-general out of office, Merkel became his successor, the first woman in that post as well.

This might well have capped her political career if it had not been for the financial scandals that forced both Kohl and his longtime heir presumptive, Wolfgang Schäuble, to resign. Although there were a number of prominent CDU politicians, among them Volker Rühe, the minister of defense, and Kohl's longtime critics, Kurt Biedenkopf and Bernhard Vogel, anxious to succeed Kohl, the party executive committee decided not to present one of the old faces. (Ironically, both Biedenkopf and Vogel were now "East Germans"; the former was the prime minister of Saxony and the latter the chief executive in Thuringia.)

Angela Merkel had a number of advantages in the race for the CDU's leadership. She had been an effective secretary-general, she was a new face, and, most important, she was one of the first CDU leaders to publicly urge the party to cut itself loose from Kohl and his scandals. In December

Gerhard Schröder decided to go on the offensive. He is reported to have exclaimed, "*Basta,* we're going to have new [federal] elections." It was an audacious gamble. At the nadir of his political fortunes the chancellor wanted to stake his future on one last roll of the dice. To obtain new elections he proposed

a constitutionally dubious maneuver: The government would introduce a vote of no confidence in the Bundestag against itself, and then ask the members of the SPD and the Greens to vote for the resolution. This would topple the government, but instead of graciously making way for Angela Merkel and

1999 she published an article in Germany's leading conservative newspaper, the *Frankfurter Allgemeine Zeitung,* urging her fellow Christian Democrats to not risk the future of the party by misguided bouts of nostalgic loyalty to past leaders.

In the spring of 2000, the CDU's executive committee asked Merkel to become a sort of roving emissary to the CDU's local and regional organizations. Her assigned task was damage control and to act as a sounding board for concerns and complaints from rank-and-file activists, but her performance was so impressive that a number of Länder organizations spontaneously nominated her as the party's next leader. When the CDU's largest Land organization, Northrhine-Westphalia, joined in the acclamation, Merkel's potential rivals withdrew their candidacies, and in April 2000 the CDU's national convention elected her chairwoman.

Since her election, Merkel has experienced both successes and failures. Her attempt to derail the Schröder government's tax reforms failed when a number of CDU-led Länder governments refused to follow her lead, but she has retained, at least for now, the loyalty of the party's powerful regional chieftains.

To Merkel's obvious disappointment, the CDU/CSU's leaders were not willing to go so far as to support her as the parties' candidate for chancellor in 2002. They turned instead to Merkel's rival, the Bavarian Prime Minister Edmund Stoiber. With the benefit of hindsight Merkel's setback in 2002 turned out to be a blessing in disguise, but it certainly did not look that way at the time. At the beginning of the campaign, most analysts, Stoiber included, expected an easy triumph for the Christian Democrats. It was not to be; Gerhard Schröder snatched victory from the jaws of defeat, giving the SPD–Greens coalition another three years in office.

Defeated in 2002 the politically fatal label of "loser" now attached to Stoiber, and the way was clear for Merkel as the CDU/CSU's candidate for chancellor in the election of 2005. In the fall of 2005 Merkel did indeed become chancellor but not quite in the way she had hoped. Because of the extremely close vote she was forced to accept a grand coalition with the Social Democrats. The last time such a political combination had governed Germany was from 1965 to 1969.

The unexpected result of the 2005 election revealed yet another facet of Merkel's political personality. She turned out to be an effective team leader under difficult circumstances. The grand coalition has been criticized for its lack of dynamic initiatives and far-reaching reforms, but the chancellor has received high marks for avoiding backbiting and acrimony within the cabinet. She has been able to establish a particularly effective working relationship with her Social Democratic counterpart in the government, Vice-Chancellor Franz Müntefering. Altogether Merkel's political life and successes constitute a remarkable achievement for a woman, who, as one colleague observed, created "a political career out of nothing."

her team, the chancellor would ask President Köhler to dissolve the Bundestag and call for new elections on September 18, 2005. The president was reluctant to accede to Schröder's request, but after some hesitation he agreed. He felt that in this case political reasons overrode constitutional doubts. Köhler recognized that to govern effectively the government needed a renewed mandate. At the same time the CDU/CSU also preferred a clear electoral decision to assuming power by default.

What followed was one of the more bizarre but also more interesting campaigns in modern German history. At the outset of the short campaign season (by law German federal election campaigns are limited to sixty days), the outcome seemed a foregone conclusion. On July 19 polls indicated that the CDU/CSU was leading the SPD by 42–27 percent. In what was clearly intended to be a farewell interview, the *Spiegel* repeatedly asked Joschka Fischer what he planned to do after the lost election. Fischer replied gamely that unlike the editors of the *Spiegel* he did not have the gift of prophesy.

In fact, the death of the SPD–Greens coalition was not quite as obvious as it appeared. Schröder relished the rough and tumble of campaigning, and he was very good at it. In his memoirs the chancellor drew an analogy to ice skating competitions: governing was like the compulsory program; campaigning was the free skating part of the competition. Merkel, in contrast, is a mediocre speaker, who always seemed uneasy with large crowds. Most analysts agreed that Schröder "won" the televised debate between the two contenders. While the chancellor single-mindedly stressed that the aims of his reform efforts had always been social justice for all, Merkel acted stiffly and attempted to present too much detail and too many nuances. By the time September 18 rolled around, Schröder was catching up fast.

But not quite fast enough. The final results were 35.2 percent for the CDU/CSU, 34.3 percent for the SPD, 9.8 percent for the FDP, and 8.1 percent for the Greens. In purely quantitative terms, the big winner was the new Left Party, which almost doubled the popular vote of the old PDS. Later analyses showed that the SPD lost 1.6 percent of its popular vote in Western Germany to the Left Party, and almost 5 percent in the Eastern Länder. Audacious to the end, Schröder promptly insisted that he was entitled to remain chancellor because he had almost won the election and if the vote had been held a week later he would have triumphed. As he put it, "the SPD had won, but it had not been victorious." That degree of political sophistry was too much not only for the Christian Democrats but also for the chancellor's own party. However narrow the margin, Merkel was the victor.

But there still remained the question of the composition of the new coalition government. For some weeks German pundits and analysts delighted in speculating about various color combinations. (German parties traditionally are associated with specific colors, so the CDU/CSU is black; the SPD and PDS, red; the Greens, green; and the FDP, yellow.) There were proposals that the new government should be red-red-green, black-yellow, or even the "Jamaican solution," black-yellow-green.

In July Merkel had proclaimed, "there will not be a grand coalition," but in October she announced, "I am looking forward to the [grand coalition]." Indeed, the two largest parties agreed to form a new government with Angela Merkel as chancellor and Franz Müntefering as vice-chancellor. When his demand that he remain chancellor was rejected, Gerhard Schröder decided not to join the new cabinet in any capacity. Instead he dropped out of politics altogether. A few weeks after the election, in a move that raised a number of eyebrows, he accepted a position as West European operations manager for Gazprom, the giant Russian natural gas producer and distributor. The eyebrows were raised even higher when news leaked out that a few weeks before leaving office Schröder's government had guaranteed a large loan to Gazprom by German private banks.

Angela Merkel, Germany's chancellor since 2005, speaking with members of the German parliament. The man second from left is Jürgen Trittin, one of the leaders of the Green Party, and the man second from the right is Gregor Gysi, one of the leaders of the Left Party. (Source: Courtesy: Wolfgang Kumm/EFE/Newscom.)

ECONOMIC AND SOCIAL DEVELOPMENTS

The contrast between future prognostication and present-day reality was especially great in the areas of economic and social developments. As noted earlier, in the heady days of 1990, not only the Kohl government but also spokespersons for private business interests confidently predicted that once the system of free enterprise was established in East Germany, the economy of the five new states would flourish in short order. The chairman of the Mercedes-Benz corporation, Edzard Reuter, claimed that in five years this region would be "the most modern part of Europe," and government experts anticipated tax revenues of 250 billion deutsche mark from the five new states within ten years. All of this was to happen without serious structural dislocations or individual hardships in either East or West Germany. In a statement that he was to regret soon after he made it, Chancellor Kohl in the summer of 1990 summed up the consensus of the experts: "No one will suffer; everyone will benefit."

In retrospect, all of these predictions seem incredibly naive, but in 1990 politicians and businesspersons alike were confident that a combination of private and public investment, coupled with large-scale labor retraining programs, would turn around the East German economy. (The entire package was given the catchy title *Gemeinschaftswerk Aufschwung Ost* ["Cooperative Enterprise for the Upswing in the East"].) Private investment was expected to be the primary vehicle for modernizing the outdated and worn-out industrial equipment. To coordinate the process of privatizing the socialized enterprises in the former GDR, the government established a new agency, the *Treuhandanstalt* (Trusteeship Agency, usually called the *Treuhand*). The agency took control of all state-owned enterprises and property in the former GDR, which for all practical purposes meant all economic assets in East Germany. Headed first by a banker, Detlev Rohwedder, and after his assassination by Birgit Breuel, a Christian Democratic official in the economics ministry, the Treuhand's mandate was to sell the enterprises under its control to private investors. Both German and foreign venture capitalists were encouraged to submit offers for the items on long "for sale" lists that the Treuhand peddled on the Internet around the world.

At the same time, the Bonn government was to do its part. It agreed to invest billions of deutsche marks to improve the infrastructure in Eastern Germany because without such facilities private investment would not be attracted to the area. The task was formidable; telephone, roads, and rail connections were all either in sad repair or completely outdated. Finally, the government would also undertake to retrain the East German workforce. Under the name of *Arbeitsbeschaffungsmassnahmen* (ABM; "measures to create work"), thousands of East German workers were sent back to school to learn the Western production techniques that they would need to find well-paying jobs in the now privately owned East German enterprises.

It became clear very quickly that this scenario did not correspond to reality. To begin with, the East German economy turned out to be in far worse shape than had been expected. In 1989 the Modrow Government had calculated the worth of properties that would be controlled by the Treuhand at 1.365 trillion deutsche mark. A year later, independent appraisers reduced that figure to 209 billion deutsche marks, and in the fall of 1992 the German finance minister Theo Waigel admitted that after selling all of the assets under its control, the Treuhand would probably close its books with a deficit of 250 billion deutsche marks.

The reason for this disappointing result was not hard to find. Virtually all of the state-owned enterprises in the GDR had not only been

Gerhard Schröder, Germany's chancellor from 1988 to 2005. Schröder was the first Social Democrat to serve as chancellor since 1982. (Source: vario images GmbH & Co.KG/Alamy.)

inefficiently managed, but they were also simply incapable of functioning at all in a competitive free-market system. As a result, the Treuhand had immense difficulties selling many of its holdings in the usual sense of the word. Often an investor took over a property only after the Treuhand agreed to assume the costs of modernizing the plant. In addition, the process of privatization in almost every case involved the dismissal of large numbers of workers. The Treuhand was certainly no moneymaker, but things were to get still worse. East Germany's industry had been primarily focused on markets in Eastern Europe and the former Soviet Union, and the Kohl government had expected that postcommunist boom times in Eastern Europe would lead to an even greater demand for East German goods. But the markets in Eastern Europe collapsed under the weight of political instability and the lack of hard currency.

By the end of 1992, economic unification seemed to be an unmitigated disaster. The Aufschwung Ost required vastly larger outlays of public investment than expected. Another budgetary pressure was the adjustment of social security payments. Public pensions in the GDR had been low, but after reunification they were adjusted upward to equal the quite generous West German schedules. All of this meant significant increases in the national debt and serious inflationary pressures. At one point inflation was above 5 percent per year, the traditional point at which in Germany widespread concern sets in. The *Bundesbank* applied the credit brake. From 1991 to the summer of 1993, German interest rates were consistently higher than those of other Western countries, but high interest rates also discouraged private borrowing and investment. And, if all these problems were not enough, in the spring of 1993, East Germany experienced a wave of labor unrest as workers insisted not only on keeping their jobs (unemployment in the five new Länder consistently hovered around 15 percent), but also on wage increases that would enable them to achieve the Western standard of living that they claimed the Kohl government had promised them.

The cost of environmental measures in the five new Länder also turned out to be far greater than expected. The GDR had not been concerned with either cleaning up the environment or keeping it clean; increased production was all that mattered. After unification West Germany's strict environmental laws also applied to East Germany. The Treuhand quickly discovered that in many cases private investors would "buy" one of its properties only if the agency, that is, the government, agreed to take over the costs of any environmental cleanup.

After first denying the reality of (or blaming each other for) the difficulties, politicians as well as labor and management leaders in the spring of 1992 began to address the problems. The result was an agreement in May 1992 called the *Solidarpakt* (Solidarity Pact). The agreement was designed to raise an additional 100 billion deutsche marks for the Aufschwung Ost without increasing the national debt. To accomplish this goal, the interested parties agreed to a package of new taxes and spending cuts. At the heart of the Solidarpakt were markedly increased consumer taxes (especially postage rates and gasoline revenues), and beginning in 1995 a 7.5 percent surcharge on the income tax. (The Kohl government refused a straight increase in income taxes because it feared this would further discourage private investment.)

Although the Solidarity Pact was widely hailed as another example of successful democratic corporatism, in practice its effect was rather more limited. The primary reason was that the agreement did not anticipate the worsening economic situation. Immediately after reunification, demand for Western consumer goods had fueled a boom in West Germany, but this was short lived. By 1992 there were signs of a beginning recession in West Germany. The downturn in the West, and the ever-increasing investment needs of the East meant that the database on which the Solidarity Pact was concluded needed to be quickly recalculated.

The news of the agreement on a new pact—more than the actual terms of the document—did have a positive effect on controlling inflation. The willingness of the economic interest groups to limit the growth of public indebtedness led the Bundesbank in the summer of 1992 to begin lowering Germany's interest rates. But that decision came too late to save the European Monetary System (EMS). The EMS was an agreement among most of the member countries of the EC to limit exchange fluctuations among their currencies to very narrow margins. After 1990 the high German interest rates led currency speculators to buy deutsche marks while selling "weaker" currencies like the British pound and the Italian lira. Eventually the EMS collapsed. Great Britain and Italy withdrew from the agreement; Spain and Portugal devalued their currencies. To salvage what was left of the EMS, the remaining partners agreed to widen the permissible exchange margins from 2.25 to 15 percent. (Ironically, after the initial turmoil the currency exchange rates of the remaining EMS members fluctuated in a very narrow spectrum—around 3 percent.)

Speculative fever in the currency markets was both a symptom and a contributing factor in plunging Germany into a severe recession in 1993–1994. Industrial production, already stagnating in the East, declined in the West. Especially the "locomotives" of the post–World War II German "economic miracle," the export of automobiles and precision machinery, experienced major difficulties.

Unemployment rose to unprecedented levels. There were almost 3.5 million unemployed in February 1993—a postwar high—and the figure reached 4 million in the spring of 1994.

The news about the German economy in the second half of the 1990s did not suggest much improvement. All of the indicators pointed to an economy beset by structural problems. The most visible difficulties were sluggish growth, a rising number of bankruptcies, and, above all, high unemployment. The average national unemployment rate hovered around 10 percent, rising to a high of 11.7 percent in March 1997, but these figures hid sharp differences between the two parts of the reunited nation. Unemployment in the East German Länder was consistently more than twice as high as it was in West Germany. In January 2001 the unemployment rate in West Germany was 8 percent, but in the East it remained disconcertingly high: 18.7 percent.

There was no dearth of explanations for the unsatisfactory performance, which contrasted dramatically with the success story of the American economy at the same time. In a national survey, taken in July 1998, the respondents blamed the problems on everything from the high cost of rebuilding the infrastructure in East Germany to lazy university students. Perhaps not surprisingly, the survey, which listed the responses of East and West Germans separately, revealed sharp differences in the views of *Ossis* and *Wessis* about Germany's economic malaise. Whereas 78 percent of the West Germans surveyed felt the moneys spent in the East were a primary reason for Germany's lackluster performance, 89 percent of the East Germans surveyed felt the major problem was the high salaries of the (West German) civil servants sent to the former GDR after reunification, and 79 percent—perhaps a legacy of communist indoctrination—were convinced "banks and major capitalists" had too much power. Remarkably similar was the number of respondents (76 percent in West Germany, 79 percent in East Germany) who believed

that the German economy was hampered by too many rules and regulations.

The analyses by experts in and out of the government agreed with some of the conclusions voiced by the "man in the street." They, too, pointed out that the cost of rebuilding the East German infrastructure was far higher than had been anticipated: some 230 billion deutsche marks (about $115 billion) between 1990 and 2000. Most of the *Aufbau Ost* ("Buildup East") was financed by the sale of treasure bonds; in 1997 the overall German public debt was a staggering 833 billion deutsche marks ($416.5 billion). In addition, the high unemployment forced the government to subsidize the unemployment insurance fund with moneys from general revenues, increasing the budget deficits still further. Finally, the experts also agreed that Germany's high taxation and excessive regulations were ill suited for the "new economy."

The debate on what Germany needed to do to rekindle the fires of the economy was not limited to the experts. The Kohl government pleaded the cause of supply-side economics: To become competitive again, Germany needed to raise productivity, lower labor costs, and attract private investors. Citing Germany's high wages, generous vacation and social-service packages, and the relatively short average workweek, the chancellor expressed fears that Germany was in danger of becoming a vast "amusement park" instead of a nation of hard workers. The government also claimed that environmental concerns had gotten out of hand, and that too many regulations prevented new construction and new investment. The federal president at the time, Roman Herzog, repeatedly used his bully pulpit to urge his countrymen to embrace the risks and opportunities of the free-market economy.

Needless to say, the critics of supply-side economics rejected this proposal. The German labor unions, traditionally a powerful segment of the economy, understandably opposed loosening the bonds of collective-bargaining agreements, but other spokespeople, too, urged restraint in abandoning the neocorporatist model, which, they argued, had for almost fifty years made Germany a land of few strikes and generally harmonious labor–management relations. Still, even labor and the SPD agreed that "business as usual" was not the answer. There needed to be short-term adjustments and a long-term restructuring of the economy. For the near future, even such radical proposals as a four-day workweek (with a corresponding reduction in wages), an idea floated by the head of the Volkswagen automobile corporation, was not rejected out of hand. In fact, at the end of November 1993, the unions agreed that the plan should be given a trial run at the Volkswagen works.

A unique factor complicating the government's economic calculations was a consequence of the agreement to introduce the new European currency, the euro, on January 1, 2002. (When the euro was introduced as the common currency of most members of the EU its value was pegged at 200 percent of the old deutsche mark.) To qualify for membership in the Euro club, a participant nation had to demonstrate that in mid-1997 its inflation rate did not exceed 1.2 percent, the annual budget deficit was not larger than 3.0 percent, and the total national indebtedness did not exceed 66 percent of the annual GDP. On the day on which the criteria were to be met, Germany (as well as virtually all other potential members of the Euro club) had difficulty meeting the deficit and indebtedness criteria, although the inflation rate was now low. The finance minister, Theodor Waigel, along with his counterparts in the EU, engaged in some very imaginative bookkeeping. (In the spring of 1997, Waigel attempted to assign the gold reserves of the Bundesbank a higher market value to reduce the government deficit, but that ploy was rejected by the Bundesbank.) A major difficulty was that the euro criteria severely constrained the government's ability to finance countercyclical measures at a time when the costs of unemployment benefits represented an ever-larger segment of the national budget.

The Kohl government pushed through some significant reforms. Recognizing, somewhat belatedly, that the era of large-scale state-owned enterprises was over, the German government converted the postal and telephone services and the federal railroads into private corporations, and it sold its share of the national airline, Lufthansa, to private investors. Unfortunately, the financial benefits to the government were substantially less than might appear at first glance. Although the government gained income from the sale of the assets, it also had to take over the debts of the state-owned enterprises to make the privatized companies attractive to private investors.

And there were other large-scale failures as well. A new, much publicized, neocorporatist "Alliance for Work" (*Bündnis für Arbeit*) remained largely a public relations effort. Gerhard Schröder commented that instead of working together to find new solutions to Germany's economic malaise, labor and management simply reiterated their well-known positions. Evidence mounted that Germany's labor costs were a major factor in the country's relative decline of productivity. By May 1996 Germany achieved the dubious distinction of having the highest labor costs among all industrialized countries: 45.52 deutsche marks ($22.76) per hour. (The comparable American figure was 25.18 deutsche marks [$12.59].) To reduce these costs and encourage private investment, the Kohl government proposed a substantial reduction of individual and corporate taxes. Because the economics and finance ministries in the Kohl cabinet were dominated by supply-side economists, the Christian Democratic tax reform was heavily weighted in favor of large incomes. Not surprisingly, the Social Democrats and the labor unions objected to this scheme, but the Länder, who have a constitutional right to be consulted if financial legislation has an impact on them, also voiced their opposition. Fearful of additional federal budget deficits that would initially result from the tax reform, Kohl's plan proposed to transfer to the states a larger share of the burden of financing a variety of social policies. Not surprisingly, the Länder objected.

The Kohl government's failure to enact meaningful tax reform contributed to its electoral defeat in September 1998, and the new Schröder cabinet was determined to learn from its predecessor's mistakes. At first glance, it appeared the demands of its coalition partner, the Greens, would complicate matters. The Greens had long demanded a so-called ecology tax, an additional levy on the consumption of gasoline and other forms of nonrenewable energy to encourage the use of public transportation and discourage energy waste. The initial package of reforms introduced by finance minister Oskar Lafontaine included the ecology tax, but the taxpayers were compensated for the new burden by a reduction of the employee and employer contributions to the social security fund. As far as the income taxes were concerned, Lafontaine proposed a reduction of the tax rate for the lowest incomes from 25.9 to 19.8 percent and for the highest incomes a reduction from 53 to 48 percent. The capital gains tax was to be reduced to 35 percent.

Lafontaine's package was shelved when the minister suddenly resigned from the cabinet in March 1999. Schröder, no friend of his cabinet colleague, claimed that Lafontaine threw in the towel when he discovered that the chancellor was not the subordinate of the finance minister. Lafontaine's successor, Hans Eichel, a former prime minister of the state of Hessen and a close ally of chancellor Schröder, went considerably further than his predecessor. Eichel's proposals included reductions of the individual income taxes by stages so by 2005 the lowest rate would be 15 percent, and the highest 42 percent. At the same time, the capital gains tax was to be reduced to 25 percent. Fortuitously there was an upturn in the economy in 1999–2000, and Eichel did not need to ask the Länder to take on additional burdens. In 2000 Germany sold goods valued at 1.2 trillion deutsche mark abroad, an increase of 17 percent over 1999. The national leadership of the CDU/CSU mounted a determined effort to derail the reforms ("too little, too late"), but they passed with comfortable majorities in both the Bundestag and the Bundesrat. Even some of the Länder governed by the Christian Democrats voted for the package.

Unfortunately, the encouraging figures from 1999–2000 did not portend long-term improvements. Instead, in the first years of the twenty-first century all of the indicators by which economists measure the robustness of an economy showed serious and chronic problems. Germany's growth rate hovered just above 0 percent, and the country had a high public debt; in July 2005 it was 1.5 trillion euros ($1.95 trillion). There was lagging domestic investment coupled with capital flight. The most visible symptom of the malaise, however, was the continuing high unemployment. In March 2005 the overall unemployment rate was 9.8 percent, but it peaked at 18 percent among workers in the East and among employees who were older than fifty-five years. In absolute terms, when the Schröder government took over in 1998, there were 3.8 million unemployed. When it left office seven years later the figure had climbed to 5 million. Numerous analysts concluded that what used to be called *Modell Deutschland* was now the "sick man of Europe."

The contours of the debate on what had happened to produce this state of affairs and what should be done to remedy it had not changed over the last decade. The political left was quick to blame the culture of U.S.-style "shareholder capitalism," with its emphasis on a rapid return on investment. Franz Müntefering's picture of hedge funds as locusts devouring assets without regard to the future was only an extreme form of this attitude. A variation on this theme was the seemingly paradoxical proposal that the way out of the high unemployment was to raise rather than cut wages. This argument postulated that in the one-sided quest to keep Germany's exports flowing, management had neglected the domestic market. Employees who were fearful of losing their job and benefits reduced their spending as consumers and depressed the home market. (This argument was not accepted by most economists, but it is true that in times of uncertainty Germans tend to save rather than consume.) Others argued precisely the opposite. In the age of globalization, Germany needed to have more U.S.-style capitalism. With its overqualified and overage workforce and an economy hampered by excessive social costs and bureaucratic regulations, Germany was losing out to its rivals. The financial black hole of subsidies to Eastern Germany remained a popular scapegoat, especially in Western Germany, as did the cumbersome German tax system.

Proposals for solutions came primarily in three areas: plans to reform the labor market; proposals for tax reform, including ways of streamlining the country's system of institutional and personal subsidies; and suggestions for reducing the maze of regulations at every level of government that was hamstringing business initiatives. Especially the Liberals focused on the numerous laws and regulations that govern hiring and firing. They wanted to abolish most of these and move to a system much closer to the American practices.

Because Schröder had promised to cut unemployment in half within his first four years in office, the SPD–Greens government prioritized reforms of the labor market. The cabinet asked a commission of experts, headed by Peter Hartz, a senior executive at the Volkswagen Corporation, to come up with a comprehensive package of reforms. The result of the commission's deliberations was a well-intentioned but complicated package of carrot-and-stick proposals. To encourage the unemployed to look for new jobs, the Hartz Commission recommended that unemployment compensation be severely cut. (Under the then current regulations, unemployed persons in Germany received about 70 percent of their final paycheck without a time limit.) At the same time the commission also recommended that the unemployed be required to accept whatever jobs were available. On the employers' side, the Hartz group proposed a series of subsidies for businesses that hired and trained (or retrained) the unemployed.

When the proposals of the Hartz Commission were made public, there was a storm of protest, especially in Eastern Germany where unemployment was highest. The critics claimed that after suffering under communism for forty years, East German workers were about to be punished again. The protestors organized Monday night marches reminiscent of the demonstrations that had toppled the GDR's communist regime. There were complaints that by reducing unemployment compensation, the Hartz Commission was trying to put the unemployed on the same level as welfare recipients. As for the requirement that the unemployed could be forced to accept available jobs, the picture of a skilled engineer suddenly forced to pick up debris in a public park made the rounds. The promised simplifications of the Hartz have also not materialized. Rather, the Social Courts (*Sozialgerichte*, a special branch of the judiciary in Germany), were overwhelmed by cases from Hartz recipients, claiming they were owed more under the regulations than they received. Conversely, the Federal Agency for Job Security sued some beneficiaries for receiving more payments than officials at the agency thought they were entitled to. The government claimed the Hartz reforms needed time to show results (the catchy slogan "Agenda 2010" was meant to suggest this), but, as it turned out, time was precisely what the Schröder cabinet did not have.

The CDU, or more precisely Angela Merkel, suggested Germany's economic problems could best be solved by comprehensive tax reforms. In 2004 Merkel asked Paul Kirchhof, a former judge on the Federal Constitutional Court and a recognized financial expert, to propose a thorough reworking of Germany's complicated tax system. Merkel also invited Kirchhof to become a member of her prospective government; Kirchhof himself expected to become the finance minister in a new Christian Democratic government. He submitted a radical plan that essentially amounted to a three-tiered flat income tax. He proposed an annual personal deduction of 8,000 euros for every taxpayer, a 2,000-euro standard deduction, and an 8,000-euro exemption for every child. The current system of myriad deductions, exemptions, and subsidies would be eliminated. The net income that remained after the standard deductions and exemptions would be tax exempt if it was less than 8,000 euros annually. Incomes between 8,000 and 20,000 euros would be taxed at 15 percent, and incomes above 20,000 euros at 25 percent.

Although Kirchhof attempted to show that under his scheme lower- and middle-income persons would actually pay less income tax than under the present system while those with higher incomes would pay more, the public was not convinced. It turned out that most people wanted to keep the certainty of their familiar deductions, exemptions, and subsidies rather than risk the uncertainty of the simplified tax structure. (Kirchhof claimed that if his proposals were adopted, anyone could fill out a tax return in ten minutes or less.)

With the arrival of the grand coalition, Kirchhof's simplified tax became moot. He did not become finance minister as he had expected; that position fell to Peter Steinbrück, a Social Democrat and former prime minister of Northrhine-Westphalia. By the end of 2006, the only tax reform implemented by the grand coalition was to relieve the employers of part of their obligations to the unemployment insurance scheme. The Bundestag raised the national sales tax, the so-called value-added tax (VAT), by 2 percent and reduced employer payments to the unemployment insurance scheme by the same amount.

Although this development was hardly the comprehensive reform package that experts and pundits had demanded, paradoxically the economic situation improved significantly with the advent of the grand coalition. Here a psychological uplift, rather than purely economic factors, were at work. Relief that the parties were no longer at loggerheads, and the immense personal popularity of Merkel (early in her tenure as chancellor she had an approval rating of 77 percent) had at least the short-term effect of replacing pessimism with optimism. There were unmistakable signs of greater consumer confidence, increased orders for goods and services, and for the first time in several years a significant decrease in the number of unemployed. In 2007 the economy grew by 2.6 percent, and in 2008 there was another growth spurt of 2.4 percent. In July 2008 there were fewer unemployed, 3.16 million, than at any time since 1992.

The good times did not last, of course. Germany could not escape the effects of the worldwide financial crisis that began in earnest in the fall of 2008. Before then the country had to deal with a home-grown financial scandal, tax evasion. For years it had been an open secret that many wealthy Germans evaded part of their tax obligations by transferring assets to secret bank accounts abroad, notably in Switzerland and Liechtenstein. Public resentment of the practice grew as the gap between the super rich and the middle classes became increasingly evident (see below, p. 377). In February 2008 Klaus Zumwinkel, the head of the now-privatized German postal service, was arrested for tax evasion. As the investigation of his case continued the prosecutors cast their net to include hundreds of other tax delinquents. There was even a minor diplomatic altercation. Germany put pressure on Switzerland and Liechtenstein to reveal the names and amounts of secret bank accounts controlled by Germans, only to be told by the Swiss that under Swiss law foreign tax evasion was not a crime. In the end, however, the Swiss and Liechtenstein authorities did agree to cooperate in the German investigation.

The tax scandal was soon overshadowed by the repercussions of the global financial crisis. Like their American counterparts, Germany's banks had many "toxic assets" on the books, the result of their participation in the frenzy for exotic financial instruments. A uniquely German aspect of the crisis was the role played by the so-called Länder banks. These are essentially the states' house banks. Their assets are the Länders' tax receipts, and their primary function is to pay the states' current obligations from civil servants' salaries to projects like road building and other infrastructure improvements. During the crisis it quickly became apparent that the managers of some Länder banks had not resisted the lure of the derivatives market. The result was threatened insolvency of several of these publicly held banks. The crisis also brought its share of high-profile bankruptcies, including Germany's largest retailer, Karstadt, and the Opel car company, then a unit of the General Motors Corporation, which was trying to sell its German subsidiary. Finally, as expected, there was rising unemployment and flat growth. The optimistic prognostications for 2008 went into the wastebasket.

The grand coalition's reaction to the crisis was what it claimed was a judicious mix of bailouts, government asset guarantees, consumer incentives, bank mergers, and a tightening of the social net. For consumers there was the German equivalent of the American "cash-for-clunkers" program. Two of the largest commercial banks, Deutsche Bank and Commerzbank, received government bailout money. The third, Dresdner Bank, was merged with the Deutsche Bank. Several of the troubled Länder banks were taken over by "healthier" neighbors. As for high-profile bankruptcies, the government pursued what its critics claimed was an erratic and irrational course. Karstadt was forced to file for bankruptcy, but the federal cabinet offered government guarantees for any purchaser of the Opel car company.

Despite considerable pressure, especially from the United States, Germany did not launch a massive stimulus package. The grand coalition claimed this was not needed. It is true that in a number of ways the impact of the economic crisis was better contained in Germany than in the United States. To begin with, Germany did not have to deal with the catastrophic effects of the housing market downturn. Most Germans do not own their home; they live in rental apartments. Then, too, the social net is more tightly woven. Germany has universal health insurance. Workers do not lose their coverage if they are unemployed. Payments to those without work also continue indefinitely. There is no need for federal legislation to periodically extend coverage.

The grand coalition's primary means of dealing with unemployment was to sponsor and pay for "short work (*Kurzarbeit*)." Under this program the government encouraged employers not to fire unneeded workers, but to put them on shortened workweeks. During the time they were not needed to perform their regular jobs they attended training programs to improve their skills. The government paid the part of the workers' wages when they were attending the training programs. Theoretically this was a win–win situation: Employers could cut their payrolls, while the workers kept their paychecks and acquired new skills as the economy revived.

In March 2009, in part to signal that the government was taking charge of the country's economic problems, Merkel appointed a new economics minister, Kart-Theodor Freiherr zu Guttenberg. A former secretary general of the CSU and a scion of an ancient Bavarian noble family, Guttenberg was young (he was only 37 at the time of his appointment), dynamic, ambitious, and very popular. The new minister rushed from Berlin to Brussels to Frankfurt, meeting with labor leaders, businessmen, and EU functionaries. At every stop he gave the impression that he was listening to the ideas presented and that he would soon present ideas of his own. As we shall see, Guttenberg did not hold office long enough to demonstrate his actual skills as economics minister.

The CDU/CSU–FDP government, which took office in the fall of 2009, inherited not only a recovering economy (especially Germany's exports were holding up surprisingly well), but also a growing national debt and a massive deficit in the federal budget. These fiscal constraints put severe limitations on the FDP's demand for tax cuts and an overhaul of the entire federal tax system. In addition, there were personal rivalries in the cabinet. The new economics minister was a Liberal, Rainer Brüderle (Guttenberg was now minister of defense), an elderly and not very forceful politician. The finance minister was the Christian Democrat Wolfgang Schäuble (he had been minister of the interior in the grand coalition), and he argued the size of the federal deficit precluded any significant tax cuts. As a result the new government's tax program was a decidedly small-bore affair. The cabinet voted to cut the VAT rate for hotel stays, and imposed a new tax on banks to provide a fund for any future bailouts, so that the taxpayer would not be burdened with these costs in the future. The tax rate for individual banks is determined by the institution's risk profile.

The first major crisis which the CDU/CSU–FDP cabinet had to confront involved not the domestic economy, but international finances. All of the EU countries were severely impacted by the global financial crisis, but the problems were worst in the PIGS nations (this not very felicitous acronym which stands for Portugal, Ireland, Greece, and Spain). Among these countries Greece faced the most acute difficulties. In the spring of 2010 Greece, a member of the Euro zone, had to admit that it was essentially bankrupt. The country had also significantly violated the criteria for euro stability.

Despite rioting in the streets of Athens, Greece not only promised to put its fiscal house in order, but it also asked for help from the other members of the euro-club. That plea was directed primarily at Germany, the EU's strongest economy. The German government's first reaction was a flat "no," and pundits rushed into the fray contending that the introduction of the euro had always been a mistake. In the end cooler heads prevailed. The EU finance ministers put together an aid package for Greece, financed partly by the EU and partly by the International Monetary Fund. As part of the package Chancellor Merkel obtained the agreement of her fellow EU leaders to rewrite the rule book on public finance in Europe so as to detect early on problems such as those encountered in Greece. In September 2010 the EU leaders announced that they had agreed on a new set of rules.

These measures succeeded in putting the German economy back on track. Exports were up, unemployment was down, and the government deficit declined because of better than expected revenues. Ironically, despite these positive indicators, the government's popularity declined. In July 2010 Merkel's cabinet had an approval rating of 34 percent, down from 48 percent when it took office in September 2009. The reasons were partly unpopular measures like premium increases for the national health insurance scheme, but analysts attributed most of the government's lack of popularity to the sense that the coalition partners spent more time bickering than governing.

FOREIGN POLICY

Reunification brought not only unexpected economic problems, but also major consequences for Germany's foreign relations. The reunited country needed to find a new place for itself in the global balance of power. It was (and continues to be) a difficult balancing act. As Henry Kissinger, the former U.S. secretary of state, once quipped, a reunited Germany was "too small to be a world power and too big to be a European power."

After reunification, the Germans undertook an intensive campaign to allay the concerns about the new Germany abroad. These efforts had three priorities. One was to settle all remaining boundary disputes; the united Germany recognized the Oder-Neisse Line as the country's permanent eastern border. A second emphasis has been to maintain and strengthen the Bonn–Paris axis as a guarantee that Germany will not embark on a new *Sonderweg* in international relations. Finally, incorporating the united Germany in a united Europe became the Kohl government's absolute first priority, earning the chancellor the sobriquet "the last great European."

Cooperation with France and the efforts to further European unity culminated in December 1991 with the Treaty of Maastricht. Primarily a Franco-German initiative, the treaty was signed at a summit meeting of the government leaders of the member states of the European Community in the Dutch city of Maastricht. The sponsors saw the agreement as a major step forward on the road to further European economic cooperation and political unity. The weighty document (it is more than a thousand pages long) provided timetables for the establishment of a European currency, the elimination of the last trade barriers in the EC, the mutual recognition of training certificates and university diplomas by the member countries, the establishment of a common European citizenship, and a name change from the European Community to the European Union.

In practice the "Maastricht strategy" did not fulfill the high hopes of its backers. It quickly became clear that Kohl and Mitterrand had neglected to prepare the groundwork for the massive basket of "Europeanization" measures envisioned by the Maastricht Treaty. Although in theory the treaty was based on the "subsidiarity principle" (which provides that decisions should always be made at the lowest possible governmental level), opponents of the agreement noted that in the absence of a strong European parliament, the Maastricht document would give the European Commission in Brussels new, unchecked powers. In Germany, fears were raised that the common European currency, the euro, would weaken the strong deutsche mark. Small nations worried about marginalization by larger powers. In a referendum, Danish voters initially ejected the treaty (they subsequently accepted it), and French voters approved it by a very narrow margin. In Germany the treaty received a vote of confidence in the Bundestag, and it survived a constitutional court challenge.

Another, in some ways equally serious problem, with the Maastricht strategy was the absence of any real concept for the EU's future political and especially its military role. Despite some platitudes about the need for common foreign and security policies of the European Union, the institutions for implementing such policies were either weak or nonexistent. Attempts to assign the European Union or the Conference on Security and Cooperation in Europe (CSCE) roles in implementing a European security policy have so far proved ineffective. A European army remains at an embryonic stage. A Franco-German military brigade (with headquarters in Strasbourg) was established, and the French and German governments hoped this would become the nucleus of a European rapid deployment defense force. But even the planned addition of a Belgian contingent was delayed by squabbles over the languages of command.

The plethora of paper plans for the future was to some extent a reflection of a leadership vacuum in the conduct of German foreign policy. In 1992 the country's longtime foreign minister, Hans-Dietrich Genscher, resigned. Genscher was the longest-serving foreign minister in any Western country as well as a man of considerable international renown. But he had suffered several heart attacks in recent years and clearly felt the need to retire from his high-profile job. (He remained honorary chairman of the FDP and a member of the Bundestag.) His successor was Klaus Kinkel, like Genscher a Free Democrat, but a much less charismatic and influential figure, both in his own party and in the cabinet.

Germany's military role outside of Europe raised even more fundamental questions. In 1992 and 1993 a fierce debate erupted over the participation of German troops in UN peacekeeping operations. When the Federal Republic joined NATO in 1955, West Germany agreed that it would not deploy any of its military forces "outside of area," which meant outside of the territory of the NATO member states. In the days of the Cold War, this made military and political sense, but in the 1990s the areas of acute security problems lay outside of the NATO area, including both Africa and southeastern Europe. (This is another reason why the British foreign minister Douglas Hurd lamented in 1989 that the Cold War was "a system with which we lived quite well for forty years.")

The Kohl government argued strongly that Germany should act as a major, but responsible, power. This includes making Bundeswehr troops available for UN peacekeeping missions. The cabinet also floated the idea of a permanent seat on the United Nations' Security Council for Germany. (There is opposition to this proposal not only in Germany itself but also among some of its European partners, who argue that "Europe" already has two permanent Security Council members, Great Britain and France.) The SPD was divided on the issue of "out of area" activism, and the Greens initially rejected using German troops in foreign military operations. In the absence of a firm parliamentary mandate, the Kohl government restricted German participation in UN operations to "peaceful" missions. In 1993 and 1994 the Bundeswehr provided medical and humanitarian aid in Cambodia and Bosnia. German ground troops were also deployed in Somalia, but only in areas where they were not likely to run into hostile forces. However, in December 1996 the Bundestag agreed that Bundeswehr troops could participate in "out of area" operations, provided they are sanctioned by the UN or NATO. Shortly afterward, at the beginning of 1997, three thousand German soldiers became part of the international troop contingent maintaining the peace in Bosnia-Herzegovina.

Germany's efforts to improve relations with the countries of Eastern Europe must be seen in conjunction with the country's efforts to make the EU a political and economic success. Since 1990 the country has provided the successor states to the Soviet bloc with massive amounts of both government and private investment to aid them in their transformation to market economies. (Volkswagen, for example, took over and modernized the Czech Škoda Motor Works.) Fears that the reunified Germany would embark on a new "Rapallo policy" (see earlier p. 299) by allying itself with Russia against the West have proved groundless.

The Germans have been especially interested in removing lingering resentments in the Federal Republic's two immediate East European neighbors, Poland and the Czech Republic. In the case of Poland, this has resulted not only in a variety of economic and cultural cooperation agreements, but also some recurrent, mostly symbolic, irritants. During the grand coalition the conservative Polish government complained about what it felt were insulting remarks about Poland in the German media and demanded an apology from the German government. Merkel's government pointedly reminded the Poles that the principle of freedom of the press prevailed in Germany.

Somewhat more serious is the ongoing debate over the mission and leadership of the "Foundation Flight, Expulsion, Reconciliation." This controversy involves the politics of memory. Germany had established this quasi-government organization to highlight both the Nazi crimes in Poland and to memorialize the plight of the ethnic Germans who had been expelled from Poland at the end of World War II. The specific issue in question is the membership of the Foundation's board of directors. The German Association of Expellees (actually descendants of the original expellees) insisted its president, Erika Steinbach, join the Foundation's board. The Poles and the FDP feared this would shift the Foundation's focus in the direction of the Germans as victims, and strenuously objected. Chancellor Merkel, who has the right to appoint the members of the board, is caught in the middle. She wants to maintain good relations with the Poles and her coalition partner, but Erika Steinbach is also a CDU member of the Bundestag and the association she heads, Association of Expellees, has traditionally maintained close ties with the Christian Democrats. Eventually Ms. Steinbach agreed not to serve on the board.

After long and difficult negotiations, Germany and the Czech Republic signed a bilateral agreement in December 1996. The pact not only settled a number of outstanding controversies but also contained mutual admissions of past wrongdoing. Germany acknowledged the immorality of the Nazis' destruction of Czechoslovakia in the 1930s, and the Czechs admitted that the expulsion of the Sudeten Germans from the country in 1945 was accompanied by unwarranted cruelties. Even so, the two sides could not agree on a full-scale settlement of private property claims. Here they "agreed to disagree."

Linking Germany's West European and East European concerns, the Kohl government acted as sponsor of the East European countries that have been seeking membership in NATO and especially the EU. Germany has supported the extension of NATO membership to Poland, Hungary, and the Czech Republic, although the Germans, like the French, would have preferred that the new membership list also include Slovenia and Romania, a proposal that the Clinton administration rejected. (Slovenia eventually did become a member of NATO.) Even more than NATO's expansion, Germany is interested in the future of the EU. The Federal Republic welcomed the decision of the European Commission in July 1997 to open negotiations for EU membership with six new applicants, including, in addition to the three new NATO members, Slovenia, Cyprus, and Estonia. These countries all joined the EU on January 1, 2004.

The Schröder government, which took office in September 1998, did not significantly change Germany's foreign policy. A stable partnership with the United States, a strengthened EU, and improved relations with the countries of Eastern Europe remained the key goals of the country's foreign relations. Surprising some observers, the new foreign minister, Joschka Fischer, quickly established himself as a skilled diplomat who moved easily among his peers. His dealings with his American counterparts during his term in office, Madeleine Albright and later Colin Powell, were especially cordial.

Inevitably, the larger Germany became more of a presence on the international stage. During the Kosovo conflict, German troops were for the first time since World War II engaged in military operations, and in the subsequent administration of this Balkan region by NATO forces, members of the Bundeswehr were fully integrated into the KFOR (Kosovo force) units. The decision to send German troops into potential harm's way was not uncontroversial. Both the SPD and the Greens have strong pacifist factions, and there was a real danger that the SPD's national congress in April 1999 would disavow the government's decision to send Bundeswehr units to the Balkans and Afghanistan. Gerhard Schröder credited the Social Democrats' leading elder statesman

and former pacifist, the eighty-year-old Erhard Eppler, with convincing the congress to back the government's position.

Out of the limelight, Germany has also continued its efforts to improve relations with both Israel and the Arab countries. Johannes Rau, the federal president elected in 1999, became the first German political leader to address the Knesset, the Israeli parliament. In another first, he spoke in German. During the time of the grand coalition, in March 2008, Angela Merkel also addressed the Knesset. In addition, during her visit to Israel the eight ministers who accompanied the chancellor held a joint session with the Israeli cabinet.

A strengthened European Union remains a primary focus of Germany's foreign relations. In fact, the desire to hasten the integration of the EU led to one of the rare missteps by Joschka Fischer. At one point, the foreign minister seemed to suggest that the EU needed a full-fledged central government. Encountering a backlash of opposition, especially in Great Britain, Fischer quickly retreated and assured the Euro-skeptics that he did not favor a European superstate. The foreign minister continued, however, to argue forcefully for a strengthened European parliament to control the various commissions in Brussels. Germany also supported the initiatives that led to the agreement in March 2000 to create a European Rapid Deployment Force (ERDF). This decision was made in the wake of the Kosovo conflict, which revealed a decided lack of European preparedness for a military emergencies. The ERDF, which was ready for deployment in 2003, consists of 60,000 soldiers drawn from the countries of the EU (13,500 from the Bundeswehr).

It required something of a balancing act to pair Germany's support for the eastward expansion of the EU with maintaining good relations with Russia. Russia sees itself as a major power in its own right and does not want to join the EU. Yet the country's leaders remain somewhat suspicious of the EU's expansion to the western borders of Russia. Especially Gerhard Schröder worked hard to continue the good personal contacts with the Russian leaders that had characterized Russo-German relations in the last years of the Kohl era.

Until the war in Iraq, relations with the United States remained largely free of friction. Both sides stressed that this is a long-term and stable partnership. An irritant that was not, strictly speaking, a matter of government-to-government relations was the long-drawn-out conflict over payments to compensate the survivors of the Nazis' program of forced foreign labor. American attorneys took the initiative in bringing several class-action suits against German businesses and the German government on behalf of these victims of Nazism, many of whom were now living in the United States. After prolonged negotiations, teams headed by a former German economics minister, Otto Count Lambsdorff (who died in 2009), and a former U.S. trade negotiator, Stuart Eizenstat, succeeded in reaching an agreement in March 2000. The pact provided for a restitution fund from which former forced laborers would be paid between 5,000 and 15,000 deutsche mark, depending on the severity of the conditions under which they had to work. The money was to come from appropriations by the German government

---

Im Mittelpunkt Guido Westerwelle (1961–)

The vice-chancellor and foreign minister in Angela Merkel's second cabinet is one of Germany's most controversial, ambitious, and successful politicians. He is also the country's first openly gay foreign minister, although, remarkably, his sexual preference is not what makes him controversial. (Incidentally, Westerwelle and his longtime partner, Michael Mronz, chose Angela Merkel's fiftieth birthday party in 2004 to make their relationship public.)

Westerwelle was born in December 1961 in the small town of Bad Honnef, not far from Bonn. He graduated with a law degree from the University of Bonn, and in 1991 entered private practice in that city. Long before then he had become active in politics. Immediately after graduating from a *Gymnasium* in Bad Honnef, he joined the FDP and that party's youth organization, the Young Liberals. Westerwelle served a national chairman of the Young Liberals from 1983 to 1988.

Unlike many of his generation, Westerwelle did not go through a youthful *Sturm und Drang* period. Except for his sexual preference, he has led a very conventional, bourgeois life. He never wavered in his political affiliation. He joined the FDP when he was nineteen years old, and he has remained a party stalwart ever since. Westerwelle rose quickly to prominence in the FDP, but his political career as a Liberal has also meant that as a big fish in a small pond he could not realize his ambition for becoming chancellor. The German Liberals are a minority party, seldom gaining more than 10 percent of the popular vote in national elections. (It must be remembered that in European political parlance the Liberals are ideologically right of center, not on the left side of the political spectrum as is the case in the United States.) The party had its best showing to date in the 2009 election. Under Westerwelle's energetic leadership the party obtained 14.6 percent of the popular vote, a respectable result, but hardly the foundation for political dominance. As a result, the FDP is condemned to junior party status in any coalition the party might enter and its leader is unlikely ever to become chancellor.

There is no doubt that Westerwelle smarts under this handicap; his dream of leading a national government is an open secret. Nevertheless, he remains committed to the FDP, and has done his utmost to increase the party's space on the political map. Westerwelle became the FDP's general secretary in 1994, and he was elected to the Bundestag in 1996. In 2001 he was elected national chairman of the party—the youngest chief in the FDP's history.

and contributions from German industry. In return, the German government and private firms would be immune from further lawsuits. The Bundestag passed the requisite legislation, appropriating the necessary funds, but there has been some difficulty in raising the matching contributions from private sources. German government leaders, including both Chancellor Schröder and the federal president, Johannes Rau, repeatedly urged industry to do its part, but the private sector was reluctant, in part because some U.S. judges have ruled that the terms of the agreement are not legally binding on potential plaintiffs, so German companies might still face future lawsuits. The real victims in all this legal squabbling, of course, are the rapidly aging survivors of Nazi exploitation.

After its reelection in 2002, the SPD–Greens coalition experienced some notable triumphs and frustrations in the conduct of Germany's foreign relations. Joschka Fischer, who continued as foreign minister in the new cabinet, remained a convinced multilateralist, who sought to reach Germany's foreign policy goals as much as possible through international institutions. These included the EU (Fischer was a vocal advocate of the failed

In cooperation with other Liberals, Westerwelle has attempted to put the FDP into the political limelight by a variety of means, ranging from the silly to the more serious. During the 2005 election campaign Westerwelle traveled around the country in a gaudily painted Guidomobil and he proclaimed the FDP to be "the fun party." At the same time, on a more serious note, the Liberals portrayed themselves as the party that favored free enterprise and individual initiatives, while accusing the Social Democrats and the Christian Democrats of safeguarding the status quo of entitlements and national sclerosis. Westerwelle also determined to keep the FDP's future options open. For most of their history the Liberals had been a junior coalition partner with the CDU/CSU, but in 2005 Westerwelle refused to announce a "coalition preference." Consequently, when the CDU/CSU and the SPD formed a grand coalition, the FDP was condemned to the status of ineffective parliamentary opposition, although Westerwelle used his position well as a vocal critic of the government.

For the 2009 election Westerwelle abandoned his earlier strategy. This time he committed the FDP to a coalition with the CDU/CSU, ruling out any other forms of political cooperation. His ploy succeeded. In October 2009 the CDU/CSU and the FDP formed a coalition government with Westerwelle as vice-chancellor and foreign minister. As Germany's chief diplomat Westerwelle has not been a notable success. To be sure, he labors under some handicaps not of his own making. The last Liberal foreign minister was Hans-Dietrich Genscher, who when he left office, was not only the longest-serving foreign minister in the Western world, but who could point to some major achievements, most notably his contribution to German reunification. But Westerwelle also created some problems of his own. His linguistic skills are not very good, and he does not seem very interested in the job, preferring instead to stir up controversy with his comments on domestic affairs. His critics also accuse him of using his travels abroad to further the business interests of his friends, rather than advance the government's international agenda. Finally, there is the formidable presence of the chancellor, Angela Merkel. She is interested in foreign affairs, and after almost six years in office she has considerable experience in international relations and is familiar with most of the world's leaders.

constitution), and the UN, where he stressed the need for effective peacekeeping missions. In fact, by 2005, except for the United States, no country had more troops stationed abroad than Germany. The fruits of Fischer's labors included EU membership for most of the former communist East European nations, and Germany's participation in the Team of Four (United States, Great Britain, France, and Germany) that worked hard to defuse the crisis over Iran's nuclear ambitions.

At the beginning of the new century tensions in the relations between the Federal Republic and the United States emerged. Schröder and Fischer, and virtually all Germans, not only expressed genuine sympathy and solidarity with the United States after the outrage on September 11, 2001, but they also supported the American military intervention to rid Afghanistan of the Taliban regime that had given aid and comfort to Osama bin Laden and the perpetrators of the attack on the World Trade Center. However, the SPD-Greens cabinet (along with most Germans and Europeans) opposed the unilateral American decision to invade Iraq. In his memoirs Schröder complained that despite lofty rhetoric, the Bush administration did not really want Europe as an equal partner in international relations. The chancellor also made Germany's opposition a campaign issue in 2002, and he quickly became a persona non grata in the White House. The chancellor's and Fischer's public opposition to the war in Iraq produced negative headlines in the United States, but it should be noted that behind the scenes the intelligence services of the two countries continued their traditional cooperation.

In contrast to the strained relationship with the United States, the SPD–Greens coalition developed a quite cordial relationship with Russia. This was partly the result of the shared opposition to the war in Iraq, but it also had economic and personal reasons. As is true for most of Western Europe, Russia supplies the bulk of Germany's natural gas needs while the Federal Republic is one of Russia's largest trading partners; the economic relationship

between them was important to both sides. In addition, President Putin of Russia and Gerhard Schröder developed a personal relationship that went beyond the normal contacts between heads of government. In fact, analysts noted that the two men shared a genuine *Männerfreundschaft* ("male bonding").

In the grand coalition that came into office in October 2005, the new foreign minister was a Social Democrat, Frank-Walter Steinmeier. He was a somewhat surprising choice. His previous position had been chief of staff of Schröder's chancellery office, which meant that Steinmeier's experience in foreign affairs was limited to the extent to which the chancellor's office was involved in the conduct of Germany's foreign relations. Some analysts concluded that Merkel accepted Steinmeier precisely because he had little expertise in foreign affairs; she wanted to be her own foreign minister. It is certainly true that after assuming office the chancellor was more in the public limelight than the foreign minister.

Not surprisingly, the grand coalition kept many of its predecessor's foreign relations priorities. Immediately after taking office Merkel underscored that she wanted to maintain the special relationship between France and Germany; her first trip outside of Germany as chancellor was to Paris to meet with President Chirac. One notable atmospheric change has been the new government's attitude toward the United States. Although the grand coalition, like the SPD–Greens cabinet, refused to engage German troops in the war in Iraq, Merkel made every effort to defuse Schröder's open antagonism toward the Bush administration. She went out of her way to establish a cordial relationship with the American president and in return was warmly received at the White House. In fact, President George W. Bush paid the chancellor the singular honor of visiting Merkel's home region in Eastern Germany.

Germany's relations with Russia were put on a somewhat less cordial footing. There were no outstanding issues to cause friction between the two countries, but for obvious reasons Merkel does not enjoy the same kind of "male-bonding relationship" as her predecessor did.

The good relations with the United States have continued after the CDU/CSU–FDP government took office. In November 2009 Merkel was accorded the honor of addressing a joint session of Congress. In sharp contrast to her usual rhetorical style, she delivered an emotionally charged and quite personal address. The chancellor expressed particularly her and Germany's gratitude for the first President Bush's unwavering support for German reunification.

The new CDU/CSU–FDP coalition has not had a particularly auspicious start in its foreign relations. The German government was severely disappointed by the lack of substantive results at the Copenhagen Climate Conference in December 2009. The German minister for the environment, Norbert Röttgen (CDU), complained bitterly that the separate agreement worked out by the Americans and the Chinese effectively undercut the attempts by the Germans and other Europeans to set definite and binding global carbon emission limits.

Another foreign relations disaster, this one with major domestic repercussions, occurred in Afghanistan. Germany contributes almost 5,000 soldiers to the international force fighting the Taliban, the third largest contingent after the American and the British contributions. In September 2009 the commander of a German unit called for American air support, which resulted in the death of a number of innocent Afghan civilians. This was bad enough. But the subsequent political fallout was the consequence of an attempted cover-up. At first everyone involved from the colonel in the field who had requested the air strike to the defense minister denied that any civilians had been hurt. But the facade crumbled fast. Investigative reporting and an independent NATO report on the incident revealed the truth. When the dust had settled, both the army chief of staff, General Wolfgang Schneiderhan, and the

newly appointed defense minister, Franz Josef Jung, resigned. Jung was replaced by the economics minister, Karl-Theodor Freiherr zu Guttenberg.

As for the new foreign minister, Guido Westerwelle, he has certainly been busy. He became a peripatetic traveler to foreign lands, although critics complained that the junkets seemed more designed to benefit the fortunes of Westerwelle's businessmen friends, who accompanied him, than to advance a coherent German foreign policy agenda. Westerwelle has also not lost his penchant for provocative utterances. He caused a storm of protest when, speaking in his capacity as vice-chancellor rather than foreign minister, he complained that some recipients of Hartz benefits could and did live like decadent Romans in the last days of the empire.

GERMAN SOCIETY TWO DECADES AFTER REUNIFICATION

In 2009 and 2010 Germany commemorated the twentieth anniversaries of two momentous events: the anniversary of the fall of the Berlin Wall in 2009 and that of national reunification a year later. There were not only the expected, somewhat self-congratulatory speeches by politicians of all stripes, but also a number of attempts to answer the question, How different was the Berlin republic from the Bonn republic?

The population continued to move from east to west and north to south. The number of people living in the areas of the former GDR declined steadily. The new Länder had a combined population of 16.43 million in 1990; ten years later that figure had fallen to 15.29 million. The favorite destinations of the Easterners were all in the West: Bavaria, West Berlin, Lower Saxony, and Northrhine-Westphalia. Interestingly, there is a gender difference in the population movement. More women than men leave the East. Especially in the generation that came of age after reunification women are attracted by the professional opportunities in Western Germany and Western Europe, while many of their male counterparts prefer the safety and familiarity of the home setting.

Problems at the beginning of the twenty-first century contrasted vividly with the euphoria that initially accompanied reunification. Pessimism was the prevailing mood in Germany at the turn of the century. Instead of the "leveled middle-class" society of the 1950s and 1960s, there was a growing gap between rich and poor: In 2005, 10 percent of the population owned 77 percent of the assets, and 9.2 percent were defined as permanently poor, which in Germany meant they were earning less than 60 percent of the median income. The introduction of the euro was blamed (not always unfairly) for the increase in the price of virtually everything. And, as we noted before, there was the inexorable growth of the unemployment figures that haunted the SPD–Greens coalition throughout its tenure.

Reunification also increased the gap between the richer and poorer regions in the country. While large tracts of Mecklenburg-Vorpommern remained what they had always been, poor and marginal agricultural land, the Hamburg region was not only the wealthiest German Land but the richest area in the entire EU region. (But the exception proves the rule: In 2009 Mecklenburg-Vorpommern created a quite successful enclave of high-tech firms clustered around the University of Wismar.)

Efforts to develop tourist attractions in the sparsely populated eastern regions have so far met with only limited success. The spending habits of Germans remained pretty much the same. East Germans now joined their West German cousins in spending more on travel and vacations than their counterparts in other European countries. Also, most Germans continued to strive after social harmony and neocorporate relations rather than antagonism and rampant individualism. Concerns about the ecology remained a priority issue. Germany mandated the most elaborate recycling program in Europe, and despite some initial grumbling, the so-called ecology tax has been widely accepted.

Much has been made of the continuing persistent differences and tensions between East and West Germans. Reunification, pundits were fond of saying, took place in the realm of politics but not in the hearts and minds of the people. Differences and mutual resentments between "Wessis," as the West Germans are colloquially called, and "Ossis," their counterparts from the five new Länder, made a mockery of "unity" in the reunited country. There were many reasons for the separateness of East and West. In the former East Germany, the euphoria of reunification gave way to complaints about the slow pace of economic recovery and the arrogance of the West Germans. Continuing revelations about the ubiquitous Stasi contacts of virtually anyone in public life in the old GDR forced numerous "native" East German politicians out of office. They were often replaced by West German "carpetbaggers," further reinforcing resentment of the Wessis.

As a result, a wave of nostalgia for "our" lost culture permeated parts of East Germany. Some enterprising entrepreneurs in the former East Germany established restaurants decorated with GDR artifacts and staffed by surly waitresses reminiscent of the former GDR's much despised restaurant and retail store monopoly, the *Handelsorganisation* ("Trade Organization"). But such developments should not be overrated. They need to be coupled with the news that when an obscure communist group called for a demonstration in East Berlin in October 2000 to protest the demise of the GDR, only seven people showed up.

What the people of Eastern Germany wanted was not a return to the communist past but a better democratic future. They certainly were concerned that all of the economic indicators continued to be lower in the East than in the West, and they resented that many West Germans treated the inhabitants of the new Länder as backward cousins. Some East Germans regretted the loss of the sense of community that was supposed to have characterized the old GDR, in contrast to the West German "push and shove society" (*Ellbogengesellschaft*). Ossis also resented that every aspect of life seemed to have to conform to West German standards. Even the old GDR's liberal law on abortions, which many in both parts of the country had hoped would become the basis for the united Germany's new national abortion law, was declared unconstitutional by the German Federal Constitutional Court. But the Wessis, too, felt they had legitimate complaints. They increasingly saw East Germany as a bottomless pit that seemed to absorb more and more resources and threatened to lower the standard of living in West Germany.

West German greed did much to sour the atmosphere between Ossis and Wessis. Immediately after reunification some West Germans filed a flurry of lawsuits demanding the return of property that had been expropriated by the Soviet and GDR authorities over the last fifty years. Here the Federal Constitutional Court eventually stepped in to help the East Germans. In a landmark decision, the court ruled that owners of property that had been taken away by the Communists were not automatically entitled to either restitution or compensation. This decision is especially important because many of these properties had in the meantime been turned into social-service institutions like kindergartens and retirement homes.

German's second attempt at *Vergangen-heitsbewältigung* ("mastering the past") encountered problems reminiscent of the difficulties that beset de-Nazification after 1945. One familiar development was the seeming tendency to punish lower-level communist officials but to leave untouched the real leaders of the old GDR regime. Erich Honecker, the SED's last leader before the *Wende,* was initially able to flee to Russia, where he took refuge in the Chilean embassy in Moscow. He was returned to Germany in January 1990 to stand trial, but before the proceedings were concluded Honecker was released from prison for health reasons and allowed to travel to Chile to live with his daughter. He died in Chile at the end of April 1994.

Erich Mielke, the former head of the hated Stasi, was sentenced (the verdict was suspended because of Mielke's poor health), but for a crime, the murder of a policeman, he had committed in 1931 as a member of the communist Red Front Fighters Association. (He died in a Berlin nursing home in May 2000.) Not until the fall of 1993 were some prominent representatives of the communist regime, such as Willi Stoph, the former prime minister, and Heinz Kessler, the former defense minister, sentenced to relatively mild prison terms.

Prosecutors have been more successful trying the military establishment of the former GDR. By the middle of 1997, several members of the East German "National Defense Council" and more than fifty officers and border guards had been sentenced to prison terms ranging up to seven and a half years in connection with the regime's order to "shoot-to-kill" persons trying to leave the GDR.

A new wave of trials took place in the spring and summer of 1996. In the most spectacular proceedings, some of the highest functionaries during the GDR's waning days, including Egon Krenz and Günter Schabowski, the SED's leader in East Berlin, were tried as criminals for authorizing the "shoot-to-kill" order. Only Schabowski expressed regret for the Wall and its consequences. The other defendants claimed they were not guilty because as GDR officials they were victims of the Cold War, merely carrying out decisions that had been made in Moscow. The court rejected the defendants' claim; they were sentenced to several years in jail. In 2003 a German court rejected Egon Krenz's request for probation. The last leader of the GDR served the full six and a half years of his sentence.

Another problem in Eastern Germany concerned the Stasi past of many of its citizens, including a number of politicians who rose to prominent positions after reunification. It became clear that the Stasi's vast army of informers included even opponents of the regime. (The last prime minister of the GDR, the Christian Democrat Lothar de Maizière, a gifted amateur musician, was accused of serving the Stasi as "informal collaborator" under the code name "Czerny.") Until more stringent regulations were issued, information about the ubiquitous cooperation of such officials with the Stasi was often released selectively by political opponents. As a result, a number of "native" East German leaders had to resign from their newly acquired political posts. The resignations left behind not only a political vacuum but also bitter accusations by many of those dismissed that the functionaries who forced them out of office did not understand the reality of life in the former East Germany; some of the victims of the new purge claimed they had cooperated with the Stasi as a cover for advancing their work against the regime.

As had been true for the Nazi era, the problem of "mastering the past" also led to a debate on how to treat the GDR as a historical entity. One view was expressed by the prime minister of Brandenburg (and former leader of the SPD), Matthias Platzeck. In May 2009 he declared, "the GDR is as dead as a dormouse," arguing it was time to concentrate on the present rather than to keep digging up the GDR past. Others insisted vehemently that on the contrary the societal repercussions of the "regime of injustice" (*Unrechtsregime*) needed to be fully explored rather than be covered with the mantle of forgive and forget.

The debate had practical as well as theoretical dimensions. Platzeck's position, for example, was motivated at least in part by concern for his political future. He headed an SPD–Left Party coalition in the state of Brandenburg, and the head of the Left Party caucus in the state legislature, Kerstin Kaiser, had to admit that she had been a Stasi informer. In her university days she had spied on her fellow students. Under the principle of forgive and forget her past was no longer relevant, but if the "regime of injustice" were to be fully exposed, her role as an active participant in the dictatorship might lead to a political scandal. Incidentally, Kaiser's own "justification" for her actions was that "everyone did it," and at the time and "we didn't know any better."

The disintegration of the Soviet system in Eastern Europe led not only to vast economic and political dislocations but also enabled the citizens of Eastern European countries to travel abroad. Many have applied for political asylum in Germany. Between 1990 and 1992 the total number of those seeking political asylum in Germany increased from 108,000 to 430,000 per year. Germany was a particularly desirable place to go because until recently the country had an extremely liberal asylum law. Virtually any foreigner could ask for political asylum in Germany, and once the application had been submitted, the individual was free to stay in Germany until his or her case was decided. Most of the applications were eventually turned down, but the judicial process usually took years, and in the meantime the asylum seekers were entitled to the benefits of Germany's social service system.

To stem the tide of asylum seekers (and to take the wind out of the sails of the right-wing extremists), the Bundestag in May 1993 passed a controversial law tightening the asylum provisions. Applicants from countries with a functioning democratic system as well as those who enter Germany from a "third country" can now be turned back without a judicial hearing. The law classifies the postcommunist countries of Eastern Europe as democratic. The legislation did have a positive effect. The number of asylum seekers declined significantly.

In the second half of the 1990s, the debate over the presence of foreigners in Germany continued with some shifts in emphasis. The Schröder government introduced legislation to make it easier for foreigners living in Germany to gain German citizenship. This led the Christian Democrats, desperate for an issue to take attention away from the scandals of Helmut Kohl, to insist that before becoming citizens foreigners needed to show that they accepted German culture as the "leading culture" (*Leitkultur*) of the country. The debate over the concept of a "leading culture" quickly became farcical with pundits and politicians asking tongue in cheek if things "typically German" included the hundreds of Italian and Spanish restaurants spread across Germany or Walt Disney's Mickey Mouse, a cultural icon just as powerful among young Germans as among American children.

While the politicians debated the esoterica of culture, businesses had other worries. Paradoxically, although high unemployment was a chronic problem, Germany also experienced a shortage of skilled workers in certain segments of the economy, notably the high-tech industry. For this reason, the Schröder cabinet proposed introducing the German equivalent of the American green card, enabling foreigners with critical skills to work in Germany for a limited number of years. Because many of these foreign technicians came from India, the Christian Democratic opposition objected to the program with the slogan "children instead of Indians." (The slogan works as a rhyme in German, "*Kinder statt Inder.*") The opposition was trying to argue that the solution to Germany's labor problems was not to import more foreigners but to raise the birthrate, which had been steadily dropping. In 1965 every German woman of childbearing age had (statistically) 2.5 children; in 2003 that number had dropped to 0.7 children. Aside from the fact that raising the birthrate was hardly a short-term solution, the whole debate was vastly overblown. Only about four hundred skilled foreign workers were covered under the green card program.

It goes almost without saying, that this controversy, as well as the debate over asylum seekers and the presence of a large Turkish ethnic minority in Germany, was grist for the mills of the right-wing extremists. There is no doubt that right-wing political extremism was the reunited Germany's most publicized problem. Some observers feared a return of "Weimar conditions." Roving bands of young toughs carrying quasi-Nazi flags and symbols (ironically most of these emblems are from imperial times—the open display of actual Nazi symbols is illegal in Germany) clearly evoked fears of 1932 all over again. The statistics were impressive and sobering.

Between the beginning of 1991 and the end of 1993, some 4,700 acts of politically motivated violence were committed in both parts of Germany. Most of these involved vandalism of various kinds, but there were also more serious incidents; in the same time span, twenty-six persons lost their lives as a result of attacks by right-wing political extremists. The most spectacular incidents took place in the spring of 1993 in the rural town of Mölln in northern Germany and in the industrial city of Solingen in the Ruhr area. Both in Mölln and in Solingen, neo-Nazis set fire to houses in which foreigners resided. In each case members of Turkish families were killed. In Solingen the outrage also led to counterviolence by Turkish youths. The problem has certainly not gone away. In 2008 the Federal Office for the Protection of the Constitution reported a 16 percent increase in politically motivated hate crimes over the previous year. Again most of the nearly 20,000 cases reported involved petty vandalism and racist graffiti, but here were 1,042 cases of arson, murder, and assault.

The perpetrators of these and other acts of right-wing violence were almost invariably so-called skinheads. Young (according to the Federal Ministry of the Interior, only 2 percent of the perpetrators were older than thirty years of age), with little education and few skills, and overwhelmingly male, they are resentful of a society that they claim has not given them the status or income they feel they deserve. The skinheads are "organized"—if that is the word—in loose bands with rapidly shifting memberships, whose primary activity consists of drinking, provocative parading, and unprovoked acts of violence. Such ideology as these groups express is limited to hatred and resentment of foreigners and Jews.

For a time, the reaction of the political establishment to the outrages was uneven. Concerned about Germany's image abroad, and anxious not to alienate potential CDU voters on the right side of the political spectrum, the Kohl government played down the level and seriousness of right-wing political violence. Indeed, some of its policies seemed to play into the hands of the extreme right.

The new asylum law, for example, appeared to suggest that the extreme right had a point: Germany really did have a "foreigner problem."

Germany, of course, does not have a national police force, and for a time some of the Länder also seemed hesitant in dealing forcefully with the activities of the skinheads. Since 1993, however, police response has been increasingly governed by what one interior minister called the policy of "zero toleration" for right-wing thugs. The police have been able to apprehend the perpetrators of political violence, and the courts have done their part in punishing the guilty individuals. A special unit of the Saxon police has had considerable success in infiltrating the right-wing scene, leading to both quick arrests and in some cases the prevention of planned incidents.

The federal president in 1993, Richard von Weizsäcker, was in the forefront of those who became personally engaged in the fight against right-wing extremism. When delivering the eulogy at the funeral for the victims of the Solingen violence, the president made an impassioned appeal for solidarity and firmness in the face of right-wing challenges to the democratic fabric of German society. A number of developments showed that Weizsäcker's appeal did not go unanswered and that the signs of a societal malaise in Germany should not be exaggerated. Overall the magnitude of right-wing extremism itself needs to be put into perspective. Although it is certainly true that pictures of skinheads throwing Molotov cocktails into a home for political refugees evoke fears of a resurrected Nazism, there have been some impressive displays of popular opposition to right-wing extremism. Since 1992 thousands participated in "chains of light" and other forms of demonstrations against xenophobia and political extremism. Carrying candles, the demonstrators (well over 100,000 in all of Germany) formed chains, at times many miles long, across the German countryside and in the major German cities. In 2009 the participants in an NPD-sponsored demonstration to protest the "bombing holocaust" of Dresden at the end of World War II were outnumbered by a counterdemonstration opposed to the NPD's initiative.

Another persistent characteristic of right-wing extremism was the large difference in the number of incidents in East and West Germany. Organized and unorganized right-wing extremism was (and is) far more prevalent in the new Länder than in the western states. The reasons were not difficult to find. High unemployment, especially among young East Germans, the heritage of an authoritarian system that vigorously denied it needed to address Germany's fascist past, and lack of exposure to foreign ethnic groups all contributed to the rise of xenophobia in the East.

The relatively smaller number of right-wing incidents of political violence in the West in turn led to a feeling in the Länder of the old Federal Republic that this was an eastern problem that did not concern them. As the outrages in Mölln and Solingen showed, this is certainly not true, and in recent years some concerted efforts by the police, the courts, and political leaders in both parts of Germany have attempted to address the problem more systematically.

There was no dearth of proposals for solutions of the country's ongoing malaise. There were calls for a renewed sense of corporatism and an invigorated sense of solidarity that should find its expression in a new "societal contract." As we saw, the SPD–Greens government attempted to reform the system of delivering social services to make it more flexible. The Christian Democrats put their faith in tax reforms and a renewed emphasis on measures to increase the birthrate. To that end they offered a series of proposals that were designed to make it easier for parents to combine work and raising a family. The minister for family and youth affairs in the grand coalition, Ursula von der Leyen (who is herself a practicing gynecologist and the mother of seven children), was a particularly tireless proponent of such policies. And there were those who contended that the prevailing mood of pessimism had psychological rather than economic causes. After all, most Germans continue to have an enviable lifestyle with good earnings, a tightly knit safety net, and benefits that exceeded those of most other countries.

In late 2005 a Hamburg advertising agency started a pro bono campaign to encourage optimism in the country: On large billboards and numerous TV spots, average Germans and celebrities proclaimed both the diversity of German society and the accomplishments of the country. The effect was mixed. Initially most respondents said the campaign made them feel good momentarily, but then reality set in again. But in the long run the effects appear to have been positive after all. In May 2009 the *Spiegel* reported that a "growing majority of Germans" were proud of their country and its reputation in the world. They had developed a "relaxed self-consciousness" (*gelassenes Selbstbewusstsein*).

The debates about the politics of memory continued. In the first years of the twenty-first century there were some major developments both in dealing with the aftermath of the East German regime and the long-standing issues associated with the Third Reich and its consequences. Although "de-Communicization" was as ineffective as the earlier de-Nazification had been and the judicial effort to deal with the crimes of the GDR's leaders was for all practical purposes over by 2006, the continuing problems of Eastern Germany fueled various forms of Ostalgie. The PDS/Left Party spearheaded protests against what it saw as the defamation of the old DDR. Among the PDS's membership, 43 percent said they saw the GDR primarily as a state that sought social justice for all, rather than as a political dictatorship. Exploiting the Ostalgie theme in a more balanced way was an interactive Museum of the GDR, which opened in East Berlin in July 2006. Here visitors could experience sitting in a typical East German apartment, complete with hidden microphones installed by the Stasi. In another part of the museum other visitors could overhear the conversations just as the secret police had done before 1989.

As part of dealing with Germany's other past, the Third Reich, the much-debated Holocaust Memorial opened in Berlin. It consists of a series of concrete columns connected by pathways that are often dead ends. Many critics derided the design as sterile, but the memorial has attracted a steady stream of visitors, whose reaction has generally been positive. There was almost unanimous praise for the Jewish Museum in the capital, which opened in May 2006. The opening ceremony featured a moving speech by the federal president, Horst Köhler. Conceived by Daniel Libeskind, the building won accolades from architectural critics for its daring design and symbolism. So did the museum's collection, which emphasizes both the vibrancy of Germany's Jewish history and the tragedy of the Holocaust.

But Jewish life in Germany is by no means limited to the past. In fact, during the first decade of the twenty-first century, Germany's Jewish community grew continuously. Fueled by a continuing influx of immigrants from the former communist countries of Eastern Europe, notably Russia, the number of Jews in Germany is now around 250,000, making it the fastest growing Jewish community in the world. The largest number of German Jews lives in Berlin, some 12,000 in 2007. But there are also vibrant Jewish communities outside of the capital. In 2006 new synagogues were dedicated in Rostock and Munich, and in September 2007 Berlin's largest synagogue was reopened after a $6.85 million renovation. The effort was worth it. The *New York Times* commented that the house of worship had been restored to its prewar splendor of "golden mosaic tiles and a star-spangled blue dome."

What experts and editorial writers quickly dubbed Germany's educational crisis ranked high among the country's societal concerns. In 2000 the Office for Economic Cooperation and Development commissioned the so-called Pisa Study to measure the effectiveness of public education in the countries of the Western world. Germany placed in the middle of the countries surveyed, ranking nineteenth in reading skills, for example. For a country that had historically taken great pride in its public education system, these were disappointing results. There were immediate cries for remedies. Because the Pisa Study had revealed significant differentiation in the results from the various Länder, educational experts proposed formulas that would equalize educational outlays among the states. Not surprisingly, the wealthier states voiced their skepticism. Another proposal called for some sort of national curriculum standards, but the Länder, led by Bavaria, objected that this would infringe on their constitutionally guaranteed right to control public education. Here, too, the initial cries of despair were unwarranted. In a new study in 2010, this one concentrating on the natural sciences, Germany had moved up to thirteenth place of the fifty-seven countries surveyed. (Incidentally, the United States ranked twenty-ninth in the same study.)

All was not well with the country's higher educational system either. Critics complained that Germany's universities, at one time the envy of the world, were now overcrowded and underfunded. As a result, the number of Nobel Prizes awarded to German scientists, for example, was declining. Ironically, in 2001 a German, Wolfgang Ketterle, did win the Nobel Prize for Physics, but he had worked at the Massachusetts Institute of Technology since 1990, giving credence to the claim that Germany's brightest scientists were leaving the country. Here, too, there were numerous proposals for reforms. Suggestions to equalize public allocations to the universities were again met with predictable opposition from the wealthier states. Germany's universities traditionally do not charge tuition, and there were proposals that tuition payments would help alleviate the universities' chronic financial problems. Needless to say, that proposal led to a number of noisy, but peaceful, student demonstrations. There were also suggestions that Germany needed to follow the American model and create a small number of elite universities, rather than cling to the myth that all German

institutions of higher learning were equally excellent. This last proposal has actually been put into effect, all be it in a modest way. In 2006 the federal education ministry selected three universities, the University of Munich and the Technical Universities of Karlsruhe and Munich, as elite institutions. This entitles them to share a $100 million federal grant over the next five years.

The environmental picture has been mixed. In 2001 the SPD–Greens coalition decided to shut down by 2020 all of Germany's nuclear reactors, except for those engaged in scientific research. This had been a long-standing demand by the Greens, and although there was some criticism of the decision in view of the rising need for energy, most Germans supported the end of nuclear energy. The CDU/CSU-FDP government that came into office in the fall of 2009 is split on the issue. The FDP generally favors nuclear energy, but the CDU/CSU is far less enthusiastic. In any case, public sentiment still does not support relying on nuclear power for Germany's energy needs.

The flood of 2002 showed the dire consequences of the GDR's longtime neglect of environmental issues. The federal government and the East German states faced the massive task of rebuilding of dikes and wetlands. Ironically, there were also proposals to make the Elbe River navigable for larger ships to increase trade with Eastern Europe, a construction project that would have destroyed many of the remaining (or rebuilt) wetlands. Yet there were also notable success stories. The Rhine, once one of Europe's most polluted rivers, has been cleaned up as a result of an aggressive international rehabilitation program. In 2006 the authorities announced that salmon had returned to the river in significant numbers.

International terrorism had a major and direct impact on Germany. Several of the perpetrators of the attack on the World Trade Center had lived in Germany as students at the Technical University of Harburg, just outside of Hamburg. In addition there was the potential threat of additional sleeper cells among Germany's Muslim population of some 3 million. The vast majority of German Muslims neither sympathized with the terrorists nor did they have any connection with radical Islam. In fact, after the attack on the World Trade Center, Germany's Muslim leaders denounced the outrages in passionate terms. But there were also a few pockets of radical Islamists, usually grouped around fundamentalist clerics. Until September 11, 2001, they operated with relative impunity because under German law the mandate of the federal and state Offices for the Protection of the Constitution did not include gathering information on religious institutions.

That changed in the wake of September 11. The minister of the interior, the Social Democrat Otto Schily, pushed through a package of laws that included, in addition to antiterror measures derived from similar programs in the United States—surveillance of suspect bank accounts, air marshals, increased border and immigration controls—authorization to monitor radical religious groups preaching hatred and violence. One of those experiencing the consequences of the new legislation was Metlin Kaplan, the so-called imam of Cologne. Kaplan had a checkered religious and political history. A native of Turkey, in 1998 he was indicted there for his alleged participation in a plot to overthrow the Turkish government. He subsequently fled to Germany and asked for political asylum, claiming he could not obtain a fair trial in Turkey. While his case was pending he established himself as the leader of a small Muslim congregation in Cologne. His so-called religious message was little more than hatred of Western culture and institutions. In October 2004 a federal court determined that Kaplan had violated his obligations under the asylum law, and he was deported to his homeland of Turkey.

The continuing danger of additional terrorist groups residing in Germany became evident in the spring of 2009. In Düsseldorf a so-called "Sauerland cell" was put on trial for conspiracy to commit acts of terrorism. The defendants were four men—two Muslim Turks and two Germans who had converted to Islam—living in a small village in the Sauerland area of Northrhine-Westphalia, hence the colloquial name of the cell. According to prosecutors the group planned bomb attacks on a number of high-profile targets, including Frankfurt airport and the American Air Force base at Ramstein in Bavaria. The men were arrested in the fall of 2009 after a six-month investigation by German and American antiterrorist agents.

The threat of terrorism had at least one fortuitous, if indirect, consequence: It forced Germany to acknowledge and deal with the "problem" of more than 7 million aliens in the country. By the end of 2006 every fifth person living in Germany was not of ethnic German stock. For many years politicians had ignored the problem. The Christian Democrats claimed, "Germany is not a land of immigrants," a slogan that was meant to suggest that the millions of guestworkers and their children and grandchildren were temporary residents in Germany who would return to their homelands in due time. That scenario had not been true for many years, but it was only the potential link between terrorism and the Muslim residents that forced the political establishment to undertake serious discussions on how to deal with the problems associated with "foreigners" in Germany.

The problem is particularly acute among the largest contingent of "foreigners" living in Germany, the ethnic Turks. By all statistical indicators Germany's Turkish minority ranks at the bottom of society: As a group it is less educated, has higher rates of unemployment, and is socially less mobile than either the "native" Germans or other immigrant groups. Recognizing the problem does not, of course, answer the questions about causes or solutions.

In 2009 a former Berlin finance senator, Thilo Sarrazin, caused a media uproar when he proclaimed the cause of the Turkish "problem" (he offered no solutions) was simple: Most Turks were neither able nor willing to integrate themselves into German society. Besides, they were not much good at anything, except perhaps running a vegetable store. Few Germans agreed with Sarrazin's extreme point of view, but other perspectives did not meet with widespread acceptance either. A year later Sarrazin, who had in the meantime become a member of the board of directors of the German Federal Bank, made headlines again. This time it was with a book, *Deutschland schafft sich ab* (Germany does away with itself). Relying on highly selective (and often erroneous) statistics, Sarrazin argued that Muslims came to Germany in order to exploit the country's generous welfare system. Once in Germany they contributed to the country's "dumbing down" because as a group Muslims are genetically inferior to "native" Germans. The publication caused another uproar. Politicians from all major parties denounced the work as inflammatory and fundamentally wrong. Sarrazin was pressured to resign from the Bundesbank, and his political party, the SPD, expelled him. But the book was also an instant best seller, with more than 600,000 copies sold in less than a month.

The moderate right insisted the immigrants needed to be fully integrated into the fabric of German society. They had to accept the German *Leitkultur* and, in addition, pass an appropriate *Gesinnungstest* ("attitude test") to show that they had embraced "Germanness." Most analysts, however, recognized that a German melting pot is unlikely. The left proposed instead to couple a minimum of integration with far-ranging cultural autonomy for the various "foreign" communities living in Germany. This concept, derided as *multi-kulti* by its opponents, would require that the immigrants learn German and accept their duties as loyal citizens of the country, but aside from these requirements the immigrants could retain their religious and cultural traditions.

But how far should cultural autonomy extend? Clearly such phenomena as "honor killings" are totally unacceptable. There have been a few instances of this crime in Germany. Here male relatives kill a female member of the family if she refuses to marry the man selected for her by the family. German law treats such crimes as murder, not justified homicide to restore the honor of the family. Similarly, the minister of the interior in the grand coalition, Wolfgang Schäuble, resisted demands by some Muslim clerics that Muslim girls be exempt from physical education in public schools. On the other hand, Germany's highest administrative court ruled in 2006 that wearing a headscarf as a public school teacher is permissible. The state of Baden-Württemberg had dismissed a Muslim schoolteacher for wearing a headscarf in class, contending that the garment was a religious symbol and therefore wearing it constituted proselytizing in the classroom. (The defendant, a native of Afghanistan, claimed that she was not proselytizing; wearing the headscarf simply made her feel "more comfortable.")

The critics of multiculturalism claimed these controversies showed that multi-kulti was an oxymoron. Cultural autonomy and national integration were simple irreconcilable concepts. But the proponents of multiculturalism produced evidence of their own. In the summer of 2006, the World Soccer Championship took place in Germany, and pictures of Muslim women, clad in traditional garb but enthusiastically waving the black, red, and gold German flag to spur on the national team, suggested cultural autonomy and national integration might not be incompatible after all. And in the 2010 World Cup competition one of the stars of the German national team was Mesul Özil, a German of Turkish descent.

In late summer 2006 the minister of the interior convened a high-level conference on Muslim–German relations. Sixty experts, thirty selected by the government and thirty by the Muslim communities, met in Berlin to address various aspects of Muslim life in Germany. The conference was not intended to recommend new legislation, and there were many disagreements on the issues, but all participants reported that they were impressed by the civility of the dialogue and expressions of goodwill on all sides.

A religious controversy of an entirely different nature involved the Catholic Church. In 2009 and 2010 the scandal of sexual abuse by some Catholic priests drew ever-widening circles. The scandal was not, of course, limited to Germany, but it had particular poignancy there, because the current pope, Benedict XVI, is a German, and in his earlier capacity as archbishop of Munich he had been directly involved in the Church's handling of a particularly serious case of sexual abuse. The constant stream of news about the abuse cases themselves as well as the Church's seeming attempt to deny the problem led to precipitous decline of the Pope's popularity in his homeland. When Benedict XVI was elected in April 2005, *Bild* ("Picture"), Germany's largest daily newspaper, in an outburst of supercilious national pride greeted the news with the banner headline, "We are Pope!" Five years later, in March 2009, a poll of Catholics, commissioned by the *Spiegel*, found that 73 percent of the respondents felt the Pope had not adequately addressed the sex scandals. Ninety-five percent answered "yes" to the question, "Should the Church ... modernize itself?"

A number of important cultural developments have occurred in recent years. In 2002 two icons of German postwar journalism died. In March, Marion Countess Dönhoff, scion of an old East Prussian aristocratic family and longtime editor of the respected Liberal weekly *Die Zeit,* passed away. She had been particularly active in encouraging a civil political culture in Germany and was instrumental in promoting German–Polish reconciliation. In November of the same year, Rudolf Augstein, a close friend of Dönhoff and the founding editor and publisher of Europe's largest-circulated newsmagazine, *Der Spiegel,* died. Augstein had founded the magazine in 1946 and had remained its editor in chief ever since then.

There were some notable architectural developments on the German landscape. In October 2005 an inaugural service was held in the rebuilt Dresden Frauenkirche (Church of Our Lady). The church had been destroyed by Allied bombs in the last months of World War II and then lay in ruins for the next forty-five years. The GDR's atheistic regime had no interest in committing resources to restoring a major church edifice, but after Germany's reunification a grassroots initiative was started to rebuild the church. The cost of 100 million euros was largely paid for by private donations; there were contributors from virtually every European country, including those who had been Germany's enemies in World War II. (One of the contributors was Wolfgang Ketterle, who donated a significant portion of his Nobel Prize to the rebuilding fund.)

A watershed in the ongoing process of rebuilding of the German capital came in 2006, when the city's building director since 1990, Hans Stimmann, retired. He had been largely responsible for recreating, especially in the former East Berlin where most of the new construction took place, what he called a "European city." By this he meant that he wanted to preserve the feel of traditional squares, piazzas, and broad avenues that characterize most large European cities. He also insisted that no building be taller than the city's highest church steeples, thereby preventing massive skyscraper construction. Stimmann was not without his critics. Some architects complained that under his aegis, mediocrity rather than bold innovation characterized the reconstruction effort. A quip made the rounds that "He saved us from the worst." To which another observer rejoined, "Yes, but also from the best."

The rebuilding of the *Museuminsel* (Museum Island) in East Berlin was a particularly apt expression of Stimmann's vision. Located on an island in the River Spree, the Museum Island had been constructed in the early twentieth century as a cluster of five neo-Baroque buildings housing sculpture, paintings, and decorative arts from ancient Egypt to the nineteenth century. Several of the buildings were badly damaged by Allied bombings and then largely neglected by the GDR authorities. After reunification the rebuilding process began in earnest. In 2001 the Old National Gallery was reopened, and in November 2006 the reconstruction of the Bode Museum was

Im Mittelpunkt Ursula von der Leyen (1958–)

Ursula von der Leyen, the minister for family, seniors, women, and youth affairs (usually abbreviated as the family ministry) in the grand coalition that took office in November 2005, personifies for many the ideal postmodern German woman because she effectively combines career, marriage, and children.

The new minister comes from a well-to-do socially and politically prominent family in Hanover. She was born on October 8, 1958, as the daughter of Ernst Albrecht, then the CFO of the world-famous Bahlsen Cookie Corporation. Albrecht later entered politics and served as Christian Democratic prime minister of the state of Lower Saxony.

After obtaining her *Abitur* in 1977, von der Leyen started out as a business administration major at the universities of Göttingen and Munich, but she later switched to medicine, obtaining her degree in 1991. From 1992 to 1996 she also attended the Graduate School of Business Administration at Stanford University. During these years her husband, Heiko von der Leyen, a biochemist and entrepreneur whom she married in 1986, was a visiting faculty member at Stanford. Upon returning to Germany she became a research fellow at the School of Medicine at the University of Hanover, where she also earned a master's degree in public health in 2002.

Von der Leyen entered politics "by the side door" (*Seiteneinsteiger*), as the Germans term it. She became a member of the CDU in 1990 but did not embark on a career in politics by going "through the front door," that is to say by standing for elected office. Rather, she made her influence felt as a member of a variety of advisory commissions that the CDU leaders appointed to guide them in formulating policy proposals. It was as a member of the CDU's advisory commission on health policy that she came to the attention of Angela Merkel, who in August 2005 asked her to become a member of the CDU/CSU's shadow cabinet, or "competency team" as Merkel preferred to call the group. With the formation of the grand coalition in the fall of 2005, von der Leyen became federal family minister.

As minister, von der Leyen embarked on a whirlwind tour of public appearances designed to highlight her activist role. Her smiling face and nonstop interviews quickly made her one of the

completed. The Bode, originally called the Emperor Friedrich Museum (to honor the then German emperor's father) when it opened in 1904, now honors Wilhelm von Bode. He was Berlin's longtime director of museums, who both designed the collection and, with the help of his friend, the Jewish banker James Simon, bought many of the pieces now on display in the Bode Museum. Bode died in 1929 and Simon in 1932.

In 2009 the last of the restored buildings on the Museuminsel was open to the public. This is the so-called *Neues Museum* (New Museum), which will house Egyptian and early and pre-historic works. The New

Museum originally opened in 1855 during the reign of the Prussian king Frederick William IV to cultivate "the most elevated interests of the people." This building was also severely damaged in World War II. The restoration and rebuilding was the work of the British architect David Chipperfield. He attempted to merge what remained of the original building with modern elements that preserved the aesthetic of the old edifice. The result, commented the *New York Times*, is a museum that looks "so beautiful and so eloquent that it short-circuits doubts and criticism." As the buildings on the Museum Island are rebuilt, most recognized personalities in the new cabinet. But her policy proposals stirred up a hornet's nest of controversy.

Her demand for more competition in the providing of healthcare services as a way of bringing down costs was hardly original, but nonetheless it aroused the ire of the political left, and her proposals for social policy reforms led to criticism from both the left and the right. Like many in the Christian Democratic camp, she had long been concerned about Germany's extremely low birthrate. (She and her husband have seven children, so any complaint about the low birthrate does not apply to her personally.) She was particularly concerned about the small family size among the middle and upper-middle classes, which typically have one or no children. As she put it, the question is not whether the wife will have a career—she will—but whether she will have children. To encourage more children in families in which both the husband and the wife are pursuing professional or managerial careers, von der Leyen proposed a series of measures to make it easier to combine career and parenthood. These included tax deductions for such child-related expenses as nannies and child care. Recognizing that the wife's career usually suffers a setback after giving birth, she also wanted to make paternal leave mandatory so the mother could continue her career path. (Ever the personification of her own policy proposals, she pointed out that by mutual agreement with her husband she took a backseat to his career until she became minister, but then he took more responsibility for raising the children.)

Not surprisingly, von der Leyen's ideas raised a storm of protest. The political left complained that her tax proposals were designed to give even more benefits to those who already had a lot; the political right objected to the mandatory paternal leave as unwanted interference by the state in private family decisions. In the end, von der Leyen had to backtrack and accept some compromises, but she remains convinced that as Germany's women attempt to combine career and family, their best model for success is the personal life of the family minister. In Merkel's second cabinet von der Leyen moved from the family ministry to the labor ministry, giving her an even larger stage for her brand of political activism.

there is also an ongoing effort to reunite the city's art treasures there. Many of the collections were separated when Berlin was divided during the Cold War.

In the first years of the twenty-first century, Germany's literary scene was marked by two very querulous scandals. For many years one of Germany's most successful and respected authors, Martin Walser, had engaged in a running feud with the country's preeminent critic, Marcel Reich-Ranicki. Walser had long complained that Reich-Ranicki used his power and influence to unfairly attack Walser's work. The author had already stirred up a controversy when in 1998 he suggested that the symbol of Auschwitz was being inappropriately used as a *Moralkeule* ("moral cudgel") to beat the Germans over the head continually and make them feel perpetually guilty. At the time many, including Reich-Ranicki, accused Walser of reawakening anti-Semitic feelings.

In 2002 Walser struck back. He wrote a book entitled *Tod eines Kritikers* ("Death of a Critic"), whose central character, André Ehrl-König, is a thinly disguised portrait of Marcel Reich-Ranicki. (In Goethe's poem the *Erlkönig*, the fictional title character lures a child to its death.) Walser endowed his title character with a variety of unpleasant personality traits, including some that critics found to be anti-Semitic stereotypes. Reich-Ranicki quickly joined the fray, describing Walser as a frustrated has-been, who has a warped personality.

The other literary uproar came in 2006 and involved Germany's most famous and respected living novelist, Günter Grass. The author of the *Tin Drum* and the recipient of the 2000 Nobel Prize for Literature, Grass had also long acted as the self-proclaimed personification of Germany's moral conscience. He repeatedly urged politicians to come clean about their Nazi past, and in 1990 he suggested that after Auschwitz, Germany's permanent national division was the appropriate punishment. Grass, in other words, was one of those whom Walser accused of using Auschwitz as a moral cudgel.

In 2006 Grass wrote an autobiography covering the first thirty years of his life. It was entitled *Beim Häuten der Zwiebel* ("While Peeling the Onion"). As is customary before publication of the book, Grass granted a number of interviews and appeared on various talk shows. Here he revealed for the first time that as an eighteen-year-old in early 1945 he had been a member of the *Waffen-SS*, Hitler's elite corps. He did not just serve in an antiaircraft unit as he had previously maintained. Grass insisted he had been drafted into the Waffen-SS, which was probably true. At the end of World War II the Waffen-SS was forcing residents of foreign countries still under Nazi control whom the Nazis defined as ethnically German to join its ranks. Grass's confession unleashed a storm of criticism, including calls for him to return his Nobel Prize. (He did not.) The critics insisted the scandal was not because of his short service in the Waffen-SS but about his long years of silence regarding this episode, while urging everyone else to be honest about their activities during the Third Reich. Grass's own explanation of his long silence was that only now could he bring himself to deal with this issue. Cynics suggested Grass had engineered the whole affair to boost the sales of his autobiography, an accusation the author vehemently denied.

PROBLEMS AND PROSPECTS

The continuing divisions in German society were dramatically laid bare by the controversies surrounding the official celebrations of the tenth anniversary of reunification. The Schröder government understandably issued optimistic reports detailing how much had been accomplished since 1990, but the actual ceremony was overshadowed by the Kohl affair and its repercussions (see pp. 351–52). The site of the official celebration was Dresden (Saxony), with that state's prime minister, Kurt Biedenkopf, acting as host. Biedenkopf was a West German and a Christian Democrat, but he was also a longtime rival and critic of Helmut Kohl. As a result, he was determined not to let the former chancellor steal the show and pointedly did not invite him to speak at the ceremony.

Kohl lashed out in anger, claiming the Social Democrats, the Greens, his enemies in the CDU, and even the German churches had dragged their heels during the dramatic months leading up to the country's reunification. Without his vision and determination, the former chancellor suggested repeatedly, the opportunity for reunification would have been lost. To compensate for his absence in Dresden, Kohl's political friends staged their own celebration in Berlin with the now-controversial leader as the main speaker. To underscore Kohl's critical role in the reunification process, they organized their memorial in a building in what had been East Berlin, the so-called Palace of Tears. During the communist era, this singularly ugly edifice had been the scene of many tearful good-byes as East Berliners had to bid farewell to their visiting relatives from West Berlin and West Germany.

The discussion about the persistent differences between Eastern and Western Germany continued to dominate much of the media discussion, both in Germany and (especially) abroad, but it should be put into perspective. It is certainly true that the hopes for a quick and complete merging of the two halves of the country were naive.

But it is also clear, as Gordon Craig noted, that the differences between Ossis and Wessis are fading, and the real problems are those facing the society as a whole. They are not differentiated by geographic area or sociopolitical heritage.

But the question remained: Was the reunited country a qualitatively different entity or merely an enlarged West Germany? In 2003 the political scientist Hans-Jörg Hennecke attempted to answer this question in a book entitled *Die Dritte Republik: Aufbruch und Ernüchterung* ("The Third Republic: New Beginnings and Disenchantment"). (The first two German republics were those of Weimar and the Federal Republic before 1990.) The author identified what he saw as "four large-scale changes." These included the internal consequences of reunification itself, the changed domestic political scene, the interlocking effects of Europeanization and globalization, and Germany's new role on the international scene.

In retrospect, there is much truth in these conclusions. It is certainly correct that reunification brought some unanticipated problems for German society as a whole. The new Germany inherited the difficulties in East Germany that the GDR had long ignored. Politically the rejuvenation of the neo-Marxist left and the explosive presence of the extreme right, especially in East Germany, were in large part the result of the gap between promise and reality of reunification. The perceived negative effects of Europeanization and particularly globalization go a long way in explaining the mood of pessimism that permeated German society for much of the last fifteen years.

On the positive side, the Third Republic is a much bigger player on the international scene. With a population of 80 million, Germany is the largest country in the EU. As Germany's participation in an increasing number of peacekeeping missions demonstrated, the reunited country's international role is significantly greater than that of the old GDR or the Federal Republic before 1990. Above all, however, the reunited Germany remains a stable democracy and a reliable partner in the European Union and the Atlantic Alliance.

CHAPTER TWELVE

Conclusion

Gordon Craig, the dean of American historians of Germany, pointed out in the early 1990s that whereas most Americans celebrate their history naively and enthusiastically, often blithely ignoring the contradictions in the country's record and at times distorting the facts, Germans continue to be very ambivalent about their history. Asked whether Germans should take pride in their history, Gerhard Schröder answered that Germans should be proud of their democratic achievements since 1945. His reply was not only historically correct and politically astute, but it also left questions about the rest of German history unanswered.

Certainly the history of modern Germany has had a disproportionately large impact on the history of Europe and the world. As we noted at the outset, much of modern German history is the story of the "German problem." Although recent scholarship has shown that in many ways the course of German history in the nineteenth century was not all that different from that of its neighbors in the West, the central fact of Germany's asymmetrical modernization remains. Modernization in Germany did not involve the simultaneous transformation of all aspects of society. Instead, Germany had a tendency to advance rapidly in some areas while lagging behind in others.

The examples of asymmetry were many. Rapid economic development in the years following unification of 1871 contrasted with the simultaneous preservation of what was essentially a premodern political system. National unification did not resolve the Reich–state problem. States' rights remained strong, which meant in practice that Prussia retained its hegemonic role in German federal affairs. The political disenfranchisement of the laboring classes was a festering sore in a country that was rapidly becoming the most industrialized nation in Europe. Traditions of anti-Semitism continued alongside what, before the rise of the Nazis, had become one of the most thriving and assimilated Jewish communities in Europe. The overall results of the modernization warp were internal tensions in the society that prevented consensual pluralism from being firmly established.

The rulers of Germany were not unaware of the problems created by asymmetrical modernization but, rather than address them forthrightly, before 1945 they repeatedly tried to use successes abroad to quell dissatisfaction with the status quo at home. The widespread and enthusiastic acceptance of the Bismarck Compromise as the price and corollary for national unification following a victorious foreign war persuaded successive sets of German leaders that the gamble should be tried again and again despite increasingly higher stakes. The primacy of domestic politics meant that Germany's involvement in World War I was not only a desperate gamble to change the international balance of power permanently but also a last-ditch attempt to keep intact the domestic balance of power. Unlike Bismarck, the rulers of Wilhelminian Germany failed in their quest. In 1918 the authoritarian social and political system that Bismarck and his successors had defended against growing opposition was defeated along with the German armies.

The political, social, and cultural pluralism that the Weimar Republic attempted to implant in place of the momentarily discredited authoritarianism had difficulty sinking its roots in German soil. Many Germans, including the old elites, associated political modernization with their own diminished status and influence, defeat in war, the loss of Germany's stature as a great power, and, perhaps most important, chronic economic and fiscal problems. In addition, the fathers of the Weimar Republic lacked the courage of their own convictions; in many spheres of public life they left the old forces in positions of real power. Consequently, despite the earnest labors of some of its leaders, real economic and social progress, and the undoubted brilliance of its cultural life, the Weimar Republic, too, fell victim to its own contradictions. In the end, it provided too little too briefly to withstand the attacks from the rise of a new form of nihilism.

Nazism had its roots in some long-standing German traditions, notably anti-Semitism and the desire for völkisch integration, but it ultimately succeeded because the Great Depression destroyed the already frayed fabric of value consensus in Germany. Even so, Adolf Hitler and his henchmen did not come to power because they promised relief from the effects of the depression to millions of Germans. In the end, Hitler became chancellor because the New Conservatives were convinced—mistakenly—that in cooperation with them the Nazis would restore the greatness of the Bismarckian and Wilhelminian past and, not incidentally, put the old elites back in their accustomed place of power and prestige.

The Third Reich represented the culmination and worst consequences of Germany's asymmetrical road to modernization. Hitler had no intention of restoring the authoritarian system of the Bismarck era; the dictator's aim was the establishment of a full-scale totalitarian society. Nazi anti-Semitism was not the relatively genteel prejudices typical of the nineteenth century, but the virulently racial variety that led logically and tragically to the physical murder of more than 6 million European Jews. Similarly, whereas Bismarck and the leaders of Wilhelminian Germany had sought to exclude from political power groups they defined as the "enemies of the Reich," the Nazis abolished all vestiges of the Rechtsstaat and established a network of terror and concentration camps that meant years of incarceration, physical maltreatment, and death for thousands of Nazi opponents.

In foreign relations, Hitler's interests went far beyond regaining the German boundaries of 1914 or even of attaining the war aims articulated by the military in World War I. The evidence is persuasive that the Nazi dictator's aim was the conquest of all of Europe and later the rest of the world. The result of this new and vastly more ambitious policy was World War II and its consequences. The stakes were immeasurably higher than in World War I, and so were the consequences of defeat. At the end of the second global conflict, German national unity had been destroyed, and the country was subjected to physical destruction on a scale unprecedented since the Thirty Years' War. Some 6 million Germans had died and another 12 million became refugees. In 1918 Germany lost some 13 percent of its pre-war territory; in 1945 fully a third of what had been Germany in 1871 was irretrievably lost. The Holocaust associated the German name with some of the worst government-sponsored outrages in any historical period.

The Reich's total defeat in 1945 finally led virtually all Germans—and not just because the victorious Allied powers insisted on it—to confront their recent past and draw appropriate lessons from it. The result was the admission, sometimes tacit, sometimes open, that in the future the politics and values of Germany needed drastic course corrections. It was a recognition that for much of its modern history Germany had been too "inner-directed." In domestic affairs, various groups in German society—not only the old Prusso-German establishment, but also the radical left and right—insisted that unless their parochial Weltanschauung were imposed on Germany, regardless of the consequences for other segments of society, history would have lost its meaning. In foreign relations "inner-directedness" led the leaders of Germany to look on the country's power and stature as ends in themselves, rather than as means to help maintain an international balance of power.

After 1945 there was an understandable tendency to replace the failed "inner-directedness" with an equally sweeping "other-directedness." Germans, both east and west of the Elbe, wanted to throw off the burden of German history before 1945 and attempt to start over again at the point of "Zero Hour." There was a temptation to draw the value base for the new beginning not from the failed past of German history but from the values of the "others," that is to say, the victorious Allies and especially the two new superpowers, the United States and the Soviet Union.

Fortunately, at least in the western half of Germany, leaders and people alike came to recognize rather quickly the futility and ahistorical nature of other-directedness. While the Communists in East Germany insisted on imposing a straitjacket of Marxist-Leninist historical determinism on the GDR, the open pluralist society of West Germany acknowledged that to establish an ongoing national identity, all Germans needed to integrate the entirety of the German past. In the Federal Republic, the components of the "other" Germany—the liberal, pluralistic, and democratic Marxist traditions—were freed and finally allowed to become the dominant forces in German society. True, these traditions also reflected the program of the Western Allies for remaking Germany, but they were not just imposed from the outside. They represented indigenous German forces that had all too often been overshadowed by the facile identification of modern German history with Prussian militarism and Nazi totalitarianism. At the same time, the foreign relations of Germany underwent a profound change. No longer major powers, the two halves of the country abandoned the quest for a hegemonic *Sonderweg* in international relations and became fully integrated into supranational power blocs, NATO and the European Union for West Germany, the Warsaw Pact and Comecon for the GDR.

For almost forty years after the end of World War II, it seemed that in their very different ways the two halves of Germany were viable societies. Of course, the Federal Republic had a political regime supported by the overwhelming majority of its people, whereas East Germany remained a one-party dictatorship, but both countries seemed internally stable and economically prosperous. But at the end of 1989, dramatic events in the GDR, coupled with the breakup of the Soviet bloc, suddenly revealed the inherent instability and weaknesses of the SED regime in East Germany. Confronted with economic difficulties beyond their control and the knowledge that the Soviet Union was unwilling to use its armed forces to perpetuate the existence of the communist regime, the aged SED leaders hastened to promise political and economic reforms. But it was too late. Quite literally, the people of East Germany in a peaceful revolution swept the regime from power.

There was suddenly talk of German reunification. The tearful scenes of East and West Germans coming together as the physical barriers between the two states crumbled seemed to indicate that there was one German people after all. As we saw, in the elections of March 1990, the big winners were the parties that promised to bring about rapid reunification. Proponents of a revitalized East Germany that would travel along a "third way" between socialism and capitalism found little support.

Although the March elections in the GDR technically confirmed only the establishment of political democracy in what was still a sovereign country, events rapidly overtook the politicians' plans and theories. True, France, Russia, and especially Great Britain wanted to slow down the reunification process, but in the summer of 1990, one dramatic development chased the other. At the beginning of July, East and West Germany agreed to economic and monetary union. In that same month Chancellor Helmut Kohl, in a remarkable feat of personal diplomacy, persuaded Mikhail Gorbachev, then the leader of the Soviet Union, that a politically united Germany that would remain a member of both NATO and the European Union was not a threat to the Soviet Union.

Throughout these dramatic months, the Kohl government had worked in close tandem with the Bush administration. Unlike France and Great Britain, the United States firmly supported German reunification, provided the reunited country remained a member of NATO and the European Union. Because this was also the desire of the West German government, the United States and the Federal Republic had no difficulty coordinating their policies. Within a few months, the seemingly impossible had become a reality: Germany was once again a united country.

After the events of October 1990, it might appear that history had come full circle. In fact, this is certainly not the case. Both the international and domestic contexts of unification in the 1990s are completely different

from those that prevailed in the 1870s. In 1871 Germany was united by force of arms, and the new nation was a global superpower, able to dominate the heart of the European continent. In 1990 unification was a peaceful process and the new nation, like the rest of Western Europe, is no longer even a fully sovereign country, much less a superpower. Integrated into the European Union, Germany and its partners have already yielded a number of important rights to the European Commission in Brussels and the European Parliament in Strasbourg. In terms of territorial dimension and military prowess, the Germany of 2001 is much smaller than that of 1871. The *Bundeswehr* of the united Germany has about half as many soldiers as the Federal Republic and the GDR together had before reunification.

Equally important, however, are the changes in German political life. The new Germany is not a country dominated by a small caste of Prussian feudal landowners and military officers. It does not have an authoritarian political system but a parliamentary democracy that enjoys the overwhelming support of both the country's elite and its population. The problems that began with the Bismarck Compromise and that haunted Germany for so long have—finally—been worked out.

And yet in one sense 1990 did contain an echo of 1871: At the end of the nineteenth century, most Germans were euphoric over national unification because they were convinced it would solve all their society's problems. Some of that same feeling prevailed briefly in 1990, only to be replaced by the realization that national unification per se is a much overrated development. But, and it is an important "but," in the aftermath of the country's reunification in 1990, no responsible German leader nor the overwhelming majority of the German people sought a solution to the country's problems in a return to the pattern of asymmetrical modernization. Instead, they are committed to political democracy, a free-enterprise economic system, and international cooperation as the means of overcoming the problems of the present. This certainly gives cause for optimism as we view Germany's future.

But to return briefly to the question posed at the outset of this chapter, was Germany in the first decade of the twenty-first century finally a "normal" nation, as the country's political leaders repeatedly insisted? Yes, and no. Until very recently most Germans were still reluctant to celebrate their nation and fearful of nationalism in general. In a debate in 2005 with the distinguished historian Heinrich-August Winkler, Joschka Fischer exclaimed, "Nationalism, that's the plague!" Yet this, too, may be changing. Some unplanned and unscientific evidence for a changing view of the nation in Germany came during the World Soccer Championship in June and July 2006. As we saw, Germany was the host nation and the motto of the event was, "Welcome Among Friends" (*Wilkommen unter Freunden*). The games were well organized, there were very few instances of hooliganism, and the Germans went out of their way to welcome the foreign players and fans. What visitors noted above all, however, was the ease with which the Germans seemed to embrace their nation and its soccer team. The country was awash in a sea of black-red-gold flags, but they were waved in a spirit of easygoing fun rather than as symbols of chauvinism and national arrogance. Germany, as the British journalist Steve Crawshaw put it, "was becoming normal in a relaxed manner."

Suggestions for Further Reading

Note: Space limitations make it necessary to limit the extent and nature of the bibliography that follows. As a result only English-language works have been included, and the annotations have been kept to an absolute minimum. An effort has been made, however, to include some of the most recent and historiographically significant works.

GENERAL WORKS

BERGHAHN, VOLKER R., ed. *Militarism: The History of an International Debate, 1861–1979.* New York: St. Martin, 1980.

BLACKBOURN, DAVID. *Water, Landscape, and the Making of Modern Germany.* New York: Norton, 2006. (A superb study of the interaction of politics, population, and the environment.)

BLACKBOURN, DAVID, AND RICHARD EVANS. *The German Bourgeoisie: Essays on the Social History of the German Middle Class from the Late Eighteenth to the Early Twentieth Century.* New York: Routledge, 1991.

BORCHARDT, KNUT. *Perspectives on Modern German Economic History and Policy.* New York: Cambridge University Press, 1991. (A series of essays by a major "revisionist" economic historian of Germany.)

CLARK, CHRISTOPHER. *Iron Kingdom: The Rise and Downfall of Prussia, 1600–1947.* Cambridge, MA: Harvard University Press, 2006.

CRAIG, GORDON A. *The End of Prussia.* Madison, WI: University of Wisconsin Press, 2003. (Brief but witty and illuminating overview of Prussia's history from beginning to end.)

———. *The Germans.* New York: Meridian, 1982.

DEHIO, LUDWIG. *Germany and World Politics in the Twentieth Century.* New York: Norton, 1959. (Superb study of the problem of hegemony in international relations.)

DEIST, WILHELM, ed. *The German Military in the Age of Total War.* Dover, NH: Berg, 1985.

ELEY, GEOFF. *From Unification to Nazism.* London: Allen & Unwin, 1986.

EVANS, RICHARD J., AND W. ROBERT LEE, eds. *The German Peasantry.* New York: St. Martin, 1986.

FREVERT, UTE. *Women in German History: From Bourgeois Emancipation to Sexual Liberation.* Providence, RI: Berg, 1989.

GREEN, ABIGAIL. *Fatherlands: State-Building and Nationhood in Nineteenth Century Germany.* New York: Cambridge University Press, 2001.

HOERDER, DIRK, AND JÖRG NAGLER, eds. *People in Transit: German Migrations in Comparative Perspective, 1820–1930.* New York: Cambridge University Press, 1995.

IGGERS, GEORG G. *The German Conception of History: The National Tradition of Historical Thought from Herder to the Present.* Rev. ed. Middletown, CT: Wesleyan University Press, 1983.

JOERES, RUTH-ELLEN B., AND MARY JO MAYNES, eds. *German Women in the Eighteenth and Nineteenth Centuries: A Social and Literary History.* Bloomington, IN: Indiana University Press, 1986. (Women's history from a feminist perspective.)

KOHN, HANS. *The Mind of the Germans: The Education of a Nation.* New York: Harper & Row, 1960. (Pioneering study of the problems and peculiarities of German nationalist thought.)

LANGEWIESCHE, DIETER. *Liberalism in Germany.* Trans. by Christian Benerji. Princeton, NJ: Princeton University Press, 2000. (Excellent survey of the subject from the early nineteenth century to the present.)

LEPENIES, WOLF. *The Seduction of Culture in German History.* Princeton, NJ: Princeton University Press, 2006.

MOSSE, WERNER E. *The European Powers and the German Question, 1848–1871.* Cambridge: Cambridge University Press, 1958.

ROSEMAN, MARK, ed. *Generations in Conflict: Youth Revolt and Generation Formation in Germany, 1770–1968.* New York: Cambridge University Press, 1995. (Series of essays comparing Germany's unifications in 1871 and 1990.)

SPEIRS, RONALD and BREUILLY, JOHN, eds. *Germany's Two Unifications: Anticipations, Experiences, Responses.* Basingstoke, UK: Palgrave Macmillan, 2005, eds.

STERN, FRITZ. *Dreams and Delusions: National Socialism and the Drama of the German Past.* New York: Vintage, 1989. (Retrospective collection of essays by one of the foremost historians of modern Germany.)

VOLKOV, SHULAMIT. *Germans, Jews, and Antisemites: Trials in Emancipation.* New York: Cambridge University Press, 2006.

CHAPTER 1: THE FOUNDERS' GENERATION, 1871–1890

ANDERSON, MARGARET LAVINIA. *Windhorst: A Political Biography.* New York: Oxford University Press, 1981.

BERLIN, ISAIAH. *Karl Marx.* 3rd ed. New York: Oxford University Press, 1963.

BISMARCK, OTTO VON. *Reflections and Reminiscences.* Trans. by A. J. Butler. New York: Howard Fertig, 1966. (Bismarck's memoirs; unreliable but indispensable.)

BLACKBOURN, DAVID. *Germany in the Nineteenth Century.* New York: Oxford University Press, 1993.

BLACKBOURN, DAVID, AND GEOFFREY ELEY. *The Peculiarities of German History: Bourgeois Society and Politics in Nineteenth-Century Germany.* Oxford: Oxford University Press, 1984.

BRAMSTED, ERNEST K. *Aristocracy and the Middle Classes in Germany: Social Types in German Literature, 1830–1900.* Chicago, IL: University of Chicago Press, 1964. (Classic study of the image of social classes in nineteenth-century German literature.)

BRECHTEFELD, JÖRG. *Mitteleuropa and German Politics: 1848 to the Present.* New York: St. Martin, 1996.

BRUFORD, WALTER H. *The German Tradition of Self-Cultivation: Bildung from Humboldt to Thomas Mann.* Cambridge: Cambridge University Press, 1975.

CARSTEN, FRANCIS L. *A History of the Prussian Junkers.* Brookfield, VT: Scolar Press, 1989.

CECIL, LAMAR. *The German Diplomatic Service, 1871–1914.* Princeton, NJ: Princeton University Press, 1977. (Important institutional history.)

CRAIG, GORDON A. *The Prussian Army in Politics.* Oxford: Oxford University Press, 1975. (Still unsurpassed analysis of the Prussian army's crucial role in shaping the social and political evolution of Germany's largest state.)

———. *Theodor Fontane: Literature and History in the Bismarck Reich.* New York: Oxford University Press, 1999. (Erudite and very sympathetic portrait of the great novelist.)

CRANKSHAW, EDWARD. *Bismarck.* New York: Viking, 1981. (The best one-volume biography in English.)

DOMINICK, RAYMOND H., III. *Wilhelm Liebknecht and the Founding of the German Social Democratic Party.* Chapel Hill, NC: University of North Carolina Press, 1982.

DORPALEN, ANDREAS. *Heinrich von Treitschke.* New Haven, CT: Yale University Press, 1957.

EDERER, RUPERT J. *The Social Teachings of Wilhelm Emmanuel von Ketteler: Bishop of Mainz, 1811–1877.*

Washington, DC: University Press of America, 1982. (Important for a Catholic perspective on German industrialization.)

FOHLIN, CAROLINE. *Finance Capitalism and Germany's Rise to Industrial Power.* New York: Cambridge University Press, 2007. (Excellent overview of the history of banking during the Founders' Generation.)

GALL, LOTHAR. *Bismarck: The White Revolutionary.* 2 vols. Trans. by J. A. Underwood. London: Allen & Unwin, 1986.

GAY, RUTH. *The Jews of Germany.* New Haven, CT: Yale University Press, 1992.

GEISS, IMANUEL. *German Foreign Policy, 1871–1914.* London: Routledge & Kegan Paul, 1976.

GERSCHENKRON, ALEXANDER. *Bread and Democracy in Germany.* Berkeley, CA: University of California Press, 1943. (Classic, if somewhat one-sided, study of the Junkers' role in retarding the political modernization of Germany.) Reprint, 1966. New Edition: Charles S. Maier, ed. Ithaca, NY: Cornell University Press, 1989.

GROSS, MICHAEL B. *The War against Catholicism: Liberalism and the Anti-Catholic Imagination in Nineteenth Century Germany.* Ann Arbor, MI: University of Michigan Press, 2004. (Attempts to put the Kulturkampf into a larger sociopolitical context.)

HAGEN, WILLIAM H. *Germans, Poles and Jews: The Nationality Conflict in the Prussian East, 1722–1914.* Chicago, IL: University of Chicago Press, 1980.

HAMEROW, THEODORE S. *The Social Foundations of German Unification, 1858–1871.* Princeton, NJ: Princeton University Press, 1972. (Still the best one-volume analysis of the causes and failures of the Revolution of 1848.)

HENDERSON, WILLIAM O. *The Zollverein.* Cambridge: Cambridge University Press, 1939. (A model of detailed analysis.)

JONES, LARRY EUGENE, AND JAMES RETALLACK, eds. *Elections, Mass Politics, and Social Change in Modern Germany: New Perspectives.* New York: Cambridge University Press, 1992.

KOCKA, JÜRGEN, AND ALLAN MITCHELL, eds. *Bourgeois Society in the 19th Century: Germany in a European Perspective.* Providence, RI: Berg, 1991.

KOSHAR, RUDY. *From Monuments to Traces: Artifacts of German Memory, 1870–1990.* Berkeley, CA: University of California Press, 2000.

KRAEHE, ENNO E. *Metternich's German Policy: The Congress of Vienna, 1814–1815.* Princeton, NJ: Princeton University Press, 1983. (Definitive work on the post-Napoleonic settlement.)

LOWE, JOHN. *The Great Powers, Imperialism, and the German Problem, 1865–1925.* London: Routledge, 1994.

MITCHELL, ALAN. *The German Influence in France after 1870.* Chapel Hill, NC: University of North Carolina Press, 1979.

———. *The Great Train Race: Railways and the Franco-German Rivalry, 1815–1914.* New York: Berghahn Books, 2000.

MOSES, JOHN A. *Trade Unionism in Germany from Bismarck to Hitler, 1869–1933.* Totowa, NJ: Barnes & Noble, 1982.

MOSSE, GEORGE L. *The Nationalization of the Masses: Political Symbolism and Mass Movements in Germany from the Napoleonic Wars through the Third Reich.* New York: Meridian, 1975. (Controversial tour de force.)

NICHOLS, J. ALDEN. *The Year of the Three Kaisers: Bismarck and the German Succession, 1887–1888.* Urbana, IL: University of Illinois Press, 1987.

PARET, PETER. *German Encounters with Modernism, 1840–1945.* New York: Cambridge University Press, 2001.

PFLANZE, OTTO. *Bismarck.* 3 vols. Princeton, NJ: Princeton University Press, 1963–1990.

PULZER, PETER. *The Rise of Political Anti-Semitism in Germany and Austria.* New York: Wiley, 1964.

RINEHART, YEHUDA, ed. *The Jewish Response to German Culture.* Hanover, NH: University Press of New England, 1985.

ROSS, RONALD J. *The Failure of Bismarck's Kulturkampf: Catholicism and State Power in Imperial Germany.* Washington, DC: Catholic University Press of America, 1998.

SHEEHAN, JAMES J. *German Liberalism in the Nineteenth Century.* Chicago, IL: University of Chicago Press, 1978. (Definitive and excellent.)

SMITH, HELMUT WALSER. *German Nationalism and Religious Conflict: Culture, Ideology, Politics, 1870–1914.* Princeton, NJ: Princeton University Press, 1995.

STEENSON, GARY P. *"Not One Man! Not One Penny!" German Social Democracy, 1863–1914.* Pittsburgh, PA: University of Pittsburgh Press, 1981.

STERN, FRITZ. *Dreams and Delusions: The Drama of German History.* New Haven, CT: Yale University Press, 1987. (An interesting mix of analysis and memoir.)

———. *Gold and Iron: Bismarck, Bleichröder, and the Building of the German Empire.* New York: Knopf, 1977.

STOLPER, GUSTAV, et al. *The Economic Development of Germany, 1870 to the Present.* Trans. by Toni Stolper. New York: Harcourt Brace Jovanovich, 1967.

TAL, URIEL. *Christians and Jews in Germany: Religion, Politics, and Ideology in the Second Reich, 1870–1914.* Ithaca, NY: Cornell University Press, 1975.

TAYLOR, ALAN JOHN PERCIVALE. *Bismarck: The Man and the Statesman.* New York: Knopf, 1955. (Controversial interpretation by the gadfly of British historians.)

VALENTIN, VEIT. *1848: Chapter of German History.* Trans. by E. T. Scheffauer. London: Allen & Unwin, 1940. (One-volume English-language condensation of the author's classic two-volume study; originally published in German in 1930.)

VICK, BRIAN E. *Defining Germany: The 1848 Frankfurt Parliamentarians and National Identity.* Cambridge, MA: Harvard University Press, 2002.

WALKER, MACK. *German Home Towns: Community, State, and General Estate, 1648–1871.* Ithaca, NY: Cornell University Press, 1971.

WAWRO, GEOFFREY. *The Franco-Prussian War: The German Conquest of France in 1870–1871.* New York: Cambridge University Press, 2003. (The most recent military history of the conflict.)

WEHLER, HANS-ULRICH. *The German Empire, 1871–1918.* Trans. by Kim Traynor. Dover, NH: Berg, 1985. (First-rate "structural" analysis by one of the leading proponents of the *Sonderweg* thesis.)

WETZEL, DAVID. *A Duel of Giants: Bismarck, Napoleon III, and the Franco-Prussian War.* Madison, WI: University of Wisconsin Press, 2001. (A study in personalities, deemphasizing military history.)

CHAPTER 2: WILHELMINIAN GERMANY, 1890–1914

ABELSHAUSER, WERNER, et al. *German History and Global Enterprise: BASF, the History of a Company.* New York: Cambridge University Press, 2004.

ABRAMS, LYNN. *Workers' Culture in Imperial Germany.* New York: Routledge, 1991.

ALLEN, ANN TAYLOR. *Satire and Society in Wilhelmine Germany: Kladderadatsch and Simplicissimus, 1890–1914.* Louisville, KY: University Press of Kentucky, 1984. (Unusual literary-political study.)

ANDERSON, MARGARET LAVINIA. *Practicing Democracy: Elections and Political Culture in Imperial Germany.* Princeton, NJ: Princeton University Press, 2000. (This and the Sperber entries are first-rate detailed studies of Wilhelminian elections.)

BALFOUR, MICHAEL. *The Kaiser and His Times.* London: Cresset Press, 1964. (Probably the most satisfactory one-volume biography of William II in English.)

BARKIN, KENNETH D. *The Controversy over German Industrialization.* Chicago, IL: University of Chicago Press, 1970.

BERGHAHN, VOLKER ROLF. *Germany and the Approach of War in 1914.* New York: St. Martin, 1973.

CECIL, LAMAR. *Albert Ballin: Business and Politics in Imperial Germany, 1888–1918.* Princeton, NJ: Princeton University Press, 1967. (Empathic biography of Germany's leading shipping magnate.)

———. *William II.* 2 vols. Chapel Hill, NC: University of North Carolina Press, 1989, 1996.

CHICKERING, ROGER. *We Men Who Feel Most German: A Cultural Study of the Pan-German League, 1886–1914.* London: Allen & Unwin, 1984.

ELEY, GEOFF. *Reshaping the German Right: Radical Nationalism and Political Change after Bismarck.* 2nd ed. New Haven, CT.: Yale University Press, 1991.

ELEY, GEOFF, AND JAMES RETALLACK, eds. *Wilhelminism and Its Legacies: German Modernities, Imperialism and the Meaning of Reform, 1890–1930.* New York: Berghahn Books, 2004.

EVANS, RICHARD, ed. *Society and Politics in Wilhelmine Germany.* London: Croom Helm, 1978.

FLETCHER, ROGER, ed. *Bernstein to Brandt: A Short History of German Social Democracy.* New York: Edward Arnold, 1987.

GAY, PETER. *Freud, Jews, and Other Germans: Master and Victims in Modernist Culture.* New York: Oxford University Press, 1978. (A collection of essays by a dean of cultural historians.)

HAU, MICHAEL. *The Cult of Health and Beauty in Germany: A Social History, 1890–1930.* Chicago, IL: University of Chicago Press, 2003.

HERWIG, HOLGER H. *The German Naval Officer Corps: A Social and Political History, 1890–1918.* Oxford: Clarendon, 1973. (Superb study of the leadership of the kaiser's favorite branch of the military.)

HEWITSON, MARK. *Germany and the Causes of the First World War.* Oxford, UK: Berg Publishers, 2004.

HULL, ISABEL V. *Absolute Destruction: Military Culture and the Practices of War in Imperial Germany.* Ithaca, NY: Cornell University Press, 2005.

KEHR, ECKART. *Economic Interest, Militarism, and Foreign Policy: Essays on German History.* Ed. by

Gordon A. Craig; trans. by Grete Heinz. Berkeley, CA: University of California Press, 1977. (Influential collection of essays by the foremost revisionist German historian of the early twentieth century.)

KELLY, ALFRED, ed. and trans. *The German Worker: Working-Class Autobiographies from the Age of Industrialization.* Berkeley, CA: University of California Press, 1987.

KENNAN, GEORGE. *The Decline of Bismarck's European Order.* Princeton, NJ: Princeton University Press, 1984. (Original interpretation by a master of diplomatic theory and practice.)

KENNEDY, PAUL. *The Rise of Anglo-German Antagonism, 1860–1914.* London: Allen & Unwin, 1980.

KITCHEN, MARTIN. *The German Officer Corps, 1890–1914.* Oxford: Oxford University Press, 1968.

LAQUEUR, WALTER. *Young Germany.* New York: Basic Books, 1962. (Places the pre-1914 youth movement within the context of the tensions of Wilhelminian society.)

LIDTKE, VERNON L. *The Alternative Culture: Socialist Labour in Imperial Germany.* New York: Oxford University Press, 1985.

MOMBAUER, ANNIKA and DEIST, WILHELM, eds. *The Kaiser: New Research on Wilhelm II's Role in Imperial Germany.* New York: Cambridge University Press, 2003.

MASSIE, ROBERT, K, eds. *Dreadnought: Britain, Germany, and the Coming of the Great War.* New York: Random House, 1991. (Massive tome on the Anglo-German naval rivalry with a focus on the personalities involved.)

MOMMSEN, WOLFGANG J., ed. *Theories of Imperialism.* Trans. by P. S. Falla. New York: Random House, 1980.

MOSSE, GEORGE L. *The Crisis of German Ideology.* New York: Grosset & Dunlap, 1964. (Controversial interpretation of the nineteenth-century intellectual roots of Nazism.)

MUNCY, LYSBETH. *The Junkers in the Prussian Administration under William II, 1888–1914.* Providence, RI: Brown University, 1944. (Still the best one-volume study in English.)

NETTL, JOHN P. *Rosa Luxemburg.* 2 vols. London: Oxford University Press, 1966. (Definitive biography of the intellectual leader of the SPD's left wing.)

NICHOLLS, J. ALDEN. *Germany after Bismarck: The Caprivi Era, 1890–1894.* Cambridge, MA: Harvard University Press, 1958.

RINGER, FRITZ K. *The German Mandarins.* Cambridge, MA: Harvard University Press, 1969. (First-rate analysis of the German academic establishment.)

RÖHL, JOHN C. G. *Young Wilhelm: The Kaiser's Early Life, 1859–1988.* Trans. by Jeremy Gaines and Rebecca Wallach. New York: Cambridge University Press, 1998. (This and the following entry constitute the first two volumes of a detailed biography by a scholar who has made the study of William II his life work.)

———. *William II: The Kaiser's Personal Monarchy, 1888–1900.* 3rd ed Trans. by Sheila de Bellaigue. New York: Cambridge University Press, 2004.

ROSENBERG, ARTHUR. *Imperial Germany: The Birth of the German Republic.* Trans. by Ian F. D. Marner. Boston, MA: Beacon Press, 1964. (Influential analysis by one of the founders of the USPD.)

RÜGER, JAN. *The Great Naval Game: Britain and Germany in the Age of Empire.* New York: Cambridge University Press, 2007.

SACKETT, ROBERT E. *Popular Entertainment, Class, and Politics in Munich, 1900–1923.* Cambridge, MA: Harvard University Press, 1982.

SCHORSKE, CARL E. *German Social Democracy, 1905–1917: The Development of the Great Schism.* Cambridge, MA: Harvard University Press, 1955. (Classic analysis of the revisionism–antirevisionism controversy in the SPD.)

SPERBER, JONATHAN. *The Kaiser's Voters: Electors and Elections in Imperial Germany.* New York: Cambridge University Press, 1997.

STACHURA, PETER D. *The German Youth Movement, 1900–1945.* New York: St. Martin, 1981.

STERN, FRITZ R. *The Politics of Cultural Despair: A Study in the Rise of the German Ideology.* Berkeley, CA: University of California Press, 1961. (Classic analysis of the antimodernist trends in Wilhelminian intellectual and political life.)

ZUBER, TERENCE. *Inventing the Schlieffen Plan: German War Planning, 1871–1914.* New York: Oxford University Press, 2002. (Controversial book claiming that the Schlieffen Plan was an invention of the German General Staff after World War I.)

CHAPTER 3: THE FIRST WORLD WAR, 1914–1918

BERGHAHN, VOLKER, R., AND MARTIN KITCHEN, eds. *Germany in the Age of Total War.* Totowa, NJ: Barnes & Noble, 1981.

BROSE, ERIC DORN. *The Kaiser's Army: The Politics of Military Technology in Germany during the Machine Age, 1870–1918.* New York: Oxford University Press, 2001.

CHICKERING, ROGER. *Imperial Germany and the Great War, 1914–1918*. 2nd ed. New York: Cambridge University Press, 2004.

DANIEL, UTE. *The War from Within: German Working Class Women in the First World War*. Trans. by Margaret Ries. New York: Berg, 1997.

DAVIS, BELINDA J. *Home Fires Burning: Food, Politics, and Everyday Life in World War I Berlin*. Chapel Hill, NC: University of North Carolina Press, 2000.

FELDMAN, GERALD D. *Army, Industry, and Labor in Germany, 1914–1918*. Princeton, NJ: Princeton University Press, 1966. (First-rate analysis of the conflict and symbiotic cooperation of the country's major interest groups in wartime. A paperback edition with a new introduction by the author was published in 1991 by Berg.)

FISCHER, FRITZ. *Germany's Aims in the First World War*. New York: Norton, 1967. (Revisionist interpretation that became a cause célèbre in the 1960s.)

FROMKIN, DAVID. *Europe's Last Summer: Who Started the Great War in 1914?* New York: Knopf, 2004. (Detailed day-by-day account of the growing crisis that led to the outbreak of World War I.)

HAGEMANN, KAREN, AND STEFANIE SCHÜLER-SPRINGORUM, eds. *Home Front: The Military, War, and Gender in 20th-Century Germany*. New York: Berg, 2002.

HAMILTON, RICHARD F., AND HOLGER H. HERWIG, eds. *The Origins of World War I*. New York: Cambridge University Press, 2003. (Covers not just Germany but all of the major powers and belligerents.)

HORN, DANIEL. *The German Naval Mutinies of World War I*. Rutgers, NJ: Rutgers University Press, 1969.

HULL, ISABEL V. *Absolute Destruction: Military Culture and the Practices of War in Imperial Germany*. Ithaca, NY: Cornell University Press, 2005.

JARAUSCH, KONRAD H. *The Enigmatic Chancellor: Bethmann Hollweg and the Hubris of Imperial Germany*. New Haven, CT: Yale University Press, 1973.

KITCHEN, MARTIN. *The Silent Dictatorship: The Politics of the German High Command under Hindenburg and Ludendorff, 1916–1918*. New York: Holmes & Meier, 1976.

KOCKA, JÜRGEN. *Facing Total War: German Society, 1914–1918*. Trans. by Barbara Weinberger. Cambridge, MA: Harvard University Press, 1985.

MORGAN, DAVID. *German Left-Wing Socialism: A History of the German Independent Social Democratic Party*. Ithaca, NY: Cornell University Press, 1975. (Definitive account of the USPD's complex ideological and organizational makeup.)

VERHEY, JEFFREY. *The Spirit of 1914: Militarism, Myth, and Mobilization in Germany*. New York: Cambridge University Press, 2000.

VINCENT, C. PAUL. *The Politics of Hunger: The Allied Blockade of Germany, 1915–1919*. Athens, OH: Ohio University Press, 1985.

WELCH, DAVID. *Germany, Propaganda and Total War, 1914–1918*. New Brunswick, NY: Rutgers University Press, 2000. (Detailed, technical, but well-illustrated study of German propaganda in World War.)

WHEELER-BENNET, JOHN. *Brest-Litovsk: The Forgotten Peace*. New York: 1939. Reprint, 1971. (Classic but still unsurpassed study of this important episode.)

WINTER, JAY, AND ANTOINE FROST. *The Great War in History: Debates and Controversies*. New York: Cambridge University Press, 2005. (The most recent survey of the historiography of guilt and blame in connection with World War I.)

CHAPTER 4: REVOLUTION, INFLATION, AND PUTSCHES: THE SEARCH FOR A NEW CONSENSUS, 1918–1923

ANGRESS, WERNER T. *Stillborn Revolution*. Princeton, NJ: Princeton University Press, 1963. (Still the best account of the KPD's repeated and abortive attempts to stage a second revolution in the early years of the Weimar Republic.)

BOEMEKE, MANFRED F., GERALD D. FELDMAN, AND ELISABETH GLASER, eds. *The Treaty of Versailles: A Reassessment after 75 Years*. New York: Cambridge University Press, 1998. (Collection of essays by French, German, and American scholars reflecting on the impact of the treaty that ended World War I.)

BURDICK, CHARLES B., AND RALPH H. LUTZ, eds. *Political Institutions of the German Revolution, 1918–1919*. Stanford, CA: Hoover Institution, 1966. (The title is misleading; the book actually contains the debates of the executive committee set up by the National Congress of Workers' and Soldiers' Councils.)

CALKINS, KENNETH R. *Hugo Haase: Democrat and Revolutionary*. Durham, NC: Duke University Press, 1979.

CARSTEN, FRANCIS L. *Fascist Movements in Austria: From Schönerer to Hitler*. Beverly Hills, CA: Sage,

1977. (Important for the Austrian background of the Nazi movement.)

———. *The Reichswehr and Politics. 1918–1933.* Oxford: Oxford University Press, 1966.

———. *Revolution in Central Europe. 1918–1919.* Berkeley, CA: University of California Press, 1972. (Puts the German events in the context of the Europe-wide post-World War I upheavals.)

DE MICHELIS, CESARE G. *The Non-Existent Manuscript: A Study of "The Protocols of the Sages of Zion."* Lincoln, NE: University of Nebraska Press, 2004.

DIEHL, JAMES M. *Paramilitary Politics in Weimar Germany.* Bloomington, IN: Indiana University Press, 1977. (The most comprehensive book on the subject.)

EPSTEIN, KLAUS. *Matthias Erzberger and the Dilemma of German Democracy.* Princeton, NJ: Princeton University Press, 1959. (Definitive biography of this important and controversial Center Party leader.)

EYCK, ERICH. *History of the Weimar Republic.* 2 vols. New York: Atheneum, 1970. (Well-written and engaging political history by a contemporary; the author was a DDP member of the Berlin city council.)

FELDMAN, GERALD D. *The Great Disorder: Politics, Economics, and Society in the German Inflation, 1919–1924.* New York: Oxford University Press, 1993.

FISCHER, CONAN. *The Ruhr Crisis, 1923–1924.* New York: Oxford University Press, 2003.

FISCHER, FRITZ. *From Kaiserreich to Third Reich.* Trans. by Roger Fletcher. London: Allen & Unwin, 1986. (A reassessment of the "Fischer thesis" by its author twenty-five years after the publication of Fischer's *Germany's Aims in the First World War.* New York: Norton, 1967)

GORDON, HAROLD J., JR. *Hitler and the Beer Hall Putsch.* Princeton, NJ: Princeton University Press, 1972. (The most detailed and satisfactory book on the subject.)

GRATHWOL, ROBERT P. *Stresemann and the DNVP: Reconciliation or Revenge in German Foreign Policy, 1924–1928.* Lawrence: University of Kansas Press, 1980.

HAMANN, BRIGITTE, AND THOMAS THORNTON. *Hitler's Vienna: A Dictator's Apprenticeship.* New York: Oxford University Press, 1999. Paperback, 2000. (Excellent study of Hitler's years in Vienna.)

HASTINGS, DEREK. *Catholicism and the roots of Nazism: Religious Identity and National Socialism.* New York: Oxford University Press, 2010. (Contends that the early Nazi Party was heavily influenced by the ideas of conservative Catholicism.)

HERTZMAN, LEWIS J. *DNVP.* Lincoln: University of Nebraska Press, 1963. (Still the best short history in English of the post-World War I conservatives.)

HUGHES, MICHAEL L. *Paying for the German Inflation.* Chapel Hill, NC: University of North Carolina Press, 1988.

HUNT, RICHARD N. *German Social Democracy, 1918–1933.* New Haven, CT: Yale University Press, 1964. (The best one-volume overall treatment of the SPD during the Weimar years; critical of the party's leadership.)

KENT, BRUCE. *Spoils of War: The Politics, Economics, and Diplomacy of Reparations, 1918–1932.* Oxford, UK: Clarendon Press, 1989.

KESSLER, COUNT HARRY. *In the Twenties.* Trans. by Charles Kessler. New York: Holt, Rinehart & Winston, 1971. (Somewhat gossipy diaries of an aesthete who traveled widely in social and political circles.)

KOLB, EBERHARD. *The Weimar Republic.* 2nd. ed. Tr. P.S. Falla and R.J. Park. New York: Routledge, 2005. (Excellent overview of the Weimar years. Especially good on methodological and historiographic problems.)

MAIER, CHARLES S. *Reconstructing Bourgeois Europe.* Princeton, NJ: Princeton University Press, 1975. (Well-done comparative analysis of German, Italian, and French society in the 1920s.)

MAYER, ARNO. *Politics and Diplomacy of Peacemaking: Containment and Counter-Revolution at Versailles.* New York: Knopf, 1967. (Controversial interpretation that argues the Versailles settlement was motivated primarily by the Allies' fear of left-wing revolutions.)

NICHOLLS, ANTHONY J. *Freedom with Responsibility: The Social Market Economy in Germany, 1918–1963.* New York: Oxford University Press, 1994.

ORLOW, DIETRICH. *Weimar Prussia, 1919–1925: The Unlikely Rock of Democracy.* Pittsburgh, PA: University of Pittsburgh Press, 1986.

SHARP, ALAN. *The Versailles Settlement: Peacemaking After the First World War.* New York: Palgrave Macmillan, 2008.

SMITH, BRADLEY F. *Adolf Hitler: His Family, Childhood, and Youth.* Stanford, CA: Hoover Institution, 1967. Reprint, 1979. (This and the next entry are superb short studies by a master of detailed analysis.)

———. *Heinrich Himmler: A Nazi in the Making, 1900–1926.* Stanford, CA: Hoover Institution, 1971.

TRACHTENBERG, MARC. *Reparations and World Politics.* New York: Columbia University Press, 1980. (Along with the Schuker entry listed under Chapter 6, one of a number of works arguing that contrary to what most Germans—and many historians—thought, the Versailles settlement was not particularly harsh on Germany.)

WAITE, ROBERT G. L. *Vanguard of Nazism: The Free Corps Movement in Post-War Germany, 1918–1923.* Cambridge, MA: Harvard University Press, 1952. Reprint, 1970. (Classic study emphasizing the proto-fascistic nature of the *Freikorps;* now somewhat eclipsed by the Diehl entry.)

WALDMANN, ERIC. *The Spartacist Uprising of 1919.* Milwaukee, WI: Marquette University Press, 1958.

WEITZ, ERIC D. *Creating German Communism, 1890–1990.* Princeton, NJ: Princeton University Press, 1997.

CHAPTER 5: FOOLS' GOLD: THE WEIMAR REPUBLIC, 1924–1930

BALDERSTON, THEO. *Economics and Politics in the Weimar Republic.* New York: Cambridge University Press, 2002.

BESSEL, RICHARD, AND E. J. FEUCHTWANGER, eds. *Social Change and Political Development in the Weimar Republic.* London: Croom Helm, 1981.

BRADY, ROBERT A. *The Rationalization Movement in German Industry: A Study in the Evolution of Economic Planning.* Berkeley, CA: University of California Press, 1933. (Classic study on the transformation of German capitalism in the second half of the Weimar years.)

BRAUNTHAL, GERARD. *Socialist Labor and Politics in Weimar Germany: The General Federation of German Trade Unions.* Hamden, CT: Archon Books, 1978.

BREITMAN, RICHARD. *German Socialism and Weimar Democracy.* Chapel Hill, NC: University of North Carolina Press, 1981. (Especially valuable for its analysis of the confrontation of the SPD and the rising Nazis.)

BULLOCK, ALAN. *Hitler: A Study in Tyranny.* London: Odhams Press, 1952. (The first scholarly biography of Hitler to appear after World War II.)

CARR, EDWARD HALLETT. *German-Soviet Relations between the Two World Wars, 1919–1939.* Baltimore, MD: Johns Hopkins University Press, 1951. Reprint, 1983.

CHILDERS, THOMAS. *The Nazi Voter: The Social Foundations of Fascism in Germany, 1919–1933.* Chapel Hill, NC: University of North Carolina Press, 1983. (One of a number of works using sophisticated quantitative methods to analyze Nazi support.)

EASTON, LAIRD M. *The Red Count: The Life and Times of Harry Kessler.* Berkeley, CA: University of California Press, 2002. (A recent and judicious biography of the Weimar Republic's most prominent aesthete.)

EVANS, RICHARD J., AND DICK GEARY, eds. *The German Unemployed, 1918–1936.* New York: St. Martin, 1987.

FEST, JOACHIM C. *Hitler.* New York: Harcourt Brace Jovanovich, 1973. (Probably the best one-volume biography.)

FOWKES, BEN. *Communism in Germany under the Weimar Republic.* New York: St. Martin, 1984.

GAY, PETER. *Weimar Culture: The Outsider as Insider.* New York: Harper & Row, 1968. (Iconoclastic interpretation of Weimar intellectual life.)

HAMILTON, NIGEL. *The Brothers Mann: The Lives of Heinrich and Thomas Mann, 1871–1950, 1875–1955.* New Haven, CT: Yale University Press, 1978.

HEBERLE, RUDOLF. *From Democracy to Nazism.* Baton Rouge, LA: Louisiana State University Press, 1945. (Pioneering study analyzing electoral support for the Nazis in the rural area of Schleswig-Holstein.)

HERF, JEFFREY. *Reactionary Modernism: Technology, Culture, and Politics in Weimar and the Third Reich.* New York: Cambridge University Press, 1984.

HESS, HANS. *George Grosz.* New Haven, CT: Yale University Press, 1974. (One of the few English-language studies of the Weimar Republic's leading caricaturist.)

JÄCKEL, EBERHARD. *Hitler's World View: A Blueprint for Power.* Middletown, CT: Wesleyan University Press, 1972. (The best short analysis of Hitler's basic ideas and motivation.)

JACOBSON, JON. *Locarno Diplomacy: Germany and the West, 1925–1929.* Princeton, NJ: Princeton University Press, 1972.

JAMES, HAROLD. *The German Slump: Politics and Economics, 1924–1936.* Oxford: Clarendon Press, 1986.

JELAVICH, JOHN. *Berlin Cabaret.* Cambridge, MA: Harvard University Press, 1993.

JONES, LARRY EUGENE. *German Liberalism and the Dissolution of the Weimar Party System, 1918–1933.* Chapel Hill, NC: University of North Carolina Press, 1988.

KATER, MICHAEL H. *The Nazi Party: A Social Profile of Members and Leaders, 1919–1945.* Cambridge, MA: Harvard University Press, 1983. (Like the Childers' entry, an analysis that makes use of sophisticated quantitative research methods.)

KRACAUER, SIEGFRIED. *From Caligari to Hitler: A Psychological Study of the German Film*. Princeton, NJ: Princeton University Press, 1947. (Pioneering study in the sociology of the cinema.)

KREIMEIER, KLAUS. *The Ufa Story: A History of Germany's Greatest Film Company, 1918–1945*. Trans. by Robert and Rita Kimber. New York: Hill and Wang, 1996.

KRUEDENER, JÜRGEN VON. *Economic Crisis and Political Collapse: The Weimar Republic, 1924–1933*. Providence, RI: Berg, 1989.

LAQUEUR, WALTER. *Weimar: A Cultural History*. New York: Putnam, 1974.

LEBOVICS, HERMAN E. *Social Conservatism and the Middle Classes in Germany*. Princeton, NJ: Princeton University Press, 1969. (First-rate analysis of the motivation underlying the antirepublican and antidemocratic attitudes of many middle-class Germans.)

MERKL, PETER H. *The Making of a Stormtrooper*. Princeton, NJ: Princeton University Press, 1980. (Well-done sociopolitical profile of the Nazis' paramilitary organization.)

MIERZEJEWSKI, ALFRED C. *The Most Valuable Asset of the Reich: A History of the German National Railway, 1920–1945*. 2 vols. Chapel Hill, NC: University of North Carolina Press, 1999. (Extremely detailed institutional history.)

MOMMSEN, HANS. *The Rise and Fall of Weimar Democracy*. Trans. by Elborg Forster and Larry Eugene Jones. Chapel Hill, NC: University of North Carolina Press, 1996.

NOAKES, JEREMY, ed. *Documents on Nazism, 1919–1945*. Atlantic Highlands, NJ: Humanities Press, 1974. (The best collection of basic primary materials in English.)

NOLAN, MARY. *Visions of Modernity: American Business and the Modernization of Germany*. New York: Cambridge University Press, 1994. (A sophisticated and controversial update of the Brady entry listed earlier.)

ORLOW, DIETRICH. *The History of the Nazi Party, 1919–1933*. Pittsburgh, PA: University of Pittsburgh Press, 1969.

PEUKERT, DETLEV J. K. *The Weimar Republic: The Crisis of Classical Modernity*. Trans. by Richard Deveson. New York: Hill and Wang, 1991.

PRIDHAM, GEOFFREY. *The Nazi Movement in Bavaria, 1923–1933*. New York: Harper & Row, 1973.

(Representative of a number of excellent analyses on the rise of the Nazis on the regional and local levels.)

RAUSCHNING, HERMANN. *Hitler Speaks*. London: Butterworth, 1939. (Revealing memoirs by an early Nazi supporter who later broke with the movement.)

REUVENI, GIDEON. *Reading Germany: Literature and Consumer Culture in Germany Before 1933*. Trans. by Ruth Morris. New York: Berghahn Books, 2006.

SCHUKER, STEPHEN A. *The Financial Crisis of 1924 and the Adoption of the Dawes Plan*. Chapel Hill, NC: University of North Carolina Press, 1976. (Like the Trachtenberg entry [in Chapter 4], this work takes a revisionist view of Versailles.)

SMALDONE, WILLIAM. *Rudolf Hilferding: The Tragedy of a German Social Democrat*. Dekalb, IL: Northern Illinois University Press, 1998. (A very sympathetic account of Hilferding's ideas by a professed American Social Democrat.)

STACHURA, PETER D. *Nazi Youth in the Weimar Republic*. Santa Barbara, CA: ABC-Clio, 1975.

TURNER, HENRY A. *Stresemann and the Politics of the Weimar Republic*. Princeton, NJ: Princeton University Press, 1963. (An important monograph that made extensive use of the Stresemann papers.)

WEITZ, ERIC D. *Weimar Germany: Promise and Tragedy*. Princeton, NJ: Princeton University Press, 2007. (The best one-volume history of the Weimar years. Especially good on culture and everyday history.)

WILLETT, JOHN. *Art and Politics in the Weimar Period: The New Sobriety, 1917–1933*. New York: Pantheon Books, 1978.

WRIGHT, JONATHAN. *Gustav Stresemann: Weimar's Greatest Statesman*. New York: Oxford University Press, 2002.

CHAPTER 6: FROM AUTHORITARIANISM TO TOTALITARIANISM, 1930–1938

ALLEN, WILLIAM S. *The Nazi Seizure of Power: The Experience of a Single German Town, 1922–1945*. New York: Franklin Watts, 1984. (Revised edition of what has become a classic in local history.)

AYÇOBERRY, PIERRE. *The Social History of the Third Reich, 1933–1945*. Trans. by Janet Lloyd. New York: The New Press, 1999. (Iconoclastic, but perceptive history of life in the Third Reich.)

BACH, STEVEN. *Leni: The Life and Work of Leni Riefenstahl.* New York: Alfred A. Knopf, 2007. (Definitive biography of Hitler's favorite filmmaker.)

BAIRD, JAY W. *Hitler's War Poets: Literature and Politics in the Third Reich.* New York: Cambridge University Press, 2008.

BARANOWSKI, SHELLEY. *Strength through Joy: Consumerism and Mass Tourism in the Third Reich.* New York: Cambridge University Press, 2004. (Excellent social history.)

BECK, HERMANN. *The Fateful Alliance: German Conservatives and Nazis in 1933, the Machtergreifung in a New Light.* New York: Berghahn Books, 2008.

BENTLEY, JAMES. *Martin Niemöller.* New York: Free Press, 1984. (Biography of one of the founders of the Confessing Church.)

BENZ, WOLFGANG. *A Concise History of the Third Reich.* Trans. by Thomas Dunlap. Berkeley, CA: University of California Press, 2006.

BINION, RUDOLPH. *Hitler among the Germans.* New York: Elsevier, 1976. (This book and the later Waite and Stern entries are representative of efforts to analyze the Hitler and Nazi phenomena with psychohistorical methods.)

BROSZAT, MARTIN. *The Hitler State: The Foundation and Development of the Internal Structure of the Third Reich.* London: Longmans, 1981.

BROWDER, GEORGE C. *Hitler's Enforcers: The Gestapo and the SS Security Service in the Nazi Revolution.* New York: Oxford University Press, 1996. (Excellent administrative history.)

CAMPBELL, BRUCE. *The SA Generals and the Rise of Nazism.* Louisville, KY: University of Kentucky Press, 2004. (A detailed study of the 178 highest-ranking storm troop leaders.)

CAPLAN, JANE, AND WACHSMANN, NIKOLAUS, eds. *Concentration Camps in Nazi Germany.* New York: Routledge, 2008. (Series of essays on the camps. Especiaally good for the newer historiography on the subject.

CONWAY, JOHN S. *The Nazi Persecution of the Churches, 1933–1945.* New York: Basic Books, 1968.

CORNI, GUSTAVO. *Hitler and the Peasants: Agrarian Policy of the Third Reich, 1930–1939.* Providence, RI: Berg, 1990.

DESCHNER, GÜNTHER. *Reinhold Heydrich.* New York: Stein & Day, 1981.

ENGELMANN, BERNT. *In Hitler's Germany: Everyday Life in the Third Reich.* Trans. by Krisbna Winston. New York: Pantheon, 1986.

EVANS, RICHARD J. *The Coming of the Third Reich.* New York: Penguin Press, 2004. (This and the following entry constitute the first two parts of a projected three-volume work that will become the best history of the Third Reich.)

———. *The Third Reich in Power, 1933–1939.* New York: Penguin Press, 2005.

FELDMAN, GERALD D. *Allianz and the German Insurance Business, 1933–1945.* New York: Cambridge University Press, 2001. (This and the Gall entry are examples of the growing field of corporate-sponsored histories written by leading professional historians.)

FISCHER, CONAN. *Stormtroopers: A Social, Economic, and Ideological Analysis, 1929–1935.* London: Allen & Unwin, 1983.

FRAENKEL, ERNST. *The Dual State: A Contribution to the Theory of Dictatorship.* New York: Octagon, 1969. (Classic study emphasizing the uneasy relationship between party and state in the Nazi system.)

FRITZSCHE, PETER. *Life and Death in the Third Reich.* Cambridge, MA: Harvard University Press, 2008. (Along with the second Koonz entry below, an attempt to explain the twisted logic that underlay Nazi notions of morality.)

GALL, LOTHAR, et al. *The Deutsche Bank, 1870–1995.* London: Weidenfeld and Nicolson, 1995.

GELLATELY, ROBERT. *Backing Hitler: Consent and Coercion in Nazi Germany.* New York: Oxford University Press, 2001.

GILES, GEOFFREY J. *Students and National Socialism in Germany.* Princeton, NJ: Princeton University Press, 1985.

GUENTHER, IRENE. *Nazi Chic? Fashioning Women in the Third Reich.* New York: Berg, 2004.

HAFFNER, SEBASTIAN. *The Meaning of Hitler.* Trans. by Ewald Osers. Cambridge, MA: Harvard University Press, 1983. (Thought-provoking attempt to assess the historic significance of Hitler and the Nazis.)

HAMILTON, RICHARD F. *Who Voted for Hitler?* Princeton, NJ: Princeton University Press, 1982. (Revisionist analysis that argues that contrary to what many scholars thought, the Nazis' electoral support was strongest not among the lower-middle classes but among upper-class and upper-middle-class Germans.)

HAYES, PETER. *Industry and Ideology: I. G. Farben in the Nazi Era.* New York: Cambridge University Press, 1987. (Definitive history of the chemical conglomerate.)

HILDEBRAND, KLAUS. *The Foreign Policy of the Third Reich.* Trans. by Anthony Fothergill. London: Batsford, 1973. (The best short treatment of the subject.)

HOFFMANN, HILMAR. *The Triumph of Propaganda: Film and National Socialism, 1933–1945.* Trans. by John Broadwin and Volker R. Berghahn. Providence, RI: Berghahn Books, 1996.

HÖHNE, HEINZ. *The Order of the Death's Head.* New York: Coward McCann, 1969.

KATER, MICHAEL H. *Hitler Youth.* Cambridge, MA: Harvard University Press, 2004.

———. *Never Sang for Hitler: The Life and Times of Lotte Lehmann, 1888–1976.* New York: Cambridge University Press, 2008. (Biography of Kurt Weil's wife and the original Jenny in the *Three Penny Opera.*)

KERSHAW, IAN. *Hitler, 1889–1945.* 2 vols. New York: Norton, 1999, 2000. (Newest and best biography of Hitler.)

———. *The Nazi Dictatorship: Problems and Perspectives in Interpretation.* London: Edward Arnold, 1985. (Particularly important for its discussion of the historiography of Nazism.)

———. *Popular Opinion and Political Dissent in the Third Reich: Bavaria, 1933–1945.* New York: Oxford University Press, 1985. (One of a number of recent works demonstrating the limits of Nazi totalitarianism as far as life for the average German was concerned.)

KINDLEBERGER, CHARLES P. *The World in Depression, 1929–1939.* Berkeley, CA: University of California Press, 1973.

KLEMPERER, KLEMENS VON. *Germany's New Conservatism.* Princeton, NJ: Princeton University Press, 1957. (Pioneering study of the New Right.)

KLEMPERER, VICTOR. *I Will Bear Witness: A Diary of the Nazi Years, 1933–1945.* 2 vols. New York: Random House, 1998–1999. (Moving diary of a German-Jewish intellectual who lived in Germany throughout the Nazi years because he was married to an "Aryan" wife.)

———. *The Language of the Third Reich: LTI—Lingua Tertii Imperii: A Philogist's Notebook.* Trans. by Martin Brady. New Brunswick, NJ: Athlone Press, 2000. (Klemperer's interesting analysis of the Nazis' perversion of the German language.)

KOONZ, CLAUDIA. *Mothers in the Fatherland.* New York: St Martin, 1987. (Important study of the Nazi women's organization.)

———. *The Nazi Conscience.* Cambridge, MA: Harvard University Press, 2003. (Interesting analysis of Nazi ideas of morality based on racial determinism.)

LEOPOLD, JOHN A. *Alfred Hugenberg. The Radical Nationalist Campaign against the Weimar Republic.* New Haven, CT: Yale University Press, 1977.

LEWY, GÜNTER. *The Catholic Church and Nazi Germany.* New York: McGraw-Hill, 1964.

MASON, TIM. *Social Policy in the Third Reich.* New York: Berg, 1990. (Makes available in English important writings of a British historian, most of whose work had previously appeared only in German.)

MOMMSEN, HANS. *From Weimar to Auschwitz: Essays in German History.* Trans. by Philip O'Connor. Princeton, NJ: Princeton University Press, 1991.

———, ed. *The Third Reich between Vision and Reality: New Perspectives on German History, 1918–1945.* New York: Berg, 2001. (A series of essays by German scholars.)

MOSSE, GEORGE L. *Nazi Culture. Intellectual, Cultural, and Social Life in the Third Reich.* 2nd ed. Madison, WI: University of Wisconsin Press, 2003.

MÜLLER, INGO. *Hitler's Justice: The Courts of the Third Reich.* Trans. by Deborah Lucas Schneider. Cambridge, MA: Harvard University Press, 1991.

MÜLLER, KLAUS-JÜRGEN. *The Army, Politics, and Society in Germany, 1933–1946.* New York: St. Martin, 1987.

NEUFELD, MICHAEL J. *The Rocket and the Reich: Peenemünde and the Coming of the Ballistic Missile Era.* New York: Free Press, 1995.

POST, GAINES. *Dilemmas of Appeasement: British Deterrence and Defense, 1934–1937.* Ithaca, NY, and London, 1993. (Argues the primary goal of the appeasers was to buy time for British rearmament, not to avoid war at all costs.)

READ, ANTHONY. *The Devil's Disciples: The Life and Times of Hitler's Inner Circle.* New York: Norton, 2004. (Breezy, popular account of Hitler's close associates. Full of not always verifiable anecdotes.)

SCHMÖLDERS, CLAUDIA. *Hitler's Face: the Biography of an Image.* Trans. by Adrian Daub. Philadelphia, PA: University of Pennsylvania Press, 2006. (Analysis of the use of Hitler's face both in Nazi propaganda and anti-Nazi caricatures.)

SEABURY, PAUL. *The Wilhelmstrasse.* Berkeley, CA: University of California Press, 1954. (Institutional analysis of the German Foreign Ministry.)

SEMMENS, KRISTON. *Seeing Hitler's Germany: Tourism in the Third Reich.* New York: Palgrave Macmillan, 2005.

Smelser, Ronald. *Robert Ley.* New York: Berg, 1988. (The only English-language biography of the head of the Nazi German Labor Front.)

Stachura, Peter D. *Gregor Strasser and the Rise of Nazism.* London: Allen & Unwin, 1983. (The only full-scale study in English of the man who, until his resignation from the NSDAP at the end of 1932, was regarded by many as one of the most influential men in the Nazi Party.)

Steinweis, Alan E. *Kristallnacht 1938.* Cambridge, MA: Harvard University Press, 2009. (The most recent account of the 1938 pogrom.)

Stephenson, Jill. *Women in Nazi Society.* New York: Harper & Row, 1981.

Stern, J. P. *Hitler: Führer and People.* Berkeley, CA: University of California Press, 1974.

Swett, Pamela E. *Neighbors and Enemies: The Culture of Radicalism in Berlin, 1929–1933.* New York: Cambridge University Press, 2004.

Tooze, Adam. *The Wages of Destruction: The Making and Breaking of the Nazi Economy.* New York: Penguin Press, 2006.

Turner, Henry Ashby, Jr., ed. *General Motors and the Nazis: The Struggle for the Control of Opel, Europe's Biggest Carmaker.* New Haven, CT: Yale University Press, 2005.

———. *German Big Business and the Rise of Hitler.* New York: Oxford University Press, 1984. (Argues convincingly that financial support from the business community for the Nazis was not nearly as extensive as often claimed.)

Waite, Robert G. L. *The Psychopathic God: Adolf Hitler.* New York: Basic Books, 1977.

Wegner, Bernd. *The Waffen-SS: Ideology, Organization, and Function.* Trans. by Ronald Webster. Oxford: Basil Blackwell, 1989.

Weinberg, Gerhard L. *The Foreign Policy of Hitler's Germany: The Diplomatic Revolution in Europe, 1933–1936.* Chicago, IL: University of Chicago Press, 1970. (Along with the volume by the same author covering the later years—cited under Chapter 7—this book is the definitive treatment of the Third Reich's foreign policy.)

Welch, David. *The Third Reich: Politics and Propaganda.* 3rd ed. New York: Routledge, 2002.

Wëtte, Wolfram. *The Wehrmacht: History, Myth, Reality.* Trans. by Deborah Lucas Schmeider. Cambridge, MA: Harvard University Press.

Ziegler, Herbert F. *Nazi Germany's New Aristocracy: The SS Leadership, 1925–1939.* Princeton, NJ: Princeton University Press, 1990.

CHAPTER 7: CONQUEST, DEATH, AND DEFEAT, 1938–1945

———. *Hitler's Beneficiaries: Plunder, Racial War, and the Nazi Welfare State.* Tr. by Jefferson Chase. New York: Metropolitan Books, 2006. (Controversial book contending that the Holocaust was in large part motivated by the Nazis' desire for controlling their victims' economic assets.)

Aly, Götz. *Final Solution: Nazi Population Policy and the Murder of the European Jews.* Trans. by Belinda Cooper and Allison Brown. New York: Arnold, 1999. (Aly is one of the foremost proponents of the functionalist school among Holocaust historians.)

Arendt, Hannah. *Eichmann in Jerusalem: The Banality of Evil.* Rev. ed. New York: Penguin, 1964. New ed., 1977. (Controversial interpretation of the Holocaust and Adolf Eichmann's role in it.)

Beck, Earl R. *Under the Bombs: The German Home Front, 1942–1945.* Lexington, KY: University Press of Kentucky, 1986.

Bellon, Bernard P. *Mercedes in Peace and War: German Automobile Workers, 1903–1945.* New York: Columbia University Press, 1990.

Black, Peter R. *Ernst Kaltenbrunner.* Princeton, NJ: Princeton University Press, 1984. (Biography of Heydrich's successor. Kaltenbrunner was the man primarily responsible for implementing the Holocaust.)

Bloch, Michael. *Ribbentrop.* New York: Crown, 1993.

Boog, Horst, et al. *Germany and the Second World War.* New York: Oxford University Press, 1999 ff. (The most comprehensive history of the Wehrmacht's operations in World War II. So far nine volumes have been published.)

Browning, Christopher R. *Ordinary Men: Reserve Battalion 101 and the Final Solution in Poland.* New York: HarperCollins, 1992. (Using much of the same documentary evidence, Browning and the Goldhagen entry [listed later in this chapter] come to widely different conclusions.)

Browning, Christopher R., and Jürgen Matthäus. *The Origins of the Final Solution: The Evolution of Nazi Jewish Policy, September 1939–March 1942.* Lincoln, NE: University of Nebraska Press, 2004. (Very detailed and judicious analysis.)

Chickering, Roger, et al., eds. *A World at Total War: Global Conflict and the Politics of Destruction, 1937–1945.* New York: Cambridge University Press, 2005.

Dallin, Alexander. *German Rule in Russia, 1941–1945.* 2nd ed. Boulder, CO: Westview, 1981.

(Originally published in 1957, this is still the best account of the Nazis' misguided and cruel occupation policies in the Soviet Union.)

ELEY, GEOFF, ed. *The "Goldhagen Effect": History, Memory, Nazism—Facing the German Past.* Ann Arbor, MI: University of Michigan Press, 2000.

EVANS, RICHARD J., ed. *The Third Reich at War, 1939–1945.* New York: Penguin Press, 2010. (The final volume of the author's masterful history of the Third Reich.)

FELDMAN, GERALD D., ed. *Networks of Nazi Persecution: Bureaucracy, Business, and the Organization of the Holocaust.* New York: Berghahn Books, 2005.

FEST, JOACHIM. *Speer: The Final Verdict.* Trans. by Ewald Osers and Alexandra Dring. London: Weidenfeld and Nicolson, 2001. (The most recent and judicious biography of Hitler's architect.)

FLEMING, GERALD. *Hitler and the Final Solution.* Berkeley, CA: University of California Press, 1984. (Important work that convincingly lays to rest any claims that Hitler did not personally order the Holocaust.)

FRIEDLANDER, HENRY. *The Origins of Nazi Genocide: From Euthanasia to the Final Solution.* Chapel Hill, NC: University of North Carolina Press, 1995.

FRIEDLÄNDER, SAUL. *Nazi Germany and the Jews: The Years of Persecution, 1933–1939.* New York: HarperCollins, 1997. (The first volume of what will undoubtedly be the definitive account of Nazi policies against the Jews.)

FRIEDRICH, JÖRG. *The Fire: The Bombing of Germany, 1940–1945.* New York: Columbia University Press, 2006. (A major contribution to the "Germans as victims" debate.)

GOLDHAGEN, DANIEL. *Hitler's Willing Executioners: Ordinary Germans and the Holocaust.* New York: Knopf, 1996. (Ambitious and very controversial new interpretation of the Holocaust.)

HASTINGS, MAX. *Armageddon: The Battle for Germany, 1944–1945.* New York: Knopf, 2004. (Detailed military history of the last year of the war that emphasizes the human aspects of the conflict.)

HEIBER, HELMUT, ed. *Hitler and His Generals: Military Conferences, 1942–1945—The First Complete Stenographic Record of the Military Situation Conferences.* Trans. by Roland Winter et al. New York: Enigma Books, 2003.

HEINEMAN, JOHN L. *Hitler's First Foreign Minister: Constantin Freiherr von Neurath, Diplomat and Statesman.* Berkeley, CA: University of California Press, 1979. (Definitive but also somewhat apologetic biography of a traditional conservative who served the Nazis to the end.)

HELMREICH, ERNST CHRISTIAN. *The German Churches under Hitler: Background, Struggle, and Epilogue.* Detroit, MI: Wayne State University Press, 1979.

HERBERT, ULRICH. *Hitler's Foreign Workers: Enforced Foreign Labor in Germany Under the Third Reich.* Trans. by William Templer. New York: Cambridge University Press, 1997.

HILBERG, RAUL. *The Destruction of the European Jews.* Rev. ed. New York: Holmes & Meier, 1985. (Remains the best, most reliable, and most detailed account of the Holocaust.)

KERSHAW, IAN. *Hitler, the Germans, and the Final Solution.* New Haven, CT: Yale University Press, 2008.

KOEHL, ROBERT L. *The Black Corps: The Structure and Power Struggles of the Nazi SS.* Madison, WI: University of Wisconsin Press, 1983.

LONGERICH, PETER. *Holocaust: The Nazi Persecution and Murder of the Jews.* New York: Oxford University Press, 2010. (Excellent account based upon the most recent archival researches. Should be used in conjunction with the Hilberg entry.)

LUKACZ, JOHN. *June, 1941: Hitler and Stalin.* New Haven, CT: Yale University Press, 2006.

MACKSEY, KENNETH J. *The Partisans of World War II.* New York: Stein & Day, 1975.

MAYER, ARNO J. *Why Did the Heavens Not Darken? The "Final Solution" in History.* New York: Pantheon, 1989. (Provocative interpretation of the Holocaust that attempts to place it in a longitudinal historical setting.)

MAZOWER, MARK. *How the Nazis Ruled Europe.* New York: Penguin Press, 2008.

MEINECKE, FRIEDRICH. *The German Catastrophe.* Cambridge, MA: Harvard University Press, 1950. (Historiographically important early attempt by a leading German historian to assess the significance of Hitler and the Nazis.)

MICHEL, HENRI. *The Shadow War: European Resistance, 1939–1945.* New York: Harper & Row, 1972.

MILWARD, ALAN S. *The German Economy at War.* London: Athlone Press, 1965. (The best one-volume account of the wartime economy.)

MÜLLER, ROLF-DIETER, AND GERD R. UEBERSCHÄR, eds. *Hitler's War in the East, 1941–1945: A Critical Asssessment.* New York: Berhahn Books, 2008.

NEUFELD, MICHAEL J. *Von Braun: Dreamer of Space, Engineer of War.* New York: Knopf, 2007. (Excellent biography of the man who was instrumental both in the V-2 program and the American space program.)

ORLOW, DIETRICH. *The History of the Nazi Party, 1933–1945.* Pittsburgh, PA: University of Pittsburgh Press, 1973.

SCHRAMM, PERCY ERNST. *Hitler: The Man and the Military Leader.* Trans. by Donald S. Detwiler. New York: Franklin Watts, 1971. (Schramm, a leading German historian, was assigned to the Wehrmacht high command as war diarist during World War II.)

SHEPHERD, GORDON. *The Anschluss.* Philadelphia: Lippincott, 1963. (Classic account of the annexation of Austria by the Third Reich.)

SPEER, ALBERT. *Inside the Third Reich.* New York: Macmillan, 1970. (Speer has been described as the friend Hitler would have had if the dictator had been capable of forming friendships; Speer was also the only one of the defendants at Nuremberg to acknowledge the evil nature of the Nazi regime and his part in it.)

STEIN, GEORGE. *The Waffen SS.* Ithaca, NY: Cornell University Press, 1966. (First-rate analysis of the Nazis' elite fighting corps.)

STEINWEIS, ALAN E. *Studying the Jew: Scholarly Antisemites in Nazi Germany.* Cambridge, MA: Harvaard University Press, 2006.

TAYLOR, A. J. P. *The Origins of the Second World War.* 2nd ed. New York: Atheneum, 1961. (Argues—not very convincingly—that World War II resulted from Hitler's miscalculations, not his premeditated intent to unleash a war of conquest.)

TREVOR-ROPER, HUGH R. *The Last Days of Hitler.* 3rd ed. New York: Collier Books, 1962. (Superior piece of detective work detailing the last days of the war in Hitler's bunker.)

WEINBERG, GERHARD L. *Starting World War II, 1937–1939.* Chicago, IL: University of Chicago Press, 1993. (The second volume of *The Foreign Policy of Hitler's Germany,* the definitive history of Nazi foreign policy.)

———. *A World at Arms: A Global History of World War II.* New York: Oxford University Press, 1994. (The best one-volume history of the World War II.)

CHAPTER 8: "CONDOMINIUM OF THE ALLIED POWERS," 1945–1949

AHONEN, PERTTI. *After the Expulsion: West Germany and Eastern Europe, 1945–1990.* New York: Oxford University Press, 2003. (Slightly misleading title; the book is really about the integration of the expellees in West and East Germany.)

ANNAN, NOEL. *Changing Enemies: The Defeat and Regeneration of Germany.* New York: HarperCollins, 1995.

BACKER, JOHN H. *Winds of History: The German Years of Lucius Dubignon Clay.* New York: Van Nostrand Reinhold, 1983.

BALFOUR, MICHAEL. *Four Power Control in Germany and Austria, 1945–1946.* London: Oxford University Press, 1956.

BALFOUR, MICHAEL, AND JULIAN FRISBY. *Helmuth von Moltke: A Leader Against Hitler.* New York: St. Martin, 1972. (Sympathetic biography of an important leader of the German resistance.)

BESSEL, RICHARD. *Germany, 1945: From War to Peace.* New York: HarperCollins, 2009. (Covers the last five months of the war and the first seven months of occupation.)

BIESS, FRANK. *Homecomings: Returning POWs and the Legacies of Defeat in Postwar Germany.* Princeton, NJ: Princeton University Press, 2006.

BLESSING, BENITA. *The Antifascist Classroom: Denazification in Soviet-Occupied Germany.* New York: Palgrave Macmillan, 2006.

CHILDS, DAVID. *The SPD from Schumacher to Brandt: The Story of German Socialism, 1945–1965.* New York: Pergamon, 1966. (Still the best short history of the postwar SPD in English.)

CLAY, LUCIUS D. *Decision in Germany.* Garden City, NY: Doubleday, 1950. (Memoirs of the American military governor who had a crucial role in determining the future fortunes of West Germany.)

CLEMENS, DIANE SHAVER. *Yalta.* New York: Oxford University Press, 1971. (First-rate account of the most controversial of the wartime Allied summit conferences.)

DAVIDSON, EUGENE. *The Trial of the Germans.* New York: Macmillan, 1966. (Detailed and fair treatment of the trial of the major Nazi war criminals before the International Military Tribunal at Nuremberg.)

EISENBERG, CAROLYN. *Drawing the Line: The American Decision to Divide Germany, 1944–1949.* New York: Cambridge University Press, 1996. (The latest attempt to explain the emergence of the Cold War and the division of Germany as consequences of the developing global conflict among the superpowers.)

FEIS, HERBERT. *Between War and Peace: The Potsdam Conference*. Princeton, NJ: Princeton University Press, 1960. (Somewhat dated but still useful account of the conference that many historians feel sealed the division of Germany.)

GALANTE, PIERRE, WITH EUGÈNE SILIANOFF. *Operation Valkyrie: The German Generals' Plot against Hitler*. Trans. by Mark Howson and Cary Ryan. New York: First Cooper Square Press, 2002.

GIMBEL, JOHN. *The American Occupation of Germany: Politics and the Military, 1945–1949*. Stanford, CA: Stanford University Press, 1968.

GLASER, HERMANN. *The Rubble Years*. New York: Paragon House, 1987.

HEARNDEN, ARTHUR, ed. *The British in Germany*. London: Hamilton, 1978. (A collection of essays especially useful on the "reeducation" efforts of the British.)

HÉBERT, VALERIE, ed. *Hitler's Generals on Trial: The Last War Crimes Tribunal at Nuremberg*. Lawrence, KS: University of Kansas Press, 2010. (Attempts to put the American war crimes trials in the context of the Cold War.)

HOFFMANN, PETER. *The History of the German Resistance, 1933–1945*. Cambridge, MA: MIT Press, 1977.

JARAUSCH, KONRAD H. *After Hitler: Recivilizing Germans, 1945–1995*. New York: Oxford University Press, 2006.

KLEMPERER, KLEMENS VON. *German Resistance against Hitler: The Search for Allies Abroad, 1938–1945*. New York: Oxford University Press, 1992.

MACDONOGH, GILES. *After the Reich: The Brutal History of the Allied Occupation*. New York: Basic Books, 2007.

MAIER, CHARLES S., et al., eds. *The Marshall Plan and Germany: West German Development within the Framework of the European Recovery Program*. New York: Berg, 1991.

MIERZEJEWSKI, ALFRED C. *Ludwig Erhard: A Biography*. Chapel Hill, NC: University of North Carolina Press, 2004.

MILWARD, ALAN S. *The Reconstruction of Western Europe, 1945–1951*. Berkeley, CA: University of California Press, 1984. (Revisionist interpretation that downgrades the significance of the Marshall Plan as a factor in the economic revival of West Germany and Western Europe.)

MOLTKE, FREYA VON. *Memories of Kreisau and the German Resistance*. Trans. by Julie M. Winter. Lincoln: University of Nebraska Press, 2003.

MOMMSEN, HANS. *Alternatives to Hitler: German Resistance under the Third Reich*. New York: Tauris, 2003.

NAIMARK, NORMAN M. *The Russians in Germany: A History of the Soviet Zone of Occupation, 1945–1949*. Cambridge, MA: Harvard University Press, 1995.

OVERY, RICHARD, ed. *Interrogations: The Nazi Elite in Allied Hands, 1945*. New York: Viking, 2001. (A documentary record of the interrogations of the major war criminals tried by the International Military Tribunal at Nuremberg.)

PETERSON, EDWARD N. *The Many Faces of Defeat: The German People's Experience in 1945*. New York: Peter Lang, 1990.

PIKE, DAVID. *The Politics of Culture in Soviet-Occupied Germany, 1945–1949*. Stanford, CA: Stanford University Press, 1992.

PRONAY, NICHOLAS, AND KEITH WILSON, eds. *The Political Re-Education of Germany and Her Allies after World War II*. Totowa, NJ: Barnes & Noble, 1985.

PUACA, BRIAN M. *Learning Democracy: Education Reform in West Germany, 1945–1965*. New York: Berghahn Books, 2009.

RÜCKERL, ADALBERT, ed. *The Investigation of Nazi Crimes, 1945–1978: A Documentation*. Trans. by Derek Rutter. Heidelberg: C. F. Müller, 1979. (An important introduction to a subject that is not well covered in English; the author was a German federal prosecutor of war crimes.)

SCHOLL, INGE. *Students against Tyranny: The Resistance of the White Rose, Munich, 1942–1943*. Trans. by Arthur R. Schultz. Middletown, CT: Wesleyan University Press, 1970. (The author is the sister of Sophie Scholl, one of the leaders of the White Rose resistance group.)

SMITH, BRADLEY F. *The Road to Nuremberg*. New York: Basic Books, 1981. (The best short introduction to the International Military Tribunal trial.)

SMYSER, WILLIAM R. *From Yalta to Berlin: The Cold War Struggle over Germany*. New York: Palgrave/St. Martin, 1999. (Good overall popular history.)

THER, PHILIPP, AND ANA SILJAK, eds. *Redrawing Nations: Ethnic Cleansing in East-Central Europe, 1944–1948*. Lanham, MD: Rowman and Littlefield, 2001. (Judicious collection of essays on a topic that still evokes passionate emotions.)

TURNER, HENRY A., JR. *Germany from Partition to Reunification*. 2nd ed. New Haven, CT: Yale University Press, 1992.

VAN HOOK, JAMES C. *Rebuilding Germany: The Creation of the Social Market Economy, 1945–1957.* New York: Cambridge University Press, 2004.

VOGT, TIMOTHY R. *Denazification in Soviet-Occupied Germany: Brandenburg, 1945–1948.* Cambridge, MA: Harvard University Press, 2000. (One of the few works treating de-Nazification in the Soviet zone in some detail.)

WETTIG, GERHARD. *Stalin and the Cold War in Europe: The Emergence and Development of the East-West Conflict, 1939–1953.* Lanham, MD: Rowman and Littlefield, 2008.

WIESEN, S. JONATHAN. *West German Industry and the Challenge of the Nazi Past, 1945–1955.* Chapel Hill, NC: University of North Carolina Press, 2001.

WILLIS, F. ROY. *The French in Germany, 1945–1949.* Stanford, CA: Stanford University Press, 1962. (Remains the only full-scale study in English of French occupation policies.)

CHAPTER 9: THE FEDERAL REPUBLIC OF GERMANY, 1949–1990

ADENAUER, KONRAD. *Memoirs.* Trans. by Beate Ruhm von Oppen. Chicago: Henry Regnery, 1966.

AUST, STEFAN. *Baader-Meinhof: The Inside Story of the R.A.F.* Trans. by Anthea Bell. New York: Oxford University Press, 2009.

BALDWIN, PETER, ed. *Reworking the Past: Hitler, the Holocaust, and the Historians' Debate.* Boston: Beacon Press, 1990. (Series of essays on the difficulty of "historicizing" Nazism in German history.)

BERGHAHN, VOLKER R. *The Americanization of West German Industry, 1945–1973.* New York: Cambridge University Press, 1986.

BETTS, PAUL. *The Authority of Everyday Objects: A Cultural History of West German Industrial Design.* Berkeley, CA: University of California Press, 2004.

BRAUNTHAL, GERALD. *The West German Social Democrats, 1969–1982.* Boulder, CO: Westview Press, 1983.

CHIN, RITA. *The Guest Worker Question in Postwar Germany.* New York: Cambridge University Press, 2007.

DEMETZ, PETER. *Postwar German Literature.* New York: Pegasus, 1970.

DIEFENDORF, JEFFRY M. *In the Wake of War: The Reconstruction of German Cities after World War II.* New York: Oxford University Press, 1993.

ERHARD, LUDWIG. *Germany's Comeback in the World Market.* New York: Macmillan, 1954. (Somewhat self-congratulatory account by the "father" of West Germany's social market economy.)

FEINSTEIN, MARGARETE MYERS. *State Symbols: The Quest for Legitimacy in the Federal Republic of Germany and the German Democratic Republic, 1949–1959.* Boston, MA: Brill Academic, 2001.

FELDMAN, LILY G. *The Special Relationship between West Germany and Israel.* London: Allen & Unwin, 1984. (An important contribution to a somewhat taboo subject.)

FINK, CAROLE, AND SCHAEFER, BERND, eds. *Ostpolitik, 1969–1974: European and Global Responses.* New York: Cambridge University Press, 2008.

FREI, NORBERT. *Adenauer's Germany and the Nazi Past: The Politics of Amnesty and Integration.* Trans. by Joel Golb. New York: Columbia University Press, 2002.

FULBROOK, MARY. *Interpretations of the Two Germanies, 1945–1990.* 2nd ed. New York: Palgrave/St. Martin, 2000.

GIERSCH, HERBERT, et al. *The Fading Miracle: Four Decades of Market Economy in Germany.* New York: Cambridge University Press, 1992.

GÖKTÜRK, DENIZ, DAVID GRAMLING, AND ANTON KAES, eds. *Germany in Transit: Nation and Migration, 1955–2005.* Berkeley, CA: University of California Press, 2007.

GRANIERI, RONALD J. *The Ambivalent Alliance: Konrad Adenauer, the CDU/CSU, and the West, 1949–1966.* New York: Berghahn Books, 2003.

GRAY, WILLIAM GLENN. *Germany's Cold War: The Global Campaign to Isolate East Germany, 1949–1969.* Chapel Hill, NC: University of North Carolina Press, 2003.

GROSSER, ALFRED. *Germany in Our Time.* Trans. by Paul Stephenson. New York: Praeger, 1971. (Insightful and sympathetic history by a leading French political scientist.)

HAFTENDORN, HELGA. *Coming of Age: German Foreign Policy Since 1945.* Lanham, MD: Rowman and Littlefield, 2006

HANRIEDER, WOLFRAM, ed. *Helmut Schmidt: Perspectives on Politics.* Boulder, CO: Westview Press, 1982.

HERF, JEFFREY. *Divided Memory: The Nazi Past in the two Germanys.* Cambridge, MA: Harvard University Press, 1997.

HUGHES, MICHAEL L. *Shouldering the Burdens of Defeat: West Germany and the Reconstruction of Social Justice.* Chapel Hill, NC: University of North Carolina Press, 1999. (Detailed study of the

Lastenausgleichsgesetz as the key to the successful establishment of the West German social market economy.)

LARGE, DAVID CLAY. *Germans to the Front: West German Rearmament in the Adenauer Era.* Chapel Hill, NC: University of North Carolina Press, 1995.

MAIER, CHARLES S. *The Unmasterable Past: History, Holocaust and German National Identity.* Cambridge, MA: Harvard University Press, 1988. (The best English-language treatment of the *Historikerstreit.*)

MARKOVITS, ANDREI S., ed. *The Political Economy of West Germany: Modell Deutschland.* New York: Praeger, 1982.

MILOSCH, MARK. *Modernizing Bavaria: The Politics of Franz Josef Strauss and the CSU, 1949–1969.* New York: Berghahn Books, 2006.

MOELLER, ROBERT G., ed. *West Germany Under Construction: Politics, Society, and Culture in the Adenauer Era.* Ann Arbor, MI: University of Michigan Press, 1997.

PAPADAKIS, ELIM. *The Green Movement in West Germany.* New York: St. Martin, 1984.

POIGER, UTA G. *Jazz, Rock, and Rebels: Cold War Politics and American Culture in a Divided Germany.* Berkeley, CA: University of California Press, 2000.

POLLOCK, JAMES K., et al. *German Democracy at Work.* Ann Arbor, MI: University of Michigan Press, 1955. (Pollock was one of General Clay's civilian political advisers.)

PRIDHAM, GEOFFREY. *Christian Democracy in Western Germany: The CDU/CSU in Government and Opposition, 1945–1976.* New York: St. Martin, 1977.

PRITTIE, TERENCE. *The Velvet Chancellors: A History of Postwar Germany.* New York: Holmes & Meier, 1979.

———. *Willy Brandt: Portrait of a Statesman.* New York: Schocken Books, 1974.

REICH-RANICKI, MARCEL. *The Author of Himself: The Life of Marcel Reich-Ranicki.* Trans. by Ewald Osers. Princeton, NJ: Princeton University Press, 2001. (Beautifully written memoirs by the undisputed dean of German literary critics.)

SCHICK, JACK M. *The Berlin Crisis, 1958–1962.* Philadelphia, PA: University of Pennsylvania Press, 1971.

SCHISSLER, HANNA, ed. *The Miracle Years: A Cultural History of West Germany, 1949–1968.* Princeton, NJ: Princeton University Press, 2001.

SCHWARZ, HANS-PETER. *Konrad Adenauer: A German Politician and Statesman in a Period of War, Revolution, and Reconstruction.* Trans. by Louise

Willmot and Geoffrey Penny. New York: Berghahn Books, 1995–1997. (Detailed and very sympathetic biography of the longtime chancellor.)

SPICKA, MARK E. *Selling the Economic Miracle: Economic Reconstruction and Politics in West Germany, 1949–1957.* New York: Berghahn Books, 2007. (Interesting analysis of the handling of the social market economy in the national campaigns of the 1950s.)

TRACHTENBERG, MARC. *A Constructed Peace: The Making of the European Settlement, 1945–1963.* Princeton, NJ: Princeton University Press, 1999. (Controversial interpretation of the Cold War that argues the key dispute was the question of nuclear arms for West Germany.)

TURNER, HENRY ASHBY, JR. *Germany from Partition to Reunification.* 2nd ed. New Haven, CT: Yale University Press, 1992.

VON WEIZSÄCKER, RICHARD. *From Weimar to the Wall: My Life in German Politics.* Trans. by Ruth Hein. New York: Bantam/Dell/Doubleday, 1999. (Memoirs of the most respected and popular of the West German postwar presidents.)

CHAPTER 10: THE GERMAN DEMOCRATIC REPUBLIC, 1949–1990

BARING, ARNULF M. *Uprising in East Germany: June 17, 1953.* Trans. by Gerald Onn. Ithaca, NY: Cornell University Press, 1972.

BOZO, FRÉDÉRIC. *Mitterand, The End of the Cold War and German Unification.* Trans. by Susan Emanuel. New York: Berghahn Books, 2009. (Detailed and judicious account of the French president's role in the German unification process.)

BURGESS, JOHN P. *The East German Church and the End of Communism.* New York: Oxford University Press, 1997.

FEINSTEIN, JOSHUA. *The Triumph of the Ordinary: Depictions of Daily Life in the East German Cinema, 1949–1989.* Chapel Hill, NC: University of North Carolina Press, 2002.

FENEMORE, MARK. *Sex, Thugs, and Rock "N" Roll: Teenage Rebels in Cold-War East Germany.* New York: Berghahn Books, 2007. Harlow, UK: Longman, 2000.

FULBROOK, MARY. *The People's State: East German Society from Hitler to Honecker.* New Haven, CT: Yale University Press, 2005.

GLAESSNER, GERT-JOACHIM, AND IAN WALLACE. *The German Revolution of 1989: Causes and Consequences.* Providence, RI: Berg, 1992.

GRIEDER, PETER. *The East German Leadership, 1946–1973: Conflict and Crisis.* Manchester, UK: Manchester University Press, 2000.

HARRISON, HOPE M. *Driving the Soviets up the Wall: Soviet-East German Relations, 1953–1961.* Princeton, NJ: Princeton University Press, 2003.

HONECKER, ERICH. *From My Life.* New York: Pergamon, 1981.

JARAUSCH, KONRAD H. *Dictatorship as Experience: Towards a Socio-Cultural History of the GDR.* New York: Berghahn Books, 1999.

MAIER, CHARLES S. *Dissolution: The Crisis of Communism and the End of East Germany.* Princeton, NJ: Princeton University Press, 1997.

MAJOR, PATRICK, AND JONATHAN OSMOND, eds. *The Workers' and Peasants' State: Communism and Society in East Germany under Ulbricht, 1945–1971.* Manchester, UK: Manchester University Press, 2002.

MCADAMS, A. JAMES. *East Germany and Detente: Building Authority After the Wall.* New York: Cambridge University Press, 1985.

PALMOWSKI, JAN, et al. *Inventing a Socialist Nation: Heimat and the Politics of Everyday Life in the GDR, 1945–1990.* New York: Cambridge University Press, 2009.

RICHTHOFEN, ESTHER VON. *Bringing Culture to the Masses: Control, Compromise, and Participation in the GDR.* New York: Berghahn Books, 2008. (One of several works claiming that control of cultural life in the GDR was less complete than either the regime or earlier scholars thought.)

SLUSSER, ROBERT M. *The Berlin Crisis of 1961.* Baltimore, MD: Johns Hopkins University Press, 1973.

SPILKER, DIRK. *The East German Leadership and the Division of Germany: Patriotism and Propaganda, 1945–1953.* New York: Oxford University Press, 2006.

ZATLIN, JONATHAN R. *The Currency of Socialism: Money and Political Culture in East Germany.* New York: Cambridge University Press, 2007. (Slightly misleading title. This is actually a sophisticated analysis of the conceptual failures of East Germany's economic management.)

CHAPTER 11: GERMANY SINCE REUNIFICATION, EUPHORIA AND DISILLUSIONMENT, 1990–PRESENT

BRADY, JOHN S., AND BEVERLY CRAWFORD, eds. *The Postwar Transformation of Germany: Democracy, Prosperity, and Nationhood.* Ann Arbor, MI: University of Michigan Press, 1999. (Series of essays attempting to put the Berlin republic into the post-1945 context.)

COHEN-PFISTER, LAUREL, ed. *Victims and Perpetrators, 1933–1945: (Re)presenting the Past in Post-Unification Culture.* Berlin: De Gruyter Verlag, 2006. (A series of articles analyzing the treatment of victims and perpetrators in post-unification literature.)

DALTON, RUSSELL J., ed. *Germany Divided: The 1994 Bundestagswahl and the Evolution of the German Party System.* Washington, DC: Berg, 1996.

FISCHER, WOLFRAM, et al., eds. *Treuhandanstalt: The Impossible Challenge.* Berlin: Akademie Verlag, 1996.

GROSSER, DIETER, ed. *Uniting Germany: The Unexpected Challenge.* Providence, RI: Berg, 1992.

HAMPTON, MARY N., AND CHRISTIAN SØE, eds. *Between Bonn and Berlin: German Politics Adrift?* Lanham, MD: Rowman & Littlefield, 1999.

JAMES, HAROLD, AND MARLA STONE, eds. *When the Wall Came Down: Reactions to German Unification.* New York: Routledge, 1992.

JARAUSCH, KONRAD H. *The Rush to German Unity.* New York: Oxford University Press, 1994.

KEANE, JOHN, ed. *Civil Society: Berlin Perspectives.* New York: Berghahn Books, 2006.

KOLINSKI, EVA. *Women in Contemporary Germany: Life, Work and Politics.* Providence, RI: Berg, 1993.

LEAMAN, JEREMY. *The Political Economy of Germany Under Chancellors Kohl and Schröder: Decline of the German Model?* New York: Berghahn Books, 2009.

LONGHURST, KERRY. *Germany and the Use of Force: The Evolution of German Security Policy, 1990–2003.* Manchester, UK: Manchester University Press, 2004.

MUNSKE, BARBARA. *The Two Plus Four Negotiations from a German-German Perspective.* Boulder, CO: Westview Press, 1995.

NIVEN, WILLIAM JOHN. *Facing the Nazi Past: United Germany and the Legacy of the Third Reich.* New York: Routledge, 2002.

OSWALD, FRANZ. *The Party That Came out of the Cold War: The Party of Democratic Socialism in United Germany.* Westport, CT: Praeger, 2002.

PECK, JEFFREY M. *Being Jewish in the New Germany.* Brunswick, NJ: Rutgers University Press, 2006.

SAROTTE, MARY ELISE. *1989: The Struggle to Create Post-Cold War Europe.* Princeton, NJ: Princeton University Press, 2009.

SCHÖNBOHM, JÖRG. *Two Armies and One Fatherland: The End of the Nationale Volksarmee.* Trans. by Peter Johnson. Providence, RI: Berghahn Books, 1995. (Fascinating diary by the West German general charged with merging the East German army into the *Bundeswehr.*)

WOODS, ROGER, ed. *Germany's New Right as Culture and Politics.* New York: Palgrave Macmillan, 2007. (An attempt to place the German extreme Right in the context of similar movements in other European countries.)

ZELIKOW, PHILIP, AND CONDOLEEZZA RICE. *Germany Unified and Europe Transformed.* Cambridge, MA: Harvard University Press, 1997. (An account of German reunification from an American perspective. At the time the book was written, the authors were members of the staff of the U.S. National Security Council.)

INDEX